SPIRIT AND
SELF IN
MEDIEVAL
CHINA

Published with the support of the School of Hawaiian, Asian, and Pacific Studies, University of Hawai'i

SPIRIT AND SELF IN MEDIEVAL CHINA

The *Shih-shuo hsin-yü* and Its Legacy

Nanxiu Qian

UNIVERSITY OF HAWAI'I PRESS

HONOLULU

Library of Congress Cataloging-in-Publication Data
Qian, Nanxiu.
Spirit and self in medieval China: the Shih-shuo hsin-yü and its legacy / Nanxiu Qian.
p. cm.
Includes bibliographical references and index.
ISBN 0-8248-2309-5 (alk. paper)—ISBN 0-8248-2397-4 (pbk. : alk. paper)
1. Liu, I-ch'ing, 403-444. Shih shuo hsin yè. I. Title: Shih-shuo hsin-yü
and its legacy.   II. Title.
DS736.L5363 Q25   2001
895.1'8240208—dc21
00-062949

Chapter 8 first appeared in *Nan Nuu: Men, Women, and Gender in Early and Imperial China*, Kononklijke Brill N.V., Leiden, The Netherlands (1999).
Chapter 9 first appeared in *Early Medieval China* 4 (1998): 49–82.
Both appear here in revised form with the permission of the publishers.

Designed by Deborah Hodgdon
Printed by The Maple-Vail Book Manufacturing Group

To Richard B. Mather

Contents

Figures

Chinese Dynasties

Shang	ca. 16th cent.–ca. 11th cent. B.C.	
Western Chou	ca. 11th cent.–771 B.C.	
Ch'un-ch'iu	770–476 B.C.	
Chan-kuo	475–221 B.C.	
Ch'in	221–206 B.C.	
Former Han	206 B.C.– A.D. 24	
Later Han	25–220	
Three Kingdoms	Wei 220–265	
	Shu 221–263	
	Wu 222–280	
Western Chin	265–316	
Eastern Chin	317–420	Hou Chao 328–352
		Ch'ien Liang 313–376
		Ch'ien Ch'in 351–394
		Hou Ch'in 384–417
		Pei Liang 397–439
Southern and	Liu Sung 420–479	Northern Wei 386–534
Northern	Ch'i 479–502	
Dynasties	Liang 502–557	Northern Ch'i 550–557
	Ch'en 557–589	Northern Chou 557–581
Sui	581–618	
T'ang	618–907	
Five Dynasties	907–960	

Northern Sung	960–1127	Liao 916–1125
Southern Sung	1127–1279	Chin 1115–1234
Yüan	1271–1368	
Ming	1368–1644	
Ch'ing	1644–1911	
Modern	1911 to date	

Japanese Periods Involved in the Japanese *Shih-shuo* Imitations

Heian 794–1185
Kamakura 1185–1333
Nambokuchō 1336–1392
Muromachi 1333–1573
Sengoku 1482–1558
Momoyama 1573–1603
Tokugawa 1603–1868
Meiji 1868–1912

Source: Suwa Tokutarō, *Nihonshi no Yōryō* (Outline of Japanese history). Tokyo: Ōbunsha, 1957.

Introduction

This book offers a comprehensive analysis of the *Shih-shuo hsin-yü* (conventionally translated as "A New Account of Tales of the World") and its literary legacy—a legacy that lasted for well over 1,600 years in China and that also extended to other parts of East Asia during this period. Compiled by the Liu-Sung (420–479) Prince of Liu I-ch'ing (403–444) and his staff around A.D. 430,[1] the *Shih-shuo hsin-yü* consists of more than 1,130 historical anecdotes about elite life in the late Han (ca. 150–220) and Wei-Chin (220–420) periods—what is generally regarded as China's early medieval period. Together, these beautifully written and artfully constructed anecdotes express what came to be known as the "Wei-Chin spirit," an outgrowth of new intellectual trends that emerged during one of the most creative and iconoclastic periods of Chinese imperial history.

The *Shih-shuo hsin-yü* also inaugurated a specific Chinese literary genre—the *Shih-shuo t'i*, which inspired dozens of imitations from the latter part of the T'ang dynasty (618–907) to the early Republican era (the early twentieth century). Most of these imitations were Chinese works, but a few were written by Japanese. What do the *Shih-shuo hsin-yü* and its various imitations tell us about the way the Wei-Chin spirit came to be transmitted and transformed across space and time? What does the *Shih-shuo t'i* reveal about changing social values, standards of behavior, and attitudes toward gender in both China and Japan? Satisfactory answers to these and other such questions require new ways of thinking about a magnificent book (and an entire genre) that for too long has been marginalized and misunderstood.

The Purpose and Significance of Studying
the *Shih-shuo hsin-yü* Tradition

Despite a general recognition of the *Shih-shuo t'i*'s place in China's literary history (and, to a lesser extent, that of Japan), the genre itself has never been adequately defined nor thoroughly studied. From the seventh century to the present, the *Shih-shuo hsin-yü* and its imitations have been categorized as *hsiao-shuo* (petty talk or minor persuasions), a pejorative classification analogous to what Confucians described as the *hsiao-tao* or the "petty path"—activities that did not measure up to Confucian standards of scholarship and/or moral attainment. The stigma of *hsiao-shuo*, with its connotations of triviality and incoherence, not only blurred the distinctive identity of the *Shih-shuo hsin-yü*, but it also dimmed the glory of the Wei-Chin spirit encapsulated within it. Complicating matters further is the fact that in modern China the term *hsiao-shuo* has come to be used as the equivalent of the Western notion of "fiction," specifically the "novel."

The *Shih-shuo hsin-yü* thus occupies a strange position in Chinese literary life. When treated as a collection of Wei-Chin cultural references and historical anecdotes, it has been highly regarded, placed in a central position, and hence well studied; but, when considered as *hsiao-shuo*, it has been ignored, marginalized, and hence underexamined. Paradoxically, the term *hsiao-shuo*, as a label of inauthenticity, has often undermined the *Shih-shuo hsin-yü*'s academic reputation, and yet the undeniable academic value of the *Shih-shuo hsin-yü* as a historical source clearly challenges the modern definition of *hsiao-shuo* as "fiction." The result has been that scholars both in China and the West have failed to see the work for itself. By forcing the *Shih-shuo hsin-yü* into one or another inappropriate category, they have created a gap in our understanding of its proper place in the Chinese literary tradition.

This study, then, fills a critical gap in both Chinese and Western language scholarship on the *Shih-shuo hsin-yü* and its imitations, viewing the whole tradition as a distinct narrative genre in its own right. It offers the first thorough study in any language of the origins and evolution of the *Shih-shuo t'i*, based on a comprehensive literary analysis of the *Shih-shuo hsin-*

yü and a systematic documentation and examination of more than thirty *Shih-shuo* imitations, many of which are still unknown to specialists in Chinese literature. As a unique Chinese genre, the *Shih-shuo t'i* does not occur in other world literatures; it emerges out of particular historical conditions, and it changes as the historical conditions change. Studying this genre can teach us about the relationships between ideology, genre, and specific historical or social contexts.

This study also contributes to the growing interest in the Chinese idea of individual *identity,* expressed in concepts such as *body, self, person,* and *gender.* These terms have received considerable attention in recent years from scholars, some of whom have employed explicitly cross-cultural approaches.[2] What the *Shih-shuo hsin-yü* and its many imitations offer is a detailed understanding of what the complex process of "self-fashioning" has entailed historically in China—specifically, how competing understandings of the "self" have been expressed in Chinese literature (and life) across the boundaries of time, space, and gender. By focusing specifically on the *Shih-shuo* genre, which provided the starting point in China for a systematic literary construction of the self (see below), we can see that contrary to certain Western assertions of a timeless Chinese "tradition," an authentic understanding of issues such as personhood and gender in China was never static; rather, it changed continually and often significantly in response to changing historical and cultural circumstances.

The *Shih-shuo hsin-yü* as "Character Writing"

What kind of a book is the *Shih-shuo hsin-yü*? The following episode provides a brief illustration of the basic characteristics of this work, its genre, and its presentation of the Wei-Chin spirit:

> When Huan Wen was young, he and Yin Hao were of equal reputation, and they constantly felt a spirit of mutual rivalry. Huan once asked Yin, "How do you compare with me [*wo*]?"
>
> Yin replied, "I [*wo*] have been keeping company with myself [*wo*] a long time; I [*wo*] would rather just be me [*wo*]." (9/35)[3]

What immediately strikes us about this episode is (1) the two characters'
burning desire for self-affirmation (the character *wo,* I/me/myself, appears
five times in a thirty-character episode) and (2) their competing understandings of what it means to be a "self." Huan Wen's (312–373) understanding of self presumes a collective, hierarchical, and standardizable
value system, in which superior status serves as the standard of judgment.
For Yin Hao (306–356), however, the self is an independent, incompara-
ble entity; to yield himself to a comparison means to erase his own identity while assuming another's. Thus he declines Huan Wen's challenge in
order to keep his own "self" intact.

Two distinct personalities emerge in this brief anecdote: Huan Wen appears arrogant and blunt. Beneath his aggressive exterior, however, he is not
very confident. He initiates a comparison and assigns himself as the standard, in order to affirm his self-worth by reference to someone else. In contrast, Yin Hao's seeming restraint only reveals his pride; he refuses to compete with Huan Wen not because he is afraid of a direct clash, but because
Huan's unsophisticated challenge merits no attention. The author does not
explicitly label these traits; we have to read between the lines. In this intense, face-to-face confrontation between the two characters, the heated
atmosphere aroused by their rivalry exposes the personalities of both parties.

This episode exemplifies some basic features of the anecdotes collected
in the *Shih-shuo hsin-yü*[4]—all of them about the daily life of real historical figures, ranging from state affairs to philosophical and poetic gatherings, from public relationships to trifling domestic matters. Most of the
episodes focus not so much on recounting the details or progression of an
event as on capturing the emotional and personal characteristics of the
participants. This concern with human personality types is further elaborated in the structure of the entire book, which classifies all the episodes
into thirty-six categories.

1. "Te-hsing"   (*Te* conduct)[5]
2. "Yen-yü"   (Speech and conversation)
3. "Cheng-shih"   (Affairs of government)
4. "Wen-hsüeh"   (Literature and scholarship)
5. "Fang-cheng"   (The square and the proper)

 6. "Ya-liang"   (Cultivated tolerance)
 7. "Shih-chien"   (Recognition and judgment)
 8. "Shang-yü"   (Appreciation and praise)
 9. "P'in-tsao"   (Ranking with refined words)
10. "Kuei-chen"   (Admonitions and warnings)
11. "Chieh-wu"   (Quick perception)
12. "Su-hui"   (Precocious intelligence)
13. "Hao-shuang"   (Virility and boldness)
14. "Jung-chih"   (Appearance and manner)
15. "Tzu-hsin"   (Self-renewal)
16. "Ch'i-hsien"   (Admiration and emulation)
17. "Shang-shih"   (Grieving for the departed)
18. "Ch'i-i"   (Reclusion and disengagement)
19. "Hsien-yüan"   (Worthy beauties)
20. "Shu-chieh"   (Technical understanding)
21. "Ch'iao-i"   (Ingenious art)
22. "Ch'ung-li"   (Favor and veneration)
23. "Jen-tan"   (Uninhibitedness and eccentricity)
24. "Chien-ao"   (Rudeness and arrogance)
25. "P'ai-t'iao"   (Taunting and teasing)
26. "Ch'ing-ti"   (Contempt and insults)
27. "Chia-chüeh"   (Guile and chicanery)
28. "Ch'u-mien"   (Dismissal from office)
29. "Chien-se"   (Stinginess and meanness)
30. "T'ai-ch'ih"   (Extravagance and ostentation)
31. "Fen-Chüan"   (Anger and irascibility)
32. "Ch'an-hsien"   (Slanderousness and treachery)
33. "Yu-hui"   (Blameworthiness and remorse)
34. "P'i-lou"   (Crudities and blunders)
35. "Huo-ni"   (Delusion and infatuation)
36. "Ch'ou-hsi"   (Hostility and alienation)[6]

All these categories are related to the observation and evaluation of people: their physical appearance, innate abilities, moral qualities, psychological traits, and emotions emerging from their political and social contact with others. This system of classification sets the *Shih-shuo hsin-yü* apart from any other collection of brief narratives in the Chinese literary tradition, thus establishing a genre known to later generations as the *Shih-shuo t'i*, which I would describe in English as *character writing*. By character writing, I mean a kind of literary narrative that focuses primarily on the categorization of human character types and the characterization of "persons."[7]

The Wei-Chin Spirit as a Collective Intellectual Aura

What is the Wei-Chin spirit? This question goes side-by-side with another one: What caused the emergence of the *Shih-shuo t'i* along with the compilation of the *Shih-shuo hsin-yü*? In his effort to trace the origin of genres within world literature, Tzvetan Todorov points out that "each era has its own system of genres, which is in relation with the dominant ideology. . . . Genres, like any other institution, reveal the constitutive traits of the society to which they belong."[8] Accordingly, the *Shih-shuo hsin-yü* emerged from, and reciprocally embodied, the Wei-Chin spirit. This spirit evolved from the close interaction and mutual reinforcement of three aspects of Wei-Chin intellectual life: namely, the dominant ideology, *Hsüan-hsüeh* (dark learning or abstruse learning), the practice of *jen-lun chien-shih* (judgment and recognition of human [character] types, more succinctly translated as "character appraisal"),[9] and the growth of self-awareness.

The focal point of this intellectual interaction was character appraisal, which started in the Later Han era as the basis of selecting officials for bureaucratic posts, when leading local scholars evaluated and recommended candidates according to Confucian moral criteria. During the Wei-Chin period, character appraisal gradually shed its political emphasis and evolved into a comprehensive study of human nature. Character appraisal incited intense competition in gentry society, nurturing in turn the growth of self-awareness that had resulted from the collapse of the Han Confucian moral codes. Self-awareness furnished character appraisal with a profusion of personalities, moving the development of this practice in the direction of psychological and aesthetic concerns. In addition, both character appraisal and self-awareness sought their theoretical basis in *Hsüan-hsüeh*, hastening the systematization of this new scholarship, which involved a rereading and reevaluating of Han Confucianism in terms of Taoism and newly imported Buddhism.[10] *Hsüan-hsüeh* brought character appraisal and self-awareness from concrete concerns about one's characteristics to an ontological, psychological, and aesthetic quest for ways to understand and to express the subtle, elusive aspects of human nature.

Character appraisal involved the entire Wei-Chin elite, each member both evaluating and being evaluated. From the perspective of the evaluator, the effort to understand human nature in general and individual personality in particular triggered profound philosophic, psychological, and ethical discussions, and the need to grasp one's elusive spirit in language and other media encouraged excursions in aesthetics, linguistics, art, and literature. From the perspective of the person being evaluated (hereafter "evaluatee"), each gentry member struggled to remain true to his or her self and to express that authentic self. This self-fashioning required a constant, often painful process of identification with and differentiation from others, along with intensely personal comparisons and competitions.

Within this intellectual context, Wei-Chin character appraisal focused on *ch'uan-shen*, or "transmitting spirit." In this process, the evaluator tried to comprehend the personality of the person being evaluated through observing his or her *shen* (spirit), and the evaluatee tried to expose the unique part of his or her personality by means of the same "spiritual" vehicle. Both parties relied heavily upon words to convey the spirit. To be sure, Chinese intellectuals had long recognized the limitations of language. In the words of the "Great Commentary" of the *I-ching* (Book of changes), "Writing does not completely express speech, nor does speech completely express ideas" (*shu pu chin yen, yen pu chin i*).[11] The *Lao-tzu* also tells us, "Those who know do not speak, and those who speak do not know" (*chih-che pu yen, yen-che pu chih*).[12] Yet instead of eschewing words, the Taoists used "all available resources of literary art" to express meanings.[13]

Following this Taoist solution to the linguistic paradox, which was later enriched by the similar concerns (and solutions) of Buddhism, Wei-Chin character appraisal contributed substantially to the literary construction of the self in China. The *Shih-shuo hsin-yü* epitomized this Wei-Chin intellectual effort. It "transmitted the spirit" of over six hundred historical figures in the book, collectively reflecting the spirit of the age. This unique Wei-Chin style and manner, sustained by an extraordinarily eccentric, sensitive, and intellectually sophisticated elite group, became known to later generations as the *Wei-Chin feng-liu* (literally, Wei-Chin winds and currents), *Wei-Chin feng-tu* (Wei-Chin winds and manner), or *Wei-Chin shen-yün* (Wei-Chin spirit consonance)—in short, what I have termed the Wei-Chin "spirit." This spirit can best be summarized as a relentless effort to realize and to manifest appropriately one's true self.

The *Shih-shuo hsin-yü* left to later generations a two-fold legacy. It transmitted a spirit that continued to inspire Chinese intellectuals to find (and express) their authentic "self." It also created a literary genre that yielded dozens of imitations. These imitations dutifully categorized collections of historical anecdotes according to the *Shih-shuo hsin-yü*'s system of classification. They also modified this model in order to conform in a more satisfactory way to their own understandings of the "self" and their respective social environments and cultural purposes. The *Shih-shuo hsin-yü* thus offered to later generations (and other societies) something other than a piece of China's mute and passive cultural heritage; instead, it made the Wei-Chin spirit an active factor in the formation (or at least expression) of the cultural values and systems of later periods.

Basic Structure of the Book

This book consists of ten chapters, divided into three parts, each of which addresses a particular theme concerning the transmission of the Wei-Chin spirit across space and time.

Part 1 shows how the late Han and Wei-Chin practice of character appraisal (*jen-lun chien-shih*) gave rise to the *Shih-shuo t'i*. Chapter 1 traces the evolution of the term *jen-lun chien-shih* from its early use as the basis for selecting officials to a comprehensive study of human nature. This evolutionary process, as indicated in chapter 2, involved a growth in self-awareness, encouraged by the debates and discussions of *Hsüan-hsüeh* in the Wei-Chin period. These debates and discussions revolved around various categories of complementary opposition such as *ming* and *shih* (name and actuality), *yu* and *wu* (something and nothing), *yen* and *i* (words and meanings), *hsing* and *shen* (body and spirit)—establishing a series of ontological, psychological, and aesthetic principles by which to recognize one's personality and to realize one's authentic self. Formed in this unique intellectual environment and designed to reflect its collective aura, the *Shih-shuo t'i* is, as chapter 3 explains at length, sui generis. To categorize it as *hsiao-shuo* is both a misclassification and a distortion.

Part 2 introduces the narrative art of the *Shih-shuo hsin-yü*, the means by which the work displayed idiosyncratic Wei-Chin personalities and transmitted the Wei-Chin spirit. Within part 2, chapter 4 examines the narrative structure of the *Shih-shuo hsin-yü* and its new taxonomy of human nature. Each of its thirty-six chapter titles summarizes and is in turn defined by the anecdotes assigned to that chapter. Together, they reflect the four major aspects of the collective Wei-Chin character: *te* (potentiality, capacity, efficacy); *ts'ai* (innate ability, talent, specialty); *hsing* (temperament, disposition, temper); and *ch'ing* (feeling, emotion, passion). All the categories involved in this taxonomy are redefined in terms of Wei-Chin *Hsüan-hsüeh* understandings of human nature. This structure also displays the linguistic paradox between the impossibility of ordering human nature with words and the necessity of doing so; hence a taxonomy of human nature oscillating between order and disorder.

Chapter 5 gives detailed attention to problems of characterization in the *Shih-shuo hsin-yü*. What, for example, bridges the conceptual gap between a cluster of linguistic signs and a "living person"? How is it possible to anchor a person's elusive "spirit" with mere words? Influenced by the Wei-Chin idea that the "self" emerges from a relentless communication (and confrontation) with others, and with Nature, the *Shih-shuo* author consistently weaves the characters in each of his anecdotes into a network of dynamic relationships. Moreover, based on the intense competition prevailing in Wei-Chin gentry society, he creatively structures many a *Shih-shuo* anecdote following what I term the "rivalry pattern," which condenses human relationships into a single basic unit. Thus, instead of offering the reader one psychological entity composed of an assortment of static personality traits, the author offers an intense psychological relationship between at least two "rivals." The tension in between generates a dynamic power that draws the reader into an open-ended reconstruction of their respective personalities.[14]

Part 3 shows how *Shih-shuo t'i* works emerged as a complement to the standard Chinese histories, focusing on the self-fashioning of the intellectual elite instead of political events. This process manifests elements of both continuity and change. On the one hand, the dozens of *Shih-shuo* imitations produced in both China and Japan over 1,600 years attest to the enduring literary importance of the *Shih-shuo t'i;* on the other hand, they reveal a subversion of the original genre, since each work evolved in response to different patterns of thought and behavior—particularly with respect to versions produced in non-Chinese environments. Because the *Shih-shuo* imitations departed from the intellectual milieu of the Wei-Chin period, and also because they served different cultural purposes, they naturally could not meet the high standards of its original work. Nonetheless, by consciously following the *Shih-shuo* model, they were able to capture and reflect at least part of its vibrant spirit.

To be sure, the *Shih-shuo hsin-yü* and its imitations did not attempt to describe all of society. Their interest fell mainly on a special group of people, the *shih,* or *ming-shih,* the "famous *shih.*" *Shih,* as a collective name for the Chinese intellectual elite, had come into existence as early as the Spring and Autumn period (ca. 720–480 B.C.), and it continued to refer to this group throughout the imperial era. Over this long period, the self-image of *shih* underwent enormous changes; thus I have tried to delineate the social identity of the *shih* at various times in terms of the materials provided by the relevant *Shih-shuo t'i* works. I have also sought guidance from various studies dealing with the intellectual life of the periods under consideration.[15] As for the rendering of *shih* and its other variants, I shall compromise between common translations in English-language scholarship and the original meanings within the Chinese context. Therefore, I shall use the terms *gentry, gentlemen,* and *intellectual elite* for *shih* as a collective social group; *gentleman* or *scholar* for individual *shih*; *scholar-official* for *shih ta-fu*; and *literati* for expressions such as *wen-shih* and *wen-jen*.

Significantly, in *Shih-shuo t'i*, the term *shih* includes women. The *Shih-shuo hsin-yü* not only records their stories in various chapters, but also dedicates to them an entire chapter, "Hsien-yüan" (Worthy beauties). In this chapter, we can see that a strong Wei-Chin flavor has permeated the word *hsien*, or "worthy," distinguishing it from its conventional signification as a Confucian moral category. Under this heading and, indeed, throughout the entire book, women are evaluated on equal terms with men. They are expected to be active, talented, articulate, and self-confident, rather than passive, mute, and submissive—standards traditionally dictated for Chinese women. Moreover, they are celebrated especially for their indispensable roles as evaluators in the character appraisal of both men and women— roles essentially denied to women prior to the Wei-Chin period. Almost all *Shih-shuo* imitations follow this tradition by including a "Worthy Beauties" chapter, and two such works, both titled *Nü Shih-shuo* (Women *Shih-shuo* [*hsin-yü*])—one by a male author and the other by a female—focus entirely on women. Although each period in Chinese history had its own particular standards for women, often defined in terms of orthodox Confucian morality, overall, under the influence of the Wei-Chin spirit, *Shih-shuo t'i* offered diverse images of women, thus providing a more complete picture of their attainments than conventional literary and historical sources.

Narratological Terms

Terms such as *character, trait, personality,* and *characterization* appear repeatedly in this book. What links this sort of English usage to Chinese reality as reflected in the *Shih-shuo hsin-yü*? Let us begin with the word *character*, since the *Shih-shuo hsin-yü* focuses squarely on the practice of character writing.

Etymologically, the English word *character* is a letter-to-letter transcription of the Greek word χαρακτήρ, which is defined as "that which is cut in or marked, the impress or stamp on coins, seals, etc."[16] Metaphorically, it means "the mark or token impressed on a person or thing, a characteristic, distinctive mark, character."[17] In its meaning "to impress," χαρακτήρ is linked to another Greek word, τύπος, which means "impression, figure, type."[18] In this sense, χαρακτήρ evolved into a narrative term, with "human types" as its referent. The Greek philosopher Theophrastus (371–287 B.C.), one of Aristotle's disciples, wrote a book titled χαρακτήρες, or "the characters," in which he categorized human character into thirty distinctive types. Many of them overlap with those among the *Shih-shuo hsin-yü* chapter titles. Because of this structural similarity between the *Shih-shuo t'i* and Theophrastan character writing, I feel especially comfortable using the English word *character,* which fully adopts the Greek word χαρακτήρ in form and in meaning,[19] in my analysis of the *Shih-shuo hsin-yü* and its imitations.

Since the mid-seventeenth century, the English word *character* gradually gained another meaning: "The sum of the moral and mental qualities which distinguish an individual or a race, viewed as a homogeneous whole; the individuality impressed by nature and habit on man or nation; mental or moral constitution."[20] This later definition of the word *character* has been widely accepted in modern times. For example, the *Dictionary of Philosophy* defines *character* as the "totality of mental traits characterizing an individual personality or self."[21]

This later meaning of *character* has also entered narrative theory. Roland Barthes thus delimits its narratological meaning: "The character is a product of combinations: the combination is relatively stable (denoted by the recurrence of the semes [voice of the person]) and more or less complex (involving more or less congruent, more or less contradictory figures [traits]); this complexity determines the character's 'personality,' which is just as much a combination as the odor of a dish or the bouquet of a wine."[22] What sets the original nature of the narrative term *character* apart from its modern sense is that the former, according to the Oxford definition, is equivalent to "type," or "trait," whereas the latter is the sum or combination of traits that determines the character's "personality"—the way that combinations of ingredients contribute to "the odor of a dish or the bouquet of a wine."

From a psychological standpoint, a "trait" may be defined as "the unit or element which is the carrier of the distinctive behavior of a man . . . a generalized response-unit in which resides the distinctive quality of behavior that reflects personality."[23] In his pioneering psycholexical study of 1931, Allport lists 17,953 trait names, such as affectionate, arrogant, brave, calculating, considerate, egoistic, guileful, hostile, humorous, hypocritical, intelligent, irascible, just, lofty, open-minded, reclusive, righteous, rude, sentimental, stingy, tactful, treacherous, vigorous, worthy, zealous, and so forth.[24] While one trait reflects a relatively persistent behavioral feature of a person, traits in combination form a unique personality.[25]

This discussion of traits should help to clarify the two senses of the narrative term *character*. Originally, *character* referred to an independent trait, but later it came to denote a variety of combinations of these traits in a single person. Corresponding to these two definitions of the narrative term *character* are two kinds of characterization: the typal characterization, and the characterization of a "person" in narrative. The former enumerates typical actions dictated by a trait in order to manifest the distinctive quality of this type. The latter, according to most Western studies, such as Barthes' and Allport's, seems to be a mere mechanical accumulation of various traits, which, as we will see later, meets a strong challenge in the *Shih-shuo hsin-yü.*

The *Shih-shuo hsin-yü* contains both kinds of characterization. If we view its episodes from the perspective of the thirty-six chapter titles, of which most are trait names, then the episodes under each chapter title will present actions that exemplify a particular human type. If we view the *Shih-shuo* episodes from the perspective of its 626 historical figures, then the anecdotes under each individual, usually traversing various chapters, will serve to reflect his or her personality. This second kind of characterization in the *Shih-shuo hsin-yü,* the creation of "persons," suggests a far more sophisticated process than what the Western narratologists cited above have delineated. By analyzing the characterization samples and reading the theoretical discussions in the *Shih-shuo hsin-yü,* we can see that a mere accumulation of traits fails to present a lifelike human figure. In order to transmit a "person's" true spirit, the author should portray him or her in relation to others. Only thus can authentic character be revealed through dynamic interhuman confrontations. To avoid confusion between the two meanings of characterization, I shall refer to the typal characterization in the *Shih-shuo hsin-yü* as the taxonomy of human nature, and use the term *characterization* only for the creation of a "person" in narrative.

Although this study adopts primarily a literary—and especially a narratological—approach, it also ventures into such diverse fields as philosophy, aesthetics, psychology, hermeneutics, and gender criticism. Each of these realms boasts a vast theoretical literature in a variety of Western languages. Although I have drawn on some of this literature in this study, I have relied predominantly upon the *Shih-shuo hsin-yü* itself for theoretical guidance because of its highly reflexive feature.

The principles that dictated the creation of the *Shih-shuo hsin-yü* and its genre came directly from its records of *ch'ing-yen,* "pure talk," or "pure conversation," the major Wei-Chin intellectual activity that incorporated discussions of *Hsüan-hsüeh,* character appraisal, and self-awareness.[26] Episodes related to pure conversation and the life of its participants dominate the *Shih-shuo hsin-yü;* hence alternative names for the work include *Ch'ing-yen lin-yu* (Wooded garden of pure conversation)[27] or *Ch'ing-yen yüan-sou* (The valleys and forests of pure conversation).[28] For this reason, my analysis of the *Shih-shuo hsin-yü* and its genre relies primarily on theories abstracted both from the theoretical statements recorded in the text and from the allegorical messages revealed in its quotidian episodes. By the same token, my examination of later imitations heavily relies upon their prefaces, commentaries, and episodes, for, as some scholars have recently noted: "Future scholarship that seeks to be global or comparative, be it literary, cultural, and historical studies, or research in the social sciences, must first develop strategies for analysis and interpretation that allow narratives of historical development different from Western ones an equal opportunity to explain the past and understand links to the present."[29]

I hope that my study of the *Shih-shuo* tradition may serve as a worthy example of a China-centered approach to the material.

Part 1

From Character Appraisal to Character Writing: The Formation of the *Shih-shuo* Genre

Introduction to Part 1:
Shih-shuo t'i, the Term and the Genre

The Grand Historian Ssu-ma Ch'ien traveled among famous mountains and huge rivers under heaven, and then completed the *Shih-chi* (Records of the grand historian) following his single will. The Left Minister Ch'ü Yüan, tortured by slanders and jealousy, chanted along the marsh bank and then composed the *Li-sao* (Encountering sorrow) following his single will. Had someone there impeded them from spelling out their thoughts and imposed upon them this or that sort of advice, neither the *Shih-chi* nor *Li-sao* could have been written. The *Shih-shuo hsin-yü* by the Liu-Sung Prince of Lin-chuan, Liu I-ch'ing, is also such a single-minded work.

During the Wei-Chin period, pure conversation was in vogue. Its subtle and systematic arguments were composed of terse words, well crafted but still full of wisdom, simple yet sophisticated. The [Wei-Chin conversationalists] bore an elegant and refined appearance and behavior, with which they commenced a new, extraordinary style. Once these words and style were put in writing, they made the reader ponder and dwell on the text without ever getting bored. The [*Shih-shuo hsin-yü*] is like the beauty in the mirror, the colorful clouds in the sky, the moisture on the surface of the ocean, and the lingering taste of olives. None of the dozens of later *Shih-shuo t'i* works can go beyond its scope.
—Ch'eng Hsü, Preface to the reprint of the *Shih-shuo hsin-yü*, 1694

The term *Shih-shuo t'i* first appeared in Ch'ao Kung-wu's (fl. mid-twelfth century) *Chün-chai tu-shu chih* (Bibliographic treatise from the prefectural studio),[1] after the early wave of *Shih-shuo* imitations arose during the T'ang-Sung periods. Although the term has since recurred often in different academic works,[2] and although *Shih-shuo t'i* as an influential genre has been historically affirmed by the *Shih-shuo hsin-yü* and its dozens of imitations, its generic characteristics remain obscure.

The *Shih-shuo hsin-yü* has remained in the category of *hsiao-shuo* in the sense of "petty talk" or "minor persuasions" since its first appearance in the "Sui Treatise."[3] Following this basic categorization, Ch'ao Kung-wu coined the term *Shih-shuo t'i* and defined the genre as "recounting . . . *yen* (words)/*shih* (events) in categories."[4] This definition thereafter has been recognized as the fundamental characteristic of the *Shih-shuo t'i*. For instance, Chi Yün (1724-1805) repeatedly refers to this description in the *Ssu-k'u ch'üan-shu tsung-mu* (Annotated catalogue of the complete collection of the four treasuries, hereafter the *Four Treasuries*) when introducing *Shih-shuo t'i* works.[5] Similarly, Lu Hsün (1881-1936) summarizes the *Shih-shuo hsin-yü* as "putting [episodes] together by categories."[6] Ning Chia-yü elaborates on these observations: "*Shih-shuo t'i* refers to a kind of structure of 'tales about people' [*chih-jen hsiao-shuo*], as represented by the *Shih-shuo hsin-yü*. It classifies the collected tales about different individuals into several categories; each presents a specific theme."[7]

All these descriptions touch on an essential feature of the *Shih-shuo t'i*—the classification of brief narratives—but they fail to characterize the genre in a more specific sense. For one thing, *hsiao-shuo* as a category in Chinese tradition has been so amorphous that it blurs different characteristics of the works lumped under it. For another, to classify human words and actions into types is by no means peculiar to the *Shih-shuo t'i*; rather, it appears to be a basic rhetorical technique used in a number of Chinese literary genres. In these cases, it is usually not the classification itself but the principles and purposes underlying the classification that delineate a specific genre.

Ch'en Yin-k'o (1890-1969) suggests that the principles that yielded the *Shih-shuo hsin-yü* classification arose from an intellectual practice prevailing during the last part of the Later Han (25-220) and the Wei-Chin period. Ch'en names it *p'in-t'i jen-lun*, or "ranking and characterizing human types," which, as I will discuss later, is only one of several of Chinese terms for character appraisal, as Chen observes: "The book of [*Shih-shuo hsin-yü*] classifies [its anecdotes] into a number of categories, and titles them with names such as the four divisions of Confucius' disciples [*K'ung-men ssu-k'o*], including (1) '*Te* Conduct,' (2) 'Speech and Conversation,' (3) 'Affairs of Government,' and (4) 'Writing and Scholarship.' Among the others there are also 'Recognition and Judgment,' 'Appreciation and Praise,' 'Classification and Embellishment,' and so forth. [This classification] obviously results from Later Han gentlemen's practice of ranking and characterizing human types."[8]

Ch'en's observation puts us on the right track for pursuing the origin of the *Shih-shuo* classification, but it leaves us with more questions than answers: What is the nature of *p'in-t'i jen-lun*? When, how, and why did it arise, flourish, and then fade? Who participated in it, with what purposes and what consequences, and upon whose standards and by which methodology? How was it related to the classification of the *Shih-shuo hsin-yü* and then the formation of the *Shih-shuo t'i*? Why did it lead to this kind of classification instead of others? My major task in Part 1, therefore, is to search for possible answers to these questions, using evidence mainly drawn from the *Shih-shuo hsin-yü* itself. Based on this exploration, I hope to redefine the *Shih-shuo t'i* as a new literary genre in its own right and with its own unique raison d'être. Such a self-invented genre, as I shall also argue, was created by and hence reveals the salient features of the Wei-Chin period.

Chapter 1

Character Appraisal:
The Foundation of the *Shih-shuo t'i*

What is Character Appraisal?

Various Chinese terms for the concept *character appraisal* circulated in late Han and Wei-Chin gentry circles. Both the *Shih-shuo hsin-yü* and the historical references quoted in its extensive and corroborative commentary by Liu Chün (462–521) abundantly document this practice.[1] In these records, character appraisal is known most fully as *jen-lun chien-shih*, with shortened forms such as *jen-lun chien*, *chih-jen chien*, *chih-jen shih*, *chih-jen*, *jen-lun*, *chien-shih*, *shih-chien*, or simply, *shih*, *chien*, or *lun*.[2] Technical actions that often accompany this practice include *p'in* (ranking), *p'ing* (commenting, evaluating), *t'i* (characterizing), and *mu* (evaluating, characterizing).[3]

To my knowledge, the term *jen-lun chien-shih* did not appear until the late Han and Wei-Chin periods. Here are some examples from Liu Chün's commentary.

> *A Variant Version of the Biography of [Kuo] T'ai* says: "[Kuo] T'ai [128–169] . . . had the perspicuous ability of *jen-lun chien-shih*. All the gentlemen within the realm whom he had characterized or ranked, some as youths and some not yet recognized (literally, yet in their home villages), later became outstanding and accomplished men—more than sixty in all. He himself wrote a book to discuss the theoretical basis of selecting scholars; but, before it had gained currency, it encountered the disorders (i.e., the Yellow Turban Revolt) and was lost."[4]

> *A Variant Version of the Biography of Ssu-ma Hui* says: "Ssu-ma Hui [d. 208] had a perspicuous ability of *jen-lun chien-shih*. While Hui was living in Ching Province he realized that the governor, Liu Piao, was of

a dark, secretive disposition, and that he would surely do injury to good men, so he kept his mouth shut and engaged in no discussions or consultations. If any of his contemporaries inquired of him about any person, he would not pass judgment, whether high or low, but would uniformly say, 'The man's excellent.'"⁵

The Spring and Autumn Annals of the Chin says: "[Wang] Yen [256–311] had a flourishing reputation, and his contemporaries attributed to him a perspicuous ability of jen-lun chien-shih. He once evaluated the gentlemen of the realm, saying: 'Wang Ch'eng is number one; Yü Ai number two; and Wang Tun number three.'"⁶

The Spring and Autumn Annals of the Chin says: "[Wang] Chi [ca. 240–ca. 285] had a perspicuous ability of jen-lun chien-shih. Since a young man, he had exceeded others in differentiating the elegant from the vulgar and the right from the wrong."⁷

Conceptualized within the above context, an early reference relevant to the jen-lun in jen-lun chien-shih may be traced back to the Li-chi (Record of rites): "A person [jen] should be compared only with those of his own category [lun]."⁸ In his commentary on this line, Tu Yü (222–284) points out that "lun is similar to lei (category or type). An official should be compared with other officials, and a gentleman with other gentlemen."⁹ As a Chin scholar, Tu Yü must have been acutely aware of the prevalence of the jen-lun chien-shih, and his interpretation of lun no doubt reflects the common understanding of the term jen-lun in his time. Confined by the text on which he comments, Tu Yü here limits lun to social ranking, but the overall idea of jen-lun referring to "human types" is clear.

As for chien-shih, Han sources have chien referring to "mirror," which "is used to observe or check one's appearance,"¹⁰ and shih, meaning "to know."¹¹ Chien and shih together signify judging (chien) and knowing or recognizing (shih) something (say, human types). Further, as a word compound, chien-shih was interchangeable with shih-chien during the Wei-Chin period. For example, Liu Chün's commentary has two accounts that relate the Chin gentleman Huan I (275–328) to this intellectual practice. One says: "Huan I had a perspicuous ability of jen-lun chien-shih,"¹² and the other says: "[Huan I's] shih-chien was clear and bright."¹³ The Shih-shuo hsin-yü also includes a chapter titled "Shih-chien," which recounts anecdotes illustrating the recognition and judgment of human types. Thus we may render *jen-lun chien-shih* into English as the "judgment and recognition of human types"—or "character appraisal" for short.

Standing by itself, *jen-lun* had two meanings during the late Han and the Wei-Chin periods. One, as discussed above, means "human types" and was often used to substitute for *jen-lun chien-shih*. The other refers to hierarchical and proper human relationships, following a usage in the *Meng-tzu*: "This gave the sage king further cause for concern, and so he appointed Hsieh as the Minister of Education whose duty was to teach the people human relationships: love between father and son, duty between ruler and subject, distinction between husband and wife, precedence of the old over the young, and [faithfulness] between friends."[14]

Both meanings co-exist in the *Shih-shuo hsin-yü* and in Liu Chün's commentary and may be differentiated only through their contexts. Consider the following two examples:

> *The Biographies of the Worthies of Ju-nan* says: "Hsieh Chen . . . intelligently recognized human types [*jen-lun*]. Even Kuo T'ai could not measure up to him in judging [people]." (Liu Chün's commentary on the *Shih-shuo hsin-yü*, 8/3)
>
> The grand tutor and Prince of Tung-hai, [Ssu-ma Yüeh], . . . in instructing his heir, P'i, wrote: "a desultory memorization of the rules of etiquette can't compare with emulating a living model of proper behavior. . . . My aide, Wang Ch'eng, is the model of [keeping] proper human relations [*jen-lun chih piao*]; take him as your teacher!" (*Shih-shuo hsin-yü*, 8/34)[15]

Here, the first example ties *jen-lun* to the typical character appraisal terms *shih* (recognizing) and *chien* (judging) and compares Hsieh Chen with the late Han character-appraisal adept, Kuo T'ai. Given such a context, we can infer that *jen-lun* means human character. The second example relates *jen-lun* to "rules of etiquette" and "proper behavior," and in this sense the term acquires a moral connotation and can be understood as "proper human relations."

The clearest example linking *jen-lun* to character appraisal is in Fan Yeh's (398–445) *Hou-Han shu* (History of the late Han), a work contemporary with the *Shih-shuo hsin-yü*, written around 430. Fan Yeh puts Kuo T'ai and Hsü Shao (150–195) in the same biography, praising Kuo as "good at *jen-lun*," and describing Hsü as "fond of *jen-lun*."[16] Fan writes: "When Hsü Shao . . . was young, he distinguished himself as having a salient reputation and integrity. He was fond of *jen-lun* and contributed a great amount of appraisal and recognition [of gentlemanly qualities]. . . . Therefore, the entire realm acclaimed Hsü Shao and Kuo T'ai the most talented in recognizing good scholars. . . . Hsü Shao and [his cousin] Hsü Ching both enjoyed high reputations in this regard, and they were fond of judging their fellow countrymen. Every month they would change their objects of ranking and characterizing; thus in Ju-nan there used to be a term 'monthly evaluation.'"[17] Judging from the unmistakable markers of character appraisal in this passage—terms such as "appraisal and recognition" (*shang-shih*), "judging" (*chiao-lun*), "ranking" (*p'in*), "characterizing" (*t'i*), and "evaluation" (*p'ing*)—*jen-lun* here undoubtedly refers to character appraisal.

The passages quoted above describe some of the most important figures in late Han and Wei-Chin character appraisal—Kuo T'ai (127–169), Hsü Shao (150–195), Ssu-ma Hui (d. 208), Wang Chi (ca. 240–ca. 285), Wang Yen (256–311), Huan I (275–328), and others—and provide some general information about this intellectual practice. First, character appraisal prospered from the late Han (Kuo T'ai and Hsü Shao's time) throughout the Eastern Chin (Huan I's time), and it was often conducted on a regular basis, such as the Ju-nan "monthly evaluation." Second, character appraisal always judged gentlemanly qualities in terms of comparisons, such as high and low, elegant and vulgar, right and wrong. In so doing, the practice served certain social and political purposes (e.g., selecting officials for government positions) and had certain personal consequences (e.g., bringing fame to some evaluatees and harm to some others). Third, character appraisal not only judged other people's inner qualities and abilities but also exposed important qualities and abilities of the evaluators themselves. Finally, most relevant to this study of the *Shih-shuo hsin-yü*, the desire to analyze the practice of character appraisal led to the compilation of works devoted to the topic, such as Kuo T'ai's work on the "theoretical basis of selecting scholars." This same desire instigated compilation of the *Shih-shuo hsin-yü,* as I shall demonstrate later in this chapter.[18] In brief, character appraisal was not merely an isolated activity; it was inextricably linked to late Han and Wei-Chin social, political, and intellectual life.

Character Appraisal as a Speech Act

How did character appraisal influence the formation of the *Shih-shuo* genre? Lu Hsün touches on this question in recounting the emergence of some works antecedent to the *Shih-shuo:*

> Scholars towards the end of the Han dynasty attached great importance to [ranking and evaluating human character] [*p'in-mu*]: fame or infamy might depend on a single expression of praise or condemnation. From the third and fourth centuries onwards, much thought was also given to the choice of words in conversation: men's talk was metaphysical and their behaviour unconventional and liberal, differing in these respects from the Han dynasty when absolute moral integrity and rectitude were the ideal. . . . After the house of [Chin] moved its capital south of the Yangtse, this fashion became even more pronounced. . . . Since this was the vogue, anecdotes and sayings were compiled from ancient records or contemporary society. Though these works contain nothing but an assortment of *bons mots* and dictums [*ts'ung-ts'an hsiao-yü*], they reflect the spirit of the age and they developed into a literary genre distinct from the tales of the supernatural.[19]

In Lu Hsün's view, the rapid popularization of character appraisal during the late Han and the Wei-Chin periods resulted in the formation of the *Shih-shuo* genre within the framework of the *Shih-shuo hsin-yü.* This process transformed character appraisal from a spoken discourse into a written one, and it eventually evolved into an independent literary genre. In this manner, late Han and Wei-Chin character appraisal functioned as a "speech act," which made possible the *Shih-shuo t'i.*

Todorov suggests that "the identity of the genre comes from the speech act that is at its base"[20]—more specifically, from the codification of the discursive properties of this speech act.[21] What kind of speech act does character appraisal entail? What features constitute its discursive properties? How do they join together to form a discourse? Consider for example a relatively "original" historical account of character appraisal that is not yet codified into a character-writing episode. It is quoted by Liu Chün from Sun Sheng's (ca. 302–373) *Tsa-yü* (Miscellaneous accounts), compiled at least a half century earlier than the *Shih-shuo:* "Ts'ao Ts'ao once asked Hsü Shao, 'What sort of person am I?' After he had asked insistently, Shao finally answered: 'An able minister in an age of order, and a treacherous warrior in an age of disorder.' Ts'ao Ts'ao laughed aloud."[22]

This episode presents a character appraisal in two parts: its text and context. The text consists of Hsü Shao's characterization of Ts'ao Ts'ao, evaluating his ability and moral qualities in two opposite political contexts, an age of order and an age of disorder. This feature establishes character appraisal as an evaluator's comment on an evaluatee's inner qualities in response to the outer world. The context consists of the relationship between the evaluator and the evaluatee and their relationship with the text. In this case, a tension exists clearly between the evaluator and the evaluatee: Hsü Shao hesitates to respond to Ts'ao Ts'ao's insistent request, finally giving Ts'ao a dichotomistic evaluation—one complementary and the other pejorative; Ts'ao at any rate accepts this contentious comment with obvious pleasure. The tension reflects the two participants' different standards and purposes, rooted in their respective social, political, cultural, and/or ethical backgrounds.

The practice of character appraisal spanned a historical period of about 350 years, from the Late Han to the end of the Eastern Chin (approximately A.D. 76–420). A close examination of its historical evolution and its interactions with other intellectual or cultural influences will expose how character appraisal eventually led to the formation of the *Shih-shuo t'i*. In what follows, I shall divide this historical period into several chronological sections, reconstruct the character appraisal practices of each section via relevant historical records and studies, and then compare these changes with the *Shih-shuo hsin-yü* accounts. I will review this evolving process by means of categories that will include the identity of the evaluators and the evaluatees, their relationships, the standards upon which the evaluations were based, and the purposes of this activity. (There is yet one more important category, the methodology of the appraisal, to be discussed in chapter 2, in relation to the evolution of the *Hsüan-hsüeh*.) In this way I hope to show how the discursive properties of character appraisal as a speech act were codified into the properties of *Shih-shuo t'i*.

A Historical Survey of Character Appraisal

Roughly speaking, character appraisal went through four different historical stages: (1) the rise of character appraisal as the basis of the Late Han selection system (ca. A.D. 76–147); (2) the morality-oriented stage, occurring with the struggle between scholar-official cliques and eunuchs, beginning with the reign of Emperor Huan and ending with the Yellow Turban Uprising (ca. 147–184); (3) the ability-oriented stage during the Han-Wei transitional period (ca. 184–239); and (4) the aesthetics-oriented stage from early Wei to the end of Chin (ca. 240–420). All these periods overlapped with each other, without clear demarcation between them.

THE RISE OF CHARACTER APPRAISAL (CA. 76–147)

The first period saw the rise of character appraisal along with the Later Han reaffirmation of the Han selection system.[23] According to Tu Yu's (735–812) *T'ung-tien* (Compendium of laws and institutions), this system was first founded in the Former Han, during the reign of Emperor Wu-ti (r. 140–87 B.C.). The selection procedure included *ch'a-chü* (the local government's "observation and recommendation") and *cheng-p'i* (the central government's "invitation and selection"), or *p'i-chao* (the central government's "selection and summons").[24] The standards of selection were known as *ssu-k'o p'i-shih* (four categories of selecting scholars), among which the first demanded that candidates "have lofty, clean, virtuous conduct and be of pure integrity," and the second demanded that candidates "be well-versed in the Confucian classics and cultivated in their moral behavior."[25] Understandably, such procedures and standards, with their strong Confucian ethical orientation, made the selection process heavily reliant upon the observations and comments of leading local Confucians. They were, after all, the most familiar with both Confucian moral teachings and the candidates' moral performance.

It was not until the reign of Emperor Chang-ti (r. 76–88) of the Later Han, however, that the government clearly emphasized the importance of local Confucians' comments and recommendations in the selection system. As Emperor Chang-ti decreed in A.D. 76: "The local selection should be based upon the candidate's accumulated merits and deeds, yet at present governors and prefects cannot tell the true from the false. Each year they recommended hundreds of the 'outstanding talents' and the 'filial and incorrupt,' yet these candidates are neither capable nor famous. To entrust state affairs to them is quite senseless. I often recall that, in the previous dynasties, gentlemen were sometimes selected from the fields, not on the basis of their pedigree."[26] The emperor felt unsatisfied because the selection had skipped the townspeople's scrutiny and operated directly through higher levels of local government and even the court. The government then had no way to find out about the candidates' moral quality. Immediately after this decree, Emperor Chang-ti mandated the restoration of the Former Han four-category standard of selecting officials. While all the selected candidates had to go through probation, those who "excelled in virtuous conduct" could assume their office directly.[27]

This decree by Emperor Chang-ti was the turning point for the Later Han selection system. It placed overwhelming emphasis on the local evaluation of candidates' moral behavior; hence the year of the decree, A.D. 76, should be taken as the "official" starting point of character appraisal.[28] As leading local Confucians' evaluations assumed increasing importance, they tended to impose more rigorous and detailed moral standards on the candidates. Consequently, the Later Han selection categories rapidly multiplied in a moral direction. Fan Yeh remarks in the *History of the Later Han:* "At the beginning of the Former Han, the emperor decreed the nomination of [gentlemen who were] worthy and outstanding and square and upright. The states and prefectures recommended [gentlemen who were]

filial and incorrupt, or of flourishing talents. . . . When it came to the Later
Han, more categories were added, such as honest and ingenuous, possessing the *Tao,* worthy and talented, frankly spoken, uniquely behaved,
loftily integrated, plain and straightforward, pure and innocent, honest and
clement, and so forth."[29]

Hence, at this early stage of "character appraisal," the local leading
scholars served as evaluators and the candidates for offices became evaluatees. The purpose of this "speech act" was to supply qualified candidates for government positions. In the process of evaluation, Confucian
moral doctrines held enormous sway. Since the early third century, this
initial stage of "character appraisal" became known as *ch'ing-i* (pure criticism), a term that, throughout the Wei-Chin and Southern dynasties periods, denoted the local comments on gentlemen based on Confucian moral
standards.[30]

Ironically, at the very peak of its moral-political function, character appraisal was already becoming an independent quest for understanding human nature—a quest increasingly removed from Han moral-political standards. Witness the selection categories listed above: The Former Han
steadfastly emphasized Confucian societal norms, such as *hsien-liang* (worthy and outstanding), *fang-cheng* (square and upright), *hsiao-lien* (filial and
incorrupt), and *hsiu-ts'ai* (flourishing talents), categories that linked a filial
son to a future good minister. The Later Han, however, introduced a number of new categories, some of which were far removed from Confucian
moral standards. Take for example the category *tu-hsing* (uniquely behaved). It prevailed among the Later Han gentry to such a degree that the
History of the Later Han contains a chapter titled "Tu-hsing lie-chuan" (Collective biographies of the uniquely behaved), devoted to many people who
did not conform to conventional social norms. Fan Yeh's preface to this
chapter comments: "Confucius said, 'Having failed to find the Middle Way,
one would, if there were no alternative, have to turn either uninhibited or
rigid [*k'uang-chüan*].' He also said, 'The uninhibited is enterprising, while
the rigid will reject certain kinds of action.' . . . Yet, if one rejects certain
kinds of action, he must stick to some others; if one is enterprising in some
way, he must be inactive in some other way. Thus, natural tendencies di-

verge, and doing and not-doing go in opposite directions."[31] One can see clearly here a self-willed and self-inventive tendency that came from and at the same time went beyond dictated norms. Fan's remarks, together with other evidence, suggest a rise in "individualism," a growing desire for self-expression, and a deviation from orthodox Confucian values in the Later Han period—all three of which presaged dominant intellectual trends in the Wei-Chin era.[32]

One indication of the distortion and decline in Late Han Confucianism was a corruption of categories (their proliferation was only a symptom of this problem, not the cause). As Fan Yeh remarks: "When ways of obtaining official positions were broadened, hypocrisy and camouflage soon gained currency."[33] Similarly, Wang Fu (ca. 85–162) wrote: "Among the officials who selected gentlemen, some nominated the stupid and boorish as Flourishing Talents, the conceited and recalcitrant as of Superior Filial Piety, the corrupt and avaricious as Incorrupt Officials, the devious and cunning as Sincere and Upright, the servile and sycophantic as Frankly Spoken, the flippant and superficial as Honest and Ingenuous, the empty and hollow as Possessing the Way, the stupid and mute as Knowledgeable of the Classics, the cruel and harsh as Clement and Considerate, the timid and weak as Martial and Fierce, and the benighted and obtuse as Resolvers of the Problematical. Name and actuality do not correspond, and what is sought for and what is offered do not match."[34]

All these problems would challenge character appraisal to a more sophisticated quest for discerning the increasingly complicated performance of human nature. Despite its evolution with the changing times, character appraisal nonetheless continued to serve as the basis of official selection, as it would more or less throughout the Wei, Chin, and Southern dynasties.[35]

THE MORALITY-ORIENTED STAGE (CA. 147–184)

The second period of character appraisal intertwined with political unrest toward the end of the Later Han, when conflict intensified between scholar-officials and the eunuchs and grandees. Fan Yeh described this political strife in the *History of the Later Han*: "During the period of the Emperor Huan (r. 147–167) and the Emperor Ling (r. 168–189), the emperors were dissolute and led the government astray. [The emperors] entrusted the state's destiny to eunuchs, with whom scholars felt ashamed to associate. Therefore commoners protested with anger, and private scholars criticized [the government] without fear. They exalted their own reputation, appraising and upholding one another, while openly commenting on lords and ministers and criticizing political leaders. The trend of extreme straightforwardness [*hsing-chih*] thereafter became current."[36]

Increasingly, character appraisal became the device for the scholar-clique partisans, the so-called *tang-jen,* to rediscipline and restrengthen the declining empire. For this new purpose, the focus of character appraisal shifted from evaluating candidates for office to two new exercises. Outside the "scholar-clique," leading partisans, who were also highly respected scholars, vehemently attacked their political opponents among eunuchs and grandees—what Fan Yeh terms "commenting on lords and ministers and criticizing political leaders." Within their own circles, these scholars closely examined the qualifications of fellow partisans in order to enhance their solidarity, and they exalted their own reputations in order to appear as Confucian moral exemplars—what Fan Yeh calls "appraising and upholding one another." Swayed by fashion, each individual scholar naturally considered gaining the favor of leading partisans as important as gaining an official position. In order to attract attention of these partisans, scholars "would certainly compete to be strange and excellent [*cheng-ch'i tou-yen*]; each wanted to surpass others with his unique behavior."[37] The trend of *hsing-chih,* or extreme straightforwardness, evidently resulted from such intense competition to be unique. It marked a rapid growth of self-awareness.

The growth of self-awareness stirred up by character appraisal also substantially changed the character appraisal enterprise. Before, the evaluators had conducted this practice according to certain regime-sanctified standards; now, with new purposes and with a great number of "extremely straightforward" evaluatees, the evaluator needed to invent an entire body of new categories, terms, and methods in order to reflect this far more complicated reality. Driven by this kind of pragmatic need, character appraisal rapidly evolved into an independent field of study. Also, the cruel persecution of the scholar-official group, plotted by the eunuchs and known in history as the "interdiction of the scholar-clique partisans" (tang-ku),[38] forced some scholars to shun specific evaluations in order to avoid exposing the good and offending the bad. Fan Yeh tells us: "Although Kuo T'ai was good at character appraisal [jen-lun], he never issued severe criticisms or concrete comments. Therefore, when eunuchs dominated the government, they could not find fault with him."[39] When concrete comments were removed from character appraisal, what remained could only be discussions of abstract principles. Thus we see the beginning of a more theoretical approach to human nature, an approach at which Kuo T'ai excelled. As the leading exponent of character appraisal in the late Han, Kuo T'ai's theoretical orientation would undoubtedly exert enormous influence on his fellow scholars.[40]

Character appraisal had thus evolved into an independent and self-contained enterprise, founded on the interaction between earlier notions of character appraisal and the growth of self-awareness, mandated by the scholars instead of being dictated by the court, and guided by its own evaluation categories instead of official standards.

Correspondingly, the Shih-shuo hsin-yü begins its account of character appraisal at this second stage and provides us with a number of concrete examples. Here are two revealing episodes, one focusing on Ch'en Fan (ca. 95–168) and the other on Li Ying (110–169):

> Ch'en Fan's words became a rule for gentlemen and his acts a model for the world. Whenever he mounted his carriage and held the reins it was with a determination to purify the whole realm. (1/1)
>
> Li Ying's manner and style were outstanding and proper, and he maintained a haughty dignity. He wished to take on himself the responsibility for the moral teaching (ming-chiao) and right and wrong [shih-fei] for the whole realm. Among the gentlemen who later progressed in office, if any succeeded in 'ascending to his hall,' they all felt they climbed through the Dragon Gate (Lung-men). (1/4)

Although character appraisal at the second stage still linked political engagement to the selection system, the Shih-shuo does not invoke this function; instead it focuses on scholars' self-discipline initiated by the scholar-eunuch conflict. With this focus, it records leading scholar-clique partisans as the evaluators, such as Ch'en Fan and Li Ying cited above. The evaluatees include (1) the political opponents of official-scholars and (2) the scholars themselves. Here, the *Shih-shuo* clearly delineates two major purposes of character appraisal: Ch'en Fan's ambition is to "purify the whole realm," which means the elimination of all enemies; Li Ying's self-assigned mission is to discipline the gentry, which leads to the competition for Li Ying's personal favor rather than for official positions.[41]

As for the standards upon which both Ch'en Fan and Li Ying assert their authority, they remain strictly within the Confucian tradition of *ming-chiao*—moral teaching or the "teaching of names."[42] The *Shih-shuo*, however, adds another term here: *shih-fei*, or "right and wrong," which suggests uncertainties. What does *ming-chiao shih-fei* mean, the right and wrong of the moral teaching, or the moral teaching of the right and wrong? If the former, then Li Ying is trying to reevaluate the conventional moral teachings in the present situation; if the latter, then Li Ying is applying conventional rules to evaluate the entire realm. In either case, *shih-fei* points to the independence and subjectivity of scholars in making judgments.

This second historic period of character appraisal ended with the interdiction of the scholar-clique partisans. Li Ying and over a hundred scholars died in jail, and some six or seven hundred others were either exiled or confined.[43] But character appraisal, now having broadened its objects and functions, survived this fatal disaster, awaiting a more prosperous period yet to come.

THE ABILITY-ORIENTED STAGE (CA. 184–239)

The third period of character appraisal witnessed the total collapse of the Han regime. The Yellow Turban Rebels (184–188) tore the entire empire asunder, and contending warlords kept it divided. This chaotic time desperately needed capable officials to help restore order. For this reason, character appraisal, still concerned with the selection of officials, emphasized political ability. From the eighth year to the twenty-second year of the Chien-an reign (196–220), a mere fifteen years in all, Ts'ao Ts'ao (155–220), the regent/prime minister of the declining Han and the founder of the future Wei regime (220–265), ordered searches for talented persons four times.[44] He theorized that "a time of peace and order honors moral behavior, whereas a time of anarchy and disorder values contributions and ability."[45] He openly advocated abandoning moral standards in favor of "selecting only those who possessed ability,"[46] including those who were "not benevolent nor filial, but capable of reigning over the state and commanding military troops."[47]

According to the *Shih-shuo*, Ts'ao Ts'ao was a man for his time: "When Ts'ao Ts'ao was young he had an interview with Ch'iao Hsüan (fl. late 2nd cent.). Hsüan told him, 'The whole realm is now in disorder, and all the warriors are struggling like tigers. Aren't you the one who will control the situation and get it in order? . . . You are really an intelligent hero [*ying-hsung*][48] in an age of disorder, and a treacherous rebel in an age of order. I regret that I am old now and won't live to see you come to wealth and honor, but I will entrust my sons and grandsons to your care.'" (7/1)

Note that Ch'iao Hsüan's appraisal of Ts'ao Ts'ao forms a symmetrical contrast with Hsü Shao's appraisal of Ts'ao Ts'ao in Sun Sheng's *Miscellaneous Accounts*, which I mentioned earlier in section 2. Hsü Shao said, "An able minister in an age of order, and a treacherous warrior [*chien-hsiung*] in an age of disorder." Ch'iao Hsüan said, "An intelligent hero [*ying-hsung*] in an age of disorder, and a treacherous rebel in an age of order." Hsü, a Confucian scholar with a "salient reputation and integrity," is critical of Ts'ao Ts'ao. By using the term *chien-hsiung*, or treacherous warrior, he accuses Ts'ao of defying Confucian values and taking advantage of chaotic times to fulfill his political ambition. Ch'iao, by contrast, is more concerned about the needs of the time. He values and admires Ts'ao Ts'ao for his unconventional qualities, which he believes will enable Ts'ao to "control the situation and get [the whole realm] in order."

These two contrary opinions typify the evolution of character appraisal during the Han-Wei transitional period. The most striking contrast lies between *chien-hsiung* and *ying-hsung*. *Chien-hsiung* had been a commonly used negative name in pre-Ch'in classics, especially the Confucian ones, to denounce evil, treacherous, and ambitious persons.[49] *Ying-hsiung*, a term from the Han,[50] was newly defined to fit the highest standard for Wei character appraisal. The Wei scholar Liu Shao (fl. 220–250) defines *ying-hsiung* in his *Jen-wu chih* (Study of human abilities) in the following way:

> Exceptionally beautiful plants are called *ying*. Animals outstanding in their groups are called *hsiung*, hence the name *ying hsiung*, for people of extraordinary scholarly and military genius. Those whose intelligence and discernment are outstanding are *ying*. Those whose courage and strength are superior to others' are *hsiung*. This is the general difference between the two. If we wish to compare their qualities, we find that they must supplement each other. Each with two parts of its own quality needs one part of the other, and then they can be completed. . . . Therefore *ying* uses its intelligence to plan the beginning and uses its discernment to see the pivot. But it waits for the courage of *hsiung* to act. *Hsiung* uses its strength to subdue the multitude and its courage to push over difficulties. But it waits till the wisdom of *ying* enables it to succeed. . . . If one has both *ying* and *hsiung*, then one can rule over the world.[51]

In this lengthy definition of *ying-hsiung*, the overwhelming emphasis is on one's political ability; moral categories, once the backbone of Han character appraisal, recede in importance. The five constant virtues, *jen* (benevolence), *chih* (wisdom), *li* (propriety), *i* (righteousness), and *hsin* (trustworthiness), which the Han had institutionalized as the standard for a gentleman, are now eclipsed by *wen* (scholarly refinement), *wu* (military talent), *ts'ung* (intelligence, cleverness), *ming* (discernment), *tan* (courage), *li* (strength), and *yung* (bravery)—qualities that are more closely associated with capability and power than with morality.

The Wei emphasis on ability inevitably broadened character appraisal from the political arena to other realms of talents. Ts'ao Ts'ao's two sons, the heir-apparent Ts'ao P'i (187–226) and his younger brother Ts'ao Chih (192–232), were both adepts and exemplars of character appraisal in this broader sense. Ts'ao P'i composed a book, *Shih-ts'ao* (Qualities of gentlemen), which, though not now extant, is listed with Liu Shao's *Jen-wu chih*, a scholarly study of character appraisal, in the same category—the "School of Names" (*Ming-chia*)—in the "Sui Treatise."[52] He also provided the earliest extant discussion of the relationship between one's writing style and personal disposition in his "Lun-wen" (Discourse on literature), which foreshadowed Liu Shao's argument concerning the connection between human nature and talents in the *Jen-wu chih* (to be discussed in chapter 4).

Ts'ao Chih, for his part, was both a theorist of character appraisal and a paragon of the talents he himself favored. Yü Huan's (third-century) *Wei-lüeh* (Brief history of Wei) includes the following anecdote, which can be viewed as Ts'ao Chih's self-appraisal:

> Han-tan Ch'un [early 3rd cent.] . . . was widely learned and well versed in literary composition. . . . Ts'ao Chih was delighted by his acquaintance with Ch'un. He invited Ch'un over, but left him alone at first. It was a hot summer day, so Chih ordered attendants to fetch water. After bathing and powdering himself, Chih, bare-headed and topless, performed the barbarian dance, "Five-Hammer Tempering," and engaged in juggling and fencing. He also recited thousands of words of humorous works [*p'ai-yu hsiao-shuo*].[53] After doing all this, he asked Ch'un: "How do you compare with me, Scholar Han-tan?" Then, putting on his clothes and hat and straightening his manner and appearance, he started discussing with Ch'un the creation of all things from the original chaos, and the significance of classifying and differentiating people [*wu*].[54] He then ranked sages, worthies, famous statesmen, and glorious gentlemen since Fu Hsi's time. He also critiqued writings, poetic expositions, and eulogies from the past to the present, and detailed the rules of political affairs. Finally he came to the discussion of military arts and tactics. At this point, Chih ordered his chef to bring in wine and dishes. All who attended were speechless, and no one rose to refute him. At dusk, when Ch'un went home, he sighed with admiration for Chih's talents [*ts'ai*], praising him as an "immortal."[55]

This episode both exemplifies the Wei ideal of a talented man and interprets the Wei concept of *ts'ai*—talent, ability, or capacity. Ts'ao Chih flaunts his talents in virtually all the categories of *ts'ai* that were conceptualized during the Wei period—political affairs, literary creation, artistic accomplishments, military arts and tactics, and philosophical reasoning, as well as character appraisal.

These *ts'ai* categories are codified in such chapter titles of the *Shih-shuo hsin-yü* as:

2. "Yen-yü"   (Speech and conversation)
3. "Cheng-shih"   (Affairs of government)
4. "Wen-hsüeh"   (Literature and scholarship)
7. "Shih-chien"   (Recognition and judgment [of human character types])
8. "Shang-yü"   (Appreciation and praise [of personalities])
9. "P'in-tsao"   (Ranking [personalities] with refined words)
20. "Shu-chieh"   (Technical understanding)
21. "Ch'iao-i"   (Ingenious art)

Not so coincidentally, the *Shih-shuo hsin-yü* starts the literature section of the chapter "Wen-hsüeh" with an account of Ts'ao Chih's legendary "Seven-Pace Poem." Similarly, the chapter "Ch'iao-i" begins with Ts'ao P'i's skill in playing pellet chess, a kind of intellectual game.

Because the late Han turmoil had driven gentlemen to migrate randomly from place to place, the tracing and investigation of candidates became extremely difficult. To deal with this problem, the Wei regime initiated a new system of selection, the so-called *chiu-p'in chung-cheng chih* (nine-rank classification [of candidates for office] by the impartial and just, hereafter the "nine-rank system"). The central government set up "impartial and just" officials in each local government to follow and observe the candidates' behavior. Theoretically, this new system continued the Han rules of selection and still relied upon *ch'ing-i,* or pure criticism—the local comments on the candidates in Confucian moral terms. In reality, however, hereditary families controlled "impartial and just" offices and gradually made the candidate's family background the basis for selection. Since the early Chin, this new system had in fact helped to keep high offices in the hands of leading clans. The *ch'ing-i* now had no actual effect on the process of designating officials, except when they were degraded.[56]

THE AESTHETICS-ORIENTED STAGE (CA. 240–420)

The period from the Wei regime's Cheng-shih reign (240–249) to the end of the Eastern Chin (317–420) marked a significant shift in both the theory and the practice of character appraisal. The changing political, social, and intellectual circumstances of the time transformed its function from an essentially pragmatic practice into a predominantly aesthetic, philosophical, and psychological one. During this period, character appraisal no longer applied to a select group of aspiring candidates for offices; rather, it extended to the entire gentry society, men and women, who became evaluators as well as evaluatees. Moreover, the standard of judgment was no longer Confucian morality (as in the Han) or timely heroism (the Ts'ao-Wei criterion); instead, people came to be judged on how genuinely they revealed themselves to others. The *Shih-shuo hsin-yü* provides an example of this shift in emphasis: "The future Emperor Chien-wen [Ssu-ma Yü (320–372), r. 371–372] talked about Wang Shu [303–368], saying, 'His ability is not particularly outstanding, and he is not at all indifferent toward glory and gain. It is only that with a small amount of genuineness and forthrightness he is capable of matching other people's abundant good qualities.'" (8/91)[57] Wang Shu does not meet any of the conventional standards we have encountered earlier in this chapter. His lack of ability suggests that he would be an inept official, and his attraction to glory and gain flies in the face of Confucian moral teachings. Yet because he forthrightly displays his real inner qualities, he wins a favorable appraisal from the future emperor, a member of the highest ruling class. This judgment signals that the gentry had already accepted a new category, "genuineness and forthrightness" *(chen-shuai)*, as a standard for evaluating personalities.

If we consider the previous standards as passive ones, based on certain "objective" rules and pragmatic purposes, then "genuineness and forthrightness" propose an active standard that does not follow such outer principles. For "genuineness" encourages one to be oneself, and "forthrightness" advocates expressing oneself openly. This new standard actually intends a nonstandard—one that allows for the evaluatee diverse and unlimited expressions of human nature and for the evaluator diverse and unlimited angles to comprehend human nature. Whereas the Han focused on moral categories and the Han-Wei transition emphasized abilities, the Wei-Chin period viewed people from all possible angles—particularly *te* (potency, potentiality, efficacy), *ts'ai* (innate ability, talent, specialty), *hsing* (temperament, disposition, temper), and *ch'ing* (feeling, emotion, passion).

The *Shih-shuo* author codified the discursive properties of Wei-Chin character appraisal into a *Shih-shuo* discourse by dividing all of the episodes into thirty-six categories. With thirty-six chapter titles, each summarizing a human type and each illustrated by the episodes included in the chapter, he created a wide-ranging treatise on human nature. It was far from complete, however, and always open to more possible categories. By offering tangible and illustrative characterizations of people, rather than abstract appraisals, the author conveyed the Wei-Chin understanding that human nature, as an autonomic and ever-changing totality, always went beyond any attempt at classification, and that any attempt at classification only provided an approximation of the person.

The author extensively transformed Wei-Chin daily-life details into appraisal episodes, for daily life most naturally and broadly links a person to the outer world and therefore authentically exposes the person's inner features through his or her responses. We can see more clearly the author's effort in this respect by comparing *Shih-shuo* episodes with pertinent sources quoted in Liu Chün's commentary. Here is one example.

> When Chancellor Wang [Wang Tao (276–339)] was appointed governor of Yang Province (Kiangsu-Anhui-Chekiang), [he kindly greeted several hundred guests]. Everyone looked happy except a guest from Lin-hai (Chekiang) named Jen and several Central Asiatics (Hu), who were not fully at ease. For this reason the chancellor came over, and as he passed by Jen remarked, "When you came to the capital, Lin-hai then was left without any people."
>
> Jen was greatly cheered by this, whereupon Wang passed by in front of the Central Asiatics, and, snapping his fingers, said, "*Lân-dźįa, lân-dźįa!*"[58] All the Central Asiatics laughed together, and the whole company was delighted. (3/12)[59]

In his commentary, Liu Chün cites Sun Sheng's (ca. 302–373) *Chin Yang-ch'iu* (Spring and autumn annals of the Chin) as one possible source of this episode: "Wang Tao was attractive and responsive in his personal relations, and there were few [ever neglected] by him. Even casual acquaintances or ordinary guests, the moment they saw him, would for the most part find themselves becoming completely open and sincere with him, and stated themselves that they were treated by Tao just as if they were old friends."[60] While the *Chin Yang-ch'iu* text appraises Wang Tao using abstract terms such as "attractive and responsive," the *Shih-shuo* episode elaborates these same features through the narration of a specific event. Although the *Shih-shuo* author does not offer additional comments, we can easily see Wang's diplomatic subtlety and political cunning in his remarks and actions. He flatters Jen because, as the head of the Northern gentry who have just immigrated to the South, Wang has to endear himself to the local elite. And he pleases the Central Asiatics in order to show the new government's willingness to embrace any possible supporters.

Sometimes, the author purposefully confounds the circumstances in order to expose the personalities of all the characters involved. The following example typifies this technique:

> Every time Shih Ch'ung invited guests for banquet gatherings he always had beautiful girls serving the wine. If any guests failed to drain their cups, he would have an attendant decapitate the girls one after the other. Chancellor Wang Tao and his cousin, the generalissimo, Wang Tun, both went on one occasion to visit Shih Ch'ung. The chancellor had never been able to drink, but with every toast forced himself to do so until he was dead drunk. Each time it came to the generalissimo's turn, however, he deliberately refused to drink, in order to see what would happen. Even after they had decapitated three girls his facial expression remained unchanged and he was still unwilling to drink. When the chancellor chided him for it, the generalissimo said, "If he [Shih] wants to go ahead and kill somebody from [his own household], what business is it of yours?" (30/1)[61]

Liu Chün quotes a relevant reference in his commentary:

> *The Records of Chancellor Wang's Moral Voices* records: The chancellor had always been held in honor by the fathers. Wang K'ai once asked Wang Tun, "I hear your cousin (Wang Tao) is a fine man, and is, moreover, a connoisseur of music. I'm going to have some female musicians perform at my place, and you may bring him along."
>
> Accordingly they went. As the girls were playing the flute, one of them had a slight lapse of memory. Wang K'ai, noticing it, had an attendant strike and kill her right in front of the steps; his facial expression remaining unchanged all the while.
>
> When the chancellor returned home he said, "I'm afraid as long as this gentleman remains in the world, we're bound to have this kind of incident."[62]

The record in *Wang's Moral Voices*, with seventy-six characters, reveals only Wang K'ai's ruthlessness; the *Shih-shuo* episode, with ninety-two characters, portrays all three men. Such efficiency results from an intentionally arranged interaction between all the characters vividly. Both Shih Ch'ung and Wang Tun appear ruthless, but Shih's cruelty is encouraged by Wang Tun's sly malice. Seeing how eager Shih Ch'ung is to show off his wealth, Wang Tun deliberately incites him into a fanatic waste of his assets. And the two men's stonehearted competition to exhibit their tenacity, at the expense of human lives, becomes even more unbearable when contrasted with Wang Tao's clemency. This specific strategy of characterization, to portray people in relation to one another, is no coincidence. Rather, as I shall explore further in chapter 5, it is rooted deeply in the logic of Wei-Chin character appraisal. Although we cannot say for certain that the author originally intended the *Shih-shuo t'i* to be a literary genre, the careful attention he gives to characterization interwoven with daily events surely had the effect of transforming dry historical records into literary narratives.

The author also tried to give more perceptibility to human inner qualities, by translating abstract appraisals into natural imagery. The following comparisons between the *Shih-shuo* episodes and their sources quoted in Liu Chün's commentary may shed light on this effort.

The *Shih-shuo hsin-yü* recounts: "Yü Ai characterized Ho Ch'iao as follows: 'In dense profusion, like a pine tree at a height of [ten thousand feet]. Though gnarled and full of knots, if used for a large building, it may serve as a beam or pillar.'" (8/15)

Liu Chün's commentary records Fu Ch'ang's (early-fourth-century) *Chin chu-kung tsan* (Eulogies of the prominent Chin gentlemen): "Ho Ch'iao always admired his maternal uncle, Hsia-hou Hsüan, as a person, and therefore he [stood out highly] among courtiers and did not mingle with the crowd. Those of his own age and class were in awe of the rigor of his manner."[63]

Thus, the *Shih-shuo* author translates the abstract appraisal of Ho Ch'iao—that "he stood out highly among courtiers and did not mingle with the crowd"—into a picturesque vision of a tall and densely foliated pine tree.

The *Shih-shuo hsin-yü* recounts: "Contemporaries characterized Chou I as: 'Unscalable as a sheer cliff'" (8/56). Liu Chün's commentary cites Sun Sheng's *Chin Yang-ch'iu*: "Chou I was rigidly correct and unapproachable. Even among his peers, no one dared to get unduly intimate with him."[64] Thus, Chou I's "rigid correctness and unapproachability" is visualized in terms of an "unscalable" cliff.

Consider also this portrayal of Hsi K'ang in the *Shih-shuo hsin-yü*: "Hsi K'ang's body was seven feet, eight inches tall, and his manner and appearance conspicuously outstanding. Some who saw him sighed, saying, 'Serene and sedate, fresh and transparent, pure and exalted!' Others would say, 'Soughing like the wind beneath the pine trees, high and gently blowing.'" (14/5)

Liu Chün's commentary quotes *Hsi K'ang pieh-chuan* (A variant biography of [Hsi] K'ang): "K'ang was seven feet, eight inches tall, with an imposing facial expression. He treated his bodily frame like so much earth or wood and never added any adornment or polish, yet [he] had the grace of a dragon and the beauty of a phoenix, together with a natural simplicity and spontaneity."[65]

Here, Hsi K'ang's "natural simplicity and spontaneity" is linked to the gentle wind.

As I shall discuss at length in chapter 2, Wei-Chin gentry members identified their ideal of human nature, genuineness, and straightforwardness with *tzu-jan,* or the spontaneity of Nature. Hence they found it most proper that natural objects signify human inner qualities; once human nature inhabits the shells of natural objects, it appropriates the perceptible qualities of Nature—its purity, freshness, loftiness, beauty, serenity, and remoteness. In this respect, too, the *Shih-shuo* author shows a strong tendency toward transforming historical records into a literary genre. Not only did he use natural imagery to portray people, but he also codified natural imagery with poetic expressions. This I shall also explore further in chapter 5.

The above survey only outlines, in a brief and general way, the historical evolution of character appraisal and the discursive transformation from character appraisal to character writing. The question of what moved character appraisal from one stage to another and what determined the path for a series of discursive transformations requires a closer examination of the cultural milieu of the Wei-Chin period, which I shall undertake in later chapters.

Chapter 2

Character Appraisal and the Formation of Wei-Chin Spirit

After the Wei nine-rank system had discharged character appraisal from its political responsibilities, what caused the practice to become even more prevalent and to evolve on its own into a multidimensional exploration of human nature? What motivated and sustained the two-hundred-year Wei-Chin desire to know, to develop, and to express one's self, leading eventually to the creation of the *Shih-shuo hsin-yü*? The answer lies in the interaction between the practice of character appraisal, the growth of self-awareness, and the evolution of the dominant Wei-Chin ideology, *Hsüan-hsüeh*.[1] All three influences contributed to the process of Wei-Chin self-fashioning and self-expression, offering terminology and methodology that, in turn, endowed the *Shih-shuo hsin-yü* with rich materials and provocative theories.

All this happened at once. For convenience I will discuss in the first section of this chapter the interaction of character appraisal with self-awareness, which problematized as well as facilitated Wei-Chin self-fashioning. In the second section, I intend to show how the Wei-Chin people, needing to use words but recognizing the inability of words to express meanings in full, negotiated their way to self-expression in collaboration with both character appraisal and *Hsüan-hsüeh*. This process resulted in disputes involving a series of complementary and oppositional philosophical concepts, derived from a great many intellectual sources, some inherited, some invented, and some imported. The whole chapter intends to illuminate the Wei-Chin spirit, not by giving definitions, but by showing how it was formed and how it operated. I shall draw evidence mainly from the *Shih-shuo hsin-yü* in order to highlight its reflexive feature, which will in turn provide a theoretical basis for my later examination of the artistic achievements of the *Shih-shuo hsin-yü*.

Character Appraisal, Self-Awareness, and Wei-Chin Self-Fashioning

In Wei-Chin times, self-awareness referred to one's self-knowledge and desire for uniqueness, and character appraisal aimed at judging and recognizing this uniqueness through language. Both collaborated in the task of defining human identity—the former from a subjective perspective, and the latter from an objective one. With a common purpose, the two cooperated as "mutual cause and effect."[2] On the one hand, the more a person desired to be different from another, the more unique characteristics he or she would display in front of the evaluator. On the other, the evaluator would analyze, evaluate, and record these unusual features with appropriate methods and terms. Thus, the growth of self-awareness enriched the content of character appraisal and impelled it to greater sophistication.

COMPARISON/COMPETITION: THE DYNAMIC OF SELF-FASHIONING

A comparison/competition dynamic drove the reciprocal relationship between self-awareness and character appraisal throughout the entire Wei-Chin era. The following *Shih-shuo* episodes illustrate this phenomenon:

> In general discussions of the relative merits of the two men, Ch'en Fan of Ju-nan and Li Ying of Ying-ch'uan, no one was able to determine which was superior and which inferior. Ts'ai Yung criticized them as follows: "Ch'en Fan is stubborn in crossing the will of his superiors, while Li Ying is strict in the management of his inferiors. Crossing the will of superiors is difficult; managing inferiors is easy."
>
> Ch'en Fan was accordingly classified at the foot of the "Three Superior Men" (*san-chün*), and Li Ying at the head of the "Eight Outstanding Men" (*pa-chün*). (9/1)
>
> The two sons of Yang Chun, the governor of Chi Province (Hopei)— Yang Ch'iao and Yang Mao—were both of mature capacity while they were still young lads with their hair in tufts. Since Chun was on friendly terms with both P'ei Wei and Yüeh Kuang, he sent the two lads to see them.

P'ei Wei's nature was magnanimous but proper, and being fond of Ch'iao for his possession of a lofty manner, he reported to Chun, "Ch'iao will come up to you some day; Mao will fall a little behind."

Yüeh Kuang's nature on the other hand was pure and unmixed, and, being fond of Mao for his possession of a spiritual discipline, he reported, "Ch'iao will undoubtedly come up to you, but Mao will become even more refined than you are."

Chun laughed and said, "The superiority and inferiority of my two sons turns out to be nothing more or less than the superiority and inferiority of P'ei Wei and Yüeh Kuang." (9/7)

These two episodes typify Wei-Chin comparative appraisals in three respects. First, Wei-Chin evaluators often drew comparisons among evaluatees so similar in social status, inner qualities, and reputation, that "no one was able to determine which was superior and which inferior." Here Ch'en Fan and Li Ying were both prominent scholar-clique partisans and role models of the late Han elite, and Yang Ch'iao and Yang Mao were brothers whose capacities rivaled each other. But because evaluators usually rendered judgments in terms of antithetically paired categories, such as *hsien-hou* (the former and the latter),[3] *sheng-fu* (the winner and the loser),[4] and *yu-lieh* (the good and the bad),[5] the connotations of superiority and inferiority naturally encouraged intense feelings of competition.

Secondly, close comparisons of this sort invited challenges not only to the evaluatees but also the evaluators—to their ability to discern subtle differences and to anchor them in proper words. In this sense, evaluators were at the same time also evaluatees; hence Yang Chun's revealing comment about his two friends, P'ei Wei and Yüeh Kuang.

Thirdly, these comparative appraisals often had specific social consequences. We have seen, for example, that Ts'ai Yung's judgment had the effect of publicly elevating Ch'en Fan to one of the most distinguished evaluative categories, while relegating Li Ying to a distinctly secondary classification. And even within the Wei-Chin family system, rivalries often affected matters such as parental favor, marital relationships, and marriage choices.[6] Competition loomed everywhere in the Wei-Chin society.

Intensifying this competition was the common practice of inviting one-on-one comparisons, in which a person would be asked to compare himself explicitly to another person or to the person who had just issued the challenge. Awkward moments like these offered a public test of one's composure as well as his ability to evaluate both himself and his rival fairly and accurately. In the chapter entitled "P'in-tsao" (Ranking with Refined Words), one-third of the comparative appraisals—about thirty episodes in all—revolve around this theme. Here are some examples:

Ku Shao [fl. early 3rd cent.] once stayed overnight conversing with P'ang T'ung [177–214]. Ku asked, "I hear you're famous [for understanding people]. Between the two of us, who is better?"

P'ang replied, "In forming and fashioning the morals of the age, or 'floating or sinking with the times,' I'm no match for you. But in discoursing on policies handed down by the ancients for the rule of kings and hegemons, or reviewing the strategic moments (of history) when 'prosperity or calamity hung in the balance (i-fu)' I would seem to be a day or so older than you."

Ku Shao, for his part, was content with this statement. (9/3)

Emperor Ming [Ssu-ma Shao, r. 323–326] once asked Hsieh K'un [280–322], "How would you rate yourself in comparison with Yü Liang?"

Hsieh replied, "As for 'sitting in ceremonial attire' in temple or hall, and making the hundred officials keep to the rules, I'm no match for Liang. But when it comes to '(living in seclusion on) a hill, or (fishing in) a stream,' I consider myself superior to him." (9/17)

Emperor Ming once asked Chou I [269–322], "How would you rate yourself in comparison with Yü Liang?"

Chou replied, "As for living in quietude beyond the cares of the world, Liang is no match for me; but when it comes to maintaining a calm dignity in hall or temple, I'm no match for Liang." (9/22)

Liu T'an [ca. 311–347] once went to Wang Meng's [309–347] house for pure conversation. At the time Wang Meng's son, Hsiu, was in his thirteenth year and was listening by the side of the couch. After Liu had left, Hsiu asked his father, "How does Intendant Liu's conversation compare with yours, Father?"

Wang Meng replied, "For sheer musical effect and elegant terminology, he's not equal to me; but when it comes to speaking out directly and hitting the mark, he surpasses me." (9/48)

Chih Tun [314–366] once asked Sun Ch'o [ca. 310–397], "How would you rate yourself in comparison with Hsü Hsün [fl. ca. 358]?"

Sun replied, "As far as exalted feelings and remoteness are concerned, your disciple has long since inwardly conceded Hsü's superiority. But in the matter of a single humming or a single intoning of poetry, Hsü will have to sit facing north." (9/54)

This sort of comparison, with its self-invented categories of analysis, moved character appraisal from a passive system to an active one. Instead of awaiting comments from others based on conventional norms, individuals could evaluate themselves and others on the basis of their own standards and values. As the above episodes indicate, these standards of evaluation were much broader than any previously court-sanctioned ones, including categories from political ability to reclusive lifestyle, from literary talents to philosophical discernment, and from inner forbearance to outer appearance. Moreover, they reveal a far more open-minded approach to knowing others and knowing the self, rejecting a superiority/inferiority formula and insisting upon the idea that each person can excel in his or her own way.

DIFFERENTIATION/IDENTIFICATION: THE DIALECTIC OF SELF-FASHIONING

The actual process of Wei-Chin self-fashioning involved one's constant differentiation from and identification with other people. I would like to illustrate this basic formula by revisiting the Yin Hao and Huan Wen rivalry introduced at the beginning of this book:

When Huan Wen was young, he and Yin Hao were of equal reputation, and they constantly felt a spirit of mutual rivalry. Huan once asked Yin, "How do you compare with me?"
Yin replied, "I have been keeping company with myself a long time; I would rather just be me." (9/35)

This episode underscores the differentiation aspect of self-fashioning. When Huan Wen asks Yin Hao, "How do you compare with me," he sets himself up as *the standard* for the comparison.[7] Yin's reply presents only an abbreviated version of his intended response, "instead of being somebody of your type, I would rather just be myself," by which Yin establishes the concept of "I" through differentiating himself from Huan Wen. Hence Yin Hao's response can be taken as an allegory that stands for a psychological truth of self-fashioning—that one establishes identity through differentiating oneself from the other(s).

Let us put this reading of Yin Hao's self-establishment alongside the following comparison between the famous Eastern Chin father-son calligraphers, Wang Hsi-chih (ca. 303–ca. 361)[8] and Wang Hsien-chih (344–388), also recorded in the *Shih-shuo hsin-yü*:

> Hsieh An (320–385) asked Wang Hsien-chih, "How would you rate your own calligraphy in comparison with that of your father (Wang Hsi-chih)?"
> Hsien-chih replied, "Of course mine isn't the same as his."
> Hsieh An said, "According to the discussions of outsiders that isn't at all the case."
> Wang replied, "How could outsiders know?" (9/75)

In their conversation, Hsieh An assumes that Wang Hsien-chih should follow in his father's footsteps. He therefore puts Hsien-chih arbitrarily into his father's category, uses his father's calligraphic achievements as *the standard,* and demands that Hsien-chih make a self-evaluation within these parameters (Fig. 2.1). Hsien-chih, however, rejects the comparison, claiming that he, as a distinguished calligrapher himself, has his own independent style; therefore he and his father are not comparable. More importantly, he, as the ultimate authority on both his "self" and his calligraphy,[9] should be the one to pass an informed judgment, not an "outsider" like Hsieh An.[10]

The principle of differentiation alone, however, cannot encompass the entirety of self-fashioning; the shaping of one's self also necessitates a process of identification. We find this principle expressed also in the Yin Hao/Huan Wen conflict. Yin insists on differentiating himself from Huan and being only himself. Huan, on the contrary, points out uncompromisingly that a pure "self" is but an illusion: "When I was young I used to play at riding bamboo horses with Yin Hao, but after I threw my bamboo rod away, he immediately picked it up. Of course he's turned out to be inferior to me" (9/38).[11] Huan Wen's seemingly childish remark exposes an important truth about self-fashioning: No matter how much we desire to be ourselves and to separate ourselves from others, the "self" cannot be cultivated in isolation. We all borrow from others, even if only uncon-

Figure 2.1. *Lan-t'ing hsü* (Preface to the Orchid Pavilion Gathering). Attributed to Wang Hsi-chih (ca. 303–ca. 361). Feng Ch'eng-su's (Early T'ang) copy. Peking Palace Museum.

sciously. The bamboo rod, then, can be taken as the symbol of certain personal traits; to pick it up means to identify oneself with its owner.

To support my reading of the "bamboo horse" episode, I would like to examine another symbol of human traits that frequently appears in the *Shih-shuo hsin-yü*—the *chu-wei,* or sambar-tail chowry. The sambar-tail chowry is a fanlike accouterment that Wei-Chin gentlemen held during pure-conversation meetings.[12] Symbolically, it was an inseparable part of the Wei-Chin gentlemen's persona, a spiritual identification, even a physical extension (Figs. 2.2, 2.3). In Yüeh Kuang's hand, it serves as a subtle surrogate of *Hsüan-hsüeh* scholarship (4/16). When Wang Yen holds it, the white jade handle is "completely indistinguishable from his hand"; hence it becomes the objectification of Wang Yen's fine qualities as a *Hsüan-hsüeh* adept (14/8). On his deathbed, Wang Meng looks at his sambar-tail chowry and laments his short life: "A [fine] person like this cannot even reach forty!" Then he gives the sambar-tail chowry to his best friend, Liu T'an. Liu, however, puts it back into Wang Meng's coffin, to show that he does not dare to identify himself with the distinguished departed (17/10).[13]

Whereas Liu T'an returns the sambar-tail chowry to Wang Meng, Yin Hao picks up Huan Wen's bamboo rod. The child Yin Hao sees something he lacks in the child Huan Wen. This lack provokes in him a desire to achieve his own wholeness. In order to fulfill this desire, the child has to identify with the one whom he admires, and then incorporate those of the

Figure 2.2. *Wei-mo pien* (Story of Vimalakīrti) (high T'ang) (detail). Tun-huang cave No. 103. East wall. It shows Vimalakīrti carrying a *chu-wei*. From *Tun-huang pi-hua* (Tun Huang wall paintings) (Peking: Wen-wu ch'un-pan she, 1959), Figure 141. In the wall paintings and reliefs of Tun-huang, Yün-kang, and Lung-men of the Southern and Northern dynasties and Sui-T'ang periods, Vimalakīrti is often portrayed as engaged in a pure conversation with the Bodhisattva Mañjuśri, with a *chu-wei* as an inseparable accouterment of his "pure conversationalist" status. See Ho Ch'ang-ch'ün, "*Shih-shuo hsin-yü* cha-chi: lun *chu-wei*" (Jotting notes on the *Shih-shuo hsin-yü*: on the term *chu-wei*). *Kuo-li chung-yang t'u-shu kuan kuan-k'an (fu-kan)* 1 (1947): 1-7.

Figure 2.3. *Kao-i t'u* (Portraits of eminent recluses). Attributed to Sun Wei (Late T'ang). Actually a fragment of *Chu-lin ch'i-hsien t'u* (Portraits of the Seven Worthies of the Bamboo Grove). Here it shows Juan Chi carrying a *chu-wei*. Shanghai Museum. (Photograph courtesy of Ho Yün-ao.) See Ch'eng Ming-shih, "Lun Sun Wei *Kao-i t'u* ti ku-shih chi ch'i yü Ku K'ai-chih hua-feng ti kuan-hsi" (On the historical background of Sun Wei's *Kao-i t'u* and its relationship with Ku K'ai-chih's artistic style), *Wen-wu* 1965.8: 16–23.

person's features that he lacks. In this way the child builds up his "self." Yin Hao's "self," of which he is so proud, is but "a hodge-podge of imaginary identifications,"[14] the identifications between his own image and that of others,[15] including the one with which he reluctantly equates himself. Even Yin Hao seems to have sensed some alienation in his "self" when he says, "I have been keeping company [*chou-hsüan*] with myself a long time; I would rather just be me." In this remark, he differentiates "I" and "myself" as if they were two people. To relate these two people, he uses a verb *"chou-hsüan,"* which means "to keep company with," "to socialize with," "to deal with," or even "to contend with," a verb indicating human relationship of both identification and competition.[16]

Again, the Yin Hao/Huan Wen conflict serves as an allegory that exposes a general truth of self-fashioning, that one can never draw a clear line between I and Thou. The formation of I is always in relation to Thou. One's self-fashioning is a dialectical process of both identification with and differentiation from the other(s). Throughout his life, a person has not only to identify himself with others, incorporating the features of others in order to establish himself; he also has to compare himself, or even compete, with others so as to distinguish himself from others. It is through this constant identification and differentiation that one recognizes himself both as a part of human society in general and as a specific individual. Consider the following *Shih-shuo* example: "When Tai K'uei went to study with Fan Hsüan, he observed everything that Fan did. If Fan was reading, he also would read. If Fan was copying a text, he also would copy a text. It was only his fondness for painting which Fan considered to be of no use, feeling that it was not proper to trouble his thoughts over such a thing. Tai thereupon painted for him illustrations for Chang Heng's *Rhyme-Prose on the Southern Capital* [*Nan-tu fu*]. After Fan had finished looking at them, he sighed in admiration and admitted that they greatly enhanced the text. It was only then that he began to appreciate the value of painting" (21/6). Here we have a delightful case of self-fashioning through both identification with and differentiation from others. Tai K'uei desires to acquire Fan Hsüan's fine scholarly qualities in order to refine himself, so he imitates Fan step-by-step. On the other hand, Tai K'uei is not satisfied with being a mere copy of Fan; he wants to establish his own unique identity. He therefore develops his own hobby, painting, in spite of his mentor's disapproval, hence establishing a more satisfactory self than his idol's.

THE ESTABLISHMENT OF A COLLECTIVE WEI-CHIN SELF

On a more general level, and to a broader extent, the differentiation/identification mechanism also contributed to the establishment of a collective Wei-Chin self. Wei-Chin gentlemen and gentlewomen, while working on the formation of their idiosyncratic personalities, unavoidably abandoned certain social conventions in favor of other values. This process is symbolically typified in a *Shih-shuo* episode concerning the breakup of a friendship between two leading Wei gentlemen, Hsi K'ang (223–262) and Shan T'ao (205–283): "When Shan T'ao was about to leave the selection bureau (in 262) and wanted to recommend Hsi K'ang as his successor, K'ang wrote him a letter announcing the breaking off of their friendship" (18/3).

This episode condenses a complicated story: Shan T'ao, upon changing his official position, recommends Hsi K'ang for his replacement—a well-intentioned offer that could easily have been arranged between the two friends in private. Hsi K'ang, however, sends Shan T'ao a public letter of rebuke, in which he severely attacks the contemporary moral-political system as confining human nature. He therefore offends the dominant Ssu-ma clan, which was then re-affirming the Confucian moral teachings as the basis of governing in order to conceal their intentional usurpation of the Wei throne—a betrayal of the very basis of the Confucian moral teachings. Hsi K'ang was soon arrested and put to death by the Ssu-mas.

By omitting both the backdrop and the consequences, and focusing instead on Hsi K'ang's action of writing an open letter to sever a friendship, the *Shih-shuo* author underscores Hsi's "unyielding integrity" in criticizing a hypocritical moral-political system.[17] He is not breaking off from Shan T'ao, but from the system that Shan T'ao represents.[18] Significantly, Hsi K'ang chooses to live in reclusion and to embrace Nature, as indicated by the title of the chapter "Ch'i-i" (Reclusion and disengagement), where the author has located this story.

Reading this episode along with the life and the works of the historical Hsi K'ang, we can understand that his defiance against prevailing norms did not arise from a momentary dissent but from a long philosophical contemplation over the authentic way of life. He summarized his vision as "transcending the moral teaching [*ming-chiao*] and following the self-so [*tzu-jan*],"[19] and he made this daring declaration in his "Shih-ssu lun" (Dispelling concealment). The main thesis of this essay, as Robert G. Henricks interprets it, "is that it is morally better to do and say what one genuinely feels, even if what one says or does goes against standard moral norms, than to hide one's feelings out of concern for what others might think."[20] Hsi K'ang rejects *ming-chiao*, for it dictates abiding by "standard moral norms," and he favors *tzu-jan,* for it expresses "what one genuinely feels." His dichotomic attitude arises from what he sees as the intrinsic needs of human nature: "The Six Confucian Classics teach us above all to restrain and direct [human nature], yet it is human nature [*hsing*] to follow one's desire [*yü*]. To restrain and direct human nature is against one's will [*yüan*], whereas by following one's desire one can gain the self-so [*tzu-jan*]."[21] Upholding the principle of "following the self-so," Hsi K'ang also maintains that one should voice one's desire openly instead of concealing or restraining it.[22] Small wonder he became a role model for the Wei-Chin effort to establish a collective self by breaking from conventional norms.

The moral-political system that the Wei-Chin gentry called into question consisted mainly of the so-called "three bonds and six rules," the basis of social order since the Han. Yü Ying-shih tells us: "The 'three bonds' refers to the relationships between ruler and subject, father and son, and husband and wife, whereas the 'six rules' pertain to those between paternal uncles, elder and younger brothers, other relatives of the same surname, maternal uncles, teachers, and friends. What is meant by these 'bonds' and 'rules'? The *Pai-hu t'ung-te lun* [Comprehensive discussions in the White Tiger Hall] provides the following answer: 'A bond gives orderliness; a rule regulates. What is greater is the bond; what is smaller is the rule. They serve to order and regulate [the relations between] superiors and inferiors, and to arrange and adjust the way of mankind.'"[23]

Numerous examples in the *Shih-shuo hsin-yü* show how intense competition can shatter the "three bonds and six rules." We have already seen, in the case of Wang Hsien-chih, how the father and son relationship could be replaced by that between two rivals in calligraphy. In this instance, Wang Hsien-chih refused to acknowledge his inferiority to his father and insisted on his own identity, an offense against filial piety.[24] Similar competition occurs between Wang Shu and his son Wang T'an-chih (330–375), causing the father to feel an irrepressible jealousy toward his own brood (see 5/47 and 5/58; to be detailed in chapter 5). This subversion of the father-son relation was particularly disturbing to the "three bonds and six rules" because, as Wu Hung points out, from the Han dynasty onward, "the parent-son relation became an analogy for the relation between ruler and subject and between Heaven and ruler," and filial piety "provided the . . . ruler with a fundamental way to govern the country and its people."[25]

Competition also occurred between brothers, subverting the principle of *t'i*—fraternal love. For example, living for years in seclusion, Wang Chan (249–295) did not want to participate in mundane affairs. His quiet personality caused his family to think of him as "half-witted." Later his nephew Wang Chi (ca. 240–ca. 285) discovered that he was actually a *Hsüan-hsüeh* adept and a talented gentleman. When Wang Chi told his father about this discovery and expressed admiration for his uncle, the father's immediate response was: "How does he compare with me?" Not daring to offend his father, Wang Chi turned the comparison against himself, replying, "He's superior to me." (8/17)[26]

Competition even entered the inner chamber, disturbing the hierarchical stability of husband and wife. Contrary to stereotype, the women we encounter in the *Shih-shuo* almost invariably challenge the Confucian doctrine that "the husband is the Heaven of the wife."[27] Here is one example. Wang Kuang (ca. 210–251) married the daughter of the famous Wei gentleman Chu-ko Tan (d. 258). When the couple exchanged words for the first time,

> Wang blurted out to his wife, "My bride's spirit and appearance are ignoble and low class, totally unlike Kung-hsiu [the courtesy name of Chu-ko Tan, literally meaning the 'Fair One']."
>
> His wife replied, "My great husband can't exactly compare with Yen-yün [the courtesy name of Wang Kuang's father, Wang Ling, literally meaning the 'Outstanding One'], either, yet he's pitting a mere woman against a magnificent hero!" (19/9)[28]

This conversation involves a multiple comparison and competition. Wang Kuang compares the bride with her father, subtly implying that he considers his wife no match for himself—he is at least as good as his father-in-law, if not better. In defending her self-esteem, the bride returns a similar comparison between the groom and his father. She argues that, if the groom cannot measure up to his father, how can he expect her to surpass her father, since hers (a magnificent hero) is superior to his (an out-

standing one). Thus the newlyweds project their competition onto their
fathers and engage in these comparisons at the expense of conventional
social relationships.

According to the "Hun-i" (Significance of marriage) in the *Li-chi* (Record
of rites), "The wedding ceremony is . . . set up to differentiate man from
woman and thereupon to establish moral connections between husband and
wife. Only when a couple is morally connected with each other can love
arise between father and son; and only when love exists between father
and son can the connections between ruler and subject be rectified. Therefore it is said that the wedding ceremony is the root of all the other rites."[29]

The "Hun-i" continues formulating another ritual ceremony supplementary to that of the wedding, a ritual that deals directly with the part
of the wife: "Once the bride has completed the ritual ceremony for a wife
[*fu-li*], [the elders] should declare to her the principle of obedience and
switch family responsibilities [from the parents-in-law] to her, so as to emphasize the principle of obedience for a wife. The [principle] of obedience
requires a wife to obey her parents-in-law and to harmonize with her sis-
ters-in-law; only then can she be considered to match her husband. . . .
Only when the wife is obedient can the family order be straightened up;
and only when the family order is straightened up can the whole household last long. Therefore, the sage kings paid special attention to a wife's
obedience."[30] In this light, one can hardly imagine a greater affront to Confucian norms of marriage than the exchange between Wang Kuang and
his wife on their wedding night. Particularly, the wife's tit-for-tat response
offends the principle of obedience, and such quarrelsomeness might have
cost her her marriage.[31]

Yet the *Shih-shuo* contains stories of comparison and competition between spouses that were far more offensive to traditional sensibilities. Here
is one:

> Wang Hun and his wife, Lady Chung (Chung Yen), were once sitting to-
> gether when they saw their son, Wang Chi, passing through the court-
> yard. With a pleased expression, Hun said to his wife, "That you have
> borne me a son like this is enough to put my mind at ease."

> Laughing, his wife replied, "If I would have gotten to marry your younger brother, Wang Lun, the sons I would have borne would definitely not have been merely like this!" (25/8)

In this case, Lady Chung openly asserts the superiority of her brother-in-law over her husband, implying that she, too, is superior to him and that she deserves a better fate.[32] She even hints at adulterous desires, challenging Confucian notions of chastity that had prevailed in Han times, only to decline in importance during the iconoclastic Wei-Chin period.[33] Later dynasties, particularly the Ming and the Ch'ing, powerfully reasserted the value of chastity, as we shall see in chapter 8; therefore we should not be surprised to find scholars such as Li Tz'u-ming (1830–1894), who bitterly criticized the "wild talk" of this particular *Shih-shuo* episode and denounced especially the "lewd words" of Lady Chung.[34]

Another example of rebellion against Confucian values can be found in the following anecdote, recorded in chapter 23, "Uninhibitedness and Eccentricity": "Juan Chi's [210–263] sister-in-law *(sao)* was once returning to her parents' home, and Chi went to see her to say good-bye. When someone chided him for this, Chi replied, 'Were the rites established for people like [us] [*wo-pei*]?'" (23/7) The *Li-chi* states, "Sister-in-law [*sao*] and brother-in-law [*shu*] are not to exchange inquiries directly with each other."[35] Juan Chi's behavior thus reflects an open disregard for *li,* or rites, which his sister-in-law obviously shares with him.

The most remarkable breakdown of conventional social relationships occurred when the positions of ruler and subject were inverted. Liu T'an, for instance, boldly considered himself to be among the first class of pure-conversation adepts, while rating the future emperor Chien-wen among the second (9/37). Here, the hallowed ruler-subject relation surrenders to the rivalry of *ch'ing-yen* scholarship.

Liu even went so far as to compare himself to Heaven:

> Wang Meng and Liu T'an met after having been separated for some time. Wang said to Liu, "You've progressed higher in rank than ever."
> Liu replied, "This is just like 'Heaven's [*t'ien*] being naturally high,' that's all." (2/66)[36]

Since antiquity, especially in the Confucian tradition, *T'ien*, or "Heaven," remained the highest authority, the superior ruling power in the entire cosmos.[37] Therefore, comparing oneself to Heaven was an act of a contemptuous irreverence, of enormous arrogance. After all, the emperor himself could only claim to be the "son of Heaven." Liu T'an's daring comparison of himself to Heaven outraged later commentators, such as Li Tz'u-ming, who wrote: "No matter how arrogant one might be, he would not compare himself to Heaven. The Chin people were so contemptuous and unrestrained that they were accustomed to self-aggrandizement. The so-called 'refined reasoning and abstruse words' which they bragged about were only something plagiarized from the Buddhist sūtras and the *Lao-tzu*. With some pretentious prattle, they confused and cheated ignorant people. They extolled their own names and tricked each other."[38]

Liu T'an's "heaven analogy," which illustrates the Wei-Chin separation from *ming-chiao,* or moral teachings, suggests another component of Wei-Chin self-fashioning: the embrace of *tzu-jan*—spontaneity, or self-so-ness. The origin of Liu T'an's daring remark comes from the following *Chuang-tzu* text: "The murmuring of the water is its natural talent, not something that it does deliberately. The Perfect Man stands in the same relationship to virtue. Without cultivating it, he possesses it to such an extent that things cannot draw away from him. It's like heaven [*t'ien*]'s being naturally high, earth naturally thick, and the sun and moon naturally bright. Do they cultivate these qualities?"[39]

In this sense, *t'ien* in Liu T'an's remark is not the anthropomorphic ruling power, "Heaven," but a material existence, "heaven," equivalent to earth, the sun, the moon, the water—in brief, anything natural. Obviously, Liu T'an identifies with the Perfect Man (*chih-jen*)—a term closely linked in the *Chuang-tzu* with the Divine Man (*shen-jen*), the Great Man (*ta-jen*), and the Sage (*sheng-jen*).[40] Although their specific meanings in the *Chuang-tzu* may differ slightly,[41] all embody self-so-ness; and the *Shih-shuo*'s frequent allusion to these personae, as in Liu T'an's "heaven analogy," reflects the Wei-Chin embrace of this central Taoist concept.[42]

A. C. Graham describes the "Great Man" in the *Chuang-tzu* in following terms: "Not only does the Great Man have a comprehensive view of the cosmos, the capacity to see himself in proportion within it is precisely what distinguishes him as a Great Man."[43]

The *Shih-shuo hsin-yü* provides an interesting illustration of one kind of proportionality, coupled with defiance of conventional norms: "On many occasions Liu Ling [d. after 265], under the influence of wine, would be completely free and uninhibited, sometimes taking off his clothes and sitting naked in his room. Once when some persons saw him and chided him for it, Liu Ling retorted, 'I take heaven and earth for my pillars and roof, and the rooms of my house for my pants and coat. What are you gentlemen doing in my pants?'" (23/6). For Liu Ling, Liu T'an, and many others, to identify with the Great Man was to transcend mundane space and to enter the spiritual void, where they could travel in their minds beyond any confinement.[44] Only under such free and natural circumstances could one's "self" grow of its own accord.

Significantly, Liu Ling was a member of the famous group of Wei-Chin gentry known as the "Seven Worthies of the Bamboo Grove" *(Chu-lin ch'i-hsien)*—a cohort that also included such notables as Juan Chi, Hsi K'ang, Hsiang Hsiu (ca. 221–ca. 300), Shan T'ao (205–283), Wang Jung (234–305), and Juan Hsien (234–305). Whether this illustrious group ever actually existed is a matter of some debate; the important point is that they served, like Chuang-tzu's "Great Man," as a tangible symbol of the Wei-Chin spirit of "freedom," and their fame spread far and wide.[45] Sun Sheng's *Chin Yang-ch'iu* tells us, for example: "At the time (ca. 260), the fame of the manner (of the 'Seven Worthies') was wafted everywhere within the seas. Even down to the present (ca. 350) people continue to intone it."[46] Under the influence of the Seven Worthies, the main stream of Wei-Chin gentry society fashioned its collective identity: a free, unrestrained spirit known as *lin-hsia feng-ch'i,* or the Bamboo Grove aura.[47]

The *Shih-shuo* author clearly aimed his ample portrayal of the Seven Worthies and their followers at a full exemplification of the Wei-Chin collective self-fashioning. He arranged the most revealing instances in the chapter entitled "Jen-tan." *Jen*—uninhibitedness—denotes an unrestrained tendency of the Taoist self-so-ness rooted in a strong sense of self-aware-

Figure 2.4. *The Seven Worthies of the Bamboo Grove and Jung Ch'i-ch'i*. Rubbing of a brick relief. South wall, tomb at Hsi-shan ch'iao, Nanking, Kiangsu. Late fourth–early fifth century. Nanking Museum. *From left to right:* Hsi K'ang, Juan Chi, Shan T'ao, and Wang Jung. (Photograph courtesy of Audrey Spiro.)

ness; and *tan*—eccentricity—denotes an intentional differentiation of one-self from the conventional world. Under these two rubrics, he detailed the Seven Worthies' outlandish behavior, presenting a scroll of some of the most colorful and idiosyncratic personalities the Chinese tradition has ever witnessed (to be detailed in chapters 4 and 5).

Character Appraisal, Abstruse Learning, and Wei-Chin Self-Expression

How did Wei-Chin self-fashioning find its expression? The inquiry evolved through the interaction between character appraisal and the evolution of *Hsüan-hsüeh*. The two were connected because of their intrinsic mutual affiliation, rather than an incidental concurrence.

Character appraisal was mainly a verbal activity; the judgment and categorization of human character types had to be conducted through language, spoken or written. With the growth of self-awareness in the transitional years from the late Han to the Wei, the flourishing of personality types demanded increasingly subtle distinctions in description. This led naturally to a metaphysical investigation of the relations between words

Figure 2.5. *The Seven Worthies of the Bamboo Grove and Jung Ch'i-ch'i.* Rubbing of a brick relief. North wall, tomb at Hsi-shan ch'iao, Nanking, Kiangsu. Late fourth–early fifth century. Nanking Museum. *From left to right:* Jung Ch'i-ch'i, Juan Hsien, Liu Ling, and Hsiang Hsiu. (Photograph courtesy of Audrey Spiro.)

and meanings. At this point, as T'ang Yung-t'ung observes, *Hsüan-hsüeh* began to be systematized. According to T'ang: "The systematization of *Hsüan-hsüeh* was grounded in disputes over the [relationship between] words and meanings. . . . The origin of this disputation emerged from the School of Names and Principles [*ming-li chih hsüeh*] of the Han-Wei period, and the School of Names and Principles originated from character appraisal."[48]

The complicated interaction between character appraisal and the evolution of *Hsüan-hsüeh* began in the late Han, when character appraisal evolved into an independent and self-contained enterprise and hence necessitated guiding theories and methodologies for understanding, discerning, and expressing human nature. Although no hard evidence has yet been found to show the existence of disputes on abstract principles at this time,[49] one can see a clear tendency of using metaphors for subtler expressions of character appraisal in the late Han. The *Shih-shuo* author sensitively seized upon this feature in his first records of this practice:

> Ch'en Fan once said with a sigh of admiration, "A person like Chou Ch'eng is truly capable of governing the state. If I were to compare him to a valuable sword, he'd be the Kan-chiang of the age." (8/1)
>
> Contemporaries characterized Li Ying as "brisk and bracing like the wind beneath sturdy pines." (8/2)

Liu Chün's commentary on this later episode provides some additional examples of metaphors taken from the Han-Wei historical records: "The *Li Family Biography* records: 'Li Ying was lofty as a mountain and pure as a deep pool. His eminent manner was highly honored. Everyone in the realm praised him saying, "Grand Warden Li of Ying-ch'uan (Honan) towers high like a jade mountain, Ch'en Fan of Ju-nan (Honan) surpasses all others like a thousand-*li* horse, and Chu Mu of Nan-yang (Honan) is cool and breezy, as when one walks beneath pines and cypresses."'"

This particular use of metaphor manifests a late Han awareness of—and an effort to deal creatively with—some fundamental problems of character appraisal. As discussed previously, the criteria of character appraisal changed substantially from the Han dynasty to the Wei-Chin period, necessitating the development of ever more sophisticated ways of describing and evaluating individuals. Court-formulated terms, such as "filial and incorrupt" or "honest and clement," no longer sufficed to express human nature fully and accurately. Thus scholars turned to metaphorical images, particularly those drawn from the natural world: landforms, sky, heavenly bodies, plants and trees, animals, water, and so forth.

Natural images liberated evaluators from the constraints of Confucian discourse, allowing them to imagine and describe the qualities of their subjects in fresh, fluid, and multidimensional ways. The following *Shih-shuo* anecdotes adduce the example of Kuo T'ai, the most proficient evaluator of the Han and Wei-Chin eras:[50] "When Kuo T'ai arrived in Ju-nan (Honan) and went to pay his respects to Yüan Lang, his carriage hardly stopped in its tracks, nor did the bells cease ringing on the harness. But when he went to visit Huang Hsien he spent a full day and two nights. When someone asked his reason, T'ai replied, '[Yüan Lang's capacity is like flowing waves, pure and easy to fetch.][51] Huang Hsien is vast and deep, like a reservoir of ten thousand *ch'ing*;[52] clarify him and he grows no purer, stir him and he grows no muddier. His capacity is profound and wide and difficult to fathom or measure'" (1/3). Comparing both Yüan Lang and Huang Hsien's personalities to water, Kuo T'ai provides an apt illustration of the way similarity and difference could be expressed in a single vivid metaphor. Despite the common denominator of water, Yüan's easily perceptible purity cannot be equated with Huang Hsien's unfathomable profundity. Using this metaphor, Kuo not only visualizes the subtlety of human nature, which has facets as complex as water. He also sets up a new standard for character appraisal: The discernible purity, as a long-standing Han moral category, cannot alone sustain one's ideal quality; human nature must maintain its self-contained and self-directed integrity. In short, the late Han conception of human nature openly and self-consciously defied the simple analytical categories of its antecedents.

We should not assume, however, that the Wei-Chin gentry adopted the method of metaphorical appraisal in a mindless or indiscriminate way, faute de mieux. Quite the contrary, only after a series of sophisticated *ch'ing-yen* debates—revolving around questions of words and meanings, names and actualities, body and spirit, and so on—did these scholars feel comfortable transforming human spirits into natural objects.

The *ch'ing-yen* debates that raged during the Wei-Chin era arose under different circumstances, involved different "schools," focused on different "classics," and were propelled by different thinkers. The table below provides a brief overview of these debates arranged according to their historical and intellectual affiliations. With the help of this table I hope to clarify, in the ensuing discussion, how the interaction between character appraisal and *Hsüan-hsüeh* enabled each side to refine itself while prompting the other side to deeper reflection and greater profundity.

NAME AND ACTUALITY

Debate over the first pair of these dichotomies, *ming* and *shih* (name and actuality), arose in the late Han and reached its peak during the Chien-an reign (196–220). It evolved in response to three main circumstances: First, as I have already discussed at length, the newly independent character appraisal necessitated its own standards and terms (*ming*) to evaluate the objects' inner qualities (*shih*). Second, the late Han frenzy for fame, which abetted fraud, further challenged character appraisal to distinguish one's real nature (*shih*) from his deceptive reputation (*ming*).[53] Third, during the Chien-an reign, Ts'ao Ts'ao desperately needed capable officials to

TABLE 1. THE *CH'ING-YEN* DEBATES OVER COMPLEMENTARY OPPOSITES

Period	Complementary Opposites	Major Schools	Classics	Major Thinkers and Their Works
Late Han (147–220)	*ming* and *shih* (name and actuality)		Confucianism: *Lun-yü, Hsün-tzu* Legalism: *Han Fei-tzu*	Wang Fu (ca. 85–162), *Ch'ien-fu lun* (Discourse by a recluse). Hsü Kan (170–217), *Chung-lun* (On the Mean).[1]
Early Wei (220–239)	*ming* and *li* (names and principles)	*Ming-li*	Confucianism: *Lun-yü, I-ching* Taoism: *Lao-tzu*	Liu Shao (fl. 220–250), *Jen-wu chih* (Study of human abilities).[2]
Wei Cheng-shih reign	*ming* and *li* *ts'ai* and *hsing* (talents and human nature)	*Ming-li*	Confucianism: *Lun-yü, I-ching* Taoism: *Lao-tzu*	Chung Hui (225–264), *Ts'ai-hsing ssu-pen lun* (Treatise on four basic relations between innate ability and human nature).
(240–249)	*yu* and *wu* (Something and Nothing)[3] *yin* and *yang* *yen* and *i* (word and idea) *pen* and *mo* (origin and end) *t'i* and *yung* (substratum and function)	*Hsüan-hsüeh*		Ho Yen (190–249), *Lun-yü chi-chieh* (Collected interpretation of the *Analects* of Confucius). Wang Pi (226–249), *Lao-tzu chu* (Commentary on the Lao-tzu), *Chou-i chu* (Commentary on the Chou changes).
Chu-lin (250–263)	*tzu-jan* and *ming-chiao* (self-so-ness and moral teachings)	*Hsüan-hsüeh*	Taoism: *Lao-tzu, Chuang-tzu*	Juan Chi (210–263), *Ta-jen hsien-sheng chuan* (Biography of the Great Man), *Yüeh-lun* (On music). Hsi K'ang (223–262), "Sheng wu ai-lo lun" (Musical sounds are without sorrow or joy), "Yang-sheng lun" (Nourishment of life).

Period	Complementary Opposites	Major Schools	Classics	Major Thinkers and Their Works
Yüan-k'ang reign (291–299)	yu and wu yen and i	Hsüan-hsüeh	Taoism: Chuang-tzu	Hsiang Hsiu (ca. 221–ca. 300), Kuo Hsiang (d. 312), Chuang-tzu chu (Commentary on the Chuang-tzu) Ou-yang Chien (ca. 265–300), "Yen chin i lun" (On words fully expressing meanings).
Eastern Chin (316–420)	yu and wu yen and i se and k'ung (Matter and Emptiness) hsing and shen (body and spirit)	Hsüan-hsüeh	Buddhism: Po-jo ching or Prajñāpāramitā Sūtras (Sūtras on the perfection of wisdom)	Shih Tao-an (312–385) Chu Tao-ch'ien (286–374) Chih Tun (314–366),* Miao-Kuan chang (Essay of marvelous view) Chu Tao-i (fl. 366–387), • "Shin erh-ti lun" (on the double truth of the spirit)

1. Makeham translates Chung-lun as "Discourses That Hit the Mark," taking "chung" as a verb (Name and Actuality, xi). I consider that "chung" here means "chung-yung," an ideal Mean between excess and deficiency.

2. T'ang Yung-t'ung takes the Jen-wu chih as an early Wei text, but Shryock believes it to be written between 240 and 250; see T'ang Yung-t'ung, "Tu Jen-wu chih," 207–208; and Shryock, The Study of Human Abilities, 2. In any case, its compilation should not be later than the early 240s when the Cheng-shih Hsüan-hsüeh began.

3. The rendering of yu/wu follows A. C. Graham, as he says: "Yu and wu when nominalised become 'what has/that in which there is (colour, shape, sound)' and what does not have/that in which there is no (colour, shape, sound)'. The least misleading English equivalents are 'something' and 'nothing'" (Studies in Chinese Philosophy and Philosophical Literature [Singapore: Institute of East Asian Philosophies, 1986], 344).

reorder the chaotic situation. His search for "human talent" (*jen-ts'ai*) necessitated accurate judgment of a candidate's innate ability (*shih*) in order to fit him to a proper bureaucratic position (*ming*).

Under such circumstances, late Han leading scholars, including Wang Fu and Hsü Kan, seriously pondered the subtle relations between name and actuality, and sought a way to reconcile them.[54] Hsü Kan, for example, systematically discussed the *ming/shih* relationship in his *Chung-lun*. For him, "the proper relationship between names and actualities is one where there is accord between them such that names faithfully represent actualities and actualities give names their meaning and significance. When name and actuality are in accord they form a whole where each partner relies on the other such that without names, actualities would not be manifest, and without actualities, there would be nothing to be manifest as names."[55]

John Makeham calls Hsü Kan's argument a "correlative theory of naming" and differentiates it from the "nominalist theory of naming" represented by such famous pre-Ch'in philosophers as Confucius, the Neo-Mohists, Hsün-tzu, Lao-tzu, Chuang-tzu, Hui Shih, and Kung-sun Lung. He argues that the nominalist theory presents the view that "it is man who arbitrarily or conventionally determines which *ming* should be applied to which *shi* [*shih*]; that is, there is no proper or correct correlation between a given *ming* and a given *shi* [*shih*] other than what has been artificially determined by man."[56] As I will show later, although Hsü Kan and his followers took "correlative theory of naming" as the ideal approach to the *ming* and *shih* relationship, pragmatism often necessitated arbitrary ways of naming. The process of Wei-Chin pure conversation involved constant debate between these two theories of naming, and the concessions and contributions made by each helped to shape the categorization scheme of the *Shih-shuo hsin-yü*.

The dispute over *ming* and *shih* in character appraisal incited discussions of other paired concepts, notably *ming/li* (names/principles) and *ts'ai/hsing* (innate abilities/human nature). The *ming/li* dispute, in its most literal sense, as Makeham points out, "referred to the discussion of the relationship between words and the abstract principles or patterns of thought represented by those words."[57] It was only natural that the *ming/shih* polarity should evolve into a *ming/li* dichotomy since *shih* (actuality) was nothing more than a cluster of thoughts awaiting the crystallization of words.

The School of *Ming-li* emerged in response to the Wei regime's call for talented people.[58] Its early stage thus focused on the pragmatic issue of how to fit candidates' talents (*shih*) to proper official positions (*ming*).[59] As one result of this early stage, Liu Shao's *Jen-wu chih* systematically detailed the relationship between one's inner nature (*hsing*), innate ability (*ts'ai*), and the official post (*jen*) that would suit him. But because of its emphasis on the political function of character appraisal, the work is not mentioned in the *Shih-shuo hsin-yü*, which focuses mainly on character appraisal as an independent intellectual practice. Nonetheless, in the formation of its own taxonomy of human nature, the *Shih-shuo* is clearly indebted to the categorization scheme of the *Jen-wu chih*, as I shall show later in chapter 4.

The *Shih-shuo hsin-yü* begins its account of the Wei-Chin philosophical debates from the later stage of the *Ming-li* School, during the Wei Cheng-shih reign (240–249). At this stage, discussions of the *ts'ai/hsing* relationship no longer focused on political considerations; rather, they turned into an enterprise of pure scholarship. The *Shih-shuo hsin-yü* includes an anecdote about Chung Hui's (225–264) *Ts'ai-hsing ssu-pen lun* (Treatise on four basic relations between innate ability and human nature), which epitomized these theoretical debates (4/5). Liu Chün recounted the basic ideas of these debates by quoting from the *Wei-chih* (Records of the Wei): "Chung Hui discussed whether *tsai* (innate abilities) and *hsing* (human nature) were identical or different, and his treatise was circulated throughout the realm. The so-called 'four basic relations' [*ssu-pen*] refer to: (1) *ts'ai* and *hsing* being *t'ung* [identical], (2) *ts'ai* and *hsing* being *i* [different], (3) *ts'ai* and *hsing* being *ho* [convergent], and (4) *ts'ai* and *hsing* being *li* [divergent]. Fu Ku favored *t'ung*, Li Feng favored *i*, Chung Hui himself favored *ho*, and Wang Kuang favored *li*."[60]

Because the original text of Chung's work is not extant, it is difficult to pinpoint all of these arguments. T'ang Chang-ju's summary is probably a plausible one: "Those who argue about whether *ts'ai* [innate abilities] and *hsing* [human nature] are identical [*t'ung*] or different [*i*] disagree with each other in their interpretation of the two concepts, *ts'ai* and *hsing*. The one who maintains that *ts'ai* and *hsing* are identical interprets *hsing* as one's "inborn nature" and *ts'ai* as the performance of one's nature. . . . The one who maintains that *ts'ai* and *hsing* are different interprets *hsing* as one's moral qualities and *ts'ai* as one's innate abilities."[61]

The importance of all these subtle arguments lies in that they moved character appraisal from a moral-political plane to an ontological one, raising questions about how to understand the elusive relationship between "name and actuality" and "nature and ability."

SOMETHING AND NOTHING

As Wei thought became ever more metaphysical, it moved farther and farther away from the sociopolitical concerns of Han Confucianism, drawing much of its intellectual sustenance from non-Confucian intellectual traditions—particularly Taoism. We should not be surprised, therefore, to find that Liu Shao applied the ideas of Lao-tzu in his *Jen-wu chih*,[62] or that Chung Hui, author of the *Ssu-pen lun*, also studied the *Lao-tzu*.[63] At this point, Wei philosopher Wang Pi, with his patron Ho Yen, embarked on a broad-scaled rearrangement of contemporary scholarship, using Taoist ideas to interpret Confucian classics. T'ang Yung-t'ung tells us: "Wang Pi was the founder of *Hsüan-hsüeh*. Yet he actually established his philosophical system by synthesizing the essence of Han Confucianism and the *Yin-Yang* School with the axioms of the School of Names and Principles, compromising them with ideas from the *Lao-tzu*, in order to probe the principles contained in Han scholarship and to clarify heretical elements. Han Confucianism thus declined, and Wei-Chin *Hsüan-hsüeh* arose."[64]

The discussion in the *Shih-shuo hsin-yü* on Wang Pi and Ho Yen immediately follows its accounts of Cheng Hsüan (127–200), the epitomizer of Han Confucianism (4/1, 4/2, 4/3), and Chung Hui, the epitomizer of Wei *Ming-li* scholarship (4/5). What the author is trying to show is that *Hsüan-hsüeh* grew out of the merger of Han Confucianism and Wei *Ming-*

li scholarship but that it went farther in the direction of metaphysics, "ignoring the study of concrete matters while emphasizing the quest for abstract principles."[65]

Wang Pi's contributions to Wei-Chin discourse can be seen in the following *Shih-shuo* anecdote:

> When Wang Pi was barely twenty, he went to visit P'ei Hui. Hui asked him, "*Wu* [Nothing] is indeed that by which all things are sustained, yet the Sage [Confucius] was unwilling to vouchsafe any words on the subject. Lao-tzu, on the other hand, expatiated on it endlessly. Why?"
>
> Wang Pi replied, "The Sage took *wu* as the permanent substratum,[66] yet *wu* is indefinable. Therefore of necessity his words applied to *yu* [Something]. Lao-tzu and Chuang-tzu, not yet free of *yu*, were continuously trying to define what they were not able to define." (4/8)[67]

Wang Pi's response here typifies his effort to apply the *Lao-tzu* dialectic to the interpretation of Confucianism, or rather to borrow the authority of Confucianism to legitimize his newly established metaphysics: an ontological quest "for a permanent substratum underlying the world of change."[68]

Wang Pi's use of the terms *yu* and *wu* is, of course, drawn from the *Lao-tzu*, where their relationship is described in the following way: "The myriad things in the world are born from Something [*yu*], and Something from Nothing [*wu*]."[69] According to the *Chin-shu* (History of the Chin): "During the Wei Cheng-shih reign [240–249], Ho Yen, Wang Pi, and their peers followed the ideas of the *Lao-tzu* and the *Chuang-tzu* and established their theory, saying: 'Heaven and Earth and myriad things all take *wu* as their origin. *Wu* is that which opens up all things and completes the task [of the creative process], and which is present everywhere. *Yin* and *yang* rely upon *wu* to transform and produce everything, and the myriad entities rely upon it to realize their forms.'"[70]

Wang Pi explicitly identifies *wu* with the *Tao,* the central concept of Taoism: "The *Tao* is a term for Nothing [*wu*]. Since there is nothing it does not pass through and nothing which does not follow it, it is called by metaphor the *Tao* [Way]."[71] So defined, *wu* becomes both the origin of the world and the Way through which the world operates. Based on this understanding, Wang Pi takes *wu* as the fundamental substratum *(t'i)* of the world, the function *(yung)* of which is to give birth to the world; hence the quest for *wu* and its connection with *yu* form the major concern of *Hsüan-hsüeh*.

Yet this *wu*, the origin of the world, is abstract and unnamable—and hence indefinable. The *Lao-tzu* states:

> There is a thing confusedly formed,
> Born before Heaven and Earth.
> Silent and void
> It stands alone and does not change,
> Goes round and does not weary.
> It is capable of being the mother of the world.
> I do not know its proper name,
> But I call it by the appellation *"Tao"*;
> If compelled to make a name for it,
> I should say "Great."[72]

In his commentary on this paragraph, Wang Pi explains why words, names, or symbols cannot express this "silent and void" *wu:* "[The reason we should name it *'Tao'*] is because we (have to) select the most comprehensive ('great') of all appellations that can be pronounced. . . . But if this (term) 'Great' becomes associated with (a notion of a definite object), then there will inevitably be distinction, and if there is distinction, then it fails to express the ultimate (truth). Hence (Lao-tzu) says: 'If compelled to make a name for it, I should say "Great."'"[73] In Wang Pi's understanding, the relation between names (or words) and *wu* reflects the relation between *yu,* Something, and *wu,* Nothing. Any name given to Nothing would associate Nothing with Something, thus distorting it by equating it to something specific.

Here we come to a pivotal problem: the inability of words to fully express ideas. Of all the dichotomies that we have encountered so far— *ming/shih* (name/actuality), *ming/li* (name/principle), *ts'ai/hsing* (innate ability/human nature), *yu/wu* (Something/Nothing), *t'i/yung* (substratum/ function), *yen/i* (word/meaning), as well as the two more pairs yet to come: *ming-chiao/tzu-jan* (moral teachings/self-so-ness) and *hsing/shen* (body/spirit)—each pair has a relatively abstract part and a relatively concrete part. Yet, as A. C. Graham points out, "for Taoists all that lacks material form is by definition *wu*";[74] thus, all these dichotomies can be molded into the *yu/wu* relationship. And since *wu* is by definition indefinable, all the abstract parts of these dichotomies—actuality, principle, human nature, substratum, meaning, self-so-ness, spirit, and so forth—are indefinable.

How, then, can we proceed? In his response to P'ei Hui, Wang Pi contends that, since *wu* is indefinable, of necessity the Sage applies his words to *yu*. In other words, the way to comprehend the immaterial, abstract part of each dichotomy is through its concrete part, and the way to grasp the idea is, after all, through the words. As Wang Pi argues in his interpretation of the *I-ching*, "To yield up ideas completely, there is nothing better than the images [*hsiang*], and to yield up the meaning of the images, there is nothing better than words [*yen*]."[75] He goes on to say, drawing upon the *Chuang-tzu*:[76] "The words are generated by the images, thus one can ponder the words and so observe what the images are. The images are generated by ideas, thus one can ponder the images and so observe what the ideas are. The ideas are yielded up completely by the images, and images are made explicit by the words. Thus, since the words are the means to explain the images, once one gets the images, he forgets the words, and since the images are the means to allow us to concentrate on the ideas, once one gets the ideas, he forgets the images."[77]

Although here the "words" and "images" refer specifically to those in the *I-ching*, Wang's intellectual ally, Ho Yen, enlarges the concept into any "words" and "images" when he says: "Since *Tao* is nameless, we may name *Tao* [or *wu*] with all the names in the world," acknowledging, however, that none of these names is truly *Tao*'s name.[78] In this sense, the "words" and "images" mentioned by Wang Pi are the names of all the manifold things in the world. Both Ho and Wang conceived of these names as mere tools for grasping ideas. The key is not to dwell upon words, symbols, forms, matter, or any kind of concrete, specific aspect of things; they are the means, but ideas are the end.

On this principle, Wang Pi laid the foundations for *Hsüan-hsüeh*. In

the words of T'ang Yung-t'ung: "Wang Pi was the first to advocate the principle of 'forgetting the words once getting the ideas' [*te-i wang-yen*]. Although
originally he meant to use it to interpret the *I-ching,* he later used it to
judge and interpret cosmological principles and human affairs. This is why
he could establish the system of *Hsüan-hsüeh.*"[79]

When Wang Pi's notion of "forgetting the words once getting the ideas"
was incorporated into the practice of character appraisal, it brought the
dynamic tension between words and ideas into the realm of body (*hsing*)
and spirit (*shen*). The problem of Wei-Chin character appraisal became
how to pursue abstract *shen* through one's perceptible behavior, remarks,
and appearance, and how to grasp abstract *shen* with tangible words in order to describe each individual personality more accurately. Wang Pi's formula, however, could not suffice to guide the rhetoric of depicting diverse
personalities, since it focused on *wu,* the dark, void, shapeless and nameless Nothing, rather than on *yu,* the colorful, nameable Something. The
bridging of the gap between the various dichotomies, *yu* and *wu, yen* and
i, hsing and *shen,* and others—had to await the intellectual engineering of
Hsiang Hsiu (ca. 221–ca. 300) and Kuo Hsiang (d. 312).

WORDS AND MEANINGS

Together, Hsiang Hsiu and Kuo Hsiang brought Wei-Chin *Hsüan-
hsüeh* to a new level of sophistication. Hsiang was the principal architect
of the process, designing the structure, so to speak, with his brilliant commentary on the *Chuang-tzu.* According to the *Shih-shuo hsin-yü,* prior to
Hsiang's time "none of the dozens of commentators on the *Chuang-tzu*
had ever been able to get the full essence of its ideas," but Hsiang Hsiu
offered such a "marvelous and insightful analysis [of this work] that
it greatly impelled the vogue of the Abstruse [Learning]." Later, Kuo
Hsiang—a person described by the *Shih-shuo* as "mean in behavior" yet
possessed of "outstanding ability"—plagiarized this study, offering an identical interpretation of the *Chuang-tzu* (4/17).

Hsiang Hsiu's commentary is no longer extant, but assuming that the
Shih-shuo is correct in identifying Kuo Hsiang's plagiarism, we can

confidently trace the ideas of the former through the writings of the latter. Among the most powerful of these ideas had to do with the relationship between *yu* and *wu*. Whereas Wang Pi and Ho Yen took the names of the multifarious "existent" things (*yu*) to be mere tools for reaching Nothing (*wu*), Hsiang and Kuo regard Something as equivalent to Nothing. In their commentary on the *Chuang-tzu,* they maintain that Nothing does not exist beyond Something, but is rather the Way of sustaining the phenomenal world. Through the Way, myriad things are born and transformed of their own accord—what Kuo Hsiang terms "self-transformation" (*tu-hua*).[80] Conversely, the rich, colorful existence and transformation of the myriad things reflect this abstract, formless, nameless, indefinable Nothing— the *Tao*, or the Way. Hsiang and Kuo express this idea in their interpretation of the notion of *"t'ien-lai"* (piping of Heaven), an analogue of *wu*, or *Tao*, in the *Chuang-tzu:*

> Is there a separate thing called the "piping of Heaven"? It is but like things [such as flutes, whistles, pipes and so forth,] made of the hollows within bamboos, and related to animate things. Altogether they form the whole Heaven. Since Nothing [*wu*] is nonexistent, it cannot produce Something [*yu*], and if Something has not yet been produced, it, in turn, cannot produce anything either. This being the case, who is it that produces production? Clod-like, it produces itself, that's all. . . . We call this the "naturally-so" [*t'ien-jan*]. The naturally-so is not created; that's why we use the word "Heaven" [*t'ien*] in speaking of it. Using the word "Heaven" in speaking of it is a means of clarifying its self-so-ness. How can "Heaven" here specifically mean that dark, void sky? . . . Heaven is the generic name for the myriad things. Since there is no such specific thing as Heaven, who is then the lord to enslave the myriad things? Thus all things are born spontaneously and have no [external] source from which they come. This is the *Tao* of Heaven.[81]

This new interpretation of the *yu/wu* relationship contributed greatly to the development of both *Hsüan-hsüeh* and character appraisal. Drawing upon it, Ou-yang Chien (265?–300) wrote a bold essay entitled "Yen chin i lun" (On words fully expressing meanings). This essay, written at the end of the third century, soon soared to the center of the *Hsüan-hsüeh* discussions, as the *Shih-shuo hsin-yü* recounts: "When Chancellor Wang Tao emigrated south of the Yangtze River (at the beginning of the fourth century), he conversed on only three topics: 'Musical Sounds Are without Sorrow or Joy' (*Sheng wu ai-lo*), 'Nourishment of Life' (*Yang-sheng*), and 'Words Fully Express Meanings' (*Yen chin-i*), and nothing else. . . . In the twists and turns of conversation, whenever anything of relevance arose, he never failed to bring them in" (4/21).

Wang Tao played a crucial role in both politics and pure conversation during the beginning years of the Eastern Chin.[82] His equation of Ou-Yang's essay with the other two—both by the leading *Hsüan-hsüeh* scholar, Hsi K'ang—shows the increasing influence of Ou-Yang's *yen chin i* theory.

In the "Yen chin i lun," Ou-yang first reconstructs the theory that words cannot fully express meanings (*yen pu chin i*) in order to prepare for his later rebuttal. The *yen pu chin i* scholars, as Ou-yang recounts, believe that the whole universe has already set itself into a natural order—manifested it automatically: "Heaven does not speak, yet the four seasons keep going around. The sage does not speak, yet his judgment and intelligence prevail. Without relying on names, forms manifest themselves, square or round, and so do colors, black or white. Therefore, names contribute nothing to things, and words have nothing to do with the principle [of the universe]."[83] According to the *yen pu chin i* scholars, the universe has its own language, a natural language, and assigns various natural names to its multifarious objects. In this view, human words are neither necessary nor sufficient to name the universe and express its order. All humanly devised forms of order, rules, or laws are artificial and false, no matter how much they claim to have imitated the natural order established by Heaven.

Contrary to the *yen pu chin i* scholars, Ou-yang stresses the importance of words: "However, people, ancient and modern, endeavor to rectify names [of things]. Sages can never eliminate words. What is the reason? Because the principle [of the universe] is conceived in the mind and cannot be expressed fully without words, and objects, though formed by themselves, cannot be differentiated without words. If we do not express our intentions with words, we cannot communicate with one another. If we do not differentiate things with names, we cannot expose our judgment and understanding. We expose our judgment and understanding, and then the names and qualities of things are differentiated. We communicate with words, and then our emotions and intentions are fully expressed."[84] Ou-yang Chien agrees with the *yen pu chin i* scholars that things naturally form themselves, but he argues that without words and names, there can be no understanding—and hence no meaning.

How can words express reality? Ou-yang Chien tells us: "In tracing the reason [why words and names are indispensable], it is not that things have natural names, or that the principle [of the universe] institutes certain expressions. We vary names in order to discriminate the substance of things. We establish different expressions in order to voice our intentions. Names change according to the substance of things, and words change according to the substance of the principle [of the universe], just as the echo responds to the sound, and the shadow follows the body. They may not be polarized into two. So if name and object, word and principle, are not two, then there is no word which is not fully expressive. Therefore I maintain that words can fully express meanings."[85] Following the theories of Hsiang Hsiu and Kuo Hsiang, that the perceivable changes of things (*yu*) can come to represent the abstract principle (*wu*) underlying these changes, Ou-Yang Chien suggests that the man-structured order, formed with appropriately varied words and names, may fully express—and hence represent—the natural order.

Ou-yang Chien's theory differs from what Makeham terms the "correlative theory of naming." He does not try to fit a name to actuality on a one-to-one basis and make the two "form a whole where each partner relies on the other such that without names, actualities would not be manifest, and without actualities, there would be nothing to be manifest as names."[86] Nor does he propose a "nominalist theory of naming,"[87] in which "it is man who arbitrarily or conventionally determines which *ming* should be applied to which *shi* [*shih*]; that is, there is no proper or correct correlation between a given *ming* and a given *shi* [*shih*] other than what has been artificially determined by man."[88] Instead, Ou-yang uses the relationship among names to reflect the relationship among things and thus equates the variation of names in a man-made system with the variation of things in the natural order. In this sense, Ou-yang Chien's theory offers a compromise between the "correlative theory of naming" and the "nominalist theory of naming."[89]

Ou-yang Chien's *yen chin i* theory provided a positive solution to the problem of *yen pu chin-i* by switching the focus from the unsolvable question of *whether* words can fully express meanings to the more constructive and down-to-earth question of *how* to make words fully express meanings. This theory later inspired the *Shih-shuo* author into a compromising taxonomy of human nature that mediated between order and disorder (to be discussed in chapter 4).

BODY AND SPIRIT

A critical issue in Wei-Chin character appraisal was the role of words in defining or delineating the relationship between *hsing* (body) and *shen* (spirit). Specifically, the question was this: Could words be used to describe one's *hsing* and thus grasp one's *shen*? Ou-yang Chien's *yen chin i* theory and the writing of Hsi K'ang (see chapter 5) offered some insights into this problem, but the solutions had to await the Eastern Chin (317–420) sinicization of newly imported Buddhism.

Ironically, this solution was based on a *Hsüan-hsüeh* misunderstanding of the relationship between two sets of philosophical terms: the Buddhist concepts of *k'ung* (*śūnyatā*; Emptiness), and its relationship with *se* (*rūpa*; visible matter), and the *Hsüan-hsüeh* categories of *wu*, Nothing, and its relationship with *yu*, Something. Emptiness is a Buddhist truth expressed repeatedly in the remarkable *Mahāyāna* collection called the *Po-jo ching* (*Prajñāpāramitā Sūtras* or Sūtras on the perfection of wisdom), a group of scriptures of various dates and lengths. The principal teaching of these sūtras, as Kenneth Ch'en sums them up, was that "the nature of the *dharma* [is] *śūnya* (void or empty)."[90] He further points out: "The *Mahāyāna* thinkers conceived of *śūnyatā* (emptiness) as meaning that the *dharmas* did not possess their own self-nature, were not ultimate facts by their own right, but were merely imagined, or came into existence depending on something else. All *saṁskṛta dharmas* were tied to conditions and were the results of many causes; they did not exist by themselves, and were said to be empty."[91]

The *Hsüan-hsüeh* concept of *wu,* or *Nothing,* and the *Mahāyāna* Buddhist *Emptiness* are two different notions. In *Hsüan-hsüeh, Nothing* represents the origin of all things. Each thing has its true, tangible existence and its own independent and specific features. By contrast, *Emptiness* as an abstract concept reflects the nature of all dharma*s* (elements of existence) and never gives birth to anything. All dharma*s,* empty and illusory by nature, come into existence either through imagination or dependency on something else.

Nothing and Emptiness also have similar features, however. Both assert an ultimate truth (or, for Nothing, the Way) underlying the phenomenal world, and both transcend words, names, and forms. Because of these similarities, Eastern Chin *Hsüan-hsüeh* adepts, or more precisely, Eastern Chin adherents of "gentry Buddhism,"[92] blurred the distinctions between the two notions and treated them as the same concept.[93] For example, the Chin gentleman Ch'ih Ch'ao (336–377) defined *Emptiness* as when "all the myriad things finally return to Nothing."[94]

Grounded in such misunderstandings, different views arose on the meaning of Buddhist Emptiness in the *Prajñāpāramitā Sūtras,* which were later referred to as the *Liu-chia Ch'i-tsung* (Six Houses and Seven "Schools").[95] Table 2 presents a summary of the basic ideas and exponents of the *Po-jo* Schools.

From the standpoint of self-expression, the three "schools of *Pen-wu* (Fundamental Nothing), *Chi-se* (Emptiness is identical with matter), and *Huan-hua* (The world is illusion) appear more important than the others. Each of the three carried its own definition of *wu* (Nothing) and *k'ung* (Emptiness), its own interpretation of the relationship between *yu* (Something) and *wu* (Nothing), *se* (matter) and *k'ung* (Emptiness), and its own way of transcending the language paradox.

The two *Pen-wu* Schools followed Wang Pi's definition of *wu,* contending that both *wu* (Nothing) and *k'ung* (Emptiness) were the origin of the phenomenal world and that they gave birth to all the elements of existence. In this view, one must directly embrace this abstract truth while avoiding entangling oneself in tangible things. *Pen-wu* masters thus reinforced Wang Pi's axiom *te-i wang-yen,* "forgetting the words once getting

TABLE 2. THE *PO-JO* SCHOOLS

Six Houses (*Liu-chia*)	Seven "Schools" (*Ch'i-tsung*)	Representatives
1 *Pen-wu* (Fundamental Nothing)	*Pen-wu* *Pen-wu i* (A variant of *Pen-wu*)	Shih Tao-an (312–385) Chu Tao-ch'ien (286–374) Chu Fa-t'ai (320–387)
2 *Chi-se* (Emptiness is identical with matter)	*Chi-se*	Chih Tun (314–366) (Ch'ih Ch'ao [336–377])
3 *Shih-han* (Retention of impressions)	*Shih-han*	Yü Fa-k'ai (ca. 310–370)
4 *Huan-hua* (The world is māya, or illusion)	*Huan-hua*	Chu Tao-i (fl. 366–387)
5 *Hsin-wu* (Emptiness of mind)	*Hsin-wu*	Chih Min-tu (fl. early fourth cent.) *Tao*-heng (fl. 360s)
6 *Yüan-hui* (Collaboration of conditions)	*Yüan-hui*	Yü Tao-sui (fl. 340s)

the idea," as a means of transcending the language paradox. They transformed Wang's phrase into *te-i wang-hsing* or *te-shen wang-hsing*, "to forget the form/body once getting the idea/spirit," using the concept for both self-expression and character appraisal.[96] A *Shih-shuo* account about Chu Tao-ch'ien, a *Pen-wu* master, typifies this approach:

> Once when the monk Chu Tao-ch'ien was present at a gathering at the villa of the future Emperor Chien-wen (Ssu-ma Yü), Liu T'an asked him, "How is it that you, a monk, are enjoying yourself within the vermilion gate?"
> Chu replied, "You naturally see it as a vermilion gate; to this indigent monk it's as if he were enjoying himself within a mat door." (2/48)

When Chu Tao-ch'ien goes to Ssu-ma Yü's villa for a pure-conversation gathering, this action thus becomes a "word" or a "form" by which Chu Tao-ch'ien "gets the idea." A monk should keep away from a vermilion gate, which symbolizes high rank and wealth, but Chu defends himself, saying that as long as he can enjoy pure conversation (as long as he gets the idea), it matters not which form it takes, within the vermilion gate or behind a mat door. Further, by establishing the vermilion gate versus mat door conflict, Chu implies that one conceptualizes things according to one's inner response to the world; consequently, one's conception of things reveals one's inner features. While Liu T'an remains captivated by the tangible form of the vermilion gate, incapable of escaping the world bustle, Chu Tao-ch'ien can see the essence of things through the form. His hermit spirit transforms a vermilion gate into a mat door.

Chu T'ao-ch'ien's *te-i wang-hsing* method seems to have also influenced his patron, Emperor Chien-wen (Ssu-ma Yü): "On entering the Flowery Grove Park (Hua-lin yüan) Emperor Chien-wen looked around and remarked to his attendants, 'the spot which suits the mind isn't necessarily far away. By any shady grove or stream one may quite naturally have such thoughts as Chuang-tzu had by the Rivers Hao and P'u.[97] [It feels as if] birds and animals, fowls and fish, come of their own accord to be intimate with men.'" (2/61)[98] Of course, the Flowery Grove Park, as the Eastern Chin imperial garden, was not at all like the Rivers Hao and P'u, where fish happily darted about, and tortoises freely dragged their tails in the mud. Yet its shady grove and stream, containing free-spirited birds and beasts, suit the emperor's mind. So he can fantasize about happiness and freedom in the wilderness (getting the idea), despite the fact that he is actually confined in this imperial garden (forgetting the form).

The axiom of *te-i wang-yen* and its variants, *te-i wang hsing* and *te-shen wang hsing,* as I shall show in a greater detail in chapter 5, tremendously influenced Wei-Chin self-fashioning and self-expression, including the ways the gentry conducted themselves—their behavior, remarks, scholarship, literary and artistic creation, and their relationship with others.[99] According to this principle, one could choose any possible way to express the "self" without entangling in any specific form.

Similarly, Chih Tun's *Chi-se* theory played a vital part in forming the Wei-Chin methodology of self-expression. His understanding of *k'ung,* Emptiness, and its relationship to *se,* matter, represents a Buddhist elaboration of Hsiang Hsiu and Kuo Hsiang's understanding of *wu,* Nothing, and its relationship to *yu,* Something.[100] Hsiang and Kuo assert in their commentary on the *Chuang-tzu* that "there is nothing which can cause a thing to be a thing";[101] rather, "all things spontaneously exist by themselves."[102] And *wu,* as a general principle, permeates and thus manifests itself in the very existence of all things *(yu).* By the same token, Chih Tun considers that *se (rūpa;* visible matter)[103] exists "as such": it does not depend upon any permanent substratum that "causes matter to be matter."[104] Based on this understanding, Chih Tun identifies matter with Emptiness. He says: "I hold that 'matter as such is Emptiness, and that matter does not (need to) be eliminated (in order to reach) emptiness.' These words express the highest (truth)."[105] According to Chih Tun, one does not go anywhere to look for Emptiness; one does not eliminate *se* in order to reach Emptiness—*se* is itself Emptiness because it lacks any substratum, and its seeming existence can only prevail as ephemeral moments in the process of causation.[106]

Chih Tun's *Chi-se* theory, an amalgamation of *Hsüan-hsüeh* and Buddhist thought, led Eastern Chin scholars to believe that no conceptual difference existed between Nothing *(wu)* and Something *(yu),* Emptiness *(k'ung)* and matter *(se).* Pursuing Chih Tun's theory, his devoted disciple Sun Ch'o composed *Yu T'ien-t'ai shan fu* (Wandering on Mount T'ien-t'ai).[107] In this imaginative rhyme-prose work, Sun embarks on an allegorical journey, seeking the ultimate truth through a literary elaboration of the beautiful landscape along the path ascending Mount T'ien-t'ai. The moment the poet reaches the summit is also the moment when he realizes that truth exists nowhere but in this perceptible world:

> We realize that *yu* can never wholly be rejected,
> That to walk with *wu* still leaves gaps.[108]
> We'll destroy both *se* and *k'ung,* and merge their traces,
> Turn at once to *yu,* and thereby gain the Way.
> . . . .
> Then we may chatter as merrily as we like all day long—
> It will be the same as utter silence, as though we'd never spoken.
> We will merge the ten thousand images through deepest
>   contemplation;
> Unwitting, we'll join our bodies with Self-so-ness.[109]

In a sudden burst of delight, by dissolving all the demarcation between

Something, Nothing, matter, Emptiness, speech, silence, and so forth, the poet finds that he has also transcended the linguistic paradox. His remarks recall the *Chuang Tzu*: "If we do not speak, then things will be all the same. Sameness, because of words, becomes differentiated; yet words are the means by which we try to make the differentiated the same again. [Therefore, I say (these words are also) no words.] Words are 'no words.' One who speaks all his life has never spoken; one who does not speak all his life has never not-spoken."[110] According to Chuang-tzu, no words, no difference; difference arises with words, and it can also be eliminated using words. In this sense, words are equal to "no words." Unlike Ou-yang Chien, who stresses that only properly used words can fully express meanings, Chih Tun and his disciples collaborate with the *Pen-wu* School in allowing for the freedom to choose any form/word for self-expression.

Chu Tao-i's *Huan-hua* theory (The world is māya, or illusion) added the final touch to the Wei-Chin methodology of self-expression. He tells us: "All *dharmas* are identical with phantoms (*huan-hua*) and are therefore named the 'worldly truth,' whereas the spirit that is in the center (heart) of a being is real and not empty. This is the principle of the highest truth. If the spirit is empty, from where can one apply the education, and by what can one cultivate the *Tao*, separate himself from the mundane world, and become a sage? Hence we know that the spirit is not empty."[111] Tao-i's theory represents another misunderstanding of Emptiness. The Buddhist doctrine of *anātmya* (nonexistence of a permanent ego, impersonality; in Chinese, *fei-shen* or *wu-wo*) denies the existence of a spirit, soul, or self, acknowledging only emptiness;[112] Chinese tradition, by contrast, stresses the transformation of the self into the sage. Without a self, or spirit, as Tao-i indicates, one loses the very subjectivity for receiving education and cultivation and achieving the sagehood. Tao-i admits that all dharmas are illusory, yet he maintains that the spirit—as the foundation of wisdom and intelligence—has to be real in order to become transformed.

If dharmas are illusory but the spirit is real, then the spirit can freely transgress the boundaries of outer forms and borrow any shape. Indeed, in an exegesis predating Chu Tao-i's, Ch'ih Ch'ao interpreted the concept of impersonality (*fei-shen*) to be when "the spirit has no constant abode, but shifts and changes without ever stopping."[113] According to Ch'ih Ch'ao and Chu Tao-i, any specific spirit can be transferred to any thing, because all things, as mere phantoms, are identical to one another in essence.[114] By the same token, any natural object, be it a mountain, a stream, a tree, a flower, the sun, or the moon, can substitute for a human body and stand for this human spirit, because a human body, also a dharma and therefore also a phantom, is essentially equivalent to any natural object.

Possibly because of this understanding or misunderstanding of Emptiness, Chin scholars widely adapted landscape descriptions for character appraisal in order to objectify the elusive human spirit.[115] Sun Ch'o, for example, applied highly personified descriptions of natural scenery in his eulogies on illustrious monks. Sun's eulogy on Chu Tao-i provides an elegant illustration of this method:

> With galloping speed he freely speaks
> In words that surely are not vain.
> Only one like Master I
> Is generous to overflowing,
> Like an orchard in spring
> Bearing fragrance and blossoms;
> Stems and branches, pliant and lush,
> With boughs and trunk, luxuriantly leafed.[116]

When Chin society acknowledged that landscape images could symbolize human personalities, Chinese landscape poetry emerged. Such poetry presented landscape as one's persona and anthropomorphic landscape descriptions as a way of self-expression. A poem by Chu Tao-i, recorded in the *Shih-shuo hsin-yü*, exemplifies the genre at its early stage:[117]

> The monk Chu Tao-i was fond of manipulating and adorning sounds and expressions. Upon his return from the capital (Chien-k'ang) to the Eastern Mountains (Chekiang), after he had passed through Wu-chung (Soochow) it chanced that snow began falling, though it was not very cold.
> On his arrival the monks asked about what had befallen him along the road, and Tao-i replied,
>
> > "The wind and frost, of course, need not be told [*pi̯ə̯u-li̯uĕn],
> > [Clouds] 'first gathering'—how dark and dense [*ts'ậm-dậm]!

Villages and towns seemed of themselves to whirl and
   evanesce [*p'iäu-p'iet]
While woods and hills then naturally turned white
   [*yâu-ńźïän]."(2/93)[118]

In his poem, Chu Tao-i carefully matches the sound with the imagery, weaving the entire poem into an effective phonetic and semantic contrast. The first three lines, describing the cold wind and frost, the dark sky and clouds, and the swirling images of villages and towns, all fall on uneven tones (tse-sheng), *piəu-ljuěn, *tsậm-dâm, and *p'iäu-p'iet, which are abrupt and brief, expressing feelings of uncertainty and anxiety. Then at the end of the fourth line comes a stable and pleasant even tone (p'ing-sheng), *yâu-ńźïän, corresponding to the overpowering whiteness of the snow.[119] Since the weather is not very cold, as the author pointedly notes, this whiteness endears rather than threatens. It overcomes darkness accumulated by the wind and forest, offering Chu Tao-i a comforting companion for his otherwise lonely and gloomy journey. Thus, Chu projects the change of his own spiritual status onto a change of the natural scene, as a traveler's excitement at viewing the purification of the universe resolves his anxiety-ridden heart.

This is the long journey that Wei-Chin Hsüan-hsüeh adepts took in order to pave the way for expressing that seemingly indefinable human nature. The Shih-shuo hsin-yü's own practice will show how the author applied these theoretical achievements to his creation and how his creation substantialized and enriched the way of Wei-Chin self-expression, adding a final touch to the formation of the Wei-Chin spirit.

Chapter 3

Shih-shuo t'i: A Sui Generis Genre

Wei-Chin character appraisal bequeathed to the *Shih-shuo t'i* obligatory discursive properties, and its nonpragmatic approach propelled the genre into a philosophical, psychological, and aesthetic quest for ideal personalities. Semantically, character appraisal implanted in the *Shih-shuo t'i* a preoccupation with the study of human nature. Syntactically, it foreshadowed the taxonomic structure of the *Shih-shuo t'i*, which classified historical anecdotes according to human character types. And verbally, the linguistic paradox that haunted character appraisal throughout the Wei-Chin era stimulated the *Shih-shuo* author to a broad search for adequate literary and artistic expressions of human nature. A new genre was in the making.

Given this direction, the author has yet to mold a concrete shape for the genre through transformation of established formulas. As Todorov points out: "From where do genres come? Why, quite simply, from other genres. A new genre is always the transformation of one or several old genres: by inversion, by displacement, by combination."[1]

Self-Claim of the Genre

Among the genres that contributed to the genesis of the *Shih-shuo t'i*, the *shuo* weighs heaviest, because it directly influenced categorization of the episodes, a feature that occupies the central attention of *Shih-shuo* readers. Scholars generally believe that the original title of the *Shih-shuo hsin-yü* was *Shih-shuo*, as first documented in the "Sui Treatise," as well as in Li Yen-shou's *Nan-shih* (History of the Southern dynasties) compiled about the same time. The title was later changed to *Shih-shuo hsin-shu* (*New writ-*

ing of the Shih-shuo) or *Shih-shuo hsin-yü* (*New account* of the Shih-shuo) because of the need to differentiate it from the Han scholar Liu Hsiang's (77–6 B.C.) *Shih-shuo* (Tales of the world).[2] Thus, when titling his work, Liu I-ch'ing chose *shuo,* a genre already in existence, to characterize the book as well as the new genre he launched. What features, then, did the *Shih-shuo hsin-yü* inherit from the genre *shuo*?

The character *shuo* has three pronunciations, with several groups of meanings. Here I cite some that are relevant to the discussion that follows:

1. **śįwat /śįwät / shuo*—to speak, to explain;
2. **śįwad / śįwäi / shuei*—to exhort, or to persuade;
3. cognate with **dįwat / įwät / yüeh,* and **d'wâd / d'uâi / tuei*—pleased, glad.[3]

And from the above three groups of meanings emerges a fourth: **śįwat / śįwät / shuo*—a genre used to explain or discuss classics, or to present certain ideas through reasoning, usually for the purpose of persuasion or advice.[4] Liu Hsieh (ca. 465–522) defines this genre in his *Wen-hsin tiao-lung* (Literary mind and the carving of dragons), "Lun shuo" (Treatise and discussion) in the following way: "The character *shuo,* to speak, or to discuss, has the meaning of *yüeh,* to please.[5] As [one of its elements,] *tui,* or to please, is a mouth and tongue [according to the "Shuo-kua" in the *Book of Changes*], the way to please is by means of one's words. When one's attempt to please goes beyond one's actual state of feeling, he is guilty of hypocrisy. For this reason Shun abhorred flattery."[6] By equating *shuo* (discussion) with *lun* (treatise), Liu Hsieh emphasizes the reasoning aspect of *shuo.* But he also points out that *shuo* differs from *lun* in having the meaning of *yüeh,* "to please." Thus, although *shuo* involves reasoning, it may easily descend from truth to fiction. This appears to be what Lu Chi (261–303) had in mind in his *Wen-fu* (Rhyme-prose on literature), when he described *shuo* as "brilliant, yet deceitful."[7]

This characteristic of *shuo,* I believe, results from the speaker/author's desire to please the listener/reader in order to drive home the argument. As Han Fei (ca. 280–233 B.C.) points out, "the difficulty of *shui* [persuading, advising, or exhorting] lies in getting to know the heart of the per-

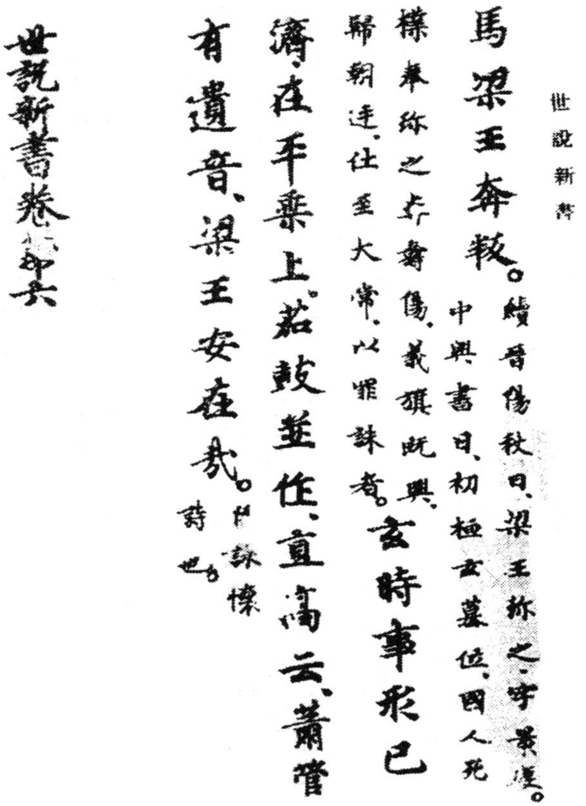

Figure 3.1. *T'ang hsieh-pen Shih-shuo hsin-shu ts'an-chüan* (Fragment of the T'ang hand copy of the *Shih-shuo hsin-shu*). Originally in 10 *chüan*. Part of an eighth-century manuscript brought to Japan perhaps as early as the ninth century and including most of *chüan* 6 (Chapters X–XIII), with the unabridged commentary by Liu Chün. Reprinted and published by Lo Chen-yü. 1916 (detail).

suaded [*so-shui*] in order to fit in with the reasoning or discussion [*shuo*]."[8] During Han Fei's time, strategists competed to persuade rulers to heed their advice, and the genre *shuo* was especially popular. The most outstanding Legalist of his day, Han Fei excelled at using historical events or legendary tales (below I will refer to them all as "tales," since the emphasis lies more in their exemplifying function than in their historical

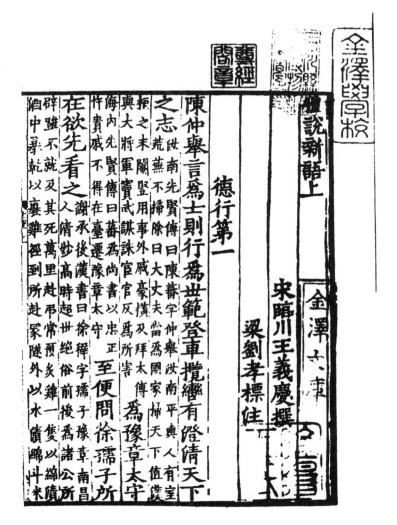

Figure 3.2. Sung edition of the *Shih-shuo hsin-yü*. Reprint of Wang Tsao's edition (thirteenth century, based on Tung Fen's 1138 edition). 5 vols. Tokyo: Sonkei Kaku or Kanazawa Bunko, 1929. Reprint, Shanghai: Chung-hua shu-chü, 1962 (*chüan* 1, 1a).

authenticity) to illustrate his arguments. This style of discussion, I suspect, is related to the *shuo* that appears in the title of the *Shih-shuo.*

In the *Han Fei-tzu,* several chapter titles, such as "Shuo-lin" (Forest of discussions), "Nei ch'u-shuo" (Inner congeries of discussions), and "Wai Ch'u-shuo" (Outer congeries of discussions), share the same character *shuo.*[9] *Shuo* in these titles means, in general, "discussions," but it actually contains two aspects: the act of telling and discussing tales and the tales as told and discussed. The chapter "Shuo-lin" is so named because "it widely narrates and discusses [*shuo*] manifold tales, which are as plentiful as trees in a forest [*lin*]."[10]

Han Fei gathers historical events and legendary tales from a wide range of sources in order to illustrate his Legalist viewpoints. This function of the tales appears especially clear in the chapters "Nei Ch'u-shuo" and "Wai Ch'u-shuo." Both contain two parts—*ching* and *shuo. Ching* presents doctrines, and *shuo* supports and explains these doctrines with tales. The *ching* part of the "Nei Ch'u-shuo" comprises thirteen passages, each bearing a two-character title accompanied by a group of tales *(shuo). Ching* and *shuo* together "illustrate how the ruler steers his subjects with strategies."[11] Likewise, the "Wai Ch'u-shuo" consists of twelve passages of *ching* supported by twelve groups of *shuo.* Together they "elucidate how the ruler observes his subjects' behavior and remarks in order to decide rewards or punishment."[12]

Han Fei's formula of the *shuo*—categorizing tales to exemplify certain arguments—inspired a number of Han writings, notably those of Liu Hsiang, the scholar who reedited the *Han Fei-tzu* and other pre-Ch'in classics that had been proscribed by the first emperor of the Ch'in dynasty (221–206 B.C.).[13] Liu's *Hsin-hsü* (New compilation of tales) and his *Shuo-yüan* (Garden of tales)—the title of which closely approximates Han Fei's *Shuo-lin*—typify this kind of writing.[14] Both the *Hsin-hsü* and the *Shuo-yüan* classify old tales and anecdotes into several chapters and name them with double-character titles. The first entry of each chapter is usually an interpretation of the title based on the Confucian classics, applying Confucian doctrines to both self-cultivation and political affairs. As Chi Yün points out, Liu Hsiang's *Shuo-yüan* and *Hsin-hsü* are "books which record anecdotes and past events for the reader's reference in following [Confucian] doctrines and orders."[15] According to their contents, Pan Ku (32–92) lists the *Shuo-yüan* and *Hsin-hsü* in the *Ju-chia* (Confucian school) under the *tzu* (Philosophers) section, in the "I-wen chih" (Bibliographic treatise) of the *Han-shu* (History of the Han; hereafter the "Han Treatise").[16]

As mentioned earlier, scholars have pointed out that the title of the *Shih-shuo hsin-yü* imitates Liu Hsiang's *Shih-shuo*.[17] Liu's *Shih-shuo* has long been lost, but, since it is listed with the *Hsin-hsü* and the *Shuo-yüan* under the Confucian School in the "Han Treatise,"[18] the three works probably share some important features. In turn, the *Shih-shuo hsin-yü* may also share something in common with the *Shuo-yüan* and *Hsin-hsü* if its style follows that of Liu Hsiang's *Shih-shuo*. Indeed, we do find a close relationship in certain chapter titles of these three works.[19]

While inheriting the *shuo* formula pioneered by Han Fei and developed by Liu Hsiang, the *Shih-shuo hsin-yü* offers a radically different system of categorization. Han Fei classifies his tales according to Legalist principles, and thus provides a series of Legalist persuasions. The *Shuo-yüan* and *Hsin-hsü* arrange their tales according to Confucian doctrines, establishing a moral guide for the reader. This purpose is revealed even more clearly in other chapter titles, such as "Chien-pen" (Establishing the foundation [of both oneself and the state]), "Li-chieh" (Building up integrity), "Tsun-hsien" (Respecting worthies), "Ching-shen" (Keeping caution), "Shan-mou" (Perfecting strategy), and so forth. The thirty-six categories of the *Shih-shuo hsin-yü*, despite their partial resemblance to the *Shuo-yüan* and *Hsin-hsü*, provide an unprecedentedly profuse list of human types.

At the same time, the *Shih-shuo hsin-yü* reflects the diminishing importance of discussion. In the *Han Fei-tzu*, each of the thirteen sections of the "Inner Congeries of Discussions" and each of the twelve sections of the "Outer Congeries of Discussions" has a subsection on "doctrine" (*ching*), in which the author directly expresses his viewpoints. In his *Shuo-yüan* and *Hsin-hsü*, Liu Hsiang shrinks the *ching* into a brief passage that opens each chapter by defining the meaning of the title. In the *Shih-shuo hsin-yü*, however, this theoretical part is condensed into the chapter title itself. This transformation of the *shuo* formula weakens the author's own

TABLE 3. SIMILARITIES BETWEEN THE CHAPTER TITLES OF *SHUO-YÜAN*, *HSIN-HSÜ*, AND *SHIH-SHUO HSIN-YÜ*

Shuo-yüan (Garden of tales)	*Hsin-hsü* (New compilation of tales)	*Shih-shuo hsin-yü*
"Kuei-te" (Exalting *te*)		"Te-hsing" *(Te* conduct)
"Shan-shuo" (Perfecting speech)		"Yen-yü" (Speech and conversation)
"Hsiu-wen" (Cultivating culture)		"Wen-hsüeh" (Literature and scholarship)
"Cheng-chien" (Honest admonition)		"Kuei-cheng" (Admonitions and warnings)
	"Tz'u-she" (Satirizing extravagance)	"T'ai-ch'ih" (Extravagance and ostentation)

voice, but encourages the reader to interpret each episode in the light of the character or behavioral type specified in the title. In this way the author intentionally allows the portraits of the idiosyncratic Wei-Chin personalities to reveal themselves.

Nonclassification or Misclassification of the Genre

The distinctive evolution and unique characteristics of the *Shih-shuo hsin-yü* have long created classification problems for Chinese bibliographers. Traditionally it has been relegated to the category of *hsiao-shuo,* a humble designation that Han historian Pan Ku lists as the last of the ten classes of the *tzu* section in the "Han Treatise."[20] He describes the category as follows: "The works of *Hsiao-shuo* probably evolved from the offices of petty officials. [They were based on] street talk and alley conversations, made up by those who engage in gossip along the roads and walkways. Confucius said: 'Though a petty path, there is surely something worth looking into. But if pursued too far, one could get bogged down; hence gentlemen do not do it.'[21] Yet gentlemen do not discard it either, for even the things which less-learned town folk can think of should be put together so as not to be forgotten, just like words of woodcutters and crazy men, of which there may be one or two worth attention."[22]

Pan Ku borrows Confucius' authority to criticize *hsiao-shuo* as a "petty path" *(hsiao-tao)*. In his postscript to the philosophers' section, Pan further states that only nine of the ten categories of *tzu* were worth examining.[23] He leaves out *hsiao-shuo* because it lacks "obvious affinity with [either] the major classical traditions or with any of the estimable schools of philosophy,"[24] and he denounces six out of fifteen *hsiao-shuo* works listed as "shallow," "absurd," or "forged," suggesting their spuriousness in origin, meaning, or factual content.[25] Inauthenticity appears to be a common stigma of the works under this rubric.

Consequently, when the "Sui Treatise" appropriated Pan's terms to define *hsiao-shuo*—that these works were nothing more than "the discussion of street talk and alley conversations"[26]—and when it documented the *Shih-shuo hsin-yü* in this category, it naturally aroused suspicion about the authenticity of the historical records included in the book. Yet at the same time that the *Sui-shu* was compiled, some of its authors also participated in the compilation of the *Chin-shu* (History of the Chin), into which they incorporated a large amount of material from the *Shih-shuo hsin-yü*.[27] To later readers, this group of historians seemed to apply a double standard to the *Shih-shuo hsin-yü:* They classified the whole book as *hsiao-shuo*, yet treated specific episodes in the book as valid historical material.

The T'ang historian Liu Chih-chi (661–721) severely criticized the *Chin-shu* compilers, complaining that while putting together a *"cheng-shih"* (official history or standard history), they should not have drawn from a source such as the *Shih-shuo hsin-yü* because it "contained obviously inauthentic historical accounts."[28] Despite the "Sui Treatise" categorization of the *Shih-shuo hsin-yü* as *hsiao-shuo*, Liu Chih-chi insisted on measuring the book against the standard of historical writing. He was not the only scholar to do so. The first commentator of the *Shih-shuo hsin-yü,* Ching Yin (fl. in the late fifth cent.), corrected about fifty historical accounts that he believed the author had distorted. In his famous commentary on the book, Liu Chün challenged the accuracy of about forty entries. And toward the end of the imperial era, Wang Hsien-ch'ien (1842–1917) maintained that the *Shih-shuo* author should not have made so many mistakes since he compiled the book not long after the time it depicted.[29]

Chi Yün was probably the first scholar who defended the *Shih-shuo hsin-yü* by clearly reminding his readers of the book's generic category. In his *Annotated Catalogue of the Four Treasuries*, which epitomizes the bibliographies written up to his time, Chi Yün argues: "Liu Chih-chi's *Shih-t'ung* (Compendium of history) seriously denounces Liu I-ch'ing's accounts [in the *Shih-shuo hsin-yü*]. Whereas Liu I-ch'ing's accounts belong to the category of *hsiao-shuo,* Liu Chih-chi examines it using the standard of historical writing. The criterion does not match the type of the text. Therefore, [Liu Chih-chi's] argument is not convincing."[30] However, Chi Yün's affirmation of the genre for the *Shih-shuo hsin-yü*—*hsiao-shuo*—does not result from his close examination of its textual features, but merely from its conventional generic attributes.

The fact that the *Shih-shuo hsin-yü* did not conform to the structure of traditional histories does not mean that it lacked historical foundations. As Richard Mather convincingly observes:

> What is clear is that nearly all of the 626 characters appearing in the pages of the "Tales of the World" are otherwise attested in the histories and other sources. Furthermore, for most incidents and remarks, allowing for literary embellishment and dramatic exaggeration, there is no good reason to doubt their reality. Only a small minority pose problems of anachronism, contradiction of known facts, gross supernatural intrusions, or apparent inconsistencies. Among the verifiable facts, for example, in Chapter II, 59, there is a record of the planet Mars (Ying-huo) reentering the "heavenly enclosure" T'ai-wei (parts of the constellations Virgo and Leo) in retrograde motion on a date corresponding to February 17, 372. This can be checked against accurate modern projections for the planetary motions of the fourth century and found to be absolutely correct.[31]

Mather further argues that, even though what actually happened or what actually was said on some historical occasions may not have been exactly as reported in the *Shih-shuo hsin-yü,* "the same accusation can be leveled at Ssu-ma Ch'ien's (145–90 B.C.) narration and dialogue in the "Records of the Grand Historian" *(Shih-chi)* and at most Chinese historiography after him. A certain amount of local color and fictionalization was more or less expected even in the standard histories."[32]

That later commentators, from Ching Yin to Liu Chün, kept amending "mistakes" in the *Shih-shuo hsin-yü* proves from another angle that the book is solidly grounded in history. It would make no sense to try to transform a fictitious work into an authentic historical one. And even in the case of "corrections" made by later commentators, some scholars defend the original text. In his *Shih-t'ung t'ung-shih* (Commentary on the compendium of history), for example, P'u Ch'i-lung (fl. 1730–1752) argues: "[Liu] I-ch'ing's book, or [Liu] Chün's corrections . . . which is the one to follow? One should not stubbornly adhere to either opinion. My humble idea is, for historical works, if there exist variant records, one should maintain the common opinions yet not abolish the variant ones."[33]

By asserting that the *Shih-shuo hsin-yü* contains mainly authentic historical records, my only purpose is to show how its features defy Pan Ku's definition of *hsiao-shuo*. I do not propose to rehabilitate the *Shih-shuo hsin-yü* as a "historical" account, because I do not think that the author ever intended to write a conventional history. To be sure, the basic units of the *Shih-shuo hsin-yü* look like biographies in miniature—each contains, if only minimally, the necessary components of a narrative: usually a single event and a few characters, all real historical figures.[34] For this reason, most scholars have considered it to be "historical" in some sense. But the overall structure of the book indicates that it is not merely a collection of biographies. In a typical historical biography, the ones contained in such books as the *Records of the Grand Historian,* the compiler collects a group of historical accounts to portray a person's life and accomplishments. In the *Shih-shuo hsin-yü,* by contrast, the author classifies biographical anecdotes to illustrate a group of human character and behavioral types. As a result, the *Shih-shuo hsin-yü* anecdotes cover a much broader spectrum of gentry life than a standard biography would. What might appear trivial in a more conventional account can underscore vividly aspects of personality that reveal different character traits and types.

The fact that the *Shih-shuo hsin-yü* contains some empirical errors does not explain its exclusion from the *shih* (history) section in the "Sui Treatise."[35] Under this section, the compilers of the "Sui Treatise" present the category "Tsa-chuan" (Miscellaneous biographies), which includes works such as Kan Pao's (fl. early fourth cent.) *Sou-shen chi* (In search of the supernatural), Liu I-ch'ing's *Yu-ming lu* (Records of the world of shadows and the human world), Yen Chih-t'ui's (531–?) *Yüan-hun chih* (Records of avenging spirits), and a certain Mr. Hsieh's *Kuei-shen lieh-chuan* (Biographies of ghosts and deities)—items that the compilers of the "Sui Treatise" describe as "fantastic and grotesque tales" *(hsü-wang kuai-tan chih shuo).*[36] Their inclusion in the same section with serious biographical writings, such as Liu Hsiang's *Lieh-nü chuan* (Biographies of exemplary women) and Hsi K'ang's (223–262) *Kao-shih chuan* (Biographies of eminent gentlemen), shows that the compilers were more concerned with the style of the work than with the authenticity of its contents.[37]

The compilers of the "Sui Treatise" were aware of the extraordinary structure of the *Shih-shuo hsin-yü* as well as the significance of that structure, but they did not know what to do with it. They could not fit the *Shih-shuo hsin-yü* into the "Histories" because it could not conform to the structural and stylistic requirements of that genre. Nor could they place it next to its possible model, Liu Hsiang's *Shih-shuo,* in the "Confucian School" under the "Philosophers" section, because the *Shih-shuo hsin-yü* was not compiled to elucidate Confucian doctrines. So the *Shih-shuo hsin-yü* found its way into the *hsiao-shuo* group under the "Philosophers" section.

Significantly, the "Sui Treatise" compilers did not denounce any of the works in their new list of *hsiao-shuo* as spurious or otherwise unreliable.[38] Although they adopted from the "Han Treatise" certain time-honored terms to define *hsiao-shuo,* their general attitude toward *hsiao-shuo* differs markedly from Pan Ku's, as the "Sui Treatise" indicates:

> *Hsiao-shuo* is the discussion of street talk and alley conversations [*chieh-shuo hsiang-yü chih shuo ye*]. The *Tso Commentary* records common people's ballads,[39] and the *Book of Songs* upholds advice from woodcutters.[40] In ancient times, sages ruled on high; historians put down [historical] records; blind men composed poems; musicians recited admonitions; ministers presented advice; gentlemen passed on [people's] opinions [to the ruler], and commoners offered criticism.
>
> In the early spring, [officials] rang wood bells while traveling around, collecting songs, ballads and poems for investigating local customs. [In order for the ruler] to correct mistakes, they recorded everything they

heard along the road. . . . Confucius said: "Though a petty path, there is surely something worth looking into. But if pursued too far, one could get bogged down."[41]

The "Sui Treatise" thus modifies Pan Ku's definition of *hsiao-shuo* considerably. First, it suggests that the sources used in the compilation of *hsiao-shuo* are indispensable to state affairs. Second, although it quotes Confucius in the fashion of the "Han Treatise," the "Sui Treatise" omits the line "gentlemen do not do it," thus reducing the stigma Pan Ku had imposed on the *hsiao-shuo* authors. Moreover, the "Sui Treatise" maintains in a postscript to the "Philosophers" section: "Confucianism, Taoism, and *hsiao-shuo* are all teachings of sages, but each has its bias. . . . If we can combine them all without leaving anything out and neutralize their biases, we can civilize people and bring order to the world [*hsing-hua chih-chih*]."[42] This assertion equates *hsiao-shuo* with the Confucian and Taoist schools, thus countering its previous marginalization from the mainstream scholarship.

The notion that *hsiao-shuo* had a role to play in guiding proper conduct resonates with a definition of the genre attributed to Huan T'an (ca. 23 B.C.–A.D. 56): "*Hsiao-shuo* writers collect episodes and little sayings, and use daily experience to exemplify their viewpoints. In this way they compose writings and write them on short blocks [*tuan-shu*].[43] With regard to guiding self-cultivation and domestic affairs [*ch'ih-shen li-chia*], writings of this kind include words of some value [*k'o-kuan chih tz'u*]."[44] Huan T'an's definition of *hsiao-shuo* also shares some common features with Han Fei's *shuo*: both illustrate viewpoints with brief narratives and petty sayings. Thus, the "Sui Treatise" may very likely have consciously linked *hsiao-shuo* (literally, "minor *shuo*") to the genre *shuo*. Viewed in this light, the phrase *"chieh-shuo hsiang-yü chih shuo ye"* in the "Sui Treatise" may best be rendered as "the *shuo* supported by street talk and alley conversations."

In other words, *hsiao-shuo*, like the other nine estimable schools of philosophy, amounts to a type of *shuo*.[45] Richard Mather describes the other *hsiao-shuo* works listed in the "Sui Treatise":

There, tucked between technical treatises on agriculture and war, it [the *Shih-shuo hsin-yü*] enjoyed the company of fictionalized biographies like the story of "Crown Prince Tan of Yen" *(Yen Tan-tzu)*. . . . Under the same heading are also listed source books for advisers to the throne, such as the "Forest of Arguments" *(Pien-lin)* or "Formulae for Those to the Right of the Throne" *(Tso-yu fang)*; jokebooks for court jesters, like Han-tan Ch'un's (third cent.) "Forest of Laughs" *(Hsiao-lin)*; and general enliveners of conversation, like the "Essential and Usable Answers for Repartee" *(Yao-yung yü-tui)*. Another work in this category very close in form to the "Tales of the World" itself was P'ei Ch'i's "Forest of Conversations" *(Yü-lin)*, which first appeared in 362.[46]

All these works are similar, Mather suggests, in providing "aids to conversation" or "enjoyable reading." Here we see an obvious connection to Liu Hsieh's definition of *shuo* in *The Literary Mind and the Carving of Dragons,* that "the character *shuo,* to speak, has the sense or meaning of *yüeh,* 'to please'." The similarity between the "Sui Treatise" *hsiao-shuo* and Han Fei's *shuo* also appears in the titles of some works. The "Forest of Arguments" *(Pien-lin),* the "Forest of Laughs" *(Hsiao-lin),* and the "Forest of Conversations" *(Yü-lin)* in the "Sui Treatise" all resemble the "Forest of Tales," or the "Forest of Discussions" *(Shuo-lin)* in the *Han Fei-tzu.* Yet none of these "forests" can be anchored next to the *Han Fei-tzu* in the Legalist School, nor do they find a place under other philosophical categories. Their concerns transgress the borders of conventional classification systems.

Because the *hsiao-shuo* classification was designed to house what was *not* a work of an estimable philosophy, it became a catch-all category in which every work found a place, yet at the same time each lost its identity. In this sense, the traditional classification of the *Shih-shuo hsin-yü* as *hsiao-shuo* became a *nonclassification* that blurred its unique characteristics.

The use of the term *hsiao-shuo* in modern times to translate the Western concept of "fiction" has created further confusion.[47] Literary historians and critics normally decide the genre of a certain work by examining its generic features, but in the case of the *Shih-shuo hsin-yü* they have forced upon it the generic features derived from the modern concept of *hsiao-shuo* (i.e., "fiction"). Thus an old stereotype has survived under a new rubric. Though many scholars consider the *Shih-shuo hsin-yü* to be an extremely valuable source on Wei-Chin history, politics, philosophy, religion, linguistics, literature and art,[48] literary historians and critics persist in labeling this collection of historical episodes as fictional.[49]

In a Class by Itself

Since the middle 1980s, Chinese scholars have begun to study the *Shih-shuo t'i* more closely,[50] seeking to redefine the genre with various names, such as *chih-jen hsiao-shuo* (*hsiao-shuo* about individuals), *i-shih hsiao-shuo* (anecdotal *hsiao-shuo*), *chin tzu-shu hsiao-shuo* (*hsiao-shuo* resembling philosophical writings), or, simply, *Shih-shuo t'i hsiao-shuo* (*hsiao-shuo* of the *Shih-shuo* genre). But all these designations reflect an uncritical acceptance of *hsiao-shuo* as a genre without clarifying the evolution of the concept, thus perpetuating the confusion. My solution to this problem is to detach the *Shih-shuo t'i* entirely from the concept of *hsiao-shuo,* either in its traditional or its modern sense. The term *Shih-shuo t'i* suffices to describe this unique genre, which arose from the Wei-Chin practice of character appraisal and took shape through the transformation of a few preceding genres—particularly *shuo* (discussion) and *chuan* (biography). The original motive for compiling the *Shih-shuo hsin-yü* was probably nothing more than a discursive reflection on human nature and an effort to summarize human behavior into abstract types. In effect, however, the description of the human world through a colorful taxonomy of human nature and a vivid characterization of "people" in narrative form created a new type of literature, which inspired many imitations over the next several centuries.

Part 2

The Narrative Art of the *Shih-shuo hsin-yü*

Introduction to Part 2:
Fictional Truth or Truthful Fiction

Order is, at one and the same time, that which is given in things as their inner law, the hidden network that determines the way they confront one another, and also that which has no existence except in the grid created by a
glance, an examination, a language; and it is only in the blank spaces of this
grid that order manifests itself in depth as though already there, waiting in
silence for the moment of its expression.
—Michel Foucault, *The Order of Things*

The basic word I-You can be spoken only with one's whole being. The concentration and fusion into a whole being can never be accomplished by me,
can never be accomplished without me. I require a You to become; becoming
I, I say You.
—Martin Buber, *I and Thou*

Later readers unanimously acclaim the *Shih-shuo hsin-yü* to be the best
of all the *Shih-shuo t'i* and a fascinating work in its own right. For instance,
Ch'ien Fen (fl. 1650s) tells us: "The dots and strokes in the *Shih-shuo hsin-
yü* are so vividly applied that they make the reader feel as if personally listening to the tasty *Shao* music played by the Musician Wei and connecting with Yin Hao and Liu T'an's abstruse thoughts. Their spirit, intelligence,
and intentions all flourish at the tip of the ink-brush . . . Had the author
not excelled in such Nature-like creativity, how could he ever have been
able to do it? Therefore, from the time of Liu I-ch'ing onward, although
each dynasty had its [*Shih-shuo t'i*] compilations, very few could continue
the tune [of the *Shih-shuo hsin-yü*]."[1]

Similar compliments pervade almost all the prefaces to the various *Shih-shuo hsin-yü* editions and imitations. Ch'ien Tseng (1629–1701) joins the chorus, praising the *Shih-shuo* characterization of Wei-Chin personalities that makes readers a thousand years later still "seem to hear them talking and laughing and to see their beards and eyebrows."[2] Mao Chi-k'o (1633–1708) goes even further, saying that the author's divine and outstanding brush portrays Wei-Chin people with such a "spiritual resemblance" (*shen-ssu*) that they "all seem ready to jump out when called upon."[3] Later readers might question the historical facts recorded in this book, but none of them ever challenged the authenticity of the Wei-Chin spirit that it transmitted.

Why did later generations of readers accept the *Shih-shuo hsin-yü* as an authentic evocation of the Wei-Chin spirit? The reason is quite simple: While reading the text, they feel as if they were "personally listening to" or "directly making contact with" the Wei-Chin people. Indeed, for the knowledge of personalities that usually demands direct contact, what can be more reliable than that acquired with our own eyes and ears? This, then, is the author's genius: He bewitched us into seeing, hearing, and connecting with individuals who are long dead. In a sense, the so-called Wei-Chin spirit is a make-believe thing, created by the narrative art of the *Shih-shuo hsin-yü*.

The *Shih-shuo*'s narrative art consists of two major parts: categorization of its episodes and characterization of its characters. The former structures the entire work by categorizing all the anecdotes into thirty-six chapters and titling them with types of human personality, behavior, or relationship; hence a taxonomy of human nature. The latter structures most of the episodes by engaging two or more characters in a rivalry pattern and exposing the dispositions of both parties through a face-to-face confrontation; hence a colorful scroll of idiosyncratic Wei-Chin personalities. The two complement each other, reflecting both the personality traits universally distributed among the Wei-Chin elite and presenting each character with a unique personality.

Chapter 4

Between Order and Disorder: The *Shih-shuo* Taxonomy of Human Nature

The Problem of Reading the *Shih-shuo* Classification

The most distinctive formula of the *Shih-shuo* genre is its classification, a "system of elements"[1] composed of both its perceptible components, including the anecdotes and the chapter titles, and an abstract syntax that links all the elements. How did the author structure this system? Why did he choose to order human nature in this particular way? What problems did he face in creating this system with language—after all, any order is ultimately a linguistic rearrangement of reality—and how did these problems affect the expression of his ideas?

The *Shih-shuo hsin-yü* offers no explicit statement about its principles of classification, so we are left to speculate. Some scholars consider the *Shih-shuo* to be an exemplification of Confucian doctrines, since the first four chapter titles, *Te-hsing* (*Te* conduct*), Yen-yü* (Speech and conversation), *Cheng-shih* (Affairs of government), and *Wen-hsüeh* (Literature and scholarship) are also known as the "four divisions of Confucius' disciples" (*K'ung-men ssu-k'o*). The groupings are as follows in the *Analects* of Confucius: "*Te* conduct: Yen Yüan, Min Tzu-ch'ien, Jen Po-niu and Chung-kung; speech and conversation: Tsai Wo and Tzu-kung; affairs of government: Jan Yu and Chi-lu; writing and scholarship: Tzu-yu and Tzu-hsia."[2]

This classification highlights certain spheres of attainment, but it does not exemplify any specific moral principle; and, as we shall see, Wei-Chin scholars did not think of these four chapters in terms of moral categories. But for later readers, especially those of modern times, *te* signified "virtue,"[3] and the first four chapters set a decidedly Confucian tone. Jao Tsung-i writes, for instance: "The *Shih-shuo hsin-yü* starts with the four divisions [of Confucius' disciples]; it originates from Confucianism. Its second *chüan*, including chapters from 'Fang-cheng' [The square and the proper] to 'Hao-shuang' [Virility and vigor] [chapters 5–13], grasps jade and embraces a virtuous tone. The first half of its last *chüan* [chapters 14–24] seems to indicate eccentric or radical people; and the second half of the last *chüan* [chapters 25–36] presents vicious and petty behavior samples. The pure and the muddy each have their allotments, and the good and the bad are clearly divided, just as grass and trees are differentiated."[4] In a similar vein, Liu Chao-yün postulates a moral hierarchy within the *Shih-shuo* system: The earlier a chapter title appears in the sequence, the higher moral value it connotes; the later, the lower.[5]

Problems of inconsistency, however, obstruct such a moralistic reading of the *Shih-shuo*. For one thing, the characters often freely cross the border between the "good" and the "bad." We see major heroes such as Juan Chi and Hsi K'ang appearing in chapter 1, "Te-hsing" (*Te* conduct), but they also occupy prominent positions in chapters 23, "Jen-tan" (Uninhibitedness and eccentricity), 25, "P'ai-t'iao" (Taunting and teasing), and 26, "Ch'ing-ti" (Contempt and insults). Wang Jung, the notorious penny-pincher whose stories form the major part of chapter 29, "Chien-se" (Stinginess and meanness), is also a genuinely filial son and an incorrupt official in chapter 1, "Te-hsing," as well as a sentimental father in chapter 17, "Shang-shih" (Grieving for the departed). Wang Tun, the treacherous and ruthless rebel whose episodes occur throughout chapters 25 to 36 and whose activities in the eyes of Jao Tsung-i present "vicious and petty behavior samples," takes up half of the episodes in chapter 13, "Hao-shuang" (Virility and vigor), which, also according to Jao, "grasps jade and embraces a virtuous tone."

Moreover, in the chapter "Te-hsing," which Jao assumes is full of Confucian content, only about half of the episodes conform with Han Confucian moral codes (filial piety, fraternal love, righteousness, benevolence, propriety, integrity, incorruptibility, and so forth). The rest celebrate other values. Thus, for example, as I discussed in chapter 1, the author seems to prefer Huang Hsien's unfathomable profundity over Yüan Lang's perceivable purity (1/3); and Ch'en Ch'en interprets his father Ch'en Shih's *te* as a capacity endowed by nature rather than as a moral faculty (1/7). Li Ying takes "responsibility for the moral teaching (*ming-chiao*) and right and wrong for the whole realm," (1/4) yet Juan Chi never passes judgment on anyone (1/15).

Some cases in the chapter "Te-hsing" transcend usually rational categories of morality, entering into the realms of emotions. Consider the following story:

> Wang Hsien-chih was critically ill. Taoists, when they offer up a petition (*Shang-chang*), must make a confession of their faults (*shou-kuo*). The master in attendance asked Hsien-chih what unusual events or [mistakes and failures (*te-shih*)][6] there had been in the course of his life
>
> Hsien-chih replied, "I'm not aware of anything, except that I remember being divorced from my wife of the Ch'ih family (Ch'ih Tao-mao)." (1/39)[7]

So strong is Wang Hsien-chih's remorse over the divorce that it keeps him from remembering any other mistakes in his life.

A letter from Wang to Ch'ih confirms his deep affection for her, although it does not fully explain the circumstances of their situation:[8] "Although we had been keeping each other's company for years, and enjoyed it all the time, still I felt frustrated that we could never love each other enough. While I was about to extend this alliance to its extreme by growing old together with you, who could have ever expected that we would be separated like this! My bosom is deeply swamped with regrets: How could I get to see you again, day and night? I weep, I sob, I toss about—nothing can restrain my grief except for death!"[9] The inclusion of this anecdote in the *Te-hsing* chapter of the *Shih-shuo* suggests that *te* here refers to much more than conventional Confucian values.

In order to understand more fully the *Shih-shuo*'s system of values, we must explore its taxonomy of human nature. I shall first introduce some major taxonomic systems that preceded the *Shih-shuo hsin-yü*, along with the principles underlying these schemes. Against this historical backdrop,

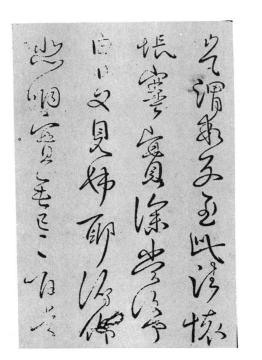 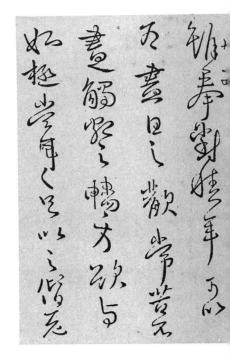

Figure 4.1. *Feng-tui t'ieh* (Letter to Ch'ih Tao-mao). Attributed to Wang Hsien-chih (344–388). From *Ch'un-hua ko-t'ieh*. Shanghai: Shanghai shu-tien, 1984.

I plan to explore the *Shih-shuo* author's own theory of understanding and classifying human nature, including his solution to the linguistic paradox that had long puzzled the participants of Wei-Chin character appraisal. Discussions of this sort will place the *Shih-shuo* taxonomy in its full intellectual and cultural context and help us to appreciate its significance, structure, and purpose.

Pre-*Shih-shuo* Understandings and Taxonomies of Human Nature

The Chinese term for "human nature" is *hsing*. The word *hsing*, as A. C. Graham explains, "is one of the few in Chinese philosophical terminology which has a very close English equivalent. It is commonly translated as 'nature', and a Chinese thinker does in fact discuss the *hsing* of a man, of a horse, of water, in very much the same contexts in which we would talk of its nature."[10] Like its English equivalent, "nature," *hsing* has several meanings. For the discussions to follow, I intend to focus on two of them. One derives from the *Analects* of Confucius: "By nature [*hsing*] we are near to each other, by practice we draw far apart."[11] Later, Hsün-tzu wrote: "That by which the living is as it is is called 'nature' [*hsing*],"[12] and again: "Whatever is so of itself [*tzu-jan*] without being worked for, is called 'nature' [*hsing*]."[13] The other meaning of *hsing* I wish to focus on is equivalent to the English words *disposition, temperament,* and/or *temper.*[14]

Among the various pre-*Shih-shuo* taxonomies of human nature, the three most relevant to my argument here include: (1) the *chün-tzu* (superior man) versus the *hsiao-jen* (inferior man) dichotomy, which pervaded pre-Han classical discourse; (2) Pan Ku's "Ku-chin jen piao" (Classification of people, past and present) in his *History of the Han,* which documented the Han "three-rank classification of people" and foreshadowed the Wei nine-rank system;[15] and (3) Liu Shao's *Jen-wu chih,* which grew out of the ardent Wei dispute over *ming* (names) and *li* (principles) and over *ts'ai* (innate ability) and *hsing* (human nature). A close analysis of these three classification systems in terms of their lineage, theoretical basis, and purposes may help us to locate the *Shih-shuo* taxonomy in its broader historical and intellectual context.

CONFUCIUS' SUPERIOR MAN/INFERIOR MAN DIVISION

The *chün-tzu* (superior man) and *hsiao-jen* (inferior man) division originally referred to two social positions juxtaposed in the earliest Chinese classics, notably the *Shih-ching* (Book of songs, or odes) and the *Shang-shu* (Book of documents). In the *Analects,* however, Confucius used them in a far more sophisticated way, as a moral classification scheme.[16] For him, the ascribed character traits of the *chün-tzu* were virtues such as *jen* (kindliness), *li* (ritual propriety), *te* (personal morality), *i* (social morality), *chih* (wisdom), and *hsin* (trustworthiness); the traits of the *hsiao-jen* were vices such as unkindness, disobedience, immorality, stupidity, insincerity, and untrustworthiness. Here are some examples of the contrasts Confucius sought to highlight and clarify, all from the *Analects:*

> The Master said, "The superior man has morality as his basic stuff and by observing the rites he puts it into practice, by being modest he gives it expression, and by being trustworthy in word he brings it to completion. Such is a superior man indeed." (XV, 18)
>
> The Master said, "The superior man is impartial and not partisan; the inferior man is partisan and not impartial." (II, 14)
>
> The Master said, "While the superior man cherishes benign rule, the inferior man cherishes his native land. While the superior man cherishes a respect for the law, the inferior man cherishes generous treatment." (IV, 11)
>
> The Master said, "The superior man understands what is righteous; the inferior man understands what is profitable." (IV, 16)
>
> The Master said, "The superior man helps others to fulfill what is good; he does not help others to fulfill what is bad. The inferior man does the opposite." (XII, 16)
>
> The Master said, "The superior man agrees without being an echo. The inferior man echoes without being in agreement." (XIII, 23)
>
> The Master said, "The superior man is easy to serve but difficult to please. He will not be pleased unless you try to please him by following the Way, but when it comes to employing the services of others, he does so within the limits of their capacity. The inferior man is difficult to serve but easy to please. He will be pleased even though you try to please him by not following the Way, but when it comes to employing the services of others, he demands all-round perfection." (XIII, 25)
>
> The Master said, "The [superior man] is at ease without being arrogant; the [inferior man] is arrogant without being at ease." (XIII, 26)
>
> The Master said, "The superior man stands in awe of three things. He is in awe of the Decree of Heaven. He is in awe of great men. He is in awe of the words of the sages. The inferior man, being ignorant of the Decree of Heaven, does not stand in awe of it. He treats great men with insolence and the words of the sages with derision." (XVI, 8)[17]

By attaching moral connotations to status terms, Confucius appropriated the dichotomy of superior man versus inferior man to suit his idea of *cheng-ming* (rectification of names). He saw his time as a period of disorder, when the actualities of things no longer corresponded to their names, and he believed that order could be restored if only names could be made right: "Let the ruler be a ruler, the minister a minister, the father a father, and the son a son," he said.[18] Fung Yu-lan explains, "if it is brought about that ruler, minister, father and son all act in real life in accordance with the definitions or concepts of these words, so that all carry out to the full their allotted duties, there will be no more disorder in the world."[19] With this goal in mind, Confucius attempted to accommodate the superior man's moral qualities (actuality) to his social status (name), contrasting the virtues he should carry with the vices he should dismiss. The *chün-tzu/hsiao-jen* division founded the moral theme for the Confucian theory of human nature, leaving open the question whether man's nature was basically good, as Mencius argued, or basically bad, as Hsün-tzu averred. Small wonder that the question of "the moral goodness or badness of human nature remains an almost exclusively Confucian preoccupation" throughout the history of Chinese philosophy.[20]

PAN KU'S THREE-RANK CLASSIFICATION OF PEOPLE

Along with the Han institutionalization of Confucianism, Confucius' moral orientation of classifying human nature pervaded Han scholarly practice. In his preface to the "Classification of People, Past and Present," Pan Ku, a leading Han Confucian scholar, immediately introduces his moral purpose of classifying people—"glorifying the good and revealing the bad, in order to admonish later generations."[21] As for how to differentiate the good from the bad, Pan Ku cites the *Analects* of Confucius for both the standard and the authority:

> Confucius said, "How dare I claim to be a sage or a benevolent man?"[22] He also said, "Only a sage could have something to do with benevolence."[23] "Without wisdom, how can one achieve benevolence?"[24] "Those who are born with knowledge are the highest. Next come those who attain knowledge through study. Next again come those who turn to study after having been vexed by difficulties. The common people, in so far as they make no effort to study even after having been vexed by difficulties,

are the lowest."[25] He also said, "You can teach those who are above average about the best things."[26] "It is only the most intelligent and the
most stupid who are not susceptible to change."[27]

According to the commentaries [on the classics], to take Yao and
Shun as examples, when Yü, Chi, and Hsieh did good [deeds] with them,
they consented to their doings, and when Kun and Huan-tou wanted to
do bad [things] with them, they put them to death. If one can do good
but cannot do bad with a person, this person can be said to be the most
intelligent [*shang-chih*]. When Lung-p'ang and Pi-kan wanted to do good
with Chieh and Chou, they were put to death, and when Yü-hsin and
Ch'ung-hou did bad [things] with them, they were approved. If one can
do bad but cannot do good with a person, this person can be said to be
the most stupid [*hsia-yü*]. When Kuan-Chung assisted the Duke Huan
of Ch'i, the Ch'i State achieved hegemony, but when Shu-tiao assisted
him, the state fell apart. If one can do both good and bad with a person,
this person can only be said to be average. According to these rules, I
have therefore arranged the order of nine ranks.[28]

Pan Ku claims direct inspiration from Confucius, but actually typifies
the Han Confucian theory of human nature, which transforms Confucius'
superior versus inferior dichotomy into a triad. His theory, known to later
times as the "three-rank classification of people," emanated from the Han
Confucian Tung Chung-shu (179?–104? B.C.). In his refutation of Mencius' assumption that "human nature is good" (*hsing-shan*),[29] Tung Chung-
shu argues: "Now note that in the Sage's [Confucius'] words, there were
originally no such expressions as 'human nature is good,' but instead 'I have
no hopes of meeting a good person.'[30] If all people's nature is good, how
can the Sage not see a good person? In considering the meaning of his
words, Confucius [obviously] means to say that it is hard to be good. Hence,
to say that all human nature is good, Mencius over-states [his case]!"[31]

Well, if Mencius went too far, what scheme would correctly define
human nature? Tung Chung-shu divided human nature into three types:
namely, that of the sage, good; that of those with very limited capacity,
bad; and that of average people, uncertain. He continues: "The nature of
the sage cannot be used to name the nature of all humans, nor the nature
of those with very limited capacity.[32] That which can be used to name human nature is the nature of average people. The nature of average people

is like a silk cocoon, or an egg. An egg needs to be incubated for twenty days to become a little chick, a silk cocoon needs to be unraveled in boiling water to become silk thread, and human nature needs to be gradually saturated with instructions and precepts to become good."[33]

Clearly, Tung Chung-shu here is trying to compromise between Mencius' categorical statement that "human nature is good" and Hsün-tzu's assertion that "human nature is bad," which stresses the function of moral teaching and moral governing in transforming the originally bad and rebellious human nature into a good and obedient one.[34] As Tung Chung-shu's follower, interpreter, and an exponent of New Text Confucianism, Pan Ku naturally took up Tung's "three-rank classification of people."[35] Pan's contemporary Wang Ch'ung (27–91), a leading scholar of Old Text Confucianism, proposed a similar classification.[36] He maintained "that those Mencius takes as having good human nature are people above the average, those Hsün-tzu takes as having bad human nature are people below the average, and those Yang Hsiung takes as having both good and bad human nature are average people."[37]

In general, Han Confucians tended to understand human nature in terms of intelligence. Those who are born wise are by nature good because they know how to follow the Way, and those who are born stupid and not willing to learn are by nature bad. A great number of people in between have the capability of receiving the sages' moral instruction and thus of becoming good.[38] The whole idea, then, is to highlight the transformative function of Confucian moral teachings.

Informed by this understanding of human nature, Pan Ku further divides each of the three ranks into three subranks—the upper, the medium, and the low—and distributes among all nine ranks about two thousand legendary and historical figures, from antiquity to the end of the Ch'in. Table 4 shows the structure of his classification and his distribution of the numbers of people, with the distinction between men and women under each rank.

Pan Ku's classification shows both the ranks of the moral hierarchy and the types (categories) of moral character. The latter, however, does not exactly correspond with the former. Pan Ku seems to have a problem

TABLE 4. PAN KU'S "CLASSIFICATION OF PEOPLE, PAST AND PRESENT"

Rank	1a Upper-upper	1b Upper-medium	1c Upper-low	2a Medium-upper	2b Medium-medium	2c Medium-low	3a Low-upper	3b Low-medium	3c Low-low
Category	The sage (*sheng*)	The benevolent (*jen*)	The wise (*chih*)						The stupid (*yü*)
Men	14	148	199	307	323	300	238	227	123
Women	0	24	6	7	7	1	2	3	8

naming people's qualities between "upper-low" and "low-low." Yet this gap in his system accords with the theory that average people can change their moral character under the ruler's transformative influence. Pan Ku's classification of human nature thus emphasizes the role of Confucian moral teachings in forming the social and political order.

Pan Ku's classification also reveals his perspectives on women. First, he evaluates them according to the same standards as men. Although the men in his list greatly outnumber women (by a ratio of 32.4 to 1), Pan Ku cannot be held entirely responsible for the overemphasis on men, since his numbers are based on the previous historical records. Second, Pan Ku includes fifty-eight women in his list, with thirty good and thirteen bad, leaving only fifteen in the middle, suggesting a skewed sample. Third, although Pan Ku does not assign a single woman to the highest rank, implying somewhat contemptuously that a woman cannot become a sage, he does include twenty-four women (the largest single group) in the second-highest category, the benevolent. Most of these benevolent women are sages' mothers, in contrast to the eight femmes fatales in the lowest rank who are mostly the consorts of the legendary tyrants.[39]

These three features create an interesting tension in Pan Ku's theory of human nature. He applies an overall didactic interpretation to human nature, emphasizing people's general mediocrity and the need for the sage's transformation, yet his sample focuses heavily on women who seem to be good by nature. He links women's benevolence to their mother's role and associates their badness with bad men, hence the suggestion that women form their moral character possibly by natural causes, through passion rather than through reason. He may have presented these perspectives unwittingly, but his rather objective viewpoint, as we shall see, is relevant to the *Shih-shuo*'s treatment of women's issues.

LIU SHAO'S CHUNG-YUNG VERSUS PARTIAL ACCOMPLISHMENT DIVISION

At the outset of his preface to the *Jen-wu chih*, Liu Shao highlights the political importance of studying human nature: "What the sages and worthies extol is nothing less than wisdom. Of all [types of] wisdom, there is nothing more valuable than knowing people. If [the ruler] can tell whether a certain individual is honest or intelligent, then various abilities may be put into proper order and all kinds of affairs may prosper."[40] For Liu Shao, then, knowing human nature and naming human types lead to the establishment of political order. Such a pragmatic approach differs somewhat from Pan Ku's moral emphasis, but it fits the major approach of the Wei School of Names and Principles, which, as already discussed in chapter 2, focuses on the relationship between one's inner nature *(hsing)*, innate ability *(ts'ai)*, and a fitting official post *(jen)*.

Like Pan, Liu Shao goes to the *Analects* of Confucius for the terminology and the mechanism of classifying people:

> Although Confucius did not test anybody and had no means to promote people, he still commented on his disciples in four divisions and classified various talents in terms of three ranks. He also commended the doctrine of the Mean [*chung-yung*] in order to distinguish the virtue of the sages.[41] He esteemed virtue in order to urge [people to] strive to obtain it.[42] He interpreted the six defects in order to warn against the deficiencies of partial abilities.[43] He examined the uninhibited and the rigid in order to bridge the gap between their abilities, and [sought to bring into balance] all those whose nature veers from the mean.[44] He hated those who look sincere but are not actually trustworthy, and pointed out that the faked appearance is difficult to preserve.[45] He also said, "Examine where one feels at home, and observe the path he takes,"[46] in order to know one's behavior. The investigation of people in the greatest detail is like this. Therefore I dare to follow the teachings of the sage in composing this work on people.[47]

Whereas Pan Ku draws from the *Analects* to support his moral analysis of human nature, Liu Shao harmonizes Confucius' words with his investigation of the connection between human nature and human abilities. Liu Shao considers both the "four divisions" and the "three ranks" to be categories of *ts'ai* (ability). In this he counters Pan Ku's typical Han moral explication of the "three ranks" while foreshadowing Wang Pi's typical Wei ability-explication of the "four divisions" (See below). Even *chung-yung*, or the Mean, which Confucius used for a moral category, comes to stand for the sage's ability in Liu Shao's *Jen-wu chih*, as we shall see.

Furnished with Confucius' terminology and drawing theoretical support from various philosophical—especially Taoist—schools,[48] Liu Shao establishes in the *Jen-wu chih* a new division of human types: namely, *chung-yung* (the man whose nature stays within the Mean), which he juxtaposes to *chü-k'ang* (the man whose nature falls short of or exceeds the Mean). In Liu's view, the man who stays within the Mean embodies the *Tao*, so "there is no name for his nature;"[49] he "is capable of infinite change, reaching the proper state as [his] limit."[50] *Chü-k'ang*, by contrast, describes an ordinary man, whose nature either does not reach *(chü)*, or strays too far from *(k'ang)*, the Mean. Consequently, his nature, not embodying the *Tao*, becomes namable.

Under the division of *Chü-k'ang*, Liu Shao distributes twelve groups of human trait names:

1. *Li-chih kang-i* (severe, strict, unyielding, and strong-willed).
2. *Jou-shun an-shu* (soft, pleasant, peaceful, and considerate).
3. *Hsiung-han chieh-chien* (fierce, brave, heroic, and robust).
4. *Ching-liang wei-shen* (refined, docile, timid, and cautious).
5. *Ch'iang-k'ai chien ching* (strong, exemplary, firm, and aggressive).
6. *Lun-pien li-i* (articulate, discriminating, reasonable, and logical).
7. *P'u-po chou-chi* (universal, broad-minded, impartial, and generous).
8. *Ch'ing-chieh lien-chieh* (clear, resolute, incorruptible, and pure).
9. *Hsiu-tung lei-lo* (eminent in action and frank).
10. *Ch'en-ching chi-mi* (taciturn, calm, subtle, and mysterious).
11. *P'u-lu ching-chin* (simple, open, direct, and forthcoming).
12. *To-chih t'ao-ch'ing* (resourceful and tactical).[51]

These categories, though not reflecting the "Mean," are not necessarily negative. They only represent objectively people's possible character traits in relation to their talents.

In short, the *Jen-wu chih* argues that a certain kind of human nature corresponds with a certain human ability and hence suits a proper post. The man whose nature stays within the Mean, "though intelligent and plain, and gifted with all kinds of abilities, does not assign himself any task." All he does is "to use his intelligence in searching for [various talented] people, and, by assigning them to appropriate posts, to achieve his own ease."[52] In other words, while staying in his position as a ruler in a Taoist fashion, he "does nothing yet nothing is left undone."[53] The man whose nature falls short of or exceeds the Mean, on the other hand, cannot be an effective ruler but might be well suited to a certain administrative position. For example, one who is severe and strong-willed carries the ability of a Legalist *(Fa-chia)* and may therefore assume responsibility for administering punishment. One who is articulate and reasonable carries the ability of a Dialectician *(Ming-chia)* and may thus be entrusted with diplomatic responsibilities. One who is brave and heroic carries military ability and may hence be a general in the field.[54]

About two decades earlier than Liu Shao, Ts'ao P'i applied a similar logic in his "Discourse on Literature." After a discussion of how one's writing style accords with one's personal disposition, Ts'ao P'i concluded: "On a basic level all literature is the same, but it acquires differences as it unfolds in its various branches. Generally speaking, memorials to the throne and disquisitions should have dignity; letters and discourses should be based on natural principles; inscriptions and eulogies should respect the facts; poems and poetic expositions should be beautiful. Each of these four categories is different, and a writer's abilities will lead him to favor some over others. Only a comprehensive talent can master all these forms."[55] Like Liu Shao, Ts'ao P'i established a dichotomy between *t'ung-ts'ai* (comprehensive talent) and *p'ien-neng* (partial ability), but he focused on literary instead of political abilities.

Despite certain differences between Confucius' distinction between superior and inferior men, Pan Ku's "three-rank classification," and Liu Shao's dichotomy between *chung-yung* and *chü-k'ang,* the three systems share at least two common features.

First, each carries a clear purpose in forming an order of human nature, and each classifies and names human types following this purpose. Confucius has in mind a political order based upon a moral regime. He therefore invents a dual name encompassing both moral character and social status and assigns to each part a group of moral or immoral trait names in order to direct people to the right and keep them from going astray. Pan Ku intends to "glorify the good and reveal the bad, in order to admonish later generations." He therefore divides people into three groups, naming the top the good/wise and the bottom the bad/stupid, leaving the middle unnamed. Thus he admonishes the average people to follow the Sages' instruction to become good; if not they will descend to the lowest category. Liu Shao's *chung-yung* versus *chü-k'ang* system seeks to place people in the proper administrative position; therefore, it employs two types of names: (a) an overall categorization (*chung-yung* or *chü-k'ang*), and (b) a subset (either "no name," for the Mean, or twelve individual trait names, for those veering from the Mean).

Second, each system consists of two counterparts that form a hierarchical yet complementary relationship. The superior man contrasts with the inferior man in the manner of the good versus the bad, the wise versus the stupid, and so forth, and so do the top group and the bottom group in Pan Ku's classification. Meanwhile, each implies the existence of the other; without the superior, good, and wise, there can be no inferior, bad, and stupid, and vice versa. Similarly, the *chung-yung* is higher than the *chü-k'ang* in terms of capacity. The former has all kinds of political abilities and is qualified to be a ruler. The latter carries partial accomplishment and suits only the position of an official. The two, then, complement each other in that the *chung-yung* measures the *chü-k'ang*, preventing the latter from going to extremes, and the *chü-k'ang* fulfills various tasks under the direction of the *chung-yung*.[56]

These two common features restrict the three classifications to relatively closed systems. Within each system, the intended purpose is to establish pertinent categories while excluding irrelevant ones. Their judgmental and hierarchical features anchor each evaluatee in a certain category and rank. Even the fluid category of "mediocre" in Pan Ku's classification can only move up or down between the good/wise and the bad/stupid extremes.

The *Shih-shuo* Understanding of Human Nature

The *Shih-shuo* scheme emerged from a tradition of tidy, closed systems of human nature such as Confucius', Pan Ku's, and Liu Shao's. But it departed from its precedents by presenting a conscious chaos, based on a rethinking of human nature and an attempt to work out proper descriptive expressions through a linguistic labyrinth. The following episode, I believe, epitomizes the *Shih-shuo*'s approach to understanding human nature:

> Yin Hao once asked, "If *tzu-jan* [self-so-ness, or being so of itself] is without intention in the matter of human endowment, then why is it that it is precisely the good men who are few and the bad many?"
>
> No one among those present had anything to say. Finally Liu T'an replied, "It's like pouring water over the ground. Just of its own accord it flows and spreads this way and that, but almost never in exactly square or round shapes
>
> All his contemporaries sighed with the highest admiration, considering it an illustrious clarification.(4/46)

Liu T'an's impertinent response to Yin Hao may easily perplex the reader, since he does not really answer why good men are few and bad many. Instead, he is trying to establish a new argument—that human nature does not have regular shapes to fit regular names such as good or bad. Thus, the episode reveals Yin and Liu's different views regarding human nature.

Yin Hao's question, "Why is it that it is precisely the good men who are few and the bad many," follows the Han Confucian approach to categorization of human nature. For instance, Pan Ku's "Classification of People" records 14 sages in contrast to 131 bad men and women. But why was this so? Han Confucians would explain that the distribution of the good and the bad among people depends on how to define these two categories. Mencius assumes that "human nature is good" merely because, as Tung Chung-shu interprets him, human beings are "better than birds and beasts"[57] because they are capable of loving their parents, whereas birds and beasts are not. For Han Confucians, however, goodness pertains to much higher standards, consisting of "conformity to the three bonds and five rules, comprehension of the principles of the eight beginnings, and the practice of loyalty, good faith, widespread love, generosity, and love of propriety [*li*]."[58] Only very few can reach this high moral standard and may be considered good. A number of people who defy these standards are surely bad; and many more are in between, awaiting the sage-kings' moral transformation. The whole enterprise of evaluating, classifying, and transforming human nature, Tung Chung-shu contends, has been set up by the will of Heaven: "What Heaven does [for human beings] goes to a certain point and then stops there. What stops inside of [a human being] is called his Heavenly [endowed nature];[59] and what stops outside of [a human being] is called the teachings of the sage-kings. The teachings of the sage-kings stay outside of human nature, yet human nature cannot but conform to them."[60]

Yet when Yin Hao revisits the same question, he faces a new premise emerging during the Wei-Chin period—"*tzu-jan* is without intention in the matter of human endowment"—as Yin puts it. From Ho Yen, Chung Hui, and Wang Pi to Kuo Hsiang, all of the major Wei-Chin *Hsüan-hsüeh* adepts interpreted Heaven as the emblem of *tzu-jan,* the self-so-ness.[61] Such a Heaven would not "control" human nature but could only let it be itself. In his commentary on Yin Hao's conversation with Liu T'an, Liu Chün accurately quotes Kuo Hsiang's interpretation of the *Chuang-tzu* concept "*t'ien-lai*" (piping of Heaven)—an analogue of *wu, Tao,* or Heaven,[62] in which Kuo concludes: "Thus all things are born spontaneously. This is the *Tao* of Heaven."[63] This new insight into the Heaven-man relationship makes it irrelevant to evaluate human nature in terms of "good" and "bad," which rely upon a mighty moral authority to set up standards and to execute judgment. If Heaven "is without intention in the matter of human endowment," who will be out there to claim the authority in shaping human nature?

Liu T'an avoids a direct answer to Yin Hao's question precisely because he sees the good and bad division as irrelevant to the Wei-Chin premise that Heaven has no control over human nature. Instead, he picks up the water analogy from the debate between Kao-tzu and Mencius over human nature. Let us look at this dispute first:

> Kao Tzu said, "Human nature is like whirling water. Give it an outlet in the east and it will flow east; give it an outlet in the west and it will flow

west. That human nature shows no preference for either becoming good
or becoming bad is like water showing no preference for either flowing
east or flowing west."

Mencius said, "It is certainly the case that water shows no preference for either flowing east or flowing west, but does it show the same
indifference to flowing upwards and flowing downwards? Human nature
being good is like water seeking low ground. There is no man who is not
good just as there is no water that does not flow downwards."[64]

What happens after water flows down and hits the ground? Liu T'an observes, "just of its own accord it flows and spreads this way and that, but
almost never in exactly square or round shapes." If, as Mencius puts it,
water tending to flow down is just like human nature tending to be good,
then exactly which shape on the ground should be named "good" and which
should be named "bad"? Water cannot form regular shapes on the ground;
likewise human nature cannot fit any artificially dictated rules. Thus conventional moral names such as *good* and *bad* are not valid in naming irregular human features.

With this new twist on the water analogy, Liu T'an establishes his understanding of human nature through a Wei-Chin *Hsüan-hsüeh* rereading
of previous interpretations—specifically those of Mencius and Han Confucians. Grounding his argument in the Wei-Chin premise of the Heaven-
man relationship, Liu T'an contends that: (1) Human nature is, as Kuo
Hsiang maintains, a "self-production" *(tzu-sheng)*, flowing "on its own accord" instead of being channeled by any outer force; and (2) human nature is neither good nor bad—it is simply amorphous and therefore unnamable, just like water—"almost never in exactly square or round shapes."
Recording that "all his [Liu T'an's] contemporaries sighed with the highest admiration, considering [Liu's response to Yin Hao] an illustrious clari-
fication," the *Shih-shuo* author points out the popularity of Liu T'an's theory among the Chin gentry and expresses his agreement with Liu's position.

With Liu T'an's water analogy, the *Shih-shuo* author also touches on
another important feature of human nature—its "communion with people
and things" *(ying-wu)*—a theory obviously adopted from Wang Pi, to be
discussed later. As noticed in Liu T'an's response to Yin Hao, the water
does not take shape until it touches the ground. By the same token, hu-

man nature shows its various aspects only when it comes in contact with its environment. In the following episode, the *Shih-shuo* author illustrates, also with a water metaphor, how one responds to the same phenomenon in different ways under different circumstances:

> While Hsieh An was in the east (i.e., in K'uai-chi, before 360), he used to travel by boat with coolies *(hsiao-jen)* pulling the boat. Sometimes they would be slow, and sometimes fast, sometimes they would stop, and at other times linger, or again they would let the boat go untended hither and yon, jolting the passengers or crashing into the shore. At first Hsieh never uttered any complaints, and people thought he was always free of anger or joy.
>
> But one time he was on his way back (by carriage) from escorting the body of his elder brother, Hsieh I (d. 358), to its burial. At sunset a driving rainstorm had come up, and the coolies were all drunk and incapable of performing their duties. At this point Hsieh, rising from the middle of the carriage, seized the carriage pole with his own hands and lunged at the driver, his voice and expression both extremely harsh. (33/14)

The author then makes a comment here—the author's only direct voice ever heard in the *Shih-shuo* text—to explain why Hsieh An's self-composure could turn into turbulence: "Even though water by nature is calm and gentle, when it enters a narrow gorge it dashes and plunges. If we should compare it to human emotions, we would certainly understand that in a harassed and narrow place there is no possibility of preserving one's composure." On the surface, this comment seems to suggest Mencius' argument that immediately follows the above quoted debate between Mencius and Kao-tzu: "Now with water, by splashing it one can make it shoot up higher than one's forehead, and by forcing it one can make it stay on a hill. But can that be said to be the nature of water? It is the special circumstances that make it behave so. That man can be made bad shows that his nature is open to similar treatment."[65]

But in comparing the two passages closely, one can see clear differences. For one thing, Mencius' water shoots up or stays on the hill against its nature because some outer force splashes or drives it. In the *Shih-shuo* author's comment, water dashes and plunges, changing from its usually calm and gentle appearance because it flows into a harassed and narrow place and hence behaves in response to this altered environment. Secondly, Mencius compares water's two different states to the two states of human nature and arbitrarily names one "good" and the other "bad," without ever explaining why smooth water represents good human nature and turbulent water represents bad human nature. In the *Shih-shuo* episode, the author compares the two different states of water to the two aspects of human nature—*te* (potency, potentiality, efficacy) and *ch'ing* (feeling, emotion, passion), exemplifying his theory with the Hsieh An anecdote.

As a leading Chin statesman, Hsieh An's extraordinary composure is the subject of some most dramatic moments in the chapter "Ya-liang" (Cultivated tolerance) of the *Shih-shuo hsin-yü*. Whether being informed of a decisive victory against foreign invaders, facing a life-death crisis in a political struggle, or encountering a violent tempest on an ocean excursion, Hsieh An's mood, expression, and demeanor always remained the same (6/27, 6/28, 6/29, 6/30, 6/35, 6/37). Understandably, a statesman needs such equanimity in order to "govern and stabilize both the court and the people" (6/28). In short, the calm and gentle feature of water aptly illustrates the rational side of Hsieh An's personality.

Yet the *Shih-shuo hsin-yü* also describes Hsieh as very sentimental and emotional. He once confessed to his close friend Wang Hsi-chih: "In my middle years [I find that] I am so affected by grief or joy that whenever I part with a relative or friend I am always indisposed for several days" (2/62). So when his elder brother passed away, his composure surrendered to intense agitation, the result of a disturbing reversal in human relations. The dashing and plunging water image accurately depicts the emotional part of his personality.

The *Shih-shuo* author does not impose any moral judgment on Hsieh An's behavior but instead presents it descriptively as a natural facet of his character. Such amoral and "natural" readings of human nature pervade the *Shih-shuo hsin-yü*. Here is another *Shih-shuo* episode, which also employs a water metaphor:

> Somebody criticized Chou I for talking and joking with relatives and friends in a crude manner, without restraint or dignity.
> Chou rejoined, "I'm like the ten-thousand-*li* Long River (the

Yangtze).[66] How could it avoid making at least one turn in a thousand *li*?" (23/25)

The turns of the Yangtze have formed naturally, and the water flowing along the river bends accordingly. Human behavior, too, follows human nature and turns in accordance with environmental changes. The entire process is autonomous rather than being dictated and scrutinized by a willful Heaven with rigorous moral standards.

Ordering Human Nature within a Linguistic Paradox

The *Shih-shuo* author's agreement with the point that human nature is like water poured over the ground, amorphous and unnamable, immediately contradicts his effort to name and organize human nature into distinctive types. This paradox is linked with the long-standing dilemma concerning the inability of words to express human nature and the fundamental needs of verbal expression in character appraisal. Only through his constant struggle with these two interwoven paradoxes did the *Shih-shuo* author eventually come to his taxonomy of human nature. And undoubtedly, the unabated *Hsüan-hsüeh* debates about complementary opposites (discussed at length in chapter 2) must have offered possible solutions to these dilemmas, evidenced by the author's conscious inclusion of the relevant episodes. Meanwhile, the author succeeded in enriching these theories with his compilation of character writing.

In his effort to define the indefinable human nature, the *Shih-shuo* author must have drawn inspiration from Wang Pi's suggestion that one may define Nothing (*wu*) in terms of Something (*yu*) and later elaborations of this theory. Drawing upon Kuo Hsiang's interpretation of the Nothing/Something relationship, the *Shih-shuo* author molds the relationship between human nature and its various manifestations into the Nothing/Something dialectic. He explains that human nature as a whole resembles the poured water, amorphous and unnamable; yet the water's shapelessness is exactly reflected by its "flowing this way and that way of its own accord"—that is, by its irregular, unpredictable shapes on the ground. By the same token, the shapelessness of human nature is reflected by its abundant, diverse manifestations.[67] Therefore, the best way to show that human nature cannot be formed into regular shapes is to exhibit how different one "self" is from others. The more different, specific "selves" the *Shih-shuo* author can depict, the more human types he can name, the more he can demonstrate the amorphous and unnamable quality of human nature. In brief, Kuo Hsiang's *yu/wu* dialectic allows the *Shih-shuo* author freedom to specify and name as many human types *(yu)* as possible while metaphysically maintaining that human nature is amorphous and unnamable *(wu)*.

Yet how to epitomize each type using accurate words remains a problem. At this stage, the *Shih-shuo* author must have drawn inspiration from Ou-yang Chien's essay, "On Words Fully Expressing Meanings." As the reader will recall, Ou-yang grounds his argument in the Hsiang Hsiu and Kuo Hsiang theory that the perceivable changes of things *(yu)* can come to reflect and represent the abstract principle *(wu)* that underlies these changes. Ou-yang thus recommends that the substance of things be differentiated by the selection of their names. And, instead of trying to fit name to actuality on a one-to-one basis, he uses the relationship among names to reflect the relationship among things, and he uses the changes in a linguistic system to reflect the changes in reality.

The philosophical understanding that human nature, as an autonomous entity, can take any shape, and the linguistic need to vary words to reflect this diversity, both require the *Shih-shuo* author to create a new system. Since such a discursive system has no precedent, the author needs to form it through (1) reconceptualizing some pre-Wei-Chin categories within the Wei-Chin intellectual context, (2) incorporating some new ones created during the Wei-Chin period, and (3) for the most part, inventing his own categories.[68]

Pre-Wei-Chin Categories

1. "Te-hsing"   (*Te* conduct)
2. "Yen-yü"   (Speech and conversation)
3. "Cheng-shih"   (Affairs of government)

4. "Wen-hsüeh"   (Literature and scholarship)
5. "Fang-cheng"   (The square and the proper)
8. "Shang-yü"   (Appreciation and praise)
9. "P'in-tsao"   (Ranking with refined words)
14. "Jung-chih"   (Appearance and manner)
15. "Tzu-hsin"   (Self-renewal)
29. "Chien-se"   (Stinginess and meanness)
30. "T'ai-ch'ih"   (Extravagance and ostentation)
31. "Fen-Chüan"   (Anger and irascibility)
33. "Yu-hui"   (Blameworthiness and remorse)

Wei-Chin Categories

6. "Ya-liang"   (Cultivated tolerance)
7. "Shih-chien"   (Recognition and judgment)
24. "Chien-ao"   (Rudeness and arrogance)
36. "Ch'ou-hsi"   (Hostility and alienation)

Shih-shuo Invented Categories

10. "Kuei-chen"   (Admonitions and warnings)
11. "Chieh-wu"   (Quick perception)
12. "Su-hui"   (Precocious intelligence)
13. "Hao-shuang"   (Virility and vigor)
16. "Ch'i-hsien"   (Admiration and emulation)
17. "Shang-shih"   (Grieving for the departed)
18. "Ch'i-i"   (Reclusion and disengagement)
19. "Hsien-yüan"   (Worthy beauties)
20. "Shu-chieh"   (Technical understanding)
21. "Ch'iao-i"   (Ingenious art)
22. "Ch'ung-li"   (Favor and veneration)
23. "Jen-tan"   (Uninhibitedness and eccentricity)
25. "P'ai-t'iao"   (Taunting and teasing)
26. "Ch'ing-ti"   (Contempt and insults)
27. "Chia-chüeh"   (Guile and chicanery)
28. "Ch'u-mien"   (Dismissal from office)

32. "Ch'an-hsien"   (Slanderousness and treachery)
34. "P'i-lou"   (Crudities and blunders)
35. "Huo-ni"   (Delusion and infatuation)

The terminology synthesis that developed was highly original, as later readers of the *Shih-shuo hsin-yü* would attest. Wu Su-kung (fl. 1662–1681), for example, tells us that "the *Shih-shuo*'s [taxonomic language] is pure and fresh, for [the work] creates most of its own terms."[69] Such freshness of language was not simply the result of the author's stylistic polish. It registers a sophisticated search for a new way to describe and categorize human nature.

The Significance of the *Shih-shuo* Taxonomy

Having located the *Shih-shuo* taxonomy within its intellectual and historical context, we may now examine its significance, structure, and purpose through a close reading of its chapter titles in relation to the text. My analysis will consider several related issues: (1) how Wei-Chin *Hsüan-hsüeh* scholars understood the concept of these chapter titles, (2) how the author defined and interpreted these categories through his deployment of episodes, (3) how the author correlated all the categories into a structure, and (4) what kind of structure he built.

Beginning with the "four divisions of Confucius' disciples," which comprise the first four *Shih-shuo* chapter titles, how did Wei-Chin *Hsüan-hsüeh* scholars understand them? Wang Pi points out in his commentary on the *Analects* that each of these divisions "cites the talents and outstanding abilities [*ts'ai-ch'ang*] [of a particular disciple]."[70] Wang's interpretation is based on the concept *te* (often translated as "virtue"), which he defines in his commentary on the *Lao-tzu*, chapter 38, as "to get" (also pronounced *te*). And "How does one get the *te*?" he asks. "By means of the *Tao*."[71]

A. C. Graham's interpretation of the interdependency between *Tao* and *te*, evidently following Wang Pi's approach, may help us to understand Wang's perspective. Graham translates *te* as "potency" and defines it as "personal capacity for the course of action which is the Way; phonetically related to *te* 'get,' opposite of *shih* 'lose'."[72] He further explains:

> A pair of concepts first prominent in the *Analects* is *Tao* "the Way" and *te* "potency." In this text *Tao* is used only of the proper course of human conduct. . . . *Te,* which has often been translated as "virtue" (to be understood as in "The virtue of cyanide is to poison" rather than in "Virtue is its own reward"[73]), had been traditionally used of the power, whether benign or baleful, to move others without exerting physical force . . . so that it becomes the capacity to act according to and bring others to the Way.
>
> The two concepts are interdependent, as later in *Lao-tzu;* a person's *te* is his potentiality to act according to the *Tao.*[74]

If *te* is one's "potentiality to act according to the *Tao,*" then *te* alone does not convey ethical or moral meaning. Whether one's act is moral or not depends on what kind of *Tao* one follows. Within the Confucian context, *Tao* undoubtedly connotes a strong moral-political sense, and this is why later scholars often interpreted *te-hsing* as a moral category. For the *Hsüan-hsüeh* adept Wang Pi, however, *Tao* is a much broader concept and therefore can be replaced with *wu* (Nothing). Thus, he argues in his commentary on the *Lao-tzu,* chapter 38: "How does one fully achieve *te*? To apply [*te*] to practical use according to *wu*. If [*te*] is applied to practical use according to *wu*, then nothing cannot be fulfilled. . . . Therefore, those who embrace the upper *te* [*shang te*] would act only according to the *Tao*. They would not *te* [make a virtue of] their *te*, nor would they stick to and use the specific. They therefore can embrace *te*, and there is nothing they cannot do. . . . Doing things according to *wu* means doing things without bias. Those who are not capable of non-striving [*wu-wei*] can only do things that belong to the categories of lower *te* [*hsia-te*], such as benevolence, righteousness, propriety, and integrity."[75]

Wang Pi's definition of *te* and its relationship with *Tao* accords with his *Hsüan-hsüeh* orientation—that the *Tao*, or *wu*, is the fundamental principle by which the myriad things fulfill themselves through their potency. In Wang Pi's words, Confucian moral categories, such as benevolence, righteousness, propriety, and integrity, occupy only a part, and, because of

their striving feature, they belong to "lower potency." It is on this understanding of *te* that Wang Pi interprets the "four divisions of Confucius' disciples" as *ts'ai-ch'ang* (talents and outstanding abilities). Therefore, I translate the category *te-hsing* into English as the "*te* conduct"—leaving *te*
untranslated—instead of the "virtuous conduct," which may easily lead to
a moral reading of the chapter "Te-hsing," and consequently of the entire
Shih-shuo hsin-yü.

Seen in this light, the moral inconsistency of chapter 1, "Te-hsing,"
which I discussed at the beginning of this chapter, becomes understand-
able. In compiling a book designed to epitomize pure conversation, the
Shih-shuo author would naturally conceptualize his terminology in a
Hsüan-hsüeh manner. Thus, in the episodes in the chapter "Te-hsing," the
concept of "*te* conduct" seems to carry two basic meanings: (1) the potentiality for acting according to whatever one considers the right way, or
Tao, which may or may not be the Confucian *Tao* (and the *te* thus achieved
may or may not be the Confucian *te*);[76] and (2) the efficacy of pressing on
with whatever one considers right regardless of any obstacles.

The following episode typifies a "Te-hsing" account with these two
meanings:

> The Prince of Liang (Ssu-ma T'ung) and the Prince of Chao (Ssu-ma
> Lun), being close relatives of the emperor, were most noble and honored
> in their time. P'ei K'ai [d. 291] each year requested from their princi-
> palities a tax of several million cash (*ch'ien*) in order to relieve the needy
> members on his mother's and father's sides of the family. Someone
> ridiculed him, saying, "How can you beg from others to perform an act
> of private charity?"
> P'ei replied, "To diminish excesses and supplement deficiencies is
> the Way of Heaven [*T'ien chih Tao*]."(1/18)

The *Tao* that directs P'ei's conduct here, what P'ei calls the "Way of
Heaven," is *not* adopted from any Confucian classics but from the *Lao-
tzu*.[77] P'ei follows his own *Tao* regardless of others' derision and therefore
shows his fortitude. As Liu Chün comments: "Once P'ei K'ai had chosen
a course of action, he moved in complete compliance with his own mind.
Even though slanderous remarks came his way, he held his ground

calmly."[78] In this sense, *te* means not only the capacity for acting according to the *Tao*, but also the capacity to act tenaciously.

In general, the *Tao* in the chapter "Te-hsing" seems quite eclectic. Li Ying's judgmental attitude toward gentlemen's moral behavior reflects long-standing Han Confucian moral teachings. By contrast, Juan Chi's non-judgmental attitude results from his understanding of *Chuang-tzu's* relativism, that there is virtually no difference between right and wrong.[79] Hsi K'ang never expresses pleasure or irritation, reflecting a Yangist/Taoist approach to life (1/16). As he writes in "Yang-sheng lun" (On nourishing life), a superior man "cultivates his nature to protect his spirit and calms his mind to keep his body intact. Love and hate do not dwell in his feelings; anguish and delight do not stay in his thoughts."[80]

As for *te* as the efficacy of acting steadfastly, the *Shih-shuo* often illustrates this idea with a comparison between two people who act according to a similar *Tao* but in different particular ways. In one case, Kuan Ning and Hua Hsin both see a piece of gold while working in the garden. The *Shih-shuo* tells us: "Kuan went on plying his hoe as though it were no different from a tile or a stone. Hua, seizing the gold, then threw it away" (1/11). Neither kept the gold, yet Hua's momentary perplexity degraded him in comparison with Kuan's never-swaying aloofness regarding wealth.[81] In another episode, a man wants to join Hua Hsin and Wang Lang in wartime. Wang takes him in despite Hua's disapproval. Later when their safety becomes threatened, Wang wants to get rid of the man, but Hua says: "This was precisely the reason I hesitated in the first place. But since we have already accepted his request, how can we abandon him in an emergency?" (1/13). In these two cases, the comparisons focus not on which *Tao* to follow—since both parties act more or less on the same principle—but rather on how insistently and consistently they are following it.

Wang Hsien-chih's deathbed episode manifests the emotional dimension of *te*. Driven by everlasting love for his ex-wife, Wang dared to speak out his regrets, regardless of the respect he had to pay to the imperial authorities who had intervened in his marriage. The inclusion of this episode in "Te-hsing" reveals the *Shih-shuo* author's rather unusual understanding of *Tao*—that as the natural path for one's life, it should include not only ideas or principles, but also feelings, emotions, and passions. Consequently, *te,* as the potentiality for acting according to the *Tao,* should follow what one *feels* to be right and not simply what one *understands* to be right. In short, the chapter "Te-hsing" sets the tone for the entire work. Wei-Chin gentlemen and gentlewomen are not defined by some outside conventional rules, but by categories more intimately related to their basic qualities as human beings. Generally speaking, these categories can be divided into four groups, each related to an aspect of human nature: namely, *te* (potency, potentiality, efficacy), *ts'ai* (innate ability, talent, specialty), *hsing* (here referring specifically to one's temperament, disposition, and/or temper, as differentiated from human nature in general), and *ch'ing* (feeling, emotion, passion). Here is how the chapters of the *Shih-shuo hsin-yü* relate to these groupings:

Te *(potency, potentiality, efficacy)*

1. *Te-hsing*	(*Te* conduct) (pre-Wei-Chin category)
5. *Fang-cheng*	(The square and the proper) (pre-Wei-Chin category)
6. *Ya-liang*	(Cultivated tolerance) (Wei-Chin category)
10. *Kuei-chen*	(Admonitions and warnings) (*Shih-shuo* invented category)
15. *Tzu-hsin*	(Self-renewal) (pre-Wei-Chin category)
18. *Ch'i-i*	(Reclusion and disengagement) (*Shih-shuo* invented category)

I group these six categories together because each of them is sustained by an inner power that enables one to act and to act firmly according to what one understands or feels is right. Within this group, *Te-hsing* in particular exemplifies this inner power; the other five elaborate this quality in various Wei-Chin contexts.

Fang-cheng (The square and the proper) was originally a Han category for selecting officials. In the *Shih-shuo hsin-yü,* it still has the traditional connotation of standing immovably by one's principles against a superior's will or in the face of peer pressure, but the concept of "principles" has been broadened. Confucian norms still affect decision making, undoubtedly, but stress also falls on the insistence of a strict Wei-Chin demarcation between a great high background (*kao-men*) and a humble one (*han-men*), as well as between Southerners (*nan-jen*) and Northerners (*pei-jen*) (5/10, 5/12, 5/13, 5/18, 5/24, 5/25, 5/27, 5/48, 5/51, 5/52, and 5/58). We also find an emphasis on the newly promoted ideal of genuineness (5/47). In one case, a governor-general's feelings for his wife triumph over his loyalty to the court, and he is labeled *fang-cheng* (5/4).

Previously, *fang-cheng* cases were built upon the conflict between two parties; if one party was named square and proper, the other consequently became unsquare and improper. In the *Shih-shuo hsin-yü*, however, the two parties in conflict can both be considered square and proper because they each insist upon their own principles (5/20, 5/29, 5/40, 5/50, and 5/66). This seemingly nonjudgmental attitude conforms to Wang Pi's *Hsüan-hsüeh* axiom that the *Tao*, or *wu*, contains any principle or feeling one chooses to follow. As long as one insists upon one's own Way, he or she should be labeled square and proper. The following episode illustrates this point:

> Although Grand Marshal Wang Yen was not on particularly friendly terms with Yü Ai, Yü continually addressed him with the familiar pronoun, "you" (*ch'ing*).
> Wang objected, "Sir (*chün*), you shouldn't call me that."
> Yü replied, "You naturally 'sir' me, and I naturally 'you' you. I naturally follow my rules, and you naturally follow yours." (5/20)

Ya-liang (Cultivated tolerance) is a newly developed Wei-Chin concept,[82] extensively elaborated in the *Shih-shuo hsin-yü* to reflect one's strong self-composure. While facing a sudden shock in life—the death of a loved one, one's impending execution, a tiger's roar, the thundering of heaven, a fire, a success, unexpected glory or insult—one's "spirit and bearing undergo no change" (*shen-ch'i pu pien*), or one's "spirit and facial expression show no change" (*shen-se pu pien*). This phrase, appearing repeatedly in the "Ya-liang" chapter, was originally used in the *Chuang-tzu* to describe the Perfect Man (*chih-jen*): "The Perfect Man may stare at the blue heavens above, dive into the Yellow Springs below, ramble to the end of the eight directions, yet his spirit and bearing undergo no change."[83]

The Wei-Chin understanding of this quality is that it tests the inner power, or *te,* of an ideal personality. Kuo Hsiang comments on the above *Chuang-tzu* passage: "When the potency [*te*] is replete within, then the spirit [*shen*] is ubiquitous without. Far and near, remote and secluded, everywhere he (the perfect man) stands is illuminated. Therefore, he can stand aloof facing the critical moment between safety and danger, and feel contented."[84] Of the various kinds of *te* conduct, self-composure was especially valued because, in order to maintain it, one had to combat one's self—one's fear, cowardice, or any kind of human weakness. Thus we can understand why *ya-liang* was conceptualized and exalted in the Wei-Chin era: With people's lives under constant threat, only those individuals with superior *te* could manage to uphold their integrity and to look calm and dignified when facing dangerous situations.

Kuei-cheng (Admonitions and warnings) and *Tzu-hsin* (Self-renewal) form a pair of concepts. *Kuei-cheng* describes one's ability to give correct advice and to give it effectively. *Tzu-hsin* responds to others' admonitions with such a high degree of forbearance and determination that one symbolically kills the old self in order to establish a new one (15/1).

Ch'i-i (Reclusion and disengagement) reflects a typical Wei-Chin trend of renouncing the world in order to maintain one's integrity, often in resistance to the allure of rank and wealth. Hsi K'ang's rejection of Shan T'ao's offer of an official position, for instance, is recorded in this chapter (18/3). And the purpose of maintaining one's integrity and living in reclusion is to cultivate oneself into the embodiment of the self-so-ness—such as a True Man *(chen-jen)* or a Great Man *(ta-jen)*—within the very bosom of Nature (18/1).

Ts'ai *(innate ability, talent, specialty)*

2. *Yen-yü*	(Speech and conversation)	(pre-Wei-Chin category)
3. *Cheng-shih*	(Affairs of government)	(pre-Wei-Chin category)
4. *Wen-hsüeh*	(Literature and scholarship)	(pre-Wei-Chin category)
7. *Shih-chien*	(Recognition and judgment)	(Wei-Chin category)
8. *Shang-yü*	(Appreciation and praise)	(pre-Wei-Chin category)

9. *P'in-tsao*	(Ranking with refined words) (pre-Wei-Chin category)
20. *Shu-chieh*	(Technical understanding) (*Shih-shuo* invented category)
21. *Ch'iao-i*	(Ingenious art) (*Shih-shuo* invented category)

This group starts with the remaining three of the "four divisions of Confucius' disciples." Although, as mentioned earlier, Wang Pi defines all four as *ts'ai-ch'ang, te-hsing* seems to denote the attitudes that guide people's general conduct, and the other three indicate more specific capabilities. The Wei emphasis on human inner ability and the Wei-Chin social, political, and cultural context greatly enriched this list of talents and abilities.

Yen-yü originally referred to the speech and conversation conducted on formal occasions, such as diplomatic events.[85] As a *Shih-shuo* category, it collects poetic sentiments from Wei-Chin daily life and witty remarks from pure-conversation gatherings. *Cheng-shih* keeps its traditional meaning of "Affairs of Government," but is updated to fit the Wei-Chin political situation. Its most famous episode is Wang Tao's remark: "People say I'm too lax [in attending to political affairs]; but those that come after me will miss this laxity" (3/15). It typifies the Wei-Chin *Hsüan-hsüeh* attitude toward political affairs: namely, that politics should take its natural course.

Wen-hsüeh originally had a much broader sense than its meaning today as "literature." According to Fan Ning (339–401), "*Wen-hsüeh* means to be well learned in the former kings' classics [*tien-wen*]."[86] *Tien-wen* here refers to all kinds of writings, from government and historical documents to literary creations. From the Wei-Chin period onward, literary writing gradually became independent from scholastic writing, and the *Shih-shuo hsin-yü* provides an early record of this process. The *Shih-shuo* author uses the first half of chapter 4 (episodes 1–65) to record Wei-Chin *Hsüan-hsüeh* discussions (including four episodes on late Han Confucian scholarship), and the second half (episodes 66–104) to record Wei-Chin literary production and criticism, plus some biographic writings. Hence for the first time in Chinese history, *wen*—literature—came to be clearly separated from *hsüeh*—scholarship.[87] This distinction in the "Wen-hsüeh" chapter was maintained throughout the entire *Shih-shuo t'i* tradition.

Shih-chien (Recognition and judgment), *Shang-yü* (Appreciation and praise), and *P'in-tsao* (Ranking with refined words) round out the picture of the Wei-Chin character appraisal. *Shih-chien* introduces the general practice of character appraisal, ranging from recognizing an "intelligent hero" capable of pacifying the realm to choosing a bosom friend adept in pure conversation. It also offers some basic approaches to the practice, including physiognomy and psychological analysis. *Shang-yü* provides many examples of character appraisal remarks, especially those with metaphorical contents. *P'in-tsao* pairs evaluatees for the purpose of making comparisons.

To these categories, the *Shih-shuo* author adds two newly invented ones: *Shu-chieh* (Technical understanding), and *Ch'iao-i* (Ingenious art). The former concentrates on Wei-Chin achievements in music, medicine, geomancy, and so forth, and the latter on art, architecture, and calligraphy. These two categories, together with the new delineation of literature elaborated in the chapter "Wen-hsüeh," testify to the powerful Wei-Chin tendency to exalt artistic and literary creations, especially those that embodied individuality.

Hsing *(temperament, disposition, temper)*

11. *Chieh-wu*	(Quick perception) (*Shih-shuo* invented category)
12. *Su-hui*	(Precocious intelligence) (*Shih-shuo* invented category)
13. *Hao-shuang*	(Virility and vigor) (*Shih-shuo* invented category)
14. *Jung-chih*	(Appearance and manner) (pre-Wei-Chin category)
23. *Jen-tan*	(Uninhibitedness and eccentricity) (*Shih-shuo* invented category)
24. *Chien-ao*	(Rudeness and arrogance) (Wei-Chin category)
27. *Chia-chüeh*	(Guile and chicanery) (*Shih-shuo* invented category)
29. *Chien-se*	(Stinginess and meanness) (pre-Wei-Chin category)
30. *T'ai-ch'ih*	(Extravagance and ostentation) (pre-Wei-Chin category)
31. *Fen-Chüan*	(Anger and irascibility) (pre-Wei-Chin category)

32. *Ch'an-hsien*   (Slanderousness and treachery)
                           (*Shih-shuo* invented category)

34. *P'i-lou*   (Crudities and blunders)
                           (*Shih-shuo* invented category)

Contrasted with the first group, which shows great inner power in controlling one's emotions, impulses, and desires, this group exhibits intrinsic characteristics irrepressible by one's will. Possibly for this reason, the *Shih-shuo* author never passes moral judgment on behavior that would later be considered "vicious and petty." Instead, we find that it is often ascribed simply to *hsing* (nature). At the same time, this third group complements the first group in underscoring the function of one's subjectivity: One controls oneself or defers to one's natural impulses; in either case, one steers oneself rather than being steered by some outer force. For example, both Wang Jung and Juan Chi observe mourning ritual for their parents in the same style—emaciated but not performing the rites. Yet the author assigns Wang's episodes to chapter 1, "Te-hsing" (*Te* conduct) (*te* group), and Juan's to "Jen-tan" (Uninhibitedness and eccentricity) (*hsing* group). For Wang, the author highlights his emaciation—his extreme grief reduces him to a skeleton (1/17, 1/20). For Juan, the author focuses on his eccentric behavior during the mourning period—he eats meat and drinks wine (23/2, 23/9), sprawls his legs apart (instead of kneeling) without weeping (23/11), and, once he feels like crying, wails until he spits up blood (23/9). The author then shows us two ways of understanding their similar behavior: (1) If we take it as one's dutiful filial expression, following one's own Way, as in Wang Jung's case, then it reveals one's *te;* and (2) if we take it as a son's natural response to his parent's death, so sad that he loses control of himself, as in Juan Chi's case, then it demonstrates his uninhibited and eccentric character.

In the chapter "Jen-tan," unrestrained behavior always occurs under the influence of wine. There are thirty-three episodes related to wine in chapter 23, three-fifths of the total (Juan Chi alone takes up seven). Most of the heroes in the "Jen-tan" chapter also appear in the chapter on "Te-hsing," including the famous "Seven Worthies of the Bamboo Grove." But whereas these gentlemen are sober in "Te-hsing," they become drunk in

"Jen-tan." Wine diminishes their self-restraint, making them more consistent with their true nature—a state they describe as "body and spirit being intimate with each other" (23/52).

Liu Ling, a prominent drinker in this chapter, considers this state to be the result of the *te*, or potency, of wine. His "Hymn to the *Te* of Wine" describes the freedom of the "Great Man":

> At this the Great Man
> Took the jar and filled it at the vat,
> Put cup to mouth and quaffed the lees;
> Shook out his beard and sat, legs sprawled apart,
> Pillowed on barm and cushioned on the dregs.
> Without a thought, without anxiety,
> His happiness lighthearted and carefree.
>
> Now utterly bemused with wine,
> Now absently awake,
> He calmly listened, deaf to thunder's crashing roar,
> Or fixed his gaze, unseeing of Mt. T'ai's great hulk.
> Of cold or heat he felt no fleshly pangs,
> Of profit or desire no sensual stir;
> He looked down on the myriad things, with all their fuss,
> As on the Chiang or Han Rivers with floating weeds.[88]

Note that the Great Man's mind resembles the Perfect Man's in the *Chuang-tzu*, self-contented and immovable by external forces. Whereas Kuo Hsiang contends that the Perfect Man achieves his aloofness from his inner potency—*te*—Liu Ling's hero, the Great Man, acquires his from wine.

Richard Mather argues that the line in the *Shih-shuo hsin-yü*, 23/52, "If for three days I don't drink any wine, I feel my body and spirit are no longer intimate with each other," parodies 4/63, "If for three days I don't read the 'Book of the Way and Its Power' (*Tao-te ching*), I begin to feel the base of my tongue growing stiff."[89] This parodic rhetoric serves a serious purpose—to give philosophical defense to a carefree lifestyle. The link between man's inner potency and the power of wine provides Wei-Chin gentlemen with an excuse for indulging themselves in drink, in order to evade the worldly bustle and to reach the status of an ideal personality—the Great Man or the Perfect Man. Thus we encounter lines such as: "Wine is just the thing to make every man naturally remote from the world" (23/35), and "Wine is just the thing which naturally draws a man up and sets him in a transcendent place [*sheng-ti*]" (23/48).

Given the transformative power of wine, drinking can yield a "famous gentleman" (*ming-shih*), as Wang Kung (d. 398) asserts: "A famous gentleman doesn't necessarily have to possess remarkable talent. Merely let a man be perpetually idle and a heavy drinker, and whoever has read the poem 'Encountering Sorrow' (*Li-sao*) can then be called a 'famous gentleman'" (23/53). In other words, wine replaces fame and contributes to a gentleman's self-fashioning. Liu Ling claims that "Heaven produced Liu Ling, and took 'wine' for his name" (23/3); Chang Han (fl. early fourth century) tells us: "Making a name for myself after death isn't as good as one cup of wine right now" (23/20); and Pi Cho (d. ca. 329) exclaims: "Holding a crab's claw in one hand and a cup of wine in the other, paddling and swimming about in a pool of wine—ah! With that I'd be content to spend my whole life!" (23/21). From an intense craving for fame to a voluntary internalization of wine as part of their natural endowment and identity, this shift shows the Wei-Chin elite's' increasing desire to maintain their natural status.

Ch'ing (*feeling, emotion, passion*)

16. *Ch'i-hsien*	(Admiration and emulation) (*Shih-shuo* invented category)	
17. *Shang-shih*	(Grieving for the departed) (*Shih-shuo* invented category)	
22. *Ch'ung-li*	(Favor and veneration) (*Shih-shuo* invented category)	
25. *P'ai-t'iao*	(Taunting and teasing) (*Shih-shuo* invented category)	
26. *Ch'ing-ti*	(Contempt and insults) (*Shih-shuo* invented category)	
28. *Ch'u-mien*	(Dismissal from office) (*Shih-shuo* invented category)	
33. *Yu-hui*	(Blameworthiness and remorse) (pre-Wei-Chin category)	

35. *Huo-ni*	(Delusion and infatuation)
	(*Shih-shuo* invented category)
36. *Ch'ou-hsi*	(Hostility and alienation)
	(Wei-Chin category)

This grouping reflects the Wei-Chin debate over the connections between *ch'ing* and *hsing* (human nature), a major topic in pure conversation that attracted the attention of almost all the *Hsüan-hsüeh* adepts. Two opposite opinions emerged from the debate: Ho Yen's position that "the sage has no *ch'ing*," and Wang Pi's argument that "the sage has *ch'ing*." Ho Shao's (b. 236) "Wang Pi chuan" (Biography of Wang Pi) tells us:

> Ho Yen claimed that the sage has no [*ch'ing*, such as] happiness, anger, sadness, and joy. His reasoning was quite refined and was expounded by Chung Hui and some others. Wang Pi, however, held different opinions from [Ho's]. He maintained: "What is more exuberant in the sage than in ordinary people is his spirit and intelligence, and what the sage has in common with the ordinary people is his five *ch'ing*. He is in exuberant spirit and intelligence so he can embrace harmony and communicate with *wu;* he has the same five *ch'ing* so he cannot respond to others without sadness or joy. The sage's *ch'ing* emerges from his response to people and things [*ying-wu*], but he does not entangle his *ch'ing* with theirs. If we were to take the sage's disentanglement as a sign that he does not commune with people and things at all, we would be quite mistaken."[90]

According to T'ang Yung-t'ung, the hypothesis that "the sage has no *ch'ing*" grew out of the *Hsüan-hsüeh* theory that if the sage follows the natural principle of Heaven, his nature will stay unstirred. In this sense, the sage has no feelings, emotions, or passion. T'ang Yung-t'ung paraphrases Ho Yen's argument: "[The sage] harmonizes his *te* with that of Heaven and Earth and joins the substratum of the *Tao*. His activities follow the natural movement of the Heavenly *Tao* and do not involve [*ch'ing* such as] joy, sorrow, happiness, and/or anger. Therefore, the sage is identical with self-so-ness [*tzu-jan*]. He follows pure principle, defers to his nature, and has no *ch'ing*."[91]

Wang Pi, too, takes the sage as the embodiment of the principle of *tzu-jan*. Yet precisely because of this, he argues, *ch'ing* as part of human nature emerges from the sage's response to people and things. T'ang Yung-t'ung explains: "Wang Pi discusses the connection between human nature and *ch'ing* in terms of its active and inactive status. Human nature is originally inactive. It becomes active in response to people and things, and thereupon it gives rise to *ch'ing* such as sorrow and joy . . . It is only natural for human beings to become active [in *ch'ing*] in response to other people and things. The sage [as a human being,] by nature should also be stirred by and respond to other people and things and in turn develop various kinds of *ch'ing*."[92]

Following Wang Pi's understanding of *ch'ing*, the *Shih-shuo* author linked *ch'ing* to human relations and emphasized two types of emotions. One type—exemplified by the chapters on "Taunting and Teasing," "Admiration and Emulation," "Favor and Veneration," "Delusion and Infatuation," and "Grieving for the Departed"—was relatively favorable. It ranged from light-hearted taunting and teasing between ruler and subject, friends, family members, and even husbands and wives to weighty matters involving life and death. The feelings aroused by these human interactions spanned the gamut from pleasure, delight, happiness, and sometimes slight embarrassment to intense adoration, love, gratitude, pain, and grief. The second group, including the chapters on "Contempt and Insults," "Dismissal from Office," "Blameworthiness and Remorse," and "Hostility and Alienation," was less positive. The feelings expressed in these categories included contempt, disgust, regret, resentment, despair, hostility, and outright hatred. The fact that the *Shih-shuo* author invented seven out of nine categories in this group suggests a heightened sensitivity toward *ch'ing* and its role in human relationships.

Life in the Wei-Chin era nourished such sensitivity. The growth of self-awareness encouraged the freer expressions of human feelings; the chaotic times underscored the capriciousness of life, thereby intensifying emotional response; and the widespread practice of character appraisal enhanced appreciation for the beauty of both people and nature. Thus, in the *Shih-shuo hsin-yü*, hearts ache for every poignantly beautiful or beautifully poignant sight, and tears drop at the sound of every melancholy song or during the reading of every sentimental poem. Heart-wrenching moments occur especially when a family member, a dear friend, or a soul mate dies. This sort of loss feels just like "burying a jade tree in the earth—how can one's feelings make peace with such a thing!" (17/9).

Release from such profound sadness requires special remedy. Death becomes an occasion for all types of passionate mourning. One approach in Wei-Chin times was to continue doing what the departed had once enjoyed. Thus playing a zither or even imitating donkey brays—gestures well beyond the boundaries of conventional ritual—became commonplace at Wei-Chin funerals. These touching moments of burying beauty in a beautiful but eccentric way are assembled in chapter 17, "Shang-shih" (Grieving for the departed), a *Shih-shuo* invented category.

Another powerful category of *ch'ing*, the love between men and women, also finds courageous and unconventional expressions in the *Shih-shuo hsin-yü*. Wang Hsien-chih's deathbed regret, introduced at the beginning of this chapter, is an example. Another example is Sun Ch'u's (d. 282) poem in memory of his late wife, which touched a friend so deeply that he commented: "I don't know whether the text is born of the feeling, or the feeling of the text, but as I read it I am sad and feel an increased affection for my own wife" (4/72).

Stories of loving couples are mainly recorded in the chapter "Huo-ni" (Delusion and infatuation), a peculiar category also invented by the *Shih-shuo* author. One story tells us:

> Hsün Ts'an [ca. 212–240] and his [beautiful] wife, Ts'ao P'ei-ts'ui,[93] were extremely devoted to each other. During the winter months his wife became sick and was flushed with fever, whereupon Ts'an went out into the central courtyard, and after he himself had taken a chill, came back and pressed his cold body against hers. His wife died, and a short while afterward Ts'an also died. Because of this he was criticized by the world [for his fatuous devotion].
>
> Hsün Ts'an had once said, "A woman's virtue is not worth praising; her beauty should be considered the most important thing." On hearing of this, P'ei K'ai [237–291][94] exclaimed, "This is nothing but a matter of whimsy; it's not the statement of a man of complete virtue. Let's hope that men of later ages won't be led astray by this remark!" (35/2)

Hsün Ts'an's affection for his wife contributes one of the most passionate love stories in the Chinese literary tradition. But his justification for this intense devotion—that he loves his wife not for her "virtue" but for her "beauty"—flies in the face of the Confucian notion that one should "value a wife for her virtue rather than for her beauty" *(hsien-hsien i se)*.[95] Hsün Ts'an's aesthetic interpretation of the husband-wife bond shocked many of his contemporaries, for the Confucian tradition regarded a harmonious relationship between husband and wife as the foundation of the Chinese social order and a virtuous wife as the key to domestic harmony.[96]

Women, too, make strong claims of love in the *Shih-shuo hsin-yü* and justify their love in their own terms:

> Wang Jung's wife always addressed Jung with the familiar pronoun "you" *(ch'ing)*. Jung said to her, "For a wife to address her husband as 'you' is disrespectful according to the rules of etiquette [*li*]. Hereafter don't call me that again."
>
> His wife replied, "But I'm intimate with you and I love you, so I address you as 'you.' If I didn't address you as 'you,' who else would address you as 'you'?" After that he always tolerated [this usage]. (35/6)

As Mather points out, "wives were apparently expected to use the more formal term, *chün*, 'my lord,'" to address their husbands.[97] Wang Jung's wife, however, asserts that using the more intimate pronoun—*ch'ing*—is her privilege as a wife. The conflict between these two pronouns, *ch'ing* and *chün*, underscores the tension between *ch'ing*, "love," and *li*, "rules of etiquette." It also distinguishes a loving wife who defines and defends her rights from an obedient wife who merely follows rules. The episode appears in the chapter "Huo-ni" (Delusion and infatuation), suggesting either that the wife is so deluded by love and so infatuated with her husband that she is willing to ignore the rules of etiquette, or that her husband, Wang Jung, is so deluded by love and so infatuated with his wife that he yields to her strong will. In either case we see the *Shih-shuo* celebration of *ch'ing* over respect for *li*.

Yü Ying-shih suggests that the wife's remark, "If I didn't address you as 'you,' who else would address you as 'you'?" reveals a growing jealousy among Wei-Chin women as well as an increasing intimacy between husbands and wives.[98] Although the Confucian tradition had long condemned jealousy as a female folly and reason enough for a man to divorce his wife,[99] in the *Shih-shuo*, for the first time, jealousy is treated as a felicitous trait of women, motivated by intense love for their husbands.[100] Influenced by the growth of self-awareness, Wei-Chin women came to feel that they had the same claim on their men's exclusive love as their men had on them.

In all, the *Shih-shuo* characters are famous in the Chinese literary tradition for being sentimental and emotional. They commend one another for "having deep feelings all the way through" (23/42), for "being sentimental idiots" (34/4), or for claiming that they themselves would "finally die because of [their] passion" (23/54). Wang Jung's defense of his immense sadness over his son's death is simple, powerful, and poignant: "A sage forgets his feelings [*ch'ing*]; the lowest beings aren't even capable of having feelings. But the place where feelings are most concentrated is precisely among people like us" (17/4).

This apology is evidently rooted in Wang Pi's theory of *ch'ing*—that "the sage's *ch'ing* emerges from his response to people and things, but he does not entangle his *ch'ing* with theirs." The Confucian tradition would expect a gentleman to cultivate his nature following the sage's model and thus repress his *ch'ing*. Wang Jung, however, openly rejects living up to the sage's standard, claiming that the expression of *ch'ing* is a natural impulse, which he shares with all common people. To detach oneself from the sage's way means to exempt oneself from conventional constraints on feelings and emotions. In this way, one's *ch'ing* may either grow into intense love and care or burn into hatred and vengeance. Emotional extremes were part of human nature. Because of this understanding of *ch'ing*, the *Shih-shuo* author could present commonly approved and commonly disapproved types of human behavior in a descriptive rather than a judgmental manner.

Women

Chapter 19, "Hsien-yüan" (Worthy beauties), an invented category focusing solely on women, includes all four aspects of human nature described above—*te, ts'ai, hsing,* and *ch'ing*. The author may have invented this category under the influence of the Han Confucian scholar Liu Hsiang's *Lieh-nü chuan* (Biographies of exemplary women), the first extant work on Chinese women.[101] But the episodes included in this chapter lack Liu Hsiang's didactic tone, which emphasizes obedience to the Confucian moral teaching.[102] As a result, the word *hsien* (worthy), once a widely used moral category in the Confucian classics,[103] acquired a new connotation.

The two authors differ from each other primarily in their attitudes toward women's intelligence. In the *Biographies of Exemplary Women*, Liu Hsiang quotes from the *Book of Songs* to condemn intelligent women: "How sad it is that an intelligent woman/Is usually an owl, a hooting owl."[104] Taking Mo Hsi to be such a wicked woman, he accuses her of influencing her husband, the legendary tyrant Hsia Chieh, with her "long tongue." He concludes that Mo Hsi's problem, as with any intelligent woman, lies in her possession of "a woman's body but a man's mind," which enables her to transcend the gender difference, to assume men's features, and to cause endless trouble.[105]

Contrary to Liu Hsiang, the *Shih-shuo* author expects a woman to have a man's mind, as exemplified in Wang Kuang's wedding-night demand, that his bride carry on her father's mental strength, emulating him both in spirit and in facial expression *(shen-se)*. The bride's tit-for-tat rebuttal to the groom, demonstrating that she is every bit her father's daughter—intelligent, eloquent, and courageous—obviously satisfies the author so that he includes this episode in the chapter "Worthy Beauties" (19/9).[106]

What kind of man's mind does the *Shih-shuo* author expect of his "worthy beauties"? Celebrating the great talent and quality of Hsieh Tao-yün, the central figure in this chapter, the author compares her to the Seven Worthies of the Bamboo Grove: "Hsieh Hsüan held his elder sister, Hsieh Tao-yün, in very high regard, while Chang Hsüan constantly sang the praises of his younger sister and wanted to match her against the other. Nun Chi went to visit both the Chang and Hsieh families. When people asked her which was superior and which inferior, she replied, 'Lady Wang's [Hsieh Tao-yün's] spirit and feelings are relaxed and sunny; she certainly has a Bamboo Grove aura [*lin-hsia feng-ch'i*]. As for the wife of the Ku family [Chang Hsüan's sister], her pure heart gleams like jade; without a doubt she's the full flowering of the inner chamber [*kuei-fang chi hsiu*]'" (19/30).[107] Nun Chi does not propose an explicit hierarchy between the two gentlewomen. Her allusion to the "Seven Worthies of the Bamboo Grove" does, however, confer superiority on Hsieh Tao-yün, for the "Bamboo Grove aura" represents the most respected of Wei-Chin character traits.[108]

Thus we see that the word *hsien* in *hsien-yüan*, "Worthy Beauties," refers to the word *hsien* in *Chu-lin ch'i-hsien*, "Seven Worthies of the Bamboo Grove," not the word *hsien* as it appears in the Confucian classics, in which it was used to depict those who possessed both *te*, Confucian moral qualities, and *ts'ai*, the capability of carrying on these qualities.[109] Consistent with the Wei-Chin redefinition of *te* as one's "potentiality to act according to the *Tao*," the Wei-Chin concept of *hsien* denoted persons who possessed both "capability and potentiality to act according to the *Tao*." In this sense, the "Seven Worthies" were named *hsien* because they followed the Taoist *Tao* of defying ritual bondage; it was "the spirit of freedom and transcendence" that created the Bamboo Grove aura. By the same token, the "Worthy Beauties" were named *hsien* because they, like the "Seven Worthies" and their *Tao*, transcended the Confucian virtues of obedience and submission that the male world had imposed upon women.

According to the episodes recorded in the "Hsien-yüan" chapter, the standards for judging a worthy gentlewoman during the Wei-Chin period included her ability to analyze human character, her literary talents, her composure in the face of difficult situations, her efforts to protect her family, and her courage to criticize and challenge her husband, brothers, and sons. Overall, the women who merited inclusion in the "Worthy Beauties" chapter of the *Shih-shuo* manifested their *te* (potency, potentiality, efficacy) primarily through their roles as protective and loving mothers, wives, sisters, and daughters. More often than not, they followed their own instincts rather than dictated principles. For example:

> Mother Chao (d. 243) once gave away her daughter in marriage. When the daughter was about to depart for her husband's home, Mother Chao admonished her, saying: "Be careful not to do any good."
>
> The daughter said: "If I don't do good, then may I do bad?"
>
> Her mother said: "If even good may not be done, how much less bad!" (19/5)

Here, the daughter is puzzled because she tries to understand the mother's admonition in terms of a conventional Confucian moral dichotomy: "good" (hao) versus "bad" (o).[110] But Mother Chao's message actually refers to a Taoist dichotomy: nonstriving (wu-wei or pu-wei) versus intentional striving (wei).[111] According to Liu Chün's commentary, Mother Chao may have been inspired by a story from the *Huai-nan tzu*,[112] which combines *Lao-tzu*'s idea of following Nature with the Yangist idea of "keeping one's natural endowment intact."[113] In any case, it seems that she intended to warn her daughter against unnecessary striving that might expose her to public scrutiny and arouse negative feelings, such as jealousy, in other people. For the mother, the daughter's personal well-being outweighed her moral obligation to society; hence Mather Chao's clever strategy of survival.

In protecting their families and coping with chaotic times, women often surpassed their men in courage, wisdom, composure, and judgment (19/1, 19/5, 19/7, 19/8, 19/10, 19/17, 19/18, 19/19, 19/20, 19/22). Take the example of Hsü Yün (d. 254) and his wife, Lady Juan. On their wedding night, Hsü refused to consummate the marriage because of the "extraordinary homeliness" of his bride. She then seized the groom's robe, scolded him for betraying Confucius' teaching about loving virtue more than sensual beauty, and shamed him into fulfilling his responsibility (19/6). Throughout their marriage, she advised Hsü wisely in dealing with political complications (19/7), but when she realized that her husband could not avoid a tragic ending, she calmly accepted reality and carefully sheltered her two sons during the crisis (19/8). All the while her "spirit and facial expression remained unchanged" (shen-se pu pien), indicating the kind of mental strength usually associated only with gentlemen, such as the Seven Worthies.

These worthy beauties displayed their ts'ai (innate ability, talent, specialty) in a variety of ways—as poets, writers, pure conversationists, and housewives—thereby earning great respect and admiration from their men as well as from society (19/11, 19/12, 19/13, 19/14, 19/16, 19/18, 19/19, 19/24, 19/30, 19/31). They also ardently participated in character appraisal, proving that they could be even better than men in this quite sophisticated practice (19/9, 19/11, 19/12, 19/26, 19/28, 19/30, 19/31). Take the case of Shan T'ao's wife, Lady Han, who offered to observe Shan's two new friends:

On another day the two men came, and his wife urged Shan to detain them overnight. After preparing wine and meat, that night she made a hole through the wall, and it was dawn before she remembered to return to her room.

When Shan came in, he asked her, "What did you think of the two men?" His wife replied, "Your own talent and taste is in no way comparable to theirs. It is only on the basis of your recognition and judgment of human character types that you should be their friend." (19/11)

What makes this story particularly interesting is that the people Lady Han evaluates are none other than three of the famous "Seven Worthies": Hsi K'ang, Juan Chi, and her own husband Shan T'ao. Although Shan was considered the most prominent character-appraisal adept of the time,[114] and despite the fact that Lady Han ranked him lower than his two friends, Shan accepted her judgment. By recounting stories such as these, the *Shih-shuo* author praises women's courage as well as their talent, for they are able to challenge the highest authority in a central realm of male-dominated practice. The author also includes in this chapter some profound contributions to character-appraisal theory made by women (19/12, 19/31), which I shall detail in chapter 5.

While prior writings tended to avoid exploring women's *ch'ing*, the chapter "Worthy Beauties" offers intimate pictures of their inner world. The women we see here are loving, but rarely tender or subservient. Their talents signal their sensitivity, especially in literary and artistic fields, and public recognition of their capabilities encourages their self-esteem. Nonetheless, their sensitivity and self-esteem often complicate their relationships with other people and cause emotional turmoil. Especially difficult for these worthy beauties is their relationship with their husbands, who occupy the center of their lives. Therefore, not coincidentally, the most talented women often seem to be the most unhappily married:

Wang Ning-chih's wife, Lady Hsieh (Hsieh Tao-yün), after going to live in the Wang family, felt a great contempt for Ning-chih. On returning for a visit to the Hsieh household, her mood was most unhappy. Her uncle, Hsieh An, hoping to comfort and relieve her, said, "Master Wang is, after all, the son of Wang Hsi-chih, and as a person in his own right isn't at all bad. Why do you resent him so much?"

She replied, "In this one household, for uncles I have (you), A-ta (Hsieh Shang), and the central commander (Hsieh Wan or Hsieh Chü), and for cousins and brothers I have Feng (Hsieh Shao), Hu (Hsieh Lang), O (Hsieh Hsüan) and Mo (Hsieh Yüan). But who would ever have imagined that between heaven and earth there actually exists someone called Master Wang?" (19/26)

Ostensibly, Hsieh Tao-yün is complaining of her husband's mediocrity compared with her uncles, brothers, and male cousins, but in fact she is comparing her husband with herself—a very talented and well-cultivated young woman and a first-rate poet.[115] The *Shih-shuo* records:

On a cold snowy day Hsieh An gathered his family indoors and was discussing with them the meaning of literature, when suddenly there was a violent flurry of snow. Delighted, Hsieh began:

"The white snow fluttering and fluttering—what is it like?"
His nephew, Lang, came back with,
"Scatter salt in midair—nearly to be compared."
His niece, Tao-yün, chimed in,
"More like the willow catkins on the wind rising."
Hsieh An laughed aloud with delight. (2/71)

Hsieh Lang, nicknamed "Hu," was among the male cousins whom Hsieh Tao-yün considered superior to her husband. His "salt-scattering" analogy, lacking poetic imagination and natural vitality, cannot rival Tao-yün's "willow catkin-rising" imagery, which brings fluffy spring into snowy winter, in literary excellence. Her message is then clear: If her husband cannot even match her male relatives' talent, how can he dream of equaling her, the most talented Hsieh child, who is fondly doted upon by her uncle, Prime Minister Hsieh An? Hsieh Tao-yün's resentment of an intellectually disappointing husband initiated a new literary theme of inner chamber lament, which would inspire a great number of bitter poems by later women writers.

Most of the women the *Shih-shuo* author recruits as "worthy beauties" defy Confucian social conventions. Wang Kuang's bride refutes her groom, and Hsü Yün's bride scolds her husband—both break the principle of obedience at the very beginning of their marriage. Lady Han puts men, including her husband, under close and critical scrutiny, and she even peeps at two male strangers all night, appraising their character—another instance of eyebrow-raising audacity![116] Hsieh Tao-yün lacks respect for her mediocre husband, in spite of the Han Confucian decree that a woman should take her husband as her Heaven.[117]

For this reason, the modern scholar Yü Chia-hsi questions the legitimacy of titling this chapter "Worthy Beauties," and he uses quotations from Chin historians to condemn Wei-Chin men for not disciplining their women.[118] Indeed, as the Shih-shuo author clearly shows us, behind almost every daring woman there stood a supportive male relation—a father, uncle, husband, son, or brother—who was willing to endorse, openly or tacitly, his female relation's unconventional behavior and remarks. Recall how Shan T'ao accepted his wife Lady Han's character appraisal and how Hsieh An comforted his niece Hsieh Tao-yün's resentment. The rationale underlying this men-women solidarity was probably drawn from a Hsüan-hsüeh understanding of human nature, which maintained that all human beings are equal and each should be true to himself or herself. If men wanted to claim Hsüan-hsüeh expertise, they would have to follow Hsüan-hsüeh principles and treat women as their equals.

By naming all these extraordinary female features "worthy," the Shih-shuo author subverts the conventional concept of hsien and creates a group of self-confident, intelligent, emotional, and strong female role models. The chapter "Worthy Beauties" thus lays the foundations for similar chapters on women in later Shih-shuo t'i works.

What emerges from this analysis of the Shih-shuo taxonomy is a sense of inconsistency—at least as judged by Confucian moral standards. The characters in the Shih-shuo hsin-yü cannot be reduced to simple stereotypes; they are multidimensional individuals, who reveal different facets of their characters under different circumstances. Thus, for example, in the "Te Conduct" chapter, Wang Jung proudly rejects others' monetary contributions because of his incorruptibility (1/21). In the "Stinginess and Extravagance" chapter, he sends his nephew a wedding gift and "later asks for its return" (29/2),[119] and he pushes his daughter to repay the money borrowed from him (29/5)—presumably because stinginess is part of his uncontrollable nature. Then, this mean father and uncle weeps bitterly over his son's death in the chapter "Grieving for the Departed." Such disparate portrayals of a character result from the author's conscious understanding of the diversity of human nature. This diversity also took the form of outright contradictions. Thus the following description: "Pien K'un said, 'In Ch'ih Yin's person there are three contradictions: (1) he's rigidly correct in serving his superiors, yet loves to have his subordinates flatter him; (2) in his private life he's pure and incorruptible, yet he's always working on grand schemes and intrigues; (3) he himself loves to read, yet he hates the learning of others'" (9/24).

Unlike his predecessors, such as Confucius, Pan Ku, and Liu Shao, who viewed the taxonomy of human nature as a means of establishing the political order, the *Shih-shuo* author seems to lack a clear-cut purpose. While Confucius and Pan Ku differentiate between the morally superior and inferior, the good and the bad, and Liu Shao makes distinctions based on differing political abilities, the *Shih-shuo* author does not apply strict rules in selecting and arranging human types. Instead, the classification of human nature seems intended for the purpose of classification itself—a project designed to reveal as many aspects of human nature as possible, no hierarchies, no judgments.

Consciously aware that words can never fully express human nature, the *Shih-shuo* author avoids the construction of an arbitrarily forged, closed system. Yet, the author feels compelled to share with readers his obsession with the personalities that constitute the Wei-Chin spirit. His compromise is to negotiate between what Makeham terms a "nominalist theory of naming" and a "correlative theory of naming."[120] On the one hand, words can never replace reality, and the assignment of any words to signify a particular reality is arbitrary. Hence, the entire *Shih-shuo* taxonomy—its naming and categorizing—can be considered a practice that follows a "nominalist theory of naming." On the other hand, the *Shih-shuo* author compiles his work through collecting and classifying historical anecdotes, in which each name for a human type—whether borrowed from an old authority, taken from some contemporary source, or invented by the author himself—is redefined or innovated to fit the changing reality. In this sense, the author seeks to construct a correlative relationship between actualities and names.

The *Shih-shuo* author thus creates a unique naming system, which vacillates between order and disorder, ever open to embrace more varieties of human types. Such a structure allows later imitators the freedom to include or exclude any categories without affecting the fundamental characteristics of the *Shih-shuo* genre. While this rather flexible structure seems a departure from relatively regulated conventional models, it may in fact faithfully reflect the unregulated reality of the human inner world. Underlying this system is a dialectical principle revealed in the following episode from the *Shih-shuo hsin-yü*:

> After Yü Ai had completed the "Poetic Essays on Thought" (*I-fu*),[121] his [cousin], Yü Liang, saw it and asked, "Do you have thoughts? If so, they're not going to be fully expressed in a poetic essay. Or don't you have thoughts? . . . If you don't, then what is there to write a poetic essay about?"
>
> Ai replied, "I am just at the point between having thoughts and not having any." (*yu-i wu-i chich-chien*). (4/75)

Of course, I am offering only one reading of the *Shih-shuo* classification here. Other interpretations, past and future, can also make sense and contribute to an understanding of the *Shih-shuo* classification of human character types. None of these explanations, including my own, will ever be complete or entirely convincing.[122] This is the beauty of the *Shih-shuo* scheme: It purports to "order" that which is by nature unlimited and beyond order. The more we want to reason about the *Shih-shuo* scheme, the more it eludes our grasp. Yet in the end, the author brings us closer than any of his predecessors to an understanding of human nature, and in so doing, he establishes the framework for later efforts to achieve the same sort of understanding.

Chapter 5

Using Body to Depict Spirit: The *Shih-shuo* Characterization of "Persons"

Along with its chapter title, each *Shih-shuo* episode comes to illustrate the human type represented by that title. Apart from its chapter title, each *Shih-shuo* episode presents a portrayal of a particular character. Over six hundred *Shih-shuo* characters freely traverse different chapters, establishing their identities through the presentation of various aspects of their lives. When we read about their loves, their sorrows, their arguments, or their rivalries, we feel transported to a real human world, where each person projects his or her unique personality. No matter how hard we try to identify all of the trait names associated with each character—and we may succeed to some extent—we can never exhaust this totality. A *Shih-shuo* character, like any person in life, is more than a mere numerical accumulation of personality traits.

Meanwhile, we may wonder: How can we regard these characters, whose identities are just clusters of words, as real people? What bridges the gap between a series of linguistic signs and a living person? Or, to put the matter more precisely, what strategies does the author employ to induce the reader to take, or mistake, characters in literature for people in life?[1] The *Shih-shuo* author seems fully aware of the difference between linguistic signs and real people. He consciously responds to the challenge of coalescing the two, solidly rooting the creation of *Shih-shuo* characters in Wei-Chin character appraisal and its interactions with Wei-Chin self-awareness and *Hsüan-hsüeh*.

Focusing primarily on the idea of *ch'uan-shen* (transmitting the spirit) of his characters, the *Shih-shuo* author adapts the complementary relationship between *shen* (spirit) and *hsing* (form or body) to the dialectic between *yen* (word) and *i* (meaning). He thus develops a unique mode of characterization—*i-hsing hsieh-shen* (using the body to depict the spirit). Here the body refers to both the human body and that of an anthropomorphized natural object or natural scene. Such "bodies" are never depicted in a static, isolated status but always in motion and in relation to others. By describing a person's body movements, gestures, postures, facial expressions, and speeches, vis-à-vis the movements of the other entities in the universe—either people or things—the author manages to transmit that person's spirit. In the following discussion, I shall first introduce the *Shih-shuo* theory of characterization, centered on a discourse of "transmitting the spirit." Then I shall discuss how the author transmits a character's spirit by depicting his or her body in two relations—that with other human beings and that with Nature.

In Relation to Others: The *Shih-shuo* Theory of Characterization

SHEN, OR SPIRIT, THE ESSENCE OF CHARACTER APPRAISAL

Character appraisal, as demonstrated in the previous chapters, is mainly a verbal practice, in which evaluators use words to express evaluatees' personalities. Among the numerous terms devoted to this practice, a most significant and widely applied notion is *shen*, or "spirit." Throughout the *Shih-shuo hsin-yü, shen* frequently appears in character appraisals:

> On the eve of Hsi K'ang's execution in the Eastern Marketplace of Loyang (in 262), his spirit and bearing [*shen-ch'i*] showed no change. (6/2)
>
> In the headquarters of the grand tutor, Ssu-ma Yüeh, were many famous gentlemen, the outstanding and unique men of the entire age. Yü Liang once said, "Whenever I saw my father's cousin, Yü Ai, in their midst, he was always naturally exhilarated in spirit [*shen-wang*]." (8/33)
>
> Wang Tun once praised his (adopted) son, Wang Ying, with the words, "The condition of his spirit [*shen-hou*] seems to be on the point of being all right." (8/49)

Wang Hsi-chih . . . in praise of Chih Tun, said, "His capacity is brilliant, his spirit keen [*shen-chün*]." (8/88)

In his "Memorial [on the Pacification of Lo-yang]" (in 356), Huan Wen wrote: "Hsieh Shang's spirit and thought [*shen-huai*] stand out above the crowd, and from his youth he has enjoyed an excellent reputation among the people." (8/103)

In various works previous to the *Shih-shuo hsin-yü*, *shen* had several different meanings,[2] but as employed in the *Shih-shuo* it usually conforms to the usage in the *Chuang-tzu*. For example, the phrase *shen-ch'i pu-pien* (spirit and bearing showing no change) in the Hsi K'ang episode just cited originates from the chapter "T'ien Tzu-fang," where *shen* means a quality of courage, vigor, or liveliness.[3] The phrase *shen-wang* (exhilarated in spirit) in the Yü Ai episode comes from the chapter "Yang-sheng chu" (Secret of caring for life), where *shen* carries a similar meaning.[4] And *shen-ming* (spirit and intelligence), another frequently used *Shih-shuo* term, originates in the chapter "Ch'i-wu lun" (Discussion on making all things equal), where *shen* stands for human spiritual intelligence.[5] Wei-Chin character appraisal not only adopted the *shen* phrases from the *Chuang-tzu*; it also invented a group of similar compounds, such as *shen-yü* (spiritual realm), *shen-se* (spirit and facial expression), *shen-tzu* (spirit and manner), *shen-feng* (the point of [one's] spirit), *shen-ch'ing* (spirit and feelings), *shen-i* (spirit and mood),[6] and *shen-chün* (divine swiftness).[7]

Although following the same basic track as in the *Chuang-tzu,* the term *shen* in Wei-Chin character appraisal merged into a new linguistic context that, in turn, affected its connotation. Despite *shen*'s frequent occurrence in the *Shih-shuo hsin-yü*, it is difficult to tell which element or category *shen* represents in relation to a specific personality. It does not belong to the categories of *te, ts'ai, hsing,* or *ch'ing*. Rather, it usually appears in a character appraisal that comments on one's entire personality, not one specific trait. For example, consider the following two commentaries on Wang Yen:

Wang Jung said, "The spirit and manner [*shen-tzu*] of the grand marshal, Wang Yen, are lofty and transcendent, like a jade forest or a jasper tree. He's naturally a being who lives beyond the reach of the wind and dust of the world." (8/16)

> Wang Ch'eng characterized his brother, Grand Marshal Wang Yen, saying, "Brother, your physical appearance bears some resemblance to the *Tao*, but the point of your spirit [*shen-feng*] is too sharp."
>
> The Grand Marshal replied, "Well, I'm certainly not as lackadaisical and easygoing as you are!" (8/27)

Wang Jung's remark indicates that Wang Yen's personality has reached the height of the *Tao*, which stands above this mundane world. Wang Ch'eng, on the contrary, complains that because Wang Yen has not sufficiently "blunted his sharpness" as Lao-tzu required, he has not attained the standard of the *Tao*.[8] Despite their different conclusions, both experts use *shen* to denote Wang Yen's entire self.[9]

Syntactically, as shown in the above episodes, *shen* is usually connected with human inner qualities—"thought," "capacity," "feelings," "mood," "bearing," and so forth—to be followed by a predicate, a statement about both *shen* and that inner aspect. The whole phrase is then used to define a person. This structure suggests that *shen* is related to personality in a way that brings one's abstract inner qualities into the view of the observer. Via *shen*, the evaluator gets to "see" the evaluatee's otherwise imperceptible human nature. Or, to put the matter differently, it is through *shen* that one's abstract personality becomes visible in the beholder's eyes. Yet *shen* does not tarry, awaiting the observer's gaze; it flashes in the beholder's eyes and then disappears:

> Huan Ssu was Wang Hun's nephew on his mother's side, and in his physical features resembled his uncle, a fact which was exceedingly distasteful to him. His paternal uncle, Huan Wen, said, "You don't resemble him all the time, but only occasionally. A constant resemblance is a physical matter, whereas an occasional resemblance is spiritual."
>
> Huan Ssu was even more displeased. (25/42)

Little is known about Wang Hun. He was probably an unlucky fellow with neither handsome physical features nor outstanding spirit; hence the nephew's resentment of his legacy.

This episode not only emphasizes the importance of *shen* in Wei-Chin character appraisal; it also juxtaposes *shen* with *hsing*, or body. In Huan Wen's understanding, whereas one's body stays perceptible and unchanged, one's *shen* appears in the beholder's eyes only momentarily. In short, *shen* is an essential but elusive quality, oscillating between visible and invisible, between spatial and temporal. The question of how to grasp one's *shen* thus became a central problem for the practice of Wei-Chin character appraisal. For the same reason, how to portray one's *shen* posed a great challenge for *Shih-shuo* characterization.

BODY VERSUS SPIRIT AND WORDS VERSUS MEANINGS

Ever since the Wei period, character appraisal had involved theoretical discussions of the relationships between a person's body, spirit, and nature. Based on the precepts of the School of Names and Principles, Liu Shao explained in his *Jen-wu chih* how the three notions were interrelated: "A person is born with a body [*hsing*], and the body embraces the spirit [*shen*]. If we [the observers] can grasp this person's spirit, we can investigate the principle and completely understand this person's nature [*hsing*]."[10] In Liu Shao's view, the spirit mediates between body and nature, making one's inner qualities visible in one's physical appearance. If the observer can apprehend the spirit, he or she may possibly understand the principle of one's human nature. But when it comes to the problem of how to grasp one's spirit, Liu Shao seems to have equated constant facial features with variable spiritual expression, therefore confining himself to a Han physiognomic understanding.[11]

Liu Shao's interpretation of the nature-spirit-body relationship represented a common position among Wei scholars. Hsi K'ang, for example, also emphasized the importance of the spirit in its relationship with the body: "The relation of spirit to body is like that of the ruler to the state. When the spirit is disturbed on the inside, the body wastes away on the outside, just as when the ruler is confused above, the state is chaotic below."[12] According to Hsi K'ang, the fluid spirit dictates and dominates the concrete appearance of the body and consequently reveals itself through changes in the body. The body and the spirit thus form a dialectically complementary relationship, in which "the body relies on the spirit to stand, and the spirit needs the body to exist."[13] Therefore, one "cultivates one's nature to protect one's spirit and calms one's mind to keep one's body intact."[14]

Hsi K'ang's understanding of the human nature-spirit-body relationship evidently follows the general *Hsüan-hsüeh* principle that *wu,* or Nothing, underlies world changes and consequently reveals itself through changes in the myriad aspects of *yu,* Something. If one's nature is equivalent to *wu,* then one's body is equivalent to the position of *yu.* For the convenience of character appraisal, it seems, Hsi K'ang and later Wei-Chin *Hsüan-hsüeh* adepts compacted the nature-spirit-body triad into the spirit-body dyad, in which spirit becomes the fluid yet visible agent of one's nature and hence stands for *wu,* and body stands for *yu.* In looking for Nothing through Something, Wei-Chin scholars developed character appraisal into a quest for the spirit through the body. As Ko Hung (284–363) put it: "In judging and evaluating a personality, observe the body and then get to the spirit."[15]

Coming to the actual practice of character appraisal, how did Wei-Chin scholars recognize the spirit in the body and give it verbal expressions? T'ang Yung-tung points out that the Wei-Chin "word-and-meaning debate" (*yen-i chih pien*) greatly helped this process.[16] As discussed in chapter 2, this debate focused on the dilemma between words' incapability of fully expressing meanings and the need for words to express meanings. As we have seen, Wang Pi recommended "forgetting the *words* once getting the idea" (*te-i wang-yen*) as a means of solving this problem. Wei-Chin *Hsüan-hsüeh* adepts, for their part, transformed this axiom into "forgetting the *body* once getting the idea" (*te-i wang-hsing*) and applied it widely to character appraisal. Here are some examples taken from the *Shih-shuo* and its contemporary sources (emphases added):

> Hsi K'ang was seven feet, eight inches tall, with an imposing facial expression. *He treated his bodily frame like so much earth or wood [t'u-mu hsing-hai]* and never added any adornment or polish, yet he had the grace of a dragon and the beauty of a phoenix, together with a natural simplicity and spontaneity [*tzu-jan*].[17]

> P'ei K'ai possessed outstanding beauty and manners. Even after removing his official cap, *with coarse clothing and undressed hair,* he was always attractive. Contemporaries felt him to be a man of jade. (14/12)

Liu Ling's body was but six feet tall, and his appearance extremely homely and dissipated, yet, detached and carefree, *he treated his bodily frame like so much earth or wood.* (14/13)

[Juan] Chi's appearance was dazzling and his vigor virile. He was proud and self-contented, deferring to his nature without restraining himself. He hardly showed happiness or anger on his face. He would either read within doors for months, or travel atop mountains or along rivers for days, forgetting to go home. He read broadly, with a particular fondness of the *Lao Tzu* and the *Chuang Tzu.* He was addicted to wine, capable of whistling, and talented in zither-playing. *When he grasped the idea, he would forget his body [hu-wang hsing-hai].*[18]

The phrase "treating one's body as earth and wood" *(t'u-mu hsing-hai)* recalls the famous *Lao-tzu* dictum, "Heaven and earth are not benevolent, and treat the myriad creatures as straw and dogs";[19] both uphold the Taoist principle of self-so-ness *(tzu-jan)* and let things be themselves. The gentlemen portrayed in the above appraisals share similar attitudes toward their bodies: They "treat them as earth or wood," they leave them untended, with "coarse clothing and undressed hair," or they simply "forget them." In any case, they neglect their bodies, thereby leading their evaluators directly to their inner selves, their "natural simplicity and spontaneity."

Meanwhile, the "natural simplicity and spontaneity" of these gentlemen are located nowhere other than in their neglected bodies. By "flaunting" these bodies, they fully express their spirit—that of *tzu-jan,* or self-soness. In other words, "forgetting the *body* once getting the idea" contains the process of "using the *body* to express the idea" as its premise. The famous Eastern Chin artist Ku K'ai-chih (341–402) applied this principle in his representational art, converting it more properly into "using the body to depict the spirit" *(i-hsing hsieh-shen),* as he explains: "No living person would greet no one or stare at nothing. In using one's body [i.e., person] to depict one's spirit, if we do not consider what the person is actually facing, the portrait will neither catch this person's liveliness nor transmit this person's spirit."[20] As a portrait painter, Ku K'ai-chih assigns himself the task of capturing and transmitting people's spirit, and he resolves to achieve this purpose by depicting the body. Yet he does not focus his attention merely on the person, but rather on the connections between the person and the outer world—even though the body may appear alone in the portrait. Ku K'ai-chih's argument exposes a crucial truth about the spirit: that it can only emerge in communion with others. Without taking into consideration what the person portrayed is "actually facing," the artist will not be able to perceive that person's spirit, much less catch it with an artistic medium.

Ku K'ai-chih's theory about "transmitting the spirit" greatly inspired the characterization in the *Shih-shuo hsin-yü* and at the same time received substantial elaboration from it. The *Shih-shuo* author collected six episodes about Ku's artistic experience in the chapter "Ingenious Art," each of which offers an elaboration of this theory. One episode records that "Ku K'ai-chih would paint a portrait and sometimes not dot the pupils of the eyes for several years. When someone asked his reason, Ku replied, 'The beauty or ugliness of the four limbs basically bears no relation to the most subtle part of a painting. What transmits the spirit and portrays the likeness [*ch'uan-shen hsieh-chao*] lies precisely in these dots.'" (21/13) Obviously, Ku would not dot the pupils until he had decided what the eyes were "staring at"—the possible people or events that would confront the person being portrayed, and the possible communication between the two parties that would draw out this person's innermost response.

But Ku would not depict every part of a human body with such a painstaking effort. He divided body parts into two groups, paying full attention to those "conveying the spirit and portraying the likeness" and neglecting those "bearing no relation to the most subtle part (the spirit) of a portrait." The *Shih-shuo* author presents two episodes that reflect such considerations:

> Wang Hui once went to visit Wang Hsi-chih's widow, Ch'ih Hsüan, and asked, "Haven't your eyes and ears suffered any impairment yet?"
> She replied, "Hair turning white and teeth falling out belong in the category of the physical body. But when it comes to eyes and ears, they are related to the spirit and intelligence. How could I let myself be cut off from other people?" (19/31)

> Wang Hui-chih once went to visit Hsieh Wan. The monk Chih Tun was already present among the company and was looking about him with

extreme haughtiness. Wang remarked, "If Chih Tun's beard and hair were both intact, would his spirit and mood be even more impressive than they are now?"

Hsieh replied, "Lips and teeth are necessary to each other, and one can't do without either of them, but what have the beard and hair to do with the spirit and intelligence?" (25/43)

Like Ku K'ai-chih, Ch'ih Hsüan and Hsieh Wan divide human body parts into two groups, distinguishing between those that merely belong to the category of the "physical body" and those that are related to "spirit and intelligence." Yet Ku, Ch'ih, and Hsieh obviously differ in their choices of the body parts. Why?

All three individuals understand that one lives in communication with the objective world, which, in turn, affects one's inner world and stimulates the expression of one's spirit. But each has a different sense of how communication functions in expressing the spirit. Ku K'ai-chih, a portrait painter, stands between his depictive target and the world. This position enables him to see both the target and what he or she "is facing," but it limits him to their very visible exchanges. Also, the portrait as visual art can capture only a certain moment of human experience. Hence Ku chooses eyes as the most important part in portraying a human being. Eyes can quickly receive and respond to outside impressions, and their every twinkling will likely contain rich meanings. The "four limbs," by contrast, usually take a longer time to complete a significant movement and therefore appear less suited to pictorial depiction.

Ch'ih Hsüan, as the target of her visitor's observation, stands at one end of the communication, with the outside world at the other. In order to expose her spirit to the world, she needs to maintain communication with the world without being "cut off." For this purpose, she emphasizes body parts that enable her to communicate with people: eyes because they watch the outer world and evoke a response and ears because they listen to the outer world and pass on the message to the mind.

Hsieh Wan stands at the other end of the communication, as the observer rather than the observed. He communicates through conversation, in order to invoke the spirit of his target, Chih Tun—one of the most out-

Figure 5.1. *Lo-shen t'u* (Nymph of the Lo River). Attributed to Ku K'ai-chih. Detail from a Sung copy. Freer Gallery.

standing pure conversationalists of the time. For him, therefore, teeth and lips also convey the spirit because they can utter Chih's inner thoughts to the outer world.

Obviously, the *Shih-shuo* author's interest lies not in which body part is most capable of transmitting the spirit but in how communication among people extracts the spirit from the body. Inspired by the pertinent arguments he has collected, particularly Ch'ih Hsüan's principle of "not cutting oneself off from others," the author resolves to portray people in relation to others.[21] For each person he pictures and each event he narrates, he considers all associated parties and depicts their interactions. In this way the author weaves an individual's appearance, remarks, and behavior into his or her relations to others, turning virtually every part of a person into a significant element related to the spirit.

Adhering to this basic principle of portraying people in relation to others, the *Shih-shuo* author translates *i-hsing hsieh-shen*, or "using the body to depict the spirit," into two strategies of characterization, each based on a different application of the word *hsing*. (1) Reading *hsing* as the form of the human body, the author tries to capture a person's spirit by depicting his or her appearance, behavior, and remarks. (2) Reading *hsing* as the form of natural objects, the author visualizes the human spirit in terms of natural imagery. I shall examine the *Shih-shuo* characterization from these two aspects in the following sections.

Using the Body to Depict the Spirit

AT THE MOMENT OF COMMUNION

Every gesture, each facial expression, all utterances in the *Shih-shuo* are rich with meaning, especially when considered in the light of other gestures, expressions, and utterances, because the author intentionally weaves his depiction of each character with that of the others. The interaction among all the participants, condensed into a short time span, intensifies every encounter, exposing human spirit with remarkable clarity.

Eyes, with their quick response and highly expressive capability, are invariably revealing in the *Shih-shuo*. For example:

> P'ei K'ai possessed outstanding beauty. One day unexpectedly he became ill. When his condition became critical (in 291) Emperor Hui (Ssu-ma Chung, r. 290–306) sent Wang Yen to visit him. At the time P'ei was lying with his face to the wall, but when he heard that Wang had arrived, having been sent by the emperor, with an effort he turned to look at him.

>   After Wang had come out, he said to others, "his [P'ei's] twin pupils
>   flashed like lightning beneath a cliff, and his energetic spirit moved vig-
>   orously. Within his body, of course, there's a slight indisposition." (14/10)

This deathbed meeting illustrates the way a proud man could draw upon
his inner resources and prior experience to impress a rival, even in the most
desperate circumstances. P'ei K'ai, well known for his attractiveness
(14/10, 14/12) and his composure (6/7), was a longtime rival of Wang Yen
(9/6). Both men were famous as character-appraisal experts (P'ei: 8/5, 8/6,
8/8, 8/14, 8/24, 21/9, etc.; Wang: 8/21, 8/24, 9/9, 9/10, 9/11 n., etc.), one
source for their rivalry. P'ei learned that the court had sent Wang to his
bedside. As a specialist in character appraisal, he knew that in order to
maintain his self-image and preserve his dignity he would have to look Wang
directly in the face. This intense moment ignited the "lightning" in P'ei's
eyes, demonstrating his vigorous spirit, even when all else was lost. Wang,
recognizing P'ei's heroic effort as an experienced evaluator himself, gave
his rival due respect.

   But eyes were not the only expressive part of the body. Even hair and
skin can carry spirit:

>   When Huan Wen subdued Shu (Szechwan, in 347), he took Lady Li,
>   the younger sister of the last ruler, Li Shih (r. 343–347), as a concubine
>   and treated her with extreme favor, always keeping her in an apartment
>   behind his study. Huan's wife, the princess of Nan-k'ang, knew nothing
>   about it at first, but after she had heard, she came with several tens of
>   female attendants, brandishing a naked sword, to attack her. It happened
>   that just then Lady Li was combing her hair, and her tresses fell, cov-
>   ering the floor. The color of her skin was like the luster of jade. Her
>   face did not change expression, and she said calmly, "My kingdom has
>   been destroyed and my family ruined. I had no wish to come here. If I
>   could be killed today it would only be what I have longed for from the
>   beginning."
>   The princess withdrew in shame. (19/21)

Under other circumstances, the depiction of Lady Li's hair and skin
might not have had much expressive strength. In this episode, however,
they become crucial elements for conveying Lady Li's spirit as "seen"
through Princess Nan-k'ang's eyes. What is it that stems the princess' fury,

causing her to withdraw in shame rather than attack? From the princess' viewpoint, we can see Lady Li's pale jadelike face, set off by her long, black, uncombed hair. This visual contrast between black and white establishes a sad and somber tone for this tragic character. A vivid figure, beautiful yet unpolished, vulnerable yet determined, desperate yet noble and utterly poised in manner, emerges from this intense confrontation with a jealous woman.[22] This episode gives the only detailed description of a woman's beauty in the *Shih-shuo hsin-yü*, which evidences that the author applies depictions of appearance only as necessary for exposing inner qualities.

Here is another illustration of how a relatively inactive part of the body can become a highly expressive element:

> At first while Hsieh An was living in the Eastern Mountains as a commoner, some of his older and younger brothers had already become wealthy and honorable. Whenever there was a gathering of the various branches of the family, it always created quite a stir among the populace.
>
> An's wife, Lady Liu, teased him, saying, "Shouldn't a great man like you be like this too?"
>
> Holding his nose, Hsieh replied, "I am afraid it is unavoidable!" (25/27)

What does Hsieh An mean by holding his nose? Yü Chia-hsi suggests that he is impudently thumbing his nose at wealth and honor.[23] Richard Mather believes that "there is an implied pun in this gesture, as popular notions equated *fu*, 'wealth' (*$pi\partial u$*), and *fu*, 'rotten' (*$b'iu$*)."[24] Thus, Hsieh An displays his disgust with the rotten smell of wealth and honor.

This is not, however, the only nose-holding episode involving Hsieh An: "Hsieh Hsüan characterized his uncle, Hsieh An, as follows: 'In his moments of leisure, without so much as even chanting aloud but merely sitting composedly tweaking his nose and looking [around], he naturally had the air of someone living in retirement among hills and lakes.'" (14/36). In this instance, nose holding appears to be a gesture of self-content rather than contempt for others, an interpretation consistent with other *Shih-shuo* episodes about Hsieh An. Although on occasion Hsieh refrained from taking office in order to avoid a power struggle at court (25/26, 25/32), he was also well aware of and contented with his administrative ability

(6/28). Thus, facing "a stir among the populace" by his brothers' wealth and honor and compelled by his wife's half-joking challenge, Hsieh An impulsively holds his nose, revealing his otherwise well-contained ambition.

Through portraying people in relation to others, the *Shih-shuo* author even turns attire into a spirit-transmitting medium. For instance:

> Whenever Wang Hsien-chih and his [elder] brother Hui-chih went to visit their maternal uncle, Ch'ih Yin, they always wore leather shoes (*lü*), and in their greetings they were most careful to observe the etiquette proper to maternal nephews. But after Yin's son Ch'ih Ch'ao died (in 377), they always wore wooden clogs (*chi*), and their deportment and manners were contemptuous and rude. When Ch'ih asked them to be seated, they would always say, "We're busy and haven't any time to sit." Once, after they had left, Ch'ih sighed, "If Ch'ao hadn't died, you rats wouldn't dare act like this!" (24/15)
>
> Wang T'an-chih did not get on at all with the monk Chih Tun. Wang called Chih a "specious sophist," and Chih characterized Wang with the words, "Wearing a greasy Yen cap[25] and a tattered-cloth single robe, with a copy of the 'Tso Commentary' tucked under his arm, chasing along behind Cheng Hsüan's carriage—I ask you, what sort of dust-and-filth bag is he, anyhow?" (26/21)

In the former episode, Wei-Chin gentlemen wore leather shoes (*lü*) and wooden clogs (*chi*) respectively for formal and casual occasions. Using the contrast between the two types of attire as a metaphor, the author juxtaposes the Wang brothers' regard and disregard for their uncle Ch'ih Yin before and after his influential son's death, thus exposing their snobbishness.

In the latter story, Chih Tun's metaphor of the old-fashioned "Yen cap" defines his long-term rival Wang T'an-chih as a stubborn and out-of-date pedant. Chih further disparages Wang by "greasing" his cap and mocking him as a poorly attired trash bag who, instead of embracing the trendy *Hsüan-hsüeh* learning, adheres to the Han Confucian scholarship of Cheng Hsüan. Whereas this abusive illustration only adds a comic touch to a diligent scholar, it reveals Chih himself as a caustic and acrimonious man.

Although Ku K'ai-chih dismisses depictions of the four limbs as "bearing no relation to the most subtle part of a portrait," relying upon verbal expressions in catching temporal changes, the *Shih-shuo* author uses body movements to good effect. Here is an amusing example: "Wang Shu was by nature short tempered. Once, while he was attempting to eat an egg, he speared it with his chopstick but could not get hold of it. Immediately flying into a great rage, he lifted it up and hurled it to the floor. The egg rolled around and had not yet come to rest when he got down on the ground and stomped on it with the teeth of his clogs, but again he failed to get hold of it. Thoroughly infuriated, he seized it and put it into his mouth. After biting it to pieces he immediately spewed it out" (31/2). In this case, the "other" involved in Wang Shu's egg-eating adventure is the egg itself. Every move Wang makes is in response to the egg, as if it were deliberately teasing him in order to reveal his famous temper.

Words and actions often complement each other in the *Shih-shuo hsin-yü*. Take, for instance, the portrayal of Huan Wen's famous confession of his ambition: "As he was reclining on his bed, Huan Wen once said, 'If I keep on like this doing nothing, I'll be the laughingstock of Emperors Wen and Ching (Ssu-ma Chao and Ssu-ma Shih).'[26] Then, after crouching and sitting up, he continued, 'Even if I can't waft my fragrance down to later generations [*liu-fang hou-shih*], does that mean I can't leave behind a stench for ten thousand years [*i-hsiu wan-tsai*]?'" (33/13) Huan Wen conscientiously puts himself under the scrutiny of history, in which he longs for a position. Fearful that he cannot meet his own expectations and that he will therefore disappoint his heroes—the Ssu-ma brothers who usurped the Wei throne and founded the Chin regime—Huan crouches, sits up, and sighs mournfully. This series of agonized movements, together with his memorable statement, leaves an unforgettable image in the mind of the reader that is far more powerful than either the utterance or the movements alone.

Huan Wen's "soliloquy" is actually a conversation with the past and the future. The *Shih-shuo* author always presents his characters' utterances with such sensitivity toward related circumstances. The following episode especially exemplifies his subtlety in this regard:

> When Jen Chan was young, he had an extremely good reputation. . . .
> As a boy and young man his spirit and intelligence were most lovable,
> and contemporaries used to say that even his shadow was good.

But from the moment he crossed the Yangtze River (ca. 307–312),[27] he seemed to lose his ambition. Chancellor Wang Tao invited the worthies of the time who had been the first to cross the river to come to Shih-t'ou (the port of Chien-k'ang), where he held a reception for Jen and treated him just as in the former days. But as soon as he saw him he felt there was a difference. After the banquet had ended and they were drinking [tea],[28] Jen suddenly asked someone, "Is this early-picked tea (*tś'ia) or late-picked tea (*mieng)?" Sensing that people were looking at him strangely, he hastened to explain himself, adding: "What I just asked was, are the drinks hot (*ńźiät) or cold (*lieng), that's all." (34/4)

This story derives its impact from the tension that exists between the "old" Jen Chan and the "new" one, defined by the changing environment. Facing Jen Chan are his old acquaintances; they have noticed that the Jen of the present differs from the Jen of their memory, yet they pretend not to notice and treat him "just as in the former days." But Jen has changed. After a chaotic time, he has lost his former "self"—his lovable spirit and intelligence, his ambition, and even his good shadow. To Jen's altered self, this attempt to recapture the good old days only presents him with an alien and uncomfortable situation—one in which he is acutely aware of his own actions and the response of others to his actions. Liu P'an-sui comments on this episode: "When Jen Chan first drinks the tea, he cannot tell if it is early-picked tea [*tś'ia] or late-picked tea [*mieng]. Once he finds out what it is, he uses quasi homophones [*ńźiät for *tś'ia and *lieng for *mieng] to cover his embarrassment. . . . At this moment, Jen Chan's bright features are displaced by dull ones, and his tongue erases his own words. We feel as if we were seeing Jen Chan right in front of our eyes, despondent and lost. This episode explains why the *Shih-shuo hsin-yü* is a masterpiece [of literature]."[29] Jen Chan's "erasing words with his own tongue" registers his futile effort in seeking a proper self-expression and anchoring his uncertain self in the others' eyes. The awareness of the others' scrutiny impels him into constant self-modification. Precisely because the author presents Jen's agonizing struggle so vividly, his every painful movement touches our "mind vision," placing him squarely before us, fully exposed.

Another case of "erasing words with one's own tongue" occurs with Emperor Ming of the Eastern Chin. While still a little child, he once attended an audience that his father, Emperor Yüan (Ssu-ma Jui, r. 317–323), granted to a man from Ch'ang-an, a northern city then occupied by barbarian invaders.

> Emperor Yüan asked the man for news of Lo-yang (Honan), sobbing all the while and letting his tears flow. His son asked, "Why does it make you cry?" Emperor Yüan then told him the whole story of the eastward crossing of the Yangtze River (307–312) and took the occasion to ask his son, "In your opinion, how far away is Ch'ang-an compared with the sun?"
>
> The boy replied, "The sun is farther away. Since I never heard of anyone coming here from the sun, we can know it for certain."
>
> Emperor Yüan marveled at him. The next day he assembled all the ministers for a banquet to report this remark, and once more he asked the same question. This time the boy replied, "The sun is nearer." Emperor Yüan turned pale [and asked abruptly], "But why did you change from what you said yesterday?"
>
> He replied, "By just lifting your eyes you can see the sun, but [even if you lift your eyes] you can't see Ch'ang-an." (12/3)

To Emperor Yüan's question, the young boy proposes two opposite answers, each pertaining to a different circumstance. On the first occasion, he addresses his answer to the man from Ch'ang-an, praising him for fleeing the enemy-occupied North and for coming to join the émigré government in the South. On the second occasion, the future emperor tailored his remark to a different audience. He erases his previous answer with a new response—"the sun is nearer"—intending to stimulate the ministers into retrieving the lost land. His remark about lifting the eyes so "you can see the sun" signifies metaphorically that Ch'ang-an has sunk into the darkness and eagerly awaits salvation from the South. By depicting Emperor Ming's "erasing words" in accordance with different circumstances, the author portrays a wise, considerate child and a capable future ruler whose seemingly childish words connote profound and portentous meanings.

By sketching intensified human interactions, the *Shih-shuo* author achieves an effect similar to Ku K'ai-chih's pictorial catches of eyes. Via each significant "twinkling," he exposes a soul beneath the appearance. But the most intensified and hence revealing moments in the *Shih-shuo* occur with "rivalry patterns" that place two individuals in dynamic competition and thus transmit the spirit of each with special force.

The rivalry pattern became the basic anecdotal structure of the *Shih-shuo hsin-yü* for at least two reasons. First, competition was a central feature of the Wei-Chin practice of character appraisal and hence integral to Wei-Chin gentry life as a whole. Second, Wei-Chin self-fashioning proceeded through a process of differentiation and identification between the I and the Thou. The rivalry pattern condenses this psychological process into a dramatic moment, when two rivals are pushed into an intense confrontation. At this point, when words, gestures, and actions are least likely to be under conscious self-scrutiny, personality traits such as arrogance, courage, composure, fearlessness, timidity, and others reveal themselves with particular clarity. Moreover, rivalry evokes contrary emotions—admiration and jealousy, respect and disdain, love and hatred. Thus the rivalry pattern enables the two parties to "see" each other, to "be seen" by each other, and to "be seen" by the reader in the fullest and most revealing light.

In this section I shall analyze four rivalry pairs, examining in each case (1) the structure of the rivalry—how the author incorporates the characters' appearance, behavior, and remarks into their rivalry relationship; and (2) the nature of the rivalry—what kinds of relationships it entails, what kinds of emotions it arouses, and what kinds of personalities it reveals.

Chung Hui (225–264) versus Hsi K'ang (223–262):

This is the most strikingly portrayed rivalry in the *Shih-shuo hsin-yü*. The author identifies both men as leading scholars of the time: Chung Hui is "thoroughly equipped with ability and reasoning powers" (24/3), and Hsi K'ang's *Hsüan-hsüeh* achievements and outstanding manner win him great fame (2/40, 4/21). The author puts the two men in the same scene when Chung Hui, desiring to get acquainted with Hsi K'ang, pays him a visit "in company with other worthy and outstanding gentlemen of the time." Hsi K'ang is "at that moment engaged in forging metal beneath a tree," totally ignoring Chung Hui's presence. When Chung Hui finally rises to go, Hsi K'ang asks him, "What had you heard that made you come, and what have you seen that now makes you leave [*Ho so-wen erh-lai, ho so-chien erh-ch'ü*]?"

Chung Hui replies, "I came after hearing what I heard, and I'm leaving after seeing what I've seen [*Wen so-wen erh-lai, chien so-chien erh-ch'ü*]" (24/3).

These two parallel remarks ignite the rivalry between Chung Hui and Hsi K'ang, which consists of three personal confrontations. In this first encounter, the similar syntactical structure of the two sets of remarks shows Chung Hui's desire to identify with Hsi K'ang, while their semantic difference reflects Chung Hui's determination to be himself. Chung Hui comes and "sees" Hsi K'ang. The latter's dignified manner, eccentric hobby, and indifference toward a group of distinguished visitors, combined with his glorious reputation, make him a coherent, attractive, and fulfilled image in Chung Hui's eyes.

Inspired by admiration for this dazzling image, Chung Hui imitates Hsi K'ang's speech. Yet he is also humiliated by Hsi K'ang's failure to greet or engage him. His anger stimulates him to competition, and he responds to Hsi K'ang's remarks with his own speech, which is at least as sophisticated as that of his rival.[30] By changing only two words of Hsi K'ang's remarks—*ho* to *wen* and *ho* to *chien*—Chung Hui has totally altered the mood of the sentence. If before it sounded haughty and somewhat satirical, like Hsi K'ang's own personality, now it becomes resentful and threatening, revealing two of Chung Hui's most prominent character traits.

In their second confrontation we learn that

> when Chung Hui had barely finished editing his "Treatise on Four Basic Relations between Innate Ability and Human Nature" (*Ssu-pen lun*), he wanted very much to have Hsi K'ang look it over. [He put the manuscript in his bosom. But as soon as he saw Hsi K'ang,][31] he became apprehensive of Hsi's objections and kept it in his bosom, not daring to bring it out.
>
> After he was outside the door he threw it back from a distance, then turned around and [ran] hastily away. (4/5)

Excited about having completed a treatise that might establish his scholarly credentials, Chung Hui is nonetheless uncertain about his talent and ability. Lacking a defined center of self, he craves authoritative approval and thus goes to Hsi K'ang, the most prestigious scholar of the time. Ironically, the one from whom he solicits support is also the one whom he wishes to surpass. Trapped in this paradoxical relationship, Chung Hui vacillates: He is anxious to achieve Hsi's approval, which will immediately elevate him to the first level, yet he is "apprehensive of Hsi's objections," which may subvert his ambition. The anticipation of rejection frustrates him, so he does not dare to bring it (the treatise) out. When the inner conflict becomes unbearable, Chung Hui escapes from the scene. Yet the desire to fulfill himself tempts him to throw his treatise—i.e., his uncertain self—back to Hsi K'ang. As long as he is driven to complete himself by outdoing his competitor, he can never escape the mixed emotions that structure all of his perceptions about his rival and himself.

The moment Chung Hui escapes from the scene is the moment when he "sees" Hsi K'ang most clearly, and this leads the reader's eyes to the latter: a dignified, haughty man, not easy to get close to, and quite intimidating. This forbidding rival is enough to repel an ambitious yet insecure young man who cannot endure the disappointment of failure. In fact, the author barely needs to describe Hsi K'ang in this episode, for he always portrays his characters in relation to "what they are facing." Through Chung Hui's reaction to Hsi K'ang, we can "see" the latter and name his traits.

In their final confrontation, it is Chung Hui's turn to be absent: "On the eve of Hsi K'ang's execution in the Eastern Marketplace of Lo-yang (in 262), his spirit and manner showed no change. Taking out his seven-stringed zither *(ch'in)*, he plucked the strings and played the *Melody of Kuang-ling (Kuang-ling san)*" (6/2). The *Shih-shuo hsin-yü* does not explicitly recount Chung Hui's role in Hsi K'ang's death, although it is implied in Chung Hui's first visit to Hsi K'ang. Driven by conflicting emotions of love and hate, admiration and jealousy, Chung Hui resolves to destroy his idol. His slanderous accusation leads to Hsi K'ang's death.[32] Now, on the eve of Hsi K'ang's execution, what does Chung Hui hope to *see* in Hsi K'ang? Fear? Despair? Regret? To his disappointment, all he can see is that Hsi K'ang is impassive. For Hsi K'ang's part, he is fully aware that he is now the subject of public scrutiny, including the scrutiny of those who engineered and ordered his execution. His seeming indifference to the dire situation is actually a courageous repudiation of those who have resented and persecuted him. Hsi K'ang has offended the Ssu-ma clan, for he has refused to serve this usurper regime and has denounced its restraining Confucian doctrines, which the Ssu-ma regime takes as its "fig-leaf" (18/3).[33] Therefore, the best way to lodge his last protest against the cruel Ssu-ma clan and to avow his unswerving integrity is to act according to his principle of "following the spontaneous," that is, *to remain himself.* Even the prospect of execution could not disturb his vibrant spirit and collected manner.

Wang Tao (276–339) and Wang Tun (266–324)
versus Chou I (269–322):

Historically, these three gentlemen were among those who fled to the south of the Yangtze River after the fall of the Western Chin, assisting Emperor Yüan in founding the Eastern Chin. Wang Tao served as chancellor, his cousin Wang Tun as generalissimo, and Chou I as vice president of the Imperial Secretariat. Their lives were therefore entangled not only with the chaotic times but also with one another.

As portrayed in the *Shih-shuo hsin-yü,* Chou I seems not to have been a capable statesman. Once when all those who had crossed the Yangtze River gathered in a suburb of the new capital, Chien-k'ang, to drink and feast,

> Chou I, who was among the company, sighed and said, "The scene is not dissimilar to the old days in the North; it's just that naturally there's a difference between these mountains and rivers and those."
> All those present looked at each other and wept. It was only Chancellor Wang Tao, who, looking very grave, remarked with deep emotion, "We should all unite our strength around the royal house and recover the sacred provinces. To what end do we sit here facing each other like so many 'captives of Ch'u'?" (2/31)

Calling Chou I and his peers "captives of Ch'u" (*Ch'u-ch'iu*),[34] Wang Tao mocked them as a group of useless men who could do nothing to save the fallen North. Moreover, he singled out Chou I for special derision. Although Wang Tao enjoyed Chou I's company and was often amused by his attractive qualities (Chou was, after all, "handsome and quick-witted, very much of a bon vivant"),[35] Chou was vulnerable—not least because of his penchant for drinking, which earned him the sobriquet "[only] Three-day-sober vice president" (23/28). Thus it happened that "Wang Tao was once drinking together with the other courtiers. Raising a colored glass [*liu-li*] bowl, he said to Chou I, 'The belly of this bowl is extraordinarily empty, yet it is called a precious vessel. Why?'" (25/14). As Liu Chün points out, Wang said this "to make fun of Chou for his lack of ability."[36]

Chou I, for his part, openly acknowledged a rivalry with Wang Tao, thinking himself the better party. He responded to Wang Tao's "glass bowl" challenge, saying: "This bowl is lustrous and luminous, genuinely clear and translucent. That's why it is precious" (25/14). Even though its belly might be "an empty cavern with nothing in it," "there is room," he asserted, "for several hundred fellows like you!" (25/18) Clearly, Chou I was proud of his genuine and pure self, considering his aesthetic qualities to be worth far more than Wang Tao's political astuteness.

But Chou I would soon change his opinion about Wang Tao. In designating the crown prince, Emperor Yüan wanted to replace his eldest son Shao with the son of his favorite concubine. Chou I and Wang Tao fought bitterly and earnestly against it, arguing that "to set aside the elder and establish the younger is already immoral in principle. Besides, Shao, being intelligent and bright as well as brave and decisive, is better fitted to carry on the succession." Emperor Yüan resolved to call in Chou and Wang first, then to issue the order behind their backs.

> After Chou I and Wang Tao had come in and had barely reached the head of the steps, the emperor sent back a counterorder for them to stop, instructing them to go instead to the eastern apartment. Chou I, not fully aware of what had happened, immediately turned around and made his way hastily back down the steps. But Chancellor Wang Tao, brushing aside the counterorder, strode directly in front of the imperial dais and said, "It's not clear why Your Majesty wishes to see your servant."
>
> The emperor remained silent and said nothing. Finally he took from his bosom the yellow paper order, tore it up, and threw it away. After this the imperial succession was finally settled.
>
> It was only then that Chou I, feeling a deep sense of shame, sighed and said, "I've always said of myself that I surpassed Wang Tao, but today for the first time I realize that I'm not his equal." (5/23)

The newly established imperial order might have been severely disturbed had it not been for Wang Tao's political sensitivity and quick response, while Chou I's sincere, trusting personality was not an asset under the circumstances. A passionate loyalist, Chou I understood Wang Tao's function in resolving the political crisis and maintaining the stability of the state. From that time onward, Chou had enormous respect for Wang Tao. So the two men kept an amicable relationship until they faced the most crucial moment in Eastern Chin history, which was dramatized and intensified by Wang Tun's participation.

Unlike his cousin Wang Tao, Wang Tun had held a high opinion of Chou I since the very beginning of their acquaintance as youths (33/8), and he predicted that Chou "would someday occupy the Three Ducal Offices [*san-ssu*]"[37]—the highest achievement for a courtier. Accompanying this recognition of Chou's great potential, however, was Wang Tun's perpetual spirit of rivalry, which made him extremely uneasy in front of his imagined rival:

> While Wang Tun was still at the Western Chin court (in Lo-yang, before 309), whenever he met Chou I he would always fan his face without being able to stop.
> Later, after they had both crossed the Yangtze River, he no longer did so. With many a sigh Wang said, "I don't know whether it is I who have progressed, or Chou who has retrogressed." (9/12)

Liu Chün reads Wang Tun's fanning his face as a gesture of fear *(tan)* and argues that a man as brazen as Wang Tun, who once deliberately made Shih Ch'ung behead his singing girls without flinching (30/1), could not be frightened in the presence of Chou I. Judging from the context, however, this gesture seems more like a sign of anxiety caused by Wang Tun's desire to surpass Chou and his frustration in not being able to do so. Indeed, although Wang almost equaled Chou in mental ability, he aimed it in a very different direction. Whereas Chou always insisted upon what he believed to be right even at the expense of his own life (5/30, 5/33), Wang liked to flaunt his valor and show his brass regardless of the cost to others (5/31, 5/32, 30/1). Therefore, in the *Shih-shuo hsin-yü*, no one ever considered Wang Tun the equal of Chou I—except, of course, Wang himself. This self-inflicted competition sent Wang Tun into nervous self-scrutiny in front of his rival, causing him to interpret nearly every change in their relationship in a self-serving way.

The two rivals eventually met as the commanders-in-chief of two opposing forces:

> After Wang Tun had rebelled [in 322] and arrived at Shih-t'ou [west of Chien-k'ang], Chou I went to see him. Wang said to Chou, "Why did you betray me?"[38]
>
> Chou replied, "Your Excellency's soldiers and chariots were violating the right. This petty official was filling in as a commander of the Six Armies (the loyalist forces), but the royal army did not succeed. In this I 'betrayed' Your Excellency." (5/33)

The two headstrong men had now reached the decisive point in their lives: Wang Tun was about to usurp the throne, regardless of the cost, and Chou I, a steadfast loyalist, was determined to die a loyalist. Although his loyalist forces had already been badly routed by Wang Tun, Chou I maintained his dignity and composure even after he had been captured. Frustrated in his attempt to subdue Chou I spiritually, Wang Tun was nonetheless hesitant to order the execution of a man he still greatly admired.

In order to understand the situation more fully, a bit more background is necessary:

> When Generalissimo Wang Tun started his revolt (in the first month of 322), his cousin, Chancellor Wang Tao, and Tao's various relations of the same generation, went to court to apologize for their deficiencies. Chou I was deeply worried over the Wangs, and when he first entered the court he wore a very worried expression. The chancellor called out to Lord Chou and said, "The lives of all of us are in your hands!"[39]
>
> Chou went directly past him without answering. After he went in, he argued vehemently to save their lives, and when they were pardoned, Chou was so pleased that he drank to celebrate. When it came time for him to emerge from the audience, the Wangs remained by the door. Chou said, "This year if we kill off all the rebel rascals, I ought to take that gold seal [of Wang Tao's] the size of a *tou*-measure, and tie it behind my elbow."[40] (33/6)

Later scholars have argued about why Chou I would not make a clear promise to Wang Tao before walking into the court. Shih Te-ts'ao's (Sung dynasty) explanation is probably the closest to the truth: "Which ruler-subject pair could have a relationship such as that between Emperor Yüan and Wang Tao? The two had stuck together, striving through all kinds of hardship and adversities. Yet, simply because of Wang Tun, Emperor Yüan became so suspicious about Wang Tao. Gentlemen felt deeply sorry about this. Therefore, When Chou I proceeded to rescue Wang Tao, he wanted it to look like it proceeded from the emperor's intention, not from his own, in order to maintain the relationship between the emperor and Wang Tao. This is why Chou I was worthy."[41] But after Chou I had emerged from the audience with Emperor Yüan, why did he joke about taking over Wang Tao's gold seal? I believe that Chou I's genuine self and his long-repressed rivalry with Wang Tao, both liberated by wine, come into play here. Overjoyed by his rescue of the entire Wang clan—possibly the greatest accomplishment in his life—Chou I for the first time tastes the joy of overpowering his rival Wang Tao and feels that he has the right to celebrate in a mischievous way.

Chou I did not understand that to Wang Tao, a professional politician, a seal, the symbol of office, weighs heavier than friendship, and that Wang's usual generosity and tolerance had been more a matter of political expediency than a manifestation of genuine personality traits. Deep down, Wang Tao was narrow minded: His political authority was not to be challenged, and his self-esteem was not to be ridiculed. Trying to make the pardon appear as if it had been on the emperor's initiative only worsened Chou I's situation. Taking Chou I's joke at face value, Wang Tao ambivalently engineered the death of his loyal friend:

> When Wang Tun reached Shi-t'ou (the port of Chien-k'ang) he asked the chancellor [Wang Tao], "Should Lord Chou be given one of the Three Ducal Offices?"
> The chancellor did not reply.
> Tun asked again, "Should he be president of the Imperial Secretariat, then?"
> Again there was no answer.
> Thereupon Tun said, "In that case, we should just kill him and be done with it."
> The chancellor still remained silent. (33/6)

As we can see here, Wang Tun still oscillates between opposite feelings toward Chou I. Now that he has power, shouldn't he offer Chou the position he once predicted for him, so that he can prove his great talent of character appraisal? Or should he just kill his long-term rival and end his spiritual torment once and for all? In the end, he opts for Chou's death, sealed by Wang Tao's silence.

It was only after Chou I had been killed that Wang Tao finally realized it was Chou who had saved his own life. With a sigh he said, "Even though I didn't kill Lord Chou myself, it was because of me that he died. Wherever he is in the nether world, I have betrayed this man!" (33/6) Wang Tun, too, wept for Chou I: "When I first met Chou in Lo-yang, the moment we met we were immediately in rapport. But it happened that the world was in turmoil, and so it has come to this!" (33/8) In a sense, Wang Tun is telling the truth, for Chou I's death was indeed the result of chaotic political circumstances and human conflicts. But by condensing these conflicts into rivalry patterns, the *Shih-shuo* author shows us that the personality of each of the three gentlemen, including Chou himself, had a role in Chou's tragic death.

T'ao K'an (259–334) versus Yü Liang (289–340):

The rivalry between T'ao K'an and Yü Liang emerged upon the death of Emperor Ming in 326. The emperor entrusted his heir-apparent, the future Emperor Ch'eng, to the young boy's maternal uncle, Yü Liang, and promoted him to be the prime minister, while excluding the powerful governor, T'ao K'an, from his last command (14/23). Suspecting that Yü had ignored the emperor's final wishes, T'ao grew resentful of Yü.[42] Their rivalry intensified during the Su Chün rebellion in 328, when Yü Liang's inept leadership threw the court into a panic and caused the young emperor to be captured by the rebels. Yü was forced to appeal for help from T'ao. T'ao blamed Yü for the tumultuous situation, saying: "Even the execution of all the Yü brothers would not be an adequate apology to make to the realm [for this situation]." (14/23) What was Yü's response to this crisis?

On the advice of a fellow courtier, who claimed to know T'ao well and assured Yü of his safety, Yü engaged himself in a face-to-face meeting with T'ao (14/23).

As soon as Yü arrived he prostrated himself [in front of T'ao]. T'ao got to his feet and stopped him, saying, "For what reason is Yü Yüan-kuei prostrating to T'ao Shih-heng?"

When Yü had finished he again made his way down to the lowest seat. Again T'ao himself demanded that Yü come up and sit with him. After he was seated, Yü finally confessed his faults and blamed himself and made his profound apologies. Quite unconsciously, T'ao found himself becoming generous and forgiving. (27/8)

Now T'ao had a reputation for being economical and frugal by nature (3/16). Thus when mealtime came,

they were eating uncooked shallots (*hsieh*), and on this occasion Yü left the white bulbs uneaten. T'ao asked him, "What are you going to do with those?"

Yü replied, "Of course they can be planted." At this T'ao heaved a large sigh of admiration that Yü was not only a cultivated gentleman, but at the same time possessed a genuine talent for administration. (29/8)

The *Shih-shuo hsin-yü* tells us that the moment T'ao K'an saw Yü, "he reversed his [negative] viewpoint. They talked and enjoyed themselves the whole day. Love and respect came to him all at once" (14/23). Yet Yü's "imposing manner and spirit" (*feng-tzu shen-mao*) were but a pretense, tactfully designed to please T'ao's eyes. With the idea of prostration, Yü Liang meant to lessen the tense rivalry by subjecting himself to T'ao K'an's superiority. The white-bulb idea indulged T'ao K'an's economical and frugal style. These actions expose Yü Liang's guileful and cunning nature. Fabricated in response to T'ao's personality, they in turn expose T'ao as a candid and trusting man, easily fooled.[43]

Wang Shu (303–368) versus Wang T'an-chih (330–375):

Wang Shu's rivalry with his son, Wang T'an-chih, occurs within a family context. On one occasion, while Wang T'an-chih was serving as Huan Wen's senior administrator (363), Huan sought T'an-chih's daughter for a marriage with his son. Under the rigorous Wei-Chin pedigree system, the distinguished Wang clan would not normally marry a daughter to a family of humble origins such as Huan Wen's.[44] Yet T'an-chih was facing his superior's request. Hesitating, T'an-chih promised to talk the matter over with his father: "Later T'an-chih returned home. Now Wang Shu was very fond of T'an-chih, and even though he was fully grown, he still used to hold him on his knees. T'an-chih then told him of Huan's request for his own daughter in marriage. In a great rage Shu thrust T'an-chih down from his knees, crying, 'I hate to see you be a fool again! Are you intimidated by Huan Wen's face? A military man, eh? How could you ever give your daughter in marriage to *him!*'" (5/58). Wang Shu's dual action, first "holding T'an-chih on his knees" and then "thrusting T'an-chih down from his knees," manifests a vacillation between his fondness of T'an-chih and his anger at him. He loves T'an-chih dearly for all his wonderful qualities: He is a successful statesman, a well-established scholar, and most important of all, his child—even if now fully grown. Thus his anger at T'an-chih seems to be mitigated by a father's indulgence: He feels unhappy seeing his son so weak in front of Huan, but he also seeks an excuse for his weakness, declaring that his son has been intimidated by Huan Wen's face. And what a frightening face Huan Wen possesses: "His temples bristle like a rolled-up hedgehog's hide, and his eyebrows are as sharp as the corners of amethyst crystal!" (14/27).

So why the father's "great rage"? What causes him to shift so quickly from one extreme to the other? The following exchange provides the answer.

> When Wang Shu was transferred to become president of the Imperial Secretariat (in 364), as soon as his affairs were in order, he immediately took up his new post. His son, Wang T'an-chih, said, "Surely you ought to have declined and dissembled a few times?"
>
> Shu rejoined, "Would you say I'm fit for this post, or not?"
>
> T'an-chih said, "Why wouldn't you be fit for it? It's only that 'being able to decline'[45] is in itself an excellent thing, and I dare say not to be neglected."
>
> Sighing, Shu said, "Since you've said I'm fit for the post, why should I still decline? People say you're superior to me, but it turns out you're not even my equal." (5/47)

After reading this episode, we see that what Wang Shu really resents is the weakness of someone judged by others to be his superior. In this sense, Wang Shu's dual action becomes a metaphor for his tormented relationship with T'an-chih. As a doting father, Wang Shu likes to "hold him on his knees." But as a jealous rival, Wang Shu unconsciously scrutinizes Tan-chih and, when he finds fault with him, "thrusts him down from his knees." To his credit, Wang Shu holds nothing back; he reveals every bit of himself—his love, his anger, and his jealousy. For this reason, Hsieh An praises him, saying: "Lift up his skin, and underneath it's all real" (8/78). T'an-chih, by contrast, weakly submits to authority and conforms to conventional norms.

Using Natural Imagery to Depict the Human Spirit

When the *Shih-shuo* author attempts to show us people "in relation to others," the term *others* refers not only to people in the human world but also to objects in nature. For one thing, the author clearly follows Wang Pi's axiom that "human nature . . . becomes active in response to people and things [*ying-wu*] and thereupon generates feelings [*ch'ing*] such as sorrow and joy."[46] For another, Wei-Chin self-fashioning embraces the *Hsüan-hsüeh* principle—*tzu-jan*, or self-so-ness—that is most accurately manifested in Nature.

Hence Nature looms large in the *Shih-shuo hsin-yü*. About one-tenth of *Shih-shuo* anecdotes employ the imagery of Nature. Some episodes expose general Wei-Chin considerations about the communion between man and Nature. Here are three examples:

> Wang Hsien-chih said, "Whenever I travel by the Shan-yin road (in K'uai-chi Commandery), the hills and streams naturally reflect and enliven each other, so vibrant that I can hardly get to appreciate and respond to them promptly. And especially if it's at the turning point between autumn and winter, I find it all the harder to express what's in my heart." (2/91)

> While Sun Ch'o was serving as Yü Liang's aide-de-camp, they went together on an outing to White Rock Mountain. Wei Yung was also among the company. Sun said of Wei, "This boy's spirit and feelings [*shen-ch'ing*] seem not at all in rapport with mountains and streams; how can he know how to write poems?" (8/107)[47]

> There was an evening gathering in the studio of the grand tutor, Ssu-ma Tao-tzu. At the time the sky and the moon were bright and clear, without even a slender trace of mist. The grand tutor, sighing, declared it to be a beautiful sight.

Hsieh Chung, who was among those present, remarked, "In my opinion, it's not as beautiful as it would be with a wisp of cloud to touch it up." The grand tutor thereupon teased Hsieh, saying, "Are the thoughts you harbor in your heart so impure that now you insist on wanting to pollute the Great Purity of Heaven (*t'ai-ch'ing*)?" (2/98)

Wang Hsien-chih's poetic sentiments exemplify how the viewer engages himself in a spiritual and emotional relationship with natural scenes. An intimate exchange with Nature, as Sun Ch'o expects of Wei Yung, could stir up the viewer's inner feelings and manifest them in the viewer's facial expression. Since a viewer appreciates a natural scene according to his or her own aesthetic standards, thereupon projecting onto it his or her inner qualities, this "human-polluted" scenery in turn becomes the visible objectification of the viewer's self. Hence Ssu-ma Tao-tzu contends that his appreciation of the "Great Purity" surpasses Hsieh Chung's "impure" ideal of beauty.

In any case, the effect of the man-Nature communication would look as if Nature were saturating man with its observable luster and thereupon making the invisible human feelings and the fluid human spirit apprehensible in the beholder's eyes. At the same time, the exponents of Wei-Chin self-expression could borrow Nature's perceivable features in order to reveal abstract human nature. Thus we find that when the *Shih-shuo* author portrays his characters "using body/form to depict spirit," natural objects lend him expressive forms.

Technically, the author links human beings to Nature mainly in three figurative modes: (1) equating the human body with a natural object, (2) locating the human body in a natural scene, and (3) inserting human spirit into a natural form. Each aims at grasping the amorphous human spirit in perceptible natural imagery.

EQUATING THE HUMAN BODY WITH A NATURAL OBJECT

Using natural imagery to portray people, the *Shih-shuo* author usually equates the human body with natural objects in a simile, exemplified by the phrase *t'u-mu hsing-hai* or "treating one's body as earth and trees"

(14/13). This process operates on the premise that only those who embody self-so-ness deserve portrayal with natural imagery such as earth and trees, and only natural imagery can provide fitting forms for the inner qualities of those who embody self-so-ness.

> Wang Tao characterized the grand marshal, Wang Yen, as follows: "High-towering (*ngâm-ngâm) the unsullied peak, standing like a cliff a thousand *jen*[48] high." (8/37)

> Contemporaries characterized Hsia-hou Hsüan as follows: "Transparently luminous (*lâng-lâng), as though the sun and moon had entered his breast." Li Feng they characterized as: "Crumbling in ruins (*d'uậi-d'âng), like a jade mountain about to collapse." (14/4)

> Shan T'ao said, "As a person Hsi K'ang is majestically towering (*ngâm-ngâm), like a solitary pine tree standing alone. But when he's drunk he leans crazily (*kuậi-ngâ) like a jade mountain about to collapse." (14/5)

> P'ei K'ai characterized Wang Jung as follows: "His eyes flash (*lân-lân) like lightning beneath a cliff." (14/6)

> Someone praised the splendor of Wang Kung's appearance with the words, "Sleek and shining (*d'âk-d'âk) as the willow in the months of spring." (14/39)

In these similes, the author mediates between abstract human inner features and perceptible natural objects through the rule of "identification by predicate."[49] The unsullied peak looks high-towering (*ngâm-ngâm) and Wang Yen looks high-towering (*ngâm-ngâm); hence the unsullied peak comes to signify Wang Yen's outstanding qualities. The sun and moon are transparently luminous (*lâng-lâng) and Hsia-hou Hsüan is transparently luminous (*lâng-lâng); hence the sun and moon come to signify Hsia-hou Hsüan's character. By the same token, willow in the months of spring is sleek and shining (*d'âk-d'âk) and Wang Kung is sleek and shining (*d'âk-d'âk); hence the willow in the months of spring signifies Wang Kung's splendid appearance. The author constructs these similes following a particular syntactic structure: subject (human) + predicate + preposition, "like" + object (natural things). The emphasis lies on the part played by the predicate, usually composed of two kinds of special adjectives. One kind is reduplicated binomes (tieh-yin tz'u) such as *si̯uk-si̯uk (sedate and dignified), *lâng-lâng (in clear tones), *si̯ə̂m-si̯ə̂m (in dense profusion), *d'âk-d'âk (clear and shining), *lâng-lâng (transparently luminous), *ngâm-ngâm (majestically towering), and *lân-lân (flashing). The other is alliterative and rhyming binomes (lien-mien tz'u) such as *·wâng-zi̯ang (vast and limitless), *d'uâi-d'âng (crumbling in ruins), and *kuâi-ngâ (leaning crazily). Traditionally, Chinese poets use these descriptive binomes to depict those qualities of things directly appealing to the observer's senses, such as sound, shape, color, texture, and so on.[50] When used in a simile between Nature and people, they pass on the sensible features of a thing to human nature.

This special syntactic structure, combined with descriptive binomes in constructing a simile, originated from the Ch'u-tz'u (Songs of the Ch'u) and abounded in the fu (rhyme-prose). For example:

> Is it better [to be aspiring like] a thousand li stallion,
> Or to [be drifting] this way and that way like a duck on water,
> Saving oneself by rising and falling with the waves?[51]

> Her body soars lightly like a startled swan,
> Gracefully, like a dragon in flight. . . .
> Dim as the moon mantled in filmy clouds,
> Restless as snow whirled by the driving wind.[52]

Thus, the author infuses not only natural beauty but also poetic subtlety into his portrayal of the Shih-shuo characters.

LOCATING THE HUMAN BODY IN A NATURAL SCENE

This figurative mode operates on the assumption that a previous process of metaphorization has implanted meanings in a natural scene. Used as the background in the present episode, this scenery comes to objectify the inner qualities of the character in the foreground. The following episode exemplifies this mode: "Ku K'ai-chih painted Hsieh K'un among crags and rocks. When someone asked why he did so, Ku said, 'Hsieh once said, "When it comes to (living in seclusion on) a hill or (fishing in) a stream, I rate myself superior to him (Yü Liang)." This fellow should be placed among hills and streams.'" (21/12). Ku K'ai-chih intends to symbolize Hsieh

K'un's aloofness from the mundane world by using the natural imagery of "hills and streams," in which Hsieh K'un himself has implanted the meaning of living in seclusion by contrasting his hermit ideal with Yü Liang's political ambition (9/17).

This figurative mode also originated from an anthropogeographic approach popular during the Wei-Chin period. Gentry members believed that one's personality was nourished by and should also match the geographic features of one's native place. So they often competed in delineating, comparing, and naming the features of both their native places and their people:

> Wang Chi and Sun Ch'u were each boasting about the beauties of their native place and the people there. Wang said,
>
>> "Our land is level [*t'an] and plain [*biwang],
>> The rivers limpid [*d'am] and clear [*ts'iäng],
>> The people incorrupt [*liäm] and correct [*t̯iäng]."
>
> Sun responded,
>
>> "Our mountains are tall-towering [*dz'uai-nguei] and crag-crested [*ts'â-ngâ],
>> The rivers mud-roiled [*ɣap-iäp] with tossing waves [*i̯ang-puâ],
>> The people rock-rugged [*luâi-luâ], with heroes aplenty [*i̯ɒng-tâ]." (2/24)[53]

The two gentlemen first implant moral significance in geographic properties and then use them to define people's personality traits. For Wang's native place, the level and plain land symbolizes fairness and honesty, and the limpid and clear river symbolizes purity; hence they breed incorrupt and correct people. For Sun's, the tall-towering and crag-crested mountains symbolize loftiness and toughness, and the heavy waves symbolize strength; hence they breed outstanding and heroic people. In his effort to harmonize human nature with the landscape, the author even rhymes the trait names of the people with the trait names of the place. Also, as Mather observes, he contrasts "the bland adjectives in double rhyme (*t'an, biwang / d'am, ts'iäng / liäm, t̯iäng) of Wang's description against the rough-textured binomes (dz'uai-nguei, ts'â-ngâ / ɣap-iäp, i̯ang-puâ / luâi-luâ, i̯ɒng-tâ) used by Sun."[54] Hence the various forms of language come to represent the various shapes of places and the various qualities of people.

This figurative expression enables the author to locate people in a metaphorized scenery and to borrow its visible features to display the character's personality. For example, snow provides often-cited background in the *Shih-shuo hsin-yü*; its metaphorical sense emerges in the following piece:

Yang Fu composed an "Ode to Snow" (*Hsüeh-tsan*), which went:

"By the (Great) Purity, it is transformed;
Riding the ethers, it flurries down.
On meeting forms, it makes them new;
On touching cleanness, it shines." (4/100)

The fact that the snow flurries down from the sky makes it the embodiment of the "Great Purity." Embracing the essence of the sky, the snow comes to cleanse all things under heaven and endows them with heavenly qualities. Thus, with the snow in the background, the character on the front stage automatically looks purified and aloof from this mundane world. By "riding a high carriage and wearing a robe of crane's plumes" in a light snow, Wang Kung makes a spectacle so impressive that Meng Ch'ang sighs in admiration: "This is truly a man from among the gods and immortals!" (16/6). If Wang Kung's celestial looks arise partially from his Taoist hermit costume, Wang Meng, wearing his ceremonial robes and walking into the office of the Imperial Secretariat, also wins Wang Ch'ia's applause: "This man no longer resembles someone living in the world!" (14/33). What does the magic? The snow! It transports Wang Meng from his earthly duties to a transcendent realm.

INSERTING THE HUMAN SPIRIT INTO A NATURAL FORM

The first two figurative modes had precedents in previous literary works, but their application to *Shih-shuo* characterization became a more conscious practice over the long-term Wei-Chin quest for transmitting the spirit. The third figurative mode emerged directly from this quest—particularly from Chu Tao-i's *Huan-hua* theory that the world is illusory, whereas the spirit is real and not empty. Here is an example: "Wang Hui-chih was once temporarily lodging in another man's vacant house and ordered bamboos planted. Someone asked, 'Since you're only living here temporarily, why bother?' Wang whistled and chanted poems a good while; then abruptly pointing to the bamboos, replied, 'How could I live a single day without these gentlemen?'" (23/46). Unlike the natural images engendered from the first two modes, the bamboos here stand as independent individuals, coming to befriend a human being on equal terms. They are infused with a human spirit while still maintaining natural features, and the human spirit assimilates their features into human qualities. This process of personification also occurs in the following two episodes:

> Liu T'an said, "In a fresh breeze under a bright moon I always think of Hsü Hsün." (2/73)
>
> Wang Kung was at first extremely fond of Wang Ch'en, but later . . . the two eventually became mutually suspicious and estranged. However, whenever either of them came upon an exhilarating experience, there would unavoidably be times when they missed each other.
> Kung was once walking after having taken medicine *(hsing-san)*, on the way to the archery hall at Ching-k'ou [modern Chen-chiang]. At the time the clear dewdrops were gleaming in the early morning light, and the new leaves of the paulownia were just beginning to unfold. Kung looked at them and said, "Wang Ch'en is surely and unmistakably as clear and shining as these!" (8/153)

These two episodes each equate a man with a natural scene whose features come to characterize the absent personality. Feeling the fresh breeze and looking at the bright moon, we join Liu T'an in appreciating Hsü Hsün's pleasant, illuminating, and poetic characteristics from both a sensuous dimension and a spiritual dimension. Similarly, with Wang Kung we apprehend Wang Ch'en's freshness and purity by enjoying the clear dewdrops and the new leaves.

Personification of Nature also transforms the man/Nature relationship into a passionate association. Wei-Chin people tend to read Nature as an understanding and admirable friend, as shown in Wang Hui-chih's obsession with bamboo and Liu T'an's indulgence in the breeze and the moon.

The same mentality also refreshes and compensates Wang Kung's tarnished friendship with Wang Ch'en. This intimacy with Nature sometimes encourages people to take a natural object as a projection of the self:

> When Huan Wen went on his northern expedition (369), as he passed by Chin-ch'eng (Kiangsu) he observed that the willows he had planted there earlier (in 341), while governing Lang-yeh Principality, had all already reached a girth of ten double spans (wei).
> With deep feeling he said, "If mere trees have changed like this, how can a man endure it?" And pulling a branch toward him, he plucked a wand, while his tears fell in a flood. (2/55)
>
> After Huan Hsüan's defeat (in 404), his personal attendant, Yin Chung-wen, returned to the capital to become consulting aide to the grand marshal, Liu Yü. His mood appeared somehow to be no longer what it was in days gone by. In front of the reception hall of the grand marshal's headquarters there was an ancient locust tree (huai) with very luxuriant foliage. On the occasion of the first of the month Yin was in the reception hall with all the others and looked intently at the tree for a long while. Sighing, he said, "The locust tree is declining; it no longer has the will to live." (28/8)

As the first anecdote makes clear, when Huan Wen planted the willow, he planted with it his ambition, and hence he made it the self-projection of an aspiring young governor. Now already an old man, his ambition still floats somewhere in the air unfulfilled.[55] Coming face-to-face with the luxuriantly mature tree is like confronting his aspiring former self, which makes his present frustration even more unbearable. In Yin Chung-wen's case, the locust mirrors his present declining situation. By lamenting for the tree, Yin spits out his resentment.

In the Shih-shuo hsin-yü, even the "purest" landscape is susceptible to this sort of human projection. For example:

> When Ku K'ai-chih returned to Chiang-ling from K'uai-chi (Chekiang), people asked him about the beauty of its hills and streams. Ku replied,
>
>> "A thousand cliffs competed to stand tall,
>> Ten thousand torrents vied in flowing.
>> Grasses and trees obscured the heights,
>> Like vapors raising misty shrouds." (2/88)

Personification occurs in the process of depiction, as the beholder evaluates Nature's beauty. While the attractiveness of a site may be the product of various factors, Ku K'ai-chih considers its vitality most impressive and tries to catch it with human categories, such as the sense of competition. In this way Ku projects his own personality onto the landscape and makes it his self-expression, from which we comprehend Ku as an energetic and restless fellow.

Quite often, the *Shih-shuo* author combines the various figurative modes in his characterizations. For example, we have seen that Wang Chi and Sun Ch'u use the features of their native places as both the similized counterparts and the symbolized background for the features of their fellow people, and Yang Fu's "Ode of Snow" is itself an independent landscape sketch serving as the pretext for snowy background. The following episode provides an example for the combination of all three modes:

> While Wang Hui-chih was living in Shan-yin (Chekiang), one night there was a heavy fall of snow. Waking from sleep, he opened the panels of his room and, ordering wine, drank to the shining whiteness all about him. Then he got up and started to pace back and forth, humming Tso Ssu's (d. 306) poem, "Summons to a Recluse" (*Chao-yin shih*). All at once he remembered Tai K'uei, who was living at the time in Shan (south of Shan-yin). On the spur of the moment he set out by night in a small boat to visit him. The whole night had passed before he finally arrived. When he reached Tai's gate he turned back without going in.
>
> When someone asked his reason, Wang replied, "I originally went on the strength of an impulse, and when the impulse was spent I turned back. Why was it necessary to see Tai?" (23/47)

Wang Hui-chih's behavior resonates with the snow scene, in which the reciprocity between man and Nature reveals Wang to be a free-spirited eccentric, with snow as the symbol of his fully liberated spirit. The snow here, of course, comprises no ordinary icy flakes; the crystals are rich in symbolic connotations, as we see in Tso Ssu's poem:

> Propped on a staff I go to summon the recluse,
> Where weed-grown paths connect the then and now.
> In the cliff cave there is no edifice;
> Amid the mountains, only his singing zither.

> White snow remains on the shadeward ridge,
> Vermilion blooms blaze in the sunward grove.[56]

Wang Hui-chih longs to merge his body into the shining white, so he opens the panels of his room, assimilating himself with the snow and acquiring the snow's purity. He orders wine because wine can help bring him to the ideal status described in Tso Ssu's poem, which transcends all of life's ordinary rules: a lofty recluse roaming freely across the border of past and present, listening to music, and enjoying an aseasonal gathering of white snow, blazing red flowers, and the sunny grove.

The metaphorized snow naturally reminds Wang Hui-chih of Tai K'uei, a famous artist living in reclusion[57] who embodies snowy purity and loftiness. The desire to see this reclusive friend drives Wang to an entire night of boating in the snowy wilderness. Through his spiritual communion with the snow on the journey, Wang feels that he has achieved all the satisfaction to be gained from meeting Tai K'uei. Hence, he no longer needs the specific form he designed for expressing his impulse, nor the physical presence of his friend. Beneath the mode of "forgetting form or body" is the mode of "using the word/body to express the idea." The form and body in the episode are thus replaced rather than forgotten—"visiting Tai K'uei" is replaced by "boating in the snowy night," and Tai K'uei is replaced by the snow.

With his unique method of characterization, the *Shih-shuo* author responds to a challenging question in narratology: "Can a character in literature be identified with people in life, or is it possible to make characters in literature as authentic as people in life?" Harold Fisch invokes Martin Buber's philosophy in order to explain the source of this problem. For Buber, human beings relate to each other basically either as I/Thou or I/It. Fisch paraphrases Buber's point: "The encounter between the I and the Thou is the fundamental event which constitutes our own existence and that of the other. But there is no judgment of the other in such an encounter. For us to sum up, judge, define, describe, it is necessary to situate ourselves in the I/It relation. But of course that does not give us the immediate knowledge of the other, the directness of relation."[58] According to Fisch's interpretation, the I/Thou encounter is the basic interhuman relation in which the I and the Thou stand equally as both subjects and objects. The encounter between the two induces a tension that elicits immediate, direct, and therefore authentic knowledge about each. The I/It relation, on the other hand, resembles the relation between Man and Thing, subject and object. The I judges and, simultaneously, the It is judged. All the knowledge about the It is expressed and modified by the I, and hence such knowledge can only be indirect and inauthentic.

The activity of characterization in literature, unfortunately, "belongs to the region of I/It, and one might conclude that as such it is doomed to inauthenticity."[59] But Fisch suggests a way to compensate for this inauthenticity: "The greatest art, whilst it cannot afford us the direct, transforming knowledge of the Thou, can point eloquently to the very absence of such knowledge, thus signifying even that which resists signification."[60] Fisch values the I/Thou relation and believes that only this relation gives direct, immediate knowledge of human personality. Yet he asserts that characterization in literature can never build up this relation within the text but can only imply it. He seems to ask the reader to reconstruct the I/Thou relation between characters through the author's original construction of characters and the reader's own experience, real or fictive, so as to acquire the absent knowledge of characters.

The *Shih-shuo* author likewise realizes the importance of interhuman relations in exposing direct knowledge of the human "self," or personality, or spirit. He therefore resolves to portray people in relation to others. As I have already suggested, by "others" he means everything that one is facing and all that one can use to build an I/Thou relationship—people as well as natural objects or natural scenes. The tension in between activates the characters' spirit and reveals it in the reader's eyes.

Moreover, because Wei-Chin character appraisal always involved intense competition, the *Shih-shuo* author condenses the I/Thou relationship into a distinctive linguistic structure—the rivalry pattern. With this pattern, he frames most of the anecdotes in the book. Thus, instead of offering the reader one psychological entity composed of an assortment of traits, the rivalry pattern provides an open-ended psychological relationship between at least two entities. The tension between the I and the Thou generates a dynamic power that differs fundamentally from the "binary principle," or principle of antithesis, that Fisch generalizes from the characterization of Theophrastan character writings. The binary principle contrasts two characters who carry two given traits opposite to each other, and "it is only through the contrastive light that they shine on one another . . . that we 'get to know' them both."[61] In the rivalry pattern, the two characters may not necessarily carry opposite traits; the author may not even clearly specify their characteristics. Their personalities only unfold through their conflicting relations. In other words, in the rivalry pattern, what really matters is not the opposite traits assigned to characters, but the conflicting relationship between characters.

Part 3

Discontinuity along the Line of Continuity: Imitations of the *Shih-shuo hsin-yü*

Introduction to Part 3:
A Category Mistake

For the distinction between a primary source and secondary literature, or between a "great Original" and its imitations, is the space in which traditional hermeneutics works. It seeks to reconstruct, or get back to, an origin in the form of sacred text, archetypal unity or authentic story. To apply hermeneutics to fiction is to treat it as lapsed scripture; just as to apply interpretation to scripture is to consider it a mode, among others, of fiction. Both points of view, it can be argued, involve a category mistake.
—Geoffrey Hartman, *The Fate of Reading*

The *Shih-shuo hsin-yü* is one of the most imitated works in the entire Chinese literary tradition. What was it about the original that impelled scholars to compose their own versions of this Wei-Chin pioneering oeuvre? What were imitators of the *Shih-shuo* trying to achieve, and how were their derivative works received by the reading public in subsequent periods?

I have been able to track down at least thirty-five imitations of the *Shih-shuo hsin-yü* and have reviewed thirty texts. For the remaining five, one is not extant and the other four have not yet been located. Each of these imitations shares with the original a basic feature: the collection and classification of historical anecdotes into human character or behavior types. They may be listed as follows:[1]

TABLE 5. IMITATIONS OF THE *SHIH-SHUO HSIN-YÜ*

	Time	Author	Title	Categories
1	T'ang	Wang Fang-ch'ing (d. 702)[1]	*Hsü Shih-shuo hsin-shu* (Continuation of the *Shih-shuo hsin-shu*), 10 *chüan*, not extant.[2]	
2		Feng Yen (fl. 742–800, *chin-shih* ca. 756)[3]	*Feng-shih wen-chien chi* (Feng's memoirs), 10 *chüan*, compiled around 800 or later.[4]	36 imitative *SSHY* types in *chüan* 9, 10
3		Liu Su (fl. 806–820)[5]	*Ta-T'ang hsin-yü* (New account of the Great T'ang), 13 *chüan*, author's preface dated 807.[6]	30 imitative types
4	Sung	K'ung P'ing-chung (fl. 1065–1102, *cs* 1065)[7]	*Hsü Shih-shuo* (Continuation of the *Shih-shuo*), 12 *chüan*, earliest extant ed. with Ch'in Kuo's preface dated 1158.[8]	38: 35 *SSHY* types + 3 imitative types
5		Wang Tang (fl. 1086–1110)[9]	*T'ang yü-lin* (T'ang forest of accounts), 8 *chüan*.[10]	52: 35 *SSHY* types + 17 imitative types
6	Ming	Ho Liang-chün (1506–1573)[11]	*Ho-shih yü-lin* (Ho's forest of accounts), 30 *chüan*, Wen Cheng-ming's preface dated 1551.[12]	38: 36 *SSHY* types + 2 imitative types
7		Wang Shih-chen (1526–1590, *cs* 1547)	*Shih-shuo hsin-yü pu* (Supplement to the *Shih-shuo hsin-yü*), 20 *chüan*, abridged from *Shih-shuo hsin-yü* and *Ho-shih yü-lin*, Wang Shih-chen's preface dated 1556, published in 1585.[13]	36 *SSHY* types
8		Chiao Hung (1541–1620, *cs* 1589)[14]	*Chiao-shih lei-lin* (Chiao's taxonomic forest), 8 *chüan*, author's preface 1585, other prefaces, dated 1587.[15]	59: 23 *SSHY* types + 22 imitative types + 14 types of things
9		Li Chih (1527–1602, *chü-jen*, 1552)	*Ch'u-t'an chi* (Writings on the pond), 30 *chüan*, published in 1588.[16]	98 imitative types
10	?	Li Hou, dates unknown	*Hsü Shih-shuo* (Continuation of the *Shih-shuo*), 10 *chüan*, with Yü An-ch'i's preface dated 1609.[17]	47: 36 *SSHY* types + 11 imitative types
11		Li Shao-wen (fl. 1600–1623)[18]	*Huang-Ming Shih-shuo hsin-yü* (Imperial Ming *Shih-shuo hsin-yü*), 8 *chüan*, with Lu Ts'ung-p'ing's preface dated 1610.[19]	36 *SSHY* types
12		Cheng Chung-k'uei (fl. 1615–1634)[20]	*Ch'ing-yen* (Pure talk), or *Lan-wan chü ch'ing-yen* (Pure talk from the Orchid-Fields Studio), 10 *chüan*, compiled 1615, 1st ed. 1617.[21]	36 *SSHY* types

Time	Author	Title	Categories
13	Chiao Hung	*Yü-t'ang ts'ung-yü* (Collected accounts from the Jade Hall), 8 *chüan*, all prefaces, including the author's, dated 1618.[22]	54: 21 *SSHY* types + 33 imitative types
14	Chang Yung (fl. late Ming)	*Nien-i shih shih-yü* (Extracts from twenty-one standard histories), also named *Chu-hsiang chai lei-shu* (The Bamboo-Fragrance Studio encyclopedia), 37 *chüan*, not seen.[23]	57 imitative types
15	Lin Mao-kuei (fl. 1591–1621)	*Nan-Pei ch'ao hsin-yü* (Southern and Northern dynasties [*Shih-shuo*] *hsin-yü*), 4 *chüan*, author's preface dated 1621.[24]	68: 14 *SSHY* types + 54 imitative types
16	Yen Ts'ung-ch'iao (fl. around 1639)	*Seng Shih-shuo* (Monks *Shih-shuo*), 24 *chüan*, author's preface, 1639; other prefaces, 1640.[25]	25 imitative types
17	Chao Yü (fl. Late Ming ?)	*Erh Shih-shuo* (Children *Shih-shuo*), 1 *chüan*, publication dates unclear.[26]	17: 8 *SSHY* types + 9 imitative types
18 Ch'ing	Liang Wei-shu (1589–1662, late Ming *cj*)[27]	*Yü-chien tsun-wen* (Distinguished accounts of the jade sword), 10 *chüan*, author's preface dated 1654, other prefaces, 1655 or 1657.[28]	34 *SSHY* types
19	Li Ch'ing (1602–1683, *cs* 1631)[29]	*Nü Shih-shuo* (Women *Shih-shuo*), 4 *chüan*, compiled early 1650s, published early 1670s.[30]	31: 7 *SSHY* types + 24 imitative types
20	Wang Wan (1624–, 1691, *cs* 1655)[31]	*Shuo-ling* (Bell of tales), 1 *chüan*, Wang's preface dated 1659, 1st ed. 1661.[32]	Not categorized
21	Wu Su-kung (fl. 1662–1681)	*Ming yü-lin* (Ming forest of accounts), 14 *chüan*, compiled 1662, 1st ed. 1681.[33]	38: 36 *SSHY* types + 2 imitative types
22	Chiang Yu-jung and Tsou T'ung-lu (both fl. early Ch'ing)	*Ming-i pien* (Compilation of Ming anecdotes), 10 *chüan*, published early Ch'ing, not seen.[34]	Unclear
23	Wang Cho (b. 1636)[35]	*Chin Shih-shuo* (Contemporary *Shih-shuo*), 8 *chüan*, author's preface dated 1683.[36]	30 *SSHY* types
24	Chang Fu-kung (fl. early Ch'ing)[37]	*Han Shih-shuo*, 14 *chüan*, published early Ch'ing, not seen.[38]	14: 10 *SSHY* types + 4 imitative types

(continued)

IMITATIONS OF THE *SHIH-SHUO HSIN-YÜ* (continued)

Time	Author	Title	Categories
25	Chang Chi-yung	*Nan-Pei ch'ao Shih-shuo* (Southern and Northern dynasties *Shih-shuo*), 20 *chüan*, not seen.[39]	Unclear
26	Yen Heng (1826?–1854)[40]	*Nü Shih-shuo* (Women *Shih-shuo*), 1 *chüan*, 1st ed. 1865.[41]	Unfinished and not categorized
27 Modern China	Hsü K'o (1869–1928)	*Ch'ing-pai lei-ch'ao* (Classified records from unofficial Ch'ing historical writings), author's preface dated 1916, 1st ed. 1917.	92, with half as imitative *SSHY* types
28	Yi Tsung-k'uei (b. 1875)	*Hsin Shih-shuo* (New *Shih-shuo*), 1 *chüan*, author's preface dated 1918.[42]	36 *SSHY* types
29 Japan Tokugawa	Hattori Nankaku (1683–1759)	*Daitō seigo* (Account of the Great Eastern World), 5 *chüan*, 1st ed. 1750.[43]	31 *SSHY* types[44]
	Rakuhokuhōsun'an Shikka	*Daitō seigo kō* (Textual studies of *Daitō seigo*), 5 *chüan*, 1751.	
30	Ōta Nanbo (Fukashi) (1749–1823) and Imai Kyūsuke (1786–1829)	*Kana Sesetsu* (*Tales of the world* in Kana), 2 *chüan*, preface dated 1824, published in 1825 under Shokusan sensei and Bunhōtei Sanboku.	27 *SSHY* types
31	Ōta Nanbo and Imai Kyūsuke	*Kana Sesetsu kōhen* (*Tales of the world* in Kana, continued edition), not seen.[45]	
32	Ōta Nanbo	*Sesetsu shingo cha* (Tea of the *Shih-shuo hsin-yü*), ca. 1770, under Yamanote no Bakajin.	4 imitative types
33	Tsunota Ken (d. 1855)	*Kinsei sōgo* (Accounts of recent times), 8 *chüan*, Tsunota's preface 1816, 1st ed. 1828.[46]	29 *SSHY* types
34	Tsunota Ken	*Shoku Kinsei sōgo* (Continued accounts of recent times), 8 *chüan*, 1st ed. 1845.[47]	27 *SSHY* types
35 Meiji	Ōta Saijirō (fl. 1892)	*Shin seigo* (New account of the world), 1892.[48]	Not categorized

1. Dates according to Chiang Liang-fu, ed., *Li-tai jen-wu nien-li pei-chuan tsung-piao* [Comprehensive chart of the dates and native places of (Chinese) historical figures as acquired from their epitaphs and biographies] (Peking: Chung-hua shu-chü, 1959), 152. For Wang's biography see Liu Hsü (887–946) et al., *Chiu T'ang-shu* [Old history of the T'ang], "Wang Fang-ch'ing chuan," 16 vols. (Peking: Chung-hua shu-chü, 1975), *chüan* 89, 9:2896–2901.

2. See Ou-yang Hsiu (1007–1072) and Sung Ch'i (998–1061), *Hsin T'ang-shu* [New history of the T'ang], "I-wen chih" [Bibliographic treatise], "Tsa-chia" [Miscellany], 20 vols. (Peking: Chung-hua shu-chü, 1975), *chüan* 59, 5:1536; and Lu Hsün, *Chung-kuo hsiao-shuo shih-lüeh*, 8:53.
3. Dates according to Chao Chen-hsin's preface to Feng Yen, *Feng-shih wen-chien chi* (Peking: Chung-hua shu-chü, 1958), iv–v.
4. See ibid., v.
5. See Ou-yang and Sung, *Hsin T'ang-shu*, "I-wen chih," "Tsa-shih" [Miscellaneous history], *chüan* 58, 5:1467.
6. See Liu Su, *Ta-T'ang hsin-yü* (Peking: Chung-hua shu-chü, 1984), 1.
7. Dates according to *Ssu-k'u chüan-shu tsung-mu*, *chüan* 120, 1:1037, s.v. K'ung P'ing-chung, *Heng-huang hsin-lun*; for his life see T'o T'o (1314–1355) et al., *Sung-shih* [History of the Sung], "Lieh-chuan" [Biographies], *chüan* 103, "K'ung P'ing-chung chuan" [Biography of K'ung P'ing-chung], *Ying-yin jen-shou pen erh-shih liu shih* ed., vols. 35–43 (Taipei: Ch'eng-wen ch'u-pan she, 1971), 41:23,604.
8. See Ch'in Kuo's preface to K'ung P'ing-chung, *Hsü Shih-shuo, Kuo-hsüeh chi-pen ts'ung-shu* ed. (Shang-wu yin-shu-kuan), i.
9. Dates according to Chou, *T'ang yü-lin chiao-cheng*, i.
10. For the compilation of *T'ang yü-lin*, see ibid., i–xxxviii.
11. Dates according to L. Carrington Goodrich and Chaoying Fang, eds., *Dictionary of Ming Biography*, 2 vols. (New York: Columbia University Press, 1976), s.v. "Ho Liang-chün."
12. See Ho Liang-chün, *Ho-shih yü-lin*, 4 vols., *Ssu-k'u ch'üan-shu* ed., " Hsü," 2a.
13. For a detailed discussion of Wang Shih-chen's compilership of the *Shih-shuo hsin-yü pu*, see chapter 7, n.14.
14. Dates according to Chiang, ed., *Li-tai jen-wu nien-li*, 462. For his life see Chang T'ing-yü (1672–1755) et al., *Ming-shih* [History of the Ming], "Chiao Hung chuan" [Biography of Chiao Hung], 28 vols. (Peking: Chung-hua shu-chü, 1974), *chüan* 288, 24:7392–7394; and Huang Tsung-hsi (1610–1695), *Ming-ju hsüeh-an*, trans. Julia Ching, *The Records of Ming Scholars* (Honolulu: University of Hawai'i Press, 1987), 196–199.
15. See Chiao Hung, *Chiao-shih lei-lin* (*Ts'ung-shu chi-ch'eng hsin-pien*, 7:569–668), "Hsü" and "Mulu."
16. See *Ssu-k'u ch'üan-shu tsung-mu*, "Tzu-pu," "Tsa chia lei," "Ts'un-mu" VIII, *chüan* 131, 1:1120; see also the "Publisher's Note" to Li Chih, *Ch'u-t'an chi*, 2 vols. (Peking: Chung-hua shu-chü, 1974), 2.
17. The *Ssu-k'u ch'üan-shu tsung-mu* contends that the book, spuriously attributed to a T'ang author, Li Hou, was actually compiled by Yü An-ch'i, a late Ming publisher; see *Ssu-k'u ch'üan-shu tsung-mu*, "Tzu-pu," "Hsiao-shuo chia lei," "Ts'un-mu" I, *chüan* 143, 2:1216.
18. Dates according to Lu Ts'ung-p'ing's preface (1610) to the *Huang-Ming Shih-shuo hsin-yü*, which puts the compilation date of this work around 1600, and the *Ssu-k'u ch'üan-shu tsung-mu*, s.v. Li's *I-lin lei-pai* [A hundred records of the forest of art], dated 1623 ("Tzu-pu" [Philosopher], "Lei-shu lei" [Classified reference], "Ts'un-mu" [Preserved titles] II, *chüan* 138, 2:1174).
19. See Li Shao-wen, *Huang-Ming Shih-shuo hsin-yü* (Yün-chien [today's Sung-chiang County, Kiangsu Province]: The Li family edition, 1610), " Hsü." See also *Ssu-k'u ch'üan-shu tsung-mu*, "Tzu-pu," "Hsiao-shuo chia lei," "Ts'un-mu" I, *chüan* 143, 2:1224.
20. The earliest date of Cheng's life is found in Chu Mou-wei's preface (undated) to Cheng's *Ch'ing-yen*, indicating the work was finished in 1615, and the latest date is found in Cheng's own preface to another work, *Erh-hsin* [Fresh words], dated 1634.
21. The only extant edition of the *Ch'ing-yen* is found in the Taiwan Central Library, included in the *Ching-shih chieh-wen* [Dispatches of the world], a 1638 collection of Cheng's four works, namely, *Ch'ing-yen*, *Ou-chi* [Random records], *Erh-hsin*, and *Chün-ch'ü* [Classification of remarkable (words)]. *Ch'ing-yen* has four prefaces and two epilogues written by Cheng's proponents, three

dated 1617 and the rest undated. See also *Ssu-k'u ch'üan-shu tsung-mu*, "Tzu-pu," "Hsiao-shuo chia lei," "Ts'un-mu" I, *chüan* 143, 2:1224.

22. See Chiao Hung, *Yü-t'ang ts'ung-yü* (Peking: Chung-hua shu-chü, 1981), " Hsü," i–v.

23. Recorded in *Ssu-k'u ch'üan-shu tsung-mu*, "Shih-pu" [History], "Shih-ch'ao lei ts'un-mu" [Historical jottings, preserved titles], *chüan* 65, 1:582.

24. See Lin Mao-kuei, *Nan-Pei ch'ao hsin-yü* (1621; reprint, Peking: Chung-kuo shu-tien, 1990).

25. See Yen Ts'ung-ch'iao, *Seng Shih-shuo* [Wan-ch'eng (today's Ch'ien-shan County, Anhwei Province): Yen-ya tzu-hang (Yen Family Publishing House), 1640], " Hsü."

26. See Chao Yü, *Erh Shih-shuo, Shuo-fu hsü* ed. This work includes 77 entries about precocious children from Han to Ming. See also Ning Chia-yü, *Chung-kuo wen-yen hsiao-shuo tsung-mu t'i-yao*, 315.

27. Dates according to Chiang, ed., *Li-tai jen-wu nien-li*, 484.

28. See Liang Wei-shu, *Yü-chien tsun-wen* (1657; reprint, 2 vols., Shanghai: Shanghai ku-chi ch'u-pan she, 1986), "Hsü." See also *Ssu-k'u ch'üan-shu tsung-mu*, "Tzu-pu," "Hsiao-shuo chia lei," "Ts'un-mu" I, *chüan* 143, 2:1225.

29. Dates according to Wang Chung-min, "Li Ch'ing Chu-shu k'ao" [A Study of Li Ch'ing's works] (*T'u-shu kuan hsüeh chi-k'an* [Library science quarterly] 2.3 [1928]:333); Chiang, ed., *Li-tai jen-wu nien-li*, puts the dates as 1591–1673. For a detailed discussion of Li Ch'ing's life, see chapter 8.

30. For a detailed discussion of the publication of Li's *Nü Shih-shuo*, see chapter 8.

31. Dates according to Arthur W. Hummel, ed., *Eminent Chinese of the Ch'ing Period*, s.v. Wang Wan, 2:840; see also *Ssu-k'u ch'üan-shu tsung-mu*, *chüan* 173, 2:1522.

32. See Wang Wan, *Shuo-ling*, prefaces respectively by Wang Wan (1659) and Wang Shih-lu (1661) (Ching dynasty ed.), 1a–2b.

33. See Wu Su-kung, *Ming yü-lin*, *Pi lin-lang ts'ung-shu* ed., with Wu's "Fan-li" [Compilation notes] dated 1662 and his own preface dated 1681, in which he indicates that the publication was delayed for twenty years. See also *Ssu-k'u ch'üan-shu tsung-mu*, "Tzu-pu," "Hsiao-shuo chia lei," "Ts'un-mu" I, *chüan* 143, 2:1225.

34. See *Ssu-k'u ch'üan-shu tsung-mu*, "Tzu-pu," "Hsiao-shuo chia lei," "Ts'un-mu" I, *chüan* 143, 2:1225.

35. Date according to Chiang, ed., *Li-tai jen-wu nien-li*, 534.

36. See Wang Cho, *Chin Shih-shuo* (Shanghai: Ku-tien wen-hsüeh ch'u-pan she, 1957), vi. See also *Ssu-k'u ch'üan-shu tsung-mu*, "Tzu-pu," "Hsiao-shuo chia lei," "Ts'un-mu" I, *chüan* 143, 2:1226.

37. See Yüan Hsing-p'ei and Hou Chung-i, eds., *Chung-kuo wen-yen hsiao-shuo shu-mu* [Bibliography of *hsiao-shuo* in classical Chinese] (Peking: Peking University Press, 1981), 361, s.v. *Han Shih-shuo*.

38. See *Ssu-k'u ch'üan-shu tsung-mu*, "Hsiao-shuo chia lei," "Ts'un-mu" I, *chüan* 143, 2:1226.

39. See Yüan and Hou, eds., *Chung-kuo wen-yen hsiao-shuo shu-mu*, 366.

40. See Yen Heng's husband Ch'en Yüan-lu's postscript to her *Nü Shih-shuo*, *Chüan-ching lou ts'ung-k'o* ed. (Shanghai: Chü-chen fang-sung shu-chü, 1920), 14a–b. Ch'en found this manuscript in 1855, the year after his wife's death, and she died before the age of thirty.

41. See Yeh Shih Li-wan's preface (dated 1865) to Yen Heng, *Nü Shih-shuo*, 1a–b.

42. See Yi Tsung-k'uei, *Hsin Shih-shuo* (2nd ed., 1922), "Hsü."

43. See Hattori Nankaku, *Daitō seigo*, 5 *chüan*, 2 vols. (Edo: Sūsanbō, 1750).

44. Ōyane Bunjirō counts 30 types, overlooking *Hōsei*; see his "Edo Jidai ni okeru *Sesetsu shingo* ni tsuite" [*New Account of Tales of the World* in the Edo period], in his *Sesetsu shingo to rikuchō bungaku* [*New Account of Tales of the World* and Six Dynasties literature] (Tokyo: Waseda Daigaku Shuppanbu, 1983), 103.

45. See Ōyane, "Edo Jidai ni okeru *Sesetsu shingo* ni tsuite," 102.

46. See Tsunota Ken, *Kinsei sōgo* (Tokyo: Shorin, 1828), publication page.

47. See Tsunota Ken, *Shoku Kinsei sōgo* (Tokyo: Shorin, 1845), publication page.
48. See Ōta Saijirō, *Shin seigo* (Tokyo: Shorin, 1892), publication page.

From this table it is evident that the *Shih-shuo hsin-yü* inspired imitations in almost all subsequent periods of Chinese history, from the T'ang Dynasty to the Republican era, as well as in Tokugawa and Meiji Japan. Yet despite this broad and sustained interest in mimesis, most *Shih-shuo* imitations received at best lukewarm reviews from Chinese scholars. As Ch'eng Hsü observed in his preface to a 1694 reprint of the *Shih-shuo hsin-yü:* "None of the dozens of later *Shih-shuo* imitations can go beyond the scope [of the original]."[2] The Ch'ing dynasty compilers of the massive *Annotated Catalog of the Four Treasuries* evaluated over a dozen imitations of the *Shih-shuo hsin-yü* and found only two to be even vaguely meritorious: Wang Tang's *T'ang Forest*—for its rather reliable historical records—and Ho Liang-chün's *Forest of Accounts*—for its "tasty elegance" (*chün-ya*).[3] As for the rest of these imitations, they either criticized them for merely recounting stale episodes or, at most, introduced their basic contents in neutral terms.[4] Lu Hsün, for his part, was amazed by the mediocre outcome overall: "As for works of the *Shih-shuo hsin-yü* type, there were many imitations . . . But, while compiling old anecdotes these works contributed nothing outstanding and different; and their accounts of current events were impaired by affectation. People nonetheless kept doing it incessantly."[5]

These remarks highlight two problems emerging from the mimetic practice of the *Shih-shuo hsin-yü:* (1) Why is it that none of the *Shih-shuo* imitations could ever match the achievements of the original work, and (2) given the first problem, why did the *Shih-shuo* imitators keep doing it "incessantly" anyway? These problems, I believe, involve what Geoffrey Hartman terms a "category mistake"—that is, a confusion of form and function and a fundamental lack of fit between the author's intention and the reader's expectation.[6]

First, the mediocrity of the *Shih-shuo* imitations resulted mainly from the imitator's adherence to the original form but divergence from the model work's function. Cultural styles register the distinction between one civilization and another.[7] Because of the difficulties of reduplicating in full that specific cultural context, imitations can hardly surpass the original. If imitations obstinately stick to the original form within a changed cultural environment and with different political, social, and intellectual concerns, they turn out to be, in Lu Hsün's words, "impaired by affectation." This yawning gap appears especially wide between *Shih-shuo* and its imitative works. The Wei-Chin cultural context, based on character appraisal, the growth of self-awareness, and the evolution of *Hsüan-hsüeh,* had no clear equivalent in later imperial times. Hence, the more the *Shih-shuo* imitations adhered to the original form in order to achieve their own cultural purposes, the less likely they were to match the literary success of the original.

Second, the persistent compilation of the *Shih-shuo t'i* works, regardless of the indifferent response from readers, was caused by the incompatibility between authorial intent and audience expectation. In contrast to other types of mimetic practice, where the model work's genre has been clearly defined before the imitation takes place—and thus the author and the reader carry similar expectations concerning the imitation—the blurred definition of the *Shih-shuo* genre left little room for shared understanding. As delineated in chapter 3, the bibliographical category known as *hsiao-shuo,* into which the *Shih-shuo hsin-yü* had been placed from the T'ang dynasty onward, implied superficiality, inauthenticity, and marginality. Although its definitions differed over time—from the Han idea of "street talk and alley gossip," to the post-Sung notion of "fictional narrative," and to the twentieth-century concept equivalent to the Western genre of the novel—it always had a certain pejorative connotation. Thus the *Ssu-k'u* compilers, in relegating the *Shih-shuo hsin-yü* and its derivatives to the category of *hsiao-shuo,* described the original work condescendingly as a good "aid for conversations" *(t'an-chu)* and expected of its imitations nothing more than the "enlargement of seeing and hearing."[8]

The authors of *Shih-shuo* imitations naturally resisted such unflattering characterizations. In their view, they were not merely "entertaining the heart" *(shang-hsin),* as Lu Hsün once remarked;[9] rather, they were doing something far more noble and important: writing history. This explains why

Shih-shuo imitators kept "doing it incessantly," despite the disappointment of their readers and the disparagement of most scholarly critics.

In making their works "historical," *Shih-shuo* imitators tended to fill in the time gaps left by previous authors. We can see this tendency clearly by rearranging the list of imitations according to the sequence of periods covered in these works.

This table shows that the *Shih-shuo* imitations together represent a five-thousand-year span of Chinese history, from legendary antiquity to the end of the imperial era. In this sense, they mirror the comprehensive chronological coverage of the standard dynastic histories (*cheng-shih*), from Ssu-ma Ch'ien's magnificent *Shih-chi* (Records of the Grand Historian) to the rather lackluster *Ch'ing Shih-kao* (Draft history of the Ch'ing).

Indeed, prefaces and postscripts to various *Shih-shuo* imitations repeatedly claimed the *Shih-shuo hsin-yü* and its derivations as part of a great tradition of historical writing. Liu Su announced in the preface and postscript of his *New Account of the Great T'ang* that he was continuing a historical writing lineage beginning with Confucius' *Spring and Autumn Annals*.[10] In his preface to K'ung P'ing-chung's *Continuation of the Shih-shuo* [*hsin-yü*], Ch'in Kuo (fl. 1158) asserted: "In collecting important parts of history, nothing is closer to perfection than the *Shih-shuo hsin-yü*."[11] Lu Shih-tao (*cs* 1538) maintained in his preface to Ho Liang-chün's *Forest of Accounts*: "It is impossible to say that [the *Shih-shuo hsin-yü*] is not an excellent history."[12] Chiao Hung, in his *Collection of Accounts of the Jade Hall*, remarks that he was simply doing a historian's job,[13] which, in the minds of many, meant the broad incorporation of materials from previous works. Yi Tsung-k'uei, who compiled the last *Shih-shuo* imitation in 1918, defended such a writing approach: "Ancient writers mostly copied from previous authors, just as Pan Ku copied from Ssu-ma Ch'ien . . . not because of intentional plagiarism, but because one cannot fabricate [historical] events. Wei Shih (fl. 12 cent.) said, 'In writing a book, whereas others wish everything coming from themselves, I wish everything coming from others.' He surely grasped what is in my mind."[14] Composed with a historical orientation, the *Shih-shuo* imitations were naturally at odds with expectations about *hsiao-shuo*—that they would be fresh and interesting, but not

TABLE 6. PERIODS COVERED IN THE *SHIH-SHUO* IMITATIONS

Author's Period	Author	Title and Publication Date	Periods Covered in the Work
Ming	Chiao Hung (1541–1620)	*Chiao-shih lei-lin* (Chiao's taxonomic forest), 8 *chüan*, 1587.	Antiquity to Yüan, ca. 3000 B.C.– A.D. 1368.
Ming	Li Chih (1527–1602)	*Ch'u-t'an chi* (Writings on the pond), 30 *chüan*, 1588.	Antiquity to Yüan, ca. 3000 B.C.– A.D. 1368.
Ming	Chang Yung	*Nien-i shih shih-yü* (Extracts from twenty-one standard histories), 37 *chüan*.	Antiquity to Yüan, ca. 3000 B.C.– A.D. 1368.
Ch'ing	Li Ch'ing (1602– 1683)	*Nü Shih-shuo* (Women *Shih-shuo*), 4 *chüan*, early 1670s.	Antiquity to Yüan, ca. 3000 B.C.– A.D. 1368.
Ch'ing	Chang Fu-kung (early Ch'ing)	*Han Shih-shuo*, 14 *chüan*, early Ch'ing.	Han, 206 B.C.– A.D. 220.
Ming	Yen Ts'ung-ch'iao (fl. around 1639)	*Seng Shih-shuo* (Monks *Shih-shuo* [*hsin-yü*]), 1640.	Han to Sung.
Ming	Ho Liang-chün (1506–1573)	*Ho-shih yü-lin* (Ho's forest of accounts), 30 *chüan*, 1551.	Han to Yüan, ca. 206 B.C.– A.D. 1368.
Ming	Wang Shih-chen (1526–1590)	*Shih-shuo hsin-yü pu* (Supplement to the *Shih-shuo hsin-yü*), 20 *chüan*, 1585.	Han to Yüan, ca. 206 B.C.– A.D. 1368.
Ming	Cheng Chung-k'uei (fl. 1615–1634)	*Lan-wan chü ch'ing-yen* (Pure talk from the Orchid-Fields Studio), 10 *chüan*, 1617.	Han to mid-Ming, ca. 206 B.C.– A.D. 1572.
Ming	Chao Yü (fl. Late Ming?)	*Erh Shih-shuo* (Children *Shih-shuo*), 1 *chüan*, publication dates unclear.	Han to mid-Ming, ca. 206 B.C.– A.D. 1572.
Sung	K'ung P'ing-chung (fl. 1065–1102)	*Hsü Shih-shuo* (Continuation of the *Shih-shuo*), 12 *chüan*, 1158 or earlier.	Southern and Northern dynasties to Five Dynasties, ca. 420–960.
Ming?	Li Hou, dates unknown	*Hsü Shih-shuo* (Continuation of the *Shih-shuo*), 10 *chüan*, late Ming?	Southern and Northern dynasties, 420–589.
Ming	Lin Mao-kuei (fl. 1591–1621)	*Nan-Pei ch'ao hsin-yü* (Southern and Northern dynasties [*Shih-shuo*] *hsin-yü*), 4 *chüan*, author's preface dated 1621.	Southern and Northern dynasties, 420–589.
Ch'ing	Chang Chi-yung	*Nan-Pei ch'ao Shih-shuo* (Southern and Northern dynasties *Shih-shuo*), 20 *chüan*.	Southern and Northern dynasties, 420–589.
T'ang	Wang Fang-ch'ing (d. 702)	*Hsü Shih-shuo hsin-shu* (Continuation of the *Shih-shuo hsin-shu*), 10 *chüan*, not extant.	Early T'ang, ca. 618–700.

Author's Period	Author	Title and Publication Date	Periods Covered in the Work
T'ang	Feng Yen (fl. 742–800)	Feng-shih wen-chien chi (Feng's memoirs), 10 chüan, ca. 800.	Early T'ang to mid-T'ang, ca. 618–800.
T'ang	Liu Su (fl. 806–820)	Ta-T'ang hsin-yü (New account of the Great T'ang), 13 chüan, 807.	Early T'ang to mid-T'ang, ca. 618–779.
Sung	Wang Tang (fl. 1086–1110)	T'ang yü-lin (T'ang forest of accounts), 8 chüan.	T'ang, 618–907.
Ming	Chiao Hung (1541–1620)	Yü-t'ang ts'ung-yü (Collected accounts from the Jade Hall), 8 chüan, 1618.	Early Ming to mid-Ming, ca. 1368–1566.
Ming	Li Shao-wen (fl. 1600–1623)	Huang-Ming Shih-shuo hsin-yü (Imperial Ming Shih-shuo hsin-yü), 8 chüan, 1610.	Early Ming to mid-Ming, ca. 1368–1572.
Ch'ing	Liang Wei-shu (1589–1662)	Yü-chien tsun-wen (Distinguished accounts of the jade sword), 10 chüan, 1657.	Ming, 1368–1644.
Ch'ing	Wu Su-kung (fl. 1662–1681)	Ming yü-lin (Ming forest of accounts), 14 chüan, 1681.	Ming, 1368–1644.
Ch'ing	Chiang Yu-jung and Tsou T'ung-lu (early Ch'ing)	Ming-i pien (Compilation of Ming anecdotes), 10 chüan, early Ch'ing.	Ming, 1368–1644.
Ch'ing	Wang Wan (1624–1691)	Shuo-ling (Bell of tales), 1 chüan, 1661.	Early Ch'ing.
Ch'ing	Wang Cho (b. 1636)	Chin Shih-shuo (Contemporary Shih-shuo), 8 chüan, 1683.	Early Ch'ing, ca. 1644–1680.
Ch'ing	Yen Heng (1826?–1854)	Nü Shih-shuo (Women Shih-shuo), 1 chüan, 1865.	Ch'ing.
Modern	Hsü K'o (1869–1928)	Ch'ing-pai lei-ch'ao (Classified records from unofficial Ch'ing historical writings), 1917.	Ch'ing to early twentieth century, ca. 1644–1915.
Modern	Yi Tsung-k'uei (b. 1875)	Hsin Shih-shuo (New Shih-shuo), 1 chüan, 1918.	Ch'ing to early twentieth century, ca.1644–1915.

necessarily convey accurate messages. Under such circumstances, category mistakes were unavoidable.

There were, however, fundamental differences between the standard histories and the *Shih-shuo* tradition. To begin with, most of the compilers of the twenty-five dynastic histories were officially commissioned to maintain the continuity of the historical records. The authors of *Shih-*

shuo imitations were exclusively private scholars who filled in historical lacunae out of a self-assigned responsibility for keeping chronological consistency and completeness.

What compelled private scholars to write "history" in such a disesteemed genre? To answer this question, we need to examine how *Shih-shuo t'i* authors and proponents perceived the difference between the *Shih-shuo t'i* and the standard histories. Liu Su, one of the earliest *Shih-shuo* imitators, discussed this difference in the postscript to his *New Account of the Great T'ang*, saying:

> Historical writings emerged a long time ago. Confucius composed the *Ch'un-ch'iu* [Spring and Autumn Annals] based on the Lu history. [The *Ch'un-ch'iu*] hailed the ruler and humbled the subject, and expelled heterodoxy and returned to rectitude. . . . It formed principles according to the meaning of [classics] and transmitted the culture in order to transform people. It was not a work just for dating and sorting [historical] events.
>
> Later authors became inept with the following problems: Ssu-ma Ch'ien intended to incorporate broad-ranged materials without making careful collations and commentaries; he downplayed the Six Classics while promoting the [works] by Huang-ti and Lao-tzu; he discriminated against scholars in favor of treacherous warriors. Pan Ku, in chronicling the rise and fall [of dynasties], praised the modern times while disregarding ancestors' virtues, and, in recounting the political transformation [of the Han regime], degraded the basis of principles while upholding the policy of punishment. Despite their shortcomings, [Ssu-ma] Ch'ien's accounts were straightforward and comprehensive, and [Pan] Ku's clear and detailed. . . .
>
> In the past, Hsün Shuang [128–190] collected Han episodes and compiled the *Han-yü* for later examples and warnings.[15] My compilation today follows this refined predecessor. It does not favor military strategies but upholds cultural virtues; it disapproves of diplomatic intrigues and condemns deception and chicanery; it expunges frivolous words in order to focus on righteousness; it reduces administrative methods in order to limit trivial matters. Those who govern the country should take people as the basis and cherish human lives following Heaven's [will]; those who cultivate themselves [literally, establish their bodies] should give priority to learning and transform [people] with culture.[16]

In justifying his compilation of a *Shih-shuo t'i* work, Liu Su looks up to Confucius' *Ch'un-ch'iu* for the model, emphasizing particularly its moral-political principles—"to hail the ruler and to humble the subject, and to expel heterodoxy and to return to rectitude." This emphasis apparently stemmed from Liu Su's desire to compile a truly historical work, for in the traditional view, any good history should provide ethical guidance. As Richard J. Smith notes, "History in China was written by scholars for scholars. As a moral drama it reflected predominantly Confucian value judgments. The history of any dynasty which was always written by its successor, was more than just a narrative record; it was also a guide to proper conduct for the present and the future."[17] Inspired by this view of history, Liu Su criticizes later authors for failing to transmit Confucian moral teachings while indulging too much in their own agendas. His targets include prominent historians such as Ssu-ma Ch'ien, who founded the genre of the standard history in the *Shih-chi,* and Pan Ku, who wrote the first standard dynastic history, the *Han-shu,* modeled after the *Shih-chi.* Liu Su's dissatisfaction notwithstanding, his criticism of the two leading historians actually summarizes the two major characteristics of a standard history— "chronicling the rise and fall [of dynasties]" and "recounting political instructions," both emphasizing historical events.

Unlike the standard history, Liu Su's work "takes people as the basis." Liu's concept of "people" includes both "those who govern the country"— that is, the ruler and his ministers—and those who are governed. A ruler/minister, he says, should "cherish human lives following Heaven's [will]." At the same time, he should also "establish himself [lit. establish his body]" *(li-shen)* through learning. In other words, a ruler/minister must be a scholar. He first cultivates himself by inscribing moral-political codes on his body; then, using the culture so acquired, he transforms the people he governs. Liu Su's work is thus intended as a guide to a scholar's self-cultivation. In order to achieve his cultural-political ends, he sees no need to cover a broad range of historical events; rather, he selects historical episodes that can "serve as later examples or warnings," making it possible for a ruler/minister to "expel heterodoxy and return to rectitude."

Liu Su's rationale for compiling his *Shih-shuo t'i* work clearly influenced later *Shih-shuo* imitators and their proponents. Ch'in Kuo's introduction to K'ung P'ing-chung's *Continuation of the Shih-shuo [hsin-yü],* which is the only extant Sung preface to a *Shih-shuo t'i* work, employs a rhetoric very similar to Liu's.[18] Ch'in wrote:

> The records in historical writings are authentic, but too comprehensive to read through without difficulty. The *hsiao-shuo* of various philosophical schools, though appealing to our eyes, are often spurious. Concise, not redundant, and authentic with reliable sources, are these not the characteristics of the *Shih-shuo* [*hsin-yü*]? This work classified previous accounts, providing for readers a summary of [history]. Since it did not get to cover the history exhaustively, some learned gentlemen started imitating and enlarging it, hence the compilation of the *Continuation of the Shih-shuo* [*hsin-yü*]. Scholar K'ung P'ing-chung searched through all kinds of histories, classified and interpreted diverse ideas, expunged superfluous words, and examined and explicated the connections between names and principles. . . . Indeed, he enhanced the luxuriant beauty of historians' [writings] and made them convenient for scholars to read. This book carries and classifies the admirable and the abominable human remarks and behavior, so that when scholars try to acquire ancient knowledge and study different [character] types, they may choose the good to follow.[19]

Like Liu Su, Ch'in Kuo stresses the didactic function of a *Shih-shuo t'i* work—its role in guiding scholars' self-cultivation, or what Liu Su terms *li-shen* (establishing oneself).

Significantly, however, Ch'in Kuo emphasizes that K'ung compiled his work through "examining and explicating the connections between names and principles [*ming-li*]." As the reader will recall, *ming-li* theory established the creative principles and thematic messages of the *Shih-shuo hsin-yü* by which the author conducted a subtle process of classifying and naming human character types. Explicitly identifying the function of *ming-li* theory in K'ung's work, Ch'in Kuo links the *Continuation of the Shih-shuo* closely to the model work's more aesthetic approach. Seen in this light, the phrase "to discriminate between the admirable and the abominable" (*ch'ü-pieh mei-o*) that Ch'in uses to summarize K'ung's work might refer to either a moral contrast between good and bad or an aesthetic contrast between beauty and ugliness. Thus Ch'in distinguishes K'ung's *Shih-shuo* imitation not only from the standard histories, which rarely give attention to such specific theoretical issues, but also from Liu Su, whose dichotomy, "to expel heterodoxy and to return to rectitude" (ch'ü-hsieh kuei-cheng), carried narrowly ethical connotations.

Ch'in Kuo's enlarged version of the Shih-shuo t'i agenda, which extended the concept of li-shen, or self-cultivation, from Liu Su's moral-political approach to aesthetic concerns, found more refined elaboration during the Ming-Ch'ing period, especially from the late Ming (1550s) to the early Ch'ing (1680s), when a frenzy over the Shih-shuo hsin-yü engendered at least nineteen Shih-shuo imitations. Lu Ts'ung-p'ing, for example, described Li Shao-wen's Imperial Ming Shih-shuo hsin-yü (1610) in the following glowing terms: "For its intimate significance, this book benefits us by exquisitely cultivating [tsu-hsiu] our bodies, minds, dispositions, and feelings; for its broader significance, this book helps us to govern the family, the state, and all under Heaven."[20] According to Lu, Li's book could guide scholars to a multidimensional refinement, because its characters were not simply colorful figures from a remote past; they were contemporary friends whose "nice conduct and beautiful remarks" could serve as an intimate source of direct instruction and inspiration.[21]

Of course, the standard histories also contained examples of gentry remarks and behavior. Why is it, then, that no critic had ever suggested that these "orthodox" works could also provide "friends" for their readers? What makes Shih-shuo t'i readers fancy that they are not reading words but talking to real people? Feng Ching (1652–1715), in his preface to Wang Cho's Contemporary Shih-shuo (1683), answers: "Someone may say: The state has its dynastic history, which can pass on big [events to later generations]. I say: No. Big [events] may carry on a person's [name], but only the fine [fragments of one's remarks or conduct] can transmit that individual's spirit. Have you ever seen the rays of the sun penetrating through a crack? Without going out to see the sun, you know the entire sun. Is this any different from transmitting one's spirit through a fragment of a remark or conduct?"[22]

What differentiates the Shih-shuo t'i from the standard histories is precisely its function of ch'uan-shen, transmitting the spirit, which embodies and enlivens the characters portrayed in the text. In order to underscore this fundamental difference between the two genres, Mao Chi-k'o (1633–

1708), another promoter of Wang Cho's work, compares the *Shih-shuo hsin-yü* with the *Chin-shu*: "In the past, people used to say that reading the *Chin-shu* was like viewing a clumsy portrait, which merely painted the body and outer appearance of a person, whereas Yin [Hao], Liu [T'an], Wang [Hsi-chih], and Hsieh [An], all imbued with elegant aura and sentiments, seem ready to jump out from the *Shih-shuo hsin-yü* when called upon. This is because the divine and outstanding writing style of the [*Shih-shuo hsin-yü*] captures the spiritual resemblance of its characters."[23] As mentioned in chapter 3, the *Chin-shu* is notorious for having incorporated a great number of *Shih-shuo* accounts, often word-for-word. That the same episode can convey the spirit of a person in the *Shih-shuo hsin-yü* but not in the *Chin-shu* reflects, of course, the effect of each respective genre. The spirits of the *Shih-shuo* characters are suffocated by the big events in the *Chin-shu*—events such as wars, political campaigns, and the "rise and fall" of dynasties.

All the prefaces and postscripts to Ming-Ch'ing *Shih-shuo t'i* equate the reading of the texts with encountering real people. Here are some examples:

> The [Liu] Sung Prince Lin-ch'uan compiled the *Shih-shuo hsin-yü* and thereby achieved imperishable reputation. Due to his effort, we can still see images of the aloof aura and elegant style of [Wei-Chin] literati after over a thousand years.[24]
>
> To this day, reading it [the *Shih-shuo hsin-yü*] still makes us feel like dancing, as if we were seeing with our own eyes [how the *Shih-shuo* characters] communicate with each other.[25]
>
> Reading it [Wang Shih-chen's *Supplement to the Shih-shuo hsin-yü*], one feels like confronting the pure uninhibitedness of Hsi K'ang and Juan Chi, listening to the *Hsüan-hsüeh* reasoning by Liu T'an and Hsü Hsün, and seeing the jade-and-pearl-like Wangs and Hsiehs.[26]
>
> Now what Master Wang Cho has collected [in his book] are [remarks] of the famous scholars of the time. Opening the volumes and enjoying the reading, we feel like meeting with [*wu-tui*] these people. In the past, people would ride for a thousand *li*, just to talk overnight with an [admirable friend]. Now we can meet such friends within an inch of wood block [print]. Isn't it thrilling![27]

This sort of excitement arises from an intellectual intimacy between the reader and the characters in the text, which offers the reader easy access to excellent friends and role models who may not be available in real life. Transcending time and space, the reader joyously "meets with" (wu-tui) his role models: His body confronts the movement of their bodies; his mind comprehends their thinking; his ears are attuned to their remarks; and his eyes appreciate their appearance. The intellectual and emotional endowment so intimately appropriated nurtures the reader in every way. This is what Lu Ts'ung-p'ing calls the "exquisite cultivation" of one's body, mind, disposition, and feelings.

Women *Shih-shuo* proponents, too, embraced the idea that *Shih-shuo t'i* characters might serve as perceivable friends and role models. As Yeh Shih Li-wan commented in her preface to Yen Heng's *Women Shih-shuo* (ed. 1865): "This volume is imbued with the lofty Bamboo Grove aura and elegant female scholars. [Reading the book,] we feel as if hearing them talking, words chiming like pearls and jade, and seeing their persons, plucking ivy branches and leaning on bamboo stems."[28] Admiration for *Shih-shuo t'i* characters often crossed gender lines. Many women took male characters for their role models and vice versa (see chapter 8).

Desire to converse with and befriend people from the past also transgressed cultural boundaries, inspiring Japanese scholars to compile *Shih-shuo* imitations. Tsunota Ken's (d. 1855) own preface to his *Kinsei sōgo* (Collected accounts of recent times) recounted:

> I once got sick and stayed alone in my studio. Twisting in bed, I felt lonesome, but no one paid me a visit. Thus, between taking medicine, I read all the recent collections of literary writings as well as miscellaneous *hsiao-shuo*. I also did some research about the authors. [As a result], famous literati and some secondary writers. . . . have each emerged with a distinct spirit and appearance. Alas, all these people are fading away from us. We cannot hear their voices, nor can we see their beards and eyebrows. Only by getting to know them as if knowing our own friends could we feel like seeing them and hearing them. Seeing these people day and night and sharing their wondrous ideas fills me with unexpected joy. I figure, rather than pleasing myself only, why don't I also please others? Besides, if I do not collect and compile these materials, how can later generations get a glimpse of the deep thoughts of these famous worthy scholars?[29]

In short, *Shih-shuo t'i* works offered something very different than conventional histories. Still "written by scholars for scholars," their purpose changed from presenting a "moral drama" to providing ethical and/or aesthetic role models. As private scholars, the authors of *Shih-shuo* imitations—men and women, Chinese and Japanese—did not have to conform to court-sanctioned, orthodox guidelines. They were not bound to respect the historical principle of "praise and blame" *(pao-pien),* nor was their concept of self-cultivation limited to official prescriptions and standard models. To these individuals, the past was a living present, infused with a spirit of vitality and authenticity derived from Liu I-ch'ing's inspirational model.

By definition *Shih-shuo* imitations operated within a framework defined primarily by the so-called Wei-Chin "spirit" which shaped elite attitudes toward self-fashioning. But the changing circumstances and personal agendas that surrounded later works often caused their authors to revise the original *Shih-shuo* scheme, affecting the selection and rewriting of individual episodes and even the recasting of Liu I-ch'ing's taxonomic system. My task in part 3 is to show how variables such as the cultural, social, and gender identities of the authors, as well as the different political and intellectual conditions under which they lived and labored, affected their final literary products, especially, their literary construction of "selves."

Chapter 6

Body and Heart:
T'ang and Sung Imitations

Establishing the Body at the Risk of the Body: T'ang Imitations

Three T'ang *Shih-shuo* imitations are found in various bibliographic records: Wang Fang-ch'ing's (d. 702) *Continuation of the Shih-shuo hsin-shu*, Feng Yen's (fl. 742–800) *Memoirs*, and Liu Su's *New Account of the Great T'ang*. Wang's work is not extant today. Feng's *Memoirs*, written in the early ninth century, mainly covers a broad range of encyclopedic entries. Only chapters 9 and 10 consist of thirty-seven T'ang historical anecdotes, divided into thirty-six imitative *Shih-shuo* categories. Liu Su's work, compiled in 807, follows the *Shih-shuo* scheme in a more rigorous way. It collects around 380 episodes about T'ang political and intellectual life under thirty imitative *Shih-shuo* categories.[1] Liu Su's own preface and epilogue clearly state his purpose and principles of compilation, making this work a very coherent and pointed piece. The writing style of *A New Account of the Great T'ang* also follows its model work, as the late Ch'ing scholar Yeh Te-hui attests: "Since Prince Lin-ch'uan compiled the *Shih-shuo hsin-yü*, later imitators have emerged from every dynasty. The T'ang dynasty inherited the aura of six dynasties, and its writing style more or less continued the fashion of the south of the Yangtze. Reading this book makes one feel that the Chin winds and currents [*feng-liu*] have not faded away from us."[2] In this section, I shall focus on Liu's *New Account of the Great T'ang*, while using Feng's *Memoir* as a supportive reference.

These early *Shih-shuo* imitations immediately introduced strong ethical overtones into the genre, as typified in Liu Su's summary of Confucius's principle for historical writing, "to hail the ruler and to humble the subject, and to expel heterodoxy and to return to rectitude." From the *Shih-shuo's* neutral classification of human character types to its early imitations' differentiation between "rectitude" *(cheng)* and "heterodoxy" *(hsieh)*, this movement marked a shift from aesthetic to ethical concerns. In this sense, T'ang *Shih-shuo* imitations changed the original genre from the character writing *of* the gentry into didactic writing *for* the gentry—from gentry self-appreciation into gentry self-cultivation—what Liu Su termed *li-shen* (establishing oneself). Nonetheless, as we shall discover later, this desire for establishing oneself in ethical terms was, ironically, often founded on the necessity of "risking oneself [lit. risking one's body]" *(wei-shen)*.[3] Such was the tenor of T'ang politics.

EXPELLING HETERODOXY AND RETURNING TO RECTITUDE

To follow what they believed to be Confucius' guidelines, both Liu Su and Feng Yen structured their imitative works through a thorough revision of the *Shih-shuo* scheme. Liu Su first elaborated what he considered as categories of *cheng*—rectitude—into a much more detailed system of classification. He expanded chapter 10, "Kuei-chen," of the *Shih-shuo* into three:

1. *K'uang-tsan*	(Rectification and assistance)
2. *Kuei-chien*	(Advice and admonition)
3. *Chi-chien*	(Intense admonition)

Chapter 5, "Fang-cheng" (Squareness and correctness), became two:

4. *Kang-cheng*	(Inflexibility and correctness)
5. *Kung-chih*	(Fairness and strictness)

Chapter 3, "Cheng-shih" (Affairs of government), was expanded into three:

7. *Ch'ih-fa*	(Handling the law)
8. *Cheng-neng*	(Ability of governing)
22. *Li-ko*	(Revision and reform)

Chapter 1, "Te-hsing" (*Te* conduct), became five, all Confucian moral categories:

6. Ch'ing-lien	(Purity and incorruptibility)
9. Chung-lieh	(Loyalty and heroism)
10. Chieh-i	(Integrity and righteousness)
11. Hsiao-hsing	(Filial behavior)
12. Yu-t'i	(Brotherly love)

Moreover, chapter 7, "Shih-chien" (Recognition and judgment), which referred to the practice of character appraisal in a neutral sense, was expanded into two:

| 13. Chü-hsien | (Selecting the worthy) |
| 14. Shih-liang | (Capacity of judgment) |

Chü-hsien (Selecting the worthy) pointed explicitly to the moral purpose of character appraisal during the T'ang period.

Liu Su expelled categories he considered "heterodox" from the original Shih-shuo hsin-yü scheme, including the following:

24. Chien-ao	(Rudeness and arrogance)
25. P'ai-t'iao	(Taunting and teasing)
26. Ch'ing-ti	(Contempt and insults)
27. Chia-chüeh	(Guile and chicanery)
28. Ch'u-mien	(Dismissal from office)
29. Chien-se	(Stinginess and meanness)
30. T'ai-ch'ih	(Extravagance and ostentation)
31. Fen-chüan	(Anger and irascibility)
32. Ch'an-hsien	(Slanderousness and treachery)
33. Yu-hui	(Blameworthiness and remorse)
34. P'i-lou	(Crudities and blunders)
35. Huo-ni	(Delusion and infatuation)
36. Ch'ou-hsi	(Hostility and alienation)

But he added two new ones:

| 21. Yü-ning | (Flattery and obsequiousness) |
| 27. K'u-jen | (Cruelty and ruthlessness) |

Compared with the purged Shih-shuo hsin-yü categories, which focus on human frailties and eccentricities primarily in private life, these two new categories have strong political connotations. Liu Su's new taxonomy of human behavior and character thus intensify the moral contrast between rectitude and heterodoxy and change the more objective and nonjudgmental *Shih-shuo hsin-yü* scheme to an explicitly normative system of classification. Liu Su even added a new pair of antithetical categories— chapter 24, "Pao-hsi" (Praise and rewarding), and chapter 25, "Ch'eng-chieh" (Punishment and warnings)—in order to enhance the Confucian principle of "expelling heterodoxy and returning to rectitude."

Feng's *Memoirs* embodies a similar taxonomic principle, in which *Fang-cheng* (Squareness and correctness) is split into two:

1. *Kang-cheng*	(Inflexibility and correctness)
6. *K'ang-chih*	(Unyieldingness and strictness)

Te-hsing (*Te* conduct) is expanded into six, also with Confucian moral meanings:

2. *Ch'un-hsin*	(Sincerity and trustworthiness)
3. *Tuan-ch'üeh*	(Dignity and honesty)
4. *Chen-chieh*	(Incorruptibility and firmness)
5. *Chien-o*	(Outspokenness)
7. *Chung-keng*	(Loyalty and straightforwardness)
8. *Ch'eng-chieh*	(Honesty and integrity)

Cheng-shih (Affairs of government) is expanded into two:

12. *Hui-hua*	(Benevolent transformation)
14. *Ch'i-cheng*	(Extraordinary governing)

Hui-hua (Benevolent transformation) pointed explicitly to the moral justification for governing.

HAILING THE RULER AND HUMBLING THE SUBJECT

The moral-political classification in T'ang *Shih-shuo* imitations manifests the authors' purpose of guiding "those who govern the country"—both the ruler and his or her ministers—to "establish themselves." Reading Liu Su's new scheme along with the episodes assigned to each category, we can see that this process of self-cultivation was by no means isolated to oneself, but a mutual definition and discipline between the ruler and the subject. Liu Su reconstructed such a dynamic relationship in a political high drama that involved Emperor T'ai-tsung (r. 627–649), the founder of the T'ang, his devoted consort, Empress Chang-sun (601–636), and his outspoken minister, Wei Cheng (580–643):

> Once T'ai-tsung stormed out of court, saying to himself: "I am going to have to kill that country bumpkin!" Empress Wen-te [Chang-sun] asked him: "Who has offended Your Majesty?" T'ai-tsung replied: "Wei Cheng is always insulting me at court, making me unable to follow myself [*tzu-yu*]." The empress retreated. Then, putting on her court attire, she stood at attention in the courtyard. Surprised, T'ai-tsung asked: "Why are you doing this?" The empress replied: "I heard that only a sage ruler can have loyal subjects. Now because Your Majesty is sage and intelligent, Wei Cheng is able to exhaust his candid words. I, your humble concubine, am waiting on you in your chambers. How can I not congratulate you on this?" Thus T'ai-tsung's wrath was dispelled.[4]

No participant feels at ease in this conflict. The emperor has to choose between losing his freedom or losing his "sagehood." The minister has to offer his loyalty at the risk of his life. Even the empress has to cut short a leisure moment shared with her husband, joining his subjects in placing the emperor under their constant scrutiny. Putting on her court attire and standing at attention to the emperor, the empress immediately transforms her inner chamber into a quasi-court, reminding the emperor that, indeed, as a ruler, he has little private life, much less personal freedom. Such is the price all the parties have to pay for establishing a collective self-identity of a newly minted empire—one in which the emperor establishes his authority as a sage and intelligent ruler, and all the others establish their affiliation to the ruler as loyal—albeit sometimes outspoken—subjects. The ruler needs to prove his or her qualifications in light of the subjects' candid criticism, and the subjects need to prove their loyalty in light of the ruler's absolute authority. Without this mutual dependence, the empire would fall apart.

This joint self-cultivation between the ruler and the subjects is motivated and intensified by a mechanism of admonition—Wei Cheng's to his emperor and Empress Chang-sun's to her husband. Admonition to the ruler was originally presented in a rather minor and mild way in the *Shih-shuo hsin-yü*, occupying only nine out of the twenty-seven entries of chapter 10, "Kuei-chen" (Admonitions and warnings).[5] It was, however, highly elaborated and promoted to the leading position in *A New Account of the Great T'ang*. A comparative analysis of two episodes, taken respectively from the *Shih-shuo hsin-yü* and *A New Account of the Great T'ang*, will show the different nature of the admonitions in each work. Both episodes record admonitions against the emperor's selection of an imperial heir, but each is presented in its own style, allowing us to probe the admonishers' motivation, the ruler/subject relationship, and the author's reason for including the episode.

The *Shih-shuo hsin-yü* episode records:

> Since Emperor Wu of Chin (Ssu-ma Yen, r. 265–299) was not fully aware of the feeblemindedness of the crown prince, Ssu-ma Chung, he held tenaciously to his intention of having him carry on the succession. The prominent ministers, for their part, mostly offered up honest counsels against it. The emperor was once at a gathering on the Ling-yün Terrace (on the palace grounds at Lo-yang) when Wei Kuan was in attendance by his side. Wishing somehow to state what was in his heart, Wei took the occasion to kneel before the emperor as though he were drunk, stroking the dais on which he was sitting, and crying, "Alas for this seat!"
>
> The emperor, although aware of what he meant, laughed and said, "Are you drunk?" (10/7)

Compared with the Wei-Chin gentry's moderate style, the T'ang gentlemen appear much more vehement regarding the same issue. Emperor T'ai-tsung encountered direct and intense opposition from his ministers on his choice of the heir apparent. T'ai-tsung picked Prince Wei, whereas his ministers, headed by the empress' brother Chang-sun Wu-chi, favored Prince Chin. Unable to make a decision, the emperor "struck his head on the dais. [Chang-sun] Wu-chi hurried to stop him [from hurting himself]. The emperor drew his knife and scared Wu-chi and the others. [Ch'u] Sui-liang snatched the knife from the emperor and handed it over to Prince Chin. Then all asked the emperor whom he wanted to select. T'ai-tsung said, 'I am willing to select Prince Chin.' Wu-chi and the others said, 'We respectively obey Your Majesty's will. If anyone disobeys, we pray to have him decapitated.'"[6]

These two episodes respectively depict the two polarities of the admonition, which, according to the *Ta-Tai li-chi* (Tai Te's [fl. first cent. B.C.] version of the *Record of the Rites*), had conventionally been conducted in five different ways: "The five ways of admonition refer to: 1. *feng-chien,* indirect admonition, 2. *shun-chien,* moderate admonition, 3. *k'uei-chien,* tentative admonition, 4. *chih-chien,* direct admonition, and 5. *hsien-chien,* risky admonition. Indirect admonition means to hint at the trouble to the ruler while seeing it start. Moderate admonition means to talk in a moderate and obedient way without irritating the ruler. Tentative admonition means to admonish the ruler according to his mood. Direct admonition means to confront the ruler with the facts. Risky admonition means to point out the threat to the state at the risk of one's life in order to protect the ruler."[7]

Wei Kuan conducts his admonition in the *feng-chien* fashion—indirect admonition. Instead of criticizing the emperor's wrong choice of a crown prince, he laments the possible loss of the dais that carries the throne. To a certain extent, Wei Kuan's style of admonition represents that of the entire Wei-Chin period. As reflected in the chapter "Kuei-chen" in the *Shih-shuo hsin-yü,* among the nine admonitions to the rulers there are as many as five indirect admonitions (10/1, 7, 12, 25, 27) and three moderate or tentative ones (10/4, 11, 12)—but only one that is direct (10/5). Liu I-ch'ing's contemporary, Fan Yeh, explained in his *History of the Later Han* why *feng* was favored during the Wei-Chin and early Six Dynasties: "The *Record of the Rites* contains five ways of admonition, and among them *feng* is the best. It expresses feelings using an object [as an allegory] and conveys intent through literary forms. Thus the one who speaks it [*feng*] has no culpability, yet it remains adequate to warn those who hear it. [*Feng*] is significant in that it can sufficiently express meanings in acceptable terms, and its reasoning can lead to the rectification [of the wrong]. What need is there to flaunt one's honesty and establish one's reputation through [intentionally] irritating the ruler?"[8]

Judging from Fan Yeh's argument, gentry of this period seem to be concerned about their own destiny as much as, if not more than, the destiny of the regime. By adopting *feng*, or indirect criticism, Wei Kuan intends to get his message across at no risk to himself, much less his family. Such a concern is also reflected in the *Shih-shuo hsin-yü*: The chapter "Kuei-chen" equates gentlemen's advice to the ruler with that to their family and friends, laying equal stress on the well-being of the royal house and that of the gentry. Also, as a rhetorical technique, *feng* originated from the Han Confucian understanding of the poetic modes of the *Book of Songs*.[9] Given this feature of *feng*, when the *Shih-shuo* author chooses to record Wei Kuan's allegorical lamentation rather than the "honest counsels" of the other ministers, he obviously has in mind a literary purpose above all else. He means to reflect the aloof and poetic Wei-Chin self that permeates even urgent political issues.

Contrary to Wei Kuan's indirect admonition, the T'ang ministers directly voice their opposition to the emperor. Indeed, their admonition takes the form of a coup d'état: The ministers grab the knife—the symbol of violence and power—from the emperor and pass it on to the prince they favor. With the knife in the prince's hand, the ministers form a threatening circle, coercing the emperor into following their advice. Had the emperor been more insistent on his own decision, Chang-sun Wu-chi and his associates would undoubtedly be accused of high treason and put to death. Their style of advice therefore amounts to the last two of the five admonitions: *chih-chien*, direct admonition, and *hsien-chien*, admonition at the risk of one's life.

Impassioned admonitions like this, which scarcely appear in the *Shih-shuo hsin-yü*, predominate Liu Su's *New Account of the Great T'ang*. Liu Su expands the *Shih-shuo hsin-yü* chapter title "Kuei-chen" into three categories and uses them to title the first three chapters: (1) *K'uang-tsan* (Rectification and assistance), (2) *Kuei-chien* (Advice and admonitions), and (3) *Chi-chien* (Intense admonitions). The entries of these three chapters constitute an increasingly intensified sequence of open admonitions to the T'ang emperors. Phrases such as "to die rather than to live shamefully," "to inflict problems [on oneself] and to endanger one's body," "to kill one's body in order to obtain righteousness," and "to spare no body in order to preserve the *Tao*"[10] prevail in these three categories, as well as admonitions included in the other chapters, divulging the T'ang gentlemen's anxiety to put their emperors on the right track.

This sort of severe criticism of the T'ang emperors naturally intensified the ruler-subject relationship and often brought reproach. Among the forty-two admonitions recorded in the first three chapters of *A New Account of the Great T'ang*, eight resulted in the admonishers' execution or exile. What compelled the T'ang gentlemen to offend the emperor at their own risk? Liu Su contributes several entries in which the T'ang gentlemen openly justify the necessity of direct and intense admonitions.

> Huang-fu Te-shen presented a memo [to T'ai-tsung], saying: "Your Majesty exhausts people by drafting them to repair the Lo-yang Palace and heavily exploits them through collecting the land-tax. Now tall chignons are in vogue, obviously influenced by Your Majesty's palace ladies." T'ai-tsung was furious, saying: "This fellow wants the court not to collect a single tax, not to labor a single person, and the palace ladies all to shave their heads, only then can he be satisfied."
>
> Wei Cheng persevered: ". . . Since ancient times, ministers presented admonitions often in emotional and extreme terms, or they wouldn't be able to persuade the ruler. Being emotional and extreme may sound like vilification. In this case, as it is said, 'A madman gibbers, and the sage judges,' it all depends on Your Majesty's judgment. Your Majesty must not punish him, otherwise who would dare say a word in the future?"
>
> Li Chün-ch'iu presented a memo, admonishing Emperor Kao-tsung [r. 650–683] not to attack Korea, saying: "One cannot talk slowly about what pains one's heart; nor can one report with ease upon urgent events. The honest man cannot conceal his true emotions. Those who receive official pay from the ruler should die for the ruler. Your subject is now receiving your majesty's pay; how dare he spare his own body!"[11]

Wei Cheng defends intense admonition as a rhetorical device, claiming that exaggeration can strengthen the power of persuasion. Li Chün-ch'iu explains it as genuine emotion—the subject's heartfelt pain stirred up by the ruler's wrongdoings, so unbearable that he can but yell it out.

Of course, as Wei Cheng points out, intensified admonitions often sound like slandering, which Fan Yeh condemned as the means for some gentlemen to "flaunt their honesty and establish their reputation through [intentionally] offending the ruler." On this matter, Wei Cheng considers it the ruler's responsibility to judge sincere criticism from vilification, and he believes the right judgment can testify to the ruler's sagehood. As for the standard of judgment, one minister suggests: "If the advice is presented for benefiting the subject's personal gains, then it's craziness; but if it is for the sake of Your Majesty's country, then it's loyalty."[12] Consideration is also given to the way a subject should deliver the criticism, in order to avoid possible misunderstandings: "Empress Wu Tse-t'ien [r. 684–704] . . . asked what is *chung*, loyalty. . . . [Cheng] Wei-chung replied: 'Your subject heard that [a loyal subject] should praise the ruler's merits in public whereas correct the ruler's wrong in private.'"[13] In so doing, ministers put themselves in a bind: In public, they were to praise the ruler and risk looking like toadies, making it impossible for them to build up their reputations as daring critics of the monarch. In front of the ruler alone, they should offer candid criticism at the constant risk of their lives. It was a tough balancing act.

Ministers could afford to take certain risks because the T'ang emperors were at least occasionally submissive:

> During the Chen-kuan reign, T'ai-tsung said to Ch'u Sui-liang: "You are in charge of the *Records of the Emperor's Daily Life*. What kind of things do you record? Does the ruler get to see it?" Sui-liang replied: "Today's *Records of the Emperor's Daily Life* . . . registers the ruler's remarks and behavior and marks good from bad for [later generations'] reference and warning, thus preventing rulers from doing illegitimate things. I've never heard of a ruler reading his own records." T'ai-tsung said: "Must you document everything bad that I do?" Sui-liang said: ". . . Whatever you do should be registered." [Another minister] Liu Chi persevered: "Even if Sui-liang were not to put it down, people under heaven will."[14]
>
> Wei Cheng once rushed back and admonished [T'ai-tsung]: "People said that Your Majesty was about to visit the south of the mountain, and already packed up for it. Yet you did not go. Why such news?" T'ai-tsung replied, laughing: "I did mean to go. Afraid that you would be unhappy, I stopped."[15]

Under these circumstances, the emperor, concerned about his image in history, voluntarily submitted to his ministers' discipline. Many admonitions recorded in *A New Account of the Great T'ang* wind up in similar ways, with emperors good-naturedly accepting their subjects' advice.

It is interesting to note that T'ang gentlemen often conceived of their loyalty to the ruler in monetary terms. The bargain was a fair one, for, as Li Chün-ch'iu put it, "Those who receive official pay from the ruler should die for the ruler's business." From the standpoint of most T'ang officials, the rewards they received were thus well deserved.[16] For example:

> Chang Wen-kuan served as one of the prime ministers [under Empress Wu Tse-t'ien]. His fellow prime ministers considered the meals provided at the council hall too delicate and requested to reduce the quality. Wen-kuan said: "These meals show the Son of Heaven's respect for chief executives and talented people. If you gentlemen feel not up to your jobs, quit so you can give way to the real talents. But don't ask to cut down our business meals in order to invite empty names [as modest or thrifty ministers]. What the state values does not lie in this."
>
> During the K'ai-yüan reign [713–741], Lu Chien was a secretary at the Imperial Secretariat. Considering some scholars at the Li-cheng Academy (the Academy in the Hall of Elegance and Rectitude) not the right choice, yet being excessively provided, he said to his fellow courtiers: "What does this Academy do for the state except spend much [of its money] in vain?" He then intended to propose its termination. Chang Yüeh, upon hearing this, said to his fellow prime ministers: "I heard that rulers from ancient times would often make mistakes in living a lavish life after achieving success. They either built towers and terraces, or indulged themselves in music and beauties. Now His Majesty [Emperor Hsüan-tsung] honors Confucianism and respects virtues. He lectures on and discusses pertinent topics himself, and issues orders to publish and collate books and recruit scholars. The Li-cheng Academy today is precisely our sage-ruler's headquarters of ritual and music, which forms the unchanging *Tao* for the future. It spends little, yet achieves a lot."[17]

It followed, then, that any imperial payment or privilege, once granted, should not be taken away for any reason. Once a prime minister under Empress Wu Tse-t'ien requested that all the officials of the central government contribute two months' salary for military purposes. A low-ranking censor presented a memo to the empress, protesting: "With your properties extending to the Four Seas, Your Majesty is rich enough to support both the state and military expenses. Why should you have to rely upon this poor official's ninth-rank salary?"[18]

Accommodating the notion of a link between loyal service and imperial payment, emperors often rewarded candid words in cash or promoted their admonishers in the T'ang bureaucracy. As Emperor Kao-tsung once said to a subject: "You inherited your family's loyal and honest tradition and are capable of contributing candid criticism. If I do not reward you abundantly, how can [such behavior] be prized and encouraged?"[19] This pragmatic justification of loyalty seems to deviate from certain basic Confucian moral teachings, such as "the superior man understands what is moral; the inferior man understands what is profitable."[20] It reveals, however, the growing reliance of T'ang gentlemen upon the regime, in accordance with the transformation of the gentry's social status during the period (to be discussed further in this section).

The fundamental purpose of mutual cultivation between the emperor and his subjects, as revealed in *A New Account of the Great T'ang,* was the establishment of a solid political system—one in which the ruler builds up his authority by following the rules and practices suggested by his humble yet often dominant subjects. The following episode exemplifies this ironic relationship: At a palace gathering with his ministers, T'ai-tsung composed a poem on reading the *Shang-shu (Book of Documents),* the Confucian classic about the governing experience of the ancient sage kings:

> Licentious, muddle-headed rulers are many;
> Self-restrained, intelligent monarchs are rare.
> Bodies are destroyed because of amassed bad deeds;
> A good reputation is built upon gathered merits.

Wei Cheng chimed in with his poem. After recounting how previous ministers disciplined their emperors, he concluded:

> Relying upon Shu-sun T'ung's ritual system,
> Then the authority of the Son of Heaven stands up.[21]

Here, T'ai-tsung identifies himself as an intelligent ruler *(ming-chün)*, while Wei Cheng assumes the identity of Shu-sun T'ung, the famous minister to the Han founder, Liu Pang. Wei points out to T'ai-tsung that the Son of

Heaven can only establish his *tsun*—authority—by relying upon *li*—the ritual-political systems—built up by his ministers. T'ai-tsung then acknowledges: "Every time Wei Cheng speaks, he disciplines me with ritual [*li*]," thus acknowledging the kind of ruler-subject relationship Wei Cheng has set up for both of them.[22]

In this sense, the T'ang idea of "hailing the ruler and humbling the subject" *(tsun-chün pei-ch'en),* in Liu Su's accounts, differs significantly from the conventional Confucian principle that "the ruler is high and the subject is low" *(chün-tsun ch'en-pei).*[23] Whereas the latter simply describes a static hierarchy defined by Confucian standards, the former tries to clarify the rather blurry relationship between the ruler and the subject that had formed in the Six Dynasties period. The aim was to make the ruler and the subject a working pair and their relationship a dynamic power balance. In this way, as I shall discuss later, the subjects were inclined to cultivate the royal authority in order to solidify the empire for their own good.

Liu Su provides a revealing illustration of the principle of "hailing the ruler and humbling the subject" in the case of Wu Tse-t'ien. Overlooking the gender difference, Liu Su equates her authority with that of other T'ang emperors, always referring to her by her imperial title, *Tse-t'ien,* or simply *shang*—Her Majesty. In his accounts of the conversations between the empress and her subjects, she refers to herself by the royal pronoun *chen,* and her subjects address her as *t'ien-tzu,* the Son of Heaven; *chün,* my lord; *pi-hsia,* Your Majesty; and so on.

Later historians have usually portrayed Wu Tse-t'ien as an aggressive, self-indulgent, and self-promoting woman, accusing her of "being a hen crowing at dawn" and "usurping the divine imperial throne."[24] Liu Su tells us that her ambition was actually approved of and encouraged by T'ang gentlemen from the very beginning. When Wu Tse-t'ien was barely a toddler, a gentleman named Yüan T'ien-kang, who was skilled in physiognomy *(hsiang-shu),* paid her family a visit: "At the moment, Tse-t'ien, dressed like a boy, was carried out by her wet nurse. T'ien-kang was astonished to see her, saying: 'This young boy's spirit and expression look profound and pure, not easy to fathom.' He asked her to try walking [*hsing*], saying: 'He has the dragon eyes and the phoenix neck, extremely distinguished.' He then observed her from various angles, saying: 'If this were a girl, she would be-come the Son of Heaven.'"[25] Gender ironies suffuse Yüan T'ien-kang's ob-servation of the future female sovereign. He mistakes Wu Tse-t'ien for a boy but notices something unfathomable about her. After "asking her to try walking [*hsing*]," he finds in her body a male royal feature—dragon eyes—and a female royal feature—a phoenix neck. Hence he announces her an androgynous, "extremely distinguished" being, surpassing both men and women, and predicts her the future Son of Heaven—should she be a girl.

Note that the line in which Yüan asks her to try *hsing* closely imitates K'uai T'ung's (fl. early 200 B.C.) physiognomic judgment of the famous Han general Han Hsin (fl. early 200 B.C.), recounted by Ssu-ma Ch'ien in his *Records of the Grand Historian*: "Judging from the features of your face, you will obtain at most the rank of marquis; judging from the features of your back [*pei*], you will become distinguished beyond verbal descrip-tions."[26] K'uai T'ung uses the word *pei* as a pun, meaning both "back" and "betrayal," advising Han Hsin to betray Liu Pang and to develop his own power. By the same token, in Yüan T'ien-kang's comment on Wu Tse-t'ien, the word *hsing* means both "to walk" and "to act." Yüan thus implies that if Wu Tse-t'ien can "act," she can become "the Son of Heaven."

In Empress Wu's later years, according to Liu Su, T'ang gentlemen not only encouraged her to act as a ruler, but also told her how:

> Chang Chia-chen, although down in his luck, had great ambition, and he was neither self-important nor self-degrading. . . . Tse-t'ien sum-moned him into the inner palace and talked to him behind a bamboo screen. Seeing Chia-chen's imposing manner and outstanding spirit, Tse-t'ien was very impressed. [Chia-chen] took the opportunity to admonish her: "Your subject was born in the wilderness, never before seeing the palace court. Now Your Majesty kindly receives me in the Heavenly court and grants me an audience. This is really something that happens only once in ten thousand generations. Yet, only a foot away, Your Majesty looks engulfed within clouds and mist. I am afraid that, in this way, something is missing in the proper relationship between the ruler and the subject [*chün-ch'en chih tao*]."[27] Tse-t'ien said: "Good," and ordered the screen rolled up. Next day, she promoted Chang censor.[28]

What is it that Chang considers missing in the proper relationship between the ruler and the subject (*chün-ch'en chih tao*)? A heartfelt mutual trust, usually transmitted through a direct eye contact between the two, now seems to be blocked by a bamboo screen. The empress consciously tries to keep up with the conventional restraint on women, offering a male subject an audience behind this symbol of segregation.[29] The subject nonetheless tells her that acting as the ruler she should assume the full authority of a [male] ruler. She should forget about her female identity or she will not be able to fully execute her authority. At the same time, Chang also underscores her female sex—not to humble her but to make her an even more distinguished monarch, one that people only encounter once in ten thousand generations.

To be sure, not all T'ang gentlemen were happy with Wu Tse-t'ien's appropriation of imperial power. Some admonished Kao-tsung not to relinquish power to Wu Tse-t'ien.[30] After Wu Tse-t'ien assumed the throne, they made sure that she appointed her own son the crown prince instead of her nephew from the Wu family, and they constantly urged her to abdicate.[31] But they also helped cultivate her authority. All their admonitions to Wu Tse-t'ien, as recorded in *A New Account of the Great T'ang*, followed the principle of "praising the ruler's merits in public" and "correcting the ruler's wrongs in private." They admonished her in the same way that they did the other emperors, implicitly admitting that she, too, deserved their life-risking admonitions. Reciprocally, Liu Su praises Wu Tse-t'ien for her willingness to take their advice, with a frequency second only to T'ai-tsung.

TRANSFORMATION OF THE GENTRY

Two historical circumstances prompted Liu Su's *Shih-shuo* imitation, focusing it on "hailing the ruler and humbling the subject" and "expelling heterodoxy and returning to rectitude." One was the early T'ang need to rectify the long-term neglect of the ruler-subject hierarchy after the collapse of the Han; the other was the middle T'ang urgency of resealing the gentry's obligation to the regime after the An Lu-shan rebellion. Both involved the T'ang "transformation of the [shih] [gentry]."[32]

The primary components in the corporate identity of the *shih* included,

TABLE 7. THE FREQUENCY OF THE SUBJECTS' ADMONITIONS
AND THE RULER'S ACCEPTANCE IN THE *TA-T'ANG HSIN-YÜ*

Ruler	Kao-tsu	T'ai-tsung	Kao-tsung	Tse-t'ien	Chung-tsung	Jui-tsung	Hsüan-tsung
Admonitions	3	31	15	21	10	3	12
Acceptance	2	31	10	17	8	2	6

as Peter Bol indicates, "office holding, pedigree, and learning"[33]—all of
which resulted from and consequently affected the gentry's relationship
with other groups, especially the ruling house. When the gentry transformed its components and structure, its members at the same time needed
to redefine their qualifications and responsibilities and to justify their social relations. Naturally, they sought to express and solidify their concerns
in writing, and the *Shih-shuo* genre provided an ideal vehicle for this purpose because of its focus on self-fashioning.

Thus, T'ang *Shih-shuo* imitations—notably *A New Account of the Great
T'ang*—registered the transformation of the gentry's social status, a change
signaled particularly by its choice of a form of admonition. The Wei-Chin
preference for indirect admonitions reflected a rather detached ruler-
subject relationship, one in which gentlemen might not rely much on the
monarchy to advance their interests. The T'ang preference for direct admonition, on the other hand, underscored the gentry's greater reliance upon
the emperor as a group: They were eager to assist the ruler in forming a
stable regime in order to assure their own status.[34]

What caused this change? During the Wei-Chin period, as discussed
in chapter 1, the nine-rank system helped to keep high offices within the
control of the great clans.[35] Their unprecedentedly influential social status, accompanied by the chaotic political situation during the Wei-Chin
and later periods of division, enabled them to manipulate the reins of imperial power. As a result, the gentry "did not rely upon the emperor (to
maintain their hereditary status); on the contrary, anyone who sought the
imperial throne had first to seek the support of the great clans."[36] An
episode in the *Shih-shuo hsin-yü* exemplifies the situation: At the New Year's

Assembly, Emperor Yüan of the Chin insisted that Chancellor Wang Tao, head of one of the greatest clans of the period, mount the imperial dais with him (22/1). Quite clearly, a gentleman during the Wei-Chin and Southern dynasties periods did not have to advance his political career through excellence in service—his pedigree would automatically move him forward. So it was during the Northern dynasties as well. But the gentry's high hereditary social status began to change under the regime of Yü-wen T'ai (505–556), the powerful regent of the Western Wei (535–559) and the founder of the Northern Chou (559–581). In A.D. 544, Su Ch'o (498–546) drafted on Yü-wen T'ai's behalf the "Six Edicts," an important document of political reform. The fourth of these read: "In the past, the selection of major state and prefectural officials has been based on candidates' family pedigrees, and thus we often cannot get worthy and good people. . . . Family pedigrees represent only the ancestors' ranks and salaries, with no guarantee of the capability of later generations. From now on, the selection process should not be limited to pedigrees, but should focus on getting the right people."[37] This decision to terminate the pedigree system had far-reaching political and social consequences, although it took a long time to implement.[38]

The Sui dynasty (581–618) continued the Northern Chou's policy of eliminating the distinction between high-ranking or "pure" (ch'ing) and low-ranking or "muddy" (cho) hereditary families in the selection system. Tu Yu observes: "From the Northern Chou onward, the selection system no longer followed the pure/muddy difference. But when Lu K'ai was appointed the minister of personnel (in 582), he and the two vice ministers, Hsüeh Tao-heng and Lu Yen-shih, differentiated between the ranks of gentlemen and selected only those from 'pure' families. Criticism therefore arose and both Lu K'ai and Hsüeh Tao-heng were ousted."[39] In order to terminate the pedigree system, Emperor Wen of the Sui (r. 581–604) abolished all the offices that took charge of localized personnel selection and returned the authority of appointment to the central government.[40] Meanwhile, in order to diminish the demarcation between the Northern and Southern hereditary clans, the Sui regime started the civil service examination system, which encouraged selection of officials based on candidates' learning and therefore gave greater opportunities for officeholding to the gentry across the country. The Sui regime carried out all these policies with a clear awareness that the pedigree system had undermined the throne's power and that the continuation of this system would endanger the newly achieved unification of China. Unfortunately for the Sui, its precipitous policies offended the great clans and to some extent quickened its fall.

Upon succeeding the Sui in 618, the T'ang regime recompiled the genealogy of the great clans and rearranged the hereditary ranks of the entire country. Although these policies appeared to reinforce the pedigree system, they actually weakened it—not only by elevating the royal house to the head of the great clans but also by affirming the absolute authority of the throne.[41] The T'ang further institutionalized the civil examination system, which, by valuing learning, challenged the claim that pedigree alone was enough to qualify men for office. As Peter Bol observes: "Any favor shown to men whose claims rested on learning alone could come only at the expense of those who, having entered through privilege, claimed pure office by virtue of their pedigree. This had begun to happen, as suggested by the inclusion of the families of those with scholarly attainment, in addition to the good families, on the clan list of 713. Once culture was no longer exclusive to some great clans, it was possible to think of a [shih] as one who had acquired or was acquiring the learning necessary to serve in government, irrespective of family background."[42]

Among the early T'ang rulers, Wu Tse-t'ien played a decisive role in carrying out political reform. She blurred, mainly through marriage, the boundaries between the royal house, her rather humble natal family, and the great clans. She ardently promoted the civil service examination system, emphasizing in particular the chin-shih degree, which prized literary creation. And, by broadly recruiting talented people, she contributed to the consolidation of the T'ang regime. According to Liu Su's account, when Wu Tse-t'ien first claimed the throne, she appointed officials "by the cartloads and bushelfuls,"[43] regardless of their family backgrounds. Gentlemen were therefore very grateful and willing to serve her, as R. W. L. Guisso points out:

The traditional historians who so frequently criticize the empress are also consistent in their admission that her abilities were great enough to attract into her service men like Ti Jen-chieh, Li Chao-te, Hsü Yu-kung, Wei Yüan-chung, and many others whose talents were hardly inferior to the ministers who had surrounded T'ai-tsung. Ssu-ma Kuang, summarizing earlier views found in the dynastic histories, says that although the empress made too many appointments, she rapidly dismissed or executed the incompetents, and that because of her decisiveness and her abilities to use reward and punishment and to recognize talent, "the brilliant and worthy of the time were all in rivalry to be employed by her." This is absolutely true, but surely it was also the case that these talented men recognized the validity and the value of many of her wider aims and desired to contribute to their achievement.[44]

The outstanding gentlemen selected by Wu Tse-t'ien devoted their service to the T'ang regime for several decades. Many of them, including Yao Ch'ung, Sung Ching, Chang Yüeh, and Chang Chia-chen, the man who advised the empress to "roll up" her screen, later became the leading statesmen of the K'ai-yüan reign under Emperor Hsüan-tsung (r. 713–756), the apex of T'ang glory.[45] In short, Wu Tse-t'ien managed to do what even T'ang T'ai-tsung had not—lay the groundwork for the destruction of the deeply entrenched pedigree system.[46]

To be sure, until the reign of Hsüan-tsung, pedigree still functioned as the main avenue for access to a political career; the civil examinations provided at most 7 or 8 percent of T'ang officials each year. It was An Lu-shan's rebellion (755–763), the suppression of which led to the dramatic rise of provincial power, that "eventually made the claim to pedigree irrelevant."[47] The social composition of the gentry thereafter gradually changed from aristocrats from great clans to scholar-officials from civil-bureaucratic families. In the words of Peter Bol, the *shih* became "a kind of cultural elite . . . composed of families that set some store in maintaining learned traditions. . . . They were of use to men with power who lacked their literary talents, knowledge of history, and repertoire of classical forms. They were good subordinates, willing to let their political aspirations depend upon those above. . . . [To] realize their political and social ambitions, the [*shih*] depended upon the ability of a higher authority to re-establish a national sociopolitical hierarchy and put them at its apex. Among all political elements, then, their interests came closest to the emperor's interests: both believed they would gain by the centralization of authority."[48]

Liu Su demonstrated this turning point in the gentry's social status with the case of Chang Yüeh (667–730), who came from a relatively undistinguished family and entered court circles through the civil examination system.[49] In the *Ch'ao-yeh ch'ien-tsai* (Comprehensive records of affairs within and outside of the court)—an account about T'ang social life written early in Emperor Hsüan-tsung's reign—author Chang Cho (c. 657–730) disparages Chang Yüeh as a *hsing-ning jen* (flatterer).[50] Previously, under the domination of the great clans, the term *hsing-ning* had referred particularly to those who had come from low gentry status (*han-men*) and had advanced themselves by flattering the higher authorities.[51] Chang Cho's contempt for Chang Yüeh obviously stemmed from the pedigree system. But in *A New Account of the Great T'ang,* compiled about fifty years after the An Lu-shan Rebellion, Chang Yüeh is promoted as a role model for the gentry; his family background seems no longer relevant.[52]

Chang Yüeh's case shows the gentry's ability to adapt in accordance with changes in its social composition and its relationship with the emperor. Once great clan status had been separated from gentry status, gentlemen became far more dependent on the ruler because now they could prove their qualifications for the gentry class only through learning and service to the emperor. Liu Su illustrated the new standards for a gentleman by reference to Chang Yüeh. Chang was chosen as the Number One scholar by Wu Tse-t'ien from ten thousand candidates at the first civil service examination held after Wu's coronation. The government documents he drafted for Her Majesty were ordered to be distributed among courtiers and foreign guests in order to "flaunt the talents obtained by a great country."[53] He served several generations of the T'ang royal house and later became one of the most able ministers under Emperor Hsüan-tsung. In Liu Su's words:

> Chang Yüeh alone resisted [the political machinations of] the Princess T'ai-p'ing faction and insisted that the crown prince [the future emperor Hsüan-tsung] perform as regent. He finally helped to pacify the [T'ai-p'ing] insurrection and became an illustrious minister. Three times he

held the leading offices of the administration, and for thirty years he was in charge of the Secretariat. Both his writing style and reasoning were refined and became even more so when he was getting old. He was especially talented at composing grand articles. He knew how to take full advantage of other officials' talents and brought in literati and scholars to assist the emperor in civilizing the people. He obtained the monk I-hsing to clarify the calendar following the *yin* and *yang* principle, in order to give correct times and seasons to people. He [advised the emperor] to offer the *feng-shan* sacrifice to Mount T'ai, to build a temple on the Sui River, to perform court rites, and to worship the Five Mausoleums. He established the Academy of the Assembled Worthies to recruit scholars. His great deeds were matchless.[54]

Liu Su thus aggrandized a dead minister to meet the contemporary ideal of a scholar-official. First and foremost, a new-style scholar-official should dedicate to the monarch his absolute loyalty, which was usually attested by his daring admonitions at any risk. When Chang Yüeh admonished Emperor Jui-tsung (r. 711–712) on behalf of the crown prince, he was barely spared exile.[55] Under this fundamental principle of loyalty, a scholar-official should display his political ability and cultural attainment in assisting the monarch to maintain a highly centralized regime. With his learning, Chang Yüeh helped the emperor to establish the ritual system, which institutionalized the social hierarchy and in turn maintained the stability of society. With his literary talent, Chang Yüeh composed ceremonial lyrics and imperial memorials, which conveyed Heaven's mandate and the emperor's voice to his subjects. With his political ability, Chang Yüeh recruited scholars and literati who, like himself, assisted the emperor to reign and to "civilize" the people.

It was no coincidence that the earliest *Shih-shuo* imitations emerged after the An Lu-shan Rebellion and that they took as their major concern the guidance of both the ruler and his or her subjects. The substantial change in the gentry's social status and the urgent need to integrate a regime that had been shattered by political turmoil required adjustment of the ruler-subject relationship and behavior. To collect and evaluate the deeds of the rulers and the gentlemen and gentlewomen who solidified the great T'ang, with standards derived from contemporary needs, would surely prove effective in achieving this purpose. When it came to the problem of how to mold these anecdotes into a structure of significance, the *Shih-shuo* genre provided a ready model, since it dealt solely with gentry life. But the aesthetic orientation of the original *Shih-shuo* genre seemed to be at odds with a predominantly ethical purpose. Under such circumstances, the transformation of the genre had to occur. Since the new-style gentry's attachment to both learned traditions and the regime demanded their commitment to Confucian ethics, an ethical flavor would saturate almost all the *Shih-shuo* imitations to come.

Establishing the Body through Cultivating the Heart: Sung Imitations

Only two Sung *Shih-shuo* imitations are extant today: K'ung P'ing-chung's *Continuation of the Shih-shuo* and Wang Tang's *T'ang Forest of Accounts.* The two authors were contemporaries and both belonged to the intellectual circle headed by the famous scholar-official Su Shih (1036–1101). K'ung P'ing-chung and his two elder brothers, K'ung Wen-chung (1038–1088) and K'ung Wu-chung (d. ca. 1097), were all close friends of Su Shih and his brother Su Che (1039–1112), joining them in intellectual interests and political activities. Huang T'ing-chien's (1045–1105) remark that "the two Sus are two linked jades and the three K'ungs form a tripod" (*erh-Su lien-pi, san K'ung fen-ting*) reflects the high regard that Sung scholars had for the literary achievements and moral behavior of these five men.[56] As for Wang Tang, his father Wang P'eng (1067–1092) was Su Shih's close friend, and his cousin Wang Hsien stood by Su Shih in his periodic political struggles.[57]

Naturally, K'ung and Wang shared with Su Shih and with each other similar ideological, historical, and literary concerns. Their two *Shih-shuo* imitations consequently complemented each other in several ways. First, the two authors used the same genre to show a common interest while avoiding the same time frame. K'ung's *Continuation* covered the time from the Liu-Sung to the Five Dynasties, while Wang's *T'ang Forest,* obviously written later,[58] focused on the T'ang period alone; hence theirs was a complementary effort, reminiscent of the relationship between Ssu-ma Ch'ien's *Records of the Grand Historian* and Pan Ku's *History of the Han*.[59]

Secondly, both works consolidated the ethical orientation established by T'ang imitations, campaigning to "establish the self" *(li-shen)* through cultivating the heart—an introspective focus encouraged by the rise of *Li-hsüeh* (Learning of Principle) in the Sung period.[60] But imitation as a cultural activity has never been a one-sided proposition. While later generations choose and efface past cultural styles to meet their own cultural purposes, past styles can also modify their potential imitators. The *Shih-shuo's* kaleidoscopic picture of Wei-Chin gentry life embraced a broad range of intellectual interests and brought together diverse literary modes. Thus, when the Sung gentry divided into scholars *(ju-shih)*, headed by Ch'eng I (1033–1107), and literati *(wen-shih)*, headed by Su Shih (see below), the *Shih-shuo* genre naturally became the literati's device for vouchsafing their understanding and construction of "self," which embraced a heart not only ethical but also literary.

INDICATING A SINCERE HEART WITH AN UPRIGHT BODY

We can see a clear inheritance of the T'ang ethical accent in Sung imitations by examining their classification systems. K'ung's *Continuation* did not depart much from the original *Shih-shuo* taxonomy. He deleted only one category, *Hao-shuang* (Virility and vigor), and added three—*Chih-chien* (Candid admonition), *Hsieh-ch'an* (Heterodoxy and flattery), and *Chien-ning* (Craftiness and obsequiousness)—all evident derivations from T'ang imitations. As Ch'in Kuo saw it, this small change served as a guide for differentiating between *mei* and *o*—"admirable" and "abominable." It is easy to see why: All three new categories consisted primarily of T'ang moral anecdotes. Old categories also tended to include more ethical entries. For example, in the chapter "Speech and Conversation," the *Shih-shuo hsin-yü* catalogued intelligent bons mots, philosophical musings, sentimental laments, or literary vignettes that might ignore Confucian moral teachings.

K'ung's *Continuation*, however, exclusively recorded remarks on governing principles or Confucian moral codes. All these changes helped accentuate the *mei-o* conflict.

Wang Tang, in his *T'ang Forest*, omitted "Quick Perception" from the original *Shih-shuo* scheme and added seventeen new categories. Seven of them—*Chung-i* (Loyalty and righteousness), *Jen-ch'a* (Trust and perspicacity), *Wei-wang* (Authority and reputation), *Wei-yüeh* (Consolation and happiness), *Yü-ning* (Flattery and obsequiousness), *Chien-luan* (Usurpation and rebellion), and *Ts'an-jen* (Cruelty and heartlessness)— underscored the *mei-o* dichotomy. Another three, *Chi-yin* (Selection and recommendation), *Wei-shu* (Designation and assignment), and *Chi-ts'e* (Strategies and policies) emphasized proper governing.[61] Wang Tang also extensively quoted from Liu Su's *New Account of the Great T'ang.* For instance, in the chapter titled "Speech and Conversation," seventeen out of forty-one episodes were extracted from Liu's most morally oriented categories—*K'uang-tsan* (Rectification and assistance), *Kuei-chien* (Advice and admonition), and *Chi-chien* (Intense admonition).

Although both the T'ang and the Sung imitations claimed to promote Confucian ethics, each favored certain values and interpretations, according to prevailing ideological and political currents. The difference can be seen in the following two episodes, taken respectively from Liu's *New Account of the Great T'ang* and K'ung's *Continuation*, both concerning T'ang T'ai-tsung:

> T'ai-tsung, having learned that many officials at the Imperial Secretariat took bribes, secretly dispatched his attendants to offer them gifts. The gate official indeed took a bolt of silk. T'ai-tsung wanted to kill him. P'ei Chü admonished: "Your Majesty uses gifts to trick the man into the crime and then quickly decides to put him to death. I am afraid this does not accord with the principles of *Tao, te* and *li* [propriety]." The man was then exonerated.[62]

> Under the reign of T'ai-tsung, a man presented a memorial, urging the emperor to expel the flatterers from his ministers. The emperor asked him who they were. The man replied, "Your subject lives among mountains and swamps and has no way to identify them. Why doesn't Your Majesty talk to all your ministers, pretending to be angry in order to test

them. Those who stick to their principles and refuse to yield are the honest ministers, whereas those who fear your temper and follow your intent are the flattering ministers." T'ai-tsung said, "If the ruler is deceitful, how can he demand his ministers' honesty? Right now I am ruling the world with 'ultimate honesty' [chih-ch'eng]. When I discovered that some former rulers used duplicity in dealing with their ministers, I always felt ashamed for them. Your plan may be good, but I do not want to adopt it."[63]

The Sung episode reinforces the T'ang emphasis on the ruler-subject hierarchy, but it differs from the T'ang episode with respect to (1) who plays the pivotal role in the ruler-subject relationship, and (2) which moral code(s) the ruler and the subject employ to rule the world and cultivate themselves. In *A New Account of the Great T'ang,* the subject assumes the role of the admonisher/educator and the ruler assumes the role of the admonished/educated. The subject talks and the ruler listens. K'ung's *Continuation* reverses the situation—the ruler no longer plays the mute and passive recipient of his subjects' candid admonition; rather, he becomes a critical authority, actively censoring his subject's suggestion and offering his own morally grounded advice. This emphasis on the ruler's active role seems clearly to rectify the Sung gentry's growing reliance upon a highly centralized imperial authority.

There is another significant difference in the two T'ai-tsung stories. In the Sung version, *ch'eng* (usually translated "sincerity")[64] emerged as a particularly prominent Confucian value. T'ai-tsung claims, in fact, that he "rules the world" with *ch'eng.* This reflects its new importance as a metaphysically grounded concept in the Sung dynasty's "Learning of Principle" or *Li-hsüeh* (see below), just as during the Han and the Wei-Chin periods *hsiao* (filial piety) occupied an analogous position in Confucian rhetoric. As shown here, T'ai-tsung's remarks clearly imitate a *Shih-shuo* instance in which Ssu-ma Chao is described as "ruling the world with *hsiao*" (23/2).

The *T'ang Forest* also valorizes the idea of *ch'eng.* For instance, Wang Tang copied an episode from *A New Account of the Great T'ang* in which the famous T'ang minister Sung Ching (663–737) is described as "relying upon *hsin* (trustworthiness) to show *ch'eng* (sincerity)." But instead of using *hsin*—one of the "Five Constant Virtues" *(wu-ch'ang)*—as the basis for *ch'eng*,[65] Wang changed the phrase into "adhering to *ch'eng* to show *hsin*,"[66] using *ch'eng* as the basis for *hsin*.

This emphasis on *ch'eng* in the writings of both K'ung and Wang can be traced to the influence of Chou Tun-i (1017–1073), a pioneer Neo-Confucian scholar who had close ties with the K'ung and Su families.[67] For Chou, *ch'eng* occupied the center of Confucian ethics: It was the "root of the sage" *(sheng-jen chih pen)*, the "root of the Five Constant Virtues" *(wu-ch'ang chih pen)*, and the "origin of one hundred kinds of [good] behavior" *(pai-hsing chih yüan)*.[68] Linking *ch'eng* to the art of government, Chou Tun-i formed his moral-political theory: "To see if one can rule the world, look how he arranges his household. To see if one can arrange his household, look how he controls himself [lit. his body]. An upright self [lit. body] indicates a sincere heart [*hsin*]. The sincere heart corrects bad behavior, and that is all."[69]

Chou's notion of *ch'eng* transformed *li-shen* (establishing the self) from the rather outward T'ang practice into a more introspective one, focusing on the cultivation of heart *(hsin)*. Naturally enough, we see this change in the *Shih-shuo* imitations of both Wang and K'ung. Indeed, K'ung opens his first chapter, "*Te* Conduct," with the following appraisal of the Liang gentleman Liu Tsun (488–535), exemplifying Chou Tun-i's idea that "an upright self indicates a sincere heart": "[Liu Tsun] loves his parents and siblings sincerely and deeply and has established himself [*li-shen*] as an upright and honest man. He contains jade-like gentleness and looks as limpid as water, always conforming words to actions. He is well versed in literature and history, with a heart as beautiful as jade."[70]

Thus, in his *Continuation of the Shih-shuo*, K'ung establishes a discourse of *ch'eng* that is applicable to various aspects of gentry life. For public affairs, he advocates the idea of "transforming people with sincerity and trustworthiness [*ch'eng-hsin*],"[71] emphasizing that a scholar-official should adhere to *ch'eng* and *hsin* himself, and then he can demand these virtues of his people: "When Yüan Te-hsiu served as the magistrate of Lu-shan county, he put a robber behind bars. It so happened that a tiger on the county border was causing atrocities. The robber appealed to kill the tiger to atone for his crime, and Te-hsiu approved his petition. The clerics contended, saying: 'The robber is tricking you to get away. Releasing a convicted criminal will inflict trouble upon yourself.' Te-hsiu said: 'I don't want to break my promise. If there will be trouble, I will take it.' Thus he released the robber. Next day, the robber carried the tiger back."[72] And for private behavior, K'ung demands that a scholar should "be honest, even when there is no one around" (*pu ch'i an-shih*, lit. "no cheating," even in a dark room where no one can see).[73]

Wang Tang in the *T'ang Forest* introduces the notion of *ch'eng* with a number of episodes about private lives. Immediately following his account of Sung Ching's demonstration of *ch'eng*, he describes T'ang Hsüan-tsung's sincere feelings toward his brothers: "Emperor Hsüan-tsung had great fraternal love for his prince-brothers. He used to think of making a long pillow and a huge quilt in order to sleep with them in the same bed. If a prince fell ill, His Majesty would be restless all day and could not eat. If his attendants persuaded him to have some food, he would say: 'My brothers are my limbs. If my limbs are out of order, my body is impaired. How could I have time to think of drinking and eating?' . . . He often got together with the princes, composing poems, drinking wine, laughing, teasing; never had he been suspicious of [his brothers]."[74] This story can be read as an allegory of *ch'eng*, in which Hsüan-tsung, as the center of the royal house, plays the sincere heart, incorporating his brothers—his extended body— with a loving, trustful bond, in order to establish a solid monarchy. In fact, Hsüan-tsung was notoriously ruthless and suspicious; he even wrongfully ordered his own sons' death.[75] But Wang Tang is trying to use him to underscore the importance of a central moral principle.

REFINING WORDS TO CONSTITUTE AN AUTHENTIC SELF

In Sung *Shih-shuo* imitations, cultivation of the heart, in accordance with the notion of *ch'eng*, guides not only gentlemen's moral-political behavior but also their scholarly learning and literary creation. K'ung's *Continuation* introduces this function in rather mysterious terms. For instance: "Cheng Cho [514–581] of the Liang was by nature refined and diligent, and was especially well versed in the three *Rituals*. When young, he once dreamed of meeting with Huang K'an [488–545] on the road. K'an said to him: 'Open your mouth, lad,' and he spat saliva in it. Cheng thereafter became much improved in comprehending the meanings and principles [of the classics]. He often suffered from a hot sensation in the heart. In the melon season, he would eat melons to calm the heart, so that he could start reading aloud as soon as he got up. He was so devoted [to learning]!"[76] Ancient Chinese believed that saliva contained one's essence.[77] By putting his saliva directly into Cheng Cho's mouth, the famous Liang Confucian scholar Huang K'an immediately passed on his best qualities—diligence, wisdom, and broad knowledge—to the young man, heating his heart with the desire to learn and moistening his throat to read.

Moral and literary inspiration could come from a variety of sources, as K'ung indicates: "Wang Jen-yü of the Chou in the Five Dynasties period [907–960] had not been willing to study until he was twenty-five years old. One night, he dreamed of cutting up his abdomen and washing his intestines and stomach with the water of the West River. Seeing the pebbles in the river all carved with seal script, he picked up some and swallowed them. Upon waking up, he found his heart and mind crystal clear and his understanding and knowledge improved daily. He composed over ten thousand poems, divided them into one hundred *chüan,* and entitled them the *Collection of the West River,* named after the river of the patterned pebbles he swallowed."[78] Here, in the same direct way that Cheng Cho swallows Huang K'an's saliva, Wang Jen-yü ingests the "patterned pebbles" of the West River. But whereas Cheng receives Huang's essence without preparation, Wang has to endure self-purification—cutting up his body and washing it thoroughly with the very water that has shaped the pebbles—in order to turn his body into a suitable residence for these imported qualities. Never before had a *Shih-shuo t'i* work had such a painstakingly acute and intimate description of self-cultivation, which, of course, shows the difficulty and subtlety of the cultivation of the heart in the arena of literary creation.

Corresponding with K'ung's mysterious accounts of scholarly and/or literary cultivation, Wang Tang explores how literary creations express a sincere heart. In his description of Chu-ko Liang's (181–234) famous "Diagram of Eight Tactics" (Pa-chen t'u), constructed with pieces of stone piled on the sandy riverbank of K'uei-chou, Wang Tang observes:

> Displayed like a pan and extending like wings, the [stone] diagram assumes the shape of a goose and the posture of a crane. Constructed with stone pieces spread on the bank, it still exists today. When the gorges are flooded and the snow melts in the three Shu areas, the river dashes and plunges. Big trees ten double spans thick, dead boughs one thousand feet long, and broken rocks and huge stones all rush down, choking the river. Water swells as high as the bank. Thunder rolls, mountains split, and stones pile up. . . . Once the flood retreats, myriad things lose their original shapes, only the diagram of little stone piles stays intact. During these six or seven hundred years, water has been brushing and pushing, yet the stone diagram has never moved. Liu Yü-hsi [772–842] says: "This is because Lord Chu-ko was sincere and intelligent, whole-heartedly determined to die for his late lord [Liu Pei]. Therefore gods protect the stone diagram, never allowing it to be changed."[79]

Wang Tang's verbal description of the stone diagram, which Chu-ko Liang created for training his troops, translates and transforms the stone piles into a literary text inscribed on the riverbank. This strong, immutable stone "document" expresses Chu-ko Liang's sincerity and intelligence (ch'eng-ming), which ingeniously designed the diagram and sustained it in the combat with the rushing water, roaring thunder, and flowing time, displaying Chu-ko Liang's wholehearted devotion to his ruler, witnessed by Heaven, Earth, gods, and man.

The two Sung Shih-shuo t'i authors' interest in the connection between ch'eng and literary cultivation can be traced to their idol Su Shih, who on many occasions discussed this relationship. Here is a relevant passage: "I heard that gentlemen in the past observed one's remarks in order to know one's personality. If the remarks could not sufficiently expose the personality, they would ask one to recite a poem in order to observe one's intent. During the Spring and Autumn period, scholar-officials all used this method to divine a person's fortune and destiny. The accordance between the prediction and the consequence could be as close as that between shadow and body, echo and sound. Isn't it because ch'eng sprouts from one's heart and there is no way to hide it, so that a single poem may foretell a person's future?"[80] For Su Shih, *ch'eng* expresses the true self in its entirety.[81] It includes, but goes beyond, the moral categories of sincerity and honesty, and in this sense it may be rendered more properly as authenticity. Sprouting from one's heart, *ch'eng* naturally flows into one's words, for which poetry is an especially effective medium of expression.

Why is it that poetry is so well suited as a means of self-expression? Su Shih addresses this question with his interpretation of Confucius' idea, *tz'u-ta,* or *ta-i,* "using words to convey fully the meaning":

> Confucius said, "If words are not refined [*wen*], they cannot go far." He also said, "If words can fully convey [the meaning], then it [refinement of the words] is enough." If we take the words that satisfy the standard of "fully conveying the meaning" as being unrefined [*pu-wen*], we are wrong. To seek the subtleties of things [*wu*] is like trying to bind the wind and catch the shadow. We may not find even one person out of hundreds of thousands who can make a certain thing comprehensible in his or her heart, much less make it comprehensible in spoken or written language. Only the words that can make things comprehensible in spoken and written language may be considered as fully conveying [the meaning]. If words really reach the point of fully conveying [the meaning], the literary works thus composed will be more than satisfactory for use.[82]

Of course, not all words that issue from one's heart can truly express the self, which is simply too subtle to catch, as illusory as wind and shadow. To seek the subtlety of one's self, as well as that of all things *(wu),*[83] to make these things "comprehensible" through the use of words, one needs to refine the words to the extent that they can discriminate shapes, colors, tastes, sounds, actions, processes—in brief, all the features of things. Only such words can satisfy the standard of *tz'u-ta* and thus be "used" to express meanings fully.[84] Once words reach *tz'u-ta,* they are *wen*—literary. Poetic words, being most refined, are the most capable of expressing the subtleties of things, among which one's self is the subtlest of all.[85]

As they linked their ethical orientation to Northern Sung *Li-hsüeh* concerns, specifically Chou Tun-i's conceptualization of *ch'eng,* Su Shih and his admirers formed their literary interest also at the instigation of *Li-hsüeh,* but from an opposite standpoint. We know of a major conflict between

the Su Shih circle and the Ch'eng I circle, known also as the struggle between the Shu and the Lo Schools. Su Shih and K'ung P'ing-chung were
especially singled out as contradicting Ch'eng I, and for this reason, Su
and K'ung's works were severely criticized by later *Li-hsüeh* scholars.[86]
The fundamental difference between Ch'eng I and Su Shih, to put the
matter somewhat starkly, lies in their respective approaches to the *Tao*—
the ultimate way.

For Ch'eng I, the Way of Heaven *(T'ien-tao)* was equivalent to the principle of Heaven *(T'ien-li)*, the mandate of Heaven *(T'ien-ming)*, and human nature *(hsing)*.[87] In the words of Peter Bol, "The moral philosophers
who established *Tao-hsüeh* (the 'Learning of the Way'), Neo-Confucianism in a narrow sense, contended that each individual was innately endowed with the patterns of the integrated processes of heaven-and-earth.
It was only necessary, then, that men realize the 'pattern of heaven' *(t'ien-
li)* that was in their own nature, for this was the real foundation for a moral
world."[88]

Ch'eng I tells us:

> Learning is to make one seek [the *Tao*] from one's inner [nature]. If one
> seeks [the *Tao*] not from inside but from outside, then [the learning one
> conducts] is not the Sage's learning. What does it mean to seek [the *Tao*]
> not from inside but from outside? It means to give the first place to lit-
> erature. Learning is to make one seek [the *Tao*] from the origin. To seek
> [the *Tao*] not from the origin but from the end is not the Sage's learning.
> What does it mean to seek [the *Tao*] not from the origin but from the
> end? It means to study details [of the outside world] and to gather in-
> stances of similarities and difference [from the outside world]. Both can-
> not benefit one's self-cultivation; therefore gentlemen will not study
> them.[89]

Ch'eng I thus argued that "composing literary pieces harms the *Tao*" *(tso-
wen hai-tao)*, for it turns scholars' attention away from their inner nature
toward the examination and depiction of external trifling things. Therefore he would never engage in the creation of "idle words" such as those
of Tu Fu: "Gliding through flowers, butterflies appear from the depths/ca-
ressing the water, dragonflies fly elegantly."[90]

Su Shih understood the *Tao* in a more or less Taoist fashion, viewing it as what "the myriad things rely upon to be themselves" and what "the myriad principles are confirmed by."[91] This *Tao* could only be "brought on" by the close study of all things.[92] In the eyes of Su Shih, literature provided the best way to "bring on" the *Tao*—by grasping the subtleties of the phenomenal world with words and introducing particular cases of human practice for the reader to intuit, not to define, the *Tao* embodied in all things.[93] Su Shih's understanding of *ch'eng* and its connection with literature is consistent with his understanding of *Tao* and the function of literature in transmitting the *Tao*. Thus, unlike Ch'eng I, Su Shih enjoys Tu Fu's "idle words," such as "Lingering, playful butterflies dance now and then/Carefree, delicate orioles chirp in harmonious flows." This couplet, visualizing Tu Fu's "aura of pure craziness and wild spontaneity,"[94] exposes the part of Tu Fu's true self that is not easily seen in his heavier poems.

For Su Shih and his followers, the *Shih-shuo* genre offered an ideal literary means to express a person's authentic self. In the first place, Su Shih's understanding of human nature accorded with that of the *Shih-shuo*: Human nature has no specific shape, it is neither good nor bad, and it can only be intuited on a case-by-case basis.[95] Second, the *Shih-shuo* genre grew out of a metalinguistic debate over whether language can fully express meanings. From the *Shih-shuo*'s taxonomic scheme to the narration of each episode, the author employs various literary means to make amorphous human personalities "comprehensible" and hence sets an excellent example in literary elaboration. Although Su Shih did not compose a *Shih-shuo* imitation, he contributed over a dozen brief essays on the *Shih-shuo* personalities,[96] plus an extensive elaboration of Ku K'ai-chih's artistic theory of "*ch'uan-shen*," transmitting the spirit.[97] He also amply used *Shih-shuo* allusions in his poetry, particularly in *tz'u*—what was then the most elegant and self-expressive literary form.[98] When his followers, K'ung and Wang, proceeded with the imitation of the *Shih-shuo,* they naturally adopted the original *Shih-shuo* scheme that more authentically reflected subtle human nature and turned away from the more didactic T'ang imitations.

Let us examine in greater detail the way K'ung and Wang emphasize the function of literature in constructing the gentry "self." One index is the relative amount of attention given to *wen* (literature) as opposed *hsüeh* (scholarship) in the *Shih-shuo* imitations discussed above. In the original *Shih-shuo* chapter on "Wen-hsüeh" (Literature and scholarship), the ratio between the entries on *wen* and *hsüeh* is 39 to 65. But it becomes 29 to 6 in K'ung's *Continuation* and 76 to 32 in Wang's *T'ang Forest*. By this statistical measure, literature assumes much greater importance in the life of the gentry in the T'ang-Sung period than at earlier times—at least as gentry life is depicted in the *Shih-shuo* imitations.

The situation is complicated, however, by the subtle interplay between literature, politics, and ethics that occurred during this particular transitional time. For instance, on the one hand, the focus on literary talent in the T'ang civil examination system promoted literature as a means of social and bureaucratic advancement, contributing to a system of patronage marked by the widespread literary practice known as *hsing-chüan* (presenting [poetry] scrolls).[99] On the other hand, the rise of *Li-hsüeh*, with its heavy emphasis on ethical responsibility, could not but have a profound effect on Sung gentlemen—even free-spirited intellectuals such as Su Shih and his followers, who were fundamentally hostile to the constant moralizing of individuals such as Ch'eng I. The result was that the T'ang-Sung literary scene as described by Kung P'ing-chung and Wang Tang lacked the aesthetic innocence of the *Shih-shuo hsin-yü*. "Bringing on the *Tao*" in Sung *Shih-shuo* imitations involved more than "idle words"; conventional values also came into play.

Let's look at some examples. In his chapter on "Wen-hsüeh," Wang Tang elaborates on Su Shih's idea that poetry can foretell one's destiny: "Candidate Li Wei composed rhyme-prose pieces such as the *Lei fu* [On tears], *Ch'ing fu* [On lightness], *Pao fu* [On thinness], *An fu* [On dimness], and *Hsiao fu* [On littleness]. Candidate Li Ho indulged himself mostly in flowers, grass, and insects. The two young gentlemen did not get far [in their political career]. [No wonder] people say that writings can foretell one's fate."[100] The titles of Li Wei's *fu* pieces manifest his rather narrow and gloomy mental states, with thoughts that linger around the dark and trivial aspects of human life. Li Ho's indulgence in delicate natural beings, too, exposes his fragile inner build. Such qualities alienate the two candidates from the more vigorous mainstream values.

In the *T'ang Forest*, Wang Tang makes literary works the major sources for character appraisal. The first episode of the chapter *Shih-chien* (Recognition and judgment) records that "two candidates of the civil service examination dazzled the capital with their literary talents, but the examiner passed them only with low ranks. He criticized them, saying: 'These fellows surely possess a flowery writing style, yet it looks frivolous [literally, their bodies look light and thin] and their literary compositions read as superfluous and extravagant. They will not make good statesmen [literally, good vessels (*ling-ch'i*)].'"[101]

By contrast, "good vessels" or "heavy vessels" can reveal the grandeur of their personalities with imposing literary themes. For instance:

> During the Chen-kuan reign, a Shu boy named Li I-fu, known as a prodigy, came to the capital. Emperor T'ai-tsung received him casually in the Shang-lin garden. It so happened that someone there caught a crow, and the emperor gave it to I-fu. I-fu immediately composed a poem as follows:
>
> > Spreading out morning clouds from the sun,[102]
> > Accompanying night yearnings of the zither,[103]
> > Although the Shang-lin Garden is full of trees
> > [The crow] will not borrow a single branch to abide.
>
> The emperor laughed, saying: "I'll lend you the entire tree." Later on he became a prime minister under Kao-tsung.[104]

Incorporating both dazzling and sentimental crow allusions into his short poem, I-fu expresses irrepressible pride and self-confidence, but not without a melancholy flavor. The crow spreads the glory of the sun over the sky, as a gentleman conveys the emperor's benevolence throughout his realm. The crow also keeps a gentleman company in his forlorn political situation. However frustrated, the crow cannot be satisfied with a humble position (one branch). The understanding emperor nods at the young prodigy's ambition, promising him a grand future.

One episode particularly manifests Wang Tang's standard of discerning a promising man of letters through his works. The early T'ang poet Lo Pin-wang participated in the rebellion against Wu Tse-t'ien and wrote a letter to the empress on behalf of the rebels:[105] "The Heavenly Empress read it. At the couplet, 'Raising moth-eyebrows, she never tolerates other beauties / Flaunting fox-charm, she casts spells on the emperor,' she smiled. Upon reading 'A pile of grave dirt is not yet dry / The six-foot tall orphan,[106] where is he?' she became very unhappy, saying: 'How can the prime minister leave out such a man!?' She regretted having missed such a talented subject."[107] The two couplets that Wang Tang cites are equally refined examples of perfect *p'ien-wen* (parallel prose), yet Wu Tse-t'ien acknowledges Lo Pin-wang's talent only in reading the second. What separates the two? The first couplet, calling the empress ugly names with narrow-minded clichés, reveals the author as a mean-spirited misogynist. The empress smiles away both the man and his attack. The second one, however, shows a devoted subject's sincere concern for the newly orphaned crown prince, exiled by his own mother. The empress, having just established her own regime, regrets the loss of a man who is not only loyal to the royal house— albeit to the wrong person—but who also has the talent to express it in a powerful way.

In short, literature—poetry in particular—provides Sung *Shih-shuo* imitations with an extremely effective means by which to show how scholars were able to attain and to express the "comprehensibility" of things— how they could, in Su Shih's memorable phrase, "bind the wind and catch the shadow." Wang Tang, for example, discussed in more than two dozens of episodes how to use words to catch subtle nuances of things and human feelings. Consider the following episodes:

> Liu Yü-hsi said: "Han Yü, Liu Tsung-yüan, and I went to listen to Shih Shih-mang interpreting Mao's commentary on the *Book of Songs*. He said, 'A mountain without grass and trees is called *ku*. Therefore the line, "Ascending the *ku*," is used to express the sadness of losing a parent, inasmuch as a mountain having no grass and trees has nothing to depend on.'"

> [A poem by] Yang Mao-ch'ing reads: "River winds along Mount K'un-lun from afar/Mountain looks like lotus buds in the autumn." This poem, entitled "Passing by Mount Hua (flower)," [compares the mountain] to lotus buds. The description is extremely accurate with its dark tranquility.[108]

Both examples exemplify the way of *tz'u-ta*: The use of one specific word can visualize sadness through a perceptible natural imagery, as shown in the first episode. And, in the second, the poet catches Mount Hua's flowery shape, quiet nature, and its dark, mysterious aura all in the image of the autumn lotus buds, simple but very appealing to the reader's imagination.

Although previous *Shih-shuo t'i* works had placed considerable emphasis on poetic events in their depictions of gentry life, never before had a *Shih-shuo* imitation included such detailed discussions of poetic rhetoric. Part of the reason for this may have been that the great outpouring of verse in the T'ang period demanded some sort of general critical response by the Sung literati, but part of the reason must surely have been the specific aesthetic sensibilities and literary inspiration of Su Shih and his circle. Su's discourse of refining words to constitute one's authentic self not only shaped the Sung works of Wang Tang and K'ung P'ing-chung, but it also influenced in significant ways the tone and style of the many Ming and Ch'ing *Shih-shuo* imitations that were to come.

Chapter 7

Things and Intent: Ming and Ch'ing Imitations

Most *Shih-shuo* imitations emerged in the late Ming and the early Ch'ing, from the 1550s to the 1680s. These works covered a longer time span (from antiquity to the early Ch'ing) and a broader range of Chinese social and intellectual life (with up to ninety-eight categories in one work) than previous *Shih-shuo t'i* works. The subgenres also expanded from general or dynastic surveys of gentry life to works focusing on specific groups, such as Chiao Hung's *Yü-t'ang ts'ung-yü* on scholars of the Han-lin Academy and Yen Ts'ung-ch'iao's *Seng Shih-shuo*, culled from three biographical works about eminent monks.[1] There were also two works on women, which I shall discuss in the next chapter, and a work about precocious children.

Not only did this *Shih-shuo* frenzy span a particular time period; it was also imbued with a strong regional flavor. Ming-Ch'ing *Shih-shuo t'i* authors and their proponents came overwhelmingly from the lower Yangtze region known as the Chiang-nan area (south of the Yangtze River), as shown in the following table:

TABLE 8. DATES AND NATIVE PLACES OF MING-CH'ING
SHIH-SHUO T'I AUTHORS AND MAJOR PROPONENTS

Name	Dates	Native Place	Connection with the *Shih-shuo t'i*
Ho Liang-chün	1506–1573	Sung-chiang Hua-t'ing (Soochow)[1]	Author, *Ho-shih yü-lin* (1551)
Wen Cheng-ming	1470–1559	Ch'ang-chou (Wu-hsien, Kiangsu)	Preface writer, *Ho-shih yü-lin*
Wang Shih-chen	1526–1590	T'ai-ts'ang	Complier, *Shih-shuo hsin-yü pu* (1556, 1585)

(continued)

Name	Dates	Native Place	Connection with the *Shih-shuo t'i*
Wang Shih-mao	1536–1588	T'ai-ts'ang	Preface writer, *Shih-shuo hsin-yü* and *Shih-shuo hsin-yü pu*
Chiao Hung	1541–1620	Chiang-ning (Nanking)	Author, *Chiao-shih lei-lin* (1585, 1587) *Yü-t'ang ts'ung-yü* (1618)
Li Chih	1527–1602	Chin-chiang	Commentator, *Shih-shuo hsin-yü pu* Editor, *Ch'u-t'an chi* (1588)
Li Shao-wen	fl. 1600–1623	Sung-chiang Hua-t'ing	Author, *Huang-Ming Shih-shuo hsin-yü* (1610)
Cheng Chung-k'uei	fl. 1615–1634	Hsin-chou (Shang-jao, Kiangsi)	Author, *Lan-wan chü ch'ing-yen* (1615, 1617)
Chang Yung	fl. late Ming	Ch'ien-t'ang (Hangchow)	Author, *Nien-i shih shih-yü* (late Ming)
Lin Mao-kuei	fl. 1591–1621	Chang-p'u	Author, *Nan-Pei ch'ao hsin-yü* (1621)
Yen Ts'ung-ch'iao	fl. ca. 1639	Wan-ch'eng (Ch'ien-shan, Anhwei)	Author, *Seng Shih-shuo* (1639, 1640)
Liang Wei-shu	1589–1662	Chen-ting (Cheng-ting, Hopeh)	Author, *Yü-chien tsun-wen* (1654, 1657)
Ch'ien Ch'ien-i	1582–1664	Ch'ang-shu	Preface writer, *Yü-chien tsun-wen*
Wu Wei-yeh	1609–1671	T'ai-ts'ang	Preface writer, *Yü-chien tsun-wen*
Li Ch'ing	1602–1683	T'ai-chou	Author, *Nü Shih-shuo* (1650s, 1670s)
Wang Wan	1624–1691	Ch'ang-chou	Author, *Shuo-ling* (1659, 1661)
Wu Su-kung	fl. 1662–1681	Hsüan-ch'eng	Author, *Ming yü-lin* (1662, 1681)
Chiang Yu-jung	early Ch'ing	Ch'ang-sha	Coauthor, *Ming-i pien* (early Ch'ing)
Tsou T'ung-lu	early Ch'ing	Heng-yang	Coauthor, *Ming-i pien* (early Ch'ing)
Wang Cho	b. 1636	Jen-ho (Hangchow)	Author, *Chin Shih-shuo* (1683)
Mao Chi-k'o	1633–1708	Sui-an (Ch'un-an, Chekiang)	Preface writer, *Chin Shih-shuo*
Chang Fu-kung	early Ch'ing?	Ch'ien-t'ang	Author, *Han Shih-shuo* (early Ch'ing)

Name	Dates	Native Place	Connection with the *Shih-shuo t'i*
Chang Chi-yung	early Ch'ing?	Hangchow	Author, *Nan-Pei ch'ao Shih-shuo*
Yen Heng	1826?–1854	Jen-ho	Author, *Nü Shih-shuo* (1854, 1865)

1. Today's name in parentheses if different from the past.

In addition to showing temporal and spatial affiliations, this table also reveals that Ming-Ch'ing *Shih-shuo t'i* authors and proponents constituted the core of what was then the most prestigious gentry group, the Chiang-nan intellectual elite, including: Wen Cheng-ming, a famous mid-Ming literatus-artist and the head of the "Four Talents of Wu" (*Wu-chung ssu-tzu*);[2] Ho Liang-chün, Wen's protégé and arguably one of the half-dozen most learned Ming scholars; Wang Shih-chen, the leading late Ming poet and head of the "Seven Later Masters" (*Hou ch'i-tzu*);[3] Wang Shih-mao (Wang Shih-chen's equally talented brother); Chiao Hung, the Number One scholar (*chuang-yüan*) of the seventeenth year of the Wan-li reign (1589); Li Chih, the iconoclastic late Ming thinker and literary critic; Ch'ien Ch'ien-i and Wu Wei-yeh (both leading figures of late Ming and early Ch'ing literature); Liang Wei-shu, Ch'ien's and Wu's close associate and himself a late Ming and early Ch'ing scholar-literatus; Li Ch'ing, a Ming loyalist scholar; Wang Wan, one of the leading early Ch'ing scholar-poets; and Wang Cho, an early Ch'ing scholar-literatus.

The social and cultural common denominator of the Chiang-nan intellectual elite set them apart from the rest of Chinese society in a number of ways. In the first place, they had a powerful sense of regional identity and local pride. Second, they were on the whole hostile to the state-sponsored *Li-hsüeh* orthodoxy of the Ming-Ch'ing period. Third, as a group they bore a political stigma: In the late Ming they were blamed for breeding "factionalism, internal dissension and an unseemly degree of attention to selfish aesthetic gratification at the expense of practical affairs"; and in the early Ch'ing they aroused the Manchu regime's continuing suspicion of the lower Yangtze region "as the heartland of tax evasion, [diehard] Ming loyalism and general insubordination."[4] Finally, they lived in an area of China that was marked by a highly developed commodity economy, in which local elites participated actively as producers, consumers, and connoisseurs. The combination of these elements produced a collective sense of cultural and intellectual distinctiveness not unlike that of their gentry counterparts in the Six Dynasties period. Thus, under very different historical circumstances, they sought to transmit their own version of the Wei-Chin "spirit."

A close reading of Ming and Ch'ing imitations of the *Shih-shuo hsin-yü* will reveal a far more sophisticated image of the Ming-Ch'ing Chiang-nan elite than most scholars have been willing to acknowledge. To be sure, they may have given what seemed to some critics to be "an unseemly degree of attention to aesthetic gratification," but their indulgence in the arts and letters was not motivated solely by selfishness, nor did it come at the expense of practical affairs. Rather, their lifestyle was built upon both their intellectual ideals and their daily life needs, which were closely linked to the commodity economy and to the distinctive culture of the area. And, although the Manchu invaders met a most determined resistance in the Chiang-nan area, the more or less depoliticized local elite eventually convinced themselves that cultural continuity exceeded the importance of Ming loyalism, however uncomfortably.

Constructing a Literati Genre: Ming Imitations

ANTI-*LI-HSÜEH* CURRENTS IN MING IMITATIONS

Scholars have repeatedly pointed out the long-term dominance of Ch'eng-Chu "Neo-Confucianism" (*Li-hsüeh* or *Tao-hsüeh*) in Ming-Ch'ing intellectual life, guided, as Benjamin Elman describes it, by a powerful "educational gyroscope" that centered on the civil service examinations. From about 1400 to 1900, the examination system reinforced Neo-Confucian orthodoxy, binding together the imperial state and gentry society.[5] Yet, one and a half centuries into the spin of this "educational gyroscope," and right in its center, opposition arose to the Ch'eng-Chu *Li-hsüeh* orthodoxy—not simply in sporadic voices, but in a well-wrought discourse implanted in a literary genre. In 1551, Wen Cheng-ming wrote a preface to Ho Liang-chün's *Forest of Accounts*, the earliest Ming imitation, in which he launched a vigorous and sharply pointed criticism of Sung *Li-hsüeh* scholarship:

> [*Ho's Forest*] . . . surely contains the ultimate principle [*chih-li*] in a literary and scholastic work, hence it is the source of righteousness. Some people may take it as fragmented, trivial, and not well organized; or they may consider it hilarious, biased, and only promoting flowery words while contributing nothing to the interpretation of the Way [*Tao*], virtue [*te*], human nature [*hsing*], and Heaven's mandate [*ming*]. Alas! Since principles of all things [*shih-li*] have no limit, how can learning ever have an end? Without being clear about principles, one may not be able to probe human nature and Heaven's mandate, but if words cannot fully convey [the meaning], by what means can the *Tao* reveal itself? Hence, to acquire broad learning and detailed understanding, one should first study the Sage's teachings, and by constituting one's authentic self [*ch'eng*] in refined words, one establishes the foundation for accumulating virtue.
>
> Limited by the learning of *hsing* and *ming*, late Sung scholars sat all day in deep, inward contemplation, believing this rigid lifestyle would suffice to cultivate the true nature and transform their dispositions. Yet their legacy left us a lot to question. They may have been beguiled by the teachings of their mentors, yet they themselves should also be faulted for simplifying the learning, making it shallow and self-contrived. They borrowed nice words to cover up their ignorance and chose to face the wall [to contemplate in isolation] without realizing that they had already fallen into vulgarity. Alas! The phrase "losing one's intent on trifles" [*wan-wu sang-chih*] has become their followers' fatal illness. Gentlemen often grieve over this.[6]

Here, Wen appropriates the accusation of *wan-wu sang-chih* (lit. losing [one's] moral intent or energy through indulgence in [trifling] things) from the *Li-hsüeh* scholars themselves. The Sung *Li-hsüeh* master, Ch'eng Hao (1032–1085), for instance, took good memory and a preoccupation with "things" to be a waste of one's moral energy.[7] He even considered "compiling a book on the good conduct of ancient people"—the kind of work traditionally categorized as belonging to the *Shih-shuo* genre—as a trifling thing to do.[8] Chu Hsi defended Ch'eng Hao's position, arguing that a focus on "trifles" would distract one from concentrating on principle (*li*).[9] And Ch'eng Hao's brother, Ch'eng I, went so far as to assert that "writing literary pieces also amounts to indulgence in trifles." Why? Because: "While writing a literary piece, one has to concentrate, or the work cannot be well crafted. But, if concentration on writing limits a scholar's *chih* [moral intent] to this [the act of writing], then how can one cultivate one's *chih* to be as great as Heaven and Earth?"[10]

In countering the charge of *wan-wu sang-chih*, Wen argues that *Ho's Forest* actually conveys the *Tao* more profoundly than the writings of *Li-hsüeh* scholars because it is not limited by the narrow parameters of Ch'eng-Chu orthodoxy.[11] Inspired by Su Shih's capacious vision, Wen maintains that the comprehension of the *Tao* requires broad and close study of all things *(po-hsüeh)*, and the transmission of the *Tao* needs refined words to elaborate the principles of things *(shih-li)*. Seen in this light, it is *Li-hsüeh* scholarship that "loses intent on trifles," not creative individuals like Ho Liang-chün. From Wen Cheng-ming's standpoint, the problem with Ch'eng-Chu followers is that their "inward" emphasis blinds them to the real *Tao* contained in the vital, colorful world.

In his preface, Wen defends not only his protégé's work but also the *Shih-shuo* genre as a whole. The significance of the *Shih-shuo*, as he sees it, lies precisely in its ability of illuminating the *Tao*, using refined words. It offers the kind of work that a scholar-literatus should engage: a combination of refined literature and solid, broad scholarship, which can serve as the "source of righteousness" and the "origin of virtue."

Wen Cheng-ming's opinions carried substantial weight, for he was then the most venerated "man of culture" *(wen-jen)* in the lower Yangtze region. Wang Shih-chen, for instance, revered him as someone "able to make the Wu area elegant, honest, and important."[12] In 1556, Wang Shih-chen compiled the *Shih-shuo hsin-yü pu* (Supplement to the *Shih-shuo hsin-yü*), culling material primarily from the *Shih-shuo hsin-yü* and adding some episodes from *Ho's Forest* in order to extend the *Shih-shuo*'s coverage to the Yüan period (1271–1368).[13] In his preface, Wang ardently praised *Shih-shuo*'s literary achievements, describing it as a highly nuanced work, written in a terse, refined style that "excited readers upon chanting its short lines, yet simultaneously drew them into lingering deep thoughts."[14] Moreover, Wang defended the *Shih-shuo* against the charge by Sung *Li-hsüeh* scholars that the "pure talk" it so amply recorded had caused the chaos of the Wei-Chin period. He argued that, if Sung scholars could not manage to resist the Mongols with *Li-hsüeh,* how could they expect Chin scholars to resist "barbarian" invaders with the pure talk?[15] Wang's *Supplement,* although adding nothing of substance to the *Shih-shuo* genre, nevertheless greatly enlarged the influence of the *Shih-shuo hsin-yü.* As Ts'ao Cheng-yung pointed out in his preface to Cheng Chung-k'uei's *Ch'ing-yen* (1617), "until the Chia-ching (1522–1566) and Lung-ch'ing (1567–1572) reigns, few scholars were aware of the *Shih-shuo hsin-yü.* They got to know it only after the publication of Wang Shih-chen's *Supplement to the Shih-shuo hsin-yü* (in 1585)."[16] As we shall see, Wang's *Supplement* also stimulated the *Shih-shuo* frenzy in Edo Japan.

One reason for Wang Shih-chen to come to this abridged project, as he explained in his preface, was his dissatisfaction with the gigantic size of *Ho's Forest,* which contained over twenty-seven hundred episodes and about a hundred thousand words—three times as many as the original work.[17] Despite Wang's call for brevity, Chiao Hung's *Chiao-shih lei-lin* (Chiao's taxonomic forest), completed in 1585 and published in 1587, covered a longer time period, from antiquity to Yüan, and was about the same size as, if not bigger than, *Ho's Forest.* Whereas all previous *Shih-shuo t'i* works had commenced with a chapter on "*Te* Conduct" or a related category, Chiao started his book with the chapter on "Pien-tsuan" (Editing and compiling), extolling scholarly erudition in compiling encyclopedic works. He also included fourteen new categories of rich, exquisite descriptions of things, ranging from garments to writing utensils (see below).

In a preface to this work, Yao Ju-shao praised *Chiao's Taxonomic Forest* as "erudite [*po*] and beautiful [*mei*]" and explained why these two features were valuable:

> One may ask: Chiao's goal in life is to obtain the *Tao,* yet this work attracts people with erudition. What is his intention? Alas, trying to tell the real *Tao,* one's mind will initially become perplexed. He has problems telling people what *Tao* is, and people have problems understanding him. The *Tao* saturated in refined writings is what people are familiar with and willing to pursue everyday. But, if no one exposes it [to people], how much good can it do? Ch'ü Po-yü advised Yen Ho upon his appointment as the tutor to the crown prince of Wei: "In your [actions

of the] body it is best to follow along with him, and in your mind it is best to harmonize with him. If he wants to be a child, be a child with him. If he wants to follow erratic ways, follow erratic ways with him. If he wants to be reckless, be reckless with him. Only wish that [your actions and mind] can meet his features in seamless coherence." In this way, the instructor is not overworked and the disciple finds an easy access [to the *Tao*]. Isn't this the way of a good educator?[18]

Following Su Shih and Wen Cheng-ming's approach, Yao's preface reiterates the point that the *Tao* is most clearly revealed in people's daily lives and in everyday objects. But he also raised a question: How can words be refined to depict the *Tao*, which actually goes beyond any verbal description? Quoting the *Chuang-tzu* idea allegorically,[19] Yao suggests that the answer is to harmonize words with the natural status of things. To achieve this harmony requires both erudition and exquisite writings; hence *po* and *mei* as the new criteria for the *Shih-shuo t'i*.

The late Ming radical scholar and literary critic, Li Chih, played a prominent role in promoting the *Shih-shuo* genre. Soon after the publication of Wang Shih-chen's *Supplement to the Shih-shuo* in 1585, Li Chih contributed a commentary to the edition. Then, based on this commentary, he published in 1588 his own *Shih-shuo t'i* work, *Ch'u-t'an chi* (Collection on the pond) by extracting episodes from the *Shih-shuo hsin-yü* and the *Taxonomic Forest* of his close friend, Chiao Hung. In compiling this work, Li Chih assigned himself the task of *ch'uan-shen,* transmitting the [Wei-Chin] spirit, and believed that *shen* could be retrieved through depicting people's relationships.[20] For this purpose, he edited the *Collection on the Pond* into five categories, namely, *Fu-fu* (Husband and wife), *Fu-tzu* (Father and son), *Hsiung-ti* (Brothers), *Shih-yu* (Mentor and friend), and *Chün-ch'en* (Ruler and subject) and further divided these five categories into ninety-nine types of human character, relationship, behavior, and knowledge.[21] Li Chih adopted the five relations from *Chiao's Taxonomic Forest*, which had been inspired by the conventional "three bonds and six rules." Significantly, however, Li turned the original sequence upside down, putting the husband and wife first and ruler and subject last. Li Chih justified this arrangement in his introduction to Category One:

Husband and wife are the beginning of people. With husband and wife, we then have father and son; with father and son, we then have brothers; and with brothers, we then have hierarchies. As long as the relationship between husband and wife is right, then none of the myriad things can go wrong. . . . Fundamentally, Heaven and Earth are [like] husband and wife; hence Heaven and Earth give rise to the myriad things. Therefore, it is clear that all under Heaven are born of Two, not One. Yet [someone] says that "One gives rise to Two, principle [*li*] gives rise to material force [*ch'i*], and the Great Ultimate [*t'ai-chi*] gives rise to the Two Modes [*yin* and *yang*] [*liang-i*]."[22] Isn't he confused? What initiates a person's life is only the *yin* and the *yang*, the life essence of man and woman. Originally, there were no such things as One and the principle, much less the Great Ultimate![23]

The quote "One gives rise to Two, the principle gives rise to material force, and the Great Ultimate gives rise to the Two Modes" evidently paraphrases a basic Sung Neo-Confucian idea—its interpretation of the origin of things.[24] By challenging it on the outset, Li Chih turns his *Shih-shuo* imitation into an anti-*Li-hsüeh* discourse. His contention is that the "natural" relationship between husband and wife is more important than the moral-political obligations stressed by the Ch'eng-Chu school. Moreover, he emphasizes the pivotal role of women in marriage, repeatedly praising talented and courageous women as "real men" or "better than men,"[25] and hence defying *Li-hsüeh* conventions and hierarchies. For Li Chih, the transmission of the Wei-Chin spirit required a defiant attitude.[26]

Since Li was one of the most influential late Ming thinkers, his writings, like those of Wang Shih-chen, fed the fires of passion for the *Shih-shuo hsin-yü*. His *Collection on the Pond* was highly popular in the late Ming, as the *Ssu-k'u* compilers later admitted,[27] and it is no accident that in the seventy years or so after his death in 1602, there were at least fifteen imitations of the *Shih-shuo*. Many of them—including Li Shao-wen's *Imperial Ming Shih-shuo hsin-yü* (1610), Cheng Chung-k'uei's *Pure Talk* (1615), Liang Wei-shu's *Jade Sword Accounts* (1654), and Wu Su-kung's *Ming Forest of Accounts* (1662)—celebrated Li Chih's legacy.[28]

Why did so many Ming *Shih-shuo* imitators and their proponents revel in iconoclasm and valorize "broad knowledge" and "refined words"? One

likely explanation is their disillusion with the Ming civil service examination system, which was based on the rigid orthodoxy of Ch'eng-Chu *Li-
hsüeh*. As Chaoying Fang suggests, Ho Liang-chün's motive for writing his
Shih-shuo imitation may well have been a desire to prove his attainment
in scholarship and literary proficiency after failing the civil examinations.[29] Fang's observation probably applies to most of the eighteen other
Ming and Ch'ing *Shih-shuo t'i* authors. Among them, only four obtained
the *chin-shih* degree (Wang Shih-chen, Chiao Hung, Li Ch'ing, and Wang
Wan), and two achieved *chü-jen* status (Li Chih and Liang Wei-shu). And
even the most celebrated degree holder of the lot, Chiao Hung, used the
Shih-shuo genre to express the long-standing frustration he felt in 1585—
four years before finally becoming the "Number One Scholar in the empire." The following episode from the beginning of *Chiao's Taxonomic Forest* is revealing: "Feng Chih of the Southern T'ang (937–975) said: 'I have
participated in civil service examinations for thirty years but haven't
achieved anything.' . . . So he returned home and built himself a studio
named 'Selecting Books.' There he compiled a work by culling the essence
from the books accumulated by nine generations of his family, altogether
208,120 *chüan*, in over 6,900 volumes."[30] We may surmise that here Chiao
Hung had his own personal experience firmly in mind, having embarked
on a similar project in 1580 after more than two decades of taking the civil
examinations without substantial success.[31]

DEFINING LITERATI IN MING TERMS

Of course, the *Shih-shuo t'i* was not simply a vehicle for expression of
frustration and dissent. It was also a way for Ming literati, who called themselves mainly *wen-shih* (gentlemen of culture) or *wen-jen* (men of culture),[32] to show their affinity with broad-ranging scholars from past eras.
Since the Wei-Chin period, the concept of literati accomplishment had
been expanded from literature and scholarship to pursuits such as painting, calligraphy, music, dancing, chanting poetry, chess, archery, medicine,
mathematics, and physiognomy. Ch'en Shou's *History of the Three Kingdoms,* along with P'ei Sung-chih's commentary, testifies to the importance

of these skills in the conceptualization of literati. For example, Ch'en praised Emperor Wen-ti of the Wei, Ts'ao P'i (r. 220–226): "He received the heavenly gifts of literary elegance and acumen. He had broad knowledge and a powerful memory and embraced both talents and skills."[33] P'ei's commentary quotes Ts'ao P'i's "Autobiography" (*Tzu-hsü*) as evidence of his extraordinary skills in archery, swordsmanship, and chess, in addition to his literary talent.[34] P'ei also recounts how Ts'ao Chih, the most celebrated Wei literatus, displayed to Han-tan Ch'un his extensive knowledge of literature, philosophy, military affairs, and politics, as well as his skills in dancing, chanting, fencing, and even juggling.

Su Shih exemplified this sort of broad-ranging talent in the Sung period. Small wonder, then, that Ho Liang-chün acclaimed him the "champion of literati for one hundred generations,"[35] providing his appreciative Ming dynasty readers with a full account of Su Shih's scholastic, literary, and artistic accomplishments.[36] With his meticulously crafted imitation of the *Shih-shuo*, Ho Liang-chün systematically posited the literati's superiority over all other members of the gentry class, expressing his long-term concern with the true value of intellectual life and, at the same time, lodging his protest against the hostile intellectual environment created by the Ming civil examination system.

Published in 1551, *Ho's Forest* was the first and the best written of all extant Ming imitations. What especially sets this work apart from other *Shih-shuo* imitations is the author's effort to update Wei-Chin concepts in Ming terms. Thus he painstakingly built up a new literati value system. The following episode from *Ho's Forest* gives us a starting point for examining Ho Liang-chün's reconceptualization of the "literati" and his relocation of their social position. The T'ang literatus, Ho Chih-chang, was assigned to be vice minister of the Board of Ritual and chosen to be a scholar of the Chi-hsien Academy (the Academy of the Assembled Worthies) on the same day. A gentleman asked the then prime minister and head of the Academy, Chang Yüeh: "Which position is more admirable, the vice minister or the Chi-hsien scholar?" Chang replied: "Since the beginning of our imperial dynasty, the vice minister has been a radiant position for gentlemen. Only those who have both outstanding reputation and substance can obtain this job. But it is, in the end, a listed official rank that has never been appreciated by the worthy people in the past. The [Chi-hsien] scholars embrace the *Tao* of the previous sage-kings and set up the right track and role models for the gentry. Only those who possess Yang [Hsiung]'s and Pan [Ku]'s skills of refining words and [Tzu] Yu's and [Tzu] Hsia's literary and scholastic talents may assume this position without feeling embarrassed. Of the two admirable positions, this is surely the better one."[37]

Using Chang Yüeh as his mouthpiece, and singling out Confucius' talented disciples, Tzu Yu and Tzu Hsia, and the two Han worthies, Yang Hsiung and Pan Ku, Ho Liang-chün seeks to set a literary standard for meaningful achievement, distinguishing between literati and mere "scholars" (*ju-shih*), men of learning but not necessarily of literary skill.[38] This explains why Su Shih and even Su's political opponent, Wang An-shih (1021–1086), receive so much attention in *Ho's Forest*, and why Sung *Li-hsüeh* scholars get such short shrift. Indeed, Ho omits Chu Hsi from his *Forest* altogether and denigrates Cheng I as nothing more than a target under the category "Contempt and Insults." One episode berates Ch'eng I for making too much of a trivial event when he admonishes the child emperor not to "destroy life," merely because the young ruler picks a willow branch. And in two other episodes, Su Shih mocks Ch'eng I for his absurd interpretation of Confucian rituals.[39] Ho defends Su Shih's harsh critique, remarking that Ch'eng I's rigid and pedantic scholarship would mislead people in the direction of "affectation and sluggishness."[40]

Worrying that the narrow *Li-hsüeh* orthodoxy would hinder scholars from obtaining broad knowledge, Ho returns to Confucius for inspiration. Wen Cheng-ming corroborates Ho, saying in his preface: "To acquire broad learning and detailed understanding, one should first study the Sage's teachings." Both men may have been under the influence of the mid-Ming literary trend of "returning to antiquity" (*fu-ku*),[41] but their hostility to the Ming examination system is also evident.[42] As Ho satirically points out, this system, fettered by Ch'eng-Chu orthodoxy, might not even be able to recognize the merit of a great scholar such as Confucius himself: "If Confucius were born today, unless he stuck to the [Ch'eng-Chu] interpretation of the Confucian classics and passed the civil service examinations, he could not be treated equally with even the lowest-ranking gentlemen."[43]

For the most part, Ho quotes Confucius in defining each of his thirty-eight categories. When no Confucian quotations are available, he turns to other famous literati: Chuang-tzu ("Living in Reclusion," "Ingenious Art"), Ch'ü Yüan ("Squareness and Correctness"), Ssu-ma Ch'ien ("Government Affairs," "Taunting and Teasing"), and even the *Shih-shuo* heroes Ho Yen ("Recognition and Judgment"), Liu T'an ("Government Affairs") and Sun Ch'o ("Reclusion and Disengagement").

Of all the thirty-eight categories in *Ho's Forest*, Ho clearly considers "Speech and Conversation" *(Yen-yü)* as the pivot.[44] The literati's superiority, he believes, is rooted in their skill with language—primarily spoken words. As Ho argues in his definition of this category: "How can we do without spoken words? Resolving problems, dissolving conflicts, answering questions, clearing away slanders, expressing sincerity, telling intentions, finding comprise among different opinions, making decisions about state affairs . . . [all rely upon speech]. How can we do without spoken words?"[45] To fulfill these discursive engagements, one needs to weave words, spoken or written, into systems of significance—an extremely difficult task that requires both scholastic and literary training. Ho reasons in his definition of "Literature and Scholarship" *(Wen-hsüeh)*: "Literature and the [grand] meaning [contained in it] are all merits created by Heaven and Earth. For those who have not obtained the essence of Heaven and Earth, how can they have a share of these merits? . . . We see them [literati] set up the meaning and compose the literary article. They make principles the trunk and words the branches, both in luxuriant growth. If [a literary composition] is not rooted in the [grand] meaning, how can it thrive? Branches and leaves may [sometimes] grow excessively abundant, but how can one do without them?"[46]

In order to make sense out of words, literature and scholarship have to work together, inasmuch as the literary composition *(wen)* and the (grand) meaning *(i)* are originally born from and bound together by Heaven and Earth. Scholastic research exposes the meaning while literary composition presents this meaning to the audience. Both are thus indispensable. Yet it was so difficult to master both subjects that "among the seventy-two Confucius' disciples who were skilled in the six arts, only two were famous for literature and scholarship."[47] This alone indicates the rarity of literati.[48]

According to Ho, literati are truly in a class by themselves, with special talents and special powers. Naturally, then, they behave in very different ways. Ho tells us: "Confucius judged gentlemen by four categories, with 'Te conduct' listed first. Thus we say, rather than convey [our intent] by empty words, we should realize it in our behavior. . . . Yet things change constantly, so responses vary accordingly. Gentlemen have numerous kinds of behavior. How can we judge them all by the same standard? The uninhibited and the rigid each go different ways; both can cultivate themselves into sagehood. The tough and the tender each carry different dispositions; as long as they persist, they will eventually reach their goals. For all kinds of considerations there is only one principle: [to act] according to *te*."[49]

Here we see that Ho's interpretation of *te* follows the *Shih-shuo* idea—that it is the potency to persist (*k'o*) in doing what one believes to be right under a given set of circumstances. This way one makes one's own rules of behavior without having to submit to anyone else's. Ho makes the case for such freedom in defining the category "Ch'iao-i" (Ingenious art):

> I read a story from the *Chuang Tzu* as follows: Lord Yüan of Sung wanted to have some pictures painted. A painter-clerk arrived late, sauntering in without the slightest haste. When he received his drawing panel, he did not stand attending at the court, but instead went straight to his own quarters. There he took off his clothes, stretched out his legs, and was sitting there naked. "Very good," said the ruler. "This is a true artist!"
>
> Later critics praised Wang Wei's paintings as being created with intellectual qualities endowed by Heaven. Alas! Only when one forgets about [the rules of] the human world can one be perfected by Heaven. Is it not that [Wang] Wei's art already entered the realm of the *Tao*? For those who only know how to follow rules without breaking them, they are mere craftsmen serving in a menial capacity and not worthy of discussing art with.[50]

In order to appreciate Ho's point more fully we should conjoin it with another episode Ho includes in "Blameworthiness and Remorse." This story tells us that one day, while T'ang T'ai-tsung was enjoying a banquet with courtiers in the imperial garden, he summoned the famous literatus-official Yen Li-pen to paint rare birds on the spot: "Yen Li-pen was then already the director of the Bureau of Honors, yet he had to prostrate himself by the left side of the pond, grinding colors and licking brushes. Looking out at the emperor's guests, he felt ashamed and embarrassed, and sweated profusely. After he went home, he cautioned his son, saying: 'Since I was young I studied hard and was lucky to have passed the civil examinations. With respect to composing poems, I can measure up to any of those [courtiers at the banquet]. But because the emperor knows me only by my painting, I have to serve in this menial capacity. I could not feel more insulted. You should learn my lesson and never practice this skill.'"[51]

Both tales involve conflict between the court and literati values. The court value system gives the ruler the privilege of making decisions as to where, when, and how to use his subject's intellectual talents. The subject should submit himself to the ruler's demands and the court's rules, regardless of his own feelings. Serving in this kind of menial capacity destroys any creative mood and subverts intellectual pride, reducing the artist to a mere craftsman.

Although the court rules have wounded Yen Li-pen's pride, Ho has little sympathy for him. Depicting Yen "grinding colors and licking brushes," Ho mimics the *Chuang Tzu* phrase, "licking brushes and mixing ink," which satirizes artists who are eager to please the ruler. Ho obviously prefers the style of the "true artist." To create real art, Ho argues, the artist should be able to walk out of the court and enter into his own quarters, where he can free himself from any bondage, visible (such as clothing) or invisible (such as court rules). His naked body identifies him with Nature, facilitating intimate contact with Heaven and Earth. Only when the artist completely forgets about the rules of the human world can he receive inspiration from Heaven and enter the realm of the *Tao*. To "embody the *Tao* in art" was thus the highest aesthetic ideal in the Ming, exemplified particularly by Wen Cheng-ming's literary and artistic accomplishments.[52]

This sort of free-spiritedness naturally invited criticism from the more conventional members of the Ming and early Ch'ing gentry—hence the charge of seeking "aesthetic gratification at the expense of practical affairs." But, were Ming aesthetes really so much above practical affairs, and what did "practical affairs" mean to them anyway? *Ho's Forest* provides an illuminating perspective on the relationship between Ming literati values and Ming material culture.

THINGS AS THE EXTENDED SELF

As we have seen, narrowly focused *Li-hsüeh* scholars relentlessly accused the Sung-Ming literati of squandering their moral energy on trifles (*wan-wu sang-chih*). But from the perspective of Ho Liang-chün and his circle, the *Tao* was in the details. In response to *Li-hsüeh* scholars, Ho increased two new categories in his *Forest*. The chapter "Po-shih" (Broad knowledge) celebrates literati's ability to recognize exotic things—strange animals, rare antiques, enigmatic poetic allusions, and so forth. The chapter "Yen-chih" (Telling the intent) defines *chih* (intent, will, ambition, or moral energy) in such a way as to link the Ming preoccupation with "things" to the ideas of Confucius himself.[53] Consider, for example, the following excerpt:

> At a private, leisure gathering, Confucius asked his disciples each to tell their *chih*, hence the saying "pursuing one's *chih* in retreat."[54] . . . Different [people], quiet or impatient, follow their own preferences. They should however seek from the Sage a middle ground for their confused opinions. Examining the *chih* of Confucius' disciples, [we find] Yu courageous and Tz'u articulate. They either cared for the people and the state or devoted themselves to ritual and musical transformation; either way, they might establish merits and pass down their names in [written] histories. Yet Confucius only said: "Oh [Yen] Hui, if you have money, I'll be your steward," and sighed agreement with Tseng Tien. Why? Because this [Confucius' opinion] shows, after all, there is difference between the high and low, and the gain and loss, of one's *chih*.[55]

Displaying an open-minded approach, Ho acknowledges that each individual may suit himself or herself with a specific *chih*, be it a moral-political ambition or an aesthetic lifestyle. This point seems clear enough.

But his stress on the cases of Yen Hui and Tseng Tien requires further elaboration.

The Yen Hui allusion refers to a conversation between Confucius and his disciples at a time of great difficulty, when the master was rejected wherever he went. According to the story, as recorded in the *Shih-chi,* whereas his other disciples offered advice that reflected "no grand *chih,"* Yen Hui presented the perfect explanation: "Master, your *Tao* is extremely great, so people under Heaven cannot accept it, though you still try to carry it on. Why should you worry about its being rejected? Its rejection only reveals you a superior man! It would be our shame if our *Tao* were not well established. If our *Tao* is already well established but cannot be accepted, then it is the ruler's shame. Why should you worry about its being rejected? Its rejection only reveals you a superior man!" Delighted, Confucius said: "Right, the son of Yen! If you have great wealth [*ts'ai*], I'll be your steward [*tsai*]!"[56]

In his commentary, Wang Su recommends reading Confucius' offer to Yen Hui as a metaphor—since Yen Hui is famously poor—an intense way "to say they share the same *chih.*"[57] In this sense, their *chih* should refer to the persistence in one's own vision of *Tao,* regardless of others' response. Yet it is at least possible that Ho had in mind a more literal reading—one that legitimated money making, despite the stigma long attached to it.[58]

An entry in the chapter entitled "Ch'iu-chih" (Pursuing the intent) from Ho's *Ssu-yu chai ts'ung-shuo* (Classified accounts from the Four Friends Studio, 1569) lends support to this view. In it, Ho applauds Fan Li's (fl. fifth cent. B.C.) *chih* for abandoning a successful political career only to become a merchant, arguing that Fan assumed this humble occupation not simply for collecting profits—since on several occasions he distributed his money among poor friends and relatives—but for showing a capacity of handling his own destiny.[59] Thus Ho Liang-chün justifies literati's financial activities as both a spiritual statement for intellectual freedom and a pragmatic means for living in retirement.

In the chapter "Yen-chih" in *Ho's Forest,* Ho records many accounts of literati's financial self-sufficiency.[60] For instance, Wang Hsi-chih, after retirement, wrote to a friend:

I've just come back from the East. The mulberry and fruit trees I had planted and grafted have now grown into full luxuriance. I take excursions among them with my sons and my grandchildren. If I see a ripe fruit, I share it among my children and then lean back to appreciate their happiness. . . . Soon I shall roam eastward with An-shih [Hsieh An, then also living in retirement], to travel among mountains and seas, and to inspect our farmlands, [making sure we have enough] to nourish our idle life. After taking care of our daily needs, I would like, now and then, to gather happily with my family and friends. We may not be able to compose poems, but we each can hold a cup of wine and talk about the crops in the fields. That may give us something to be happy about [lit. to clasp our hands for]. . . . Such is the sole purpose [chih-yüan] of my old age![61]

Wang, the most celebrated calligrapher of all time and hence a man accustomed to leisurely refinement, takes pleasure in being able to manage the family finances. The lifestyle he has chosen indicates a pragmatic attitude toward earning a living in retirement, when a government salary is no longer available to him.

The Tseng Tien allusion conveys a somewhat different message. In this story, as recorded in the *Analects,* Confucius turns to Tseng Tien after listening to three of his other disciples expressing their political ambitions *(chih)* and asks about Tseng's *chih.* Tseng responds:

"In late spring, after the spring clothes have been newly made, I should like, together with five or six adults and six or seven boys, to go bathing in the River Yi and enjoy the breeze on the Rain Altar, and then to go home chanting poetry."
The master sighed and said, "I am all in favour of Tien."[62]

Here, Tseng Tien emphasizes the intellectual and aesthetic side of a literati life: poetry, music, leisurely outings, literary gatherings, and so forth.

Taken together, the Yen Hui and Tseng Tien allusions point to a *chih,* sanctioned by the Sage himself, that involves political detachment, economical self-sufficiency, and intellectual spiritual satisfaction. Ho describes this sort of lifestyle in several essays in the "Yen-chih" chapter, such as the following one by Hsiao Ta-huan (fl. mid-sixth cent.):

I built a small cottage among the woods and surrounded it with walls in a secluded place. Nearby I view smoke and mist; faraway I watch winds

and clouds. . . . An orchard spreads behind the house, so that by opening the window I can enjoy flowers; a vegetable garden extends in front
of the door, so that by sitting under the eaves I may inspect the irriga-
tion. Two *ch'ing* of paddy field provide meals; ten *mu* of mulberry trees
and hemp supply clothing.[63] Three or five female servants weave; four
or so male servants farm. Making cheese and herding sheep, in accordance with P'an Yüeh's [247–300] intent;[64] feeding chickens and plant-
ing millet, in response to old man Chuang-tzu's words. . . . A friend comes
from afar, and we comment on past and present; farmers pass by, we exchange farming skills. All this satisfies me, and I am overwhelmed with
happiness.[65]

In this alluring essay, the author builds pragmatic and intellectual elements
into each other, not only in his life but also in his literary structure. In reality, the cottage and the garden extend into the wilderness and the walls
bring nature into the household. In the text, allusions make words descriptive of the visible scenery and also expressive of invisible ideas. Thus,
rising smoke from the house chimney and diffusing mist in the valley refer to the satisfying spiritual atmosphere enjoyed by Hsiao, as well as the
actual scenery. Similarly, whirling winds and clouds (*feng-yün*) signal not
only the changeable weather but also a hostile political environment that
is now, fortunately, far away from him.[66] Within this open yet private space,
he combines home management with scholastic learning and poetic creation, discussing history with friends and farming skills with neighbors with
equal ease and pleasure.

When sacrifices have to be made, physical comfort surrenders to spiritual satisfaction. Here is an illuminating example: "Yang Pao, though poor,
loved calligraphy, paintings, and rare antiques, and he filled his bags with
collections [of these items]. He could only afford to provide rough clothes
and coarse food for his several female attendants, but they performed wonderful singing and dancing anyhow. Lord Ou-yang [Hsiu] [1007–1072] once
wrote him a poem with the line, 'sitting on a three-legged chair, conducting music,' which is an authentic portrayal [of Yang Pao's life]."[67] The point
is not, of course, that Yang Pao is mean to his attendants—he himself only
gets to sit on a broken chair. Rather, it is that the family, though not well-
to-do, manages to maintain a rich intellectual life, with wonderful artistic

collections and beautiful music. More important, Yang Pao makes sure to share his spiritual enjoyment with close friends, including Ou-yang Hsiu, the leading literatus of his time. Although Ou-yang's poem taunts Yang good-naturedly, it is also dotted with amusement and appreciation.

The Yang Pao episode also reveals how collecting things was an essential component of literati life in the eyes of Ho Liang-chün. About one-fifth of the 164 episodes that Ho collected in "Yen-chih" are devoted to this theme. What made "things" so important to literati, and how were they related? Before answering these questions, we need to examine what kinds of things attracted the literati's attention. Here is a good example: "Lord Ou-yang [Hsiu] said: 'I have collected one thousand [i-ch'ien] chüan of ancient model pieces of calligraphy,[68] ten thousand [i-wan] chüan of books, one [i-chang] zither, one set [i-chü] of chess, and I often serve myself one jar [i-hu] of wine, with my own person getting old among all these things. These are my six 'ones' [liu-i].' Thus he called himself 'Six-One Retired Scholar' (Liu-i chü-shih). He wrote an autobiography under this title and had it inscribed on a stone tablet."[69]

All of the items on Ou-yang's list were popular with literati collectors. So were other "things," including antiques, paintings, writing utensils, and natural items such as mountains, rivers, rocks, plants, and animals—all related to literati's lifestyle.[70] Sometimes connoisseurs gave up basic living supplies in order to acquire such things. One gentleman left his family starving for a decade while he pursued a political career at the capital; yet in the end, all he brought home was an ink stick made by the famous Southern T'ang artisan Li T'ing-kuei, a bamboo painting by the Sung literatus-artist Wen T'ung, and a pile of historical draft by Ou-yang Hsiu. Another gentleman was caught in a tempest while boating home and lost all his belongings, except for a precious copy of Wang Hsi-chih's calligraphy, which he managed to rescue at the risk of his own life. He then inscribed the following words on the scroll: "I am willing to sacrifice my life to protect this priceless treasure."[71]

Among the most collectible things for the literati were their own kind, for their admirable talents, cultural refinement, and entrancing personalities. Thus literati collected literati as friends, guests, and especially connoisseurs. K'ung Jung (153–208) "loved talented gentlemen and always felt he had not gathered enough of them." Po Chü-i (772–846) collected and classified his peers into "empty-door friends" *(k'ung-men yu)*, "mountains and streams friends" *(shan-shui yu)*, "poetry friends" *(shih-yu)*, and "wine friends" *(chiu-yu)* and enjoyed life with them accordingly. If literati could afford it, they entertained friends with delicate food and wine in addition to intellectual activities. If they were relatively poor, they lured guests with rare books and delightful stories, thus "detaining them all day even under protest." On occasions when they could not find satisfactory companions in the world of the living, they searched elsewhere. Ho tells us, for example, of literati who would encircle a dead gentleman's grave with their gardens, worshipping him with flowers and drinking with him daily. He also recounts stories of scholars who sought companionship with beloved role models from history. Chao Ch'i (d. 201) painted the portraits of four great historical heroes and then added his own as the leading figure of this handsome collection,[72] and Ou-yang Hsiu simply collected himself.

The following episode from *Ho's Forest* underscores the importance of literati connoisseurship, focusing on the eccentric late Yüan artist Ni Tsan (1301–1374):

> Ni Tsan's home had a "Pure Mystery Pavilion" and a "Cloudy Forest Hall." The "Pure Mystery" was especially well constructed. Ni planted emerald *wu-t'ung* trees in front of the building and surrounded it with strangely shaped rocks. Inside he stacked ancient calligraphy and famous paintings. Guests with no taste would not be allowed. Once a foreigner came to pay tribute [to the throne] and stopped at Wu-hsi [where Ni lived] en route. Having heard about Ni, he wished to meet with him, bearing one hundred *chin* of aloes as a present.[73] Ni sent out word that he had just left for a drink of spring water at the Hui Hill. Next day, the foreigner came again, and again Ni excused himself to go out viewing plum blossoms. Unable to see Ni, the foreigner lingered around the house. Then Ni secretly ordered the "Cloudy Forest" opened and let him in. In the east wing of the hall were ancient jade ornaments, and in the west wing were antique bronzes. Amazed, the foreigner asked the butler: "I heard of another building named the Pure Mystery Pavilion. May I take a look at it?" The butler said: "Not everyone is allowed. Besides, my master is not home, so I have no permission to take you in." The foreigner bowed several times to the pavilion and then left.[74]

The "Pure Mystery Pavilion" displays a first-rate gallery, where Ni Tsan collects the best architecture, gardening, and art, and matches them with equally elegant visitors. A foreigner comes, and his desire to see Ni, fused with his fragrant gift, signals a potential guest. But Ni needs to verify his qualifications. With a meticulously designed plan and himself as the bait, he seduces the foreigner into revealing his taste. Ni's mysterious absence, with exquisite excuses such as "drinking spring" and "visiting plum blossoms," only intensifies the foreigner's desire to see him, and, by virtue of his persistence, the foreigner proves his good taste, thereby gaining access to the "Cloudy Forest." Although he gets to see neither Ni nor the "Pure Mystery Pavilion," he is acquainted with Ni's eccentric personality and artistic sensitivity; thus his farewell salute to the "Pure Mystery" is actually paid to its "absent" owner.

Undoubtedly Ni was there all along, behind the scene, enjoying the show he had so elaborately staged. He refused, however, to grant his foreign "guest" access to the "Pure Mystery Pavilion," possibly because his taste did not reach that high level. Clearly, Ni had established a hierarchy of connoisseurship, with himself—as both artist and object—at the apex. And although Ni was a collector of people, so to speak, only Nature deserved his artistic attention. "Nobody in this world," he once wrote, "is worthy of my brush."[75]

The contrast between Ming literati conceptions of the value of "things" and Sung Neo-Confucian views can be illustrated by two anecdotes, each involving an inkstone. The first is from the *Chu-tzu yü-lei* (Classified quotations of Master Chu Hsi) and the other is from the "Yen-chih" chapter, *Ho's Forest*:

> Master Shang-ts'ai (Hsieh Liang-tso) used to own a great number of wonderful antiques. [But] in order to concentrate on learning, he gave up all of them. Later he even gave a good inkstone to somebody else.[76]
>
> Hu Tan made an inkstone, several square feet in size, and inscribed one side with the words: "Hu Tan of the Sung made this inkstone of the Han and named it Spring and Autumn." He left instructions to bury it with him after his death.[77]

Hsieh Liang-tso was one of Ch'eng Hao's loyal disciples—so devoted, in fact, that he gave up everything his mentor had labeled *wan-wu*—broad knowledge, literary writing, and rare antiques. He also warned later scholars against indulgence in trifles.[78] Chu Hsi highlights the sacrifice of Hsieh's inkstone precisely because this object symbolizes self-indulgent literary activity. Hu Tan, by contrast, not only makes an inkstone but also keeps it beyond death. The achronological inscription on the stone might be self-mockery (indicating that he was too poor to own an antique inkstone), a self-boast (that he was capable of making a treasure), or an expression of his ambition (*chih*)—his intention to compile a historical writing, the *Han Spring and Autumn Annals*. In any case, both the inscription and the disposition of the inkstone reflect his wholehearted embrace of literati values.

Ming *Shih-shuo* imitations often depict "things" in this symbolic fashion, presenting them as the emblems of literati intellectual capability, moral conscience, and aesthetic taste, as well as the utensils for creating such emblems.[79] Such episodes effectively illustrate the newly minted values of the literati—their craving for broad knowledge, their efforts to pass on this knowledge with literary and artistic creations, and their desire for a free and beautiful lifestyle separated from the mainstream value system. This separation is exemplified in the following episode from *Ho's Forest*:

> Lu Ch'i and Feng Sheng ran into each other on the street, each carrying a bag. Lu Ch'i opened Feng Sheng's bag and found only an ink stick, so he laughed out loud. Feng Sheng solemnly responded: "[The ink stick is made of] smoke from the Heaven Summit mixed with the brain of needlefish. The Master of the Golden Stream [referring to himself] obtained it and uses it to copy an ancient version of [Ch'ü Yüan's] 'Encountering Sorrow.' Compared with your carrying three hundred silk-veined name cards and enslaving yourself to fame and profit, which is better?" Feng Sheng then searched Lu Ch'i's bag and indeed found three hundred name cards in it.[80]

The confrontation between the ink stick and the name card illustrates the conflict between two value systems. The ink stick is linked to scholarship, literature, art, and all other intellectual achievements; the name card joins fame, profit, and social connections. The ink stick is made of pine smoke and fish brain, essences of Nature; name cards are composed of silk-veined paper, an artificial material. The recluse living by the Golden Stream (Chin-hsi Tzu) plans to use the ink to copy an ancient version of "Encountering Sorrow" and thus continue a long-standing tradition of literary refinement and scholarship; the "slave of fame and profit" (*ming-li nu*) will carry hundreds of name cards and search for official positions around the capital. In each case, the "thing" describes the man.

In Ming *Shih-shuo* imitations, the relationship between literati and things is one of mutual definition and refinement. Literati infuse their intrinsic and intangible qualities into things through creating, using, and/or appreciating them—hence things become their extended selves. At the same time, things adorn literati with their external and material qualities acquired from natural endowment and/or human embellishment. In his *Imperial Ming Shih-shuo*, Li Shao-wen details this process through the mouthpiece of the late Ming artist Ch'en Chi-ju (1558–1639):

> Incense makes one secluded; wine makes one remote; rock makes one outstanding; zither makes one silent; tea makes one fresh; bamboo makes one cold; the moon makes one lonely; chess makes one idle; a vine staff makes one lofty; water makes one empty; a cloud makes one unrestrained; a sword makes one melancholy; a rush mat makes one meditative; a beauty makes one tender; a monk makes one detached; flowers make one lyrical; and bronzes and stone steles make one ancient.[81]

This piece of prose offers a typical literati reading of things. Its litany—including antiques, utensils, drinks, natural objects, and people—accords with the fourteen categories listed in *Chiao's Taxonomic Forest*, epitomizing the Ming literati's favorite possessions.[82] Every word has been carefully chosen to link the quality of the thing to the sensibility of the person. Therefore, the scent of incense, often arising during zither playing, sutra chanting, or poetry composing, at once awakens one to and mesmerizes one into the memory of such reclusive moments. The smell of wine, redolent with psychological solace and poetic excitement, distances one from reality with its power of intoxication. The moon, which once shone over one's happy gatherings with loved ones, becomes a reminder of loneliness. The water, a symbol of Taoist change and Buddhist emptiness, casts one adrift into the eternal void. The cloud, which wanders aimlessly in so many poems, now draws one's eyes to unrestrained space. The sword, burning with ambition on its blade, can cause sadness as one recalls the blood spilled by that ambition. The monk, whether talkative or quiet, preaches the irrelevance of the world. In short, only broad learning, enthusiastic observation, and aesthetic judgment can bring so much meaning and beauty into things, turning them into material markers of the literati's cultural status.

To be sure, using "things" as an extension of "self" harkens back to the sambar-tail chowry sentiments that appear in the original *Shih-shuo hsin-yü* (see chapter 2). Not until the Ming, however, did any *Shih-shuo t'i* work give so much self-conscious attention to this particular process. And because of their preoccupation with "things," Ming *Shih-shuo t'i* authors, like the late Ming literati more generally, continued to be criticized. As Craig Clunas observes: "In the early Qing [Ch'ing] the term "man of culture" (*wen ren* [*jen*]) almost came to be used ironically, implying a class of self-absorbed, studiedly amateurish dilettanti who had, by putting theatricals or garden design on a par with government, brought about their own nemesis."[83]

But the Ming literati's "impracticality" actually arose from very practical needs—namely, the necessity of preserving their social status in the face of mounting pressure from the civil service examination system. Benjamin Elman notices that from the Sung dynasty onward, the state increasingly used the examinations to confine and regulate the power of elites.[84] Effective ways to control the selection process included supervising the ratio between successful and failed candidates and imposing a regulated examination curriculum. Thus, when Ch'eng-Chu *Li-hsüeh* became state orthodoxy, and "the likelihood of licentiates passing higher examinations entitling them to civil appointments became more formidable,"[85] those who had had broader intellectual interests, such as Wen Cheng-ming and Ho Liang-chün, were naturally disadvantaged. What should these people do? Should they yield to Neo-Confucian orthodoxy in order to seek offices, or should they insist upon being *wen-jen,* men of culture, regardless of the consequences? If they chose the latter path, could they survive by operating only within a moral-cultural framework?

Here Ming economic changes came into play. As indicated earlier, the beginning of the Ming *Shih-shuo* frenzy coincided with the beginning of China's second commercial revolution, which spanned the late Ming (1550–1644) and the high Ch'ing (1680–1820) periods and created the most sophisticated and productive economy in the world.[86] This highly commoditized economy intensified the movement of goods, including literary and artistic products created by literati. This newly increased trade in commodities offered the literati opportunities for financial survival, but it did not really lower their social rank. Richard John Lufrano explains: "The great economic changes of the second commercial revolution gave wealth greater weight in the determination of social status, thus heightening the unreality of the traditional ranking system [scholar, peasant, artisan, and merchant] and inspiring some writers and theorists to conceptualize a new ranking system that would better reflect the importance of commerce and the merchant."[87] Thus the new economic environment worked to the advantage of the literati. As Clunas points out:

> Paintings by those with regional and or national reputations were valuable from the minute they were painted and could enter the commodity market at any time after they had left the possession of the original recipient. This was true even of the work of the classic exemplars of the 'scholar-amateur' model in art, such as . . . Wen Cheng-ming. . . . Their work was particularly prized by the art market, paradoxically for its associations with a denial of the possibility of treating a work of art like a commodity. James Cahill has written: "learning and a high level of culture theoretically placed one outside the marketplace, where one's creations were not for sale; but in a strictly practical sense, the fruits of learning were objects of value, marketable commodities just as were the productions of the artisan." This ambivalence applied equally to calligraphy and literary skills. Wen Cheng-ming was himself well aware of this ambivalence, and the multitude of anecdotes surrounding his life include the claim that, at the same time as he refused to paint to order for politicians, foreigners or merchants, he would give works to needy friends or relations as a form of subsidy, in the knowledge that they would be sold immediately.[88]

With this economic/cultural leeway and supported by their literary and artistic creations-turned-into-commodities, Ming literati, after being detached from the orthodox Ch'eng-Chu system, managed to reaffirm their values while maintaining financial self-sufficiency. Thus Ho Liang-chün could include financial management as part of the literati *chih* and talk comfortably about the one hundred *chin* of aloes paid as an "entrance fee" to Ni Tsan's gallery. By the same token, both Li Shao-wen and Chiao Hung could gloat over how much cash, silk, or gold people offered to obtain a certain Ming literatus-artist's works.[89] In their view at least, taking money did not vulgarize the literati status; on the contrary, the more money a literati product brought, the more that sum would say about the elegant taste embedded in the object.

Seen in this light, it was no accident that a *Shih-shuo* frenzy emerged in late Ming Chiang-nan, the heart of China's second "commercial revolution."[90] The *Shih-shuo t'i* opened an ideal space for Ming literati, not only by providing them with a vehicle for attacking the narrow emphasis of Ch'eng-Chu *Li-hsüeh,* but also by giving them an opportunity to collect, classify, and portray diverse and colorful personalities—people just like themselves. The *Shih-shuo* genre became a sanctuary where new values could be freely discussed and openly celebrated, where Ming literati could, in effect, sit naked, like the "real artist" who had been summoned by Lord Yüan of Sung.

With and within the Alien: Ch'ing Imitations

In 1644, elegantly decadent and self-absorbed Ming literati suddenly found themselves under Manchu rule. The Manchu conquest of China inaugurated three embarrassing centuries of alien domination for the Chinese gentry. Entangled in unfamiliar problems caused by racial, cultural, and political conflicts, the gentry's identity and value system faced a new challenge. How were Chinese literati affected by this very difficult and delicate situation, and how did they cope with it?

Yi Tsung-k'uei's *New Shih-shuo* account of P'u Sung-ling's (1640–1715) life presents a revealing picture of the situation. Yi believes that P'u's outstanding work *Liao-chai chih-i* (Strange tales from Make-Do Studio) was not included in the court-commissioned *Ssu-k'u ch'üan-shu* (Complete collection of the Four Treasuries) because: "One of its tales, titled 'Lo-sh'a hai-shih' [Rākṣāsas and the Ocean Bazaar], satirizes the Manchus and the [Ch'ing] government. For instance, the story suggested that women's imitation of men's clothes followed the Manchu custom.[91] This, along with some other details, such as that the beautiful [people] could not be accepted [by the court], and the uglier one was, the higher one ascended [in hierarchy], caused the book to be banned."[92] The "Rākṣāsas and the Ocean Bazaar" tells of a young scholar-turned-merchant who travels to an alien country where the political structure is the same as China's, yet the standard for judging beauty and ugliness is totally the opposite. Hence, whereas beautiful people (from a Chinese viewpoint) are rejected by the court, ugly ones are recruited into the government. This brief story, and Yi's explanation of why the Ssu-k'u compilers rejected the Liao-chai chih-i, epitomize the problems and sentiments of the gentry during the Ch'ing period.

The Manchus, well aware of their status as foreign conquerors and outnumbered about a hundred to one by the Han Chinese, feared social disorder of any sort and were hypersensitive to racial issues. As a result, they made a conscious effort to suppress works that seemed to have an anti-Manchu flavor and coerced the Han Chinese literati into changing their literary styles.[93] As Yi Tsung-k'uei observes, "Because of this stern censorship, [the Han Chinese literati] would deeply conceal their intent, subtly conveying them by means of ghost or fox-spirit stories or sophisticated allegories."[94] Under these difficult circumstances, the Shih-shuo genre, along with the literati value cultivated in Ming imitations, offered the Chinese gentry a spiritual asylum. At least six of the nine Ch'ing Shih-shuo imitations were composed in the first four decades of Manchu rule.[95] These forty unsettling years spanned from the 1644 conquest of the Ming capital, Peking, to the Ch'ing regime's harsh suppression of the San-fan rebellion in 1682. In between, Ming loyalists offered continual resistance to the Manchu invaders and the Ch'ing regime made constant efforts to tempt or coerce Chinese intellectuals into its service.[96]

Such a chaotic and repressive environment might seem unlikely to nurture the Shih-shuo genre, but there are at least two possible explanations for its flourishing at this time. One is that several authors had started their works during the late Ming *Shih-shuo* frenzy, and their enthusiasm for this sort of writing became even stronger in the wake of the Manchu conquest. Forced to live under "barbarian" conquerors, many Chinese intellectuals found comfort in preserving Chinese cultural and historical traditions. Secondly, the literati value advocated by Ming *Shih-shuo* imitations showed how literati could depoliticize their works, enabling them to carry on a life of their own, relatively independent of unsettling political shifts. Either way, the imitation of the *Shih-shuo hsin-yü* helped some early Ch'ing literati to cope with the pain caused by the shocking dynastic change.

The first Ch'ing *Shih-shuo* imitation, Liang Wei-shu's *Accounts of the Jade Sword* (1654), illustrates both ameliorative functions. According to Liang's own preface, he had started collecting savory Ming remarks and anecdotes during the last years of the Ming and had virtually completed the work upon its collapse. Now, a decade after the fall of Ming, his sons, fearing the scattering of a manuscript full of materials as rare "as stars and phoenixes,"[97] decided to have the book printed.

The three promoters of Liang's work, Wu Wei-yeh, Ch'ien Ch'ien-i, and Ch'ien Fen, all strongly emphasized in their prefaces the importance of composing histories during a transitional period. Wu Wei-yeh recalled that he, too, had embarked on a *Shih-shuo t'i* project when serving in the Ming court, but had to destroy the draft in order to avoid causing trouble in the intense late Ming factional struggle. Then, "Before long the world fell into pieces, and lords, ministers, and my old friends almost all died or disappeared in the incidents. Those who were lucky enough to survive, such as myself, became dizzy in the head because of all the sufferings we endured. Sometimes, with a group of people, we tried to recollect one old event or another, but no one could remember a thing. It was then that I began to regret the loss of my draft."[98] At a time when "historical writings have been in short supply for a long time, and no one can tell when a historical work will be available,"[99] as Ch'ien Fen characterized it, historical writings such as Liang Wei-shu's *Accounts of the Jade Sword* appeared especially precious. Without such efforts, Ch'ien Ch'ien-i argued, crucial moments of the Ming history would fall into oblivion: "Who would interpret correctly the ambiguous [government] records of the Wan-li [1573–

1620] and Ch'ung-chen [1628–1644] reigns? And the new accounts of
the Lung-wu [1645–1646] and Yung-li [1647–1661] reigns would have no
evidence."[100]

Mentioning the two Southern Ming reigns, the Lung-wu and the Yung-
li, Ch'ien related Liang's work to the sensitive issue of the remnant Ming
loyalists who were still fighting the Manchus in the South. It would be
misleading, though, to assume that Ch'ien was issuing a patriotic call for
the restoration of the Ming, or to take Wu's preface as a loyal tribute to
the past Ming rulers. Ch'ien and Wu had been leading Ming literati-
officials, but they eventually participated in the Manchu government. Although Liang Wei-shu, also a Ming courtier, did not personally serve the
Ch'ing, his son and nephew assumed important official positions with the
new dynasty. Liang's request that both Ch'ien and Wu write prefaces to
his work indicates his acceptance of the dynastic change. His resignation
is also reflected in the dating of each preface according to the Ch'ing calendar, a concession no true Ming loyalist would accept.

By assigning themselves the task of reconstructing the Ming history,
Liang and his promoters found a "noble" rationale for their lack of loyalty
to the fallen regime. There were precedents for such choices. Ch'ien Fen
related in his preface the story of the former Yüan Han-lin scholar Wei Su
(1303–1372), who, after surviving the Yüan, tried his best to recover the
Yüan history.[101] According to some more detailed accounts of the story,
Wei Su was about to commit suicide at the fall of his dynasty but was convinced to live when a monk said to him, "Should your lordship die, the history of the [Yüan] would die with you."[102] Similarly, Liang and his promoters
convinced themselves to transmit Ming records for Ch'ing reference. As
Ch'ien Fen suggested in his preface: "If the authorities sincerely want to
solicit and consult [historical] writings or records, to whom, then, should
they turn but to this gentleman [Liang]?"[103]

Kai-wing Chow analyzes the psychology that made this sort of decision possible—even attractive—in the early Ch'ing period: "By identifying with [Chinese] culture rather than with the Ming regime, Chinese
literati could justify their participation in the Manchu government. Belief
in the universality of Chinese culture and one's commitment to preserv-

ing it under an alien regime could help mitigate the sense of guilt of those who served the Manchus."[104] This rationale had deep roots in the "literati value" developed in the Ming and fully expressed in Ming *Shih-shuo* imitations. Those who died for the Ming or participated in the resistance to the Ch'ing were mostly scholars who were bound by rigid Neo-Confucian moral-political imperatives. But for Ming literati such as Ch'ien Ch'ien-i and Wu Wei-yeh, the establishment of a literati value depoliticized their position and helped, eventually, to dissolve their commitment to the fallen regime.

Liang Wei-shu's work did not provide to later generations a full picture of Ming intellectual life. He chose to ignore the accounts of Ming loyalist campaigns and to focus on the fulfillment of Ming "literati values," which included, among other things, a complete exclusion of Neo-Confucian scholarship from literati life. While late Ming *Shih-shuo* imitators still showed respect for Wang Yang-ming (Wang Shou-jen 1472–1529), the founder of the *Hsin-hsüeh* (Learning of the mind) doctrines, Liang mocked both the *Li-hsüeh* and the *Hsin-hsüeh* masters. Here are two examples:

> T'ang Shun-chih had sincerely believed Chu Hsi. Then one day he suddenly said, "I feel none of Master Chu's interpretations [of the Confucian classics] is correct."[105]

> When [Wang] Yang-ming was lecturing at Ling-yin Temple on the West Lake, he strongly denounced Hui-weng's (Chu Hsi's) interpretations [of the Confucian classics]. An old monk in the audience asked, "During your licentiate time, did you gentleman ever follow Chu's commentary to compose your essays?" Yang-ming replied, "This was what the court institutionalized for selecting scholars; how could I not follow?" The old monk said, "Why didn't you use your own interpretations?" Yang-ming said, "Had I done so, I would not have passed the examinations." The monk laughed, saying: "Then Lord Wen's [Chu Hsi's] interpretations were your precious ship. How could you abandon it once you have ferried across the Ocean of Misery?"[106]

Both Chu Hsi and Wang Yang-ming were institutionalized role models for the gentry, worshipped along with Confucius under Ming imperial decrees.[107] Once Liang tarnished their sacred images, whom would he choose for their replacement? Liang recommended the maverick scholar

Li Chih. He suggested, through Chiao Hung's mouth, that "even though [Li Chih] may not be considered a sage, he may, at least, be labeled *k'uang* [crazy or wildly enthusiastic] and be seated next to the Sage [Confucius]"[108] Liang chose Li Chih as the leading literati figure because of his *k'uang*, which was rooted in Li's "child mind" theory of literature *(t'ung-hsin shuo)*. Li Chih believed that true literature can only grow out of passion and emotions so intense that they drive the writer crazy—"raving, yelling, shedding tears, and wailing uncontrollably."[109] For this reason, Li Chih advocated exempting literati from scholarship, advising a friend: "I would like you, my revered elder brother, not to talk about scholarship. Talking about scholarship suffocates numerous pleasant enjoyments. Human life naturally has the means to fulfill itself in the world; why should we add one more such thing [as scholarship]? To take Master [Li] K'ung-t'ung [Li Meng-yang (1473–1529)] and Master [Wang] Yang-ming for example, they lived at the same time, [Wang] was an expert in the scholarship of *Tao* and *te* and [Li] excelled at literature. Ten million generations from now, their essence and glory will still flourish. Why talk about *Tao* and *te* in addition to [literature]? Will people emulate Master K'ung-t'ung less than they emulate Master Yang-ming?"[110] In Li Chih's view, scholarship was concerned with fundamental philosophical principles, whereas the role of literature was to provide "enjoyment." Although Li Chih remained an ardent exponent of Wang Yang-ming's *Hsin-hsüeh* school and although his "child mind" theory relied heavily upon Wang's ideas, he wanted to detach scholarship from literati identity in order to preserve literature from the harmful effects of false speculation and specious reasoning.[111]

Liang Wei-shu's support of Li Chih's conception of literature finds clear expressions in his account of T'ang Hsien-tsu (1550–1617), who composed the drama *Mu-tan t'ing* (Peony pavilion): "The grand secretary, Chang Wei (fl. 1594–1597), once said to T'ang, 'With your reasoning and arguing talents, you may hold the sambar-tail chowry and ascend the tiger-rugged altar [to preach *Li-hsüeh* doctrines], and you would not be inferior to the [Sung *Li-hsüeh*] Masters Lien [Chou Tun-I], Lo [Ch'eng Hao and Ch'eng I], Kuan [Chang Tsai], and Min [Chu Hsi]. Yet you linger amidst emerald

flutes and red castanets. Won't you be laughed at by other scholars?' T'ang
replied, 'I discuss scholarship with you all the time, but nobody understands. While you talk about *hsing* [human nature], I talk about *ch'ing* [hu-
man feelings and emotions].' Chang had no response."[112]

Here, T'ang suggests that drama is equal to *Li-hsüeh* scholarship.
Clearly, he builds up this argument by drawing on Li Chih's contention
that, as long as it was created with "child mind," drama can yield the "ultimately great literature" *(chih-wen)* and can convey the *Tao* of the sages.[113]
Liang lends support for T'ang's point by citing the first emperor of the Ming,
Chu Yüan-chang (r. 1368–1398), who once compared Kao Ming's (1310–
1380) drama *P'i-pa chi* (Story of lute) to delicate food and the Confucian
classics to five grains—both equally indispensable for a well-balanced
diet.[114] At the same time, Liang affirms Li Chih's emphasis on the role of
literature in providing enjoyment, approvingly citing T'an Yüan-ch'un's
(1586–1631) characterization of his fellow Ching-ling poet Chung Hsing
(1574–1624): "This fellow is not [simply] a friend, but something that can
be used for entertainment all day long."[115]

With his *Account of the Jade Sword,* Liang Wei-shu transmitted Ming
literati values to early Ch'ing *Shih-shuo* imitations, notably Wang Wan's
Bell of Tales and Wang Cho's *Contemporary Shih-shuo,*[116] published respectively in 1661 and 1683. Both works focused exclusively on Ch'ing
literati life, and significantly, neither contributed a single episode to the
ruler/subject relationship.[117] It is hard to tell whether the two authors intended to emphasize the literati's transcendence of the ruler/subject hierarchy, or whether they simply borrowed this transcendental mood to mitigate the embarrassment of expressing loyalty to a "barbarian regime." In
any case, for the first time since the T'ang transformation of the gentry,
the emperor was absent in a *Shih-shuo* imitation.

This depoliticization of literati life is clearly reflected in the two authors'
choice of characters. Both concentrated on their personal associations—
Wang Wan on his literati friends in the capital, such as his rival, the
renowned early Ch'ing poet Wang Shih-chen (1634–1711), and Wang Cho
on his local peers in Hangchow. Thus both conveniently avoided involv-

ing a number of early Ch'ing scholars who remained loyal to the Ming, such as Huang Tsung-hsi (1610–1695), Ku Yen-wu (1613–1682), Wang Fu-chih (1619–1692), Chu Shun-shui (1600–1682), and Wan Ssu-t'ung (1638–1702), to name just a few.

Wang Wan's *Bell of Tales* was not categorized; so he concentrated exclusively on literary and artistic activities and eccentric lifestyles. He may have intentionally omitted the categorization so that he would not have to address moral-political questions. Wang's depoliticizing and amoralizing approach of literati life appears clearly in his portrayal of the notorious late Ming literatus-official Kung Ting-tzu (1615–1673), who first surrendered to the rebel marauder Li Tzu-ch'eng (fl. mid-seventeenth cent.) and then served the Ch'ing court. Yi Tsung-k'uei, whose *New Shih-shuo* also covered early Ch'ing life, could forgive similar Ming "traitors" such as Ch'ien Ch'ien-i and Hung Ch'eng-ch'ou (fl. mid-seventeenth cent.), but never the treacherous Kung. Yet Wang Wan treated Kung like a mentor, as if all of his political and moral twists during the Ming-Ch'ing transition did not in any way defile this man's literary grace.[118]

Since both Wang Wan and Wang Cho wrote about people related to their own lives, they naturally became characters in their respective *Shih-shuo t'i* works, thus adding a new feature to the genre. While Wang Wan, ever cautious, portrayed himself only in a matter-of-fact fashion, Wang Cho used the opportunity for aggressive self-promotion. Among all *Shih-shuo* imitators, no one recruited more supporters than Wang Cho—altogether seventeen proponents wrote prefaces for him. Indeed, he drove the literati's self-affirmation to such an extreme that he made himself a role model in his own work: "Wang Cho is widely learned and well versed, and his fame extends across the entire east side of the Yangtze River. . . . Scholar-officials passing through Wu-lin county would initially pay him a visit and engage him in friendship. Halting their carriages in front of his house, they often could not bear to leave."[119] According to Wang Cho, his friends sought to acquire his literary writings "like gluttonous apes looking for fruits," and so great was his aesthetic appeal that people felt that while in his presence they were "casually facing a chrysanthemum that arouses the beholder's delicate appreciation."[120]

Such extreme self-appreciation made Wang Cho a laughingstock in the eyes of more traditional scholars, who for two millennia had upheld modesty as a fundamental virtue of the superior man *(chün-tzu)*. The *Ssu-k'u* compilers thus criticized the *Contemporary Shih-shuo* in the following terms: "Its appraisals seem overly exaggerated. In a sense, this is a work that solicits reputation and provokes solidarity, similar to the style of Ming poetry clubs. The inclusion of the author's own episodes especially violates the standard [of the *Shih-shuo* genre]."[121] Wang Cho's arrogance, however, seems not to have troubled later *Shih-shuo* imitators. Yi Tsung-k'uei, for one, praised the *Contemporary Shih-shuo* for its "tasteful and everlasting words and meanings," which he considered "comparable to Prince Lin-ch'uan's [*Shih-shuo hsin-yü*]."[122] Yi consciously emulated Wang Cho's precedent and made himself a character in his *New Shih-shuo.*

Although early Ch'ing *Shih-shuo* imitators followed their late Ming predecessors in promoting literati values, the two periods differed from each other in terms of aesthetic moods. If Ming literati preferred *lo,* or pleasure, then early Ch'ing literati seemed overwhelmed with *ch'ou,* or melancholy. Wang Cho recounts:

> When Wu Chin temporarily stayed at Shan-yin, he thought of Lin Ssu-huan who was then also wandering about without a permanent residence. At that moment Wu only felt that:
>
>> A thousand cliffs competed to stand in melancholy [*ch'ien-yen ching-ch'ou*],
>> Ten thousand torrents vied in shedding tears [*wan-ho cheng-lei*].[123]
>
> Hsü Ching-chih once by mistake said "the fur is exhausted and the gold is worn" [*ch'iu-ching chin-pi*] instead of "the gold is exhausted and the fur is worn" [*chin-ching ch'iu-pi*], and all the guests there laughed at him. Hsü said, "If the skin does not exist, where should the hair attach itself? Doesn't this mean that 'the fur is exhausted'? Who could expect that the well-tempered steel would ever become pliable? Doesn't this mean that 'the gold (metal) is worn'?"[124]

It is clear that Wu Chin's poetic remark mimics the famous *Shih-shuo* lines, "A thousand cliffs competed to stand tall / Ten thousand torrents vied in flowing" *(ch'ien-yen ching-hsiu, wan-ho cheng-liu)* (*Shih-shuo hsin-yü,*

2/88). Similarly, Hsü Ching-chih's defense of his slip of the tongue, "the fur is exhausted and the gold is worn," follows the *Shih-shuo* bon mot, "to rinse the mouth with rocks and to pillow the head on the streams" *(shu-shih chen-liu)*.[125] The replacement of a few words suffices to transform the Chin ecstasy about a reclusive lifestyle into early Ch'ing lamentation over a permanent residence forever lost. The once-proud men of letters, who considered themselves the masters of Chinese culture and the owners of the natural world, now had to submit to an alien ruler or else wander about, like a piece of hair, with nowhere to attach: "We are like cuckoos, the melancholic [*ch'ou*] kind that exists naturally between Heaven and Earth."[126]

Early Ch'ing literati were doomed to despondency. Their belief in a "literati value" that transcended the ruler/subject relationship excused them from dying for the Ming regime, but it never grew strong enough to free them from their sense of guilt over cutting themselves off from the fallen dynasty. After all, their detachment from rigorous Confucian moral standards was more a reaction to the confinement of *Li-hsüeh* than a rebellion against Confucianism itself; they never abandoned the basic Confucian value system. On the other hand, the early Ch'ing literati's pride in being "Chinese" forbade them from serving a regime of different cultural origin, costing them their social status, their comfortable lifestyle—and possibly their lives. Suspended in uncertainty about their identity, their future, and the meaning of life, the early Ch'ing literati could only assuage their guilt and pain through artistic and literary creations. Suffusing the entire universe with their melancholy mood, they found comfort in the preservation of Chinese culture. This was probably the best they could do for the Chinese tradition, and the best they could do for themselves.

Chapter 8

Milk and Scent: Women *Shih-shuo*

Two Ch'ing *Shih-shuo* imitations, both entitled *Nü Shih-shuo* (Women *Shih-shuo*), deal entirely with women: One is by the male writer Li Ch'ing (1602–1683),[1] composed in the early 1650s, and the other is by a woman, Yen Heng (1826?–1854), published a decade or so after her death. Li's work includes 759 stories about remarkable women from antiquity to the end of Yüan, collected from both historical and legendary writings and categorized into thirty-one types. Yen managed in her short lifetime to collect seventy-nine unclassified entries about women poets and artists from the early Ch'ing to her own time—mainly residents of the Chiang-nan area, especially her hometown, Hangchow.

In spirit and in form, the two *Nü Shih-shuo* elaborate on the "Hsien-yüan" (Worthy beauties) chapter in the *Shih-shuo hsin-yü*, which, as part of the *Shih-shuo* legacy, finds its place in almost all imitations. These chapters, including the two *Nü Shih-shuo*, form a "Hsien-yüan" tradition at once divergent from and complementary to the tradition of the *Lieh-nü chuan* (Biographies of exemplary women) in the dynastic histories, begun by the Han Confucian scholar Liu Hsiang (77–6 B.C.). Whereas the *Lieh-nü* tradition "illustrates the virtues associated with proper womanly behavior in Confucian families"[2]—often exemplified by female docility and obedience—the *Hsien-yüan* tradition mostly portrays strong-willed and outspoken gentlewomen who may or may not have followed the Confucian patriarchal model. Therefore, one must ask, in reading works of the *Hsien-yüan* tradition: In whose voice are these strong-willed women speaking—their fathers' or their own? What is expressed in that voice, how is it constructed, and why is it constructed in this particular way?

As discussed at length in chapters 2 and 4, the "Hsien-yüan" chapter in the *Shih-shuo hsin-yü* literally demands that women model themselves

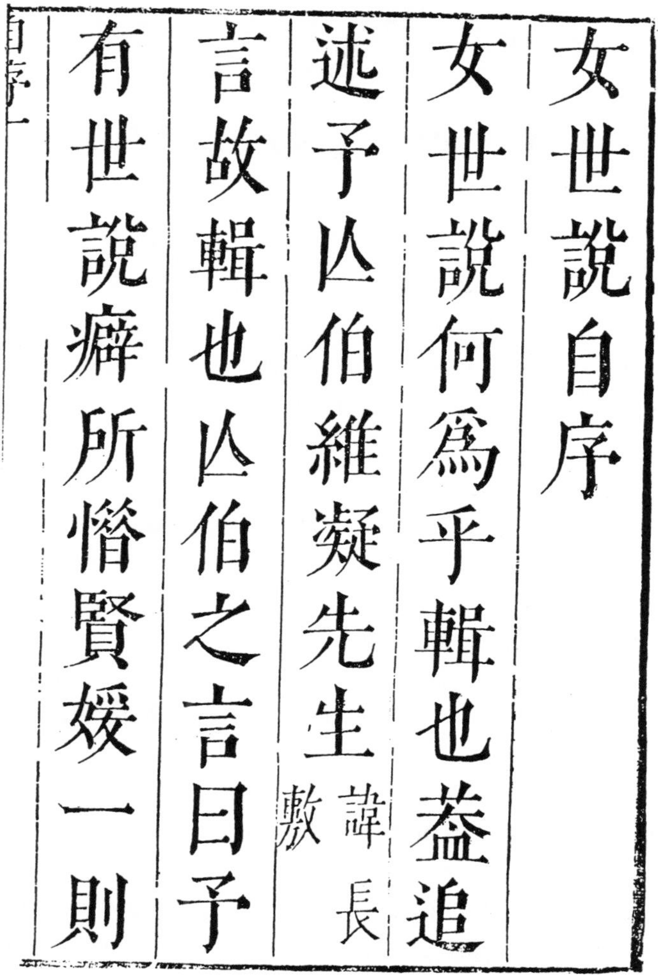

女世說自序　女世說何爲乎輯也益追　述予厶伯維疑先生　言故輯也厶伯之言目予　有世說癖所憎賢媛一則

薛長　敷

Figure 8.1. Li Ch'ing's (1602–1683) preface to his *Nü Shih-shuo* (early 1670s) (1a).

after their fathers in spirit, manners, and talents. It sets up Hsieh Tao-yün as a role model for Wei-Chin women and describes her as deeply imbued with the "Bamboo Grove aura" *(lin-hsia feng-ch'i),* thus surpassing the "full flowering of the inner chamber" *(kuei-fang chi hsiu).* Here the "Bamboo Grove aura" refers expressly to the "Seven Worthies of the Bamboo Grove,"

Figure 8.2. Yen Heng's (1826?–1854) *Nü Shih-shuo* (1920 edition) (1a).

who embody the most esteemed characteristics of Wei-Chin gentlemen: philosophical depth, poetic talent, and artistic expertise, combined with a carefree and lofty lifestyle.

Emulating the "Seven Worthies" did not, however, make Hsieh Tao-yün or other Wei-Chin women blind followers of patriarchal values, much less of the Confucian system as a whole. After all, the ideological basis of *lin-hsia feng-ch'i*—namely, *Hsüan-hsüeh*—emerged from a critical Wei-Chin rereading and reevaluation of Han Confucianism. In the process,

Hsüan-hsüeh incorporated Taoism and Buddhism, both of which undermined notions of Confucian hierarchy and preached equality and free-spiritedness for all individuals. Based on the understanding that things are and should be equally themselves, the Bamboo Grove aura as a manifestation of the Wei-Chin spirit transcended gender difference and was applicable to both men and women. In a sense, the Wei-Chin spirit was a coproduct created by both men and women, and it was this cooperation between the two genders and their shared critical attitude toward conventional patriarchal values that sustained the *Hsien-yüan* tradition and foreshadowed the creation of the two *Nü Shih-shuo*.[3]

What is striking about the two *Nü Shih-shuo* is that they each tried to construct a distinctive female value system, even though the two authors had somewhat different agendas and occupied different social and gender positions. There is no evidence that Yen Heng ever saw Li Ch'ing's *Nü Shih-shuo,* most probably because Li's works had been officially banned during the Ch'ing period.[4] Nonetheless, the two authors concurred in their disappointment with men in particular and with the conventional patriarchal value system in general, and each sought an alternative. Viewing the world from the standpoint of women, they became sensitive to the way women's lived bodily experiences often conflicted with the cultural meanings inscribed on the female body.[5] Thus, they tended to consider the significance of women's lives not so much from the Confucian orthodoxy inscribed on the female body—with which they became more or less disillusioned—but rather from the standpoint of the female body itself. Taking as their point of departure the relationship between the female body and the world, they examined how women struggled to have their voices heard amidst generally repressive social circumstances. For this reason, each independently constructed version of women's values mutually interpreted and mutually elaborated the other. Occupying the center of this joint construction were two pivotal elements associated unmistakably with the female body—*ju,* milk, and *hsiang,* scent—the fluid and penetrating essence of which connected the female body to the rest of the world.

In the following discussion, I plan first to explore how and why each of the two authors appropriated the female body as a cultural metaphor to express their dissatisfaction with mainstream male values. Then I shall examine the female value systems established in the two works. Due to the gender difference between the two authors, their ways of constructing each system came from opposite directions. Li Ch'ing, a man and a self-assigned protector of Chinese culture, stood as the "owner" of the culture. He borrowed the female body and encultured its natural qualities in order to criticize corruption and inadequacy in the world of men. Thus, female virginity became the symbol of political and cultural purity, and women's milk and scent values were transformed into an ideal combination of ethics and aesthetics. Since Li Ch'ing could not uproot himself entirely from his socio-gender position as an elite male, his milk/scent scheme unavoidably fell into a conventional nurturing/alluring dichotomy, even though he elevated women's nurturing feature (milk) to the highest realm of virtue and shifted women's alluring feature (scent) from a sensual to a spiritual focus. In either case, man still stood as the subject/appreciator and woman as the object/appreciated.

By contrast, Yen Heng, a woman, presented the female body in terms of its own internal transitions and contradictions, caught between flowering talent in youth and burdensome responsibilities after marriage. In order to resolve these conflicts, Yen Heng reclaimed culture in terms of a woman's life. Such a mentality led Yen Heng to feminize literary creation into childbirth and to bring milk and scent into mutual refinement and reinforcement in her "flower and kitchen poetics." Yen Heng's positive resolution offers fascinating insights into elite female consciousness during the nineteenth century. Yet the milk and scent values, both generated from the female body and therefore expected to coexist, were often coerced into mutual exclusion by larger social forces and frameworks.

The Female Body as a Cultural Metaphor

FEMALE VIRGINITY AND CULTURAL PURITY

With his *Nü Shih-shuo*, Li Ch'ing made an effort to preserve the purity of China's cultural identity in the face of the Manchu conquest. Li

Ch'ing attained his *chin-shih* degree in 1631 and served the Ming court until its fall in 1644. After that he retreated to his hometown, T'ai-chou, and spent the rest of his life writing and doing historical research. The *Nü Shih-shuo* was among the several works he completed during this period.[6] Upon its publication, Li Ch'ing's disciple, Lu Min-shu, wrote a preface questioning his mentor's motive in composing such a work: "How has it come about that you, with your heroic brush and tongue, have composed a book for women? . . . Is it because you alone considered women of this world to be teachable and thus composed this edition to tell them that to be a virtuous beauty you must behave as such; to be a talented beauty you must behave as such; and to be a talented and virtuous beauty, devoid of licentiousness, treachery, jealousy, and cantankerousness, you have to take your guidance from such and such?"[7]

To this seemingly rhetorical question, Li Ch'ing answered: "No, no, I am myself still an unmarried virgin [*ch'u-tzu*]; how could I presume to educate all married women [*fu*] under Heaven?"[8] A *ch'u-tzu,* or unmarried virgin, would certainly be unqualified to educate a *fu,* or married woman, on how to be a good wife. Since Li is a man, his blurring of the gender difference clearly invests his answer with something other than its literal meaning. On a metaphorical level, *ch'u* means "at home," in contrast to *ch'u,* "away from home." Within gentry circles, the *ch'u/ch'u* dichotomy has always referred to the conflict between "being away from home (to serve the court)" and "remaining at home (and not serving the court)." Given Li Ch'ing's political environment, one may easily interpret his *ch'u-tzu* versus *fu* allegory as expressing contempt for Han Chinese scholar-officials who polluted their "virginity" by serving the Manchus.

It was not uncommon for Ming gentlemen to equate their moral or political purity with female virtues. Li Ch'ing's virgin allegory resonates with several Ming *Shih-shuo* accounts. One example often cited recounts that Yang Shou-ch'en (1425–1489) "held himself aloof and never pursued further advancement in official positions." When people urged him to do so, he declined, saying: "I am like a widow who has kept her chastity for thirty years. . . . How can I remarry now that I am already white-haired?"[9]

In China's literary tradition, comparing a gentleman's political standing to a woman's sexual status may be traced to the pre-Ch'in period. Prior to the Ming, however, the analogy almost invariably likened an estranged, exiled subject to an abandoned wife.[10] The purity of the female body came into play because of the growing sanctification of women's chastity in late imperial times. Sung *Li-hsüeh* scholars intensified the issue to the point that they considered the purity of the female body to come before its vitality—to be preserved, if necessary, at the expense of the latter. As Ch'eng I put the matter: "To die of hunger is a trifling matter, to lose [one's] chastity is a grave matter."[11] During the Yüan period, the cult of widow-chastity included the practices of self-mutilation and suicide as "a formal or public display of fidelity at the time of the husband's death."[12] Also under the Yüan, "formal specification of the criteria of age and social status for virtuous widows began in 1304."[13] By Ming imperial edict, a woman's chastity could bring honor and reward to her family.[14]

The purity of the female body thus became a symbol not only of the highest ethical status, but also of the difficulty of attaining that status. Gentlemen who had imposed this hardship on women inversely borrowed the symbol of the female body to engender their political purposes, either to proclaim their own political chastity or to "shame men who were unwilling to rise to the same heights of virtue."[15] In this sense, Li Ch'ing's virgin allegory suggests that he intended his *Nü Shih-shuo* to shame disloyal males by contrasting them with more righteous females. Indeed, if women, with weaker bodies, could adhere to the traditional value system, why couldn't men? Li underscores this theme in the following episode: "Wu Hsi surrendered Shu to the Tartars. The general of Hsing-chou, Li Hao-i, plotted to exterminate him. He bid farewell to his wife, Ma, saying, 'Limit daily expenses and take good care of yourself!' Ma scolded him, saying, 'You are about to kill the traitors for the court; why still bother yourself with your family? I will not humiliate the Li family name!' Ma's mother also said, 'Go, fight! Alive you shall be heroes, and dead, heroic ghosts!' Hao-i happily said, 'Even women can be so [brave], not to mention us men!'"[16]

In his *Nü Shih-shuo,* Li Ch'ing devotes two entire chapters—"Chieh-

i" (Chastity and righteousness) and "I-yung" (Determination and courage)—to women's vehement resistance to invasions of their bodies, home-
towns, states, and country. From empresses to peasant women, from grand-
mothers to young girls, women of all classes and all ages react righteously
to such threats: They either kill their enemies or kill themselves.[17] Even
courtesans, who are not expected to maintain their purity, choose death
instead of abandoning their bodies to traitors or invaders.[18] By recruiting
such individuals into the shrine of chaste women, Li Ch'ing accentuates
his scorn for the men who surrendered China to the Manchus.

FEMALE FERTILITY AND LITERARY CREATIVITY

Disappointment with men seems to have also permeated Yen Heng's
Nü Shih-shuo. Li Ch'ing's bitterness is easy to understand, for, as I have already indicated, his original purpose in compiling this work was to humiliate the men who polluted their own cultural identity. But what about Yen?

Yen Heng—courtesy name Tuan-ch'ing—was a native of Jen-ho (in today's Hangchow, Chekiang province). Apparently from an elite family that
paid great attention to her education, Yen was "talented in embroidery, poetry, and music."[19] Her marriage also seems to have been an excellent
match. Her husband, Ch'en Yüan-lu (studio name: Hung-chu tz'u-jen, or
Red-Candle Poet), a native of Ch'ien-t'ang (also part of today's Hangchow),
was himself a talented man, an "ideal" husband for an intellectual woman.[20]
After Yen's death, Ch'en edited Yen's *Nü Shih-shuo* and appended to it a
touching postscript. By conventional criteria, her life appears to have been
full and satisfying. What, then, caused Yen's resentment?

Due to an untimely death, Yen Heng did not get to preface her works,[21]
so we have no way to penetrate directly into her motivation for literary creations. Her close friend, Yeh Shih Li-wan, provides some clues, however.
In a preface to Yen's *Nü Shih-shuo,* Yeh candidly criticizes Ch'en for not
encouraging his wife's intellectual ambition until it was too late:

> Always keeping inkstones and brushes next to pots of cosmetics, and oc-
> casionally writing in mornings or evenings, Lady Yen created words
> sufficient to embellish the ancient and advise the present. Red-Candle
> Poet only feasted on her beauty reflected in the mirror, shoulders and

eyebrows [*chien-mei*] side by side; but ignored the literary talent [*san-tuo*] borne in her belly [*fu-p'i*],[22] with which she was gestating [*yün*] a [women's] history.[23]

In elegant parallel prose, Yeh Shih Li-wan juxtaposes pots of cosmetics with writing utensils and one female body part, eyebrows, with another, belly. The link between these elements suggests several inner-chamber mechanisms that represent respectively the conventional expectations of husbands and wives in their married lives. Whereas eyebrows provide a site of inner-chamber pleasure typified by a man painting his wife's eyebrows, the belly, where a woman conceives her child, is a site of familial responsibilities.[24] Ordinarily a wife would beautify—or allow her husband to beautify—her eyebrows with cosmetics so she could attract her man's sensual attention, which would lead to the reproduction of offspring in her belly. Yen Heng's ambition, according to Yeh Shih Li-wan, included but went beyond this marriage routine. Tucking inkstones and inkbrushes among pots of cosmetics, she intended not only to enhance her outer beauty but also to express her inner beauty by writing about women.

Using *yün*—the same word for conceiving and carrying a child—to indicate Yen Heng's conception of a writing project, Yeh Shih Li-wan metaphorically equates female fertility with women's literary creativity, underscoring the equal importance of both endeavors. Hence she reprimands men for paying too much attention to women's beauty and not enough to their minds.

Yeh Shih Li-wan's remarks prove her a sensitive and honest reader of her dead friend's work. Her use of the female fertility metaphor resonates with and corroborates Yen Heng's bitterness, as we see in the following episode:

Mao T'i, courtesy name An-fang, was a native of Jen-ho and was married to Hsü Hua-cheng. Before long her father-in-law abandoned the family and became a monk, and her husband frequently left home to travel. Prompted by the changes of the times and the decay of things, she created beautiful poems. Nearing forty she was still childless. Her younger sister-in-law picked up a piece of the herb called *I-nan* [Bring-me-a-son], saying: "Sister-in-law, why don't you write a poem about this to invite good fortune?" She replied: "Poetry is my spirit and intelligence [*shen-ming*]. Composing poems amounts to giving birth to a son." Her poem, "Snow," has a line: "One night, all turns boundlessly white."[25]

In Yen Heng's view, Mao T'i's men have betrayed her, offering no protection, no assistance, and no support. Thus she chooses the line, "One night, all turns boundlessly white" to illustrate Mao T'i's chilly perception of the tragic changes occurring in her world, where no one—particularly no man—is in sight. Mao T'i is therefore forced into creating a family on her own, through poetry—the only thing that keeps her company and makes her "fertile." She literally engenders poetry into her "spirit and intelligence" and then clones this most important part of her body into a poetic child, instead of relying upon a man's help to conceive a son.[26]

Both Yen Heng and her proponent Yeh Shih Li-wan closely link culture to women's lived bodily experiences, specifically childbirth (including the conception)—the most painful yet most significant passage of a woman's life. They use childbirth as a central metaphor to link two important aspects of a woman writer's existence: biological and literary creation. The comparison underscores the intimacy that a writing woman feels for her literary creation—a feeling as intense as if poetry were her own child, inseparable from her own body and life.

Indeed, in Yen Heng's *Nü Shih-shuo,* the portrayal of writing women's lives often blurs the distinction between household routine and cultural creation. These women weave their lived bodily experiences into poetic and artistic themes, tucking their writing tools and artistic products into dressers and sewing kits, amidst cosmetics and needlework. In this way their writing instruments, poetic and artistic themes, and cultural products literally become parts of the female body, radiating a powerful female essence, as Yen Heng suggests in the following episode:

In the Half-Cocoon Garden, Deer City, a young girl inscribed a *chüeh-chü* poem on the wall with her hairpin. It reads:

In the moonlight I arrive, delicately leaning on my maid;
Pear blossoms, white as snow, dot the dark moss.

Red silkworms industriously exhaust the melancholy silk;
Who split the cocoon, woven with shared effort?

She attached the character *"P'i"* after the poem, which suggests that she
may have wanted to sign her whole name, but did not get to do it.[27]

The culture-body intimacy is flaunted particularly in the writing tool
that the young girl uses to inscribe the poem—a hairpin closely connected
to her body—instead of a conventional writing brush. The characteristics of the female body are also revealed clearly in the poem. The first
line, "In the moonlight I arrive, delicately leaning on my maid," indicates
another female body part—bound feet that prevent a woman from walking freely on her own; hence she underscores the difficulty of making an
excursion to this spot. The central image, a cocoon woven by two silk-
worms with "melancholy silk"—*ch'ou-ssu,* punning *ch'ou-ssu,* "melancholy
thoughts"—is the symbol of despairing love.[28] The metaphor clearly arises
from women's routine experience of weaving. The young girl "weaves"
a fabric of meaning that is poignantly beautiful, suggesting several sad
possibilities—that she has come to an old tryst spot, mourning for a long-
lost relationship; that she has come upon a place whose name reminds
her of a lamentable episode; or that she is waiting in vain for a lover to
show up. While this sort of heartbroken experience occurs often as a poetic theme, this one stands out with a clear female voice. In order to make
her thoughts known to later times, the girl feminizes the poetic inscription—
traditionally used by men to leave their traces in history—with her own
bodily features, thus appropriating this "male" cultural activity for female
self-expression.

In contrast to this daring exposure of her gender, the girl seems hesitant to reveal her name. The ending thus adds a dramatic twist to this brief
narrative, making the reader speculate as to why she did not finish the sig-
nature. Was she interrupted by an outer force, or did she consider "sign-
ing one's name" improper for a woman? Her name also fills us with wonder, for the character *p'i* is often used in transliterating Buddhist terms
from their original Sanskrit. Is there a Buddhist dimension to this story,
and if so, what is it? We can only speculate that in this case, and no doubt

in many others, a tension existed between women's desire to have their voices heard and the repressive sociocultural circumstances that often denied women this privilege.

Milk Ethics and Scent Aesthetics in Li Ch'ing's *Nü Shih-shuo*

UPSETTING MEN'S ORDER

Li Ch'ing's first impulse may have been to vent his anger at disloyal scholars by invidious comparison with women, but in the process he became increasingly serious about portraying women in their own right, not simply as the mute foils of men. As clear evidence of this concern, Li Ch'ing's women speak forthrightly, often claiming that they are acting on their own volition rather than blindly following conventional norms. Thus, although many women remain widowed or even commit suicide after their husbands' death, they justify their behavior in personal terms; few admit to having answered men's calls to "chastity."[29] The following episode provides an apt example:

> While King Chuang of Ch'u was traveling in Yün-meng, Lady Ts'ai and Lady Yüeh were in attendance. The king suggested that the three of them vow to live and to die together. Lady Ts'ai agreed. Lady Yüeh said, "When Your Highness acquired me in my humble place of origin, in exchange for silk and horses, you did not obligate me to die with you." Later on the king became ill. It so happened that there were red clouds surrounding the sun like flying birds. The diviner took it to be a bad omen harmful to the king. Some suggested that they "transfer the harm" onto generals or ministers. The king rejected this advice, saying, "They are my arms." Lady Yüeh said, "How great is your kingly virtue! For this reason I would like to follow you [to death]. Our past journey was for licentious pleasure, therefore I dared not promise [to die with you]. Now Your Highness has returned to propriety. All the people in the country would be willing to die for you, not to mention myself, your humble concubine. I am willing to die for your righteousness, not for your pleasure."[30]

Lady Yüeh's noble voice changes the significance of her possible death. Had she not spoken, she would die a mute object, no different from the silk and horses that the king traded for her. Once she spoke, however, she elevated herself to the same level as all the people in the country. If she should die, then, she would die not merely as the king's slave, but as an individual dying for the righteousness she believed in.

Once Li Ch'ing's women break silence, their subjectivity as strong and independent women emerges. Whereas strong women may demonstrate strength by merely following rules made by others—typically by men in a patriarchal tradition—strong and independent women challenge the mechanisms of male control in the process of promoting their own principles. In Li Ch'ing's *Nü Shih-shuo,* women have together formed a new value system by deconstructing prevailing male values, including moral, political, and aesthetic judgments. An examination of this deconstructive and reconstructive process might begin with the following episode: "After King Hsiang of Ch'i died, King Chao of Ch'in sent an envoy with a jade-link puzzle to the queen [of King Hsiang], saying: 'Ch'i is full of wise men. Is there anyone who knows how to solve this puzzle?' The queen showed the puzzle to all the courtiers, but none knew how to disentangle it. The queen thereupon used a hammer to break the link. She dismissed the Ch'in envoy, saying: 'I have respectfully solved the puzzle.'"[31] In the Confucian tradition, jade symbolizes the virtue of a superior man *(chün-tzu)*—hence it is the sign of patriarchal privilege.[32] The jade-link puzzle, made by order of the aggressive King Chao of Ch'in, links male wisdom and ambition to this already very powerful emblem. Sending this puzzle to Ch'i, which has just lost its king, Ch'in issues a challenge to Ch'i's male wisdom and a threat to Ch'i's patriarchal privilege. Since Ch'in devised this entire diplomatic ploy following male rules, the puzzle can only confound those who act upon the same standards, such as the Ch'i courtiers. When the queen views the jade link from a perspective other than that of her courtiers, the puzzle immediately becomes unproblematic. Symbolically, what the queen smashes is not simply a jade link but a power system suffused with male values.

This episode becomes a paradigm for Li Ch'ing's deconstruction of a male-dominant world. When this world excludes women from the center of power, it provides them with opportunities to disregard male rules—and even makes it possible for them to attack the male system itself. Notice how the following story calls into question the very benevolence of Heaven—a central Confucian concept: "Girl Kao, posthumously entitled 'Min,' the 'Commiserated,' was seven years old when her father, Kao Yen-chao, surrendered to the state [of the T'ang] and Li Na ordered her whole family slaughtered. . . . On the eve of execution, her mother and brother, thinking that Heaven was divine and intelligent, worshipped Heaven before their last moment. The girl said, 'If Heaven is indeed divine and intelligent, how can it allow my loyal and righteous family to be wiped out? What kind of wisdom does Heaven have that deserves our worship?' She alone would not pay respect [to Heaven] but instead cried to the west for her father. Saluting her father several times, she then went to her death."[33]

The women in Li's Nü Shih-shuo also ridiculed various confinements men forced upon them—for example, foot-binding, which imposed spiritual constraints in a physical form. A son asked his mother, "Why do the women of rich households usually bind their feet?" She replied: "I have heard that gentlewomen in the past would not walk out of their inner chambers, and, if they had to, they would take a carriage. Since they had nothing to do with feet, they had them bound. Although women were confined like this, there still occurred in later times the [love] affair [hsing, lit. walk] at Sang-chung and the elopement [pen, lit. run] from Lin-ch'iung. When Fan Chü said, 'to bind one's feet and not to enter Ch'in,' he was using a female metaphor."[34] Li Ch'ing of course knew when foot-binding started and recorded the event in the Nü Shih-shuo: Li Yü (937–978), the last ruler of the Southern T'ang, ordered his concubine Yao-niang to bind her feet "in the form of a hooklike crescent moon" and to dance on a lotus-shaped platform.[35] However, he moves the custom back some two thousand years and emphasizes its moral rather than its sensual purpose—namely, that men invented foot-binding in order to prevent women from walking or running down the road to debauchery.

Moreover, crossing the boundaries of authorship and gender, Li Ch'ing alters Fan Chü's words in the Chan-kuo ts'e (Intrigues of the warring states) into a line from Li Ssu's (?–208 B.C.) "Shang-shu Ch'in Shih-huang" (Admonition to Ch'in Shih-huang), asserting that Fan Chü/Li Ssu are "using a female metaphor." The following are the two men's remarks in the original texts:

Fan Chü:

If all [gentlemen] under Heaven saw me, your subject, die for devoting loyalty [to Your Majesty], they would shut their mouths and bind their feet [kuo-tsu], daring not to come to Ch'in.[36]

Li Ssu:

[Your Majesty would then] make all gentlemen under Heaven dare not to go west. They would bind their feet [kuo-tsu] not to enter Ch'in.[37]

As we can see, the phrase kuo-tsu pu ju Ch'in in Fan Chü/Li Ssu's original texts refers to men's "hesitation to serve Ch'in." Asserting it as a female metaphor, Li Ch'ing moves kuo-tsu from its original male/political context into a female/moral context.

The form of such an anachronistic account of history—a verbal collage assembled with shredded cultural fragments—thus parodies the male discourse of mutilating the female body. If men invented foot-binding to ensure women's virtue, women might advise men to do the same in order to ensure their righteousness. In this episode, we can easily detect Li Ch'ing's anger toward Ming scholars who surrendered to the Manchus: They should have bound their feet to keep them from "walking" or "running" down the road to political debauchery!

INVENTING A WOMEN'S ORDER

Disillusioned with most of his fellow gentlemen, Li Ch'ing employs women as alternative cultural agents, using their distinctive voices to express his own opinions. Looking into the fundamental differences between women and men, Li tries to reconcile unique female qualities with his own value system. In this effort, he finds that milk and scent, which link the female body closely to the rest of the world, can give that world an easy access to an understanding of women.

Although milk value and scent value often coincide, Li's *Nü Shih-shuo* usually associates milk with moral concerns and scent with aesthetic issues. In human life, *ju*—milk—is produced by *ju*—breast-feeding—which links a mother to her child in the process of *chü*—nurturing. Hence in Li's *Nü Shih-shuo*, breast-feeding comes to signify the maintenance of life and serves as the symbol of humanity. For example, a mother insists upon breast-feeding her infant son one last time before both are put to death—a powerful protest against the savage punishment of clan elimination (*mieh-tsu*).[38]

At one point, the process even exceeds gender boundaries: "When Minister Pi Kou's [fl. 713–741] stepmother died, his two half sisters were still infants. He breast-fed them, and milk came out from his breasts. Upon his death, his two sisters cried grievously until they fainted. They said, 'People in the past said that it was the mother who nurtured us. Now our elder brother breast-fed us, and he was thus our surrogate mother. In order to repay his favor of nurturing, we ought to mourn for him as for our mother.' They hence paid him [a] three-year [mourning ritual]."[39] This episode revises an earlier anecdote in Liu Su's *New Account of the Great T'ang*. Liu originally categorized this mythical story under "Yu-t'i" (Brotherly love), defining Pi Kou's virtuous conduct, however extraordinary, as still a male behavior. And the two sisters justified their unusual manner of grieving also in terms of a brother-sister relationship.[40] Li Ch'ing, however, disregards Pi Kou's sex by classifying this behavior under "Shu-te" (Female virtues), and he has the two sisters claim Pi Kou to be their surrogate mother and hence to be honored as a birth mother. Thus Pi Kou, although male in sex, becomes female in gender.[41]

This episode dramatizes a fundamental connection between the body and culture, as Judith Butler points out:

> Considering that "the" body is invariably transformed into his body or her body, the body is only known through its gendered appearance. It would seem imperative to consider the way in which this gendering of the body occurs. My suggestion is that the body becomes its gender through a series of acts which are renewed, revised, and consolidated through time. From a feminist point of view, one might try to reconceive

the gendered body as the legacy of sedimented acts rather than a pre-
determined or foreclosed structure, essence or fact, whether natural, cultural, or linguistic.[42]

The body is understood to be an active process of embodying certain cultural and historical possibilities.[43]

Obviously, Li Ch'ing's purpose in relating this story in this particular way
is not to show how a man's body can perform a woman's biological function, but to exalt a female virtue, tz'u—motherly love—as a cultural value
that transcends gender differences. In Li Ch'ing's view, tz'u, a moral category exemplifying the quality of nurturing and typified by the operation
of breast-feeding, should be considered the most fundamental and universal value of the human world. He articulates this idea through the voice
of Empress Wu Tse-t'ien, who argued for a three-year mourning period for
the mother even while the father was still alive. She said: "A mother to her
child devotes the deepest love. She locates the child in a dry and warm
place whereas she herself dwells in wet; she swallows bitterness while emit-
ting sweet [milk]. Nothing could surpass such extreme love, so it should
be greatly rewarded."[44]

According to the I-li (Etiquette and ritual), the three-year period was
originally designed to mourn for a ruler or a father. Children were to observe a three-year mourning for their mother—in a lesser ritual form—
only when the father had already died.[45] By upgrading the mourning ritual for the mother, Empress Wu formally institutionalized the value of
tz'u—motherly love. Acknowledging her effort in promoting this fundamental moral value, Li Ch'ing brings the notoriously ruthless female sovereign into the chapter "Jen-hsiao" (Benevolence and filial piety).

Li Ch'ing subsequently contrasts the patriarchal moral system of the
ruler with the female moral system of the mother. The two clash when a
minister/son commits treason, a signal of the bankruptcy of certain values upon which the minister/son has established himself. Who should take
the blame for corrupting him? The ruler accuses the mother of misguid-
ing the son. The mother protests: "I, your humble maid-servant, am not
guilty. I heard that when a son is young, he is the [mother's] son, but af-

ter he has grown up, he becomes the [mother's] friend. I managed to raise a son for Your Highness, and Your Highness chooses him to be your minister. This man is Your Highness' minister, not my son anymore. It is that Your Highness has a rebel-minister, not that I have a rebel-son."[46] Here, the mother clearly separates the two systems; each, she contends, has its own value structure. Her system contains only natural categories such as mother, child, and friend, which usually form peaceful relationships of the nurturing to the nurtured, the loving to the loved. The ruler's system, on the other hand, contains artificial elements that form power relationships such as between the ruler and the minister, the lord and the servant. Such a structure unavoidably anticipates violent treason and rebellion. While with his mother, the son is a loving child and friend. Once he enters the ruler's court, he has the capacity to be a violent rebel. Therefore, the mother and her milk value have not made the ruler's minister into a rebel-son; rather, the ruler and his power system have corrupted the mother's loving son into becoming a rebel-minister.

Similar to the milk value, the scent value also builds upon something emitted from the female body, but scent links the female body to others in ways very different from those of milk. In traditional "aromatic and glamorous" (hsiang-yen) stories, women's scent provokes male desires for the female body. Li Ch'ing adapts many of these stories in his Nü Shih-shuo and always veils his beauties with a swirl of fragrance.[47] He nonetheless transforms the original sensual appeal of the female scent into a spiritual one, thus entirely changing its effect on the man-woman relationship. As one episode relates: "T'ang Princess T'ai-p'ing loved the 'Essay on Yüeh I' [composed by the Wei literatus Hsia-hou Hsüan and rendered calligraphically by Wang Hsi-chih]. Empress Wu gave her a brocade bag [to contain it]. Later an old woman threw the bag into the fire, and the fragrance lasted for several days."[48] What is the source of this strong aroma? Is it the princess' touch? Is it the empress' brocade bag? Is it the beauty of Wang Hsi-chih's calligraphy? Or is it the literary eminence of Hsia-hou Hsüan's essay that depicts Yüeh I's heroic qualities? The answer is as ambiguous as the smell is indistinct.

Metaphorically, the aroma may arise from the heated intercourse between the princess and the empress' female scent and Hsia-hou and Wang's male talents. Li Ch'ing thus introduces the idea that the female scent can ignite the blaze of male talent. In Li's *Nü Shih-shuo,* literati often solicit such magic power from the female touch. For instance: "The Ku-tsang prefect Chang Hsien's concubines were daily on duty in his studio. Those reading books were named 'Spreading-Fragrance Courtesans' [Ch'uan-fang chi]; those attending his essay writings were named 'Ink-Fairies' [Mo-o]; and those in charge of his poetic manuscripts were named 'Double-Purity Masters' [Shuang-ch'ing tzu]."[49] The line "Those reading books were named 'Spreading-Fragrance Courtesans'" *(tsou-shu che hao* Ch'uan-fang chi*)* forms a symmetry, equating *shu*—books—with *fang*—fragrance. Male literati, accustomed to seeking sensual pleasure from the female body (typified by concubines and courtesans), now rely upon the female mind to transform books into fragrance, or await the female scent to penetrate into cultural activities and to help brew intellectual elegance. Either way, "fragrance" becomes the sign of enhanced aesthetic achievements.

From sensual to spiritual, the transformation of women's "scent" proceeded along with their increasing participation in intellectual life. Li Ch'ing devotes four entire chapters to women's artistic and literary activities, including "Ju-ya" (Scholarly elegance), "Chün-ts'ai" (Outstanding talents), "Ying-hui" (Prominent intelligence), and "I-ch'iao" (Art and ingenuity). In these chapters, women freely roam through all kinds of cultural fields—historical writing, scholastic learning, poetry, painting, calligraphy, music, medicine, geomancy, divination, even archery and military arts—often surpassing men. In addition to these shared categories, women master their own special domains of weaving, embroidery, and sewing in which men can hardly compete.[50]

Women's unique contributions invited men's growing recognition of female talents, hence the following peculiar form of celebration: "At the household of the Hsü-chou governor and Minister Chang Feng-chien, courtesans were well read. People who borrowed Chang's books often found powder and rouge stains stamped like seals [yin] on the volumes."[51] Li Ch'ing endorses the female touches. Since to stamp seals on books or paintings indicates possession, the episode presents both a female claim and a male acknowledgment that women are genuine connoisseurs and owners of culture whose scent graces cultural products and whose participation enriches cultural life.[52]

Flower and Kitchen Poetics in Yen Heng's *Nü Shih-shuo*

Yen Heng dedicated her *Nü Shih-shuo*, the only *Shih-shuo* imitation written by a woman, almost exclusively to Ch'ing women's poetic and artistic achievements. Therefore, in addition to the records of women's daily life, the work also contains a great number of comments on women's poetry and art. Yen Heng then faced a problem that had never before occurred to any *Shih-shuo* imitator: Upon which standard should she measure women's works? Yen Heng chose not to follow the conventional rules set up mainly by men. Guided by her own lived bodily experience, she established an evaluative discourse, a "female poetics," deliberately weaving flower imagery and nurturing themes into artistic and poetic creation. As a result, Yen Heng's *Nü Shih-shuo* suggests a female value system that also contains scent and milk elements but, as we shall see later, differs from Li Ch'ing's version in structure and approach.

FEMINIZING THE MALE POETICS

Flower imagery pervades Yen Heng's portrayal of women, occupying about two-fifths of all the anecdotes. These anecdotes are closely linked to women's life passages through mysterious, empathetic connections. Thus, a hortensia flower dropped into a mother's dream portends the birth of a talented daughter, and red crab apple petals transforming into white mourns the suicide of a chaste woman. Plum blossoms will not bloom unless their beloved beauty comes; orchids wilt when their mistress passes away. Women also give flowers mutual care. They rejoice while flowers are blooming, and pine away while flowers are withering.[53] In Yen Heng's *Nü Shih-shuo,* flowers are at once women's alter egos and soul mates. As such, they naturally enter women's poetic and artistic creations as the dominant images. Yen Heng's women depict flowers via all kinds of artistic media, including poetry, painting, embroidery, paper cuts, and so forth, sometimes quite inventively.[54] And women's descriptions of flowers are often the "portrayals of themselves" (tzu hsieh-chao).[55]

Mysteriously, the flowers they create, like real ones, emit sweet scent that serves literally or metaphorically as an unmistakable sign of a "female" cultural identity. For example, a young woman artist paints roses that "are illustriously colorful and can also generate fragrance." When she displays her works in the springtime, butterflies come to dance around and cannot be waved away.[56] This close connection between women and flowers in both nature and culture manifests itself particularly in the following episode: "Liang Ying, courtesy name Mei-chün (Lady Plum), by nature loved plum blossoms. She had a Plum Studio; on its four walls she inscribed over a thousand ancient and contemporary poems about plum blossoms. When no plum blossoms were in sight, she would view them from the walls, saying, 'How can any painting come up to this!' She also compiled a volume of ancient poetic lines on plum blossoms. Lady Lin Ya-ch'ing entitled it Fragrance from Every Word [tzu tzu hsiang]."[57]

Liang Ying's Plum Blossom Poetry Studio (Mei-hua shih-wu) evidently emerged from the long-standing plum cults dating from the Sung period (960–1279), particularly in Chiang-nan—the native place of Liang Ying and her beloved flowering plum.[58] The idea of building such a studio bears the influence of Sung scholars' plum worlds, which can be "as small as a flowering branch in a crystal vase or a single tree in a courtyard, [or] as large as the plantations of a suburban villa or [a] mountain retreat." And the way to appreciate plum blossoms follows the principle of what Maggie Bickford terms a "cultural chain reaction."[59] Bickford elaborates: "The interaction between the individual's encounter with the flowering plum in nature, his flowering-plum experience (comprising his own present and past together with received precedents or analogs), his contemplation and creation of flowering-plum ideals in literature, and his material realization of those ideals in pictorial form and in the man-made environment is characteristic of Sung plum appreciation."[60]

Unlike the male literati's plum worlds, Liang Ying builds her studio not with real plum trees but with poetic texts about flowering plum, and she "views" the blossoms by means of words rather than gazing on real flowers. The effect of appreciation she thus achieves, as Liang Ying brags, goes beyond the expressive aptness of paintings, for she not only "sees" the colors and shapes but also "smells" the fragrance of the flowers; hence the title of Liang's volume of poems. This multidimensional blend of sensory and reading experience can only emerge from body-and-soul indulgence in a blur of physical and literary beauty, which results from a woman's intuitive identification with the flowers that bloom both in nature and in culture.

But Yen Heng's exaltation of flower imagery and intimate comparison between flowers and women's qualities challenge the conventional masculine poetics that marginalizes flower imagery, especially if it analogizes flowers to the female body. For example, the Chin poet/critic Yüan Hao-wen (1190–1257) ridicules the Sung poet Ch'in Kuan's (1049–1100) style as "girls' poetry" (nü-lang shih), simply because Ch'in links flower imagery to women.[61] As he elaborates in the "Biography of Wang Chung-li" (Wang Chung-li chuan): "I used to study with the gentleman. Once I asked him how to compose poems. He used Ch'in Guan's poem, 'Spring Rain,' as an example, saying, 'His poetic lines, "Passionate peonies are filled with spring tears/Languid roses recline among evening branches," are not unskillful. But, compared with Han Yü's (768–824) "Banana leaves are big and gardenia flowers fat," "Spring Rain" reads more like a woman's poem. Why should one waste his energy on learning a woman's style?'"[62] Yüan and Wang disparage Ch'in Kuan not because his poems are "unskillful," but because his couplet sounds too feminine compared with the lines from Han Yü's poem "Shan-shih" (Mountain stone):

> I ascend the hall and sit on the terrace, in the ample new rain;
> Banana leaves are big and gardenia flowers fat.[63]

Although also depicting plants and flowers in the rain, Han Yü uses adjectives ta, big, and fei, fat, to create strong, "masculine" images. Ch'in Kuan's flowers, by contrast, create very different moods: Raindrops fall on peony petals like tears dwelling on pink cheeks; and rose branches, saturated with water, recline like tender waists. Consistent with their gender-oriented criticism, Yüan and Wang dismiss these tearful, languid images, celebrating instead Han Yü's "manly" images. Thus the complicated critique of poetry is reduced to a masculinity-versus-femininity dichotomy. Han Yü's style is associated with men and is therefore good, and Ch'in Kuan's is associated with women and is therefore bad. Obviously, for Yüan Hao-wen and Wang Chung-li, poetics has a gender—and it is male. However deserving of a sophisticated critique, once Ch'in Kuan associates himself with women, he alienates himself from male poetics.

Yen Heng, a learned scholar and poet, must have been familiar with Yüan Hao-wen's criticism of Ch'in Kuan. She does not defer to Yüan Hao-wen's poetic authority, however; rather, she relentlessly champions flower imagery in portraying the female body and in reflecting women's destiny. Refusing to accept the idea that poems thus composed merely present an inferior version of male poetry, Yen Heng believes that female poetics complements and amplifies male poetics, creating a literary culture that is more beautiful and "fragrant" than it would otherwise be. For instance, in the Plum Studio episode mentioned earlier, the scent of words clearly comes from Liang Ying's rearrangement of culture, which so intensifies its beauty that each word she has chosen generates fragrance. Hence Yen Heng tells us that female touch has enhanced the aroma of Chinese culture.

Yen Heng's version of female poetics complements male poetics not only with its scent value, but also with its milk value. As she also recounts in the Plum Studio episode, whenever the outer world becomes inhospitable and there are "no plum blossoms in sight," Liang Ying "views" flowers on the wall, between the poetic lines she has collected and preserved. Thus this "female" cultural entity, created by a woman's love for Nature and culture, provides shelter for both. Again, the nurturing feature included in Yen Heng's female poetics comes from women's lived bodily experience. Yen Heng's women read, write, and comment on poetry based on their life as poets, scholars, and women. Their life as women brings their nurturing nature into their literary and artistic creativity. The following episode is especially revealing in this respect: "Yüan was Yüan Mei's [1716–1797] aunt. When Mei was young, he used to read the 'Great Edict' in the *Book of Doc-*

uments and was quite frustrated by its tongue-twisting features. His aunt then would come to his help by reading with him. She used to comment on ancient people. Among them, she disliked Kuo Chü, so she composed a poem to criticize him."[64] Yüan's qualities as a loving nurturer, a learned scholar, and a sensitive poet are wonderfully woven into a child-protective network. Her scholarly ability enables her to guide a child through the difficult learning of the *Book of Documents,* and she condemns Kuo Chü, one of the twenty-four paragons of filial piety, because he achieved his reputation at the risk of his son's life.[65]

As nurturers, women are closely affiliated with the kitchen, where they store and cook food for their families. The kitchen thus becomes an emblem of women's care, a soul-stirring place that understandably provides a poetic site for a woman-poet. Yen Heng presents the following touching episode: "I do not know who Ch'en K'un-wei is. Once Lord Sang, the minister of Public Works, bought a copy of the *Poems of a Hundred Yüan Poets,* to which [a postscript by Ch'en], in small handwriting, was attached. It reads, 'On the day of Double Ninth, the year of Ting-ssu, our kitchen had no rice. I picked up the *Poems of a Hundred Yüan Poets* to sell in order to provide my family with some meals. Unable to bear [the pain of] letting it out of my hands, I composed this long regulated poem [to commemorate the event].'"[66]

This episode reveals a chilly dilemma in a writing woman's life: Her milk value and scent value may often be in conflict, and she may have to sacrifice one to maintain the other (I shall return to this theme later). As shown here, she has to trade the *Poems of a Hundred Yüan Poets,* possibly a treasure from her dowry,[67] in exchange for rice to feed her family. Torn between love for family and love of poetry, Lady Ch'en assuages her anxiety and sorrow in a long poem. Such a process of poetic creation reaffirms a general rule in Chinese literary tradition—that "a poet emerges from sorrow" *(ai-yüan ch'i sao-jen).*[68] The kind of sorrow that Lady Ch'en feels is uniquely a woman's. A gentleman would rarely have any "kitchen" frustrations, since, as Mencius says, "a gentleman should keep a distance from the kitchen."[69] Yet women—Lady Ch'en and Yen Heng alike—consider the kitchen no less noble than the imperial court.

Yen Heng includes an episode that launches a criticism directly at those gentlemen who "keep a distance from the kitchen": "Chin Shih-shan, courtesy name Hsüeh-chuang, was precocious by nature. When she was a young girl, her mother taught her short poems. To the poetic line 'The water boils on the bamboo stove, and the fire has just turned red,' Shih-shan commented, laughing: 'If the water is already boiling, how can the fire have just turned red?'"[70]

Whoever composed this poetic line had everything right according to traditional (male) poetics, including syntactic rules, phonetic rules, and so on. But its semantic illogicality had not been detected until the poem entered the inner chambers, simply because no male had "kitchen knowledge."

With this "kitchen criticism," Yen Heng teaches her readers some general truths. When men marginalize women into certain realms—kitchens, for instance—they estrange themselves from these indispensable realms and doom themselves to incomplete knowledge about the world. For women, being "marginalized" to places where men never go allows them to see things that men can never see, things that are usually closely related to the nurturing of human lives. Thus, while women bring their nurturer's experience into their literary and artistic creation and criticism, they play nurturers not only of life, but of human knowledge as well.

Empowered by a mastery of knowledge exceeding that of men, at least in certain important respects, Yen Heng's women exhibit strong self-esteem; they have something to teach men and therefore deserve to be mentors and critics. Yen relates the story of a bridegroom who writes a poem to his bride on their wedding night, with the line: "In front of the mirror stand, the female disciple salutes [me]." Rejecting the groom's self-serving assumption of mentorship, the bride protests, boldly saying: "Why don't you change 'female disciple' [*nü men-sheng*] into 'female teacher' [*nü hsien-sheng*]?"[71] She thus accepts the ritual of endorsing a teacher-disciple relationship between husband and wife but rejects the protocol that deems the husband more learned. Instead, she contends that, in front of the mirror stand, the centerpiece of the inner chamber and hence the center of the female domain, women comprehend more than men.[72]

At least some men in late imperial times accepted and supported female poetics. Indeed, the "female teacher" story recounted above got into broad circulation in the eighteenth century through at least two written versions, including one by Yüan Mei,[73] whom Yen Heng greatly admired as a leading promoter of women poets and poetry.[74] Yen Heng also indicates male intellectuals' acknowledgment of female poetics in the following episode:

> In the courtyard of the Ch'ü-chou Villa, the crab apple flowers were in full bloom in the snow of October. The famous scholars [ming-shih] of the time all wrote poems about the event, and among them Hsü Hsüeh-t'ang [literally, Hsü the Snow Crab Apple] composed the best. A poem in Wang Hang's [courtesy name Hsi-hao, 1704–?] "Miscellaneous Poems from Chin-men" reads:
>
> > A lady scholar with tousled hair, eyebrows unpainted,
> > Sent me an extremely beautiful [yen-chüeh] poem on the crab apple flower.
> > Using a jade scale to measure talented men,
> > She surpasses Wan-erh, of days of old, in the tower.
>
> [A poem] written for Hsüeh-t'ang.[75]

Wang Hang's poem alludes to a myth about the early T'ang prodigy Shang-kuan Wan-erh (664–710). On the eve of her birth, Wan-erh's mother dreamed that Heaven gave her daughter a jade scale to measure talented men.[76] Later, Wan-erh grew up to be a famous poet and was chosen the imperial critic responsible for ranking the top-rated male poets such as Sung Chih-wen (d. 712) and Shen Ch'üan-ch'i (d. 729).[77] Comparing Hsüeh-t'ang to Wan-erh, Wang Hang asserts Hsüeh-t'ang's superiority over men as both a poet and a critic, based solely on a reading of her crab apple poem. In other words, a single flower poem can transform a male poet's aesthetic perspective.

This episode also shows how women poets can redirect the male gaze with their literary achievements. When Wang Hang first views Hsüeh-t'ang's female body, he sees only her "unpainted eyebrows." They indicate her disinterest in the cultural convention of adorning herself to please men, hence a rejection of male access to her body.[78] At the same time, the absence of "painted eyebrows" lures the male gaze to the exploration of this missing part and thus moves it from her body to her poem, from her outer beauty to her inner beauty. Correspondingly, Wang uses *yen-chüeh*— extremely beautiful—a word usually used to describe women's physical attractiveness, to describe her female poetics. Thus, Hsüeh-t'ang's "un-painted eyebrows" subvert the long-standing cultural meanings inscribed on the female body and give women equal opportunities to enter into a poetry contest with men, a competition in which both genders are equally considered *ming-shih*—famous scholars.

Linking the female body to a poem through a flower image, the "snow crab apple," Yen Heng portrays a female poet who is named after the flow-ers she writes about and whose poem reflexively describes her flowerlike inner qualities. Thus, on a metaphorical level, Yen Heng builds an emblem to female poetics that harmonizes the female body, women's lived bodily experiences, nature, and poetry all at once.

YEN HENG'S "TENDER THOUGHTS" POEMS AND THE FEMALE POETICS

How about Yen Heng's own poems? Do they reflect the female poet-ics she so painstakingly constructed? Although Yen left only seventeen po-ems from her "Tender Thoughts Hermitage," they are enough to show a close affinity with the lifestyle of the literary women celebrated in the *Nü Shih-shuo*. There are records of her poetic outings, always attending her mother-in-law and always in the company of female in-laws and cousins— a clear emulation of the Banana Garden women's poetry club of early Ch'ing Hang-chou, whose stories occupy one-tenth of Yen Heng's *Nü Shih-shuo*.[79] On these occasions, Yen Heng inscribed poems wherever she went, often with a hairpin.[80] We also have her poetic correspondence with other writing women, inscriptions on female artists' works, and, of course, ac-counts of her own solitary moments, imbued with poetic sentiments.

Yen's tender thoughts, saturated with women's values and embellished with flower imagery, are particularly condensed in the following two po-ems, joined under the title, "While sorting old embroidery patterns, I found a lotus petal inscribed with a poem in small regulated script by Lady Chin Ts'ai-chiang, the mother of my mother-in-law":

Her purity of bamboo grove aura soared above the others.
Her new poems spread all over the Jade Lake.
Picking up flowers to try out the wearing-flower script,
Her style surpassed the rocky [*lin-hsün*] T'ai-hua [Mountain]
      in the autumn.

Daughter Hsieh's gauze veil, Daughter Ts'ai's zither,
A motherly instruction resurfaces after a long time.
Yet I hide it again deeply in a jade case,
So as not to stir up my aging lady's sadness for her mother.[81]

These two poems present an interesting juxtaposition of flowers and
rocks. First, Yen Heng surrounds her grandmother-in-law, Lady Chin Ts'ai-
chiang, with well-wrought flower imagery. This pure lady-poet picked up
a delicate lotus petal on the Jade Lake one summer day, and inscribed a
poem on it with *tsan-hua ko* (wearing-flower script), a lovely calligraphic
style that looks "like a beauty wearing flowers, dancing and laughing in
front of a mirror stand."[82] She then gave the inscribed petal to her daughter as a mother's instruction, possibly on her wedding day, and the daughter naturally preserved it along with her most precious embroidery patterns.
When the granddaughter-in-law uncovered this piece of family treasure,
her sensitive heart immediately recognized and embraced its perfect combination of poetic beauty, calligraphy, delicate writing material, and the
poet herself. But, as a filial daughter, she could not be unconcerned with
her aging mother-in-law's feelings.

All this is as tender as the lotus petal. Why, then, does the fragile summer lotus convey a rocky *(lin-hsün)* message of autumn? How is the Jade
Lake linked to Tai-hua Mountain? The answer to these questions can be
found in the actual instruction inscribed on the lotus petal, as Yen Heng
reveals in the first line of the second poem: "Daughter Hsieh's gauze veil
and Daughter Ts'ai's zither." At first glance, Lady Chin seems to recommend that the daughter polish her young talents following the two brilliant prodigies, Hsieh Tao-yün and Ts'ai Yen [Wen-chi] (fl. late Han). Yet,
instead of alluding to Hsieh Tao-yün's youthful wit, typified by the well-
known line about "willow catkins" *(liu-hsü),* Lady Chin emphasizes Hsieh's
middle-age accomplishment, represented by the "gauze veil." According

to the *History of the Chin,* "Lieh-nü chuan," Hsieh Tao-yün's talented younger brother-in-law Wang Hsien-chih was once trapped in a "pure-conversation" debate. Covering her face with a gauze veil, Tao-yün took his place and defeated the opponent.[83] Comparable to Hsieh Tao-yün's "gauze veil," Ts'ai Yen's "zither" refers not to the musical talent of her youth[84] but to a series of zither lyrics attributed to her mature years, the famed "Hu-chia shih-pa p'ai" (Eighteen melodies of the Hu pipe). These poems depict her twelve painful years in captivity by the Hsiung-nu and the Han people's sufferings at the time.[85]

There is one more relevant reference. In the Chinese tradition, water symbolizes wisdom and mountains symbolize benevolence.[86] Thus, the transition from the summer on the Jade Lake to the autumn of T'ai-hua Mountain constructs a mother's design for her daughter's life passage—a passage from flowery youth into fruitful middle age and from a talented girl to a benevolent woman who transforms her wisdom into the strength to protect her family. In the process, the flower's tenderness meets the rock's toughness. If flowers symbolize women's features as creators and nurturers, rocks symbolize their inner strength as protectors.

By including Ts'ai Yen as a role model in her motherly instructions *(i-hsün),* Lady Chin, along with her interpreter Yen Heng, carries a standard quite different from that of men. For instance, the Ming scholar Ho Liang-chün, the author of *Ho's Forest,* criticized Ts'ai Yen in his preface to the "Hsien-yüan" chapter: "Ts'ai Wen-chi lost her chastity to the Northern court (the Hsiung-nu), and gentlemen feel ashamed for her. Even though she had outstanding literary talent, what about her is worth mentioning?"[87] Following the *Hsien-yüan* tradition, Ho appreciated writing women and readily admitted Ts'ai's outstanding talent in literature.[88] He nonetheless rejected Ts'ai Yen in the end, criticizing her for "losing her chastity" *(ju-shen,* lit., defilement of her body). Thus he identified a tension between a woman's literary talent and her moral behavior (in his definition, of course), anticipating Chang Hsüeh-ch'eng's (1738–1801) similar understanding of women. Chang, a contemporary of Lady Chin, acknowledged the literary talent of Ts'ai Yen and Hsieh Tao-yün, but found Ts'ai's life problematic and considered Hsieh to have "strayed from the middle path."

Neither was therefore capable, in Chang's view, of transmitting the *Tao* of ancient China.[89]

The divergent evaluations of Ts'ai Yen and Hsieh Tao-yün, proposed respectively by Lady Chin and her male opponents, Ho and Chang, underscore an important point made by Susan Mann: "Women's learning invoked sharply different reactions from learned men. At one extreme was Chang Hsüeh-ch'eng's ideal, a moral instructress whose family roles (whether maternal, wifely, or daughterly) at once desexed her and endowed her with power and autonomy. The other extreme was Yüan Mei's ideal, a young passionate aesthete whose frail body and sexual naiveté signaled her vulnerability and dependency."[90] For Chang, "Women's poetic voice . . . smacked of lewdness: it was the voice of the courtesan," while in Yüan's view, "a learned woman's highest achievement was to write poetry." Yüan "found young female poets appealing because the child's mind represented spontaneity, simple diction, and pure emotion: 'The poet is one who has not lost her childlike mind.'" In brief, for a variety of learned men—Ho Liang-chün, Chang Hsüeh-ch'eng, and Yüan Mei among them—the "two classical models—the moral instructor and the brilliant prodigy . . . represented competing ideals of erudite womanhood that were impossible to reconcile."[91]

Learned women saw the matter differently. For Chin Ts'ai-chiang and her granddaughter-in-law, Yen Heng, women's learning could and should embrace all values: moral instruction and poetic creation, milk and scent, existing together in mutual definition, refinement, and reinforcement. The two were an exemplary couple for this reconciliation. Chin, the moral instructor, brought scent value into her motherly instruction by writing it in a poetic form, in refined calligraphy, and symbolically on a flower petal. Yen, the brilliant prodigy, followed Chin's advice, pursuing not only the scent but also the milk values. Two poems found in Yen Heng's Tender Thoughts collection, standing as a pair of self-portraits, speak of this effort. One is entitled "In Praise of the Glass Beauty":

> Clean as ice, pure as water,
> Her words, jade and pearl, fascinate the four sides.
> Don't say that her body looks truly fragile;

Her mind is by nature extraordinarily bright.
Too delicate to stand against the wind;
So illusory as if walking on the moon.
She keeps me company in the lonely inner chamber;
Behind the crystal screen, in the soundless night.[92]

Using the translucent imagery of glass, Yen Heng simultaneously materializes the abstract concepts of *chieh,* clean, and *ch'ing,* pure, into a delicate female body and abstracts a female body into an ethereal spirit. The resulting poetic entity has both sensuous and spiritual appeal. Her ice body chimes, describing a refined poet who emits poetic lines like jade and pearls, every word a musical note. Her crystalline flesh allows viewers to see into her mind, as bright and pure as the glowing water. Her fragile figure shivers in the wind, a sensitive creature, easily affected by the changing environment. She blends into the moonlight, ready to absorb Nature into herself and to dissolve herself into Nature: pure, clean, delicate, fragile, sensitive—a most vivid portrayal of a female poetic spirit!

Yet this ice body does not embrace a poetic spirit only. It also possesses a fiery passion. Ice and fire clash, triggering heroic sentiments that thunder out of Yen Heng's Tender Thoughts Hermitage:

The pure wind of the universe has its rocky toughness [*lin-hsün*];
"Luckily" my fair body belongs to the golden inner chamber.
I have the desire to sing and cry for people;
Only by mistake others call me a poet.[93]

In this poetic confession of Yen Heng's moral/literary ambition, the rugged word *lin-hsün* appears again. It substantiates Yen Heng's "fair body in a golden inner chamber"—her "glass beauty" aspect—linking it with a "desire to sing and cry for people." This interpretation of *lin-hsün* reinforces Yen Heng's reading of Chin Ts'ai-chiang's "motherly instructions" and establishes the core of Yen Heng's female poetics, which combines ethics with aesthetics. Ethically, *lin-hsün* extends a woman's protection of her family to all people. Aesthetically, *lin-hsün* demands the powerful poetic expression of such a nurturer's concerns.

Under the new "rugged" poetic standard, *lin-hsün,* we can see even more clearly why Yen Heng and Chin Ts'ai-chiang celebrate Ts'ai Yen in

spite of men's depreciation of her. As women themselves, they have a very
different sense of what virtue is and how to arrange the order of virtuous
categories. While men almost invariably take chastity as a woman's primary virtue, Chin Ts'ai-chiang and Yen Heng place greater value on
women's capacities as nurturers and protectors. Yen Heng occasionally
praises women's chastity, but chastity is not the focus of her *Nü Shih-shuo*.
As a matter of fact, she never discriminates against courtesans but pays
them equal respect for their moral behavior—such as loyalty—and artistic achievements.[94] Thus, Ts'ai Yen embodies perfectly the idea of *lin-hsün*
inasmuch as she, with outstanding literary talents, heroically bears the bur-
den of her own and other people's sufferings.

Although we find no further elaborations of *lin-hsün* in Yen Heng's
poems, several episodes in her *Nü Shih-shuo* exemplify this concept. One
salutes the late Ming loyalist and courtesan-poet Li Yin (1616–1685),
describing her poetic style as "thoughtful, melancholy, imposing, and
powerful, stronger than that of any heroic man."[95] Another expresses the
Ming loyalist-poetess Wu Shan's "jade tree and bronze camel lament"[96]
over the tragic fall of the dynasty and the incapability of retrieving the
lost land.[97] Had Yen Heng not died so young, she would certainly have
included more blazing records of *lin-hsün,* blasted from the "pure wind
of the universe."

Confined in a "golden inner chamber," however, Yen Heng's *lin-hsün*
ambition remained limited to her family. (Here the tension between
women's lived bodily experiences and the cultural meanings inscribed on
the female body is so intense that Yen Heng cynically describes herself
"lucky" to be a woman.) Most of Yen Heng's poems therefore depict daily
life against a poetic, flowery background. Consider the following representative poem, "Chanting Inner Thoughts: In Harmony with the Master
of Spring Sound Pavilion, following his original rhyme":

> Too exquisite, the shadows of the *t'u-mi* roses!
> Every time thinking of you, I feel lost.
> Longing for you, I consult the Ch'u Diviner;
> Feeling cold, I send you the Wu coat.

Seeing my little daughter, I miss my son;
Attending the mother-in-law, I tidy my emerald hairpin.
Only the Moon Goddess knows my thoughts;
Deep in the night, shining over the sleepless, in separate places.[98]

This poem, evidently addressed to her husband, depicts a virtuous and loving wife, mother, and daughter-in-law, who alone takes care of the family. On a late spring night, her thoughts embrace the absent husband and son, both far away from home. The *t'u-mi* flowers retreat into the dim moonlight, leaving their shadows to beguile her eyes and diffusing their scent to remind her of some intimate moment. One more spring has passed, yet the husband is not yet back. Home alone and lovesick, she has no desire to beautify herself. She must, however, tidy her hair while attending her mother-in-law, in an effort to keep up a normal life for the old and the young. Caring, tender, and loving—in both a spiritual and a sensuous sense—this is the married life that Yen Heng has resolved to maintain. But even this humble ambition will soon clash with reality, and the fragile glass will eventually be shattered.

Conflict between Milk and Scent

Yen Heng, following Chin Ts'ai-chiang's "motherly instructions," struggles to combine milk value with scent value. On occasion we find similar cases in Li Ch'ing's *Nü Shih-shuo*.[99] Overwhelmingly, however, Li and Yen highlight a disturbing dilemma for women: Although both values emanate from the female body, a woman finds it extremely difficult to maintain the two at the same time. Often she must either sacrifice her scent value in order to be a dutiful wife and mother or abandon the milk value for the sake of literature and art.

What causes this dilemma? Scent and milk should naturally coexist unless some intruding force drives them apart. Marriage seems one such force. Those who quit aesthetic pursuits in order to concentrate on being a mother, a wife, and a daughter-in-law face painful decisions, as Li Ch'ing records: "Fu Jo-chin's wife, Sun, was skillful in creating poems. However, she did not often compose them and, [when she did,] she frequently burnt her poetic manuscripts. Her family advised her to preserve the drafts, but she said, 'I occasionally [compose poems] just for myself. A woman should concentrate on weaving in order to be filial and respectful [to her in-laws]. Poetic writing is not something [a married woman] should do.'"[100]

For those who insist on upholding their aesthetic ideals, the choices are also difficult: "Miss Yeh-lü, named Ch'ang-ko, was talented in writing poetry and prose. She vowed not to marry, saying: 'A girl cannot rhyme if she is not pure.'"[101] What is it about marriage that threatens women's creativity and scares Ch'ang-ko away from going through a normal life passage? Following her own reasoning, it seems that sexual contact with the male body pollutes female purity (virginity), thus destroying female talent. Ch'ang-ko's worship of virginity as the origin of women's creativity and her disgust with the male body are themes repeated elsewhere in the two Nü Shih-shuo. Yen Heng records that a girl named Ink Maiden decides to sleep all her life with a painting of bamboo by a famous woman artist, as if worrying that a male artist would defile the bamboo, the symbol of purity and integrity.[102]

In another example adduced by Li Ch'ing, "Sung T'ing-fen's five daughters were all smart and literary. . . . They were by nature plain and pure, and disliked wearing perfume, cream, or cosmetics. They wanted to stay unmarried so they could glorify the Sung family with their scholarship."[103] In addition to their persistent esteem of chieh, purity, as the warrant for literary creation, the Sung sisters also offer another reason for defending their virginity—they want to glorify their natal family rather than the family of some "outsider." The defense of physical purity thus becomes a defense of intellectual nobility, motivated, perhaps, by an implicit fear: They may be open to possible humiliation by marrying into an inferior intellectual lineage. This anxiety can be traced back to the story of Hsieh Tao-yün, whose lamentation over marrying an intellectually inferior husband foreshadows a similar sorrow for later generations.[104]

Being unmarried offers a woman relative freedom to reject undesirable men and to associate with those suitable for her spiritual and intellectual needs. Li Ch'ing recounts the following two stories:

Yüan Hao-wen's younger sister, who was both literary and beautiful, entered the Taoist clergy. Chang P'ing-chang desired to marry her, so he proceeded to pay her a visit. Upon his arrival, [Priestess Yüan] was fixing the ceiling with her own hands. She stopped to meet him. P'ing-chang asked if she had written any poems lately. Yüan instantly replied, "Yes, I just obtained a couplet:

> Bid the newly arrived pair of swallows,
> Move your nest elsewhere, to a carved beam."

Stricken with fright, P'ing-chang retreated.[105]

Ts'ao Miao-ch'ing, a native of Ch'ien-t'ang, would not marry even at thirty. She was outstanding in both literature and personal character. Once she took her poems and essays and, accompanied by an old nanny, visited Yang Wei-chen [1296–1370] on Tung-t'ing Mountain in T'ai-hu Lake. Singing poems and playing the zither for Yang, she depicted her melancholy mood over desolate mountains and rivers. Attuned to the zither melodies of "Crying Ospreys" [Kuan-chü] and "Morning [Flying] Pheasants" [Chih chao(-fei)], she brought her poems into harmony with the "White Snow" [Pai-hsüeh] stanzas.[106] [Yang] Wei-chen appreciated her so much that he edited and prefaced the *Collection of Ts'ao's Melodies*.[107]

In the first anecdote, Priestess Yüan, by entering a Taoist temple, has simultaneously found a fortress to protect her virginity and a literary salon in which to meet fellow poets. And by fixing the ceiling, obviously broken by the intruding swallows that sought to build their love nest, she makes a symbolic gesture of rejecting any sort of sexual advances. At the same time, by receiving a male visitor and discussing her poem with him she shows her willingness to communicate with potential male friends. Furthermore, as the case of Ts'ao Miao-ch'ing and Yang Wei-chen reveals, when such a friendship indeed develops, the intense spiritual intercourse of the two will throw them into ecstasies of mutual understanding and appreciation. (Note that the two zither melodies, "Crying Ospreys" and "Morning (Flying) Pheasants," are both love songs.) For an intellectual woman, nothing can be more rewarding in life than this.[108]

Yet men like Yang Wei-chen are rare. Ideal men seem mostly to have lived in the past, keeping women company merely as historical images, enshrined in texts and portraits. Both Li Ch'ing and Yen Heng touch on women's idolization of such male role models:

Woman Pai of Suchow was widowed at twenty. She built a shrine at the northeastern corner of her house. In the shrine she hung the portraits of Su Shih and Ch'en Liang (1143–1194) and painted their life stories on the wall. She regularly offered them burning incense and cleaned the shrine herself.[109]

> Li Yin . . . imitated the painting style of Pai-yang Shan-jen. She carved a small statue of her idol with aloe wood to worship him.[110]

And, of course, Yen Heng's own story adds to the painful record of women's destiny: Even her own literatus husband proved to be incapable of meeting her spiritual needs. Poor woman Yen; although she was not unhappily married in most respects, her situation could be no better than Ink Maiden's. All her life, she slept "alone" with her manuscripts, longing for intellectual understanding and appreciation.

In short, the two *Nü Shih-shuo* mark the difficulty of harmonizing scent value and milk value. For many women, it was simply too frustrating to bring their scent value through the passage of marriage and then merge it into motherhood. For intellectual women, the only way out was to retain their virgin status in order to maintain their scent value. Yet even this "pure" aesthetic choice was largely a literati ideal that existed most vividly in an illusory world such as that of Prospect Garden in *Dream of the Red Chamber*.[111] In a sense, Li Ch'ing's *Nü Shih-shuo* foreshadows, and Yen's resonates with, the aesthetics of this great novel: the mysterious fragrance whirling around the most talented and beautiful maidens, the homage to women's virginity as the origin of genius and purity (against men's general pollution), the female dominance over literary and artistic matters, and a spiritual intimacy and equality between talented women and a few understanding men. At the same time, Li's work predicts, and Yen's proves, the inevitable disillusion of this aesthetic system following the collapse of the garden, the fortress of women's order.

Chapter 9

An Alien Analogue: The Japanese Imitation *Daitō seigo*

The *Shih-shuo t'i* inspired imitations not only in imperial China but also in Tokugawa and Meiji Japan.[1] Ironically, the closest imitation of the *Shih-shuo hsin-yü* in late imperial times can be found in Japan rather than in China. It is Hattori Nankaku's *Daitō seigo*, or *An Account of the Great Eastern World,* a work that presents an animated scroll of Heian (794–1185) and Kamakura (1185–1333) personalities. Written entirely in classical Chinese and furnished with its model work's taxonomic scheme and linguistic style, the *Daitō seigo* physically looks very much like the *Shih-shuo hsin-yü.*[2] Moreover, it spiritually resembles the *Shih-shuo hsin-yü* by focusing on people's personalities and emotions. In a sense, the *Daitō seigo* stands out as the only imitation of the *Shih-shuo hsin-yü* that presents human personalities objectively, independent of moral or political judgments.

Why should the *Daitō seigo* resemble its model work so closely when other imitations did not? Hattori's student, Tei Mō'ichi (Udono Shinei) (1710–1774), addresses this problem in his preface to the *Daitō seigo.* He first contemplates why the *Shih-shuo hsin-yü* towers above all of its imitations: "From my point of view, Prince Lin-ch'uan's (Liu I-Ch'ing) achievement is indeed unique, towering over a thousand years. . . . Is it because there was no more Prince Lin-ch'uan, or there was no more Chin period? Why is it that [the *Shih-shuo hsin-yü* tradition] was so difficult for later authors to follow? . . . The Chin trend upheld competitions in pure conversations. Anyone who participated in this practice would cast pearl[-like arguments] and receive jade[-like refutations]. Pearls and jades spread along the roads, shining over one another. When it came to Prince Lin-ch'uan's time, he was able to collect them as his own treasure, whereupon he compiled the *Shih-shuo hsin-yü.*"[3]

Tei Mō'ichi goes on to argue that the *Daitō seigo* emanated from a time similar to the Chin period and an author as talented as Prince Lin-ch'uan. Consequently, the *Daitō seigo* outshone Chinese imitations, such as *Ho's Forest*, becoming the closest analogue of the *Shih-shuo hsin-yü.*[4] I agree with Tei Mō'ichi and intend to explain the affinity between the two works in terms of their authorship and historical background. I believe, however, that their similarity resulted not from a "coincidence," as Tei suggests, but rather from Hattori Nankaku's intentional compilation of the Daitō episodes following the spirit of the Wei-Chin era and the model of the *Shih-shuo.*

Hattori Nankaku's Life and Time

Hattori Nankaku was a scholar of the Chinese Classics, a writer of Chinese verse, and a literatus-painter of the middle Tokugawa or Edo period.[5] Although the Chu Hsi School of Neo-Confucianism (*Tao-hsüeh* or *Li-hsüeh*) was then state orthodoxy,[6] Hattori Nankaku was himself affiliated with an unorthodox Confucian school known as Ancient Learning (*Koga-kuha*). Its major premise was that "the essence of Confucianism was to be comprehended, not by studying what later scholars such as the Sung philosophers said, but by going directly to the texts of the ancient philosophers."[7] With this basic assumption, the Ancient Learning scholars launched their broad-ranging criticism of Chu Hsi's philosophy.

Hattori Nankaku's mentor, Ogyū Sorai (1666–1728), one of the most radical thinkers among the unorthodox Confucians, particularly opposed Chu Hsi's position that principle, *li*, governs human nature. Against the Chu Hsi scholars' insistence that one's imperfect material endowment (*kishitsu*) could be fashioned into a sage's personality that embodies *li*, Ogyū Sorai argued that one's endowment could never be changed: "One receives a material endowment [disposition] from Heaven and parents. To say that one's disposition may be changed and that human beings are responsible for changing it is the Sung Confucians' absurd idea and is totally unreasonable. One's disposition cannot be changed in any case. Rice will always stay rice, and beans always beans."[8]

Precisely because rice and beans maintain their natural status, Ogyū Sorai continues, their different functions make the world work. For Ogyū Sorai, Chu Hsi scholars strove in vain to change human beings by following certain prescriptions because they were trying to change rice into beans and beans into rice—in the end creating something that was neither rice nor beans. Ogyū Sorai thus argues that human dignity can best be achieved by urging the free development of individuality and by promoting the diversity of human personalities.[9]

As one of the two most prominent disciples of Ogyū Sorai, Hattori Nankaku steadfastly championed the Sorai School's beliefs. His compilation of a *Shih-shuo* imitation obviously provided a means by which to advocate his mentor's ideas. For one thing, the Wei-Chin theme of "being one's self," as elaborated in the *Shih-shuo hsin-yü*, conformed closely to Ogyū Sorai's conception of unchangeable human dispositions—the idea that rice should stay rice and beans should remain beans.[10] As Tokuda Takeshi observes, the *Shih-shuo* taxonomy of human nature tends to present human nature objectively, free of any moral restraint: "Among the well-known thirty-six categories of the *Shih-shuo hsin-yü*, . . . the second half includes "Uninhibitedness and Eccentricity," "Rudeness and Arrogance," and "Taunting and Teasing" to "Extravagance and Ostentation," "Slanderousness and Treachery," "Delusion and Infatuation," and "Hostility and Alienation." These categories vividly depict those lively human figures who abandon [Confucian] moral standards and [in so doing] develop a theme about straightforward personalities which does not appeal to Neo-Confucians."[11] Seen in this light, it was only natural for Hattori Nankaku to mount Heian and Kamakura personalities within a *Shih-shuo* frame, since, as we will see, the former provided the most illustrious examples of "rice and beans" in Japanese history, and the latter helped to highlight the diverse qualities of these "natural" human beings, which was exactly what Ogyū Sorai wanted.

An imitation of the *Shih-shuo hsin-yü* would also have reflected the Ancient Learning belief that ancient texts carried more truth about Confucianism than did the Chu Hsi interpretations. When Ancient Learning scholars undertook to refute Chu Hsi's ideas, they usually sought support in Han or pre-Han Chinese classics. The *Shih-shuo hsin-yü,* although a later source, would be acceptable for Hattori Nankaku for two reasons: (1) The *Shih-shuo hsin-yü* had appeared in China seven hundred years earlier than Chu Hsi's works, and (2) although the *Shih-shuo hsin-yü* consisted of *Hsüan-hsüeh* principles that were based mainly on the ideas of *Lao-tzu* and *Chuang-tzu* and were therefore often opposed to the Han Confucian moral teachings, it nonetheless upheld Confucius himself as the greatest of all the sages.[12] Thus Hattori Nankaku could claim that the *Shih-shuo hsin-yü* represented the "true" inheritance of Confucianism.

Hattori Nankaku's enthusiasm for the *Shih-shuo hsin-yü* was obviously stirred up by the Tokugawa frenzy over this work. The *Shih-shuo hsin-yü* was probably introduced to Japan around the early seventh century, when Japan started sending envoys systematically to China. The earliest bibliography of Chinese books in Japan, *Nihonkoku genzai sho mokuroku* (Catalogue of current books in Japan), compiled around the end of the ninth century, already registered the *Shih-shuo* [*hsin-yü*]. A T'ang era manuscript of the book has also been preserved in Japan, which may have been imported during the Heian period.[13] In any case, the *Shih-shuo hsin-yü* has certainly influenced Japanese intellectuals since the Heian period. For instance, Monk Kūkai (774–835), a famous early Heian scholar and poet, was very fond of this work. He inscribed his screen with passages from the *Shih-shuo,* presented a poem to the prime minister entitled "Shōfu Buntei shitoku *Sesetsu shingo* shi" (Poem on my first reading of the *Shih-shuo hsin-yü* at the Literary Pavilion in the prime minister's residence), and he extensively quoted from the *Shih-shuo hsin-yü* in his *Sankyō shiki* (Guide to the three religions).[14]

It was not until the Tokugawa period, however, that Japanese scholars expanded their interest in the *Shih-shuo hsin-yü* from simply alluding to it as an inspiring source to extensively studying the entire work. As a result, the Tokugawa period produced at least six imitations, three translations, and about twenty works focusing mainly on its phonetic, semantic, and textual elements. One reason for this passionate devotion to the work was the importation of Wang Shih-chen's *Supplement to the Shih-shuo hsin-yü* in the late seventeenth century.[15]

Early Tokugawa society welcomed the *Supplement to the Shih-shuo* for three main reasons. (1) As one of its major policies, the early Tokugawa Bakufu encouraged the teaching of Confucianism through a reading of classic Chinese texts. The *Supplement to the Shih-shuo* incorporated a great amount from *Ho's Forest,* a work that conveyed a relatively stronger Confucian moral message than the *Shih-shuo hsin-yü.* It therefore enabled a possible—if somewhat forced—moral interpretation of the entire work to meet the contemporary Japanese need for Confucian education. (2) Along with the trend of learning the Chinese classics, scholars as well as the literate public showed a growing interest in reading Chinese novels and stories, which were comparatively easy to understand and beneficial in terms of learning the Chinese language. The *Supplement to the Shih-shuo* fit this demand because both the *Shih-shuo hsin-yü* and *Ho's Forest* contained tasteful stories and meaningful remarks. (3) The *Supplement to the Shih-shuo* also satisfied the eagerness of Tokugawa readers to absorb a large amount of information about China relatively painlessly. In twenty *chüan,* the *Supplement to the Shih-shuo* recounted altogether fifteen hundred years of gentry life in China. In addition to the Wei-Chin period covered in the *Shih-shuo hsin-yü, Ho's Forest* supplied a great many episodes from the Han to the end of the Yüan (ca. 206 B.C.– A.D. 1368). Although Hattori Nankaku's own interest was obviously focused on the *Shih-shuo hsin-yü* itself, as can be seen in Tei Mō'ichi's preface, there seems no reason to deny that his interest was ignited by the general Tokugawa frenzy for the *Supplement to the Shih-shuo.*

The Daitō Period

What Hattori Nankaku called the Daitō period included both the Heian and Kamakura eras. Historically, the two eras differed significantly: The former was an aristocratic society dominated by the Fujiwara family; the latter was a newly arisen samurai society led by the Minamoto Shoguns. The author's primary focus is on the life of Heian aristocratic intellectu-

als, although it extends into the Kamakura period. To avoid possible confusion, I will follow the author in referring to the two eras covered in the
Daitō seigo as the Daitō period.

Why did Hattori Nankaku choose to compile Daitō anecdotes instead
of those from any other Japanese historical period? In his preface to the
Daitō seigo, Hattori emphasizes the similarity between the Daitō and the
Wei-Chin periods and explains how and why the two were alike:

> During our medieval period, the Fujiwara clan monopolized the central
> government. The rich and the glorious almost all came from this family.
> Only by nepotistic opportunities could the royal descendants or grandees
> be admitted into this high society, not to mention those from less im-
> portant families, who could only achieve official posts through either the
> Fujiwaras' promotion or marriage connections with them. As for com-
> moners, they happily stayed in the mud—nobody dared to desire to as-
> cend the blue sky. Thus the Fujiwaras were crowded in the cabinet and
> ministries for generations, occupying different offices. For three or four
> hundred years, the realm was controlled by one single family. This fam-
> ily's glory even surpassed that of the Wangs and the Hsiehs [who shared
> power] in the Chin dynasty, and who, like refined jades and fragrant or-
> chids, each had their own styles. In general, however, the [Daitō] senti-
> ments harmonized with the sophisticated Chin ideals, and the [Daitō]
> remarks were attuned to the beautiful Chin tones. This was probably be-
> cause body vitality [*taiki*] may be transplanted from one place to another
> and human essence [*bussei*] may be put to multiple uses—all the result
> of natural conditions. The two places (China and Japan) were ten thou-
> sand *li* apart, and the two periods (Chin and Daitō) were several hun-
> dred years separated, [yet] how similar their elegant styles and lofty ideals
> look![16]

Although Hattori Nankaku explains this transspatial and transtemporal similarity in terms of a natural diffusion of bodily vitality and human essence,
a careful reading of his preface suggests that the Daitō free spirit and aesthetic orientation grew out of an inner logic of political-cultural connection in Japan that paralleled the Chin situation. This connection featured
an association between the dissolved imperial authority, the ascendancy of
the privileged clan(s), and the rise of an aristocratic culture that carried
strong aesthetic characteristics, as can be seen in the historical writings of
the Heian and Kamakura periods as well the *Daitō seigo* itself.[17]

From a reading of the *Daitō seigo* we learn that during the Daitō period, the emperors lost their power first to the Fujiwara regency (ca. 858–ca. 1158) and then to the Kamakura shogunate (1185–1333). As a result, the emperors were relegated mainly to ceremonial and cultural activities instead of conducting state affairs. This alteration of imperial duties clarifies why most entries in chapter 4, "Bungaku" (Literature and scholarship), involve the literary talent and aesthetic taste of the emperors themselves (see 4/1, 4/4, 4/7, 4/9, 4/10, 4/16, 4/21, etc.) and why Emperor Ichijō's (r. 986–1011) idea of "obtaining [talented] people" *(tokujin)*—a quality usually associated with administrative skill—referred only to obtaining people of letters.[18]

Since the heads of the big clans (mainly referring to the Fujiwara family)[19] also headed the regency to the emperors, important posts became their hereditary possessions. Consequently, the male members of the Fujiwara clan as well as other privileged families developed strong aristocratic consciousness. In short, they believed that pedigree and birth determined everything. The following *Daitō seigo* episode typifies this mentality:

> Fujiwara no Kintō (966–1041) was about to resign from the position of major counselor [Hattori's commentary to this sentence reads: "During the reign of Kankō (1004–1011), his lordship could not get along well with (the authorities)"].[20] He first asked court secretaries to pen a resignation memorial for him, but none of the drafts satisfied him. He then went to Ōe no Masahira (952–1012) for help. Masahira promised [to draft it], but went home worried. His wife, Lady Akazome, was surprised and asked why. He told her that he had difficulty in ascertaining the major counselor's real intent. The wife advised, "His lordship is always posing. The other court secretaries probably did not mention his pedigree and birth and therefore dissatisfied him." Masahira gladly accepted her advice. When Kintō opened the draft and read phrases such as, "Your subject descends directly from five generations of prime ministers," and "Since his ancestor, Lord Chūjin," etc., he was very pleased and decided to use the draft.[21]

Understandably, men from such noble families could be extremely snobbish and smug, disdaining all rules and regulations. Since the Daitō male aristocrats did not have to prove competency in state affairs in order to advance their political careers, they had time to develop their interests in art, music, and literature—the kinds of talents that were especially appreciated by the imperial court. Their pride and arrogance naturally found ready expression in works of art and literature that were diverse, sentimental, and free willed—the common denominators of Daitō aesthetics and Daitō character appraisal.

As for the Fujiwara daughters, they were destined to marry emperors and royal descendants[22] so that the Fujiwaras could keep their authority over the imperial family.[23] As the future consorts of cultivated emperors, the Fujiwara girls had to be well educated. By the same token, the ladies in attendance to the imperial consorts, also from privileged families, were usually selected for their intelligence. The special political function and superior personal qualities of the Daitō aristocratic women thus awarded them relative equality with men. For example, a Heian critic compared the famous woman *waka* poet, Ono no Komachi (fl. ca. 834–877), with five male *waka* poets, commenting impartially on the strong as well as the weak points of each individual. Similarly, when Emperor Ichijō bragged about his ability to "obtain people," the "people" consisted of four male courtiers and fourteen palace ladies, all renowned for their literary talents. Among them was Lady Murasaki Shikibu (978–1016?), author of the great *Genji monogatari (Tale of Genji)*.[24]

According to Hattori Nankaku's description, the Daitō people seemed to yield to their natural impulses and feelings rather than to obey the rules of propriety. Their uninhibitedness transcended political and moral codes. A few random examples taken from the *Daitō seigo* should convey the general mood. One anecdote tells us that during the reign of Engi (901–922), Great Minister of the Left Fujiwara no Tokihira clashed on almost every political issue with Great Minister of the Right Sugawara no Michizane. The latter liked laughing—a personality quirk he could not (and did not try to) overcome. Once, stirred by an official's amusing manner, he laughed so hysterically that he could no longer handle court affairs; thus he left all the decisions for his political opponent to make.[25] The famous gentleman/writer, Minamoto no Takakuni (1004–1077),[26] always displayed such a proud air that he would spur on a pony right in front of his lordship Uji (Regent/Prime Minister Fujiwara no Yorimichi, fl. 1017–1067)—behavior that was considered extremely improper and offensive. To defend himself, Takakuni said, "What I ride is not a pony, but live clogs [*katsugeki*]."[27]

Guiding this trend of free self-expression in the *Daitō seigo* was the Daitō people's general preference for naturalness, usually exemplified by the vivacity of Nature: "When Fujiwara no Nobunori (fl. ca. 1000) was dying, a monk preached the doctrine of *Chū'u* (the mid-state between life and death) in order to rectify his thoughts [about death]. Nobunori said, 'What does it look like to be in the state of *Chū'u?*' The monk said, 'It seems that one walks toward dusk and gets lost in the wilderness.' Nobunori then asked, 'If it is in the wilderness, shouldn't there be grass and woods dyed with autumn colors and insects singing randomly?' The monk replied, 'There should be.' Nobunori said, 'Then, [to be in the state of] *Chū'u* is not too bad.' The monk felt despondent and left."[28] According to Buddhist belief, *Chū'u* represents a vague, indefinable position between life and death, a nonstatus rather than a status.[29] In order to give Nobunori easy access to the understanding of this difficult concept, the monk explains this nonlife state in terms of the life state and hence puts himself in a dilemma. For Nobunori's part, he craves life to the last minute and struggles to implant life's colorful and noisy qualities on a faceless and soundless death. His voluntary attachment to the mortal world shows a strong desire for the naturalness of life and, at the same time, a denial or a rejection of death.

Within this natural, lively world, the Daitō people desired that all things remain pristine and that nothing be artificially changed. "Fujiwara no Tadatomo found a shelter against rain at the gate of the East Temple (Tōji). There a bunch of beggars gathered next to him. Either hunchbacked or with twisted limbs, they all looked ugly and abnormal. Their abnormality amused Tadatomo at the beginning. Pretty soon, however, Tadatomo lost his interest and became disgusted with them. When he went home, he ordered the removal of all the grafted plants kept in his greenhouse that he had loved, saying, 'How could I ever again love [these plants] that look like the beggars?'"[30] We may assume that the craft of grafting plants involves the technique of twisting the branches into certain shapes against their natural growth, as is often practiced in Chinese gardening.[31] In this episode, the association of deformed human bodies with twisted plants suggested to Tadatomo an unnatural alteration of Nature's patterns.

Clearly, the Daitō style bears a distinctively Japanese character. Compared with the Wei-Chin style, the Daitō style appears more intuitive and instinctive and therefore less contemplative. Whereas the backbone of the Wei-Chin style—the trend toward self-esteem—evolved mainly from an ontological meditation on human value, the Daitō self-esteem grew directly from the status consciousness of Daitō aristocrats, from their imputed blue blood. Moreover, the Wei-Chin style emerged from a conscious opposition to Han Confucian doctrines and developed in discussions surrounding both Wei-Chin *Hsüan-hsüeh* and character appraisal, whereas the Daitō style had no previously dominant ideology either to follow or to oppose. Consequently, Daitō culture sufficed to stir the free development of personalities and hence prepared the groundwork for character writing, but it lacked a theoretical foundation for systematizing these materials. Hattori Nankaku managed to fill this theoretical gap by arranging the Daitō anecdotes into a coherent character-writing scheme—a worthy successor to the pioneering project of Liu I-ch'ing.

Fitting the Daitō Spirit to the Wei-Chin Scheme

Of course, in collecting Daitō anecdotes from various Japanese classics[32] and rearranging them under the *Shih-shuo* taxonomy, Hattori Nankaku faced the problem of how to accommodate Daitō stories to an alien system. He made every effort to incorporate the *Shih-shuo hsin-yü* style into the *Daitō seigo,* including the following attempts!

First, the most obvious effort is that he categorized 354 anecdotes into thirty-one categories out of the original thirty-six *Shih-shuo* types. Hattori Nankaku explains this imperfect imitation in his preface: "I attach the relevant chapter titles to the entries I select, rather than selecting entries to fit the titles; therefore I leave out some titles that lack entries. It is not my intention to follow strictly [the original *Shih-shuo hsin-yü* scheme] step-by-step."[33] Yet this loose imitation actually adheres quite closely to the principles of the *Shih-shuo* taxonomy of human nature, which upholds flexi-

bility in categorizing human character types without forcing any restric-
tive rules upon the process. Such an open system results from a negotia-
tion between the *Hsüan-hsüeh* understanding that human nature is by nature indefinable and unnamable and the objective of understanding human
nature in terms of distinctions.

Second, Hattori Nankaku rewrote all of the entries in a Six Dynasties
prose style characteristic of the *Shih-shuo hsin-yü*.[34] This style brought the
flavor of the spoken language into the written language by broadly em-
ploying *chu-tzu*—or *joji*—aid-words. Aid-words themselves have no substantial meanings, "functioning only to supplement or 'aid' the essential
characters" in a sentence.[35] As an Ancient Learning scholar, Nankaku was
well versed in Chinese philology. He was the earliest Japanese scholar to
notice this prose feature of the *Shih-shuo hsin-yü,* and he intentionally incorporated a great number of different aid-words from the *Shih-shuo hsin-
yü* into the *Daitō seigo,*[36] including *tou* (all, totally), *fu* (again, also), *ping*
(both, all), *nai* (thus), *ning* (would rather), *yü* (want to, desire to), *ch'ieh*
(and also), *i-fu* (also-also), *i-i* (also because), *fang-chin* (just now), *erh-hou*
(from now on), *erh-i* (that's it), and so on. None of these words have substantial meanings in Chinese; the English translations I have provided here
sound much stronger than they should. The function of these aid-words
is to mollify the intense structure of substantial words in the written language and to create a linguistic atmosphere closer to spoken language. As
a result, Yoshikawa Kōjirō maintains, "the prose becomes more supple
rhythmically, and also more subtle in what it is able to convey. It comes
nearer to the rhythms and modulations of speech, with the attendant ad-
vantages and disadvantages of greater prolixity. As with speech, its subtleties sometimes become vagueness."[37] This confused cluster of subtlety
and vagueness was, presumably, advantageous to narrative works such as
the *Shih-shuo* and the *Daitō seigo* since the atmosphere of spoken language
usually helps to create more lifelike characters.

Third, Hattori made a substantive effort, I believe, to ground many
Daitō personalities in the Wei-Chin standard of *chen-shuai* (being genuine
and straightforward), or *shinsotsu* in its Japanese pronunciation. Consider
the following story: "On the day when Hōjō Yasutoki (1183–1242) directed

public affairs, there was a legal case (between A and B). A made every effort to defend himself. When it came to B's turn, his self-defense was brief but very convincing. A was very frustrated, sighing, 'Gosh, I lost!' The onlookers all laughed at A. Yasutoki alone, however, appreciated him, saying, 'One who issues a lawsuit would usually reject admitting his own fault even though he knows it, and would make endless excuses to defend himself. I have been judging lawsuits for a long time, but never before have I seen anyone who was so ultimately genuine and straightforward [*shin-sotsu*] as this man.'"[38] *Chen-shuai* in the *Shih-shuo hsin-yü* actually intends a nonstandard rather than a standard, because being "genuine and straightforward" means being ultimately one's self. It consequently allows Hattori Nankaku the freedom to portray all kinds of personalities.

Most of the anecdotes that Hattori Nankaku collected provide trivial details about Daitō intellectual life, and many seem to have no particular significance. For example, Sugawara no Fumitoki (fl. early Heian) composed a poetic line, "The seacoast wind evinces strength, yet willows are still stronger." His elder brother mocked him, saying, "Well, the word 'stronger' is indeed stronger [but vulgar]." Fumitoki pondered a long time over a better word but could not find one. So he asked his brother what word he would use. The brother said, "I don't know either."[39] Stories of this kind have no political or moral meanings. Although the entry belongs to the "Literature" chapter, it makes little or no contribution to literature or art—both Fumitoki and his brother do not appear poetic enough even to fix a poetic line. Its existence among other *Daitō seigo* entries can be explained solely by its "pure" presentation of an outspoken and honest—yet imprudent and untalented—personality. In other words, the significance of this otherwise insignificant entry lies exactly in its confirmation of the *Daitō seigo* as a *Shih-shuo t'i* work, one focusing on the "natural" portrayal of human character.

Fourth, Hattori Nankaku selected and rewrote many Daitō anecdotes following the *Shih-shuo* models. A side-by-side comparison may help us to see the interplay of the Daitō spirit and the *Shih-shuo* formula.

> On the seventh day of the seventh month Hao Lung went out in the sun and lay on his back. When people asked what he was doing, he replied, "I'm sunning my books." (*Shih-shuo hsin-yü*, "P'ai-t'iao," 25/31)

The Abbot of Tōji sent a message to Prime Minister Fujiwara no Yorimichi (fl. 1017–1067), saying, "My library of Buddhist classics collapsed. I would like your lordship to have it
fixed." The prime minister had great respect for the abbot and
immediately sent him his steward and some workmen. The abbot looked very unhappy, saying, "Go back to tell your lord: If
he cannot even figure out such a small matter, how can he manage the affairs under Heaven?" The steward and workmen returned the message to the prime minister. The latter thought
about the meaning and could not get it. After a while, an old
maid said, "The abbot must have referred to his belly as the library." The prime minister therefore sent delicious food to the
abbot. The abbot was delighted and sent back his thanks: "After receiving the materials your lordship kindly donated, my library has been fixed." (*Daitō seigo,* "Gengo" [Speech and con-
versation], *chüan* 1, 11a)

The above Hao Lung story recorded in the *Shih-shuo hsin-yü* was based
on a long-standing Chinese custom that, on the seventh day of the seventh month, people would put on a grand sunning of their wardrobes and
books. Hao Lung, so poor that he has nothing to flaunt, exposes his belly
to the sunshine, saying, "I'm sunning my books (where memory is stored),"
thus showing his typical Wei-Chin intellectual pride and his contempt of
mundane vanity.[40] The *Daitō seigo* episode here is a close *kambun* [Chi-
nese] rendering of a Japanese text taken from the *Shoku yotsugi* (Continued tales of generations), originally written in the kana syllabary.[41] Although
we cannot be sure that the author of the *Shoku yotsugi* knew of the Hao
Lung story, we can be certain that this story provoked Hattori to include
the tale of the abbot in his *Daitō seigo.*

By rendering the *Shoku yotsugi* account into terse Chinese prose, Hattori transformed it into a typical *Shih-shuo*-style account. In a similar way
he revised the semantic meanings of the original Japanese texts in order
to make them more consistent with the *Shih-shuo* model. Compare the
following two episodes:

Huan Hsüan once went to call on Yin Chung-k'an while the latter was
resting in the apartment of a concubine. Yin's servants made excuses for
him but did not notify him. Huan later mentioned this incident to Yin,
who replied, "I didn't sleep with my concubine, and even if I did, wouldn't
I 'worship worthies instead of loving beauties' [*hsien-hsien i-se*] [i.e.,

Wouldn't I leave my concubine and come out to receive my gentlemen visitors]?" (*Shih-shuo hsin-yü*, "Yen-yü," 2/103)

Fujiwara no Sanetada had been a widely renowned worthy scholar since his youth. Yet he was infatuated with beautiful women. Once, seeing a beauty passing by, he went out of his door to court her. A passerby said, "Should a worthy also enjoy such pleasure?" He answered, "Loving a beauty changes one into a worthy" [*iro o iro toshi, ken ni kaeyo*]. (*Daitō seigo*, "Gengo," *chüan* 1, 8b)

This *Daitō seigo* episode translates a story from the *Jikkunshō* [Treatise of ten rules]. In the original text, the scholar phrases his self-defense as "through womanizing one becomes a worthy" (*jōji ni kenjin nashi*).[42] Hattori cunningly changes it into "loving a beauty changes one into a worthy" (*iro o iro toshi, ken ni kaeyo*), which reverses, both syntactically and semantically, the well-known Confucian teaching, "worship worthies instead of loving beauties" (*ken o ken toshi, iro ni kaeyo*).[43] In this way, Hattori links the Sanetada story to Yin Chung-k'an's explanation as recorded in the *Shih-shuo hsin-yü*. This inventive translation illustrates Hattori's effort to absorb the *Shih-shuo* flavor in the re-creation of each episode.

Precisely because Hattori upholds *shinsotsu*—being genuine and straightforward—the *Daitō seigo* retains its genuine Japanese originality and flavor. Even for stories written in emulation of the paradigmatic entries in the *Shih-shuo hsin-yü*, we may still recognize certain distinctive Japanese characteristics. The narrative structure of a story about competition between two artisans, for example, emulates entirely that of a *Shih-shuo hsin-yü* episode about Chung Hui (225–264) and Hsün Hsü (d. 289), yet the specific elements are revealingly different. Chung Hui, a skillful calligrapher, imitates Hsün Hsü's handwriting and writes a letter to Hsü's mother, demanding a precious sword that Hsü keeps with her. By this means, Hui steals away the sword. To get even with Hui, Hsü paints Hui's late father on the wall of the gatehouse of Hui's newly built mansion, portraying "his clothes, cap, and features just as they were when he was alive." When Hui sees the portrait, he is "greatly affected and upset, and as a result the mansion remains empty and abandoned" ("Ch'iao-i," 21/4).

In another *Daitō seigo* episode, architect Hida (fl. ca. 850–858) fools

the painter Hyakusai Kawanari (fl. ca. 850–858) with the complex structure of a small hall he has designed. To get even with Hida, Kawanari then
invites him home for a visit. The narrative relates that when Hida walked
in, "he suddenly saw inside of the front porch a corpse lying on the ground,
utterly deformed and stinking. Startled and scared, the architect was about
to turn back and leave. At this point [he heard] the host laughing inside.
The architect then took a closer look at the dead body and found it merely
a still-life painting on a screen. Only then did he realize it was not the real
thing" (Daitō seigo, "Kōgei" [Ingenious art], chüan 4, 15a).[44]

Even if we juxtapose the two episodes without citing their sources,
one can still easily recognize the cultural identity of each by the features
of the two paintings involved. Hsün Hsü's retaliation against Chung Hui
was based on two Chinese traditions: (1) the code of filial piety, to which
the Chinese people always adhered, even during the relatively liberal Wei-
Chin period; and (2) the function of the decoration of the gate, gatehouse,
or front porch, which usually introduces the features of the entire building. To place an ancestor's portrait in the gatehouse would turn the building into a memorial to the dead and would thus forbid the offspring any
practical use of the place. No matter how far Hsün Hsü meant to go in
his revenge, he would never paint a dead body anywhere. But for Hyakusai Kawanari, the most famous Japanese court artist of the Montoku reign
(850–858), there seems to be no rule against adorning the front porch with
a dead body painting. Kawanari designs his revenge by choosing what he
considers the most startling and frightening image.

Such a daring motif as the decaying body—vigorous, powerful, and re-
alistic to the point of being grotesque—later became rather popular during the Kamakura period when paintings of female cadavers were used to
illustrate the uncertainty of life in preaching Buddhist doctrines. Gail Chin
discusses in great detail this motif in Kamakura paintings: "While the symbol of the female cadaver can be traced back to early Buddhist India, there
are no paintings or literary evidence of paintings of a female corpse in pro-
gressive stages of decay from the Indian subcontinent. . . . From T'ang
(618–906) and Five Dynasties (907–960) there remain certain poems describing bodily decay found in the cave temples of Tun-huang, and there

are fragments of wall painting of the corpse, but this requires further investigation (Kawaguchi 1964). The decomposing cadaver is a topic of discussion in Chih-i's (538–597) *Mo-ho chih-kuan* (The Great Calming and Contemplation, T. 1911, 46. 121a–122b) . . . but now it is only in Japan that paintings of the topic are commonly found."[45] The fact that the decaying-body paintings can only be found in Japan is not accidental. This sort of painting must have emerged from some long-standing artistic inclination in the Japanese tradition. More central to my point, Hattori, although quite knowledgeable about both the Wei-Chin and Daitō periods, did not try to modify the content of his stories to fit the Chinese mentality. The uniqueness of the *Daitō seigo*, I think, rests in Hattori Nankaku's intentional maintenance of the natural originality of the Daitō anecdotes.

In addition to maintaining the original flavor of the Daitō episodes while fitting them to the *Shih-shuo* scheme, Hattori also strove to rewrite and refine them with his own aesthetic ideal of human nature and his own artistic and poetic tastes. This innate tension between Daitō culture, the Wei-Chin spirit, and Nankaku's values gave the *Daitō seigo* its own unmistakable identity.

The following anecdote, taken from the *Daitō seigo*, captures Nankaku's efforts to modify the Daitō material with *Shih-shuo* nuances and his own artistic sensitivity:

> At [Fujiwara no] Toshitsuna's (fl. mid-eleventh cent.) garden, Fushimi, mountains and streams were superbly beautiful. Grass, woods, and pavilions manifested a natural taste. Sometimes, when people came to visit, Toshitsuna would have his men playing the role of travelers passing through the mountains for his guests to view from afar. He claimed that his Fushimi surpassed any other famous garden.
>
> On a clear morning after a snowfall, Lord Uji (Regent/Prime Minister Fujiwara no Yorimichi, Toshitsuna's father) intended to make an excursion. The lord said to his attendants, "Toshitsuna often brags about his villa [Fushimi]. Let's visit him on impulse [*jōkyo*], just to give him a surprise. Isn't it good fun!" He thereupon ordered a ride [to Toshitsuna's garden]. When he and his attendants arrived at the garden, however, the gate was locked and nobody was in sight, only the whiteness of snow shining over the paths. All complained that Toshitsuna was not prepared for viewing the snow scenery, or for entertaining guests. One attendant

knocked at the door and loudly announced several times the arrival of his lordship. Not until after a long time did they see an usher appear from a side gate. The attendant scolded him, "His lordship has come. Why did you take so long to answer the door?" The usher replied, "My master forbids us from stamping about on the snow, so I had to come by a roundabout route along the mountain. Excuse me for not having greeted his lordship sooner." All appreciated [Toshitsuna's caution], saying, "This is much better than hastily coming to open the door and to make a mess of the snow."

The lord then walked in and enjoyed the snow scene. After a while, his followers complained to the host, saying, "Since his lordship is here, why don't you throw a banquet for us?" The lord, laughing, urged his followers to press even harder. . . . The host then stood up and ordered the utensils. Soon they saw ten male and ten female servants, all dressed in bright colors, with the one who carried the keys leading the way uphill, and all the others lined up after him, each stepping in the footprints of the person ahead of him/her. Afterwards they came back, each bringing a piece of table silver. Now the tail turned into the head and the head the tail, following the original track on the snow. All the visitors enjoyed the scene from afar. Thus the banquet was ready. All had a wonderful time [*kashō,* literally, wonderful visualization] that day, and the lord was extremely contented.[46]

This episode, actually a lengthy note to an anecdote about Toshitsuna's pride in his garden, rewrites a record of the *Shoku yotsugi.*[47] Hattori keeps its basic plot—Lord Uji's surprise visit at his son's garden on a snowy day, and Toshitsuna's management to minimize the possible disturbance of the natural whiteness—to reflect the carefree and exquisite lifestyle of Heian aristocrats. Meanwhile Hattori revises this episode by (1) bringing in a *Shih-shuo* touch, as typified in his use of the term *jōkyo,* "on impulse," and (2) adding in his own artistic design, as typified in his use of the term *kashō,* "wonderful visualization." Neither term, nor any details in support of these two ideas, are found in the *Shoku yotsugi* text. Thus Hattori recreates this story into one of the most profound and meaningful *Daitō seigo* episodes, expressing his ideal of human nature.

By putting the word *jōkyo* into Lord Uji's mouth, Hattori compares this episode with a *Shih-shuo* story and thus draws a parallel between the lord's visit with his son on a snowy morning, "on impulse," and Wang Hui-chih's visit with his friend Tai K'uei on a snowy night, also "on impulse" (*ch'eng-*

痕鑰公家乃陪至速之怪莊言雪旅莊曰大
而先曰士物客今應應門其後裝山已東
行焉賤十亦貴衆門門無俄清過水是世
既後器人賤主皆者者賞乘朝山皆樓話
乃者何婢耳人佳曰徐雪與欲以勝託卷
杯一害子設日賞公自待驚有爲州此之
盤行但十有厨曰命旁客其所遽木境七
銀魚須人一傳殊至徑之不遊觀園佳
器上饌皆二尋勝矣出備意觀既亭賞
人山耳束杯到狼君門從亦謂自盡之
擎先主裝盤矣藉何從者是左稱自儲
一者人鮮都且遽不者呵佳右名然那
物已乃麗在山隔設呵曰號曰園有可
而跡起者山林無盛曰公皓俊踰客一
返後取一倉之路饌公至漫綱宅時目
則皆其人遙供器公入久而常宇或總
最踐俄提隔器　笑賞　已以治使之
後其見倉無　　時雪　皆莊公人伏
　　　　　　　移迎　　　則値　見

hsing) (Shih-shuo hsin-yü 23/47) (See chapter 5). Hattori's link between the two snowy visits immediately imbues the Daitō snow with the profundity of its *Shih-shuo* model.[48] He further supports this implantation of meaning with the following detail: Lord Uji did not notify Toshitsuna about his visit in advance, nor did Toshitsuna know that his father was coming, yet one side expected to be well received and the other was well prepared for entertaining the guest. Who, then, played the messenger between the father and the son? It was the snow. Here snow functions as a commonly understood cultural code among the Daitō elite. Hattori further explains the snow's symbolic nature in the following episode: "[Urabe] no Kaneyoshi (known as Yoshida Kenkō, 1283–1350) said, 'Once on a snowy morning, I happened to write to my friend about some business. In haste I did not get around to mentioning the snow. My friend replied, "You didn't even ask about the snow—you are not my friend!"'"[49] The seemingly illogical association of snow with friendship suggests that, for Kaneyoshi's friend at least, snow is an indicator of one's personality. A person who cares for snow would surely have some quality in common with it—purity, beauty, poetic feelings, etc.—and would thereby be a worthy friend. This strong desire to identify people with Nature allows us to read the Toshitsuna episode as a metaphor. Toshitsuna's endeavor to preserve the snow's natural status from being disturbed is equivalent to maintaining the intrinsic innocence of human nature. It is through such a mentality and endeavor that the idiosyncratic Daitō personalities thrive.

While both episodes project the gentlemen's ideal of lofty personality onto the shining whiteness of the snow, the gentlemen in each episode have their own ways of "spending the impulse." As discussed at length in chapter 5, the *Shih-shuo* description of Wang Hui-chih's snowy journey follows the Wei-Chin *Hsüan-hsüeh* principle of *te-i wang-yen* (forgetting the words once getting the idea), which emphasizes the purpose rather than the means to achieve the purpose. As for Hattori, a painter, he intends his characters to "spend their impulse" through *kashō,* a "wonderful visualization" of an animated landscape painting composed of both the snow scene and people.[50]

With a painter's artistic sensitivity, Hattori seizes upon a detail from the *Shoku yotsugi* record: Toshitsuna has his men playing the part of travelers passing through the scene in order for his guests to have a "view from afar." He then mounts this "live" landscape-painting structure within a snow scene, with its sprinkling of small human figures among mountains and streams. He also adds to it sensuous touches that were not in the original text, such as the colorful clothing of the servants, the shining silver in their hands, and the elegant trace on the snow drawn by their meticulously designed steps. While reading this episode, the reader feels both inside and outside a picture. Inside the picture, the reader joins Toshitsuna's guests and "watches" a colorful line composed of the twenty servants, rhythmically moving in the shining whiteness. The otherwise stark stillness is instantly animated and full of vitality. Outside the picture, the reader views this scroll of Heian aristocratic life as a portrayal of idiosyncratic Daitō personalities who are as pure as the white snow and as lively as that colorful line. For a painter, to present something "visible" is always at the core of his artistic concern. With the help of his artistic talent and sensitivity, Hattori Nankaku successfully manages to make invisible human nature visible.

In a curious and complex way, then, Hattori is both like and unlike other *Shih-shuo* imitators. In common with all of them, he compiled the *Daitō seigo* to achieve his own cultural purposes. Yet his end product conformed more closely to the basic model created by Liu I-ch'ing than that of any other *Shih-shuo* imitation. As I have tried to argue, however, this does not mean that Hattori and Liu were intellectually identical. Liu inventively created the *Shih-shuo hsin-yü* and its genre to register a two-century-long contemplation of human nature and the diverse personalities it engendered. But he did not invent the Wei-Chin spirit that inspired his creation and reflexively presented itself through this creation. Hattori, on the other hand, borrowed the *Shih-shuo hsin-yü* framework to restructure and rewrite diverse Daitō personalities. By celebrating the "authentic" Japanese values he thus created, Hattori intended to challenge the rigid Chu Hsi orthodoxy that Tokugawa society had borrowed from China. In this sense, the so-called Daitō spirit presents a phantom flower, cultivated by a genius named Hattori Nankaku.

Chapter 10

New and Old:
The Last Wave of
Shih-shuo Imitations

The last wave of *Shih-shuo* imitations, Hsü K'o's *Ch'ing-pai lei-ch'ao* (Classified records from unofficial Ch'ing historical writings) and Yi Tsung-k'uei's *Hsin Shih-shuo* (New *Shih-shuo*), emerged soon after the 1911 Republican Revolution. The two works were finished only two years apart, in 1916 and 1918 respectively, but the two authors' motivation and purpose of compilation differed greatly.

Although claimed as a *Shih-shuo* imitation, Hsü K'o's *Ch'ing-pai lei-ch'ao* looks more like an encyclopedic work. With 13,500 Ch'ing historical anecdotes classified into ninety-two categories, it covers almost every aspect of Ch'ing China: its geographical features, social, political, and economic systems, art, religion, and culture, as well as about fifty *Shih-shuo*-style human character types. The inclusion of some new categories, such as *wai-chiao* (diplomacy), *chung-tsu* (races), *tsung-chiao* (religions), *hui-tang* (societies and parties), *mi-hsin* (superstition), *tung-wu* (animals), *chih-wu* (plants), *k'uang-wu* (minerals)—as well as various groups of lower-class people, such as *yen-ssu* (eunuchs), *yu-ling* (actors), *ch'ang-chi* (prostitutes), *hsü-i* (clerics), *nu-pi* (servants and slaves), *tao-tsei* (robbers and thieves), *kun-p'ien* (swindlers), and *ch'i-kai* (beggars)[1]—indicates the author's desire to take into account the various political, social, and cultural changes of his time.

Overall, Hsü K'o's purpose was to write a conventional historiographical account of the Ch'ing. Both Hsü and his proponent, Chu Tsung-yüan, stated in their prefaces that they were simply recording the rise and fall of the previous dynasty while the memory was still fresh but all the taboos were gone.[2] Chu summarized the Ch'ing achievements in the following way: "Because [the Ch'ing rulership] could see what the Ming had neglected, it intentionally avoided the Ming flaws in its ritual and political systems, promoted scholarship, and respectfully placed worthy Confucians [in proper offices]. . . . Consequently, the Confucian gentle manner became the national vogue, and each generation was thronged with scholar-officials who admired the [Confucian] moral teachings and righteousness."[3] Hsü K'o likewise celebrated the Ch'ing in his preface and "compilation notes." For example, he recorded the last Empress Dowager Lung-yü's "virtue of yielding from modesty" (*jang-te*) as she agreed to the abdication of the child emperor Hsüan-t'ung (r. 1909–1911).[4]

Clearly, Hsü K'o and Chu Tsung-yüan intended to establish a fair record of the Ch'ing dynasty in Chinese history—yet for whose reference? In the past, the purpose of compiling such an account was to provide information to the new ruler. We can recall how Liang Wei-shu and his three preface authors, Wu Wei-yeh, Ch'ien Ch'ien-i, and Ch'ien Fen, promoted Liang's *Accounts of the Jade Sword* as a guidebook for the succeeding regime. Hsü K'o and Chu Tsung-yüan, however, seemed to lack such ambition, despite the ambitious range and size of the *Ch'ing-pai lei-ch'ao*. Hsü K'o claimed to be offering his book solely for the reference of scholars, so that they would not have to rely upon foreign sources in composing histories of the Ch'ing.[5] Hsü's modesty came from his sense that an entirely new era had dawned, and he could not determine how to connect the old and the new—and therefore what to offer the new.

Compared with Hsü and Chu's perplexity, Yi Tsung-k'uei appeared much more assertive about his purpose in compiling a *Shih-shuo* imitation. His *New Shih-shuo* strictly adhered to the original *Shih-shuo* categorization scheme, yet the word "new," or *hsin,* separated it from any of its predecessors. It marked Yi's participation in the collective "historical consciousness" of a revolutionary period, when Chinese intellectuals appealed to the word *hsin* as a challenge to the past and a guide to the future.[6] As Yi explains in his "Li-yen" (Compilation notes):

This book is basically a work of *hsiao-shuo,* an aid to conversation. But teachers of ethics may use the chapters of *"Te* Conduct," "The Square and the Proper," "Cultivated Tolerance," "Warnings and Admonitions," etc., for their reference. Teachers of Chinese may use the chapters on "Literature and Scholarship," "Ranking with Refined Words," "Appreciation and Praise," etc., for their reference. The entire book can serve as a general reference for teachers of history. As for the chapter "Affairs of Government," it sets the rules for bureaucrats; "Speech and Conversation" is a guide for legislators; "Worthy Beauties" provides a good teacher for gentlewomen; "Quick Perception" is a treasure-trove for military men. These are the additional functions [of my work].[7]

This statement of purpose displays an effort to fit the old to the new. Yi Tsung-k'uei tries to match traditional categories with new cultural and political concepts invented or imported amidst dramatic cultural and political changes.

Somewhat ironically, Yi describes his work as *"hsiao-shuo,"* despite its rigid historical formula. This seeming accommodation to the conventional categorization of the *Shih-shuo* genre amounts less to an expression of modesty than to a daring claim of self-importance, in accordance with the new meaning bestowed on *hsiao-shuo.* Among those who aggressively championed the *hsiao-shuo* genre during the transitional period from the late Ch'ing to the early Republican era, Liang Ch'i-ch'ao (1873–1929) probably exerted the strongest influence on Yi.[8] In his two essays on *hsiao-shuo,* Liang equated the genre with the Western concept of novel or fiction and emphasized its function in bringing China into a new mode: "If we want to make new the people of a nation, we must first make new the fiction of this nation. Therefore, if we want to make new the morality [of a nation], we must first make new its fiction; to make new the religion [of a nation], we must first make new its fiction; to make new the politics [of a nation], we must first make new its fiction; to make new the customs [of a nation], we must first make new its fiction; to make new the learning and art [of a nation], we must first make new its fiction. Even up to the point of making new the people's minds and personalities, we must first make new the fiction. Why is it so? Because fiction possesses an inconceivable power to guide humanity."[9] Yi Tsung-k'uei's description of the role of his *New Shih-shuo* accords with Liang's description of the function of new *hsiao-shuo*—a reference for teaching ethics, literature, and history and a guidebook for people's behavior and remarks.

Yi's definition of *people,* as specified in his preface, still focused on the gentry. But in addition to the original gentry components—*kuan-liao* (officials) and *hsien-yüan* (gentlewomen)—Yi added *chiao-yüan* (professors, teachers), *i-yüan* (members of the national assembly), and *chün-jen* (military officers). These new elements reflect the changes of gentry composition at the beginning of the twentieth century. As Ernest P. Young observes: "We find a new range of prestigious occupations—military officer, newspaperman, politician, engineer, scientist, even lawyer—but recruited largely from the same class which had in the past aspired chiefly to roles in education and the government bureaucracy."[10] This "new range of prestigious occupations" can be found throughout the *New Shih-shuo,* showing Yi Tsung-k'uei's sensitivity toward the gentry transformation in the midst of cultural and political turbulence, where new elements and new structures entangled ineluctably with the old. Thus, with grand expectations of the *hsiao-shuo*'s capacity, Yi Tsung-k'uei consciously offered his *New Shih-shuo* to guide the Chinese gentry into a new era.

The questions for us to explore in this chapter are then: What did Yi Tsung-k'uei mean by "new"? How did he conceptualize "new"? Why did he define "new" this way instead of another? How is this "new" related to the Chinese tradition—particularly to the *Shih-shuo* tradition? And finally, what is the significance of this "new" to the transition from tradition to modernity?

The "New" in the *New Shih-shuo*

Yi Tsung-k'uei compiled the *New Shih-shuo* at the dawn of the New Culture era. The abolition of the civil service examinations in 1905 had "eliminated the institutional reinforcement of orthodox Confucian values." Termination of the imperial system and severance from an alien sovereign further rid the Chinese elite of many traditional taboos in politics and culture. The gentry now felt that they had become the masters of their lives and their culture and could freely discuss and organize the best ways of preserving and improving Chinese culture. Meanwhile, the Chinese elite also found itself standing at a crossroads, "search[ing] for new values and institutions in the midst of political chaos, social unrest, widespread demoralization, and foreign imperialism."[11]

Quo vadis? This was the question facing the Chinese elite as well as Yi Tsung-k'uei, who had taken on himself the responsibility of leading the gentry through this chaos. An anecdote in the New Shih-shuo captures the dilemma: "Wang K'ai-yün [1832–1916] was an aged and erudite scholar with a sense of humor. In the winter of the year Hsin-hai [late 1911–early 1912], the Republic of China was established, and gentlemen competed to cut off their queues and wear Western-style clothes. It happened that Wang was celebrating his eightieth birthday, and guests flocked to his house. Wang was still wearing Ch'ing clothes and cap. The guests laughed and asked him why. Wang said: 'My clothes are surely foreign styled, but are yours Chinese? [In my opinion,] only when you wear an opera costume can you be counted as having restored the Han style.' The guests had no way to refute him."[12]

Queue cutting symbolized the eager divorce of Chinese patriots from an alien regime, which they blamed for the humiliations China had endured at the hands of Japan and the West. But after the Chinese had shed the Manchu stigma, what clothes should they wear and which way should they go? The elite had undergone a rapid transformation and were now confronting a possible deformation. Their original identity had faded, alive only in theatrical fabrication, yet their new identity remained uncertain. The co-staging of Western suits, Manchu clothes, and Chinese opera costumes on the birthday of an old famous gentleman at the dawning of the Republican China dramatizes this joyful yet perplexing moment.

With Wang K'ai-yün's costume metaphor, Yi Tsung-k'uei cautions the Chinese elite that abandoning one alien style only to adopt another is still a form of foreign subjugation. He knew all too well that radical New Culture intellectuals were prepared to abandon Chinese tradition entirely, in order to pursue their social Darwinist modernizing agenda. Wrote Yi:

Recently [1915], gentlemen such as Ch'en Tu-hsiu, Hu Shih, Ch'ien Hsüan-t'ung, and Fu Ssu-nien have started editing the journal *New Youth* [Hsin ch'ing-nien], by which they have initiated the idea of a Literary Revolution and advocated using the vernacular for writing. Hu says: "Dead language cannot give birth to live literature. If China wants live literature, we must use the vernacular; we must use the [modern] Chinese language [*kuo-yü*, literally, national language],[13] and we must write literature in the [modern] Chinese language." Ch'en strongly upholds a fundamental solution by overthrowing Confucianism and reforming [Chinese] ethics. Ch'ien urges the abolition of the Chinese language and the adaptation of an artificial language that has simple and clear grammar, unified pronunciation, and refined etymology. Fu wants to excavate the very fundamental follies of Chinese academia, saying that all the Chinese scholarship for thousands of years has been that of the *Yin-yang* school, and all the literature has been that of shamanism. "If we do not eradicate these follies," says Fu, "our culture will naturally stand in opposition to Western culture." Upon reading these gentlemen's contentions, it seems that they all take the old literature to be dead literature and intend to wipe it out.[14]

Many New Culture intellectuals completely turned their backs on Chinese tradition. To them Western values were supreme—the only standard by which to measure "progress." Yi recognized the radically iconoclastic nature of the New Culture Movement and had a certain sympathy for the iconoclasts, but he deplored their one-sidedness and argued for a judicious balance between "old" and "new," a middle ground between Chinese tradition and Western-inspired modernity. He suggested that "if [the Literary Revolution] can cast off its biases and promote itself gradually, it may not be impossible for [this movement] to serve as a turning point in improving our culture."[15]

Thus Yi Tsung-k'uei offered his *New Shih-shuo* to exemplify the very balance he recommended. In this sense, Yi Tsung-k'uei's "new" seems to mean a new attitude that allowed him to discuss delicate political, racial, and cultural differences in a "neutral" way, as he delineated in his "Compilation Notes":

> This book aims at fair and proper judgment. The author of a recently published work, *Ch'ing-pai lei-ch'ao*, with obvious bias names Hung [Hsiu-ch'üan] [1812–1864] and Yang [Hsiu-ch'ing] [fl. mid-nineteenth

cent.] as rebels,[16] lists Sun [Yat-sen] [1866–1925] and Huang [Hsing] [fl. early twentieth cent.] among bandits.[17] Works such as *Man-Ch'ing pai-shih* [Unofficial history of the Manchu-Ch'ing dynasty] and *Ch'ing-kung mi-shih* [Inside stories of the Ch'ing court], on the other hand, go overboard in their denunciation of [the Manchus] out of racial discrimination. This book is meant to clarify all these [erroneous opinions]. . . .

The famous Ch'ing Confucian scholars were divided into the Ch'eng-Chu and the Lu-Wang Schools; the scholarship of the Confucian classics was divided into Han Learning and Sung Learning; the ancient-style prose was divided into the T'ung-ch'eng and the non-T'ung-ch'eng Schools; and poetry was divided into the Han, Wei, T'ang, and Sung styles. Each marked its own boundaries, extolling itself and disdaining the others. This book includes all of them in order for the reader to glance at the currents of the entire dynasty. The author has absolutely no prejudice against any particular sect.[18]

Conveying such "fair and proper" attitudes, Yi Tsung-k'uei intended the *New Shih-shuo* to be a paradigm of fairness, a cultural form neutral in the midst of raging controversies. Therefore, he adhered to a formula based upon the *"san-shih"* principles of the *Spring and Autumn Annals*[19]—even supplying each character with a brief biography. As a result, the *New Shih-shuo* accounts were so tightly constructed and historically grounded that Ts'ai Yüan-p'ei (1868–1940) praised them for having "no word without a source."[20] On the other hand, Yi also wanted to "establish a private history that conveys his personal opinion," pressing "praise and blame." Eventually, he expected to compile a work that "balances all kinds of opinions and harmonizes both the elegant [*ya*] and the common [*su*] culture."[21] Using this "balanced" agenda to evaluate the gentry of the Ch'ing and the early Republican China, Yi Tsung-k'uei tried to work out a "new" value system for the Chinese elite.

The period that Yi dealt with was one of the most turbulent in Chinese history, from the Manchu conquest of China in 1644 to the eve of the May Fourth Movement in 1919. These three hundred years were characterized by the constant Han Chinese rebellions/revolutions against "barbarian" dominance, involving a variety of political, social, economic, intellectual, racial, cultural, and gender clashes and crises.

In the *New Shih-shuo*, Yi's "fair and proper criteria" eliminated, for the first time in Ch'ing history and in Chinese history generally, the difference between races (the Manchus and the Han people), political factions (the Taiping rebels and the Ch'ing court; imperial officials and the republican revolutionaries), ideologies (Confucianism and various newly imported westernisms), and scholastic and poetic schools. His neutral attitudes yielded an unprecedentedly balanced world of the Chinese gentry in the *New Shih-shuo,* which simultaneously embraced all kinds of cultural standards across time and space. For instance, the late Ming loyalists and the early Ch'ing ministers are equally admired for their uprightness *("Te* Conduct"). The Taiping rebel-prince Shih Ta-k'ai (1831–1863) stands right alongside the suppressor of the Taiping Rebellion, Tseng Kuo-fan (1811–1872), as a skilled writer of prose ("Literature and Scholarship"). Ch'ing Confucian scholarship and its mortal enemy, the New Culture Movement, both receive praise for marking a turning point in the development of Chinese culture ("Literature and Scholarship"). And a young lady named Hsü Shu-hsin (fl. late 1890s) earns plaudits for being both a filial daughter and a courageous opponent of foot-binding ("Worthy Beauties").

How did Yi Tsung-k'uei present his self-proclaimed "fair-minded" account of this period? What clashes and differences did he choose to erase, and what clashes and differences did he thus underscore? Yi's accounts of the three punctuating moments of this period—namely, the Ming-Ch'ing transition, the Taiping Rebellion, and the 1911 Republican Revolution— offer some of the most dramatic episodes for our perusal, when the gentry was forced into harsh choices between fellow Chinese who were apparently willing to subvert China's cultural tradition and alien invaders who claimed to be the protectors or reformers of Chinese culture. By examining these accounts we can see the author's standards of evaluating the gentry and piece together the eclectic value system expressed in his approval and disapproval.

The *New Shih-shuo* starts at the moment when the rebel marauder Li Tzu-ch'eng caused the collapse of the Ming and hence gave the Manchus an excuse to invade China and to "legitimize themselves as the protectors of China's cultural heritage."[22] This crisis split the Ming gentry into three portions—those who maintained loyalty to Ming, those who surrendered to the Manchus, and those who surrendered to Li Tzu-ch'eng. Each group in turn received a different treatment from Yi Tsung-k'uei.

Yi Tsung-k'uei offers highest homage to the gentlemen and gentle-women who died for or stayed loyal to the Ming. He pays particular respect to the Ming loyalist-scholars, such as Huang Tsung-hsi, Ku Yen-wu, and Wang Fu-chih, who spent the rest of their lives studying Confucian classics, living in poverty and reclusion. Yet, also according to Yi Tsung-k'uei, these scholars' loyalty to the Ming and devotion to the Chinese cultural tradition did not hinder them from encouraging their sons, nephews, and disciples to serve the Ch'ing.[23] For example, after the fall of the Ming dynasty, Ku Yen-wu's mother starved herself to death;[24] Ku himself rejected the Ch'ing court's repeated summonses and six times vowed his loyalty at the last Ming emperor's tomb.[25] Meanwhile, the same Ku Yen-wu instructed his nephew, Ch'ing Grand Secretary Hsü Yüan-wen (1634–1691), to link governing with literary creation and scholastic research in order to serve the new regime more efficiently: "Only when you have the intent to establish the state [system] and to govern the common people can you ascend mountains and travel along rivers [for composing poems]; only when you have the strategy to benefit the world and to comfort people can you study the past and discuss the present."[26]

Similarly, although Huang Tsung-hsi relentlessly rejected invitations from the Ch'ing court, at the request of Hsü Yüan-wen he encouraged his student Wan Ssu-t'ung and his son Huang Pai-chia (fl. early Ch'ing) to participate in the compilation of the court-commissioned *History of the Ming*.[27] Here we see a clear pattern that Yi Tsung-k'uei draws for the Ming loyalists: Despite their own commitment to the fallen dynasty, for the sake of the continuation of the Chinese cultural tradition and the stability of society, they allow their descendants to collaborate with the new regime.

Yi launches severe criticism at those famous Ming gentlemen who surrendered to the Manchus, such as Ch'ien Ch'ien-i, Wu Wei-yeh, and Hung Ch'eng-ch'ou ("Contempt and Insults"), but not without a certain sympathy and understanding. He even contributes three lengthy episodes to their apology ("Blameworthiness and Remorse"). He defends Wu Wei-yeh as follows: "When Wu Wei-yeh became critically ill, he wrote a poem, which read: 'Twenty years living in disgrace / How to redeem myself from this sin?' Sad and sorrowful, he regretted that he did not die [for the Ming]. The pain he had swallowed was unspeakable. After [the Ming fell in] 1644, his mother was still alive. So when the [Ch'ing] court once and again summoned him, he had to bite his lips to serve [the new dynasty]. His inner thoughts naturally differed from those who desired wealth and rank, such as Ch'ien Ch'ien-i and Kung Ting-tzu."[28]

According to Yi Tsung-k'uei, Wu Wei-yeh was forced to serve the Ch'ing because he had to attend his mother, a forgivable excuse in the name of Confucian filial piety. This separates him from those who surrendered to the Ch'ing for acquiring rank and wealth, such as Ch'ien Ch'ien-i. But despite his harsher criticism of Ch'ien, Yi still finds his later remorse convincing and acceptable:

> [Ch'ien] retreated to his native place and entertained himself with poetry. Regretting having ever lost his integrity, he published his collective scholastic works, denouncing [the Manchu habit of] head shaving and the Manchu language. His essays such as the "Preface to the Miscellaneous Poems Written after Drinking at the High Party Hall" read: "Hearing the barbaric song, Ch'ih-lo, only increases my sadness; under the tent-like sky, what is the harm to be drunk?" His poems such as . . . "The Yen Memorial": "Forests still echo T'ang wailing / Stream clouds forever protect Han clothes." The "Miscellaneous Thoughts on the West Lake": "Songs and dances dream of flowers—previous dynasties' sorrow / Heroes restore the Han—later generations' longing." . . . A sort of attachment to the old dynasty often flows between the lines. No wonder his books were banned and the printing blocks destroyed after his death.[29]

Yi also applies the same apologetic strategy to the case of Hung Ch'eng-ch'ou, the most notorious Ming traitor, who, after being captured by the Manchus, assisted them in the conquest of China. Yet in Yi's account, Hung not only redeemed his treason, he even contributed greatly to the Han people:

> Hung . . . after being mocked and scolded [by Ming loyalists], regretted the wrong he had done. After the Manchus and the Hans became one family, he asked for a secret audience [with the Ch'ing sovereign] and recommended the Banner people not to make a living by themselves but instead to rely upon the Han people. Thereafter the Manchus and the Hans lived separately. The Han people could work in peace as farmers, artisans, and merchants, . . . whereas the Banner people knew nothing

New and Old 349

about making a living. They relied upon the Hans like infants rely upon their wet nurses. Thus, [upon the 1911 revolution, the Han] people and soldiers together overthrew the Manchu throne in but a few months. Such is Hung's contribution to the Han people. He is somehow a man who knows how to amend his ways.[30]

Contrary to his mercy for those who surrendered to the Ch'ing, Yi's most ferocious denunciation falls on those who surrendered to Li Tzu-ch'eng:

> Li T'ai-hsü . . . served as a minister during the Ch'ung-chen reign [1628–1644]. Upon the fall of the [Ming] dynasty [1644], he did not die but instead surrendered to Li Tzu-ch'eng. After the Ch'ing dynasty was founded he fled home. A chü-jen named Hsü Chü-yüan . . . wrote a drama. It told that after [Li] T'ai-hsü and Kung Ting-tzu surrendered to the rebels, they heard that the Ch'ing troops were entering [the capital]. They then fled to the South. While arriving at Hangchow, they were closely pursued by the [Ch'ing] soldiers, so they hid under the legs of the iron statue of Lady Wang, the wife of [the Southern Sung minister] Ch'in Kuei. It so happened that Lady Wang just had a miscarriage. After the soldiers passed by and the two gentlemen came out, both had blood on their heads.[31]

Ch'in Kuei and his wife were about the most hated couple in Chinese history, because of their roles in the wrongful death of the loyal general Yüeh Fei. Set against such a historical backdrop, the scene appears extremely abusive: Smearing Lady Wang's womb-blood on the two gentlemen's heads makes them the very miscarried fetuses of this evil woman, the doubly corrupted evil seeds—what could be more insulting than this? When Li and Kung saw this drama, they both wailed, saying: "Our reputation and integrity have collapsed to the ground like this—what else can we say?"[32]

Comparing Yi Tsung-k'uei's attitudes toward the three gentry groups in the Ming-Ch'ing transition, we can see at least two common denominators: One is Yi's definition of the gentry value, and the other is Yi's anti-Manchu complex. For Yi the gentry value rests upon its moral principles and its scholastic, literary, and artistic achievements. His anti-Manchu sentiments arise from this cultural value package—namely, his contempt for the backward "barbarian" culture. Yet this "barbarian" regime had also claimed to protect Han culture and had more or less kept its promise throughout the Ch'ing period.

Taking all these complications into consideration, Yi Tsung-k'uei forms his standards of judgment. He highly commends the Ming loyalists mainly for their efforts to preserve the Chinese cultural tradition, including their compromise with the Manchus for this purpose. He denounces the Ming gentlemen who either surrendered to or served the Ch'ing, but forgives them if (1) they served the Ch'ing because of some moral dilemma, such as in Wu Wei-yeh's case; (2) they later regretted their betrayal and put their regrets in literary or artistic form, such as in Ch'ien Ch'ien-i's case; or (3) they regretted their betrayal and presented strategies benefiting the Han Chinese, such as in Hung Ch'eng-ch'ou's case. For Yi Tsung-k'uei, it seems, the gentlemen in such cases may have betrayed their regime, but they did not betray their culture. But Yi disdains Li Tzu-ch'eng and his followers as ignorant peasantry, the *tsei* (rebels) or *k'ou* (bandits) who dared to revolt against the legitimate regime of their own racial and cultural heritage. Thus Yi considers gentlemen who surrendered to Li Tzu-ch'eng as having committed double treason—to their regime and to their culture—and therefore as unforgivable. This culturally oriented mentality foreshadows Yi's invention of the history and his evaluation of the gentry of the next two historical moments.

The Taiping Rebellion (1850–1864) was also a peasant uprising against a "legitimate" regime. Its anti-Manchu program and Western-inspired ideology, however, anticipated the 1911 Republican Revolution, and it was therefore hailed by the Republican Revolutionaries, including Yi Tsung-k'uei. In order to fit his celebration of the Taiping Rebellion to his own value system, Yi rewrote it into a "gentry revolution" by portraying its leaders as outstanding gentlemen. He thus salutes the Taiping prince, Shih Ta-k'ai: "Shih Ta-k'ai, with both his literary and military talents, rose in revolution but failed. People circulated his 'War Proclamation' [*hsi-wen*], which reads: 'Can we bear to see our lofty nation's garment polluted by barbarians? Heroes of the Central Land, restore our rivers and mountains!' His spirit and vitality surpassed the entire generation. They also transmitted the ending couplet of his poem, 'Expressing Inner Thoughts': 'Our ambition not yet fulfilled, people already suffer / In the Southeast, tears everywhere.' Such are really a benevolent man's kind words. They would surely shame those war mongers [the Manchus and their Han generals] to death."[33]

In Yi's description, Shih Ta-k'ai embodies all the best gentlemanly features. He rises in revolution out of patriotic sentiment—to overthrow a "barbarian" (*i-ti*) regime and to restore the lost land. His concern about common people's sufferings over his own political ambition typifies the Confucian moral code of *jen*—benevolence. Moreover, his superb literary achievements put a dazzling touch on his princely moral qualities, making him an even more convincing role model for the gentry.

Yi portrays another Taiping prince, Li Hsiu-ch'eng (d. 1864), in a similar manner: "Li Hsiu-ch'eng was well versed in literature and fond of literati. While stationed at Soochow, he used to boat in the moonlit night and to compose poems over the wine cup. After [the Taiping capital] Chinling [Nanking] had been besieged for a long time, Li often stared westward and sighed, appearing sorrowful. He composed two *lü-shih* poems, entitled 'Sentiments of the Time,' which are full of virility and vigor, no less than Ts'ao Ts'ao's heroic poems."[34] The scenes depicted in this episode locate Li Hsiu-ch'eng in a typical poetic environment, elevating him to the same status as the famous gentleman-warrior Ts'ao Ts'ao. Characterizing Shih Ta-k'ai and Li Hsiu-ch'eng as benevolent leaders and talented literati, Yi Tsung-k'uei seeks to redefine the Taiping Rebellion as a Han Chinese gentry revolution, designed to restore the rightful Han Chinese sovereign as well as the traditional Han Chinese culture.[35]

By radically redefining the Taiping Rebellion as a gentry revolution, Yi equates the Taiping leaders with Ch'ing scholar-officials, blaming the latter for resisting the former. For example, he writes of the Ch'ing scholar-general P'eng Yü-lin (1816–1890), who fought against the Taipings in the Chiang-nan area:

Upon his [P'eng Yü-lin's] death, Wang K'ai-yün mourned him with matched verses [*lien*],[36] saying:

"For poetry and wine he's naturally a famous man,
Plus his official merits, oh, so splendid!
All this forever increases the price of his plum paintings.

A towering ship desires to waft across the ocean.
Sighing, I lament my hero has passed on;
How can I bear to recount his bloody battles in Chiang-nan?"

The "plum painting" line refers to his talent in painting plum blossoms. [In the line] not bearing to recount those "bloody battles," Wang implies disapproval of P'eng's slaughtering his compatriots.[37]

Using this matched verse, Yi sets up a pattern for evaluating the Ch'ing gentlemen who pacified the Taipings, such as Tseng Kuo-fan, Li Hung-chang (1823–1901), and Tso Tsung-t'ang (1812–1885). He celebrates their cultural achievements but denounces their ruthless repression of people's anti-Manchu outcry. He writes in his "Compilation Notes": "As for civil wars, I dare not mention them at all, in case it would sound like praising the slaughter of our compatriots."[38]

On the other hand, Yi Tsung-k'uei highly commended the gentlemen who were willing to help the Taiping rebels: "Wang T'ao once presented a letter to Li Hsiu-ch'eng, the Taiping Prince of Loyalty. The letter was several thousand characters long, and each of the characters could put the Ch'ing troops to death, yet [Li Hsiu-ch'eng] turned it down. [Wang] thereafter traveled to the Southern Pacific Islands and eventually stayed in Hong Kong. Upon hearing about [this letter], Li Hung-chang appreciated Wang and intended to recruit him as an adviser. Several times Li Hung-chang sent messengers to Wang, but Wang modestly refused. In his response to Li Hung-chang, he wrote: 'My heart has long turned into ashes, and I am too old to serve. When [the burning stalks are] cooking [the beans of] the same roots, how dare I intensify [the fire]?'"[39] Wang T'ao devoted to the Taipings his loyalty and his wisdom, embodied in the advice he gave to Li Hsiu-ch'eng, which, according to Yi Tsung-k'uei, "topped any other strategies plotted in the interests of the Taiping Kingdom."[40] Disheartened by Li Hsiu-ch'eng's rejection, Wang T'ao put himself into exile, as any loyal subject would do under the circumstances. Yet when Li Hung-chang urged him to serve the Ch'ing court, Wang T'ao reproached him as "the burning stalks . . . cooking the beans of the same roots." In short, Yi fully justifies Wang's support of the Taipings and his rejection of Li Hung-chang's overtures, because the former fought on behalf of the Han Chinese whereas the latter defended a barbarian regime.

As shown in Wang T'ao's story, Yi valorizes the gentlemen proponents of the Taipings for their willingness to help with their wisdom, including the newly acquired knowledge from the West. For example, Jung Hung (aka Yung Wing), one of the first Chinese students overseas, came back from America and paid a visit to Hung Hsiu-ch'üan, suggesting that he (1) develop diplomatic relations [with the West], and (2) buy ships [from the West]. Hung, however, did not take his advice. Recounting this story, Yi sighs: "The *Kuo-yü* [Conversations from the states] says: 'Those who can gain the [support of the] *shih* [intellectual elite] prosper, and those who cannot fail.' True, true!"[41] Yi then concludes that the Taipings could not take advantage of such advice because "the Manchus' vitality and fortune [*ch'i-yün*] had not been exhausted, so the Han Chinese were doomed to fail."[42] For Yi, Heaven's mandate still played a critical role in dynastic change.

In Yi's view, the 1911 Republican Revolution represented the best values of the past and the present and the best features of China and the West. It also recruited the best gentry role models. In his portrayal, the Republican Revolutionaries were sincere gentlemen of high moral character—ardent fighters who devoted their lives to noble goals and accomplished poets who dipped patriotic pens into their own blood. His description of the Nan-she (Southern Poetry Club) members especially touts this new value system: "Recently (1909), a poetry club named Nan-she, the Southern Society, emerged from the southeast. Composed of the great revolutionaries, it focuses on the study of literature and advocates righteousness and integrity. Its famous members, such as Huang Hsing, Sung Chiao-jen, Ch'iu Liang, Ning T'iao-yüan, Ch'eng Chia-ch'eng . . . and so forth, are all well-known literary champions. Each year they publish two huge volumes of [poems and literary essays] . . . and most of them are either cynical, indignant criticisms against reality or noble and sorrowful self-expressions, similar to Tu Fu's poetic history."[43]

Yi Tsung-k'uei attached to this description an extensive note detailing the biographical background of each member mentioned in the episode—twenty-four in all. Reading them sheds valuable light on Yi's conception of "new" gentry values. For instance:

> Huang Hsing, a native of Shan-hua, Hunan, was by nature sincere and honest. . . . He had been quite in favor of nationalism [*min-tsu chu-i*]. Later he went to Japan and, with Chang T'ai-yen, Sun Yat-sen, Sung

Chiao-jen, and others, organized the T'ung-meng hui to prepare for revolution. He headed uprisings in Chen-nan and Canton, which, though not successful, shattered the Manchus' nerves. In the ninth month of the year Hsin-hai [1911], he went to Hupeh as the commander-in-chief of the revolutionary troops. Soon Chin-ling [Nanking] was reinstated [as the capital] and the temporary government [of the republic] was established. He [Huang] was selected the Grand Marshal. . . . In the Kuei-ch'ou [1913] Incident, he foresaw Yüan Shih-k'ai's [1859–1916] failure in his self-destructive monarchical attempt and left [Nanking] for Japan and America. Upon Yüan's death he came back to live in Shanghai and died a year later. All his life he disciplined himself rigorously. He liked reading Tseng Kuo-fan's poetry and prose, saying: "Although Tseng's intent differs from mine, his way of self-discipline is strict. I should take him for a model."[44]

Sung Chiao-jen lost his father while young. He was poor, but extremely filial to his mother. . . . Later, hunted by the Ch'ing court because of his involvement in revolution, Sung fled to Japan. He missed his mother, often crying from night till dawn.

[Yi's note to this episode reads:] Sung Chiao-jen was a native of T'ao-yüan, Hunan. . . . He organized the T'ung-meng hui in Japan with Sun Yat-sen and Huang Hsing, advocating revolution [ko-ming chu-i]. After the establishment of the Republic [of China], he was appointed minister of Agriculture and Forestry. He later resigned to organize the Kuomintang [the Nationalist Party], because he favored a party cabinet. [For this reason] the Yüan Shih-k'ai government grew increasingly hostile to him. In 1913, he was assassinated in Shanghai. Those who knew him grieved over his death.[45]

Ch'iu Liang was a native of Hsiang-yin, Hunan. He announced the independence of Shansi in support of the 1911 Republican Revolution. In 1913, he published the *Democratic Daily* in Peking to berate Yüan Shih-k'ai. In 1915, Yüan's partisans enticed him to Peking and murdered him.

Ning T'iao-yüan, a native of Li-ling, Hunan, was by nature honest and straight, and well versed in poetry and prose. He joined the T'ung-meng hui while young. In the P'ing-Li Incident, he was imprisoned in Changsha for three years, where he drank wine, wrote poems, and sang with a metal-and-stone-toned voice. After he was released, he went to Peking to be the editor-in-chief of the *Imperial Daily*. He was articulate and outspoken, attacking the [Ch'ing] government without fear. When the Wuch'ang Uprising took place [in 1911], he rushed between Hunan and Hupeh, working on both Li Yüan-hung's and T'an Yen-k'ai's staffs. Soon he was assigned to be the director of the San-fo Railroad Bureau. After Sung Chiao-jen's assassination, he resigned from his office, fled to Shanghai, and telegraphed T'an Yen-k'ai, urging him to announce independence. The Yüan government secretly ordered his arrest. He was then murdered in Wuchang.

Ch'eng Chia-ch'eng was a native of Anhwei. In 1915, he failed in his attempt to assassinate Yüan Shih-k'ai and was promptly executed.[46]

Yi seems to have a clear agenda in writing these biographical notes. The common denominators he uses to introduce Nan-she members include: (1) They were both poets and revolutionary fighters who used poetry to record their revolutionary strife, first against the Manchu regime and then against Yüan Shih-k'ai's monarchical attempt; (2) they maintained traditional Confucian values, such as filial piety, loyalty, and righteousness, but meanwhile embraced Western values. Among the twenty-four poets introduced here, many studied abroad, and half of them were members of the newly constituted, Western-styled National Assembly (chung-i yüan) and National Deliberative Assembly (ts'an-i yüan). The inclusion of the director of a railroad bureau and a mathematician shows the gentry's ability to incorporate advocates of Western knowledge. Moreover, many Nan-she poets employed new Western-style newspapers in advocating revolutionary ideas and attacking their enemies. Here again, Yi depicts the gentry not only as ardent preservers of Chinese culture but also as open-minded intellectuals, capable of embracing new values and entertaining new options.

This eclectic value system also applied to gentlewomen. The chapter "Worthy Beauties" in the New Shih-shuo collected the stories of the most diversified women paragons in Chinese history. In addition to the traditional categories such as devoted mothers, virtuous wives, filial daughters, erudite scholars, and creative poets and artists, Yi also included women warriors, loyalists, educators, and revolutionaries, notably martyrs such as Ch'iu Chin (1875–1907) and Li Jun, wife of the famous late Ch'ing reformer T'an Ssu-t'ung (1865–1898). Here, Yi Tsung-k'uei eloquently describes Li's tragic death:

T'an Ssu-t'ung's wife Li Jun was well versed in the "Inner Principles" [of the Book of Rites] as a young girl, and she was broadly learned. T'an once sighed with admiration for her intelligence. She collected the "Biographies of Women" from all dynastic histories and to each attached a commentary. On the wife of the Ming minister, Yang Chi-sheng [1516–1555], she commented: "At that moment partisans of the evil faction dominated the court, and the political situation was extremely dark. No matter how much Lady Yang tried to defend her husband, even petitioning a dozen times, she would have no way to reach the emperor. The only thing she could have done was to tie the petition to her hair and to hide a dagger in her bosom and then to commit suicide on behalf of her husband at the gate of the imperial palace. In that way she might have moved the emperor." Right after T'an Ssu-t'ung died a martyr for the 1898 Reform, Lady Li took a sedan chair into the Hunan governor's office. She knelt down on the ground wailing, and then took a dagger out of her sleeve and cut her throat. Her blood spilled onto Governor Ch'en Pao-chen's [1831–1900] official gown; thus she died.[47]

Although Li Jun's death looks like one more tragic suicide a widow commits after her husband's death, the place where she chooses to die upgrades and updates this traditional ritual. She rejects dying silently in her private chamber, as tradition would have it. Rather, she follows her own suggestion to Yang Chi-sheng's wife—killing herself in a public place, the governor's office—hence offering a public defense for her husband and a fearless outcry against the ruthless government. Her blood inscribes her statement on the governor's official gown—a highly symbolic gesture that registers a woman's heroic interference in public affairs. Li Jun's suicide thus defies the "Inner Principles," which taught women "not to talk about public affairs" (pu yen wai).[48] In describing Li Jun's heroic death, Yi Tsung-k'uei provides one of the most touching moments in Chinese women's history, when an intellectual woman both follows and transcends her cultural tradition, dying simultaneously for her husband and for her nation.

Conceptualizing the "New" in Terms of the "Old"

Yi Tsung-k'uei may have recognized the special historical moment that was his, but he did not appoint himself to lead people down a new path in the fashion of the radical New Culture intellectuals. Their concept of "new" differed distinctly from Yi's, as Lydia H. Liu indicates:

The inaugural issue of the journal *Xin chao* [Hsin-ch'ao] (Renaissance or New Tide), published by students at Beijing [Peking] University at the peak of the New Culture movement, carried a polemical piece by Chen Jia'ai [Ch'en Chia-ai], entitled "Xin" [Hsin] (New). This article spelled out the rhetoric of modernity in a series of tropes. "The new is singular, and the old is plural," said the author. "The former is singular for being absolutely unique, whereas the latter is plural for being open to infinite multiplication." Armed with the figure of inflective grammar, the author then proceeded to elaborate his point about old and new using the metaphor of genealogy: "It takes two, man and wife, to make a single son at a time (even twins come one after the other). Conversely, parents that give birth to the son were in turn brought into the world by the grandparents, who owed their lives to the great-grand parents *ad infinitum*." Far from being a treatise preaching filial piety, the essay tried to make the point that "old" ideas, like the older generation, were bound to be replaced by "new" ones, which the author defined in the rest of the essay as singular, unique, modern, and therefore superior.[49]

Yi's idea of "new" embraced the very feature that Ch'en considered old—namely, its openness to "infinite multiplication." As we have just seen, Yi's "fair and proper" attitude allowed him to juxtapose eclectic—very often contradictory—values, which he put in order by means of the *Shih-shuo* scheme of classification. By examining several interrelated new concepts highlighted in the text, we may see how he invested them with different values and accentuated them with a *Shih-shuo* flavor, thus revealing his conception of the "new."

Ko-ming. This is a crucial marker of "new" in the *New Shih-shuo*, used to characterize the Taiping Rebellion and, in particular, the 1911 Republican Revolution. It employs one of the "return graphic loans" which, according to Lydia H. Liu, refer to "classical Chinese-character compounds that were used by the Japanese to translate modern European words and were reintroduced into modern Chinese."[50] Yi, once a Chinese student in Japan and therefore well acquainted with the Japanese usage of *ko-ming*, or *kakumei*, clearly uses this term in its modern sense to translate the European concept of "revolution." For instance, he frequently compares the 1911 Revolution to the 1776 American Revolution and, more typically, combines *ko-ming* with another modern term—*chu-i*.

His interpretation of *ko-ming* nonetheless adheres closely to its Chinese traditional meaning, the righteous power shift in the name of Heaven's mandate, as described in the *I-ching*: "Just as Heaven and Earth make use of Radical Change so that the four seasons come to pass, so did Tang [T'ang] and Wu bring about radical change in the mandate to rule in compliance with the will of Heaven and in accordance with the wishes of mankind."[51] Understanding *ko-ming* in this rather conventional way, Yi blames the Taipings' failure on its destiny decided by Heaven's will.[52] Furthermore, he classifies the 1911 Revolution entries mainly under "*Te* Conduct," equating this *ko-ming* with those of T'ang and King Wu, whose revolts against tyrannical rulers were justified as moral conduct in the Confucian tradition. He compares Sun Yat-sen to George Washington because they both "abandoned [the opportunity of ruling] all under Heaven as if abandoning a pair of old shoes,"[53] suggesting Taoist aloofness from worldly gains rather than a bourgeois revolutionary ideal.

Chuan-chih. This word compound is another "return graphic loan" borrowed from the Japanese word *sensei,* used to translate the Western concept of "autocracy."[54] Yi Tsung-k'uei employed this term to characterize Manchu rule in order to justify the gentry's outcry—which he often labeled as "revolution." He used it only on two occasions, but each reflected the political, cultural, economic, and racial conflicts between the Ch'ing regime and the Han Chinese gentry. Here is one episode:

> Upon the Ch'ing troops entering the border [of Ming China], the Ch'ing government required the Han Chinese to shave [the front of] their hair. K'ung Wen-piao, a former prefect [and a descendant of Confucius], presented a memorial to the court, saying: "Following Your Majesty's edict, . . . the head of the K'ung clan already had all four generations shaving the hair after leading us to report to our ancestral temple. Yet, I, your subject, think that the late Sage was the inventor of the ritual . . . and nothing in the ritual exceeds the importance of the costume. The Sage's costume has been preserved by his descendants. From the Han to the Ming, the political system might vary, but, for two thousand years, the style of our ritual costume has never changed. To have it changed, I am afraid, might harm Your Majesty's principle of honoring Confucianism and the *Tao.* Whether we should grow our hair back and restore our ancestral costume depends on Your Majesty's sage judgment." The

emperor decreed: "Shaving hair is a strict edict, and no offender should be tolerated. K'ung Wen-piao has committed a capital offense pleading for his hair. His life may be spared in consideration of his being the Sage's descendant. But, 'Confucius was the sage whose actions were timely.'[55] [K'ung Wen-piao's] defiance blemished his ancestor's *Tao* of acting according to the times. Make sure that he is dismissed from office and never again be appointed to any position!" Alas, there is surely no way to argue with an autocratic [*chuan-chih*] ruler who excessively abuses power![56]

Under the excuse of keeping intact the core of the Confucian tradition (the ritual costume, fu-chih), K'ung Wen-piao challenges the Manchu regime's claim to be continuing the Han Chinese tradition. An interesting argument unfolds. On K'ung Wen-piao's part, he emphasizes a two-thousand-year cultural tradition that has never undergone any change, regardless of the changes in the political system. The Ch'ing emperor, citing none other than Confucius himself, contends that culture, too, should go through changes along with the changes of the political situation. The real conflict at stake, evidently, falls between the Manchu ruler's effort to subordinate the Han Chinese tradition to his own political system and the gentry's request to maintain its cultural tradition on its own terms.

The other episode reads:

Chin Sheng-t'an [d. 1661] had been famous for his literary talents since his youth. He was by nature uninhibited, eccentric, and outspoken. . . . He participated in the 1660 Wailing Temple Incident [*k'u-miao an*] under the Shun-chih reign. All the participants were later arrested, put to trial, and sentenced to death; their families were put in slavery, and their properties were confiscated.

[Yi's note:] The trial of the Wailing Temple Incident took place under the following circumstances: Jen, a native of Shansi and the magistrate of Wu County, bullied the Wu people into paying their taxes in advance. [Wu] licentiates, Hsüeh Erh-chang and the others, stirred by the people's agony, rang the bells, beat the drums, and wailed at the Confucius Temple. Hundreds of scholars joined them. . . . Later they were arrested and put to trial, . . . and eighteen scholars were executed. Alas, under an autocratic [*chuan-chih*], abusive bureaucracy and strict literary inquisitions, unless retreating in reclusion, few, if any, literati could escape their fatal destiny, much less an uninhibited scholar like Chin Sheng-t'an![57]

This episode concerns another basic principle of the gentry: In addition to protecting the Chinese cultural tradition, they are also obligated to protect their fellow people's interests. Indeed, by protecting other people, they fulfill the responsibility of continuing the codes of Chinese culture—specifically the code of *jen*, or benevolence. This episode also reflects the conflict between the literati's carefree lifestyle and the rigorous governmental repression. Yi records the Chin Sheng-t'an episode in the chapter "Jen-tan" (Uninhibitedness and eccentricity), identifying Chin with his free-spirited Wei-Chin predecessors, such as Hsi K'ang, who was also executed by an autocratic government. Even the way they faced death was aesthetically identical. Just as Hsi K'ang plucked the zither before his execution, Chin remained high spirited until the last minute. He left the following words to his wife: "It tastes extremely delicious to eat soybeans along with pickled vegetables. I cannot die without passing on this recipe to later generations!"[58]

Using the term *chuan-chih* with its newly acquired Western connotations, Yi attacks the Ch'ing government mainly because it violates the fundamental values that the gentry has traditionally upheld—the need to feel that they are the bearers of the culture and the guardians of the Chinese people's interests (and their own!). This feeling was highly sensitized under an alien regime. So, once this autocratic system has been lifted and the gentry feel unprecedentedly free, any sort of autocratic monarchy becomes utterly unbearable—even it is of the Han Chinese gentry's own racial makeup. Seen in this light, we should not be surprised to find how ardently Yi opposed Yüan Shih-k'ai's monarchical attempt.[59] He contributed a number of records to those who fearlessly fought against Yüan, particularly to those killed in this campaign, such as the five Nan-she poets introduced above.

I-hui. As the ardent enemy of autocracy, Yi was naturally fascinated with newly imported constitutional ideas, including *i-hui, kuo-hui, i-yüan* (all equivalent to "national assembly," "parliament," or "congress"), *i-yüan* (assembly members), and so forth.[60] With irrepressible excitement, he tells us:

> The National Assembly [*tzu-cheng yüan*] was the constitutional institution implanted at the end of the Ch'ing dynasty. Its members were either appointed by the emperor or elected by the people. It created a new system unprecedented in the thousands of years Chinese tradition. At the moment [when the council first gathered,] the spirit and feelings of its members [*i-yüan*] looked energetic and vivacious.
>
> In 1913, the National Assembly [*kuo-hui*] [of the Republic of China] was officially inaugurated. The first meeting was held on April 8. There were about eight hundred members [*i-yüan*], known as the "eight hundred arhats."[61]

Precisely what is attractive to Yi Tsung-k'uei about this new system? We can see in his writings a particular preoccupation with *yen-shuo* (public speech),[62] which legitimized the gentry's right to articulate its views in public. He describes three speeches given at the first meeting of the Ch'ing National Assembly: "The first was a member's call for impeachment against Prince Ch'ing, the second was Liu Tse-hsi's report on the budget, and the third was Yang Tu's interpretation of the new law codes. Each presented tens of thousands of words. The audience was all in high spirits, and the journalists were all exhausted in taking notes."[63] Of these three speeches, Yi especially hailed the call for impeachment against Prince Ch'ing, who was then head of the "Chün-chi ch'u" (Council of State), which was the executive branch of the Ch'ing government. Yi elaborates in a note that when a member who was elected by the people (*min-hsüan*) accused the prince of "dictating state affairs and taking bribes in governmental operations," his "voice thundered like a booming bell and all the participants applauded with their approval."[64] Here the form of the impeachment is as significant as its content. For the first time in Ch'ing history, and in Chinese imperial history as well, the gentry publicly criticized the government through a legitimate, official channel.

Yi describes at length how, during the political turmoil of the early Republican period, the gentry broadly applied this new tool of *yen-shuo*:

> Shanghai is a cultural center where political theorists often give public speeches [*yen-shuo*] and thereby influence public opinion. In 1913, Sung

Chiao-jen gave a speech at the local branch of the Nationalist Party, enumerating the failure of the Yüan Shih-k'ai government. In 1916, Sun Yat-sen spoke at the Chang Garden about the Five-Rights Constitution. Each time they would spend hours elaborating their ideas. Those among the audience all sighed in admiration.

Liang Ch'i-ch'ao is a great political theorist of today, skilled in presenting persuasive, entertaining speeches. In 1916, he interpreted in public [yen-shuo] the constitutional principles at the Tiger District Bridge. Not only did his proponents all express enormous admiration, even his enemies had no way to refute him.[65]

Yi Tsung-k'uei may have considered the form *yen-shuo* to be a Western concept. Yet his way of presenting *yen-shuo* anecdotes echoes various *Shih-shuo* accounts of late Han "private scholars' fearless criticism" *(ch'u-shih heng-i)* and Wei-Chin "pure conversations," when gentlemen openly reproached the government and debated over philosophical topics and political issues at public gatherings. Also, in a manner reminiscent of the original *Shih-shuo,* Yi not only conveys the contents of these speeches but he also pays equal attention to the style of the speakers and the response of the audience, which he often recounts in *Shih-shuo* terms. For example, in indicating that at the first meeting of the Ch'ing National Assembly the audience was all "high spirited" *(shen-wang),* he adopted the term *shen-wang* from the *Shih-shuo*'s characterization of Yü Ai (8/33). His praise of Sung Chiao-jen and Sun Yat-sen's persuasive speeches reminds us of Liu T'an's water analogy, which also makes the audience "sigh in admiration." Most revealingly, his account of Sun Yat-sen's presidential inauguration speech resembles a *Shih-shuo* episode almost word-for-word:

Sun Yat-sen, after being elected the first president of the Republic of China by the representatives from seventeen provinces, set out wine and threw a banquet in Chin-ling [the temporary capital of the Republic of China, Nanking]. All the heroes and worthies of the Southeast came in droves. Sun had always had a martial disposition and vigorous air, and moreover on this particular day his voice and intonation rang out heroically as he told about the successes and failures from antiquity to the present, and the future of the world and the nation. His manner was rugged and flintlike [*luậi-lâk] and the whole company sighed [uninter-ruptedly] in appreciation.[66]

> After Huan Wen had pacified Shu (in 347), he gathered his aides and officers and set wine before them in the palace of Li Shih (the last ruler of Shu). All the local gentry of Pa and Shu (Szechwan) came in droves. Huan had always had a martial disposition and vigorous air, and moreover on this particular day his voice and intonation rang out hero-ically as he told how from antiquity to the present "success or failure have proceeded from men," and survival or perdition are bound up with hu-man ability. His manner was rugged and flintlike (*luậi-lâk) and the whole company sighed [uninterruptedly] in appreciation. (Shih-shuo hsin-yü, 13/8)

This portrayal of Sun Yat-sen mimics the Shih-shuo portrayal of Huan Wen, but it expands the focus to include not only the nation's destiny but also world affairs.

P'ing-yün. Yi employs p'ing-yün to express a fair and proper attitude toward evaluating historical and contemporary affairs. Under this general principle, he invokes a pair of new concepts—t'ung-pao (compatriots) and kuo-min (citizens)—to equalize the status of all the people within the newly established Republic of China.

T'ung-pao had been traditionally used to indicate brothers of the same parents and people of the same country—and, presumably, of the same race. Yi Tsung-k'uei has, however, re-conceptualized this term by in-cluding the Manchus among the Chinese people in order to mediate the deep-rooted practice of "racial discrimination" (chung-tsu chih-chien). Yet as we have seen, anti-Manchu bias pervades Yi's account of the Ch'ing dynasty. Only after the 1911 Revolution did Yi claim that the Manchus, too, were part of the newly established Republic of China—a minority group of t'ung-pao (compatriots) affiliated with the Han majority. This em-ployment of t'ung-pao suggests more a victor's hauteur toward the defeated enemy than a historian's fairness toward his fellow people.

Kuo-min has its origin in the Tso Commentary, but it emerged as the Chinese equivalent of the Western notion of "citizen" at the end of the Ch'ing period. It became broadly used under Yüan Shih-k'ai's presidency (1912–1916), registered in terms such as "kuo-min hsüeh-hsiao," the official name for primary-level schools.[67] This use of the term indicates its application to the entire population of the republic. Yet according to Yi's account in the following episode, both the president and his ministers seem to have had a problem understanding the term in this way:

> Chang Chien [1853–1926] is simple and quiet, but sometimes he comes up with a witty bon mot that can make people smile. When Yüan Shih-k'ai was secretly plotting his monarchical attempt, Mr. Chang confronted him. Yüan tried hard to explain it away as a rumor, saying: "If the citizens [kuo-min] were to decide the [imperial] system for the nation, the one most qualified for the throne should be [former] Emperor Hsüan-t'ung, and the second should be Duke Yen-sheng (Confucius' descendant). If we were to look for a descendant of the Ming royal house [with the Chu family name], then Minister of Interior Chu Ch'i-chin, Chih-li Commissioner Chu Chia-pao, and Chekiang General Chu Jui should all be considered qualified candidates. Why me?" Mr. Chang smiled, saying: "So would the opera singer Chu Su-yün also be qualified for the throne?" Yüan was upset about this conversation for days.[68]

This conversation takes place under a republican system. Against such a backdrop, the search for candidates for the throne should be conducted among all citizens of the republic. Yet the president seems to acknowledge only the gentry as *kuo-min,* and Chang Chien, the minister of Agriculture and Commerce, includes an actor as a "candidate" only in jest. Yi Tsung-k'uei is of a similar mind. Disdainful of the common people, his *p'ing-yün* attitude appears fair only when applied to the gentry. Outside of gentry circles, class discrimination precedes racial issues, but within the gentry, an anti-Manchu bias persists.

Continuing the "Old" in terms of the "New"

By combining "old" with "new," Yi put himself at odds with the radical New Culture activists. The first issue of the *New Youth* (September 1915) published Wang Shu-ch'ien's article "Hsin-chiu wen-t'i" (The problem of new and old), which drew an uncompromising line between the two: "New and Old are absolutely incompatible; the words of the compromisers prove that they don't understand either the New or the Old. They are the criminals of the New World and the petty thieves of the Old. All problems of the present stem from the fact that the banners of New and Old are unclear. The reason for this is that the definitions of New and Old are unclear."[69] Yi was familiar with the *New Youth* and its iconoclastic agendas, but he chose a different path. Why?

In order to understand why Yi chose to connect "new" to "old" rather than to sever the two, we need to look into his background. According to Yi's self-introduction in his preface, he was born into a gentry family and educated by his father and his uncle. Thus, like any gentry youth, Yi was well versed in the Chinese classics and, as he himself put it, "extremely addicted to [*k'u-shih*] the *Shih-shuo hsin-yü.*" Yi's otherwise regular, conventional education was interrupted by the turmoil toward the end of the Ch'ing period, and he found himself among those who went to study in Japan at the beginning of the century. Coming back after the establishment of the Republic of China, Yi was elected one of the first members of the National Assembly. After Yüan Shih-k'ai dispersed the assembly, he stayed in Peking and composed the *New Shih-shuo.*[70]

Like many Chinese elite activists at the turn of the century, Yi was well acquainted with the "old" and at the same time exposed to the "new." But he felt that the "old" cultural tradition had never been fully developed because of the repression of an autocratic and barbaric political system. Yi embodied his frustration in recounting Wang Chung's (1745–1794) "three regrets": First, that Nature creates people yet makes them dependent on clothing and food and causes them to die before reaching a hundred years of age; second, that he had neither two wings to fly into the nine clouds nor four hooves to gallop a thousand *li*; and third, that the ancient people left behind only their writings but not their spirit for him to communicate with."[71] A leading scholar of the Evidential Research (K'ao-cheng) School, Wang Chung devoted his life to textual criticism.[72] His desire to know the spirit of the ancients grew out of his search for the authentic meaning of ancient writings. Since the school of Evidential Research had sprouted from Ming loyalist-scholars such as Ku Yen-wu and their iconoclastic effort to continue the Chinese tradition under Manchu repression, it linked the desire for scholastic freedom to the desire for spiritual freedom. This episode thus communicates, in an allegorical way, a gentry member's long-term ambition for being the owner of his life, his person, and the culture that is the extension of his spirit.

The termination of the Ch'ing regime and the introduction of "new" options offered the best opportunity for the gentry to fulfill its ambition. But they could see the greatness of the "new" only through their old lenses. For this reason, they picked up the values in the new system that best suited their old longings; hence their enthusiasm for "revolution," "anti-autocracy," the parliamentary or congressional system, and so forth. Their agenda was to return the nation and its culture to its legitimate stewards—the Han Chinese gentry—and to allow them to move China ahead through incorporating the best values—the way they had always imagined. Their anti-autocratic campaign aimed at preventing China from falling back into the iron grip of any dictator—witness their vehement battle against Yüan Shih-k'ai—and their obsession with the congressional system was intended to represent the gentry as the collective leader of the nation. For Yi Tsung-k'uei and his ilk, "new" was not the termination of "old" but rather its continuation.

Yi thus represents the gentry at a transitional time, optimistic, eager to welcome a new era, but perplexed about exactly what to do with it. Yi's unsettled thoughts about an unsettled time manifest themselves in the ironic ending of the chapter "Literature and Scholarship." This chapter, which presents his contemplation of China's future as part of a thorough survey of Ch'ing elite culture, could have ended with his neutralization of the radical *New Youth* agendas, quoted earlier in this chapter. But Yi added one more episode that not only disturbs the chronological order but also undermines the serious tone of the longest and best-written chapter in his book:

> The "poetry bell" [*shih-chung*] is a variant of "linked verse" [*lien-chü*]. No one knows when it started. It flourished fully during the T'ung-chih and Kuang-hsü reigns (1862–1908). . . . It is also unknown as to why it came to be called "bell." Famous lines passed on to this day are mostly in the style of "describing objects" [*fu-wu*], such as:

>> Ten thousand *li* of streams and mountains go to the Red
>> Emperor—Hsiang Yü

One life of virtue is ruined by Crimson Maiden—Ying-ying
General Great-Strength is all courage—Chao Yün
Ducal Son the scoundrel originally had no guts—crab
Hero under the groin wearing a red scarf—sanitary napkins
Names on the wall covered with green gauze—a memorial
    tablet

And that is it.[73]

Among all Chinese literary games, the "poetry bell" was among the most difficult. Yet it was also an utterly inconsequential art form. As illustrated here, all the objects are randomly thrown together, linked only by rhythm, rhyme, parallelism, and other technical rules.[74] Thus we see unrelated things standing side by side: Hsiang Yü, defeated by Liu Pang (the Red Emperor), is paralleled with the romantic affair of Ying-ying, facilitated by Hung-niang (Crimson Maiden); the legendary general Chao Yün is matched with, of all things, a crab; and a pile of sanitary napkins, designed to protect female bodies, is linked to a tablet of men's names that honors male deeds. That this mischievous group of trivial poetic lines should appear next to the weighty New Culture Movement forms the strangest reading moment in the *New Shih-shuo*. In one episode, culture is taken as a matter of life or death for the entire Chinese nation.[75] In the other, poetry, the finest Chinese literary form, becomes a mere game for literati to play with. The irrational linking of the "poetry bell" and the New Culture Movement reflects the author's (unconscious?) confusion about a complex reality that was full of contingencies.

The *New Shih-shuo* is not very successful as character writing per se. The author seems unconcerned with the many philosophical, psychological, and aesthetic issues bearing on questions of human nature, but concentrates primarily on the collective character of the Ch'ing and early Min-kuo gentry. Exactly because of his eclectic account of gentry behavior and remarks, however, Yi Tsung-k'uei successfully reveals the uncertain social status and cultural identity of the Chinese elite from the end of China's imperial era to the beginning of its modernity.

Conclusion: The Self and the Mirror

The *Shih-shuo* tradition reveals an intimate and inextricable connection between the "self" and the "other." Although the *Shih-shuo* genre arose from the Wei-Chin elite's desire to express themselves on their own terms, as if the opinions of others did not matter, in fact they and their successors never stopped adjusting their images, trying to present an ideal self to others. The *Shih-shuo* tradition clearly reflects this effort in its never-ending revision of the genre—in its expansion of categories, reclassification of episodes, and rewriting of accounts—all so that the intellectual elite could dazzle their audience—and themselves—with the vision of a perfect self.

What was this "self?" In the *Shih-shuo hsin-yü*, the most often used pronouns standing for the "self" include *wo* (appearing 163 times), *tzu* (131 times), *wu* (58 times), *chi* (45 times), and *shen* (11 times).[1] Hsü Shen (A.D. 30–124) defines these terms in his *Shuo-wen chieh-tzu* (Interpretation of words):

> *Wo,* I/me/myself, refers to one's body as one's self.
>> *Tzu,* self, means nose, and [the written character] resembles the shape of a nose.
>> *Wu,* I, is used to refer to [one's] self, [signified by] the pictographic radical, *k'ou* (mouth).
>> *Chi,* self, means the center of [the body] and resembles a human belly.
>> *Shen,* I, means the spine [of the human body].[2]

All these definitions refer explicitly to the human form, with an acute awareness of the way in which the body serves as a concrete marker distinguishing the "self" from the "other."[3] According to the *Shih-shuo hsin-yü*, the most important and reliable record of Wei-Chin linguistic changes,[4] the Wei-Chin period preferred body-related pronouns for the "self" to those not defined in such physical terms, such as *"yü¹,"* I, which only appears five times in the *Shih-shuo*, and *"yü²,"* I/my, which appears only twice (see glossary for Chinese characters).[5]

This broad usage of body-related pronouns of the self suggests that genuine "selfhood" could only emerge through personal association with others—through intense contact and close communion that involved the entire range of human emotions and other mental activities. Such an understanding of the self clearly arose from the Wei-Chin practice of character appraisal, in which the evaluator discerned each individual self through observing its performance in relation to others, and the evaluatee exposed his or her genuine self through a spontaneous and natural response to the world. On such occasions, the self existed in the physical contact of one's body with the eyes of others. This fundamental definition of self makes it impossible for one's self to exist on its own.

Because of this understanding of the self, the mirror metaphor abounds in the *Shih-shuo hsin-yü,* when people become "mirrors"—in particular, "water mirrors" *(shui-ching)*—for those around them to assure the existence of a self and to check on and improve the quality of this existence. Here are some examples:

> This man is a water mirror [*shui-ching*] to other men. Looking into him is like rolling away the clouds and mist and gazing at the blue sky. (8/23)[6]

> When did you ever see a bright mirror [*ming-ching*] wearied by frequent reflections, or a clear stream roiled by a gentle breeze? (2/90)[7]

What features made a water mirror a popular metaphor in Wei-Chin character appraisal?[8] The Chin gentleman Hsi Tsao-ch'ih characterized its connotation: "The water is utterly level so that even an evil person will follow its example; the mirror is utterly clear yet an ugly person is not angry at it. The water mirror reflects every detail of an object but never causes resentment because it has nothing to hide."[9]

In poetic diction, Wei-Chin pure conversationalists compared eminent gentry members to the "water mirror" because it could reflect the flaws of the person facing it and set up a fair, pure, and honest example for the person to rectify his or her self. The mirror metaphor of this function was continuously prevalent in the *Shih-shuo* imitations[10] and found profound elaborations in Wang Tang's *T'ang Forest,* which quotes T'ang T'ai-tsung as saying: "We use bronze as a mirror to straighten our clothes and cap, the past as a mirror to understand [the causes] of the rise and fall of states, and a person as a mirror to recognize our merits and faults. I have always maintained these three mirrors to prevent myself from making mistakes."[11]

In these mirror allegories, "I/we" uses the past and the "other" as the standard to check the present and the "self." But "I/we" is by no means a mute receiver of the past and the other's rules. Rather, it has to decide exactly what rules to follow before abiding by any. Thus, "I/we" stands as the subject and locates itself in the "here and now," examines, evaluates, names, and categorizes the past and the "other" according to its own experiences and in terms of its own needs. On the other hand, the past and the "other" are not mute either. The allegory of a human water mirror, be it individual or collective, arises precisely from the idea that it also has identity and subjectivity. It actively displays its own pure, fresh qualities and at the same time honestly reflects the features of the one facing it, hence offering the present and the self a model for emulation, an equal for comparison, and a rival to be challenged. The relationship of both sides of the mirror is one of mutual definition and justification. This mirror approach was applied to both the evaluation of the *Shih-shuo hsin-yü* and to the creation and assessment of its imitations.

Evaluating the *Shih-shuo*

As mentioned in the introduction, previous studies have placed the *Shih-shuo hsin-yü* in a peculiar and paradoxical position vis-à-vis China's literary history, both highly centralized and utterly marginalized. These ambivalent evaluations of the *Shih-shuo hsin-yü* have resulted from the interaction between the intrinsic features of cultural evaluation as a "present" activity and the characteristics of the *Shih-shuo hsin-yü* as a "past" cultural system.

According to Richard J. Smith, the formation of cultural systems and the evaluation of these systems involve—implicitly or explicitly—a process of classification: "Although the term 'culture' is sometimes used . . . with respect to collective artistic, literary, and technical accomplishments, it refers fundamentally to classification—the naming and arranging of things, ideas, and activities into coherent systems of meaning. Viewed in this light, cultural analysis becomes the evaluation of these systems, their interrelationships, and their social manifestations. The trick, of course, is to avoid imprisonment by one's own set (or sets) of conceptual categories."[12] Smith's warning of avoiding "imprisonment by one's own set (or sets) of conceptual categories" suggests that such confinement is usually the case. Any cultural analysis, however "objectively" oriented, inevitably carries its own purposes and embodies its own temporal and spatial concerns. Consequently, any cultural critique tends to rename and rearrange old conceptual schemes in an attempt to reconcile them with present objectives.

The past and the "other," as objects examined, are thus unavoidably in tension with the "now" and the "I." With their sets of names and categories, they await the corresponding interpretation of the "now" and the "I" following the same taxonomic principles. The "now" and the "I," with their own taxonomic principles, dissolve or deconstruct original taxonomies to fit their own "concrete situation." The appraisal of the *Shih-shuo hsin-yü* and its genre typifies the tension between the initial creation of a cultural system and its later evaluations, as reflected in three major forms, each a distortion of the original.

First, as discussed at length, the *Shih-shuo hsin-yü* presents a taxonomy of human nature par excellence. Yet ever since the compilation of the "Sui Treatise," Chinese bibliographers have relegated the *Shih-shuo hsin-yü* to *hsiao-shuo*—a category that overlooks its taxonomy of human nature and hence does not suffice to express the unique origins and highly distinctive identity of the work. The bibliographic scheme in the "Sui Treatise" failed to register the *Shih-shuo hsin-yü* under a more appropriate classification apparently because of its own concrete situation. The grand scheme, which contained 14,466 books and fifty-one categories, was intended mainly to proclaim the great T'ang ambition of continuing and comprehending the entire Chinese cultural tradition. But, limited to a contemporary understanding of distinctiveness and order, it could not discern the individual features of each book included.

A second distortion of the *Shih-shuo hsin-yü* occurred with subsequent imitations of the book. As will be discussed more fully below, the *Shih-*

shuo hsin-yü's taxonomy of human nature became the "trademark" of its genre and the feature that intrigued later imitators, who either fully adopted or highly elaborated the original categorization system. In so doing, they usually transported it to a context and put it to some cultural purpose quite distinct from its original aesthetic, psychological, and hermeneutic concerns. This deviation from the original intention also confused its generic identity. When imitators and their proponents struggled to disavow the label of *hsiao-shuo,* they only succeeded in relabeling *Shih-shuo t'i* works as "historical" writings. This further blurred the identity of the *Shih-shuo hsin-yü.*

A third type of distortion surfaced when scholars used the *Shih-shuo hsin-yü* as "source material." This academic approach involved dismantling the original arrangement of the *Shih-shuo hsin-yü* and redistributing its contents as evidence to support various cultural interpretations. Thereby the *Shih-shuo hsin-yü* achieved its greatest distinction as an indispensable "historical" source on the Wei-Chin period, but only at the expense of fragmenting its individuality into piles of cultural footnotes. Under the fractured glare of each compartmentalized episode, the overall significance of the *Shih-shuo hsin-yü* as a unique contribution to Chinese culture vanished.

These understandings and misunderstandings, interpretations and misinterpretations, do not really diminish the significance of the *Shih-shuo hsin-yü.* On the contrary, the perpetual scholarly uncertainty about the work attests to an irrepressible eagerness for comprehending a rich and fascinating cultural system whose unique features go beyond conventional classification and demand further explication. The "Sui Treatise" could only register the *Shih-shuo hsin-yü* under the vague classification *hsiao-shuo;* yet, compared with all other clear-cut, well-defined categories, *hsiao-shuo* became a distinctive marker of *Shih-shuo hsin-yü*'s "otherness" and a sign of the bibliographers' frustration over expressing its "otherness." Similarly, the persevering imitations of the *Shih-shuo hsin-yü* may have distorted its original intention as a taxonomy of human nature; yet they clearly exposed the book's never-fading charm to the readers of later generations. By the same token, the use of the *Shih-shuo hsin-yü* as a historical source may have dismantled its narrative structure, but it also built up its other identity as the most conclusive cultural source of the Wei-Chin period. In short, from such confusion the *Shih-shuo hsin-yü* emerges to carry certain qualities that characterize a classic: its "otherness," indicating a "product of individual genius"; its influence on later *Shih-shuo t'i* works, demonstrating its "perpetual contemporaneity"; and its broad coverage of Wei-Chin culture, making it an "index of civility."[13]

Although no authority in China ever claimed the *Shih-shuo hsin-yü* as a classic, celebrations of its classic qualities frequently appeared in the prefaces to its numerous editions and other academic works. The early Ch'ing scholar Ch'eng Hsü, for instance, wrote glowingly: "The Grand Historian Ssu-ma Ch'ien traveled among famous mountains and huge rivers under Heaven, and then completed the *Shih-chi* following his single will *(ku hsing i i)*. The Left Minister Ch'ü Yüan, tortured by slanders and jealousy, chanted along the marsh bank and then composed the *Li-sao* following his single will. Had someone there impeded them from spelling out their thoughts and imposed upon them this or that sort of advice, neither the *Shih-chi* nor *Li-sao* could have been written. The *Shih-shuo hsin-yü* by the Liu-Sung Prince of Lin-chuan, Liu I-ch'ing, is also such a single-minded work."[14] By equating the *Shih-shuo hsin-yü* with the *Shih-chi* and the *Li-sao*, Ch'eng Hsü connects the book directly to the most celebrated works in the Chinese literary tradition. In his view, all were the products of the author's "individual genius" rather than the fruits of a collective mentality. The individuality and originality of the three works can be seen in the fact that each initiated a new genre of Chinese literature: The *Shih-chi* created the "biographical history" *(chi-chuan t'i)*; the *Li-sao* inaugurated the "songs of Ch'u" *(Ch'u-tz'u)*; and the *Shih-shuo hsin-yü* produced the *Shih-shuo* genre *(Shih-shuo t'i)*.

One might argue that every great and influential work must be the product of a single will, but clearly not every single-willed work is great and influential. Since evaluation is a "contemporary" cultural activity applied to a "past" cultural system, the "greatness" of a classic can only make sense in relation to the present. As Frank Kermode maintains: "The doctrine of classic as model or criterion entails, in some form, the assumption that the ancient can be more or less immediately relevant and available, in a sense contemporaneous with modern—or anyway that its nature is such that it can, by strategies of accommodation, be made so. . . . What is being contested is a received opinion as to the structure of the past and of its relation to the present. It is a question of how the works of the past may retain identity in change, of the mode in which the ancient presents itself to the modern."[15]

In the case of the *Shih-shuo hsin-yü*, how does the author present his work to the modern? What constitutes the *Shih-shuo hsin-yü*'s "perpetual contemporaneity?" More precisely, what is it about Liu I-ch'ing's individual genius that allows the *Shih-shuo hsin-yü* to retain its identity while simultaneously participating actively in the ongoing present. As Ch'eng Hsü tells us: "During the Wei-Chin period, pure conversation was in vogue. Its subtle and systematic arguments were composed of terse words, well crafted but still full of wisdom, simple yet sophisticated. The [Wei-Chin conversationalists] bore elegant and refined appearance and behavior, with which they commenced a new, extraordinary style. Once these words and style were put in writing, they made the reader ponder and dwell on the text without ever getting bored. The [*Shih-shuo hsin-yü*] is like the beauty in the mirror, the colorful clouds in the sky, the moisture on the surface of the ocean, and the lingering taste of olives. None of the dozens of later *Shih-shuo t'i* works can go beyond its scope."[16]

According to Ch'eng Hsü, the *Shih-shuo hsin-yü* is an index of Wei-Chin pure conversation and character appraisal, but by no means a mechanical one. Liu I-ch'ing's creative talent arranges the Wei-Chin intellectual experience into a written system—a taxonomy of human nature that can perpetually converse with later generations because questions concerning human nature will always arouse interest. Ch'eng's four analogies—the "beauty in the mirror," the "colorful clouds in the sky," the "moisture on the surface of the ocean," and the "lingering taste of olives"—present descriptions of the dynamic relationship between the text and the reader. In the course of this intimate contact, the text caresses the reader's senses: dazzling the eyes with beautiful colors, moisturizing the skin with freshness, and entertaining the tongue with delicacy. Meanwhile, the images of reflected beauty, floating clouds, vaporizing moisture, and lingering taste—things that seem to be within one's reach yet can never be fully embraced—also imply the inexhaustibility of this reading experience. Both the Wei-Chin era and Liu I-ch'ing's individual genius are so unique that "none of the dozens of later *Shih-shuo t'i* works can go beyond [the *Shih-shuo hsin-yü's*] scope." Thus, the *Shih-shuo hsin-yü's* "perpetual contemporaneity" dwells in the renovative contact between a brilliant text and its insatiably inquisitive readers. With its classic qualities, the text enchants as well as puzzles, making the reading process of the *Shih-shuo hsin-yü* a lasting delight, generation after generation.

This dynamic contact between the text and the reader also suggests that, in the process of evaluation, a great work never remains a mute object, passively awaiting the examiner's inevitable effacement. Rather, it exerts its power and influence over later readers with its unique cultural values, thereby forever reasserting its identity. Liu Hsi-tsai (1813–1881) clearly recognizes this function of the text in his celebration of the *Shih-shuo hsin-yü*: "The strategies of prose composition and stylistic preferences changed after the emergence of the *Chuang-tzu* and the *Lieh-tzu;* they changed again after the import of the Buddhist sutras, and yet again after the completion of the *Shih-shuo hsin-yü.* Few would not read these books, and, once they were read, few would not become addicted to them and transform themselves following these works."[17]

Like Ch'eng Hsü, Liu Hsi-tsai places the *Shih-shuo hsin-yü* among the most relentlessly influential works in the Chinese cultural tradition. The powerful contemporaneity of such great works allows them to communicate with the modern and at the same time compels the modern to transform with them. A similar interactive process was at work with imitations of the *Shih-shuo,* although it took somewhat different forms and had somewhat different purposes.

Imitating the *Shih-shuo*

By choosing the *Shih-shuo* genre for fulfilling their mission of *li-shen*—establishing the body or self-cultivation—later *Shih-shuo* imitators immediately involved themselves in a network of mutual revision. Departing from character appraisal, the intellectual basis for the *Shih-shuo* genre, and taking the genre to be a variety of history instead of character writing, later *Shih-shuo t'i* authors disengaged themselves from *Shih-shuo*'s ontological inquiries as to what self is and how to express the self with language. Yet by appropriating the genre, they unwittingly assumed the literary principles embedded in the basic features of a character writing, including the idea of shaping the unshapeable selves in a flexible taxonomy of human nature and the notion of manifesting elusive personalities in the tension of rivalry. The responsibilities left for them, therefore, were to decide (1) what kind of self they wanted to fashion under various different historical and cultural circumstances, and (2) how to fashion that self.

For this purpose, later *Shih-shuo t'i* authors used the *Shih-shuo* genre as both a collective mirror and a collection of individual mirrors. The collective mirror offered a historical point of reference for them to locate their social, political, cultural, and/or economic position. The individual mirrors offered role models for them either to emulate or to challenge. Each specific group of the gentry, during a specific time period and in a specific space, then developed a set of new agendas in revising the original genre to fit their newly fashioned literary selves.

T'ang imitations emerged amid the gentry's transformation from aristocrats to degree holders/bureaucrats for the purpose of establishing the gentry's strong bond to the ruler. In this sense, the *Shih-shuo hsin-yü* and its genre offered T'ang imitators only a negative reference—namely, the Wei-Chin gentry's detachment from the royal house. T'ang imitations therefore altered the aesthetic and psychological orientation of the *Shih-shuo* to fit a new ethical scheme, and they chose role models only from T'ang gentlemen, such as Wei Cheng, a paragon of loyalty, and Chang Yüeh, the epitome of T'ang intellectual achievements and a specimen of the T'ang transformation of gentry status.[18] Yet it is clear that the moral-political high drama of the T'ang imitations, which emphasized loyal subjects in tension with strong-willed rulers, followed the *Shih-shuo* rivalry pattern. Moreover, the revision of the *Shih-shuo* scheme resulted from the great flexibility and subversive potential of the scheme itself. In other words, T'ang *Shih-shuo* imitations drew upon the *Shih-shuo* legacy in their attack on this legacy.

Sung imitations emerged after both the transformation of the gentry and the institutionalization of the examination system had reached a stable point. Since the T'ang-Sung examinations privileged literary creativity, Sung literati-scholars enjoyed one of the most dynamic and prosperous periods of literature and art in Chinese history. Confronting the rise of Sung *Li-hsüeh,* Sung literati-scholars felt the need to emphasize the rich, colorful literary presentation of the *Tao,* in contrast to the dull, narrow-minded *Li-hsüeh* preaching of the *Tao.* For this purpose, they went back to the aesthetically oriented *Shih-shuo* scheme, and they also looked to the successful T'ang degree holders for poetic inspiration. But lacking the Wei-Chin obsession with self-exposure and the T'ang dramatization of moral-political conflict, the tension of personalities grew weak in Sung imitations. We thus see more descriptions of social fashion and poetic styles than portrayals of characters.

Ming *Shih-shuo* imitations arose from a new set of political, cultural, and economic conditions, coupled with the literati's growing resentment over the narrow-minded and repressive orthodoxy of the Ming examination system. The Yüan-Ming establishment of Ch'eng-Chu *Li-hsüeh* as the center of the state's "educational gyroscope" and the rapid expansion of lower degree holders deprived many talented and free-spirited literati the opportunity of officeholding. On the other hand, the growth of a commodity economy offered literati the possibility of making a living from their literary and artistic talents. Under the circumstances, literati needed to redefine their identity in terms of separation from the mainstream values of degree and officeholding and in favor of an artistic lifestyle enabled by economic independence.

The first and the best Ming *Shih-shuo* imitator, Ho Liang-chün, established this sort of literati identity by redefining the *Shih-shuo* categories in terms of new Ming cultural priorities. He powerfully asserted the literati's superiority over other intellectual groups, brought in property management as a positive component of literati life, and promoted role models who fashioned their own destinies rather than being manipulated by others. Reflecting the growth of the Ming commodity economy, a new emphasis on "things"—as both artistic products and the utensils used to make these products—became part of a Ming literatus-artist's sense of his extended self. The Ming depoliticization of literati identity, in turn, provided the early Ch'ing literati with an asylum for cultural survival, as amply illustrated in Ch'ing *Shih-shuo* imitations.

The respective authors of the two women *Shih-shuo,* one a man and the other a woman, both lived during the late imperial era and each endeavored to construct a female value system that reflected their disappointment with men and with conventional patriarchal values. They both identified defiant voices in the worthy beauties of the *Shih-shuo hsin-yü,* but because of differences in their gender, social position, and cultural outlook, their interpretations of women's lives naturally conflicted, even as they overlapped in significant respects. Occupying the center of this joint venture were two pivotal elements associated unmistakably with the female body—milk and scent—the fluid and penetrating essences that connected the female body to the rest of the world.

Japanese imitations, represented by Hattori Nankaku's *Daitō seigo,* borrowed the *Shih-shuo* genre in order to oppose another cultural construction that had been borrowed from China, Chu Hsi's *Li-hsüeh* school, which the Tokugawa state adopted as its official orthodoxy. Focusing on debates about human nature, Hattori Nankaku crafted his *Shih-shuo* imitation to present what he considered to be Japan's "true" intellectual identity. By carefully adhering to the *Shih-shuo*'s taxonomy of human nature, its rivalry patterns, and its terse, refined writing style, the *Daitō seigo* provided an ideal vehicle for revealing the authentic self of the free-spirited Heian aristocrats that graced its pages.

The last wave of *Shih-shuo* imitations marked China's transition from the late imperial period to the republican era. The Chinese intellectual elite was ecstatic that, finally, they were able to carry on their own value system without having to submit to a repressive regime. Yet they were immediately confronted with the coercive Western influence, introduced into China with its overpowering military force and technology on the one hand and its seductively sophisticated culture on the other. This compelling cultural intrusion, under the beguiling name of "New," instantly turned the Chinese elite's never fully achieved intellectual-political ambition "Old." Perplexed, the Chinese elite looked back to find a starting point within the Chinese tradition, and once again, some of them picked up the forever fresh, self-contented, and unorthodox frame of the *Shih-shuo* tradition. They wondered whether the free spirit that saturated this tradition might not, after all, have close affinities with Western individuality and whether Old and New might not yield a productive middle ground between each other.

Throughout Chinese history, across time, gender, and space, the *Shih-shuo* tradition, with its spiritual freedom, intellectual sophistication, literary refinement, and refreshing iconoclasm, offered the most defiant members of the Chinese elite a flexible and comfortable space in which to operate whenever they felt unduly constrained. In that intellectual and cultural space, they did not have to answer to any authoritative voice but could focus instead on nurturing their idiosyncratic selves according to their own values. As a means for achieving this liberating end, the *Shih-shuo* genre retained its vitality for well over a thousand years, providing a mirror to the elites of each period to assist them in their self-fashioning, as well as providing a reflection of their times for us today.

The Lure of the *Shih-shuo hsin-yü*

The reading of a great work drives the text and the reader into a relationship of intense conflict, in which the reader imposes his or her own rules of classification in an attempt to absorb the text into that reader's own conceptual system. The text, meanwhile, rejects such absorption and attempts to seduce the reader with its own cultural values. This situation recalls the conflict between Yin Hao and Huan Wen with which I commenced this study of the *Shih-shuo hsin-yü*. When Huan Wen challenges Yin Hao, asking "How do you compare with me?" he uses his own standard to evaluate Yin Hao. Yin Hao, on the other hand, rejects being imprisoned by Huan Wen's set of conceptual categories and insists on being himself. This conflict between Huan Wen's projection of the self onto the "other" and

Yin Hao's refusal to be effaced into the "other," as discussed at length in chapters 2 and 5, enacts mutual assimilation and differentiation and results in the exposure and fulfillment of both identities.

The *Shih-shuo hsin-yü* invites precisely such intense engagements; indeed, my study provides yet another example of the struggle. No single engagement, including mine, may accurately reflect the entire reality of the *Shih-shuo hsin-yü*. The significance of the cultural encounter, however, lies more in the process than in the product. The more the *Shih-shuo hsin-yü* lures us into the struggle to know it, the more we appreciate its value as an inexhaustible source of inspiration—one that arouses our interest over time and across space. Despite the frustration of trying to free ourselves from its intellectual labyrinth, the constant ecstasy of immersion in its inestimable beauty and wisdom teaches us ever more about both the *Shih-shuo hsin-yü* and ourselves.

Notes

Introduction

1. The *Shih-shuo hsin-yü* has been conventionally attributed to Liu I-ch'ing since its first official entry in the "Ching-chi chih" [Bibliographic treatise] of the *Sui-shu* [History of the Sui] (hereafter the "Sui Treatise") completed in 656. Lu Hsün (1881–1936), however, suggests that Liu had only sponsored the work of his staff; see his *Chung-kuo hsiao-shuo shih-lüeh* [Brief history of Chinese *hsiao-shuo*], in *Lu Hsün ch'üan-chi* [Complete works of Lu Hsün], 10 vols. (Peking: Jen-min wen-hsüeh ch'u-pan she, 1957), 8:48. Hsiao Hung, on the other hand, maintains that the *Shih-shuo hsin-yü* was mainly compiled by Liu I-ch'ing with the help of Yüan Shu and Ho Chang-yü; see her "*Shih-shuo hsin-yü* tso-che wen-t'i shang-ch'üeh" [On the authorship of the *Shih-shuo hsin-yü*], *Kuo-li chung-yang t'u-shu-kuan kuan-k'an*, 14.1 (1981):8–24. Other important studies on this topic include Kawakatsu Yoshio, "*Sesetsu shingo* no hensan o megutte" [On the compilation and editions of the *Shih-shuo hsin-yü*], *Tō-hōgakuhō* 41 (1970):217–234; Richard B. Mather, "Introduction to *A New Account of Tales of the World*," *A New Account of Tales of the World*, xviii; and Chou I-liang, "*Shih-shuo hsin-yü* ho tso-che Liu I-ch'ing shen-shih ti k'ao-ch'a" [*Shih-shuo hsin-yü* and a study of the author Liu I-ch'ing's life], originally in *Chung-kuo che-hsüeh shih yen-chiu* 1 (1981), collected in Chou I-liang, *Wei-Chin Nan-pei ch'ao shih lun-chi hsü-pien* [Continued collection of essays on the history of the Wei, Chin, Southern and Northern dynasties] (Peking: Peking University Press, 1991), 16–22. I shall maintain the conventional attribution and leave this problem open for further consideration. For the compilation date of the *Shih-shuo hsin-yü*, see Kawakatsu Yoshio, "*Sesetsu shingo* no hensan o megutte," 217–234.

2. Pioneer works on this topic include Donald J. Munro, ed., *Individualism and Holism: Studies in Confucian and Taoist Values* (Ann Arbor: Center for Chinese Studies, University of Michigan, 1985); Tu Wei-ming, ed., *The Living Tree: The Changing Meaning of Being Chinese Today* (Stanford: Stanford University Press, 1994); David L. Hall and Roger T. Ames, *Thinking through Confucius* (1987), *Anticipating China: Thinking through the Narratives of Chinese and Western Culture* (1995), and *Thinking from the Han: Self, Truth, and Transcendence in Chinese and Western Culture* (1998), all with State University of New York Press at Albany, to name just a few.

3. The citation "9/35" stands for "Chapter 9/Entry 35" of the *Shih-shuo hsin-yü*. The English translation of the *Shih-shuo hsin-yü* and Liu Chün's (462–521) commentary is based mainly on Richard B. Mather, trans., *A New Account of Tales of the World* (Minneapolis: University of Minnesota Press, 1976). In order to make the reading less confusing, I will indicate retranslations and major modifications, but not minor changes. My retranslations and modifications, as well as translations of Liu Chün's commentaries not included in Mather's *Tales of the World,* are based on Yü Chia-hsi, *Shih-shuo hsin-yü chien-shu* [Commentary on the *Shih-shuo hsin-yü*], 2 vols. (Shanghai: Shanghai ku-chi ch'u-pan she, 1993). Both Yü and Mather numbered each entry, so references to the *Shih-shuo hsin-yü* text will give only the chapter and entry numbers, except in discussions about textual or translation problems. Unless otherwise stated, all translations of the other texts are mine.

4. The modern edition of the *Shih-shuo hsin-yü* contains 1,130 episodes. The original edition possibly carried more. The number was reduced, according to Tung Fen's colophon to the 1138 block-print edition, by the Sung scholar Yen Shu (991–1055), who claimed to have "completely eliminated all redundancies" of the *Shih-shuo* texts and Liu Chün's commentary; see Mather, *Tales of the World,* xxvii. Yü Chia-hsi, too, points out Yen Shu's "arbitary elimination" of Liu's commentary; see Yü, *Chien-shu,* 1:530, 2:632, etc.

5. "Te-hsing" is conventionally translated "Virtuous Conduct"; for a discussion of this particular rendering, see chapter 4.

6. According to Wang Tsao (thirteenth century), "*Shih-shuo hsü-lu*" [Preface to the *Shih-shuo hsin-yü*], the Sung (960–1279) editions of the *Shih-shuo hsin-yü* differ with one another in the number of the chapters—respectively, 36, 37, 38, and 39. Wang believes that 36 is the correct number. See the reprint of Wang Tsao's edition of the *Shih-shuo hsin-yü,* 5 vols. (Tokyo: Sonkei Kaku or Kanazawa Bunko, 1929), 4:1a–3a.

7. I have borrowed the term *character writing* from the *Shih-shuo t'i,*s closest Western counterpart—the Theophrastan character writing; see my introduction to this tradition below.

8. Tzvetan Todorov, "The Origin of Genres," *New Literary History* 8 (1976):163. Todorov did not give a clear definition of the term *ideology* in this essay. Judging from the context, his understanding seems similar to that of Terry Eagleton, who defines ideology as "a body of ideas characteristic of a particular social group or class" (Terry Eagleton, *Ideology: An Introduction* [London: Verso, 1991], 1).

9. I have adopted this term from Yiming Tang's translation of *renlun* [*jen-lun*], a short form of *renlun jianshi* [*jen-lun chien-shih*]; see his "Voice of Wei-Jin [Chin] Scholars: A Study of *Qingtan* [*Ch'ing-t'an*]" (Ph.D. diss., Columbia University, 1991), 129; see also my discussion of the term in chapter 1.

10. For a detailed discussion of the evolution of *Hsüan-hsüeh* and its interaction with Wei-Chin character appraisal and self-awareness, see chapter 2.

11. Wang Pi (226–249) made this comment on the following passage: "Confucius said: 'Writing does not completely express speech, nor does speech completely express ideas.' If so, is it true that we cannot get the Sage's idea?" (*Chou-i* [*cheng-i*] [(Or-

thodox commentary on) Book of changes], "Hsi-tz'u" I, in Juan Yüan [1764–1849], ed., *Shih-san ching chu-shu* [Commentaries on the thirteen Chinese classics] [1826; reprint, 2 vols., Peking: Chung-hua shu-chü, 1979], 1:82). The passage here already constructs the paradox between words' inability to express ideas completely and the eternal need of words to express ideas.

12. *Lao-tzu*, ch. 56, in Wang Pi, *Wang Pi chi* [*chiao-shih*] [(Commentary on) Complete works of Wang Pi], commentary by Lou Yü-lieh, 2 vols., Vol. 1: *Lao-tzu Tao te ching chu* [(Commentary on) Lao-tzu Tao te ching] (Peking: Chung-hua shu-chü, 1980), 147–148.

13. A. C. Graham, *Disputers of the Tao: Philosophical Argument in Ancient China* (La Salle, IL: Open Court, 1989), 199–200.

14. Baruch Hochman holds that the reader's reading activity is the "final cause" of the characterization. He maintains: "The emphasis on our activity is crucial, because it reminds us that the whole which is the literary work is not only the sum of its parts, and more than the sum of its parts, but also a conjuring of absent, nonexistent parts. A work of literature is an entity made up of things not there, referred to by the words that constitute the text. Even the things 'not there'—houses, people, events—are 'there' only insofar as we fabricate them in consciousness out of what we bring to their perception: that is, out of our experience, and out of what we bring from our experience to the work we are reading" (*Character in Literature* [Ithaca: Cornell University Press, 1985], 33).

15. For example, from Yü Ying-shih's *Chung-kuo chih-shih chieh-ts'eng shih-lun* [Historical studies of Chinese intellectual class] (Taipei: Lien-ching shih-yeh ch'u-pan kung-ssu, 1980) for the early period to Wei-Chin, Peter Bol's *"This Culture of Ours": Intellectual Transitions in T'ang and Sung China* (Stanford: Stanford University Press, 1992) for T'ang-Sung, and Richard J. Smith's *China's Cultural Heritage: The Qing* [Ch'ing] *Dynasty, 1644–1912* (Boulder: Westview Press, 1994) for the Ch'ing, to cite just a few.

16. Henry George Liddell and Robert Scott, *Greek-English Lexicon*, abridged and revised by James Whiton (Oxford: Oxford University Press, 1871), s.v. "χαρακτήρ."

17. Ibid.

18. *The Compact Edition of the Oxford English Dictionary* (Oxford: Oxford University press, 1971), s.v. "type."

19. See *The Compact Edition of the Oxford English Dictionary*, s.v. "character."

20. Ibid.

21. Edited by Dagobert Runes (Totowa, NJ, 1975), 230; as quoted in Seymour Chatman, *Story and Discourse* (Ithaca: Cornell University Press, 1978), 120.

22. Roland Barthes, *S/Z*, trans. Richard Miller (New York: Noonday Press, 1974), 67. Seymour Chatman argues that "Richard Miller confuses what is already a difficult text by translating French 'traits' as 'figures'" (*Story and Discourse*, 116, n. 22), so he puts "[trait]" after "figures" when quoting this passage (ibid., 115). Here I follow his correction. See ibid., 107–138, for a more detailed discussion of these terms.

23. Gordon W. Allport, "What is a Trait of Personality?" *Journal of Abnormal and Social Psychology* 25 (1931):368.

24. Gordon W. Allport and Henry S. Odbert, "Trait-Names: A Psycho-Lexical Study," *Psychological Monographs* 47.1 (Princeton, NJ: Psychological Review, 1936), 38–171 passim.

25. See ibid., 368–372; also see Chatman, *Story and Discourse*, 120–126.

26. Also known as *ch'ing-t'an* (pure talk or pure conversation), a rather confusing Han and Wei-Chin term overlapping in meaning with another contemporary term, *ch'ing-i* (pure criticism). I shall stick to *ch'ing-yen* in my following discussion since the *Shih-shuo hsin-yü* uses this word only for "pure conversation" (see 2/70, 4/28, 9/48, etc.). For a detailed discussion of the differences between *ch'ing-i, ch'ing-t'an,* and *ch'ing-yen,* see Yiming Tang, "The Voice of Wei-Jin [Chin] Scholars," "Appendix: Ch'ing-t'an yü ch'ing-i k'ao-pien" [Study of pure criticism and pure conversation], 310–317; see also his *Wei-Chin ch'ing-t'an* [Wei-Chin pure conversation] (Taipei: Tung-ta t'u-shu ku-fen yu-hsien kung-ssu, 1992).

27. See Huang Po-ssu (1079–1118), "Pa *Shih-shuo hsin-yü* hou" [Epilogue to the *Shih-shuo hsin-yü*], in his *Tung-kuan yü-lun, Ssu-k'u ch'üan-shu* ed., *chüan* b, 12a.

28. See Chou Hsin-ju's preface to the *Shih-shuo hsin-yü,* 1828 edition.

29. Theodore Huters, R. Bin Wong, and Pauline Yu, eds., *Culture and State in Chinese History: Conventions, Accommodations, and Critiques* (Stanford: Stanford University Press, 1997), "Introduction," 26.

Introduction to Part 1

1. See Ch'ao Kung-wu, *Chün-chai tu-shu chih* (1884; reprint, 4 vols., Taipei: Kuang-wen shu-chü, 1967), 2:771.

2. See, for example, Yung-jung, Chi Yün et al., eds., *Ssu-k'u ch'üan-shu tsung-mu* (also known as *Ssu-k'u ch'üan-shu tsung-mu t'i yao*) [Annotated catalogue of the complete collection of the Four Treasuries] (1822; reprint, 2 vols., Peking: Chung-hua shu-chü, 1965), *chüan* 141, 2:1196 and *chüan* 143, 2:1226; see also Ning Chia-yü, "Shih-shuo t'i ch'u-t'an" [Tentative study of the *Shih-shuo* genre], *Chung-kuo ku-tien wen-hsüeh lun-ts'ung* 6 (1987):87–105.

3. See Wei Cheng (580–643) et al., *Sui-shu,* 6 vols. (Peking: Chung-hua shu-chü, 1973), 4:1011.

4. See Ch'ao, *Chün-chai tu-shu chih,* entry of the *T'ang yü-lin* [T'ang forest of accounts]: "[the *T'ang yü-lin*] imitates the *Shih-shuo t'i,* recounting famous words [*ming-yen*] of the T'ang in categories" (*chüan* 13, 2:771). Wang Hsien-ch'ien's commentary on this entry quotes a variant, *shih* (events), for *ming-yen* (famous words) (ibid). The *T'ang yü-lin* text consists of both events and words.

5. See Yung-jung, Chi Yün et al., eds., *Ssu-k'u ch'üan-shu tsung-mu, chüan* 140, 2:1182; *chüan* 141, 2:1196, 1204; and *chüan* 143, 2:1216, 1222, 1223, 1224, 1225, and 1226.

6. See Lu Hsün, *Chung-kuo hsiao-shuo shih-lüeh*, 8:47.

7. Ning, "*Shih-shuo t'i* ch'u-t'an," 87.

8. Ch'en Yin-k'o, "T'ao Yüan-ming chih ssu-hsiang yü ch'ing-t'an chih kuan-hsi" [T'ao Yüan-ming's thought and its relations with pure conversation], in *Chin-ming kuan ts'ung-kao ch'u-pien* (Shanghai: Shanghai ku-chi ch'u-pan she, 1980), 180.

Chapter 1: Character Appraisal

1. Liu Chün's commentary is considered the best among the commentaries on the *Shih-shuo hsin-yü*. It "cites relevant passages—passages which were often drastically abridged by eleventh-century editors—from over 400 works (unofficial histories and biographies, family registers, local gazetteers, etc.) from the Later Han through Liu Chün's own times. Since most of these works are now lost, the quotations from them in Liu's and other similar commentaries such as P'ei Sung-chih's commentary on the *San-kuo chih* provide valuable supplementary material and occasional corrections to the idiosyncratic accounts in the *Shih-shuo hsin-yü*" (*The Indiana Companion to Traditional Chinese Literature*, 1986 ed., s.v. "*Shih-shuo hsin-yü*," by Richard B. Mather).

2. See *Shih-shuo hsin-yü*, 1/5, 2/34, 4/98, 7/16, 8/13, 8/58, 8/100, 9/3, 9/13, 21/9 etc.; Liu Chün's commentary on the *Shih-shuo hsin-yü*, 1/8, 1/18, 1/30, 1/32, 1/33, 2/9, 2/25, 2/32, 2/55, 2/74, 2/99, 3/6, 3/17, 4/74, 4/91, 5/12, 5/15, 7/16, 7/22, 8/3, 8/17, 8/22, 8/27, 8/65, 8/97, 8/98, 9/3, 9/11, 9/15, etc.

3. See mainly *Shih-shuo hsin-yü*, chapters 8 and 9, both the text proper and Liu Chün's commentary.

4. Liu Chün's commentary on the *Shih-shuo hsin-yü*, 3/17; cf. Mather, *Tales of the World*, 88–89, n. 1 to 3/17.

5. Ibid., 2/9; cf. Mather, *Tales of the World*, 31–32, n. 1 to 2/9.

6. By Sun Sheng (ca. 302–373); ibid., 9/11; cf. Mather, *Tales of the World*, 252, n. 1 to 9/11.

7. Ibid., 8/17; my retranslation.

8. *Li-chi* [*cheng-i*] ([Orthodox commentary on] Record of rites), "Ch'ü li II" [Detailed interpretation of rites], *Shih-san ching chu-shu*, *chüan* 5, 1:1268. Li Hsien's (651–684) commentary on the term *jen-lun* in Fan Yeh (398–445), *Hou-Han shu* [History of the Later Han], 12 vols. (Peking: Chung-hua shu-chü, 1965), "Kuo T'ai chuan" [Biography of Kuo T'ai], quotes this line from the *Li-chi* as well as Cheng Hsüan's (127–200) commentary on the line: "*lun* is similar to *lei* (category or type)" (*chüan* 68, 8:2226). Another early source of *jen-lun* is found in the *Chuang-tzu*, "Chih pei-yu" [Knowledge roams north]: "Fruits and melons, each have their patterns and principles. Human types too, difficult as they are, have their order" (Kuo Ch'ing-fan [1845–1891], ed., *Chuang-tzu chi-shih* [Collected commentaries on the *Chuang-tzu*], 4 vols. [Peking: Chung-hua shu-chü, 1961], *chüan* 7b, 3:744–745). Burton Watson translates *jen-lun* here as "human relationships" (*The Complete Works of Chuang Tzu*

[New York: Columbia University Press, 1968], 240); judging from its context, which discusses different human qualities, I believe *jen-lun* here refers to "human types."

9. *Li-chi cheng-i, chüan* 5, 1:1268.

10. Mao commentary on the *Shih-ching* [Book of songs], "Po-chou" [Cypress boat], quoted in Tuan Yü-ts'ai (1735–1815), *Shuo-wen chieh-tzu chu* [Commentary on *Interpretation of words*] (1815; reprint, Shanghai: Shanghai ku-chi ch'u-pan she, 1981), s.v. *Chien*.

11. Hsü Shen (30–124), *Shuo-wen chieh-tzu* [Interpretation of words] (1873; reprint, Peking: Chung-hua shu-chü, 1963), s.v. *Shih*.

12. *Hsü Chiang-chou pen-shih* [Basic story of Hsü Ning], quoted in Liu Chün's commentary on the *Shih-shuo hsin-yü*, 8/65.

13. *Huan I pieh-chuan* [Separate biography of Huan I], ibid., 1/30.

14. *Meng-tzu* [*chu-shu*] [(Commentary on) Mencius], V, 4, *Shih-san ching chu-shu*, 2:2705; trans. D. C. Lau, *Mencius* (Penguin Books), IIIA, 4, 102.

15. These translations are all mine. Mather does not differentiate these two meanings of *jen-lun* in the *Shih-shuo hsin-yü* and Liu Chün's commentary. For instance, he translates *jen-lun* respectively as "human relations" and "human relationships" in Liu Chün's commentary on 8/17 and 8/27, which, according to the texts proper, should stand for "human types."

16. Fan Yeh, *Hou-Han shu*, "Kuo Fu Hsü lieh-chuan" [Biographies of Kuo T'ai, Fu Jung, and Hsü Shao], *chüan* 68, 8:2226 and 2234. The three, Kuo T'ai, Fu Jung, and Hsü Shao, are placed together mainly because they enjoy a common reputation as experts of *jen-lun chien-shih*. The eulogy of this collective biography reads: "Kuo T'ai embraced the treasure of profound recognition and well-versed judgment. . . . Fu Jung [was good at] judging true qualities, and Hsü Shao [was good at] character appraisal" (*chüan* 68, 8:2236).

17. Ibid., *chüan* 68, 8:2234–2235.

18. For the evolution of character appraisal from concrete evaluation to abstract theorization, see Ch'en Yin-k'o, "Hsiao-yao yu Hsiang-Kuo i chi Chih Tun i t'an-yüan" [Study of Hsiang [Hsiu]-Kuo [Hsiang] and Chih Tun's interpretations of *Chuang-tzu*, "Hsiao-yao yu"], *Ch'ing-hua hsüeh-pao* 12 (April 1937):309–314.

19. Lu Hsün, *Chung-kuo hsiao-shuo shih-lüeh*, 8:46, trans. Yang Hsien-yi and Gladys Yang, *A Brief History of Chinese Fiction* (Peking: Foreign Languages Press, 1976), 66–67, with modifications bracketed.

20. Tzvetan Todorov, "The Origin of Genres," *New Literary History* 8 (1976):169. Todorov, however, does not give the term *speech act* a clear definition. He seems to take it as a self-evident name for any kind of human action of speech, such as a prayer or a storytelling. He also points out that, while any genre originates from a certain speech act, not any speech act can work into a genre.

21. See ibid., 164–165.

22. Liu Chün's commentary on *Shih-shuo hsin-yü*, 7/1.

23. In a broader sense, character appraisal as practical characterology appeared as early as in the *Shang-shu* [Book of documents], "Yao-tien" [Canon of Yao], which contains a detailed account of selection of officials according to the candidate's moral disposition, including Yao's discussion with his courtiers about whom to promote and why, and his inspection, assignment, and/or dismissal of the candidate. See *Shang-shu* [*cheng-i*] [(Orthodox commentary on) Book of documents], "Yao-tien," *Shih-san ching chu-shu*, *chüan* 2, 1:122–123. My discussion here is limited to the periods when the term *jen-lun chien-shih* was actually applied to this practice.

24. All these terms frequently appear in Fan Yeh, *Hou-Han shu*, and Tu Yu (735–812), *T'ung-tien* [Compendium of laws and institutions]. See, for example, *Hou-Han shu*, "Tso Chou Huang lieh-chuan" [Biographies of Tso Hsiung, Chou Chü, and Huang Ch'iung] (*chüan* 61, 7:2015–2044); "Tang-ku lieh-chuan" [Biographies of the interdicted scholar-clique partisans] (*chüan* 67, 8:2183–2224); "Kuo Fu Hsü lieh-chuan" (*chüan* 68, 8:2225–2237); and Tu Yu, *T'ung-tien*, "Hsüan-chü I" [Selection I] ([Shanghai: Shang-wu Yin-shu kuan, 1935], *chüan* 14, 73–75). In these sources, *ch'a-chü* sometimes refers to the observations and recommendations by the central government officials. Also, T'ang Yung-t'ung differentiates *ch'a-chü* from *cheng-p'i*, saying: "In the Han dynasty, *ch'a-chü* was the way for choosing among average gentlemen, whereas *cheng-p'i* was for promoting extraordinary persons" (T'ang Yung-t'ung, "Tu Jen-wu chih" [Reading the Study of Human Abilities], in *Wei-Chin Hsüan-hsüeh lun-kao* [Preliminary discussions of the abstruse learning of the Wei-Chin period], originally published by Jen-min ch'u-pan she [Peking: Jen-min wen-hsüeh ch'u-pan she, 1957], collected in *T'ang Yung-t'ung hsüeh-shu lun-wen chi* [Peking: Chung-hua shu-chü, 1983], 199).

25. Tu Yu, *T'ung-tien*, *chüan* 13, 73.

26. Ibid., 74.

27. Ibid.

28. T'ang Chang-ju points out:

The system of selection in the Later Han judged a candidate by his moral behavior, which came from his practice of Confucian doctrine. In other words, "a good understanding of the Confucian classics causes good behavior." What Confucianism advocated was a moral order that extended from the family to society. The starting point was anchored in one's moral behavior toward his family members, then to his townspeople. Later Han gentlemen believed that this was the basis from which one could observe a certain individual. . . . Therefore, criticism from one's clansmen and townspeople became the major or even the only basis for the selection. ("Chiu-p'in chung-cheng chih-tu shih-shih" [A tentative interpretation of the *Chiu-p'in chung-cheng* system], *Wei-Chin Nan-pei ch'ao shih lun-ts'ung* [Collected essays on the history of the Wei, Chin, Southern and Northern dynasties] [Peking: San-lien shu-tien, 1955], 86)

29. Fan yeh, *Hou-Han shu*, "Tso Chou Huang lieh-chuan," *chüan* 61, 7:2042.

30. See Yiming Tang, "The Voice of Wei-Jin [Chin] Scholars," "Appendix: Ch'ing-t'an yü

ch'ing-i k'ao-pien," 310–317; T'ang Chang-ju, "Ch'ing-t'an yü ch'ing-i" [Pure criticism and pure conversation], in *Wei-Chin Nan-pei ch'ao shih lun-ts'ung*, 289–297; and Chou I-liang, "Liang-Chin Nan-ch'ao ti ch'ing-i" [Pure criticism in the Chin and Southern dynasties), *Wei-Chin Sui-T'ang shih lun-chi* 2 (1983):1–9.

31. Fan Yeh, *Hou-Han shu*, "Tu-hsing lie-chuan," *chüan* 81, 9:2665.

32. In his discussion of the Wu Liang Shrine carvings (created A.D. 151), Wu Hung suggests that the "individual preferences" in picking up artistic motifs and depictions of stories and omens for the carving design "signified the beginning of individualism in Chinese art." Yet, as he also points out: "At this stage . . . individualism could be realized only through a manipulation of conventional forms" *(The Wu Liang Shrine: The Ideology of Early Chinese Pictorial Art* [Stanford: Stanford University Press, 1989], 230). Late Han desire for self-expression was also strongly revealed in the "Nineteen Old Poems" [*Ku-shih shih-chiu shou*]; see Wang Yao, "Wen-jen yü chiu" [Literati and wine], in *Chung-ku wen-hsüeh shih lun-chi* [Collected essays on the history of medieval Chinese literature] (Shanghai: Shanghai ku-chi ch'u-pan she, 1982), 29–30. "Nineteen Old Poems" had tremendous sway on the Wei-Chin gentry. See, for example, *Shih-shuo hsin-yü*, 4/101. See also Yü Chia-hsi's commentary on the *Shih-shuo hsin-yü*, 1/17, about the Later Han influence on the Wei-Chin intellectual trend.

33. Fan Yeh, *Hou-Han shu*, "Tso Chou Huang lieh-chuan," *chüan* 61, 7:2042.

34. Wang Fu, *Ch'ien-fu lun* [Essays by a recluse], "K'ao-chi" [Examining the standing] *(Chu-tzu chi-ch'eng* ed. [Peking: Chung-hua shu-chü, 1954, 1986], 28–29); trans. John Makeham, *Name and Actuality in Early Chinese Thought* (Albany: State University of New York Press, 1994), 107–108.

35. See Yiming Tang, "The Voice of Wei-Jin [Chin] Scholars," "Appendix: Ch'ing-t'an yü ch'ing-i k'ao-pien" 310–317; T'ang Chang-ju, "Ch'ing-t'an yü ch'ing-i," 289–297; and Chou I-liang, "Liang-Chin Nan-ch'ao ti ch'ing-i," 1–9.

36. Fan Yeh, *Hou-Han shu*, "Tang-ku lieh-chuan," *chüan* 67, 8:2185.

37. Yü Ying-shih, "Han-Chin chih chi shih chih hsin tzu-chüeh yü hsin ssu-ch'ao" [Self-awareness of the literati and the new tide of thought in the Han-Chin period], in *Chung-kuo chih-shih chieh-ts'eng shih-lun*, 236.

38. See Fan Yeh, *Hou-Han shu*, "Tang-ku lieh-chuan," *chüan* 67.

39. Fan Yeh, *Hou-Han shu*, "Kuo Fu Hsü lieh-chuan," *chüan* 68, 8:2226

40. Ch'en Yin-k'o believes that Kuo T'ai started the exploration of the theoretical principles of *jen-lun chien-shih;* see his "Hsiao-yao yu Hsiang-Kuo i chi Chih Tun i t'an-yüan," 309–310. See also Yü Ying-shih, "Han-Chin chih chi shih chih hsin tzu-chüeh yü hsin ssu-ch'ao," 239.

41. Both consequences can be confirmed by historical records. Ch'en Fan was famous for extolling his fellow scholars and openly criticizing his political opponents. He also attempted to clear up the realm physically—in A.D. 168, he organized the attack upon the eunuchs and was killed in the ensuing fighting. See the *Shih-shuo hsin-yü*, 1/1, 8/1, 8/2, 8/3, both the text proper and Liu Chün's commentary; and Fan Yeh, *Hou-Han shu*, "Ch'en Wang lieh-chuan" [Biographies of Ch'en Fan and Wang Yün], *chüan*

66, 8:2170. Li Ying was one of the leading scholar-officials during the period. He served for years as governor or prefect of several states and prefectures. As the head of these various local administrations, his responsibilities included selecting officials. Also, as a leading scholar, Li Ying's ability and authority in character appraisal would overwhelm any challenge. Both his position and his ability made him famous in promoting qualified candidates. Kuo T'ai, for example, was among many who built up their reputations through Li Ying's recommendation. See Fan Yeh, *Hou-Han shu*, "Tang-ku lieh-chuan," *chüan* 67, 8:2191–2197; "Kuo Fu Hsü lieh-chuan," *chüan* 68, 8:2225; and Yüan Shan-sung, *Hou-Han shu*, quoted in Yü Chia-hsi's commentary on the *Shih-shuo hsin-yü*, 1/4.

42. T'ang Chang-ju defines *ming-chiao* as setting up *chiao* (teaching) according to *ming* (names or doctrines): "It includes the political system, selection of officials, education and transformation with rites and music, etc." ("Wei-Chin Hsüan-hsüeh chih hsing-ch'eng chi ch'i fa-chan" [The formation and evolution of Wei-Chin *Hsüan-hsüeh*], in *Wei-Chin nan-pei ch'ao shih lun-ts'ung*, 312; also see 316); Yü Ying-shih believes that *ming-chiao* should be understood "in terms of the order of relations between people, among which the most important are the relations between ruler and subject, father and son." ("Ming-chiao wei-chi yü Wei-Chin shih-feng ti yen-pien" [Crisis of the Confucian moral teaching and the evolution of Wei-Chin intellectual style], in *Chung-kuo chih-shih chieh-ts'eng shih lun*, 332); Makeham maintains that *ming-chiao* "may be understood to have two senses. One is 'the ethos that fosters the cultivation of a virtuous reputation'; the other is 'the moral teaching that champions the cultivation of a particular virtue: filial respect and submission *(xiao [hsiao])*'" *(Name and Actuality*, 100). For the definition of *ming-chiao*, see also T'ang Chang-ju, "Wei-Chin ts'ai-hsing lun ti cheng-chih i-i" [Political significance of the Wei-Chin theory of human ability and nature], in *Wei-Chin nan-pei-ch'ao shih lun-ts'ung*, 301; Ch'en Yin-k'o, "T'ao Yüan-ming chih ssu-hsiang yü ch'ing-t'an chih kuan-hsi," 182; T'ang Yung-t'ung, "Wei-Chin Ssu-hsiang ti fa-chan" [Development of Wei-Chin thought], in *T'ang Yung-t'ung hsüeh-shu lun-wen chi*, 298; Richard B. Mather, "Individualist Expressions of the Outsiders during the Six Dynasties," in Munro, ed., *Individualism and Holism*, 199; and Ying-shih Yü, "Individualism and the Neo-Taoist Movement," in Munro, ed., *Individualism and Holism*, 136. As we shall see later, *ming-chiao* is an important notion in *Hsüan-hsüeh*, always appearing in opposition to *tzu-jan* ("the self-so," "spontaneity," or "naturalness").

43. See Fan Yeh, *Hou-Han shu*, "Tang-ku lieh-chuan," *chüan* 67.

44. The dates of these four orders are respectively the eighth year (203), fifteenth year (210), nineteenth year (214), and twenty-second year (217) of the Chien-an reign; see Ch'en Shou (233–297), *San-kuo chih* [Records of the Three Kingdoms], *Wei-shu* [History of the Wei], "Wu-ti chi" [Basic annals of Emperor Wu], 5 vols. (Peking: Chung-hua shu-chü, 1959, 1982), *chüan* 1, 1:32, 1:44, and P'ei Sung-chih's (372–451) commentary, 1:24, 1:49–50; see also T'ang Chang-ju, "Wei-Chin ts'ai hsing lun ti cheng-chih i-i," 303–304.

45. Ts'ao Ts'ao's order issued in the eighth year of the Chien-an reign, quoted in P'ei Sung-chih's commentary, *San-kuo chih, Wei-shu*, 1:24.

46. Ts'ao Ts'ao's orders issued in the fifteenth year of the Chien-an reign, *San-kuo chih, Wei-shu*, 1:32.

47. Ts'ao Ts'ao's order issued in the twenty-second year of the Chien-an reign, quoted in P'ei Sung-chih's commentary, *San-kuo chih, Wei-shu*, 1:49.

48. Mather translates *ying-hsung* as "brave warrior." For an explanation of my rendering, see below.

49. See, for example, *Hsün-tzu* [*chi-chieh*] [(Collected commentaries on) *Hsün-tzu*], ch. 5, "Fei-hsiang" [Refuting physiognomy], *Chu-tzu chi-ch'eng* ed., *chüan* 3, 56.

50. See Pan Piao (3–54), "Wang-ming lun" [On ruler's mandate], in *Wen-hsüan* [Selections of refined literature], ed. Hsiao T'ung (501–531), commentary by Li Shan (d. 689), 3 vols. (Peking: Chung-hua shu-chü, 1977), *chüan* 52, 3:719.

51. Liu Shao, *Jen-wu chih* (early sixteenth century; reprint, Peking: Wen-hsüeh ku-chi k'an-hsing she, 1955), *chüan* B, 10–12; trans. based on J. K. Shryock, *The Study of Human Abilities: The Jen wu chih of Liu Shao* (New Haven: American Oriental Society, 1937), 127–129.

52. See Wei Cheng et al., *Sui-shu*, *chüan* 34, 4:1004. For a detailed discussion of the "School of Names," see chapter 2.

53. *P'ai-yu hsiao-shuo*, literally "jester's petite talks," should refer to humorous writings. Ts'ao Chih especially showed off his talent in this respect possibly because Han-tan Ch'un was the author of the *Hsiao-lin* [Forest of jokes], one of the early collections of jokes. See Wang Yao, "Fang-shih yü hsiao-shuo" [Alchemist and *hsiao-shuo*], in *Chung-ku wen-hsüeh shih lun-chi*, 105; see also Ts'ao Wen-hsin, "Chien-an hsiao-shuo k'ao pien" [Study of Chien-an *hsiao-shuo*], *Huai-pei mei-shih yüan hsüeh-pao (She-k'o pan)* 1988.4:92.

54. During the Wei-Chin period, *wu*, in addition to its meaning of "thing," was often taken as an alternative of *jen*, "person," of which many examples are shown in the *Shih-shuo hsin-yü* and other contemporary works, such as Liu Shao, *Jen-wu chih* (*chüan* A, 5); see Liu P'an-sui (d. 1966), *Shih-shuo hsin-yü chiao-chien* [Commentary on the *Shih-shuo hsin-yü*], *Kuo-hsüeh lun-ts'ung* 1.4 (1928):102–103.

55. *Wei-lüeh* [A brief history of Wei], as quoted in P'ei Sung-chih's commentary on the *San-kuo chih, Wei-shu*, "Han-tan Ch'ün chuan" [Biography of Han-tan Ch'ün], *chüan* 20, 3:603.

56. See Tu Yu, *T'ung-tien*, "Hsüan-chü II," *chüan* 14, 77–81, especially 78; see also T'ang Chang-ju, "Chiu-p'in chung-cheng chih-tu shih-shih," 85–126.

57. My retranslation; cf. Mather, *Tales of the World*, 233–234.

58. Mather's original note: "This is evidently a Chinese approximation for some Central Asian or Prakrit version of the Buddhist Sanskrit greeting, *Rañjanī* meaning something like 'Good cheer'" (*Tales of the World*, 86, n. 3 to 3/12).

59. Modification bracketed.

60. Liu Chün's commentary on the *Shih-shuo hsin-yü*, 3/12; modification adopted from

Chou I-liang and Wang I-t'ung, "Ma-i *Shih-shuo hsin-yü* shang-tui" [Discussion of Richard B. Mather's translation of the *Shih-shuo hsin-yü*], *Ch'ing-hua hsüeh-pao* 20.2 (1990):214.

61. Modification bracketed.

62. Liu Chün's commentary on the *Shih-shuo hsin-yü*, 30/1.

63. Ibid., 8/15.

64. Ibid., 8/56; my retranslation.

65. Ibid., 14/5.

Chapter 2: Character Appraisal and the Formation of Wei-Chin Spirit

1. For discussions of the fuller political, social, and economic context, see, for example, Chou I-liang, *Wei-Chin nan-pei ch'ao shih lun-chi hsü-pien*; Kawakatsu Yoshio, *Rikuchō kizokusei shakai no kenkyū* [A study of Six Dynasties aristocratic society] (Tokyo: Iwanami shoten, 1982); T'ang Chang-ju, *Wei-Chin nan-pei ch'ao shih lun-ts'ung*; Wang Chung-lo, *Wei-Chin nan-pei ch'ao shih* [A history of the Wei, Chin, Southern and Northern dynasties], 2 vols. (Shanghai: Shanghai jen-min ch'u-pan she, 1979 [Vol. 1] and 1980 [Vol. 2]); Albert E. Dien, ed., *State and Society in Early Medieval China* (Stanford: Stanford University Press, 1990); Charles Holcombe, *In the Shadow of the Han: Literati Identity and Society at the Beginning of the Southern Dynasties* (Honolulu: University of Hawai'i Press, 1994), to cite just a few.

2. Yü Ying-shih observes: "Character appraisal and self-awareness interacted as mutual cause and effect. Only when individuality grew fairly mature, could character appraisal become increasingly subtle and eventually establish an independent subject. This is why character appraisal prevailed after the mid-Eastern Han. On the other hand, the development of *jen-lun chien-shih* must have also contributed enormously to the growth of self-awareness" ("Han-Chin chih chi shih chih hsin tzu-chüeh yü hsin ssu-ch'ao," 237). See also his "Individualism and the Neo-Taoist Movement," 126.

3. See also *Shih-shuo hsin-yü*, 9/9.

4. See, for example, *Shih-shuo hsin-yü*, 2/51, 5/15, 5/23, 5/47, 6/15, 9/2, 9/35, 9/39, 9/40, 9/45, 9/48, 9/53, 9/57, 9/73, 9/74, 10/19, 25/12, 25/33, etc.

5. See, for example, *Shih-shuo hsin-yü*, 1/13, 4/38, 5/18, 6/26, 6/29, 9/7, 9/9, 9/15, 9/52, 9/71, 9/81, 19/30, etc.

6. See, for examples, *Shih-shuo hsin-yü*, 1/29, 6/19, 19/26, etc.

7. Italics are used for emphasis, here and after.

8. Dates according to Yü, *Shih-shuo hsin-yü chien-shu*, 2:631–632, n. 4 to 16/3.

9. As John Timothy Wixted points out, "there was no clear-cut distinction between a man's character and his [artistic] works. . . . A man and his works had been considered inseparable in earlier Chinese thought" ("The Nature of Evaluation in the *Shih-*

392 Notes to Pages 48–53

p'in [Grading of poets] by Chung Hung [A.D. 469–518]," in Susan Bush and Christian Murck, eds., *Theories of the Arts in China* [Princeton, NJ: Princeton University Press, 1983], 232); Wixted's original note: "Ssu-ma Ch'ien, when writing about Confucius and Ch'ü Yüan, said he could imagine what sort of men they were from their writings (*Shih chi* [Records of the Historian], 49, p. 1947 and 84, p. 2503)."

10. An obvious rivalry existed between Wang Hsien-chih and Hsieh An, who was also a capable calligrapher; see Chang Huai-kuan, *Shu-tuan* [Judgment on calligraphy], *chüan* B, quoted in Yü, *Shih-shuo hsin-yü chien-shu*, 1:538, n. 1.

11. My retranslation.

12. For an introduction to the origin and function of *chu-wei*, see Mather, *Tales of the World*, 56, n. 2 to 2/52. See also Ho Ch'ang-ch'ün, "*Shih-shuo hsin-yü* cha-chi: lun *chu-wei*" [Jotting notes on the *Shih-shuo hsin-yü*: On the term *chu-wei*], *Kuo-li chung-yang t'u-shu kuan kuan-k'an (fu-kan)* 1 (1947):1–7.

13. See also Yü, *Shih-shuo hsin-yü chien-shu*, 2:641, n. 2. About the similar symbolic function of a sambar-tail chowry, see also *Shih-shuo hsin-yü*, 2/52, 4/22, and 4/31.

14. An assertion by Jacques Lacan, as quoted in Jacques-Alain Miller, "Jacques Lacan: 1901–1981," *Psychoanalysis and Contemporary Thought* 7.4 (1984):621.

15. I find that Jacques Lacan's psychological conception of the mirror stage is helpful for analyzing the formation of "self" in the *Shih-shuo hsin-yü*. This mirror-stage theory starts with a drama like this: A small child contemplates himself in a mirror and develops his earliest sense of ego by seeing an integrated self-image. Three points derived from this situation are important to my topic. First, the mirror situation suggests that "we arrive at a sense of an 'I' by finding that 'I' reflects back to ourselves by [means of] some object or person in the world. This object is at once somehow part of ourselves—we identify with it—and yet not ourselves, something alien" (Terry Eagleton's interpretation of Lacan's theory of the mirror stage, *Literary Theory: An Introduction* [Minneapolis: University of Minnesota Press, 1983], 164–165). Second, this alienation initiates in the "I" a desire to complete itself by identifying itself with this alien, integrated image. As Lacan points out: "At the same time as it prefigures its alienating destination[,] it is still pregnant with the correspondences that unite the I with the statue in which man projects himself, with the phantoms that dominate him, or with the automaton in which, in an ambiguous relation, the world of his own making tends to find completion" (Jacques Lacan, "The mirror stage as formative of the function of the I as revealed in psychoanalytic experience," *Ecrits: A Selection*, trans. from the French by Alan Sheridan [New York: W. W. Norton, 1977], 2–3). Third, because this alienation separates the "I" from its self-image in the mirror, the "I" "entertains a profoundly ambivalent relationship to that reflection. It loves the coherent identity which the mirror provides. However, because the image remains external to it, it also hates that image" (Kaja Silverman's interpretation of Lacan's theory, *The Subject of Semiotics* [New York: Oxford University Press, 1983], 158).

16. See *Tz'u-yüan* [Etymological dictionary]. Revised ed. (s.v. *Zhou*).

17. As Liu Chün points out by quoting from the [*Hsi*] *K'ang pieh-chuan* [A variant biography of Hsi K'ang]: "Wouldn't [Hsi K'ang] know that Shan would not use an offi-

cial position as a token of friendship? He just wanted to signal his unyielding integrity in order to silence those who intended to recommend him [to the court]" (my translation).

18. As also recorded in the *Shih-shuo hsin-yü*, Shan T'ao seemed to bear no personal resentment against Hsi K'ang, but instead took good care of Hsi's son after his death (3/8). Thus the *Shih-shuo* author tells us that Shan T'ao actually understood Hsi K'ang's real reason for cutting off their relationship.

19. Hsi K'ang, "Shih-ssu lun" [Dispelling concealment], in *Hsi K'ang chi [chiao-chu]*, [(Commentary on) *Collected Works of Hsi K'ang*], edited by Tai Ming-yang (Peking: Jen-min wen-hsüeh ch'u-pan she, 1962), *chüan* 6, 234.

20. Robert G. Henricks' introduction to Hsi K'ang, "Shih-ssu lun," in *Philosophy and Argumentation in Third-Century China: The Essays of Hsi K'ang,* translated with introduction and annotation by Henricks (Princeton, NJ: Princeton University Press, 1983), 107; see also Donald Holzman, *La Vie et la Pensée de Hi K'ang* (Leiden: E. J. Brill, 1957), 122, n. 2.

21. Hsi K'ang, "Nan 'tzu-jan hao-hsüeh lun'" [Questioning "one naturally likes to learn"], in *Hsi K'ang chi [chiao-chu]*, *chüan* 7, 261.

22. Henricks interprets the meaning of the two central concepts, *kung* and *ssu*, in Hsi K'ang's "Shih-ssu lun" as follows: "*Kung* in the essay is 'unselfish,' and *ssu* is 'self-interest.' But Hsi K'ang also uses *kung* to mean 'be open,' 'go public,' while *ssu* means to keep things to oneself" (*Essays of Hsi K'ang*, 107). Henricks, however, translates the title of "Shih-ssu lun" as "Dispelling Self-Interest." After a close reading of the essay, I believe that *ssu* here mainly means to conceal things because of certain concerns, as opposed to *kung* as entire openness, hence my rendering of the title, "Dispelling Concealment."

23. Ying-shih Yü, "Individualism and the Neo-Taoist Movement," 121. For the Han institutionalization of the "three bonds" *(san-kang)* as Confucian moral codes, see also Wu Hung, *The Wu Liang Shrine*, 169–170.

24. According to Confucius' teachings, a filial son should always follow his father's model and should not change his father's ways even after the father's death. In the words of the *Analects*: "If, after three years of one's father's death, one makes no changes to his father's ways, he can be said to be a filial son" (*Lun-yü [chu-shu]*, I, 11 [number follows Yang Po-chün, *Lun-yü i-chu* (Annotated translation of the Analects of Confucius) (Peking: Chung-hua shu-chü, 1980), here and after], *Shih-san ching chu-shu*, 2:2458).

25. Wu Hung, *The Wu Liang Shrine*, 180.

26. I translate the sentence *"Ho ju wo"* as "How does he compare with *me*" instead of Mather's "How does he compare with *us*." See Mather, *Tales of the World*, 215.

27. *I-li [chu-shu]* [(Commentary on) Etiquette and ritual], "Sang-fu" [Mourning ritual], *chüan* 30, *Shih-san ching chu-shu*, 1:1106.

28. Mather's commentary on this episode: "A later commentator, who refers to himself as 'Your servant' [*ch'en*], writes: 'Wang Kuang was a famous gentleman; how could

he have spoken lightly of his father-in-law? The story is untrue!'" (*Tales of the World*, 345).

29. *Li-chi* [*cheng-i*], *Shih-san ching chu-shu, chüan* 61, 2:1680–1681.

30. Ibid.

31. The most commonly cited wrongdoings that would cause a woman to be divorced by her husband include: (1) failure to produce a male heir, (2) adultery, (3) disrespect to husband's parents, (4) quarrelsomeness, (5) stealing, (6) jealousy, and (7) vicious disease; see, for example, Ho Hsiu's commentary on the *Ch'un-ch'iu kung-yang chuan* [*chu-shu*] [(Commentary on) Kung-yang commentary on the spring and autumn annals], the twenty-seventh year of Duke Chuang, *Shih-san ching chu-shu, chüan* 8, 2:2239.

32. The historical Chung Yen was an expert in physiognomy and a famous poet. Liu Chün's commentary on the *Shih-shuo hsin-yü*, 19/16, quotes the *Fu-jen chi* [Collection of women's works]: "Lady Chung possessed literary ability, and her poems, poetic essays, hymns, and obituaries have become current in the world" (trans. Mather, *Tales of the World*, 349). According to the "Sui treatise," the five-*chüan* collection of Chung Yen's literary works was extant in the Liang dynasty; see Wei Cheng et al., *Sui-shu*, "Ching-chi chih," IV, *chüan* 35, 4:1070.

33. For a detailed discussion of Han—particularly Later Han—emphasis on women's chastity, see Wu Hung, *The Wu Liang Shrine*, 176–177. Wu Hung also notes a radical change in attitudes concerning women's morality from the Han to the Wei-Chin period. He compares the virtuous women portrayed respectively on the wall of the Wu Liang Shrine (established in 151) to a lacquer screen excavated from the tomb of [Ssu-ma Chin-lung] (d. 484), finding that, while the designer of the Wu Liang carvings took women's chastity as the central motif, "the designer [of the Ssu-ma Chin-lung screen] seemed less interested in the moral issue of chastity" (*The Wu Liang Shrine*, 173–177). Neither is chastity a major concern in the *Shih-shuo hsin-yü*. The author records only one case about a widow's devotion to her deceased husband, out of love rather than fidelity to the moral code (19/29), and he holds high regard for Lady Chung, including her as a major character in the chapter entitled "Hsien-yüan" [Worthy beauties].

34. See Li Tz'u-ming's comment on this episode, quoted in Yü, *Shih-shuo hsin-yü chien-shu*, 2:789.

35. Quoted in Liu Chün's commentary on the *Shih-shuo hsin-yü*, 23/7, trans. James Legge, *Li Ki*, I, 77, in Mather, *Tales of the World*, 374.

36. Liu Chün's commentary cites an earlier version of this episode from P'ei Ch'i (fl. second half fourth cent.), *Yü-lin* [Forest of tales]: "Wang: 'You've made great progress lately.' Liu: 'Do you look up?' Wang: 'What do you mean?' Liu: 'If you didn't look up, how could you estimate the height of Heaven?'" (Mather, *Tales of the World*, 62).

37. See *Lun-yü*, II, 4; III, 13; VI, 8; IX, 11; XI, 8; XIV, 37 and 38; XVI, 8; etc. See also Fung Yu-lan, *A History of Chinese Philosophy*, trans. Derk Bodde, 2 vols. (Princeton, NJ: Princeton University Press, 1973), 1:30–31.

38. Quoted in Yü, *Shih-shuo hsin-yü chien-shu*, 1:125–126, n. 3 to 2/66.

39. *Chuang-tzu*, Chapter 21, "T'ien Tzu-fang," Kuo, ed., *Chuang-tzu Chi-shih, chüan* 7b, 3:716, trans. based on Watson, *Complete Works of Chuang Tzu*, 226, and Mather's commentary on the *Shih-shuo hsin-yü*, 2/66.

40. These Taoist notions of perfection, spirituality, greatness, and sageliness have nothing to do with Confucian values, although Confucians employed similar terms in describing degrees of moral refinement.

41. For the meaning of *chih-jen*, see, mainly, *Chuang-tzu*, Chapter 21, "T'ien Tzu-fang"; for *shen-jen*, see *Chuang-tzu*, Chapter 1, "Hsiao-yao yu" [Free and easy wandering]; for *ta-jen*, see *Chuang-tzu*, Chapters 17, "Ch'iu-shui" [Autumn floods], 24, "Hsü Wu-kuei," and 25, "Tse-yang"; see also Graham, *Disputers of the Tao*, 204–211.

42. In a very general sense, chapter 6, "Ya-liang" [Cultivated tolerance] seems to exemplify the *chih-jen* ideal; chapter 14, "Jung-chih" [Appearance and manner], the *shen-jen* ideal; and chapter 23, "Jen-tan" [Uninhibitedness and eccentricity], the *ta-jen* ideal.

43. Graham, *Disputers of the Tao*, 206.

44. Juan Chi's *Ta-jen hsien-sheng chuan* [Biography of the Great Man] also presents a Wei-Chin elaboration of the "Great Man" ideal in the *Chuang-tzu*; in Yen K'o-chün (1762–1843), ed., *Ch'üan shang-ku san-tai Ch'in Han San-kuo Liu-ch'ao wen* [Complete prose from antiquity to the Six Dynasties] (Kuang-ya shu-chü ed.; reprint, 4 vols., Peking: Chung-hua shu-chü, 1958), Vol. 2: *Ch'üan San-kuo wen* [Complete prose of the Three Kingdoms], *chüan* 46, 5a–11a. See also Donald Holzman, *Poetry and Politics: The Life and Works of Juan Chi (A.D. 210–263)* (Cambridge: Cambridge University Press, 1976), 185–226.

45. On the broad influence and the problem of the existence of this group, see Mather, *Tales of the World*, 371, n. 1 to 23/1. See also Ho Ch'i-min, *Chu-lin ch'i-hsien yen-chiu* [Study of the Seven Worthies of the bamboo grove] (Taipei: Chung-kuo hsüeh-shu chu-tso chiang-chu wei-yüan hui, 1966); and Nanking po-wu yüan, "Nanking Hsi-shan ch'iao Nan-ch'ao mu chi ch'i chuan-k'o pi-hua" [A Southern dynasty tomb and its brick reliefs at Hsi-shan ch'iao, Nanking], *Wen-wu* 1960.8-9:37–42.

46. Liu Chün's commentary on the *Shih-shuo hsin-yü*, 23/1.

47. See *Shih-shuo hsin-yü*, 19/30.

48. T'ang Yung-t'ung, "Yen-i chih pien" [Discernment of the relations between words and meanings], in *Wei-Chin Hsüan-hsüeh lun-ka*, collected in *T'ang Yung-t'ung hsüeh-shu lun-wen chi*, 215.

49. Kuo T'ai's work on the basis of selecting scholars possibly involved theoretical discussions but was lost; see the discussion of this issue in chapter 1.

50. See *Shih-shuo hsin-yü*, 3/17.

51. The present version of the *Shih-shuo hsin-yü* has only Kuo T'ai's appraisal of Huang Hsien. The reference to Yüan Lang is interpolated from Liu Chün's commentary, which indicates that both appraisals were recorded in the *Kuo T'ai pieh-chuan*. Judg-

ing from the context of the entire episode, which obviously suggests a comparison between the two evaluatees, I believe that the *Shih-shuo* author originally included both appraisals, but Yüan Lang's part was later cut by Yen Shu. See also Fan Yeh, *Hou-Han shu*, "Huang Hsieh chuan" [Biography of Huang Hsien], *chüan* 53, 6:1744, and Li Hsien's commentary on this biography, *chüan* 53, 6:1745, n. 6.

52. 1 *ch'ing* = 15.13 acres.

53. See T'ang Yung-t'ung, "Tu *Jen-wu chih*," 202–203.

54. See ibid., 203, and Makeham, *Name and Actuality*, 4.

55. Makeham, *Name and Actuality*, xiii–xiv.

56. Ibid., xiii.

57. Ibid., 191–192.

58. The School of *Ming-li* (Names and Principles) or *Ming-chia* (School of Names) in the Wei-Chin period differed from the *Ming-chia* in the pre-Ch'in period. Although both concentrated on "distinguishing names and analyzing principles" (*pien-ming hsi-li*), the pre-Ch'in school focused on logical analysis of general principles through the differentiation of terms, whereas the Wei-Chin school focused on the criticism of personalities. Thus, the "Ming-chia" category in the "Sui Treatise" replaces the two major works of the pre-Ch'in School of Names recorded in the *Han-shu* [History of the Han], "I-wen chih" [Bibliographic treatise]—the *Hui-tzu* and the *Kung-sun Lung-tzu*—with Liu Shao's *Jen-wu chih* and Ts'ao P'i's *Shih-ts'ao*. See Pan Ku (32–92), *Han-shu*, 12 vols. (Peking: Chung-hua shu-chü, 1962), *chüan* 30, 6:1736; and Wei Chen et al., *Sui-shu*, *chüan* 34, 4:1004; see also T'ang Yung-t'ung, "Tu *Jen-wu chih*," 196–213; and Fung, *History of Chinese Philosophy*, 2:175–179.

59. See T'ang Chang-ju, "Wei-Chin ts'ai hsing lun ti cheng-chih i-i," 309.

60. Yü, *Shih-shuo hsin-yü chien-shu*, 1:195; my translation.

61. T'ang Chang-ju, "Wei-Chin ts'ai-hsing lun ti cheng-chih i-i," 300. Notes Richard B. Mather: "The conformists (those who maintain that *ts'ai* and *hsing* are *t'ung* or *ho*) apparently maintained that if a person possessed ability, his nature would automatically allow him to perform ably in office. If such a person were to decline to apply his ability in the service of the state on grounds of not wishing to violate his inborn nature, he would immediately be deemed disloyal or at least morally reprobate" ("Individualist Expressions of the Outsiders during the Six Dynasties," 203). See also T'ang Yung-t'ung, "Yen-i chih pien," 214–232.

62. See T'ang Yung-t'ung, "Tu *Jen-wu chih*," 210–213.

63. See ibid., 209.

64. T'ang Yung-t'ung, "Yen-i chih pien," 214. Yü Ying-shih considers Wei *Hsüan-hsüeh* to have resulted from multiple origins, but mainly as a development of the late Han "simplification of Confucianism" (*ju-hsüeh chien-hua*); see his "Han-Chin chih chi shih chih hsin tzu-chüeh yü hsin ssu-ch'ao," 275–305, particularly 301.

65. T'ang Yung-t'ung, "Yen-i chih pien," 214. The *Shih-shuo* author underscores this radical break by his use of typical *Hsüan-hsüeh* terms such as *t'an* (conversation), *t'an-*

k'o (conversationalist), *li* (hypothesis, argumentation), *nan* (refutation), and later *hsüan* (abstruse), *hsüan-yüan* (abstruse and remote), *hsüan-feng* (abstruse wind), *hsüan-lun* (abstruse discussion), *hsüan-yen* (abstruse conversation), *ch'ing-yen* (pure conversation), etc.; see mainly *Shih-shuo hsin-yü,* chapter 4, "Wen-hsüeh."

66. Observes Ch'en Li (1810–1882): "Wang Pi discusses the doctrines of *Lao-tzu* and *Chuang-tzu* yet regards Confucius as superior to the two Taoist philosophers. His axiom that 'the Sage (Confucius) takes *wu* as the permanent substratum,' however, is still derived from the *Lao-tzu* and the *Chuang-tzu*" (*Tung-shu tu-shu chi* [Reading notes from the Eastern Studio], 16, quoted in Yü, *Shih-shuo hsin-yü chien-shu,* 1:199, n. 2 to 4/8). See also Fung, *History of Chinese Philosophy,* 2:168–175.

67. My retranslation; cf. Mather, *Tales of the World,* 96.

68. E. Zürcher, *The Buddhist Conquest of China,* 2 vols. (Leiden: E. J. Brill, 1959), 1:87.

69. *Lao-tzu,* ch. 40; Chinese text according to Wang pi, *Lao-tzu Tao te ching chu* [(Commentary on) Lao-tzu Tao te ching], in *Wang Pi chi [chiao-shih]* [(Commentary on) Collected works of Wang Pi], commentary by Lou Yü-lieh, 2 vols. (Peking: Chunghua shu-chü, 1980), 1:110.

70. Fang Hsüan-ling (578–648) et al., *Chin-shu* [History of the Chin], "Wang Yen chuan" [Biography of Wang Yen], 10 vols. (Peking: Chung-hua shu-chü, 1974), *chüan* 43, 4:1236; see also Zürcher, *Buddhist Conquest of China,* 1:89.

71. Wang Pi, *Lun-yü shih-i* [Interpretation of *Lun-yü*], in *Wang Pi chi [chiao-shih],* 2:624; trans. Graham, *Studies in Chinese Philosophy and Philosophical Literature* (Singapore: Institute of East Asian Philosophies, 1986), 345.

72. *Lao-tzu,* ch. 25, *Wang Pi chi chiao-shih,* 1:63; see also D. C. Lau, trans., *Lao Tzu Tao Te Ching* (Penguin Books, 1963), 82; and Zürcher, *Buddhist Conquest of China,* 1:89.

73. Wang Pi, *Lao-tzu Tao te ching chu,* in *Wang Pi chi [chiao-shih],* 1:64; trans. Zürcher, *Buddhist Conquest of China,* 1:89.

74. Graham, *Studies in Chinese Philosophy,* 346.

75. Wang Pi, *Chou-i lüeh-li* [General remarks on *Chou-i*], "Ming-hsiang" [Clarifying the images], in *Wang Pi chi [chiao-shih],* 2:609; trans. Richard John Lynn, *The Classic of Changes: A New Translation of the I Ching as Interpreted by Wang Bi [Pi]* (New York: Columbia University Press, 1994), 31.

76. *Chuang-tzu,* "Wai-wu" [External things]: "The fish trap exists because of the fish; once you've gotten the fish, you can forget the trap. The rabbit snare exists because of the rabbit; once you've gotten the rabbit, you can forget the snare. Words exist because of ideas; once you've gotten the idea, you can forget the words" (Kuo Ch'ingfan, ed., *Chuang-tzu chi-shih,* 4:944; trans. based on Watson, *Complete Works of Chuang Tzu,* 302).

77. Wang Pi, *Chou-i lüeh-li,* in *Wang Pi chi [chiao-shih],* 2:609; trans. Lynn, *The Classic of Changes,* 31.

78. Ho Yen, "Wu-ming lun" [On namelessness], quoted in Chang Chan's (fl. ca. 370) *Lieh-tzu chu* [Commentary on the *Lieh-tzu*], *Chu-tzu chi-ch'eng* ed., 41.

79. T'ang Yung-t'ung, "Yen-i chih pien," 215.

80. See Kuo Hsiang's commentary on *Chuang-tzu,* "Ch'i-wu lun" [Discussion on making all things equal], Kuo, ed., *Chuang-tzu chi-shih,* 1:111–112.

81. Kuo Hsiang's commentary on *Chuang-tzu,* "Ch'i-wu lun": "[The piping of Heaven] blows through the myriad [hollows], each in a different way, letting each be itself" (Kuo, ed., *Chuang-tzu chi-shih,* 1:50). See also Mather, *Tales of the World,* 116, n. 1 on 4/46.

82. For Wang Tao's role in early Eastern Chin life, see mainly *Shih-shuo hsin-yü,* chapter 3, "Cheng-shih," and chapter 4, "Wen-hsüeh."

83. Ou-yang Chien, "Yen chin i lun," in Ou-yang Hsün (557–641) ed., *I-wen lei-chü,* 4 vols. (Shanghai: Shanghai ku-chi ch'u-pan she, 1965, 1982), *chüan* 19, 1:348.

84. Ibid.

85. Ibid. My translation of the last three sentences borrows from Mather's translation of Liu Chün's commentary on the *Shih-shuo hsin-yü,* 4/21: "Names change according to objects; words are transformed in dependence on principles. They may not be polarized into two. So if name and object, word and principle, are not two, then there is no word which is not fully expressive." On Ou-yang Chien's "Yen chin i lun," see also James J. Y. Liu, *Language—Paradox—Poetics: A Chinese Perspective,* ed. Richard John Lynn (Princeton, NJ: Princeton University Press, 1988), 3–37, especially 30–33.

86. Makeham, *Name and Actuality,* xiii–xiv.

87. According to Makeham, "we may note that Ouyang Jian [Ou-yang Chien] is clearly a nominalist and that he rejects the position held by (Xu Gan) [Hsü Kan] that 'things have naturally appropriate names,' evidencing that by the latter half of the third century the correlative position was under attack" (ibid., 192).

88. Ibid., xiii.

89. Ou-yang Chien's *yen chin i* theory shows the clear influence of Hsün-tzu's essay, "Cheng-ming" (On the correct use of names), whose wisdom, as Graham summarizes it, is that "the function of names is to 'point them [objects] out' from each other, by assimilating them to and differentiating them from other objects" (Graham, *Disputers of the Tao,* 263). But, as Graham also points out, "Hsün-tzu like the Later Mohists thinks of objects as concrete bits of stuff" (ibid.), and, as a nominalist, he believes that the name should fit actuality on a one-to-one basis—unlike Ou-yang, who locates things in systems and corresponds them with systems of names. Cf. a major paragraph from the *Hsün-tzu* essay, "Cheng-ming":

> When with differences in expression and divergence in thought we communicate with each other, and different things are obscurely confounded in name or as objects, the noble and the base will not be clarified, the same and the different will not be distinguished; in such cases intent will inevitably be hampered by failure to communicate, and action will inevitably suffer from frustration and obstruction. Therefore the wise made for them apportionments and distinctions

and instituted names to point out objects, in the first place in order to clarify noble and base, secondly to distinguish same and different. When noble and base are clarified, and same and different distinguished, intent is not hampered by failure to communicate and action does not suffer from frustration and obstruction. This is the purpose of having names. (Trans. Graham, *Disputers of the Tao*, 263)

90. Kenneth Ch'en, *Buddhism in China* (Princeton, NJ: Princeton University Press, 1964), 59.

91. Ibid., 59–60.

92. During the mid-Eastern Chin period, "gentry Buddhism" reached its peak. Different from Buddhism as a popular cult, gentry Buddhism had a "distinctly rational and intellectual flavor"; its ideal was not "the quiet surrender to the power of a superhuman savior, but in the first place the realization of Chuang-tzu's 'equality of all things,' the pursuit of the wisdom of the sage who 'reflects' on all phenomena without ever leaving his state of trance-like non-activity, a wisdom which in these circles is vaguely equated with the hazy concepts of *nirvāna, prajñā, samatā, tathatā* and *bodhi* all merged into one" (Zürcher, *Buddhist Conquest of China*, 1:73–74). For the formation of gentry Buddhism in China, see Zürcher, 1:71–75.

93. As Graham points out, "Chinese Buddhism at first confused the Void (*śūnyatā*) with the *wu* of Taoism, but later learned to deny that it is either *yu* or *wu*" (*Studies in Chinese Philosophy*, 348).

94. Ch'ih Ch'ao, "Feng-fa yao" [Essentials of religion], in Seng Yu, *Hung-ming chi*, 5 vols. (*Ssu-pu ts'ung-k'ang* ed.), *chüan* 13, 4:9a; see also Zürcher, *Buddhist Conquest of China*, 1:172–173.

95. *School* is actually a misleading word. In the time of the fourth century, there existed no "school" in the proper sense of the word, but different interpretations of a doctrine. See Stanley Weinstein, "Buddhism, Schools of: Chinese Buddhism," *The Encyclopedia of Religion,* ed. Mircea Eliade, 16 vols. (Macmillan, 1987), 1:482–487. For a detailed discussion of the "Six Houses and Seven 'Schools'," see T'ang Yung-t'ung, *Han Wei Liang-Chin Nan-Pei-ch'ao fo-chiao shih* [History of Buddhism of the Han, Wei, Chin, and Southern and Northern dynasties], 2 vols. (Peking: Chung-hua shu-chü, 1955, 1963), 1:229–277, and "Wei-Chin *Hsüan-hsüeh* liu-pieh lüeh-lun" [Brief study of the scholarly trends of Wei-Chin *Hsüan-hsüeh*], *Wei-Chin Hsüan-hsüeh lun-kao, T'ang Yung-t'ung hsüeh-shu lun-wen chi*, 233–244; Walter Liebenthal, trans. *Chao Lun, The Treatises of Seng-chao*, with introduction, notes and appendices (Hong Kong University Press, 1968), 54–63, 133–150; Tsukamoto Zenryū ed., *Jōron kenkyū* [Study of *Chao-lun*] (Kyoto: Hōzōkan, 1955), 15–16; Zürcher, *Buddhist Conquest of China*, 1:71–159; and Ch'en Yin-k'o, "Chih Min-tu hsüeh-shuo k'ao" [Study of Chih Min-tu's theory], *Chin-ming kuan ts'ung-kao ch'u-pien*, 141–167.

96. The first extant example of "forgetting the body once getting the idea" (*te-i wang-hsing*) can be found in Fang Hsüan-ling et al., *Chin-shu*, "Juan Chi chuan" [Biography of Juan Chi]: "Juan Chi . . . read extensively and was especially fond of reading the *Lao-tzu* and the *Chuang-tzu*. . . . When he grasped the idea (merging his

spirit into the *Tao*), he would forget his physical body" *(chüan* 48, 5:1359). But the methodology had long permeated Wei-Chin gentry life, and similar expressions had long circulated in Wei-Chin writings; see T'ang Yung-t'ung, "Yen-i chih pien," 225–228.

97. Mather's original note:

> See *Chuang-tzu* XVII, 19b (Watson, pp. 188–189): Chuang-tzu and Hui Shih were once strolling on the bridge over the River Hao (Anhui), when Chuang-tzu remarked, "See how the minnows dart in and out so free and unconcerned. Such is the pleasure that fish enjoy." Hui-tzu replied, "You aren't a fish. How do you know what pleasures fish enjoy?" Chuang-tzu said, "You aren't me. How do you know I don't know what pleasures fish enjoy?" Ibid., 18b–19a (Watson, pp. 187–188): Chuang-tzu was once angling in the River P'u (Shantung), when the King of Ch'u sent two great officers to visit him there, hoping to tie Chuang-tzu down with responsibility for his entire realm. Chuang-tzu, still holding his rod without looking around, answered them, "I hear that in Ch'u you've got a sacred tortoise who's been dead for three thousand years and is wrapped in a napkin preserved in the ancestral temple. Would this tortoise rather be dragging his tail in the mud, or would he rather have his bones preserved and honored?" The two great officers replied, "He'd rather be dragging his tail in the mud." "Then be off with you! I'd rather drag my tail in the mud, too."

98. Mather's original note: "Ibid., IX, 8b–9a (Watson, p. 105): In an age of perfect virtue men live together with birds and animals."

99. See T'ang Yung-t'ung, "Yen-i chih pien," 217–232.

100. For Chih Tun's superb scholarship on the *Chuang-tzu,* see the *Shih-shuo hsin-yü,* 4/32 and 4/36; for his creation of the *Chi-se* theory, see 4/35.

101. Kuo Ch'ing-fan, ed. *Chuang-tzu chi-shih,* 3:754, Kuo Hsiang's note.

102. Ibid.

103. Zürcher defines matter as *"pars pro toto* for the five *skandhas,* i.e., the sum of all subjective and objective phenomena" *(Buddhist Conquest of China,* 1:123).

104. "Those who speak about matter must only (realize) that matter is matter as such (without any substratum). For how would matter be dependent on anything which causes matter to be matter in order to become matter?" (Seng-chao's introduction to *Chi-se* tenet, as quoted in Seng-chao, "Pu chen-k'ung lun" [On the false Emptiness], in Yen K'o-chün ed., *Ch'üan shang-ku san-tai Ch'in Han San-kuo Liu-ch'ao wen, Ch'üan Chin wen* [Complete prose of the Chin], *chüan* 164, 11ab; trans. Zürcher, *Buddhist Conquest of China,* 1:123).

105. Chih Tun, *Miao-kuan chang* [Essay of marvelous view], quoted in Hui Ta's *Chao-lun shu* [Interpretation of *Chao-lun*]; trans. Zürcher, *Buddhist Conquest of China,* 1:123.

106. For Chih Tun's *Chi-se* theory, see T'ang Yung-t'ung, *Han Wei liang-Chin Nan-Pei ch'ao fo-chiao shih,* 1:254–263; "Wei-Chin *Hsüan-hsüeh* liu-pieh lüeh-lun," 237–240;

Zürcher, *Buddhist Conquest of China*, 1:123-30; Tsukamoto Zenryū, ed., *Chōron kenkyū*, 15–16; and W. Liebenthal, trans., *Chao Lun*, 55–56, 138–143.

107. The *Shih-shuo hsin-yü* includes an episode about Sun Ch'o's writing of *Yu T'ien-t'ai shan fu* (4/86).

108. Burton Watson's original note on these two lines reads: "Both Taoism and Buddhism teach the student, as a step in his training, to give up concepts of being and purposive action and embrace those of nothingness and non-action; but true enlightenment comes when he can transcend such dualistic thinking and accept things as they exist. The remainder of the poem plays in paradoxical terms on these ideas of transcendence and acceptance" (*Chinese Rhyme-prose* [New York: Columbia University Press, 1971], 85).

109. Hsiao-t'ung, ed., *Wen-hsüan, chüan* 11, 1:166; see also Watson, *Chinese Rhyme-prose*, 85.

110. *Chuang-tzu* [*chi-shih*], 4:949; trans. James J. Y. Liu, *Language—Paradox—Poetics*, 12, with modifications bracketed. For the textual problem and the interpretation of this passage, see Liu, 12–13.

111. Chu Tao-i, "Shen erh-ti lun" [On the double truth of the spirit], quoted in T'ang, *Han Wei liang-Chin Nan-Pei ch'ao fo-chiao shih*, 1:266; see also Zürcher, *Buddhist Conquest of China*, 1:144, and Liebenthal, 149.

112. See Hans Wolfgang Schumann, *Buddhism: An Outline of Its Teachings and Schools*, trans. Georg Feuerstein (Wheaton, IL: Theosophical Publishing House, 1973), 124 and 144; Zürcher, *Buddhist Conquest of China*, 1:100.

113. Ch'ih Ch'ao, "Feng-fa yao," in Seng Yu, *Hung-ming chi, chüan* 13, 4:9a; trans. Zürcher, *Buddhist Conquest of China*, 1:172–173.

114. As Schumann understands, "The Emptiness of every being which is identical with the Emptiness of all others, possesses all the characteristics of the essence" (*Buddhism: An Outline of Its Teachings and Schools*, 144).

115. See mainly *Shih-shuo hsin-yü*, chapters 2, "Yen-yü" (Speech and conversation), 8, "Shang-yü" (Appreciation and praise), and 14, "Jung-chih" (Appearance and manner).

116. Quoted in Liu Chün's note to *Shih-shuo hsin-yü*, 2/93, trans. Mather, 72; also in Hui Chiao, *Kao-seng chuan* [Biographies of eminent monks], "Chin Wu Hu-ch'iu Tungshan si Chu Tao-i" [Biography of Chu Tao-i], (Peking: Chung-hua shu-chü, 1992), *chüan* 5, 208.

117. For a more detailed introduction to Chu Tao-i's life, see his biography in *Kao-seng chuan, chüan* 5, 206–208; see also Zürcher, *Buddhist Conquest of China*, 1:144–145.

118. Archaic pronunciations are reconstructed according to Bernhard Karlgren, *Grammata Serica, Bulletin of the Museum of Far Eastern Antiquities Stockholm*, no. 12, 1940 (reprint, Taipei: Ch'eng Wen, 1971), 999a, 470b, 647e, 619n, 1157e, 311a, 1039j, 217a.

119. The tones of *ļiuĕn, dâm, p'iet,* and *ńźjän* follow *Sung-pen Kuang-yün* [The Sung edition of the enlarged version of the Rhyme Book] (reprint, Peking: Chung-kuo shu-tien, 1982), 380, 423, 475, and 117.

402 Notes to Pages 84-85

Chapter 3: *Shih-shuo t'i*

1. Tzvetan Todorov, "The Origin of Genres," *New Literary History* 8 (1976):161.

2. Mather observes:

> It seems that the original title of the book was simply "Tales of the World" (*Shih-shuo*), the name by which it appears in the bibliographical sections of the Sui and T'ang dynastic histories, as well as in citations in the early-seventh-century encyclopedias *Pei-t'ang shu-ch'ao, Ch'u-hsüeh chi,* and *I-wen lei-chü.* But to distinguish it from an earlier work of the same name, now lost, by Liu Hsiang. . . , it soon acquired the added words "*New Writing* of Tales of the World" (*Shih-shuo hsin-shu*), the title by which it is cited in the ninth-century miscellany *Yu-yang Tsa-tsu* (IV, 7a) by Tuan Ch'eng-shih. This title is confirmed by the oldest surviving manuscript fragment of the work, the so-called "T'ang fragment," written in the calligraphic style of the eighth century and covering most of the sixth *chüan* of the ten-*chüan* version (Chapters X through XIII). The present title, "*New Account* of Tales of the World" (*Shih-shuo hsin-yü*), seems to appear for the first time in Liu Chih-chi's "Compendium of History" (*Shih-t'ung,* 17.2b, SPTK ed.), which was first published in 710. It is indiscriminately mixed with the other two titles in citations appearing in the early Sung encyclopedias, *T'ai-p'ing kuang-chi* and *T'ai-p'ing yü-lan,* of 983, but thereafter the work is consistently referred to by its present title." (*Tales of the World,* xxvii)

> See also Yung Jung, Chi Yün et al., eds., *Ssu-k'u ch'üan-shu tsung-mu, chüan* 140, 2:1182; Liu Chao-yün, "*Shih-shuo t'an-yüan*" [Search for the origin of the *Shih-shuo hsin-yü*], *Sinkiang ta-hsüeh hsüeh-pao (She-k'o pan)* 1979.1:7. Some argue, however, that *Shih-shuo hsin-yü* is the original title, abbreviated to *Shih-shuo* solely for convenience; see, for example, Chou Pen-ch'un, "*Shih-shuo hsin-yü* yüan-ming k'ao-lüeh" [Brief study of the original title of the *Shih-shuo hsin-yü*], *Chung-hua wen-shih lun-ts'ung* 1980.3:43–47.

3. Archaic pronunciations are reconstructed according to Karlgren, *Grammata Serica,* 324q, 324o, and 324a; and *Tz'u-yüan,* 4 vols. s.v. *Shuo/shui/yüeh.*

4. See *Tz'u-yüan,* s.v. *Shuo/shui/yüeh;* and Liu Hsieh, *Wen-hsin tiao-lung,* "Lun shuo" (*Wen-hsin tiao-lung* [chu], *chüan* 4, 1:326–358). Cf. Vincent Yu-chung Shih, trans., *The Literary Mind and the Carving of Dragons* (Hong Kong: Chinese University Press, 1983), 198–211. *Shuo* of this variety extensively appeared in book titles contained in the first official bibliography, the "I-wen chih" of the *Han-shu.* In the following discussions, I will attach the proper phonetic transcription to the character on each of its appearances.

5. Vincent Yu-chung Shih's commentary on this line reads: "The character *shuo* is composed of two elements: *yen* (to speak) on the left, and *tui* (to please) on the right. Hence *shuo* has two senses: to speak and to please. Later, the *yen* radical is replaced by a heart radical, when it is taken to mean 'to please' and is pronounced *yüeh.* But the original form persists, though its pronunciation is identical with *yüeh,* when it means 'to please'" (*The Literary Mind,* 207, n. 21).

6. Liu Hsieh, *Wen-hsin tiao-lung* [*chu*], *chüan* 4, 1:328; see also Shih, *The Literary Mind*, 205–207.

7. *Wen-hsüan*, 1:241.

8. *Han Fei-tzu* [*chi-chieh*] [Collected interpretations of *Han Fei-tzu*], "Shui-nan" [Difficulty of persuasion], ed. Wang Hsien-shen, *Chu-tzu chi-ch'eng* ed., *chüan* 4, 60.

9. See ibid., *chüan* 7–*chüan* 14, 125–262.

10. Ssu-ma Chen's (T'ang dynasty) commentary on Ssu-ma Ch'ien (145–ca. 86 B.C.), *Shih-chi* [Records of the Grand Historian], "Han Fei lieh-chuan" [Biography of Han Fei], 10 vols. (Peking: Chung-hua shu-chü, 1959), *chüan* 63, 7:2148.

11. Ibid.

12. Ibid.

13. See Pan Ku, *Han-shu*, "I-wen chih," *chüan* 30, 6:1701; see also Liu Hsiang, *Han Fei Tzu shu-lu* [Bibliographic record of the *Han Fei Tzu*], in Yen K'o-chün ed., *Ch'üan shang-ku san-tai Ch'in Han San-kuo Liu-ch'ao wen*, vol. 1: *Ch'üan-Han wen* [Complete prose of the Han], *chüan* 37, 6a–b.

14. This type of writing also includes the late Han scholar Ying Shao's *Feng-su t'ung-i* [General interpretation of customs], and so forth.

15. Yung Jung, Chi Yün et al., eds., *Ssu-k'u ch'üan-shu tsung-mu*, *chüan* 91, 1:772.

16. See Pan Ku, *Han-shu*, "I-wen chih," *chüan* 30, 6:1727.s

17. See Lu Hsün, *Chung-kuo hsiao-shuo shih-lüeh*, 8:47; Liu Chao-yün, "Shih-shuo t'an-yüan."

18. See Pan Ku, *Han-shu*, "I-wen chih," *chüan* 30, 6:1727.

19. Liu Yeh-ch'iu suggests that the *Shih-shuo hsin-yü* was influenced by Liu Hsiang's *Hsin-hsü* and *Shuo-yüan* in style. Ning Chia-yü further elaborates Liu's idea and points out the similarity between the chapter titles of *Hsin-hsü, Shuo-yüan,* and *Shih-shuo hsin-yü*. Table 3 is basically adopted from Ning's essay. See Liu Yeh-ch'iu, *Wei-Chin Nan-Pei ch'ao hsiao-shuo* [Wei, Chin, and Southern and Northern dynasties *hsiao-shuo*] (Shanghai: Shanghai ku-chi ch'u-pan she, 1978), 22–23, and Ning, "'Shih-shuo t'i' ch'u-t'an," 87–90.

20. Liu Hsin's (d. 23) *Ch'i-lüeh* [Seven bibliographic categories] first set up this genre under the section of the "Philosophers." Liu Hsin's taxonomic scheme, including his definitions of genres, was later incorporated into the "Han Treatise" and overshadowed Chinese bibliographies throughout the imperial era. See Pan Ku, *Han-shu*, "I-wen chih," *chüan* 30, 6:1701.

21. *Lun-yü* [*chu-shu*], XIX, 4, *Shih-san ching chu-shu*, 2:2531; a comment by Tzu-hsia, with no reference to *hsiao-shuo*.

22. Pan Ku, *Han-shu*, "I-wen chih," *chüan* 30, 6:1745; translation mainly based on *The Indiana Companion to Traditional Chinese Literature*, 1986 ed., s.v. "Hsiao-shuo," by Kenneth Dewoskin; see also Laura Hua Wu, "From *Xiaoshuo* [*hsiao-shuo*] to Fiction:

Hu Yinglin's Genre Study of *Xiaoshuo,*" *Harvard Journal of Asiatic Studies* 55.2 (1995):340.

23. See Pan Ku, *Han-shu,* "I-wen chih," *chüan* 30, 6:1746. The ten philosophical schools listed in the "Han Treatise" include (1) *Ju-chia* (Confucian School), (2) *Tao-chia* (Taoist School), (3) *Yin-yang chia* (Yin-yang School), (4) *Fa-chia* (Legalist School), (5) *Ming-chia* (School of Names), (6) *Mo-chia* (Mohist School), (7) *Tsung-heng chia* (School of Diplomatists), (8) *Tsa-chia* (Miscellaneous School), (9) *Nung-chia* (Agricultural School), and (10) *Hsiao-shuo chia* (*Hsiao-shuo* School); see ibid., *chüan* 30, 6:1724–1746.

24. *The Indiana Companion to Traditional Chinese Literature,* 1986 ed., s.v. "Hsiao-shuo," by Kenneth Dewoskin.

25. See Pan Ku, *Han-shu,* "I-wen chih," *chüan* 30, 6:1744.

26. Wei Cheng et al., *Sui-shu,* "Ching-chi chih," *chüan* 34, 4:1012.

27. The "Shih-chih" [Ten treatises] of *Sui-shu* (actually the ten historical treatises of five dynasties: the Liang, the Ch'en, the Northern Ch'i, the Northern Chou, and the Sui), including the "Ching-chi chih," were compiled from 641 to 656. At least three scholars, Ling-hu Te-fen, Li Ch'un-feng, and Li Yen-shou (fl. mid-seventh cent.) involved in the compilation of the "Ten Treatises" also participated in the compilation of the *Chin-shu* during 646–648. See the prefaces to the *Sui-shu* (1:i) and the *Chin-shu* (1:i) by the editors of the Chung-hua shu-chü edition.

28. Liu Chih-chi, *Shih-t'ung* [*t'ung-shih*] [(Commentary on) Compendium of history], commentary by P'u Ch'i-lung, 2 vols. (Shanghai: Shanghai Ku-chi ch'u-panshe, 1978), *chüan* 17, 2:482.

29. See Wang Hsien-ch'ien, "*Shih-shuo hsin-yü hsü*" [Preface to the *Shih-shuo hsin-yü*], in *Shih-shuo hsin-yü,* 4 vols. (Ch'ang-sha: Ssu-hsien chiang-she, 1891), 1:1a–b.

30. Yung Jung, Chi Yün et al., eds., *Ssu-k'u ch'üan-shu tsung-mu, chüan* 140, 2:1182.

31. Mather, *Tales of the World,* xiii–xiv.

32. Ibid., xiv.

33. P'u Ch'i-lung, ed., *Shih-t'ung t'ung-shih, chüan* 17, 2:482.

34. Structuralist theory argues that each narrative has two parts: "a story, the content or chain of events (actions, happenings), plus what may be called the existents (characters, items of setting); and a discourse, that is, the expression, the means by which the content is communicated" (Seymour Chatman, *Story and Discourse,* 19).

35. The "Sui Treatise" categorizes all the books it has recorded into four sections, namely, *ching* (classics), *shih* (history), *tzu* (philosophy), and *chi* (prose and poetry, plus Taoist and Buddhist religious sūtras); see Wei Chen et al., *Sui-shu, chüan* 32–35, 4:903–1104.

36. Ibid., *chüan* 33, 4:982.

37. See ibid., *chüan* 33, 4:974–982.

38. The "Sui Treatise" lists twenty-five titles under the *hsiao-shuo* category; none of them repeats any of the fifteen titles listed under the same category in the "Han Treatise"; see ibid., *chüan* 34, 4:1011–1012.

39. See the *Tso-chuan*, the twenty-eighth year of Duke Hsi.

40. See the *Shih-ching*, "Ta-ya," "Pan."

41. Wei Cheng et al., *Sui-shu*, "Ching-chi chih," *chüan* 34, 4:1012.

42. Postscript to the *tzu* section, Wei Chen et al., *Sui-shu*, *chüan* 34, 4:1051.

43. Quoting Wang Ch'ung, *Lun-heng*, "Hsieh-tuan," Chiang Tung-fu maintains that, in the Han dynasty, writings other than Confucian teachings, which were written on the two-foot and four-inch long blocks, were written on one-foot blocks and therefore were called *tuan-shu;* see his "Chung-kuo hsiao-shuo kuan ti li-shih yen-chin" [Evolution of the Chinese perspective on *hsiao-shuo*], *Tientsin shih-ta hsüeh-pao (She-k'o pan)* 1992.1:56.

44. Huan T'an (24 B.C.–A.D. 56), *Hsin-lun* [New essay] (not extant), quoted from Li Shan's commentary on Li Ling, "Tsa-shih" [Miscellaneous poems], in Hsiao T'ung, ed., *Wen-hsüan*, *chüan* 31, 2:444; see also Kenneth Dewoskin's translation of this fragment in *The Indiana Companion to Traditional Chinese Literature*, 1986 ed., s.v. "*Hsiao-shuo.*" The *Sui-shu* compilers must have known about Huan T'an's definition of *hsiao-shuo* because the "Sui Treatise" includes Huan T'an's *Hsin-lun* in the "Confucian School" under the "Philosophers" section (*Sui-shu*, *chüan* 34, 4:998).

45. One may note the remarkable resemblance between Han Fei's opinion about *shuo* and Pan Ku's account of the operation of the nine estimable philosophical schools: "[The nine schools] all arose at the time when the [Chou] kings' principles declined and the lords of states endeavored to assume power. Each ruler of the time had his own likes and dislikes of ruling methods. Therefore, these nine schools arose simultaneously. Each school developed itself [in] one direction and promoted what it was good at. The scholars of each school galloped from one state to another, presenting their views to meet the lord's needs" (Pan Ku, *Han-shu*, "I-wen chih," *chüan* 30, 6:1746).

46. Mather, *Tales of the World*, xiv.

47. J. A. Cuddon defines fiction as "a vague and general term for an imaginative work, usually in prose. At any rate, it does not normally cover poetry and drama though both are a form of fiction in that they are moulded and contrived—or feigned. Fiction is now used in general of the novel, the short story, the *novella (qq.v.)* and related genres" (J. A. Cuddon, *A Dictionary of Literary Terms* [Penguin Books, 1982, 1987], s.v. "Fiction"). For detailed discussions of the evolution of the *hsiao-shuo* concept, see Wang Ch'i-chou, "Chung-kuo hsiao-shuo ch'i-yüan t'an-chi" [Tracing the origin of Chinese *hsiao-shuo*], *Wen-hsüeh i-ch'an* 1985.1:12–23; *The Indiana Companion to Traditional Chinese Literature*, 1986 ed., s.v. "*Hsiao-shuo,*" by Dewoskin; Chiang Tung-fu, "Chung-kuo hsiao-shuo kuan ti li-shih yen-chin," 55–62; Yang I, *Chung-kuo ku-tien hsiao-shuo shih-lun* [On the history of classical Chinese *hsiao-*

shuo] (Peking: Chung-kuo she-hui k'o-hsüeh ch'u-pan she, 1995); and Wu, "From *Xiaoshuo* to Fiction, 339–371.

48. Examples of this kind are too numerous to cite. Listed here are just a few representative works: Ch'en Yin-k'o, "Hsiao-yao yu Hsiang-Kuo i chi Chih Tun i t'an-yüan," "Shu *Shih-shuo hsin-yü* wen-hsüeh lei Chung Hui chuan Ssu-pen lun shih-pi t'iao hou" [On the episode "When Chung Hui had barely finished editing his *Treatise on the Four Basic Relations between Innate Ability and Human Nature*" in the "Wen-hsüeh" chapter in the *Shih-shuo hsin-yü*], *Chin-ming kuan ts'ung-kao ch'u-pien*, 41–47, "Chih Min-tu *hsüeh-shuo k'ao*," "T'ao Yüan-ming chih ssu-hsiang yü ch'ing-t'an chih kuan-hsi"; Donald Holzman, *Poetry and Politics: The Life and Works of Juan Chi* (Cambridge: Cambridge University Press, 1976); Mather, "Individualist Expressions of the Outsiders during the Six Dynasties"; T'ang Yung-t'ung, *Wei-Chin Hsüan-hsüeh lun-kao;* Tsung Pai-hua, "Lun *Shih-shuo hsin-yü* ho Chin-jen ti mei" [On the aesthetics of the *Shih-shuo hsin-yü* and the Chin people], *Hsing-ch'i p'ing-lun* 10 (January 1941):8–11; Yü Ying-shih, "Han-Chin chih chi shih chih hsin tzu-chüeh yü hsin ssu-ch'ao," "Ming-chiao wei-chi yü Wei-Chin shih-feng ti yen-pien," "Individualism and the Neo-Taoist Movement"; and E. Zürcher, *The Buddhist Conquest of China*, 1:81–145, for which Zürcher acknowledges that the *Shih-shuo hsin-yü* is the "main source" (ibid., 1:93).

49. For example, Y. W. Ma cites the *Shih-shuo hsin-yü* as an example of fictional work, or of the fictional group of *pi-chi*, in Chinese literature; see *The Indiana Companion to Traditional Chinese Literature*, 1986 ed., s.v. "Fiction" and *"Pi-chi,"* by Y. W. Ma.

50. Important works of this kind include Ning Chia-yü, "*Shih-shuo t'i* ch'u-t'an," 87–105; and Yang I, "Han Wei Liu-ch'ao *Shih-shuo t'i* hsiao-shuo ti liu-pien" [The evolution of the *Shih-shuo t'i hsiao-shuo* during the Han, Wei, and Six Dynasties], *Chung-kuo she-hui k'o-hsüeh* 1991.4:85–99.

Introduction to Part 2

1. Ch'ien Fen's "Preface" to Liang Wei-shu (1589–1662), *Yü-chien tsun-wen* [Distinguished accounts of the jade sword], 2 vols. Reprint of the 1657 Tz'u-lin t'ang edition (Shanghai: Shanghai ku-chi ch'u-pan she, 1986), 1a–b.

2. Ch'ien Tseng, *Tu-shu min-ch'iu chi* [Records of a diligent reader] (Peking: Shu-mu wen-hsien ch'u-pan she, 1983), 78.

3. Mao's preface to Wang Cho, *Chin Shih-shuo*, v.

Chapter 4: Between Order and Disorder

1. Michel Foucault, *The Order of Things: An Archaeology of the Human Sciences* (New York: Vintage Books, 1973), xx: "A 'system of elements'—a definition of the segments by which the resemblances and differences can be shown, the types of variation by which those segments can be affected, and, lastly, the threshold above which there

is a difference and below which there is a similitude—is indispensable for the establishment of even the simplest form of order."

2. *Lun-yü* [*chu-shu*], XI, 3, *Shih-san ching chu-shu,* 2:2498.

3. For the etymological origin of the concept of *te,* see Donald J. Munro, *The Concept of Man in Early China* (Stanford: Stanford University Press, 1969), 185–197; for its meaning in Confucianism, see ibid., 106, 108–109, 125, and 147.

4. Jao's preface to Yang Yung, *Shih-shuo hsin-yü chiao-chien* (Hong Kong: Ta-chung shu-chü, 1969), i.

5. See Liu Chao-yün, "*Shih-shuo* t'an-yüan,*" 8. The chapter order of the *Shih-shuo hsin-yü* seems to have remained undisturbed since the day the book was compiled (Liu Chao-yün's arguments are obviously based on this assumption). Mather believes: "Although Tung Fen in his colophon to the 1138 block-print edition, which is the ancestor of all modern texts, states explicitly that Yen Shu (991–1055), whose version he followed, had reduced an original forty-five chapters *(p'ien)* to the present thirty-six by 'completely eliminating all redundancies,' I find it difficult to believe that he actually disturbed the order of Liu I-ch'ing's text, since the chapter titles and numbers in the T'ang fragment correspond exactly to those of the modern text" ("Introduction" to *Tales of the World,* xxvii).

6. Mather translates *te-shih* as "successes and failures." Chang Yung-yen maintains that *te-shih* is a *p'ien-cheng fu-tz'u* (leaning compound) meaning *kuo-shih,* mistakes and failures *(Shih-shuo hsin-yü tz'u-tien* [Dictionary of the *Shih-shuo hsin-yü*] [Chengtu: Szechwan jen-min ch'u-pan she, 1992], s.v. *Te).*

7. Mather's note to this episode: "In the version of this story quoted from *TPYL* [*T'ai-p'ing yü-lan*], 641, Hsien-chih says, 'I have nothing to confess. It's only my having sent away the daughter of the Ch'ih family which causes me regret'" (*Tales of the World,* 19).

8. Liu Chün offers two references in his commentary regarding this unfortunate situation: (1) Wang Hsien-chih had been married to Ch'ih Tao-mao and later divorced her, and (2) he was decreed to marry Princess Yü-yao. It is, however, unclear whether these two events were related.

9. *Ch'un-hua ko tieh* [Ch'un-hua collection of calligraphy], *chüan* 9, quoted in Yü, *Shih-shuo hsin-yü chien-shu,* 41, n. 3 to 1/39.

10. Graham, *Studies in Chinese Philosophy,* 7.

11. *Lun-yü* [*chu-shu*], XVII, 2, *Shih-san ching chu-shu,* 2:2524; see also Graham, *Studies in Chinese Philosophy,* 18.

12. *Hsün-tzu* [*chi-chieh*], ch. 22, *chüan* 16, 274; trans. Graham, *Studies in Chinese Philosophy,* 15.

13. Ibid.

14. For a survey of various theories of human nature in the history of Chinese philosophy, see Wang Ch'ung (27–91), *Lun-heng* [Balanced discussions], "Pen-hsing" [Fundamental human nature], *Chu-tzu chi-ch'eng* ed., 28–30; Graham, *Studies in Chi-*

nese Philosophy, 7–66; and Wang Pao-hsien, *Cheng-shih Hsüan-hsüeh* (Chi-nan: Ch'i-lu shu-she, 1987), 363–411.

15. The Wei nine-rank system adopted Pan Ku's hierarchical approach—but not his good/bad distinction—classifying candidates for official posts by their pedigree, moral qualities, and abilities; see Tu Yu, *T'ung-tien, chüan* 14, 77. Ko Hung's (284–363) *Pao-p'u tzu,* "Hsing-p'in" [Ranking of personalities], also followed the Han classification but simplified it into a good versus bad dichotomy, with thirty-nine good types and forty-four bad types; see *Pao-p'u tzu wai-p'ien [chiao-chien]* [(Commentary on) *Pao-p'u tzu,* the outer chapters], commentary by Yang Ming-chao, 2 vols. (Peking: Chung-hua shu-chü, 1991), *chüan* 22, 1:532–548.

16. Kung-ch'üan Hsiao writes:

> The term "superior man" [*chün-tzu*] is to be found in the *Odes* and the *Documents;* it was by no means an invention of Confucius. . . . However, in the *Odes* and the *Documents,* the term refers to a social position and not to the individual's moral character. . . . Confucius's use of the term *chün-tzu* in the *Analects* includes exclusive references to status, exclusive references to character, and uses in which the reference is to character and status simultaneously. . . . It may be inferred that the first of Confucius's meanings in his use of the term "superior man" completely follows that encountered in the *Odes* and the *Documents,* while his second meaning must have been his own invention, and the third meaning follows the old usage but slightly alters its import. The old meaning of the word contains the general implication that the man who possessed rank should cultivate his virtue, while Confucius tended towards an emphasis on the cultivation of virtue in order to acquire rank. (*A History of Chinese Political Thought,* 2 vols., trans. F. W. Mote [Princeton, NJ: Princeton University Press, 1979], 1:117–119).

17. In, respectively, *Shih-san ching chu-shu,* 2:2518, 2462, 2471, 2504, 2508, and 2522; cf. D. C. Lau, trans., *The Analects,* 134, 73, 74, 122, 123, and 140.

18. *Lun-yü* [*chu-shu*], XII, 11, *Shih-san ching chu-shu,* 2:2503–2504; cf. Derk Bodde, in Fung, *History of Chinese Philosophy,* 1:60.

19. Fung, *History of Chinese Philosophy,* trans. Bodde, 1:60.

20. Graham, *Studies in Chinese Philosophy,* 18.

21. Pan Ku's opening paragraph is as follows:

> Since the written language had been invented, what our ancestors could get to know is recorded in the classics and their commentaries. Until T'ang [Yao] and Yü [Shun], emperors and kings had titles and posthumous titles [to comment on their deeds] whereas their assistants did not [i.e., the classics and their commentaries would make comments on the rulers' behavior but not on their assistants]. Yet the philosophers did make some comments on them [the assistants]. Although these comments were not by Confucius, they were recorded in various writings, with the eventual purpose of glorifying the good and revealing the bad, in order to admonish later generations. Therefore, I broadly incorpo-

rated this kind of material into my classification of people (*Han-shu, chüan* 20, 3:861).

22. *Lun-yü* [*chu-shu*], VII, 34, *Shih-san ching chu-shu*, 2:2484; trans. Lau, *Analects*, 90.

23. This line, quoted in a rather out-of-context manner, was extracted from the following conversation in the *Analects*: "Tzu-kung asked, 'If there were a man who gave extensively to the common people and brought help to the multitude, what would you think of him? Could he be called benevolent?' The master said, 'It is no longer a matter of benevolence with such a man. If you must describe him, "sage" is, perhaps, the right word'" (ibid., VI, 30, *Shih-san ching chu-shu*, 2:2479; trans. Lau, *Analects*, 85).

24. Ibid., V, 19, *Shih-san ching chu-shu*, 2:2474.

25. Ibid., XVI, 9, *Shih-san ching chu-shu*, 2:2522; trans. Lau, *Analects*, 140.

26. Ibid., VI, 21, *Shih-san ching chu-shu*, 2:2479.

27. Ibid., XVII, 3, *Shih-san ching chu-shu*, 2:2524; trans. Lau, *Analects*, 143.

28. Pan Ku, *Han-shu, chüan* 20, 3:861.

29. See *Meng-tzu* [*chu-shu*], XI, 2, *Shih-san ching chu-shu*, 2:2748.

30. *Lun-yü* [*chu-shu*], VII, 26, *Shih-san ching chu-shu*, 2:2483.

31. *Ch'un-ch'iu fan-lu* [Luxuriant dew of the spring and autumn annals], "Shih-hsing" [Substantial nature], *Ssu-pu ts'ung-k'an* ed., *chüan* 10, 7b–8a.

32. See *Lun-yü* [*chu-shu*], XIII, 20, *Shih-san ching chu-shu*, 2:2508.

33. *Ch'un-ch'iu fan-lu*, "Shih-hsing," *chüan* 10, 7b–8a; see also Fung, *History of Chinese Philosophy*, 2:37.

34. See *Hsün-tzu* [*chi-chieh*], chapter 23, "Hsing-o" [Human nature is bad], *Chu-tzu chi-ch'eng* ed., *chüan* 17, 293; see also Burton Watson, trans., *Hsün-tzu: Basic Writings* (New York: Columbia University Press, 1963), 162–163.

35. Fung Yu-lan points out that Pan Ku's *Po-hu t'ung* [Comprehensive interpretation of classics from White-Tiger Hall] "represents the theories of the New Text school, and much of it agrees with the doctrines of Tung Chung-shu" (*History of Chinese Philosophy*, 2:22).

36. For the difference between the New Text and the Old Text schools of Han Confucianism, see ibid., 2:7–167, particularly 133–136.

37. Wang Ch'ung, *Lun-heng*, "Pen-hsing," 30.

38. See *Hsün-tzu* [*chi-chieh*], chapter 23, "Hsing-o," *chüan* 17, 295–300, and "Ch'üan-hsüeh" [Encouraging learning], *chüan* 1, 11–12; see also Watson, trans., *Hsün-tzu*, 166–171 and 22–23. For Tung Chung-shu's theory of human nature, see his *Ch'un-ch'iu fan-lu*, "Shen-ch'a ming-hao" [Profound examination of names and titles] and "Shih-hsing," *chüan* 10, 1a–7a and 7a–8b.

39. Nü-wa, the legendary mother of the Chinese people, is an exception among the benevolent women in that she is not associated to any man (*Han-shu, chüan* 20, 3:864).

And Yu-hsin is an exception among the bad women in that she is the sage Yü's mother (ibid., 3:876).

40. Liu Shao, *Jen-wu chih*, "Preface," 3.

41. *Lun-yü* [*chu-shu*], VI, 29, *Shih-san ching chu-shu*, 2:2479: "Supreme indeed is the Mean as a moral virtue!" (trans. Lau, 85).

42. Referring to Confucius' words in *Lun-yü* [*chu-shu*], XI, 19, *Shih-san ching chu-shu*, 2:2499: "[Yen] Hui has probably reached the perfection of [virtue]"; for the interpretation of this line see Yang Po-chün, *Lun-yü i-chu*, 1:115–116.

43. *Lun-yü* [*chu-shu*], XVII, 8, *Shih-san ching chu-shu*, 2:2525: "The Master said, 'Yu, have you heard about the six qualities and the six attendant faults?' 'No.' 'Be seated and I shall tell you. To love benevolence without loving learning is liable to lead to foolishness. To love cleverness without loving learning is liable to lead to deviation from the right path. To love trustworthiness in word without loving learning is liable to lead to harmful behavior. To love forthrightness without loving learning is liable to lead to intolerance. To love courage without loving learning is liable to lead to insubordination. To love unbending strength without loving learning is liable to lead to indiscipline'" (trans. Lau, 144–145).

44. *Lun-yü* [*chu-shu*], XIII, 21, *Shih-san ching chu-shu*, 2:2508: "Having failed to find moderate men for associates, one would, if there were no alternative, have to turn to be uninhibited and rigid. The uninhibited is enterprising, while the rigid will reject certain kinds of action." Cf. Lau, 122.

45. See *Lun-yü* [*chu-shu*], VIII, 16, *Shih-san ching chu-shu*, 2:2487.

46. *Lun-yü* [*chu-shu*], II, 10, *Shih-san ching chu-shu*, 2:2462: "Look at the means a man employs, observe the path he takes and examine where he feels at home. In what way is a man's true character hidden from view?" (trans. Lau, 64).

47. Liu Shao, *Jen-wu chih*, "Preface," 4; cf. Shryock, trans., *Study of Human Abilities*, 3.

48. T'ang Yung-t'ung points out that Liu Shao's *Jen-wu chih* adopts Taoist principles; see "Tu *Jen-wu chih*," 209–213.

49. Liu Shao, *Jen-wu chih*, *chüan* A, 6.

50. Ibid., *chüan* A, 7, trans. Shryock, *Study of Human Abilities*, 102.

51. Ibid.; trans. cf. Shryock, *Study of Human Abilities*, 102–103.

52. Ibid., *chüan* A, 12; "Preface," 4.

53. *Lao-tzu*, ch. 37, in *Wang Pi chi chiao-shih*, 1:91.

54. See Liu Shao, *Jen-wu chih*, *chüan* A, 7-12, Shryock, *Study of Human Abilities*, 102–111.

55. Hsiao T'ung, ed., *Wen-hsüan*, *chüan* 52, 3:720; trans. Stephen Owen, ed., *An Anthology of Chinese Literature* (New York: W. W. Norton, 1996), 360–361.

56. See Liu Shao, *Jen-wu chih*, *chüan* A, 6–12.

57. Tung Chung-shu, *Ch'un-ch'iu fan-lu*, "Shen-ch'a ming-hao," *chüan* 10, 6a.

58. Ibid.; trans. Bodde, Fung, *History of Chinese Philosophy*, 2:36. For Tung Chung-shu's explication of the "three bonds" *(san-kang)*, see ibid., 2:42–43. Tung, however, did not explicate the meaning of the "five rules" *(wu-chi)*, which were later elaborated into "six rules" *(liu-chi)* by Pan Ku in his *Pai-hu t'ung-te lun* (see ibid., 2:43–44). For Pan Ku's definition of the "three bonds and six rules," see Ying-shih Yü's introduction quoted in chapter 2.

59. I believe the character *hsing* (nature) is missing here in the original Chinese text, judging from the similarity between this passage and one in Tung Chung-shu, *Ch'un-ch'iu fan-lu*, "Shen-ch'a ming-hao": "What Heaven does [for human beings] goes to a certain point and then stops there. What stops inside of [a human being] is called his Heavenly [endowed] nature; and what stops outside of [a human being] is called human affairs. Human affairs stay outside of human nature, yet human nature cannot but complete itself along with them" *(chüan* 10, 4b).

60. Tung Chung-shu, *Ch'un-ch'iu fan-lu*, "Shih-hsing," *chüan* 10, 7b; see also Fung, *History of Chinese Philosophy*, 2:34.

61. For detailed discussions of Han and Wei-Chin interpretations of the *Tao* of Heaven and its connection with human nature, see T'ang Yung-t'ung, "Wang Pi sheng-jen yu ch'ing i shih" [Interpretation of Wang Pi's hypothesis that the sage has emotions], *Wei-Chin Hsüan-hsüeh lun-kao, T'ang Yung-t'ung hsüeh-shu lun-wen chi*, 254–263; and Wang Pao-hsien, *Cheng-shih Hsüan-hsüeh*, 363–389.

62. Liu Chün quotes, with slight variation from the *Chuang-tzu [chi-shih]*:

> The *Chuang-tzu* says: "As for the piping of Heaven, it blows through the myriad openings, each in a different way, letting each be itself." Kuo Hsiang's *Commentary* says: "Since Nothing [*wu*] is nonexistent, it cannot produce Something [*yu*], and if Something has not yet been produced, it, in turn, cannot produce anything either. This being the case, who is it who produces production? Clod-like it produces itself, that's all. If it is not produced by a Self [*wo*], and if a Self does not produce other objects [*wu*], and objects do not produce a Self, then they are just so of themselves [*tzu-jan*], that's all. We call this the 'naturally-so' [*t'ien-jan*]. The naturally-so is not created; that's why we use the word 'Heaven' [*t'ien*] in speaking of it, because this is a means of clarifying its self-so-ness."

63. Kuo, ed., *Chuang-tzu chi-shih*, 1:50.

64. *Meng-tzu [chu-shu]*, XI, 2, *Shih-san ching chu-shu*, 2:2748; trans. D. C. Lau, *Mencius* (Penguin, 1970), 236–237. For detailed discussions of this paragraph and the Mencian theory of human nature, see Lau, trans., *Mencius*, Appendix 5, 235–243; and Graham, *Studies in Chinese Philosophy*, 7–66.

65. *Meng-tzu [chu-shu]*, XI, 2, *Shih-san ching chu-shu*, 2:2748; trans. Lau, *Mencius*, 237.

66. 1 *li* = 0.3 mile.

67. Liu Chün suggests that Liu T'an's analogy between human nature and poured water is derived from Kuo Hsiang's above commentary on the *Chuang-tzu*. Liu Chün's suggestion is very possibly correct, since the basic idea expressed in Kuo Hsiang's *Commentary on the Chuang-tzu*, the so-called *tu-hua* (self-transformation), is one of the

major *Hsüan-hsüeh* trends that flourished during Liu T'an's time. See Kuo, ed., *Chuang-tzu chi-shih*, 1:111; see also T'ang, "Wei-Chin Hsüan-hsüeh liu-pieh lüeh-lun," 233–244; Fung, *History of Chinese Philosophy*, 2:207–210.

68. See Morohashi, Tetsuji, *Daikanwa jiten* [The great Chinese-Japanese dictionary], 12 vols. (Tokyo: Taishūkan-shoten, 1960).

69. Wu Su-kung, *Ming yü-lin* [Ming forest of accounts] (*Pi lin-lang ts'ung-shu* ed., 1681), "Fan-li" [Compilation notes], 1b.

70. Originally quoted in Huang K'an (488–545), *Lun-yü i-shu*, which was in turn quoted in Liu Pao-nan (1791–1855) *Lun-yü cheng-i* [(Orthodox commentary on) The Analects of Confucius], *Chu-tzu chi-ch'eng* ed., *chüan* 14, 239.

71. Wang Pi, *Lao-tzu Tao te ching chu*, in *Wang Pi chi* [*chiao-shih*], 1:93. Wang Pao-hsien points out that Wang Pi's interpretation of the relationship between *Tao* and *te* is that between *t'i* (substratum) and *yung* (function), and *te* is inferior and affiliated to *Tao*, different from Han Confucians' juxtaposition of *Tao* and *te* as two equally important concepts; see his *Cheng-shih Hsüan-hsüeh*, 213–230.

72. Graham, *Disputers of the Tao*, 497.

73. Shryock also notices these two meanings of *te*, as he says: "The English word virtue means 'goodness,' and also 'power, force, energy.' So does the Chinese term" (*Study of Human Abilities*, 31).

74. Graham, *Disputers of the Tao*, 13.

75. Wang Pi, *Lao-tzu Tao te ching chu*, in *Wang Pi chi* [*chiao-shih*], 1:93-94; see also Richard John Lynn, trans., *The Classic of the Way and Virtue: A New Translation of the Tao-te ching of Laozi* [*Lao-tzu*] *as Interpreted by Wang Bi* [*Pi*] (New York: Columbia University Press, 1999), 119–127.

76. Murakami Yoshimi has also discussed diverse Wei-Chin understandings and performances of *te* as reflected in the *Shih-shuo hsin-yü* and believes such diversity results from the Wei-Chin pursuit of *chen*, sincerity or genuineness; see his "Gi Shin ni okeru toku no tayōsei—*Sesetsu shingo* no shisō" [On Wei-Chin diversity of *te*—*Shih-shuo hsin-yü*'s thought], in *Suzuki Hakushi koki kinen tōyōgaku ronsō* [Collected essays on East Asian Studies in celebration of Dr. Suzuki's seventieth birthday] (Tokyo: Meitoku shuppansha, 1972), 549–570.

77. *Lao-tzu*, ch. 77, *Wang Pi chi chiao-shih*, 1:186.

78. Trans. Mather, *Tales of the World*, 11.

79. See Juan Chi, "Ta Chuang lun" [On understanding Chuang-tzu], in Yen K'o-chün, ed., *Ch'üan shang-ku san-tai Ch'in Han San-kuo Liu-ch'ao wen*, vol. 2: *Ch'üan San-kuo wen*, *chüan* 45, 8a–11b; see also Donald Holzman, *Poetry and Politics: The Life and Works of Juan Chi* (*A.D. 210–263*) (Cambridge: Cambridge University Press, 1976), 99–109.

80. In *Hsi K'ang chi* [*chiao-chu*], *chüan* 3, 146; trans. Henricks, *Essays of Hsi K'ang*, 24; see also 11–12 for Henricks' discussion of the connection between Hsi K'ang's approach of nourishing life and that in the *Chuang-tzu* and popular Taoism. For the

Yangist fidelity to one's nature and life and the connection between Yangism and Taoism, see Graham, *Disputers of the Tao*, 56–59.

81. See *Lun-yü* [*chu-shu*], VII, 16, *Shih-san ching chu-shu*, 2:2482.

82. The earliest example of "ya-liang" cited in Morohashi, *Daikanwa jiten*, 11:996, is in Yang Hsiu (175–219), "Ta Lin-tzu hou chien" [Letter to the Marquis Ling-tzu (Ts'ao Chih)].

83. Kuo, ed., *Chuang-tzu chi-shih, chüan* 7b, 3:725; trans. Watson, *Complete Works of Chuang Tzu*, 231.

84. Ibid.; see also Watson, *Complete Works of Chuang Tzu*, 231.

85. See Liu Pao-nan, *Lun-yü cheng-I, chüan* 14, 238.

86. As quoted in Wang Shu-min, "*Shih-shuo hsin-yü* wen-hsüeh p'ien pu-chien" [Supplementary commentary on the chapter "Wen-hsüeh" of the *Shih-shuo hsin-yü*], *Nanyang ta-hsüeh hsüeh-pao* [Nanyang University journal] 8–9 (1974/1975):12.

87. As Li Tz'u-ming points out in his note to episode 4/66, the *Shih-shuo* author's "intention is to divide all the episodes here. Before this, all belongs to scholarship, and after this, all belongs to literature" (quoted in Yü, *Shih-shuo hsin-yü chien-shu*, 1:244, n. 1 to 4/66). According to Li Yen-shou, *Nan-shih*, in 438–439, Emperor Wen of the Liu-Sung (r. 424–453) ordered four academies institutionalized—namely, *Ju-hsüeh* [Confucian learning], *Hsüan-hsüeh* [Abstruse learning], *Shih-hsüeh* [Historiographic learning], and *Wen-hsüeh* [Literature?] (6 vols. [Peking: Chung-hua shu-chü, 1975], *chüan* 2, 1:45–46). Scholars usually take this record as evidence for the earliest date at which the term *wen-hsüeh* was separated from scholarship and came to stand for literature only, similar to today's concept of *wen-hsüeh*. But what *wen-hsüeh* means in the *Nan-shih* is unclear. For the sake of accuracy, I would like to take the *Shih-shuo hsin-yü*, which was certainly compiled before 433 (when Hsieh Ling-yün [385–433] was executed, of whom the *Shih-shuo hsin-yü* has a favorable account), as the first solid record indicating the separation of literature—*wen*—from scholarship—*hsüeh*. For the *Shih-shuo hsin-yü*'s function in the evolution of the concept *wen-hsüeh*, see also Fu Hsi-jen, "*Shih-shuo* ssu-k'o tui *Lun-yü* ssu-k'o ti yin-hsi yü shan-pien" [The *Shih-shuo hsin-yü*'s continuation and variation of the four divisions in the *Analects of Confucius*], *Tan-chiang hsüeh-pao* 12 (March 1974):120–122; Wang Shu-min, "*Shih-shuo hsin-yü* wen-hsüeh p'ien pu-chien," 12; Cheng Hsüeh-t'ao, "Tu *Shih-shuo hsin-yü* wen-hsüeh p'ien cha-chi" [Notes on reading the *Shih-shuo hsin-yü*], *Hsü-chou shih-fan ta-hsüeh hsüeh-pao* 1982.2:9–14; and Liu Chao-yün, "*Shih-shuo* chung ti wen-hsüeh kuan-tien" [Literary viewpoint in the *Shih-shuo*], *Sinkiang ta-hsüeh hsüeh-pao* (*Che-hsüeh she-hui k'o-hsüeh*) 1985.3:97–98.

88. Quoted in Liu Chün's commentary on the *Shih-shuo hsin-yü*, 4/69; trans. Mather, *Tales of the World*, 129–130, n. 2 to 4/69.

89. See Mather, *Tales of the World*, 391, n. 1 to 23/52.

90. Quoted in P'ei Sung-chih's commentary on *San-kuo chih, Wei-shu*, "Chung Hui chuan" [Biography of Chung Hui], 3:795.

91. T'ang Yung-t'ung, "Wang Pi sheng-jen yu ch'ing i shih," 255.

92. Ibid., 258.

93. Mather's note: "Ts'ao P'ei-ts'ui, d. ca. 240. The daughter of a cousin of Ts'ao Ts'ao who was married to Hsün Ts'an. His extreme devotion to her and frank admiration for feminine beauty shocked his contemporaries" *(Tales of the World,* 579).

94. The original Chinese text has only "P'ei-ling" (Director P'ei). Whereas Mather takes it as referring to P'ei Wei (267–300) *(Tales of the World,* 485), Yü Chia-hsi attributes it to P'ei K'ai *(Shih-shuo hsin-yü chien-shu,* "Index," 43, s.v. P'ei K'ai). I follow Yü's designation because not only were P'ei K'ai's dates closer to Hsün Ts'an's, but also he was famous for sticking to the pattern of etiquette (see *Shih-shuo hsin-yü,* 23/11).

95. *Lun-yü [chu-shu],* I, 7, *Shih-san ching chu-shu,* 2:2458. Mather points out that Hsün Ts'an's remark is a parody of this phrase *(Tales of the World,* 485, n. 1 to 35/2). My translation follows Yang Po-chün's interpretation *(Lun-yü i-chu,* 1:5, n. 2 to I, 7).

96. See Yang Po-chün's discussion of this matter, *Lun-yü i-chu,* 1:5, n. 2 to I, 7.

97. Mather's note to the *Shih-shuo hsin-yü,* 35/6, *Tales of the World,* 488.

98. See Yü Ying-shih, *Chung-kuo chih-shih chieh-ts'eng shih-lun,* 346.

99. See the "seven rules for divorcing a wife" *(ch'i-ch'u chih t'iao)* cited in chapter 2, n. 31.

100. See also the case of Hsieh An's wife, Lady Liu. Although denigrated as a stereotype of jealousy in a contemporary source, Yü T'ung-chih's *Tu-chi* [Records of jealousy], she is highly regarded in the *Shih-shuo hsin-yü* as a worthy woman for preventing her husband from indulging too much in singing girls (19/23). See also Yü Chia-hsi's commentary on this episode.

101. See Marina H. Sung, "The Chinese *Lieh-nü* Tradition," in Richard W. Guisso and Stanley Johannesen, eds., *Women in China* (Youngstown, NY: Philo Press, 1981), 63–74.

102. See Liu Hsiang's prefaces to the seven chapters of the *[Ku] Lieh-nü chuan* [Biographies of (Ancient) exemplary women], *Ts'ung-shu chi-ch'eng hsin-pien* ed. (101:672-705), "Mu-lu" [Table of contents], i–ix.

103. For example, it appears in the *Lun-yü* twenty-five times; see Yang Po-chün, *Lun-yü i-chu,* 303.

104. *Shih-ching,* "Ta-ya," "Chan-yang," quoted in Liu Hsiang, *[Ku] Lieh-nü chuan, chüan* 7, 190.

105. Ibid., 189. Liu Hsiang describes Mo Hsi: "Mo Hsi was Hsia Chieh's consort. She had a beautiful appearance but lacked virtue; reckless and evil, she did not follow the Way. She had a woman's [body] but a man's mind, and, [like a man,] she carried a sword and wore a cap." The original text has *hsing,* "behavior," rather than *hsing,* "body" or "form." Since the phrase "carrying a sword and wearing a cap" is used more to describe her appearance, I believe *hsing* (behavior) here is a "phonetic loan character" *(chia-chieh tzu)* for *hsing* (body or form).

106. For the bride's father Chu-ko Tan's deeds and personality, see *Shih-shuo hsin-yü,* 9/4. See also chapter 2 for a more detailed discussion of this episode.

107. My retranslation.

108. Notes Yü Chia-hsi: "This episode comments that Lady Wang, though a woman, car-ries a gentleman's style, and therefore Lady Ku cannot come up to her. . . . That Tao-yün, as a woman, has a Bamboo Grove aura is enough to prove her a female gentle-man. As for [Nun Chi's] comment that Lady Ku is the full flowering of the inner chamber, it only indicates that she is an outstanding woman, that's all. Although [the *Shih-shuo* author] does not specify who is superior and who is inferior, the difference reveals itself. This is the beauty of the Chin rhetoric" (*Shih-shuo hsin-yü chien-shu*, 2:698, n. 1 to 19/30).

109. As typified in the *Shang-shu* [*cheng-i*] [(Orthodox commentary on) Book of docu-ments], "Ta-Yü mo" [Counsels of the Great Yü]: "No men of virtue and talents [*hsien*] will be neglected away from court; and the myriad States will all enjoy repose" (*Shih-san ching chu-shu*, *chüan* 4, 1:134); trans. Legge, *The Chinese Classics*, Vol. III, *The Shoo King*, 53; see also *Lun-yü*, IV, 17; VI, 11; XV, 14; etc.

110. See, for example, *Lun-yü*, II, 19, 20; III, 25; XII, 22, 28; XVI, 11; XX, 2; etc.

111. *Lao-tzu*, ch. 37, *Wang Pi chi* [*chiao-shih*], 1:91.

112. For Liu Chün's commentary and Yü Chia-hsi's interpretation of this episode, see the *Shih-shuo hsin-yü chien-shu*, 2:669–671.

113. *Huai-nan tzu*, "Shuo-shan" [Interpreting the mountain]: "There was once a person who was giving her daughter to marriage. She instructed her daughter: 'You go! Be careful not to do any good.' The daughter said: 'If I don't do good, then may I do no-good?' The mother responded: 'If even good may not be done, how much less no-good!' This instruction is meant to keep the daughter's natural endowment intact" (*Chu-tzu chi-ch'eng* ed., *chüan* 16, 274). For an introduction to Yangism see Graham, *Disputers of the Tao*, 53–59; for the inclusion of Yangism in the *Huan-nan tzu*, see ibid., 54.

114. Shan T'ao was appointed the head of the Selection Bureau because of his perspic-uous "recognition and judgment of human character types"; see Fang Hsüan-ling et al., *Chin-shu*, "Shan T'ao chuan" [Biography of Shan T'ao], *chüan* 43, 4:1223; and *Shih-shuo hsin-yü*, 18/3.

115. The "Sui Treatise" records the two-*chüan* collection of Hsieh Tao-yün's literary works (*chüan* 35, 4:1070). For a detailed discussion of Hsieh Tao-yün's poetic accom-plishments in relation to a widespread interest in and respect for women's poetic tal-ents during the Six Dynasties, see Kang-i Sun Chang, "Ming-Qing Women Poets and the Notions of 'Talent' and 'Morality'," in Huters, Wong, and Yu, eds., *Culture and State*, 244–245.

116. A similar story also tells how Hsieh An's wife Lady Liu peeps at her husband's guests and then criticizes Hsieh An for befriending unworthy men. For this reason, she con-tends, her husband cannot come up to her brother, Liu T'an. On hearing her words, Hsieh An appears "deeply embarrassed" (*Shih-shuo hsin-yü*, 26/17).

117. Since the Han dynasty, "husband" has also been called *so-t'ien*, meaning "what [a wife] takes as her heaven"; see P'an Yüeh (247–300), *Kua-fu fu* [Rhyme-prose on a

widow], in Hsiao T'ung, ed., *Wen-hsüan, chüan* 16, 1:233; see also Li Shan's commentary on the term.

118. See Yü Chia-hsi, *Shih-shuo hsin-yü chien-shu*, 2:663, n. 1 to the title "Hsien-yüan."

119. Mather's original translation of this line, *"hou geng tse chih,"* is "afterward proceeded to send him a bill for it"; retranslation according to Chou and Wang, *Ma-i shang-tui*, 246.

120. For the definitions of these two terms see Makeham, *Name and Actuality*, xiii–xiv.

121. The text appears in Yü Ai's biography, Fang Hsüan-ling et al., *Chin-shu, chüan* 50, 5:1395; Mather has rendered the text into English *(Tales of the World*, 132–133, n. 1 to 4/75).

122. For example, based on Jao Tsung-i's moral reading of the *Shih-shuo* classification, Fu Hsi-jen believes that the *Shih-shuo* author takes the "four divisions" as the guideline *(ching*, lit., warp) and the other thirty-two chapter titles as its elaboration *(wei*, lit., weft), and tries to distribute all the *wei* categories under the four *ching*; see his "*Shih-shuo* ssu-k'o tui *Lun-yü* ssu-k'o ti yin-hsi yü shan-pien," 101–123.

Chapter 5: Using Body to Depict Spirit

1. Paraphrasing Rawdon Wilson's "The Bright Chimera: Character as a Literary Term" *(Critical Inquiry* 5 [1979]:725–749), Baruch Hochman specifies the four causes that form the entire process of characterization: material, efficient, formal, and final. Hochman says: "The material cause, as Wilson sees it, is the writer, in whose imagination characters take form. The efficient cause is the text, within which the characters are projected. The formal cause is the artifice that forms, generates, or precipitates character within the text, so that it is 'there' in the text for us to appropriate. And the final cause is the impact on us of those figures, an impact that has deep moral and psychological roots and implications in human experience" *(Character in Literature*, 32).

2. Such as referring to divine beings in the *Chou-li* and Ch'ü Yüan's "Chiu-ko" [Nine songs] and mysterious things in the *I-ching*; see *Tz'u-yüan*, s.v. *Shen*.

3. *Chuang-tzu*, "T'ien Tzu-fang": "The perfect Man may stare at the blue heavens above, dive into the Yellow Springs below, ramble to the end of the eight directions, yet his spirit and bearing [*shen-ch'i*] undergo no change" (Kuo, ed., *Chuang-tzu chi-shih, chüan* 7b, 3:725; trans. Watson, *Complete Works of Chuang Tzu*, 231).

4. *Chuang-tzu*, "Yang-sheng chu": "The swamp pheasant has to walk ten paces for one peck and a hundred paces for one drink, but it doesn't want to be kept in a cage. In high spirits [*shen-wang*], it ignores [mundane issues such as] why good is regarded as good" (My translation following Kuo Hsiang's commentary; see Kuo, ed., *Chuang-tzu chi-shih, chüan* 2a, 1:126; see also Watson, *Complete Works of Chuang Tzu*, 52).

5. *Chuang-tzu*, "Ch'i-wu lun": "To wear out your spirit and intelligence [*shen-ming*]

trying to make things into one without realizing that they are all the same" (Kuo, ed., *Chuang-tzu chi-shih, chüan* 1b, 1:70; see also Watson, *Complete Works of Chuang Tzu,* 41). The term appears in the *Shih-shuo hsin-yü,* 4/44, 19/31, 21/8, 25/43, 34/4, etc.

6. *Shih-shuo hsin-yü,* 6/36, 6/3, 8/16, 8/27, 19/30, 6/29.

7. *Shih-shuo hsin-yü,* 2/63, in which Chih Tun uses this word to describe his horses, but with a clear intent to analogize the "divine swiftness" of horses with that of the human mind; see Mather's commentary on this episode.

8. *Lao-tzu,* ch. 4, "The *[Tao]* is empty, yet use will not drain it. / Deep, it is like the ancestor of the myriad creatures. / Blunt the sharpness; / Untangle the knots; / Soften the glare; / Let your wheels move only along old ruts" (*Wang Pi chi chiao-shih,* 1:10, trans. Lau, 60). See also Mather, *Tales of the World,* 220, n. 1 on 8/27.

9. Both Wang Jung and Wang Ch'eng were famous adepts of Wei-Chin character appraisal. See Fang Hsüan-ling et al., *Chin-shu, chüan* 43, 4:1235, on Wang Jung; and Wang Yin, *Chin-shu* [History of the Chin], quoted in Liu Chün's commentary on the *Shih-shuo hsin-yü,* 8/27, on Wang Ch'eng.

10. Liu Shao, *Jen-wu chih, chüan* A, 5.

11. See ibid., *chüan* A, 1–5; see also T'ang Yung-t'ung, "Tu Jen-wu chih," 196–197.

12. Hsi K'ang, "Yang-sheng lun," *Hsi K'ang chi [chiao-chu], chüan* 3, 145; trans. based on Henricks, *Essays of Hsi K'ang,* 23–24.

13. Ibid., 146; trans. ibid., 24.

14. Ibid.; trans. ibid.; see also *Chuang-tzu,* "Yang-sheng chu." Hsi K'ang here seems to take *hsing* (human nature) and *hsin* (mind) as synonyms, both standing for one's inner self.

15. Ko Hung, *Pao-p'u tzu wai-p'ien [chiao-chien],* "Ch'ing-chien" [Pure judgment], *chüan* 21, 1:512.

16. See T'ang Yung-t'ung, "Yen-i chih pien," *T'ang Yung-t'ung hsüeh-shu lun-wen chi,* 226.

17. "Hsi K'ang Pieh-chuan," quoted in Liu Chün's commentary on the *Shih-shuo hsin-yü,* 14/5.

18. "Juan Chi chuan," Fang Hsüan-ling et al., *Chin-shu, chüan* 48, 5:1359. I treat this account as basically a Wei-Chin record because, as I mentioned in chapter 3, the compilation of the *Chin-shu* in Early T'ang heavily relied upon the *Shih-shuo hsin-yü* and many Wei-Chin sources.

19. *Lao-tzu,* ch. 5, translation based on Wang Pi's interpretation of the chapter; see *Wang Pi chi chiao-shih,* 1:13. Lau, citing *Chuang-tzu,* translates *ch'u-kou* as "straw dogs" (*Lao Tzu Tao Te Ching,* 61).

20. Ku K'ai-chih, "Wei Chin sheng-liu hua-tsan" [Eulogies of the portraits of the Wei-Chin elite], in Chang Yen-yüan (fl. 847–862), *Li-tai ming-hua chi* [Records of the masterpieces of art from the previous dynasties], (Peking: Jen-min Mei-shu ch'u-pan she, 1963), *chüan* 5, 118.

21. In the Western tradition, Jean-Paul Sartre explains how one is defined by his relation to the other: "In a word, my apprehension of the Other in the world as probably being a man refers to my permanent possibility of being-seen-by-him; that is, to the permanent possibility that a subject who sees me may be substituted for the object seen by me. 'Being-seen-by-the-Other' is the truth of 'seeing-the-Other.' Thus the notion of the Other can not under any circumstances aim at a solitary, extra-mundane consciousness which I can not even think. *The man is defined by his relation to the world and by his relation to myself*" (emphasis mine) (*Being and Nothingness: An Essay on Phenomenological Ontology*, trans. Hazel E. Barnes [New York: Philosophical Library, 1956], 257).

22. Liu Chün quotes in his commentary on this episode a similar story recorded in Yü T'ung-chih, *Tu-chi*:

    After Huan Wen had pacified Shu, he took the daughter of Li Shih as a concubine. The princess (Huan's wife), a ferocious and jealous woman, knew nothing about it at first, but after she knew she went with drawn sword to Lady Li's apartment, wishing to cut off her head then and there. When she saw Lady Li, the latter was at the window combing her hair. Staying her hand, she faced the princess, her spirit and expression calm and sedate. When she spoke, her words were extremely sad and poignant, whereupon the princess, throwing away her sword, came forward to embrace her, crying, "Dear child, even *I* feel affection for you as I see you; how much more must that old rascal!" And from that time on she befriended her. (Trans. Mather, *Tales of the World*, 353)

23. See *Shih-shuo hsin-yü chien-shu*, 2:802, n. 2 to 25/27.

24. Mather, *Tales of the World*, 412, n. 2 to 25/27.

25. In his commentary on this episode, Li Tz'u-ming quotes Fang Hsüan-ling et al., ed., *Chin-shu*, "Wu-hsing chih" [Treatise of the five elements], to point out that the Yen cap (*yen-ch'ia*) was a Wei fashion and therefore was out of date in the Eastern Chin. See Yü, *Shih-shuo hsin-yü chien-shu*, 2:841, n. 1 to 26/21.

26. Mather's original note: "Ssu-ma Chao and Ssu-ma Shih were the second and eldest sons respectively of Ssu-ma I, and the real founders of the Chin Dynasty. Ssu-ma Shih deposed the Wei ruler, Ts'ao Fang (r. 240–254) in 254, and Ssu-ma Chao killed his puppet successor, Ts'ao Mao . . . in 260. Chao's son, Yen, then accepted the abdication of Ts'ao Huan (r. 260–265), and mounted the throne as Emperor Wu of Chin (r. 265–290)" (*Tales of the World*, 477).

27. The "moment he [Jen Chan] crossed the Yangtze River" refers to the time when "the refugees from the Western Chin court at Lo-yang . . . emigrated to the Yangtze Delta during the barbarian invasions of the North between 307 and 312" (Mather's commentary on the *Shih-shuo hsin-yü*, 2/31, *Tales of the World*, 45).

28. Modification according to Chou and Wang, "Ma-i *Shih-shuo hsin-yü* shang-tui," 250.

29. Liu P'an-sui, *Shih-shuo hsin-yü chiao-chien*, 105–106.

30. To compete with others in presenting intelligent remarks was fashionable in the Wei-

Chin era, especially when two gentlemen first met; see *Shih-shuo hsin-yü,* 25/9 and chapter 2, "Yen-yü."

31. My modification follows an alternate text of this episode; see Yü, *Shih-shuo hsin-yü chien-shu,* 1:195, the emendation on 4/5; and Wang Li-ch'i, "*Shih-shuo hsin-yü* chiao-k'an chi,*"* in *Shih-shuo hsin-yü* (Tokyo: Sonkei Kaku or Kanazawa Bunko, 1929; reprint, 2 vols., Peking: Wen-hsüeh ku-chi k'an-hsing she, 1956), 2:18; see also Morino Shigeo, "Toku *Sesetsu shingo* zakki: Bungaku hen" [Notes taken from reading the chapter "Literature and Scholarship" in the *Shih-shuo hsin-yü*], *Chūgoku chūsei bungaku kenkyū* 2 (1962):47.

32. Liu Chün's commentary to 6/2 quotes Chung's accusation against Hsi from the *Chin Yang-ch'iu:* "Today the imperial way is clear and enlightened, and the winds of its morality are wafted to all within the Four Seas. . . . But Hsi K'ang does not subject himself to the Son of Heaven above, nor does he serve the princes and nobles below. He despises the times, is arrogant towards the world, and is of no use to his fellows. Unprofitable to the present age, he is a baneful influence on its morals. . . . Today, if Hsi K'ang is not executed, there will be no means of purifying the Royal Way" (trans. Mather, *Tales of the World,* 180).

33. *Shih-shuo hsin-yü,* 18/3: "When Shan T'ao was about to leave the selection bureau (in 262) and wanted to recommend Hsi K'ang as his successor, K'ang wrote him a letter announcing the breaking off of their relationship." In the letter, Hsi K'ang wrote that he could not endure the restraints of Confucian doctrines, and he "criticized T'ang (the founder of Shang) and Wu (the founder of Chou), and belittled Chou (the sage duke of Chou) and Confucius"; see Liu Chün's commentary and Hsi K'ang's "Yü Shan Chü-yüan chüeh-chiao shu" [Letter to Shan T'ao to break off the friendship], *Hsi K'ang chi [chiao-chu],* chüan 2, 122; see also Mather's commentary on this episode. The *Shih-shuo hsin-yü* openly recounted Chin's usurpation of the Wei throne; see 33/7 and 5/8.

34. Alluding to a story in the *Tso-chuan,* Ch'eng 9 (Legge 5:371): A man from Ch'u was captured in a battle; he missed his country but could not do anything about it. See Mather, *Tales of the World,* n. 3 to 2/31, 45–46.

35. Mather's biographical note on Chou I, *Tales of the World,* 512. See also the *Shih-shuo hsin-yü,* 2/40.

36. Trans. Mather, *Tales of the World,* 408.

37. According to another historical source of this episode, quoted in Liu Chün's commentary on 33/8; trans. following Chou and Wang, *Ma-i shang-tui,* 249.

38. Mather's original note: "Chou I had once been a protégé of Wang Tun in 313, when he was fleeing for his life; see TCTC [*Tzu-chih t'ung-chien*] 88.2802" (*Tales of the World,* 167, n. 1 to 5/33).

39. Mather's original note: "According to CS [*Chin-shu*] 69.19b, Liu Wei, the principal object of Wang Tun's revolt, had urged that the entire Wang clan be exterminated" (ibid., 473, n. 2 to 33/6).

40. Mather's original note: "The gold seal was Wang Tao's emblem of office as director of works and chancellor" (ibid., n. 3 to 33/6).

41. Shih Te-ts'ao, *Pei-ch'uang chih-kuo lu* [Records of witty words from the north window], *chüan* A, as quoted in Yü, *Shih-shuo hsin-yü* chien-shu, 2:900, n. 1 to 33/6.

42. See Liu Chün's commentary to 14/23.

43. As an afternote to support this reading of the two personalities: Although T'ao helped Yü to pacify the rebels and to return to power, Yü executed T'ao's son after T'ao's death. See Fang Hsüan-ling et al., *Chin-shu*, "T'ao K'an chuan" [Biography of T'ao K'an], *chüan* 66, 6:1780; Yü, *Shih-shuo hsin-yü* chien-shu, 2:640, n. 2 to 17/9.

44. See Yü, *Shih-shuo hsin-yü chien-shu*, 1:333, n. 2 to 5/58.

45. Mather's note to this quote: "See 'Book of Documents,' *Yao-tien* I, 1 (Legge III, 15): Yao was respectful and able to decline," *Tales of the World*, 172.

46. T'ang Yung-t'ung's interpretation, "Wang Pi sheng-jen yu ch'ing i shih," 258.

47. Both Yü Chia-hsi and Mather take Sun's comment on Wei Yung as a statement rather than a question (see Yü, *Shih-shuo hsin-yü chien-shu*, 1:478, and Mather, *Tales of the World*, 237). I believe, however, Sun Ch'o here is inquiring about Wei's ability to compose landscape poems, inasmuch as an outing in the Wei-Chin period usually involved this sort of poetic activities. For example, two famous outings, respectively taking place in 296 and 353, resulted in two anthologies of poems: the *Golden Creek Poems (Chin-ku shih)* and the *Orchid Pavilion Poems (Lan-t'ing shih)* (see *Shih-shuo hsin-yü*, 9/57, 16/3, and Liu Chün's commentary on both accounts). The historical figure Sun Ch'o witnessed the transitional time from *hsüan-yen shih* (abstruse-word poetry) to *shan-shui shih* (landscape poetry). His *Yu T'ien-t'ai shan fu* (Wandering on Mount T'ien-t'ai) manifests the Eastern Chin attempt to define *wu* (Nothing) in terms of landscape descriptions (see Richard B. Mather, "The Mystical Ascent of the T'ien-t'ai Mountains: Sun Ch'o's *Yu T'ien-t'ai shan fu*" [*Monumenta Serica* 20 (1961):226–245]; and Watson, trans., *Wandering on Mount T'ien-t'ai*, in *Chinese Rhyme-prose*, 79–85).

48. 1 *jen* = 8 feet.

49. I borrow this expression from Tzvetan Todorov; see his *Poetics of Prose* (Ithaca: Cornell University Press, 1977), 126.

50. For a more detailed discussion about the nature of "alliterative and rhyming binomes" and "reduplicated compounds," see Liu Hsieh, *"Wu-se"* [The physical world], in *Wen-hsin tiao-lung* [chu], *chüan* 10, 2:693–694; Wang Li, *Ku-tai Han-yü* [Classical Chinese language], 4 vols. (Peking: Chung-hua shu-chü, 1962), 1:79 and 2:502; and David R. Knechtges, trans. with annotations, *Wen Xuan* [*Wen-hsüan*], *or Selections of Refined Literature*, 2 vols. (Princeton, NJ: Princeton University Press, 1982), 2:2–3.

51. "Pu-chü" [Divining where to stay] in the *Ch'u-tz'u*, Hung Hsing-tsu, *Ch'u-tz'u pu-chu* (Shanghai: Shanghai ku-chi ch'u-pan she, 1979), 114–115, trans. David Hawkes, *The Songs of the South* (Penguin Books, 1985), 205, with modifications.

52. Ts'ao Chih, *Lo-shen fu* [Goddess of the Lo], in Hsiao T'ung, *Wen-hsüan*, 1:270, trans. Watson, *Chinese Rhyme-prose*, 56.

53. For similar practice see also *Shih-shuo hsin-yü*, 2/26, 2/72, 2/94, etc. The archaic pronunciations are reconstructed by Mather, *Tales of the World*, 43, n. 1 to 2/24.

54. Ibid.

55. Liu P'an-sui's commentary on this episode: "[Huan Wen's] weeping over the willow must have taken place in 369. . . . At the time he was already a sixty-year-old man. Looking at the luxuriant foliage of the willow, he lamented over his not yet fulfilled ambition of usurping the throne. Viewing [the willow] today and recalling the past, he could not help feeling an irrepressible sadness" (Quoted in Yü, *Shih-shuo hsin-yü chien-shu*, 1:115).

56. Quoted in Liu Chün's commentary on this episode.

57. *Shih-shuo hsin-yü,* 18/12: "Since Tai K'uei was sharpening his integrity in [reclusion] in the Eastern Mountains (Chekiang), and his elder brother, Tai Tun, was desirous of establishing his merit as a 'suppressor of evil' *(shih-o),* the grand tutor, Hsieh An, said to Tun, 'How vastly different you two brothers are in your ambition and work!' Tun replied, 'In the case of this petty official, I "can't endure the misery of poverty," while in the case of my younger brother, "it doesn't alter his happiness".'"

58. Harold Fisch, "Character as Linguistic Sign," *New Literary History* 21.3 (spring 1990):605. See also Martin Buber, *I and Thou,* trans. Walter Kaufmann (New York: Charles Sribner's Sons, 1970), 62.

59. Fisch, "Character as Linguistic Sign," 605.

60. Ibid.

61. Ibid., 598.

Introduction to Part 3

1. I consider these works *Shih-shuo* imitations because: (1) They followed the *Shih-shuo* structure and writing style; (2) their authors and/or preface writers claimed affinity with the *Shih-shuo* genre; and/or (3) they were identified as *Shih-shuo* t'i works in later scholastic works, such as Yung Jung, Chi Yün et al., *Ssu-k'u chüan-shu tsung-mu;* Juan Fu, *Ssu-k'u wei-shou shu-mu t'i-yao* [Bibliography of books excluded from the Four Treasuries), appended to *Ssu-k'u chüan-shu tsung-mu;* Lu Hsün, *Chung-kuo hsiao-shuo shih-lüeh;* Chou Hsün-ch'u, *T'ang yü-lin chiao-cheng* [Commentary on the T'ang forest of accounts], 2 vols. (Peking: Chung-hua shu-chü, 1987); etc.

2. Ch'eng Hsü, "Ch'ung-k'o *Shih-shuo hsin-yü* hsü," *Shih-shuo hsin-yü* (Kuang-ling: Yü-ho t'ang, 1694), 1a.

3. *Ssu-k'u ch'üan-shu tsung-mu,* "Tzu-pu," "Hsiao-shuo chia lei" II, *chüan* 141, 2:1196, 1204.

4. See Ibid., *chüan* 143, 2:1216–1226.

5. Lu Hsün, *Chung-kuo hsiao-shuo shih-lüeh,* 8:53.

6. Geoffrey Hartman, *The Fate of Reading* (Chicago: University of Chicago Press, 1975), 17.

7. See Thomas M. Greene, *The Light in Troy: Imitation and Discovery in Renaissance Poetry* (New Haven: Yale University Press, 1982), 7: "The temporality of language

is . . . linked with the temporality of human customs and styles—'mores et habitus'—and with that of other human works—'alia nostra opera' (translated . . . as 'characteristics'). . . . Dante was evoking through Adam's voice the mutability not merely of specific words and dialects but of styles, the 'mores et habitus' of culture, those styles by which civilizations in their temporality can be distinguished from one another." Also see Greene's note on this passage.

8. *Ssu-k'u ch'üan-shu tsung-mu,* "Tzu-pu," "Hsiao-shuo chia lei" I, *chüan* 140, 2:1182.

9. Lu Hsün, *Chung-kuo hsiao-shuo shih-lüeh,* 8:46.

10. Liu Su, *Ta-T'ang hsin-yü,* "Yüan-hsü," 1, and "Tsung-lun," 202.

11. K'ung P'ing-chung, *Hsü Shih-shuo,* "Hsü," i.

12. As included in Chang Wen-chu's 1585 edition of the *Shih-shuo hsin-yü pu,* 6a.

13. Chiao Hung, *Yü-t'ang ts'ung-yü* [Peking: Chung-hua shu-chü, 1981], v. Very often, promoters of *Shih-shuo* imitations would also make bold claims in favor of the author. Ch'in Kuo emphasized the importance of K'ung P'ing-chung's *Continuation of the Shih-shuo* in "enhancing the luxuriant beauty of historians' [writings]" (K'ung, *Hsü Shih-shuo,* "Hsü," i). Kuo I-o (fl. 1618) characterized Chiao Hung's *Accounts of the Jade Hall* as "a miniature history of the Han-lin Academy members" (*Yü-t'ang ts'ung-yü,* iii). Ch'ien Fen (fl. 1657) praised Liang Wei-shu's *Distinguished Accounts of the Jade Sword* as "superior to average dynastic or family histories" (Liang Wei-shu, *Yü-chien tsun-wen,* 18). And Ch'ien Ch'ien-i (1582–1664) likewise considered Liang's work to belong to the category of history (ibid., 21–29).

14. Yi Tsung-k'uei, *Hsin Shih-shuo* (2nd edition, 1922), "Li-yen" [Compilation notes], 1a–1b.

15. See Fan Yeh, *Hou-Han shu,* "Hsün Shuang lieh-chuan" [Biography of Hsün Shuang], *chüan* 62, 7:2057.

16. Liu Su, *Ta-T'ang hsin-yü,* "Postscript," 202–203.

17. Smith, *China's Cultural Heritage,* 136.

18. Such discrimination between the standard history and the *Shih-shuo t'i* prevailed throughout the *Shih-shuo* tradition, even as reflected in Satō Tan's preface to Tsunota Ken, *Kinsei sōgo:* "The standard history records the important events and deeds concerning a dynasty's order and disorder, rule and law, as well as worthy, corrupt, loyal, treacherous, obedient, deceitful, just, and unjust human types. As for fragmented samples of remarks and conduct, which the standard history does not include but which may reveal the admirable and abominable features of the current custom and people's mind, *hsiao-shuo* will follow and keep records. This is why *hsiao-shuo* can never be abolished" (1a–b). Of course, here Satō still keeps the conventional categorization of *Shih-shuo t'i* as *hsiao-shuo.*

19. Ch'in Kuo's preface to K'ung P'ing-chung, *Hsü Shih-shuo,* "Hsü," i.

20. Li Shao-wen, *Huang-Ming Shih-shuo hsin-yü,* " Hsü," 2b–3b.

21. See ibid., 3b.

22. Feng Ching's preface to Wang Cho, *Chin Shih-shuo,* " Hsü," iii.

23. Mao Chi-k'o's preface to Wang Cho, *Chin Shih-shuo,* " Hsü," v.

24. Chu Mou-wei's preface to Cheng Chung-k'uei, *Ch'ing-yen* (1615), 1a–2b.

25. Wang Shih-mao's (1536–1588) preface to Wang Shih-chen, *Shih-shuo hsin-yü pu,* in Chang Wen-chu's 1585 edition, 1b.

26. Wang T'ai-heng's postscript to Wang Shih-chen, *Shih-shuo hsin-yü pu,* in Chang Wen-chu's 1585 edition, 1b. "Jade and pearl" allude to *Shih-shuo hsin-yü,* 14/15: "Someone went to visit Grand Marshal Wang Yen. He happened to arrive when Wang Tun, Wang Jung, and Wang Tao were also present. Passing into another room, he saw Wang Yen's younger brothers, Wang Yü and Wang Ch'eng. Returning, he said to the others, 'On today's trip wherever I cast my eyes I saw tinkling and dazzling pearls and jade.'"

27. Ting Peng's preface to Wang Cho, *Chin Shih-shuo,* " Hsü," iv.

28. Yeh Shih Li-wan's preface to Yen Heng, *Nü Shih-shuo,* " Hsü," 1a. "Plucking ivy branches and leaning on bamboo stems" alludes to Tu Fu's (712–770) poem, "Chia-jen" [The beauty]. It portrays a lofty and beautiful woman who, in a chaotic time, chose to live a reclusive life, plucking ivy branches to mend her thatched hut and keeping company with bamboo trees; see *Tu-shih [hsiang-chu]* [Comprehensive commentary on Tu Fu's poems], commentary by Ch'iu Chao-ao (Ch'ing), *Ssu-k'u Ch'üan-shu* ed. (reprint, Shanghai: Shanghai ku-chi ch'u-pan she, 1992), *chüan* 7, 24a, 223.

29. Tsunota Ken's preface to the *Kinsei sōgo,* 1a.

Chapter 6: Body and Heart

1. Other similar collections of T'ang historical anecdotes include Liu Su (fl. mid-eighth cent.), *Sui-T'ang chia-hua* [Remarkable anecdotes of Sui and T'ang], Chang Cho (ca. 657–730), *Ch'ao-yeh ch'ien-tsai* [Comprehensive records of affairs inside and outside of the court], and Li Chao (fl. early ninth cent.), *T'ang kuo-shih pu* [Supplement to the T'ang history], etc., but none of them has a classification of the *Shih-shuo* type.

2. Yeh Te-hui's colophon to Liu Su, *Ta-T'ang hsin-yü,* 208.

3. The term appears in Liu Su, *Ta-T'ang hsin-yü,* "Kang-cheng" [Inflexibility and correctness], *chüan* 2, 29.

4. Liu Su, *Ta-T'ang hsin-yü,* "Kuei-chien," *chüan* 1, 13; see also Howard J. Wechsler, *Mirror to the Son of Heaven: Wei Cheng at the Court of T'ang T'ai-tsung* (New Haven: Yale University Press, 1974), 126.

5. These nine include three admonitions to the powerful usurpers Wang Tun (10/12) and Huan Hsüan (10/25, 27).

6. Liu Su, *Ta-T'ang hsin-yü,* "K'uang-tsan," *chüan* 1, 5.

7. Quoted in Li Hsien's commentary on Fan Yeh, *Hou-Han shu,* "Li Yün chuan" [Biography of Li Yün], *chüan* 57, 7:1854, n. 1.

8. Fan Yeh, *Hou-Han shu,* "Li Yün chuan," *chüan* 57, 7:1853.

9. See the "Great Preface to *Book of Songs*" (Shih ta-hsü), *Mao-Shih* [*cheng-i*], *Shih-san ching chu-shu*, *chüan* 1, 1:269, 271. For more interpretation about *feng* as a poetic mode or rhetorical technique, see Stephen Owen, *Readings in Chinese Literary Thought* (Cambridge: Harvard University Press, 1992), 46 and 586–587; see also John Louton, "Mei Sheng," in *The Indiana Companion to Traditional Chinese Literature*, s.v. "Mei Sheng."

10. Liu Su, *Ta-T'ang hsin-yü*, "Chi-chien," *chüan* 2, 25. "Kang-cheng," *chüan* 2, 29 and 30; "Chung-lieh," *chüan* 5, 73.

11. Ibid., "Chi-chien," *chüan* 2, 21 and 23.

12. Ibid., *chüan* 2, 19.

13. Ibid., "Cheng-neng," *chüan* 4, 65.

14. Ibid., "Kung-chih," *chüan* 3, 41. For *ch'i-chü chu* [Records of the emperor's daily life], see Liu Chih-chi, *Shih-t'ung*, "Shih-kuan chien-chih" [Establishment of historian offices]; and Tu Yu, *T'ung-tien*, "Chih-kuan" III.

15. Liu Su, *Ta-T'ang hsin-yü*, "Ts'ung-shan" [Following good], *chüan* 9, 137–138.

16. As reflected in the *Shih-shuo hsin-yü*, Wei-Chin gentlemen never made as explicit monetary demands as T'ang officials did for their service to the emperor. For example, Hsieh An once asked the young people in his family why the Chin emperor Wu (Ssu-ma Yen, r. 265–290) usually bestowed meager gifts to his leading minister Shan T'ao. Hsieh Hsüan replied: "It is probably because the recipient's desires were few, which made the giver forget about the meagerness of the gift" (2/78). Whereas Wei-Chin scholars' seeming indifference toward monetary rewards was caused by complicated economic and political conditions of the time, some of them possibly developed this attitude based on their *Hsüan-hsüeh* beliefs. For instance, Wang Yen was said to have "always esteemed the 'Abstruse and Remote' [*hsüan-yüan*] . . . and never let the word 'cash' [*ch'ien*] pass his lips" (10/9).

17. Liu Su, *Ta-T'ang hsin-yü*, "Shih-liang," *chüan* 7, 102, and "K'uang-tsan," *chüan* 1, 11.

18. Ibid., "Kung-chih," *chüan* 3, 43.

19. Ibid., "Chi-chien," *chüan* 2, 23.

20. *Lun-yü*, IV, 16.

21. When Liu Pang founded the Han dynasty, Shu-sun T'ung set up the court ritual for him. See Ssu-ma Ch'ien, *Shih-chi*, "Shu-sun T'ung lieh-chuan" [Biography of Shu-sun T'ung], *chüan* 99, 8:2722-3; and Pan Ku, *Han-shu*, "Shu-sun T'ung chuan," *chüan* 43, 7:2126–2128.

22. Liu Su, *Ta-T'ang hsin-yü*, "Wen-chang" [Literary composition], *chüan* 8, 123.

23. *Li-chi* [*cheng-i*], "Yüeh-chi" [Record of music]: "As Heaven is high and earth low, the positions of the ruler and the subject are so determined" (*Shih-san ching chu-shu*, *chüan* 37, 2:1531).

24. Liu Hsü et al., *Chiu T'ang-shu*, "Tse-t'ien huang-hou pen-chi" [Annals of Empress Tse-t'ien], *chüan* 6, 1:133.

25. Liu Su, *Ta-T'ang hsin-yü,* "Chi-i" [Recording the strange], *chüan* 13, 193.

26. Ssu-ma Ch'ien, *Shih-chi,* "Huai-yin hou lieh-chuan" [Biography of Marquis Huai-yin], *chüan* 92, 8:2623.

27. I translate *chün-ch'en chih tao* as "the proper relationship between the ruler and the subject" based on the following paragraph in the *Li-chi* [*cheng-i*], "Li-ch'i" [Ritual vessels]: "The *Tao* between the father and the son, and the moral obligation between the ruler and the subject, refer to their proper relationships" (*Shih-san ching chu-shu, chüan* 23, 2:1431).

28. Liu Su, *Ta-T'ang hsin-yü,* "Chü-hsien," *chüan* 6, 96–97.

29. *Ch'ui-lien,* a term referring to a female sovereign attending court behind a bamboo screen, seems to have started with Wu Tse-t'ien. Liu Hsü et al., *Chiu T'ang-shu,* "Kao-tsung pen-chi" [Annals of Emperor Kao-tsung], records: "Every time His Majesty [Kao-tsung] attended court, Heavenly Empress [later Empress Tse-t'ien] would sit in back of the throne, behind a bamboo screen. State affairs, important or trivial, would be reported to her [before each hearing]. Inside and outside the court, people referred to both the emperor and the empress as the 'Two Sages'" (*chüan* 5, 1:100). Seen in this light, Chang Chia-chen's advice to Wu Tse-t'ien, clearly taking place after Kao-tsung's death, urges her to assume an independent status as the ruler.

30. See Liu Su, *Ta-T'ang hsin-yü,* "Chi-chien," *chüan* 2, 23–24.

31. See ibid., "K'uang-tsan," *chüan* 1, 6–7; and "Chi-chien," *chüan* 2, 25–26.

32. Peter Bol, *"This Culture of Ours": Intellectual Transitions in T'ang and Sung China* (Stanford: Stanford University Press, 1992), 32. Bol defines the term *shih:* "During most of the six (seventh–twelfth) centuries dealt with here, those who called themselves *shih, shih-jen, shih-ta-fu* dominated Chinese politics and society. As [*shih*] they were members of the elite rather than of the commonalty (*shu*) or of the populace (*min*). As a group their function was to serve (*shih*) in government rather than to farm the land, work as craftsmen, or engage in trade. And they supposed that they had the education and talent necessary to serve in government and guide society" (ibid., 4).

33. Ibid.; see also 34.

34. Bol delineates the change of *shih*'s identity during this period and its continual impact on the Sung dynasty: "In the seventh century, the *shih* were an elite led by aristocratic great clans of illustrious pedigree; in the tenth and eleventh centuries, the *shih* were the civil bureaucrats; and finally, in the southern Sung, they were the more numerous but rarely illustrious local elite families who provided bureaucrats and examination candidates" (*This Culture of Ours,* 4). Bol uses the word *aristocratic* to characterize the gentry from Wei-Chin to early T'ang. But as Charles Holcombe notes: "China's medieval elite was certainly 'aristocratic,' in Patricia Ebrey's sense of possessing 'hereditary high social status, independent of full court control,' but it did not constitute a feudal aristocracy and was therefore not at all what the term usually implies in a European context" (*In the Shadow of the Han,* 8). He suggests that "the early medieval Chinese great families might more accurately be described as hereditary or partially hereditary bureaucrats than as aristocrats" (ibid., 7). For Ebrey's ar-

gument, see *The Aristocratic Families of Early Imperial China: A Case Study of the Po-Ling Ts'ui Family* (Cambridge: Cambridge University Press, 1978), 10.

35. For the formation of the gentry into hereditary clans that possessed both office holding and pedigree (learning and talent were assumed) from the late Han to the Wei-Chin periods, see T'ang Chang-ju, "Chiu-pin chung-cheng chih-tu shih-shih," 118–126; Yü Ying-shih, "Tung-Han cheng-ch'üan chih chien-li yü shih-tsu ta-hsing chih kuan-hsi" [The connection between the establishment of the Eastern Han regime and great clans], in his *Chung-kuo chih-shih chieh-ts'eng shih-lun,* 109–184; and Holcombe, *In the Shadow of the Han,* 6–8.

36. T'ang Yung-t'ung and Jen Chi-yü, *Wei-Chin Hsüan-hsüeh chung ti she-hui cheng-chih ssu-hsiang lüeh-lun* [Brief study on sociopolitical perspectives in Wei-Chin *Hsüan-hsüeh*] (Shanghai: Shanghai jen-min ch'u-pan she, 1956), 25. For the dominance of the great families over the court during the Eastern Chin and Southern dynasties, see also Holcome, *In the Shadow of the Han,* 6–8.

37. Ling-hu Te-fen (583–666) et al., *Chou-shu* [History of the Chou], "Su Ch'o chuan" [Biography of Su Ch'o], 3 vols. (Peking: Chung-hua shu-chü, 1971), *chüan* 23, 2:386.

38. See Ch'en Yin-k'o, *Sui-T'ang chih-tu yüan-yüan lüeh-lun kao* [Draft of a brief discussion of the origins of Sui-T'ang political systems] (Peking: Chung-hua shu-chü, 1963), 96.

39. Tu Yu, *T'ung-tien, chüan* 14, 81. See also Wei Cheng et al., *Sui-shu,* "Lu K'ai chuan" [Biography of Lu K'ai], *chüan* 56, 5:1384.

40. See Tu Yu, *T'ung-tien, chüan* 14, 81. Ch'en Yin-k'o also points out that "while the prefects in the Northern Chou might appoint their subordinate officials, . . . the Sui regime put all [the authority of appointment] under the central offices of selection. This is the feature of the centralization of the Sui political system" (*Sui-T'ang chih-tu yüan-yüan lüeh-lun kao,* 87).

41. See Bol, *This Culture of Ours,* 40–41.

42. Ibid., 44–45.

43. Liu Su, *Ta-T'ang hsin-yü,* "Hsieh-hsüeh" [Humor and teasing], *chüan* 13, 189.

44. R. W. L. Guisso, *Wu Tse-t'ien and the Politics of Legitimation in T'ang China* (Bellingham: Program in East Asian Studies, Western Washington University, 1978), 136.

45. Liu Hsü et al., *Chiu T'ang-shu,* "Lu Chih chuan" [Biography of Lu Chih]: "[Lu] Chih presented a memorial, saying: 'In the past, Empress Dowager Tse-t'ien . . . promoted [officials] with trust and looked for [talented men], never getting tired.'. . . Yet she also rigorously checked on their proficiency and rapidly promoted or demoted them. . . . Thus, when she was alive, she was praised for her intelligence of knowing people, and [thanks to her effort], her successors got enough [capable] gentlemen to use" (*chüan* 139, 12:3803). In Ou-yang and Sung, *Hsin T'ang-shu,* "Li Chiang chuan" [Biography of Li Chiang], Li remarks: "Although Empress Wu appointed too many officials, all the famous statesmen in the K'ai-yüan reign came from her selection" (*chüan* 152, 15:4842). See also Ch'en Yin-k'o, "Chi T'ang-tai chih Li Wu Wei

Yang hun-yin chi-t'uan" [Account of the marriage clique of the Lis, Wus, Weis, and Yangs], *Chin-ming kuan ts'ung-kao ch'u-pien*, 254–255.

46. As Ch'en Yin-k'o points out: "T'ai-tsung, though a rare hero, was still restrained by the tradition and not [able to reform] without hesitation. Wu Chao [Wu Tse-t'ien] came from a lower family [*han-tsu*] background in Shan-tung [so she did not have to be as restrained by the tradition as T'ai-tsung]. Once she seized upon political power, she . . . switched the center of China to Shan-tung, promoted the civil service examination system, particularly the *chin-shih* degree that focused on literary composition, and selected talented people; hence she destroyed the aristocracy of the Southern and Northern dynasties" ("Li Wu Wei Yang hun-yin chi-t'uan," 248–249).

47. See Bol, *This Culture of Ours*, 44–45.

48. Ibid., 51–52.

49. See *The Indiana Companion to Traditional Chinese Literature*, s.v. "Chang Yüeh," by Paul W. Kroll.

50. Chang Cho, *Ch'ao-yeh ch'ien-tsai* (Peking: Chung-hua shu-chü, 1979), *chüan* 5, 125.

51. *Hsing-ning* first appeared as *ning-hsing* in Ssu-ma Ch'ien, *Shih-chi*, to title a chapter about those who achieved the emperor's favor through flattery. As a chapter title it was thereafter adopted in later biographical histories. In the Southern dynasties, the word acquired a new meaning, referring to humble family background. See Ssu-ma Ch'ien, *Shih-chi*, *chüan* 125, 10:3191–3196; and Li Yen-shou, *Nan-shih* (History of the Southern dynasties), 6 vols. (Peking: Chung-hua shu-chü, 1975), *chüan* 77, 6:1913–1945.

52. See Liu Su, *Ta-T'ang hsin-yü*, "K'uang-tsan," *chüan* 1, 10–11.

53. Ibid., "Wen-chang," *chüan* 8, 127.

54. Ibid., "K'uang-tsan," *chüan* 1, 10. Liu Su also recorded a comparison between Chang Yüeh and the most celebrated T'ang gentleman, Wei Cheng, saying: "Contemporary opinion considered Chang Yüeh to have surpassed Wei Cheng in erudition and judgment" ("Shih-liang," *chüan* 1, 103).

55. See ibid., "K'uang-tsan," *chüan* 1, 8–9.

56. See Chou Pi-ta's (1126–1204) preface to *Ch'ing-chiang san K'ung chi* [Works of the three K'ungs from Ch'ing-chiang] (*Ssu-k'u ch'üan-shu* ed.); T'o T'o et al., *Sung-shih*, "Lieh-chuan" *chüan* 103, "K'ung Wen-chung chuan" [Biography of K'ung Wen-chung], "K'ung Wu-chung chuan," and "K'ung P'ing-chung chuan," *Ying-yin jen-shou pen erh-shih liu shih* ed., 9 vols. (Taipei: Ch'eng-wen ch'u-pan she, 1971), 41:23,603–23,604; see also Ch'eng Ch'ien-fan and Wu Hsin-lei, *Liang Sung wen-hsüeh shih* [History of Sung literature] (Shanghai: Shanghai ku-chi ch'u-pan she, 1991), 188. A great number of records of the intimate correspondence between the K'ungs and the Sus can be found in their poems and other writings.

57. For Wang Tang's connection with the Su Shih circle, see Chou, *T'ang yü-lin chiao-cheng*, i–iv.

58. Chou Hsün-ch'u makes this observation according to Wang Tang's note to *T'ang yü-lin*, *chüan* 5, Entry 729, quoting from K'ung P'ing-chung's *Hsü Shih-shuo;* see *T'ang yü-lin chiao-cheng*, iii–iv and 2:499.

59. See also ibid. for the complementary relationship between the two Sung imitations.

60. For the place of *Li-hsüeh* in the Confucian intellectual tradition, see Fung, *History of Chinese Philosophy*, 2:407 ff.

61. The other categories include: *Shih-hao* [Hobbies], *Li-su* [Customs], *Chi-shih* [Recounting events], *Pien-t'an* [Penetrating talks], *Tung-chih* [Zoology and botany], *Shu-hua* [Calligraphy and painting], and *Tsa-wu* [Miscellaneous things]. See Wang Tang, *T'ang yü-lin* [*chiao-cheng*], "*T'ang yü-lin* yüan hsü-mu" [Original table of contents of the *T'ang yü-lin*], 2.

62. Liu Su, *Ta-T'ang hsin-yü*, "Kuei-chien," *chüan* 1, 13.

63. K'ung P'ing-chung, *Hsü Shih-shuo*, "Yen-yü," *chüan* 1, 9.

64. For the various meanings of *ch'eng*, such as honesty, sincerity, frankness, authenticity, and trustworthiness, see *Erh-ya* [*chu-shu*], "Shih-ku" (*Shih-san ching chu-shu*, *chüan* 1, 2:2569).

65. Liu Su, *Ta-T'ang hsin-yü*, "Jung-shu" [Tolerance and leniency], *chüan* 7, 109–110.

66. Wang Tang, *T'ang yü-lin* [*chiao-cheng*], "Te-hsing," *chüan* 1, no. 3, 1:2.

67. A close friend of their father, Chou Tun-i had a strong influence upon the K'ung brothers. K'ung Wen-chung showed great respect for both his scholarship and personality in his "Chi Chou Mao-shu wen" [Elegiac prose for Chou Tun-i], *Ch'ing-chiang san K'ung chi*, *chüan* 19a–b, and "Chi mu wen" [Elegiac prose presented at (Chou Tun-i's) tomb site], appended to *Chou Yüan-kung chi* [Collected works of Chou Tun-i] (*Ssu-k'u ch'üan-shu* ed.), *chüan* 8, 1a–2a. K'ung P'ing-chung expressed similar feelings for Chou Tun-i in his poem "T'i Lien-hsi shu-t'ang" [Inscription on the Lien Stream Studio (Chou's studio)], as quoted in Hou Wai-lu, *Sung-Ming li-hsüeh shih* [History of Sung-Ming Neo-Confucianism], 2 vols. (Peking: Jen-min ch'u-pan she, 1984), 1:80–81. Wang Tang probably accepted Chou's influence through the Su Shih circle because Su Shih, like most of his contemporaries, greatly admired Chou. See Su Shih, "Mao-shu hsien-sheng Lien-hsi shih ch'eng Tz'u-yüan jen-ti" [Poem on Mr. Chou Tun-i's Lien Stream, presented to my kind younger friend, Tz'u-yüan], appended to *Chou Yüan-kung chi*, *chüan* 7, 3a–b.

68. Chou Tun-i, *T'ung-shu* [Comprehending the changes], in *Chou Yüan-kung chi*, *chüan* 1, 9b, 11b.

69. Ibid., *chüan* 1, 37a.

70. K'ung, *Hsü Shih-shuo*, "Te-hsing," *chüan* 1, 1.

71. Ibid., "Te-hsing," *chüan* 1, 6.

72. Ibid.

73. Ibid., *chüan* 1, 7.

74. Wang Tang, *T'ang yü-lin* [*chiao-cheng*], "Te-hsing," *chüan* 1, no. 4, 1:3.

75. Because of a palace power struggle, Hsüan-tsung removed his crown prince Li Ying and ordered his death along with his two brothers; see *Hsin T'ang-shu,* "T'ai-tzu Ying chuan" [Biography of Crown Prince Li Ying], *chüan* 82, 12:3607–3608; see also Liu Su, *Ta-T'ang hsin-yü,* "Ch'eng-chieh," *chüan* 11, 172–173.

76. K'ung, *Hsü Shih-shuo,* "Wen-hsüeh," *chüan* 2, 26.

77. Nathan Sivin points out in his *Traditional Medicine in Modern China* that saliva in traditional Chinese medicine belongs to the category of "dispersed body fluids"—*chin-yeh*—which "is a general term for all normal moisture and fluids in the body [excluding blood and semen], important substances for the maintenance of vital activity" (Ann Arbor: University of Michigan Press, 1987, 243); see also 147.

78. K'ung, *Hsü Shih-shuo,* "Wen-hsüeh," *chüan* 2, 29.

79. Wang Tang, *T'ang yü-lin* [*chiao-cheng*], "Wen-hsüeh," *chüan* 2, no. 225, 1:141–142; Chou Hsün-ch'u points out in his commentary that this episode is quoted from Liu Yü-hsi's *Liu Pin-k'o chia-hua lu* [Admirable remarks by Liu Yü-hsi]. The same episode in the *T'ai-p'ing kuang-chi* [Broad records of the T'ai-p'ing Reign], *chüan* 374, under *Chia-hua lu,* does not have Liu Yü-hsi's comment. The modern text of *Liu Pin-k'o chia-hua lu* does not even have this episode. Therefore I suspect that Liu's comment regarding the connection between *ch'eng* and certain literary expression was added, or at least revised, by Wang Tang.

80. Su Shih, "Hsieh Mei Lung-tu shu" [Letter of thanks to the Lung-tu Scholar Mei], *Su Shih wen-chi* [Complete prose of Su Shih], 6 vols. (Peking: Chung-hua shu-chü, 1986), *chüan* 49, 4:1424.

81. In his "Chung-yung lun shang" [On the mean, I], Su Shih defines *ch'eng* as the basis of *hsing,* human nature:

    The *Record* [*of the Rites*] says: "From *ch'eng* to achieve *ming* (intelligence) is called *hsing* (human nature). . . ." What does *ch'eng* mean? It means to be fond of something. If one is fond of something, one feels self-confident. Thus we say [this person is] *ch'eng.* What does *ming* mean? It means to know something. If one knows something, one becomes intelligent. Thus we say [this person is] *ming.* . . . In talking about our likes and dislikes, nothing can be more obvious than our fondness of beautiful women and disgust with stinky odor. This is human nature. To be fond of the good as much as of the beautiful, and to feel disgusted with the bad as much as with the stinky odor, this is the sage's *ch'eng.* Therefore, the *Record* says: "From *ch'eng* to achieve intelligence is called human nature." (*Su Shih wen-chi, chüan* 2, 1:60–61)

82. Su Shih, "Yü Hsieh Min-shih t'ui-kuan shu" [Letter to Judge Hsieh Min-shih], in *Su Shih wen-chi, chüan* 49, 4:1419.

83. Peter Bol interprets Su Shih's *wu* as "historical categories of human affairs" (*This Culture of Ours,* 260). I, however, consider it a much broader concept in Su Shih's works, including both human affairs and objects.

84. Kuo Shao-yü understands Su Shih's concept of "use" (*yung*) as "a use without purpose, a natural use, and a use beyond any utilitarian claim" (*Chung-kuo wen-hsüeh*

p'i-p'ing shih [History of Chinese literary criticism] [Shanghai: Hsin wen-i ch'u-pan she, 1957], 170).

85. Evidently, the *I-ching* axiom, "refining words to constitute one's *ch'eng*," provided the theoretical basis for Su Shih and his close followers—K'ung P'ing-chung, Wang Tang, and the others—in considering the significance of *ch'eng* and its literary expression. See *Chou-i* [*cheng-i*], "Ch'ien," *Shih-san-ching chu-shu, chüan* 1, 1:15.

86. *Ssu-k'u chüan-shu tsung-mu, chüan* 120, 1:1037: "In our research we find that K'ung P'ing-chung and his contemporaries, Liu An-shih and Su Shih, and Lin Li and T'ang Chung-yu in the Southern Sung, behaved no less than superior men. But because K'ung P'ing-chung, Liu An-shih, and Su Shih contradicted Master Ch'eng I, and Lin Li and T'ang Chung-yu were contradicting Master Chu Hsi, *Li-hsüeh* scholars have treated them like bandits and enemies."

87. Ch'eng I said: "[Heaven's] principle, [human] nature, and [Heaven's] mandate, the three are not different. Once one has fully understood [Heaven's] principle, one has also comprehended [human] nature, and once one has comprehended [human] nature, one knows Heaven's mandate. Heaven's mandate is Heavenly *Tao*. Put in use, it is then called [Heaven's] mandate. [Heaven's] mandate means [Heaven's] creation and transformation" (*Erh-Ch'eng i-shu* [Posthumously published works of the two Ch'engs], *Ssu-k'u ch'üan-shu* ed, *chüan* 21b, 2a). See also Ma Chi-kao, *Sung Ming li-hsüeh yü wen-hsüeh* [Sung-Ming Neo-Confucianism and literature] (Ch'ang-sha: Hu-nan shih-fan ta-hsüeh ch'u-pan she, 1989), 36–38.

88. Bol, *This Culture of Ours*, 2.

89. *Erh-Ch'eng i-shu, chüan* 25, 6b. See also Ma, *Sung Ming li-hsüeh yü wen-hsüeh*, 38.

90. Ibid., *chüan* 18, 95a–96a.

91. Han Fei-tzu, "Chieh-Lao" [Interpreting the *Lao-tzu*]. Kuo Shao-yü in his *Chung-kuo wen-hsüeh p'i-p'ing shih* cites this couplet to interpret Su Shih's *Tao* (168). Su Shih himself, however, never explicitly defines his *Tao*, possibly because he considers *Tao* an uncertain, indefinable concept. As he says:

The sages knew that *tao* was difficult to speak of. Therefore they borrowed yin and yang to speak of it, saying "one yin and one yang are what is meant by *tao*." One yin and one yang is a way of saying yin and yang have not yet interacted and things have not yet come into being. There is no metaphor for the approximation of *tao* more exact than this. As soon as yin and yang interact they bring things into being. At first they make water. Water is the juncture of (being) [Thing] and (non-being) [Nothing]. It begins to separate from (non-being) [Nothing] and enter into (being) [Thing]. Lao Tzu recognized this. His words were: "The highest good is like water" and also "Water is close to *tao*." Although the virtue of the sages can be spoken of with names, it cannot be circumscribed by one thing, just as is the case with water's not having constant form. This is the best of the good; it is "close to *tao*" but it is not *tao*. Now when water has not yet come into being and yin and yang have not yet interacted and through the whole expanse there is not a single thing, yet we cannot say that there is nothing there—this truly is the approximation of *tao*. (Su Shih, *Tung-p'o I-chuan* [Tung-po's commentary on the *Book of Changes*], "Hsi-tz'u," *Ssu-k'u ch'üan-shu* ed., *chüan* 7, 10a–b; trans. Kidder Smith Jr. et al., *Sung Dynasty Uses of the I Ching* [Princeton, NJ: Princeton University Press, 1990], 78; for Su Shih's understanding of *Tao*, see also ibid., 72–81)

92. Su Shih, "Jih yü" [On finding an analogy for the sun]; Su Shih further explains: "What does 'brought on' mean? Sun Wu said, 'Those skilled at war bring the others on; they are not brought on by the others.' Tzu-hsia said, 'The various artisans master their trades by staying in their workshops; the superior man brings his tao on by learning.' When it arrives on its own without anyone seeking it, is this not what 'bring on' is all about?" (*Su Shih wen-chi, chüan* 64, 5:1981; trans. Bol, *This Culture of Ours*, 275).

93. See also Bol's discussion of "Jih yü": "Su was skilled at placing larger issues in the context of actual practice, but it was a skill born of the belief that abstract ideas were meaningfully experienced in the particular. Tao, as the ultimate source, can be intuited in experience but not defined; it can be realized by learning gradually and incrementally how to do something oneself, not by simply following a set of instructions. The danger is that shih will think tao can be known apart from things, as something transcendent. It is transcendent (and thus beyond definition), but it is also immanent in things and affairs" (Bol, *This Culture of Ours*, 276).

94. Su Shih, "Shu Tzu-mei Huang Ssu-niang shih" [Inscribing Tu Fu's poem, "Huang the Fourth Lady"], *Su Shih wen-chi, chüan* 67, 5:2103.

95. Su Shih says: "*Ch'ing* [feelings, emotions, passion, etc.] arises when *hsing* [human nature] becomes active. Tracing [*hsing*] up it reaches *ming* [Heaven's mandate], and tracing down it reaches *ch'ing*. All this is nothing but *hsing*. Hsing and *ch'ing* possess no difference between the good and the bad" (*Tung-p'o I-chuan*, "Shih ch'ien" [Interpretation of *Ch'ien*], *Ssu-k'u ch'üan-shu* ed., *chüan* 1, 5a).

96. See *Su Shih wen-chi, chüan* 65, 5:2021–2028.

97. See ibid., *chüan* 70, 5:2214–2215.

98. See Su Shih, *Tung-p'o yüeh-fu* [chien] [(Commentary on) The *Tz'u* poems of Su Shih], commentary by Lung Yü-sheng (Taipei: Hua-cheng shu-chü, 1990), 31, 40, 42, 93, 174, 242, 245, 286, 300, 302, 319, 326, 349–350, 368, and 369. Using *Shih-shuo* allusions seems to have been popular among tz'u poets of the Sung; even the fastidious Li Ch'ing-chao (1084–?) directly quoted the *Shih-shuo* lines, "Clear dewdrops gleaming in the early morning light/New leaves of the paulownia just beginning to unfold" (8/153), into her poem; see *Li Ch'ing-chao chi* [chiao-chu] [(Commentary on) The collected works of Li Ch'ing-chao], commentary by Wang Chung-wen (Peking: Jen-min wen-hsüeh ch'u-pan she, 1979), *chüan* 1, 49. Hsin Ch'i-chi (1140–1207) was also famous for quoting and alluding to the *Shih-shuo hsin-yü*; see *Chia-hsüan tz'u* [*pien-nien chien-chu*] [(Commentary on the chronologically edited) *Tz'u* poems of Hsin Ch'i-chi], commentary by Teng Kuang-ming (Shanghai: Shanghai ku-chi ch'u-pan she, 1978), *chüan* 1, 11, 31, 33, 57–58, 60; *chüan* 2, 101, 105, 108, 110, 112–113, 119, 121, 126, 128, 139, 149, 152, 153, 157, 206, 230; *chüan* 3, 273; *chüan* 4, 306, 307, 312, 313, 316, 317, 324, 329, 335, 337, 339–340, 340–341,

350, 361, 385, 389–390, 391, 405, 413, 427, 428, 432–433; *chüan* 5, 454, 457, 481, 483, 494, 511; *chüan* 6, 521, 523; and *chüan* 7, 545.

99. Wang Tang frequently recounts tales of patron-protégé relationships involving *hsing-chüan*. Here are two examples from the *T'ang yü-lin*:

> Po Chü-i went to the capital to attend the civil service examination. After arriving there, he brought his poems to visit the Secretary Ku K'uang. Noticing his name ["Chü-i" on the poetry scroll], Ku stared at him and said: "Right now rice is expensive; living [*Chü*] here isn't easy [*i*]." Upon opening the scroll and reading the first poem: "Grass on the Hsien-yang plain / Withers and sprouts every year / Wildfire cannot burn it all / Spring wind blows, it grows back," Ku sighed with admiration, saying: "Since you can compose such words, living here will be easy." He recommended him around, and thus helped Po to establish his reputation. ([*chiao-cheng*], "Shang-yü," *chüan* 3, no. 412, 1:277)

> Li Ho visited Han Yü with his poems. Han Yü, then in charge of the Imperial Academy, was extremely tired after seeing off a guest. The butler presented Li Ho's poetry scroll. Han Yü read it while loosening his belt. Upon reading the first two lines, "Black clouds crush, the city wall seems to collapse / Armour shines, like golden scales open to the sun," he immediately put the belt back on and ordered the butler to invite [Li] in. ([*chiao-cheng*], "Shang-yü," *chüan* 3, no. 413, 1:278)

> For the impact of the T'ang civil service examination system—particularly the practice of *hsing-chüan*—on T'ang literature, see Ch'eng Ch'ien-fan, *T'ang-tai chin-shih hsing-chüan yü wen-hsüeh* [Literature and the *chin-shih* candidate literary portfolios] (Shanghai: Shanghai ku-chi ch'u-pan she, 1980).

100. Wang Tang, *T'ang yü-lin* [*chiao-cheng*], "Wen-hsüeh," *chüan* 2, no. 238, 1:151.

101. Ibid., "Shih-chien," *chüan* 3, no. 372, 1:247. Wang Tang here alludes to Pan Ku, *Han-shu*, "Mei Fu chuan" [Biography of Mei Fu]: "Gentlemen are the important people [lit. heavy vessels] of the state. With them, the state is stable [lit. heavy]; without them, the state is unstable [lit. light]" (*chüan* 67, 9:2919).

102. The ancient Chinese myth holds that there is a three-foot crow in the sun; see *Tz'u-yüan*, s.v. *San*.

103. Kuo Mao-ch'ien, *Yüeh-fu shih-chi*, "Ch'in-ch'ü ko-tz'u" [Lyrics of the zither songs IV]: "Li Mian, *Interpretation of the Zither Melodies*: 'Crow Crying at Night' was composed by Ho Yen's daughter. When [Ho] Yan was first put in jail, there were two crows living on the roof of his house. His daughter said: 'The cry of a crow brings good news, so my dad will be exonerated.' She thereupon composed this melody" (*chüan* 60, 3:872).

104. Wang Tang, *T'ang yü-lin* [*chiao-cheng*], "Shang-yü," *chüan* 3, no. 409, 1:275.

105. The Hsü Ching-yeh Rebellion, taking place in 684; see *Chiu T'ang-shu*, "Tse-t'ien huang-hou chi," *chüan* 6, 1:117.

106. "Six-foot tall orphan" (*liu-ch'ih chih ku*) (this "foot" is equal to only about seven inches

today; see *T'zu-yüan*, s.v. *Liu*) refers to Wu Tse-t'ien's son Li Hsien, the future emperor Chung-tsung (r. 684, 705–710), who assumed the throne in 684 after Kao-tsung's death but was immediately abolished and put in exile by his mother. See *Chiu T'ang-shu*, "Tse-t'ien huang-hou chi," *chüan* 6, 1:116–117.

107. Wang Tang, *T'ang yü-lin* [*chiao-cheng*], "Wen-hsüeh," *chüan* 2, no. 180, 1:116.

108. Ibid., no. 199, 1:127; no. 213, 1:135.

Chapter 7: Things and Intent

1. Hui Chiao, *Kao-seng chuan* [Biographies of eminent monks], Dao Hsüan, *Hsü Kao-seng chuan* [Continued biographies of eminent monks], and Tsan Ning, *Sung Kao-seng chuan* [Biographies of Sung eminent monks].

2. Including also Chu Yün-ming (1461–1527), T'ang Yin (1470–1524), and Hsü Chen-ch'ing (1479–1511).

3. Led by Li P'an-lung (1514–1570) and Wang Shih-chen.

4. Craig Clunas, *Superfluous Things: Material Culture and Social Status in Early Modern China* (Cambridge: Polity Press, 1991), 169 and 168.

5. See Benjamin A. Elman, "Political, Social, and Cultural Reproduction via Civil Service Examinations in Late Imperial China," *Journal of Asian Studies* 50.1 (February 1991):8; and Stephen J. Roddy, *Literati Identity and Its Fictional Representations in Late Imperial China* (Stanford: Stanford University Press, 1998), 18. Elman also summarizes the Ming institutionalization of *Tao-hsüeh* under Emperor Yung-lo (r. 1403–1424) in "The Formation of 'Dao Learning' as Imperial Ideology during the Early Ming Dynasty." He notes, for example, that "Zhu Di [Chu Ti] actively promoted Confucian studies, especially the Southern Song (1127–1279) Confucian persuasion known as *Daoxue* [*Tao-hsüeh*] (Dao Learning), which had become the core curriculum of the civil service examinations in 1313 during the Yuan [Yüan] dynasty (1280–1368) and since 1384 during the Hongwu [Hung-wu] reign. Zhu's own *Shengxue xinfa* [*Sheng-hsüeh hsin-fa*] (The methods of the mind in the sages' teachings), completed in 1409 and presented to his designated successor, was emblematic in his mind of the unity of the *daotong* [*Tao-t'ung*] (orthodox transmission of the Dao) and the *zhitong* [*chih-t'ung*] (statecraft legitimacy) that he claimed for his reign" (in *Culture and State in Chinese History*, ed. Huters et al., 60).

6. Wen Cheng-ming's preface to *Ho shih yü-lin*, *Ssu-k'u ch'üan-shu* ed., "Hsü," 1b–2a.

7. Ch'eng Hao's rebuke to Hsieh Liang-tso (1050–1103), in Chu Hsi ed., *Shang-ts'ai hsien-sheng yü-lu* [Quotations of Master Shang-ts'ai (Hsieh Liang-tso)] (*Tz'u-yüan*, s.v. *Wan*).

8. *Erh-Ch'eng i-shu*, Hsieh Liang-tso's recollection of Ch'eng Hao: "While studying with [Master] Lo-chung [Ch'eng Hao], I compiled the good deeds of ancient people into a volume. The master saw it, saying I was 'squandering moral energies on trifles' [*wan-wu sang-chih*]" (*chüan* 3, 2b).

9. Ibid. Famous late Ming literatus-artist Ch'en Chi-ju (1558–1639) remarked that the *Li-hsüeh* scholars of his time even "took reading history as a matter of *wan-wu sang-chih.*" See his *K'uang-fu chih-yen* [A crazy man's remarks], 1607 edition, *chüan* 2, 5a.

10. *Erh-Ch'eng i-shu, chuan* 18, 95a.

11. Ho Liang-chün, for his part, pointed out that refined literature could both serve sociopolitical goals and express personal feelings, while "inward contemplation" *(fan-kuan nei-chao)* could at most benefit one's own body and mind. Literature might guide one to pursue sensual pleasure, but highly isolated meditation could cause one to neglect one's responsibilities. Comparatively speaking, then, bad literature was less damaging than isolated meditation, for "licentiousness only corrupts one's own person; neglecting responsibilities harms one's family and country" (Ho, *Ssu-yu chai ts'ung-shuo* [Classified accounts from the Four Friends Studio] [Peking: Chung-hua shu-chü, 1959, 1983], *chüan* 4, 30).

12. Cheng Chung-k'uei quotes Wang Shih-chen's words in *Ch'ing-yen, chüan* 5, 2a.

13. The earliest edition of the *Shih-shuo hsin-yü pu* was published by Chang Wen-chu in 1585. It includes a preface by Wang Shih-chen, dated 1556, indicating that he compiled the *Shih-shuo hsin-yü pu* by extracting from the *Shih-shuo hsin-yü* and the *Ho-shih yü-lin.* It also has two prefaces by Wang's younger brother Wang Shih-mao, dated respectively 1580 and 1585, detailing Wang Shih-chen's compilation and Chang Wen-chu's editing and publication of the work. The compilers of the *Ssu-k'u ch'üan-shu tsung-mu,* who evidently did not see this early edition, asserted that the work was spuriously attributed to Wang Shih-chen based on a Ch'ing edition with Chang Fu's preface dated 1676. Wang Chung-min, according to the Chang Wen-chu edition, confirms that Wang compiled the work and criticizes the *Ssu-k'u* compilers' hasty conclusion; see his *Chung-kuo shan-pen shu t'i-yao* [Bibliography of Chinese rare books] (Shanghai: Shanghai ku-chi ch'u-pan she, 1982), 391.

14. Wang Shih-chen's preface to the *Shih-shuo hsin-yü pu,* 2a.

15. Ibid., 2b.

16. Ts'ao Cheng-yung's preface to Cheng Chung-k'uei, *Ch'ing-yen,* 1b.

17. The *Ssu-k'u ch'üan-shu tsung-mu* says that the *Ho-shih yü-lin* incorporated all of the anecdotes in the *Shih-shuo hsin-yü,* but, in fact, Ho excluded almost all of them.

18. Yao Ju-shao's preface to Chiao Hung, *Chiao-shih lei-lin* (*Ts'ung-shu chi-ch'eng hsin-pien* ed.), 1–2. Yao quotes Ch'ü Po-yü's advice from the *Chuang-tzu,* "Jen-chien shih" [In the human world] (*Chuang-tzu* [*chi-shih*], 1:165); see also Watson, *Complete Works of Chuang Tzu,* 62.

19. In the original story, Ch'ü Po-yü advises Yen Ho how to lead the crown prince, a cruel and reckless man, to the right path without getting himself in trouble; see *Chuang-tzu* [*chi-shih*], 1:164–166.

20. See Li Chih's prefaces to *Ch'u-t'an chi,* 2 vols. (Peking: Chung-hua shu-chü, 1974), 1–4.

21. For example, the category of *Fu-fu* includes the following subcategories: *Ho-hun* [Mar-

riage], *Yu-hun* [Ghost marriage], *Sang-ou* [Loss of a spouse], *Tu-fu* [Jealous women], *Ts'ai-shih* [(Women's) talents and knowledge], *Yen-yü* [(Women's) speech and conversation], *Wen-hsüeh* [(Women's) literature and scholarship], *Hsien-fu* [Worthy husbands], *Hsien-fu* [Worthy wives], *Yung-fu* [Virile husbands], *Su-fu* [Vulgar husbands], *K'u-hai chu-ao* [Miserable women], and *Pi-an chu-ao* [Immortal women]. For more detailed information about the *Ch'u-t'an chi* and its connection with Li's commentary on the *Shih-shuo hsin-yü pu*, see *Ch'u-t'an chi* and Wang, *Chung-kuo shan-pen shu t'i-yao*, 340 and 391.

22. The translation of these Neo-Confucian terms is based on Wing-tsit Chan, *A Source Book in Chinese Philosophy* (Princeton, NJ: Princeton University Press, 1963), 463, 489, 491, 589–591, and 784.

23. Li Chih, *Ch'u-t'an chi*, 1.

24. See Chan, *A Source Book in Chinese Philosophy*, 463, 489, 491, and 589–591; Hou Wai-lu, *Sung-Ming li-hsüeh shih*, 1:384.

25. See Li Chih, *Ch'u-t'an chi*, *chüan* 2, 26, and *chüan* 4, 56.

26. See Li Chih's prefaces to *Ch'u-t'an chi*, 3–4.

27. *Ssu-k'u ch'üan-shu tsung-mu*, *chüan* 131, 1:1120. The publication of the *Li Cho-wu p'i-tien Shih-shuo hsin-yü pu* [Supplement to the *Shih-shuo hsin-yü* with commentary by Li Chih] in Japan, 1694, also inspired Japanese scholars into broad-scaled study and imitation of the *Shih-shuo hsin-yü*; see Kawakatsu Yoshio, "Edo jidai ni okeru *Sesetsu* kenkyū no ichimen" [An aspect of the study of the *Shih-shuo hsin-yü* during the Edo period], *Tōhōgaku* 20 (1960):2; and Ōyane Bunjirō, *Sesetsu shingo to rikuchō bungaku*, 92.

28. See, for example, Li Shao-wen, *Huang-Ming Shih-shuo hsin-yü*, "Wen-hsüeh," *chüan* 2, 12b–13a, and "P'in-tsao," *chüan* 4, 16a.

29. Ho Liang-chün never passed the provincial examinations, and he was very critical of the commentaries by Chu Hsi; see Goodrich and Fang, eds., *Dictionary of Ming Biography*, s.v. Ho Liang-chün.

30. Chiao Hung, *Chiao-shih lei-lin*, "Pien-tsuan," *chüan* 1a, 2.

31. See ibid., Chiao's colophon to the "Mulu," 3.

32. These two terms were not new in the Ming time, however. During the Han, they were used to denote scholars who had broad knowledge and were talented in composing essays, either literary or theoretical. For *wen-shih*, see Han Ying, *Han-shih wai-chuan*, 7; for *wen-jen*, see Wang Ch'ung, *Lun-heng*, "Ch'ao-ch'i" [Surpassing the extraordinary]: "Those who can interpret and edit classics to present to the court and to put in records, or can establish theoretical arguments and compose essays, are literati [*wen-jen*] and erudite scholars" (*Chu-tzu chi-ch'eng* ed., 135). See also Ts'ao P'i, *Tien-lun*, "Lun-wen" [On literature]: "Literati [*wen-jen*] have looked down upon one another since ancient times" (Hsiao T'ung, ed., *Wen-hsüan, chüan* 52, 3:720).

33. Ch'en Shou, *San-kuo chih*, *Wei-shu*, "Wen-ti chi" [Annals of Emperor Wen-ti, *chüan* 2, 1:89–90.

34. P'ei Sung-chih's commentary on this passage.

35. Ho, *Ssu-yu chai ts'ung-shuo, chüan* 23, 206.

36. See ibid., *chüan* 3, 26, *chüan* 23, 206, *chüan* 28, 259–261, *chüan* 29, 263–264, etc. For similar usage of *wen-jen* or *wen-shih*, see ibid., *chüan* 23, 204, 208, and 211, and *Ho-shih yü-lin, chüan* 8, 11a, 18a, and *chüan* 9, 5b, etc.

37. Ho, *Ho-shih yü-lin, chüan* 5, 7b.

38. See *Ho-shih yü-lin, chüan* 7, 1a, Ho's definition of "Wen-hsüeh."

39. *Ho-shih yü-lin, chüan* 28, 20b–21a, 19ab.

40. Ho's note to the episode.

41. For the Ming *fu-ku* movement, see Kuo, *Chung-kuo wen-hsüeh p'i-p'ing shih,* 297–348.

42. Wen did not take the civil examinations in his early life. At the age of fifty-three he obtained the rank of consultant in the Han-lin Academy through local government recommendation and an examination held by the Ministry of Personnel (see Goodrich and Fang, eds., *Dictionary of Ming Biography,* s.v. Wen Cheng-ming). As already mentioned (note 29), Ho never passed the provincial examinations, and he was very critical of the commentaries by Chu Hsi (see ibid., s.v. Ho Liang-chün).

43. *Ho-shih yü-lin, chüan* 24, 12a, definition of "Ch'ung-li."

44. Wen Cheng-ming observes: "Although the *Ho's Forest* is divided into thirty-eight categories, tracing its features and grasping its crucial points, the chapter on 'Speech and Conversation' is certainly its crux [*tsung*]" (Wen's preface to *Ho-shih yü-lin,* 1b).

45. Ho's definition of the category "Yen-yü," *Ho-shih yü-lin, chüan* 4, 1a.

46. Ho's definition of the category "Wen-hsüeh" [Literature and scholarship], *Ho-shih yü-lin, chüan* 7, 1a–b.

47. Ibid., 1a.

48. The six arts include rites, music, archery, driving of chariot, calligraphy, and mathematics; see *Chou-li [chu-shu]* [(Commentary on) The Book of Chou rites], "Ti-kuan" [The ministry of earth], "Pao-shih" [Tuitor], *chüan* 14, *Shih-san ching chu-shu,* 1:731. Here Ho makes a deliberate "category mistake": "literature and scholarship" do not belong to the "six arts" but to the "four categories of Confucius' disciples." This intentional error intensifies the contrast of the not-that-ordinary many (Confucius' seventy-two prize disciples) with the extraordinary few, who, by possessing the essence of Heaven and Earth, obtain the authority to interpret the *Tao.*

49. *Ho-shih yü-lin, chüan* 1, 1a, definition of "Te-hsing."

50. Ibid., *chüan* 23, 19ab, definition of "Ch'iao-i." See also *Chuang-tzu [chi-shih],* "T'ien Tzu-fang," *chüan* 7b, 3:719–720; and Watson, *Complete Works of Chuang Tzu,* 228, text and note.

51. *Ho-shih yü-lin,* "Yu-hui," *chüan* 30, 3a.

52. See Li, *Huang-Ming Shih-shuo hsin-yü,* "Ch'i-hsien," *chüan* 5, 19b.

53. The chapter "Yen-chih" (2 *chüan*) is one of the six longest chapters in *Ho's Forest*. The others are "Te-hsing" (3 *chüan*), "Yen-yü" (2 *chüan*), "Wen-hsüeh" (3 *chüan*), "Fang-cheng" (2 *chüan*), and "Shang-yü" (2 *chüan*).

54. *Lun-yü,* XVI, 11.

55. *Ho-shih yü-lin,* "Yen-chih," *chüan* 10, 1a–b.

56. Ssu-ma Ch'ien, *Shih-chi,* "K'ung-tzu shih-chia" [Hereditary House of Confucius] (*chüan* 47, 6:1932).

57. Wang Su's commentary: "*Tsai,* the man who manages [another's] property. By saying 'I'll be your *tsai*,' [Confucius] meant that he was sharing the same *chih* with Yen Hui" (ibid.).

58. Such as condemned in the *Shih-ching,* "Ta-ya" "Chan-yang": "[As wrong] as that [the trick of] selling at triple profit, / A superior man should have any knowledge of it; / A woman who has nothing to do with public affairs / Leaves her work of tending silk-worms and weaving" (*Mao-shih [cheng-i], chüan* 18, 1:577–578); also in the *Lun-yü:* "The superior man understands what is righteous; the inferior man understands what is profitable" (IV, 16). To link Confucius to money conflicts a more conventional image of the Master, who sees wealth and rank as floating clouds (see *Lun-yü,* VII, 16).

59. See Ho, *Ssu-yu chai ts'ung-shuo, chüan* 30, 272.

60. See *Ho-shih yü-lin,* "Yen-chih," *chüan* 10, 6a–b, 21b; *chüan* 11, 2b, 10a–11b, 13a–b, etc.

61. Ibid., "Yen-chih," *chüan* 10, 20b–21a.

62. *Lun-yü,* XI, 26; trans. Lau, *Analects,* 110–111.

63. 1 *ch'ing* = 15.13 acres, and 1 *mu* = 1/6 acre.

64. A reference to P'an Yüeh's idea expressed in his *Hsien-chü fu* [On idle life]. See Fang et al., *Chin-shu,* "P'an Yüeh chuan" [Biography of P'an Yüeh], *chüan* 55, 5:1504–1505.

65. *Ho-shih yü-lin,* "Yen-chih," *chüan* 11, 10a–b; see also *chüan* 10, 6a–7a, 12a–b, 21b, 26a–b; *chüan* 11, 16a–b.

66. The expression *Feng-yün,* winds and clouds, has been used to refer to the turmoil of politics since as late as the Six Dynasties period; see *Tz'u-yüan,* s.v. *Feng.*

67. *Ho-shih yü-lin,* "Yen-chih," *chüan* 11, 19b–20a; see also 25b.

68. Referring to Ou-yang Hsiu's collection of calligraphy, including both original works and rubbings; see *Ssu-k'u ch'üan-shu tsung-mu, chüan* 86, 1:733, s.v. Ou-yang Hsiu, *Chi-ku lu.*

69. *Ho-shih yü-lin,* "Yen-chih," *chüan* 11, 19b.

70. See *Ho-shih yü-lin,* "Yen-chih."

71. See ibid., "Huo-ni," *chüan* 30, 24a, and 24b–25b.

72. Ibid., "Yen-chih," *chüan* 10, 8a; *chüan* 11, 15b, 25b, 1b–2a, 7a; and *chüan* 10, 6a.

73. 1 *chin* = 1.1 pound.

74. *Ho-shih yü-lin,* "Chien-ao," *chüan* 26, 22b–23a.

75. Cheng, *Ch'ing-yen,* "Ch'ing-ti," *chüan* 9, 5b.

76. Chu Hsi, *Chu-tzu yü-lei, Ssu-k'u ch'üan-shu* ed., *chüan* 101, 18a. Giving up writing utensils as a symbolic gesture of concentrating on contemplation seems to have come from the Ch'an Buddhist tradition, as Chiao Hung recorded in *Chiao-shih lei-lin,* "Shih-pu" [Buddhism]: "Li Mi went to Mount Heng to take the Ch'an master, Ming Tsan, as his mentor. Ming Tsan told him: 'Those who are willing to study with me should first break their brushes and inkstones'" *(chüan* 8, 375).

77. *Ho-shih yü-lin,* "Yen-chih," *chüan* 11, 20a.

78. See *Erh-Ch'eng i-shu, chüan* 3, 2b.

79. See, particularly, *Ho-shih yü-lin,* "Yen-chih," "Huo-ni"; *Chiao-shih lei-lin,* "Wen-chü" [Writing utensils], "Tien-chi" [Books], "Sheng-yüeh" [Music and musical instruments], "Hsün-liao" [Incense materials]; and Li, *Huang-Ming Shih-shuo hsin-yü,* "Ch'i-i."

80. *Ho-shih yü-lin,* "Yen-yü," *chüan* 5, 9a.

81. Li, *Huang-Ming Shih-shuo hsin-yü,* "Ch'i-i," *chüan* 5, 33b.

82. The fourteen categories of things in the *Chiao-shih lei-lin* include: chapter 46, *Kung-shih* [Palaces and chambers], 47, *Kuan-fu* [Garments], 48, *Shih-p'in* [Food], 49, *Chiu-ming* [Wine and tea], 50, *Ch'i-chü* [Utensils], 51, *Wen-chü* [Writing accessories], 52, *Tien-chi* [Books], 53, *Sheng-yüeh* [Music and musical instruments], 54, *Hsün-liao* [Incense materials], 55, *She-yang* [Nutrition], 56, *Ts'ao-mu* [Plants], 57, *Niao-shou* [Animals], 58, *Hsien-tsung* [Immortals], and 59, *Shih-pu* [Buddhist monks].

83. Clunas, *Superfluous Things,* 168.

84. Elman, "Political, Social, and Cultural Reproduction," 13–14.

85. Ibid., 14. Elman also points out: "By 1400, for example, it is estimated that there were thirty thousand licentiates [*sheng-yuan (yüan)*] out of an approximate population of sixty-five million, a ratio of almost one licentiate per 2,200 persons. In 1700, there were perhaps 500 thousand licentiates in a total population of 150 million, or a ratio of one licentiate per three hundred persons" (ibid.).

86. For a convenient overview of the development of commerce in late imperial China, see Richard John Lufrano, *Honorable Merchants: Commerce and Self-Cultivation in Late Imperial China* (Honolulu: University of Hawai'i Press, 1997), 23 ff; Clunas, *Superfluous Things,* 5; Timothy Brook, *The Confusions of Pleasure: Commerce and Culture in Ming China* (Berkeley: University of California Press, 1998); and Smith, *China's Cultural Heritage,* 37–38.

87. Lufrano, *Honorable Merchants,* 37.

88. Clunas, *Superfluous Things,* 119.

89. One episode tells that people throughout the country competed to obtain Kao Ping's (1350–1423) poems and paintings, offering him so much cash and silk that they often surpassed his annual income at the Han-lin Academy (see Li, *Huang-Ming Shih-*

shuo hsin-yü, "Ch'iao-i," *chüan* 6, 18a; and Chiao Hung, *Yü-t'ang ts'ung-yü,* "Ch'iao-i," *chüan* 7, 256). Also, Hsia Ch'ang's (1388–1470) paintings of bamboo and rocks were so famous that even people from Korea and Japan would come to buy them with gold (see Li, *Huang-Ming Shih-shuo hsin-yü,* "Ch'iao-i," *chüan* 6, 21b).

90. The Chiang-nan area, particularly the city of Suchow, where most of the *Shih-shuo* imitators and their proponents gathered, was China's commercial center in the Ming-Ch'ing period. See Clunas, *Superfluous Things,* 145, and Lufrano, *Honorable Merchants,* 23 ff.

91. Yi Tsung-k'uei mistakes this detail from another *Make-do Studio* tale, "Yeh-ch'a kuo" [Country of devils]; see *Liao-chai chih-i,* 2 vols. (Shanghai: Shanghai ku-chi ch'u-pan she, 1979), 1:148.

92. Yi Tsung-k'uei, *Hsin Shih-shuo,* "Wen-hsüeh," *chüan* 2, 18b.

93. For the literary inquisitions of the early and high Ch'ing period, see Liang Ch'i-ch'ao (1873–1929), *Chung-kuo chin san-pai nien hsüeh-shu shih* [History of Chinese learning of the recent three hundred years], in *Liang Ch'i-ch'ao lun Ch'ing-hsüeh shih liang-chung* [Two works by Liang Ch'i-ch'ao on the history of Ch'ing learning] (Shanghai: Fu-tan ta-hsüeh ch'u-pan she, 1985), 107–108 and 118; see also R. Kent Guy, *The Emperor's Four Treasuries: Scholars and the State in the Late Ch'ien-lung Era* (Cambridge: Harvard University Press, 1987), 16–34, 157–200.

94. Yi Tsung-k'uei, *Hsin Shih-shuo,* "Li-yen," 2–3.

95. Among the nine Ch'ing imitations, three—Chiang Yu-jung and Tsou T'ung-lu, *Ming-i pien,* Chang Fu-kung, *Han Shih-shuo,* and Chang Chi-yung, *Nan-Pei ch'ao Shih-shuo*—were not seen. The two *Nü Shih-shuo* respectively by Li Ch'ing and Yen Heng will be discussed in chapter 8. This section will then focus on Liang Wei-shu, *Yü-chien tsun-wen,* Wu Su-kung, *Ming yü-lin,* Wang Wan, *Shuo-ling,* and Wang Cho, *Chin Shih-shuo.*

96. Liang Ch'i-ch'ao divides these forty years into three periods in terms of the Manchu regime's policy toward Chinese scholars: (1) 1644–1653, temptation, tempting Chinese intellectuals with academic degrees and official ranks; (2) 1654–1671, repression, when several wide-scale persecutions of Chinese intellectuals occurred; and (3) after 1672, a time of conciliation. See Liang, *Chung-kuo chin san-pai nien hsüeh-shu shih,* 106–107.

97. Liang Wei-shu, *Yü-chien tsun-wen* (1657; reprint, 2 vols., Shanghai: Shanghai ku-chi ch'u-pan she, 1986), "Hsü," 31.

98. Ibid., 3–4.

99. Ibid., 16–17.

100. Ibid., 23.

101. See ibid., 17.

102. Chiao Hung, *Yü-t'ang ts'ung-yü,* "Tsuan-hsiu" [Compiling and editing], *chüan* 4, 127.

103. Liang Wei-shu, *Yü-chien tsun-wen,* " Hsü," 18.

104. Kai-wing Chow, *The Rise of Confucian Ritualism in Late Imperial China: Ethics, Classics, and Lineage Discourse* (Stanford: Stanford University Press, 1994), 45.

105. Liang, *Yü-chien tsun-wen,* "Wen-hsüeh," *chüan* 3, 28a.

106. Ibid., "Kuei-chen," *chüan* 7, 19a.

107. Liang's own commentaries on "Wen-hsüeh," *chüan* 3, 28a and 1b, indicate respectively that Chu Hsi and Wang Yang-ming were offered sacrifices in the Confucian temple under Ming imperial decrees.

108. Liang, *Yü-chien tsun-wen,* "Shang-yü," *chüan* 6, 21a.

109. Li Chih, "T'ung-hsin shuo" [Essay on the child mind], *Fen-shu, chüan* 3, as quoted in Kuo, *Chung-kuo wen-hsüeh p'i-p'ing shih,* 351.

110. Li Chih, "Yü Kuan Teng-chih shu" [Letter to Kuan Teng-chih], as quoted in Ma, *Sung-Ming li-hsüeh yü wen-hsüeh,* 177–178.

111. For Li Chih's connections with the Wang Yang-ming school and his literary theory, see Kuo, *Chung-kuo wen-hsüeh p'i-p'ing shih,* 349–351; and Chun-shu Chang and Shelley Hsueh-lun Chang, *Crisis and Transformation in Seventeenth-Century China: Society, Culture, and Modernity in Li Yü's World* (Ann Arbor: University of Michigan Press, 1992), 162–163.

112. Liang, *Yü-chien tsun-wen,* "Kuei-chen," *chüan* 7, 3b–8a.

113. See Kuo, *Chung-kuo wen-hsüeh p'i-p'ing shih,* 351.

114. Liang, *Yü-chien tsun-wen,* "Wen-hsüeh," *chüan* 3, 10a.

115. Ibid., "Shang-yü," *chüan* 6, 2b.

116. Ting P'eng, one of the proponents of Wang Cho's *Chin Shih-shuo,* mentioned Liang's *Yü-chien tsun-wen* as a major contemporary *Shih-shuo t'i* work; see *Chin Shih-shuo,* "Hsü," 4.

117. Wang Wan briefly mentioned the Shun-chih emperor's (r. 1644–1661) appreciation of Kung Ting-tzu, only for extolling Kung's literary talent without really making a case of sociopolitical engagement between the ruler and the subject; see Wang, *Shuo-ling,* 16a.

118. See ibid., 16a–b, 22a–b.

119. Wang Cho, *Chin Shih-shuo,* "Wen-hsüeh," *chüan* 3, 34.

120. Ibid., "Yen-yü," *chüan* 2, 18.

121. *Ssu-k'u ch'üan-shu tsung-mu, chüan* 143, 2:1226.

122. Yi, *Hsin Shih-shuo,* "Li-yen" [Compilation notes], 2a.

123. Wang, *Chin Shih-shuo,* "Yen-yü," *chüan* 2, 20.

124. Ibid., 21.

125. *Shih-shuo hsin-yü,* 25/6: "When Sun Ch'u was young he wanted to become a recluse. Speaking of this once to Wang Chi, he intended to say, 'I'll pillow my head on the rocks and rinse my mouth in the streams.' Instead, he said by mistake, 'I'll rinse my

mouth with rocks and pillow my head on the streams.' Wang asked, 'Are streams something you can pillow on, and rocks something you can rinse with?' Sun replied, 'My reason for pillowing on streams is to "wash my ears," and my reason for rinsing with rocks is to "sharpen my teeth".'"

126. Wang, *Chin Shih-shuo,* "Yen-yü," *chüan* 2, 18.

Chapter 8: Milk and Scent

1. These dates in Wang, "Li Ch'ing Chu-shu k'ao," are confirmed by Li Ch'ing's postscript, dated 1676, to a 5-*chüan* edition of the *Nü Shih-shuo,* in which Li signed himself as "the seventy-five [*sui*] old man." They are also consistent with Huang Tsung-hsi, *Ssu-chiu lu* [Memoir of old acquaintances], in which Huang recounts: "In the year 1673, I sent the gentleman [Li Ch'ing] a letter to T'ai-chou. The gentleman replied, 'I have been living at home for about thirty years, and now I am about seventy-three *sui* old'" (in *Huang Tsung-hsi ch'üan-chi* [Complete works of Huang Tsung-hsi], 12 vols. [Hangchow: Chekiang ku-chi ch'u-pan she, 1985], 1:367). For Li Ch'ing's life, see Huang, ibid.; Wang, ibid.; and *Ssu-k'u ch'üan-shu tsung-mu,* Appendix 1, "Ssu-k'u ch'e-hui shu t'i-yao" [Bibliography of the purged and destroyed books from the Four Treasuries], 2:1839–1840, 1843–1844.

2. Susan Mann, *Precious Records: Women in China's Long Eighteenth Century* (Stanford: Stanford University Press, 1997), 2.

3. Susan Mann observes: "Eighteenth-century writers especially praised the female poets of the Six Dynasties period, and they often cited stories from the literary lives of characters in *A New Account of Tales of the World* [*Shih-shuo hsin-yü*]"—especially "Xie Daoyun [Hsieh Tao-yün] of willow catkin fame" (ibid., 91).

4. See Wang, "Li Ch'ing chu-shu k'ao"; and "Ssu-k'u ch'e-hui shu t'i-yao," 2:1839–1840, 1843–1844.

5. I am indebted to Katie Conboy's comments in her introduction to *Writing on the Body: Female Embodiment and Feminist Theory:* "At first glance, the answer to Simone de Beauvoir's question—'What is a woman?'—appears simple, for is the female body not the marker of womanhood? The body has, however, been at the center of feminist theory precisely because it offers no such 'natural' foundation for our pervasive cultural assumptions about femininity. Indeed, there is a tension between women's lived bodily experiences and the cultural meanings inscribed on the female body that always mediate those experiences" (Katie Conboy et al., eds. [New York: Columbia University Press, 1997], "Introduction," 1).

6. About the publication of Li Ch'ing's *Nü Shih-shuo,* the *Ssu-k'u ch'üan-shu tsung-mu* does not include its record. Wang, "Li Ch'ing Chu-shu k'ao" (337), quotes Ku Chieh-kang, *Ch'ing-tai chu-shu k'ao* [Study of Ch'ing works], saying that "There exists printed edition(s)," but neither Wang nor Ku provide specific records. Yüan and Hou, *Chung-kuo wen-yen hsiao-shuo shu-mu,* records an 1825 edition, with four proper *chüan* and a *chüan* of addenda (*pu-i*), published by the Ching-i chai. Of only two editions I have seen (Nanking Library)—one 4 *chüan* and the other 5 *chüan*—

neither bears the publisher's name nor the publication date. In his 1673 letter to Huang Tsung-hsi, Li Ch'ing noted: "I hereby present you several printed copies of my humble works, in order for you to know that, during these thirty years, I whiled away each day by working incessantly on these books" (Huang, *Ssu-chiu lu*, 1:367). Hence we may infer that by this time, while Li was approaching the age of seventy-three (note that Confucius was said to have died at the age of seventy-three), he had already finished his major works and put them in print. The 4-*chüan Nü Shih-shuo* was probably among these publications. It bears two prefaces, respectively by Li Ch'ing and Lu Min-shu. Li's preface indicates that he compiled the *Nü Shih-shuo* in his early fifties. Lu recounts how Li Ch'ing showed him the manuscript of the *Nü Shih-shuo* along with his other four most important works and asked for his prefaces. The 5-*chüan* edition was possibly a later one. It kept the identical print of the original 4 *chüan* and added a *chüan* of addenda (*pu-i*) along with Li Ch'ing's 1676 postscript, explaining why he compiled this extra *chüan*. It also replaced Lu Min-shu's implicitly anti-Manchu preface with a nonpolitical one by Li Ch'ing's uncle, Li Ssu-ching. All these three prefaces are undated (Li dated his postscript "ping-ch'en" [1676] without indicating the reign title), possibly because Li, Lu, and Li's uncle, as Ming loyalists, rejected using the Ch'ing calendar.

7. Li Ch'ing, *Nü Shih-shuo,* ca. 1673 ed., Lu Min-shu's preface, 5a–6a.

8. Ibid., Lu Min-shu's preface, 6a–b.

9. Li Shao-wen, *Huang Ming Shih-shuo hsin-yü,* "Te-hsing," *chüan* 1, 3b; see also Cheng Chung-k'uei, *Ch'ing-yen,* "Fang-cheng," *chüan* 3, 9b–10a; and Chiao Hung, *Yü-t'ang ts'ung-yü,* "Fang-cheng," *chüan* 5, 159.

10. See, for example, Ch'ü Yüan's *Li-sao* [Encountering sorrow] and Ts'ao Chih's "Tsa shih" [Miscellaneous poems].

11. *Ch'eng-shih i-shu, Ssu-pu pei-yao* ed., *chüan* 22B, 3a; trans. Marina H. Sung, "The Chinese *Lieh-nü* Tradition," in *Women in China: Current Directions in Historical Scholarship,* eds. Richard W. Guisso and Stanley Johannesen (Youngstown, NY: Philo Press, 1981), 72.

12. Jennifer Holmgren, *Marriage, Kinship and Power in Northern China* (Aldershot, UK: Variorum, 1995), 184. Holmgren notes that these practices were confirmed as a formal display of fidelity by "further contact with northern culture after the collapse of the T'ang empire, along with the legalistic approach to the vow of celibacy during Yüan" (184). As Holmgren points out, "the assimilation of non-Han ideas on the afterlife gradually modified the Chinese perception of widow-suicide to the point where self-immolation upon the death of the husband was seen as a highly appropriate display of fidelity to the deceased" (188).

13. Mark Elvin, "Female Virtue and the State in China," *Past and Present* 104 (1984):123.

14. See Marina H. Sung, "The Chinese *Lieh-nü* Tradition," 72.

15. Katherine Carlitz, "Desire, Danger, and the Body," in *Engendering China: Women, Culture, and the State,* eds. Christina K. Gilmartin et al. (Cambridge: Harvard University Press, 1994), 111.

16. Li Ch'ing, *Nü Shih-shuo*, "Shu-te" [Female virtues], *chüan* 1, 8a.

17. See ibid., "Chieh-i" [Chastity and righteousness], *chüan* 1, 30a–41a; and "I-yung" [Determination and courage], *chüan* 2, 12a–20a.

18. See ibid., "Chieh-i," *chüan* 1, 39a-b.

19. Ch'en Yüan-lu's postscript to Yen Heng, *Nü Shih-shuo,* 14a.

20. The Ch'ing poet Chang Wen-t'ao's (fl. 1790–1800) wife expressed an intellectual woman's ideal about marriage in the following lines: "It's a blessing to be a talented man's wife / Even reduced [by poverty] as thin as a plum blossom." See Yi Tsung-k'uei, *Hsin Shih-shuo,* "Wen-hsüeh," *chüan* 2, 31a.

21. In addition to the unfinished *Nü Shih-shuo,* Yen Heng also left seventeen poems collected, possibly by her husband, under the title *Nen-hsiang an ts'an-kao* [Remnants of poems from Tender Thoughts Hermitage], 1 *chüan,* 1st ed. 1865, *Chüan-ching lou ts'ung-k'o pen* ed. (Shanghai: chü-chen fang-sung yin-shu chü, 1920). Yen Heng's poetic accomplishment won praise from later critics. Hsü Shih-ch'ang (1855–1939), for instance, included eight of her seventeen poems in his *Wan-ch'ing i shih-hui* [Collected poems from the Twilight Cottage], 4 vols. (1928; reprint, Peking: Chung-kuo shu-tien, 1989), *chüan* 192, 4:797–798.

22. *San-tuo,* "three a lots," refers to the ways of improving literary writings. Ch'en Shih-tao (1053–1101), *Hou-shan shih-hua* [Poetry talks of Hou-shan]: "[Ou-yang] Yung-shu (Ou-yang Hsiu) says that there are three 'a lots' in improving literary writings: to read a lot, to write a lot, and to discuss a lot" (Ho Wen-huan [fl. 1770], ed., *Li-tai shih-hua,* 2 vols. [Peking: Chung-hua shu-chü, 1980], 1:305).

23. Yeh Shih Li-wan's preface to Yen Heng, *Nü Shih-shuo,* 1a.

24. The most famous story of painting the wife's eyebrows is recorded in Pan Ku, *Han-shu,* "Chang Ch'ang chuan" [Biography of Chang Ch'ang], *chüan* 76, 10:3222.

25. Yen Heng, *Nü Shih-shuo,* 1b. Yen possibly quoted this episode and Mao's poetic line from Wu Hao's *Kuo-ch'ao Hang-chün shih-chi* [Collected Hangchow poems from the reigning dynasty], 32 *chüan* (1800; reprint, Ch'ien-t'ang: Ting-shih, 1874), *chüan* 30, 13a-b.

26. Dorothy Ko has discussed Mao T'i's case in her *Teachers of the Inner Chambers: Women and Culture in Seventeenth-Century China* (Stanford: Stanford University Press, 1994), 243. Commenting on Mao's remark, "Poetry is my god and spirit [*shen-ming*]; I give birth to sons through the act of writing," Ko writes: "Biological procreation perpetuated the male line of descent; literary creation vindicated the woman writer's existence as an individual and opened a gateway to immortality. Mao Anfang's [An-fang's] individualistic vision is not anti-patrilineal family in intent. Her statement implies that motherhood need not be a woman's only goal in life. But if Mao had had biological sons, she probably would have seen her mission as poet as compatible with that as mother." Thus Ko, adopting a rather optimistic tone, sees Mao's self-imposed poetic mission as one more alternative in a woman's life, compatible with her possible motherhood, whereas I see poetry as Mao's only way to sustain herself after becoming disillusioned with men. Also, I translate *shen-ming* as "spirit and intelligence"

following its general usage and meaning in the *Shih-shuo hsin-yü*. A most relevant example is recorded in the chapter "Hsien-yüan" (see *Shih-shuo hsin-yü*, 19/31, and Mather, *A New Account of Tales of the World*, 355).

27. Yen Heng, *Nü Shih-shuo*, 6a-b.

28. See *Tz'u-yüan*, s.v. *T'ung*.

29. Some of these chaste women stories intend to mock men's hypocrisy and selfishness. One episode tells that the Chin ducal son, Ch'ung-erh, took many wives during his exile. Upon leaving Ti for Ch'i, he said to his Ti wife, Chi-k'uei, "Wait for me. If after twenty-five years I do not come back, then remarry." Chi-k'uei replied, "I am already twenty-five, to wait for another twenty-five years, I will be in my coffin. Please let me wait for you anyway" (Li Ch'ing, *Nü Shih-shuo*, "Chieh-i," *chüan* 1, 30a-b).

30. Ibid., "Chieh-i," *chüan* 1, 30b.

31. Ibid., "I-yung," *chüan* 2, 12a. Li Ch'ing quotes this episode from the *Chan-kuo ts'e* [Intrigues of the warring states], "Ch'i-ts'e" [Intrigues of Ch'i] VI. See *Chan-kuo ts'e*, 3 vols. [Shanghai: Shanghai ku-chi ch'u-pan she, 1985], *chüan* 13, 1:472–473.

32. See *Li-chi* [*cheng-i*], "Yü-tsao" [Jade embellishment]: "Without a [good] reason to [do otherwise], the superior man keeps his jade [pendant] with him. The superior man compares his virtue to [the quality of] the jade" (*Shih-san ching chu-shu, chüan* 30, 2:1482). See also *Mao-shih* [*cheng-i*], "Ch'in-feng" [Odes of Ch'in], "Hsiao-jung" [Little militant]: "I miss my lord; he is as gentle as the jade." Cheng Hsüan's commentary on this line is: "The jade has five virtues" (*Shih-san ching chu-shu, chüan* 6, 1:370). *Li-chi*, "P'in-i" also enumerates the virtues of a gentleman that jade symbolizes (see *Shih-san ching chu-shu, chüan* 63, 2:1694).

33. Li Ch'ing, *Nü Shih-shuo*, "Jen-hsiao" [Benevolence and filial piety], *chüan* 1, 14a-b. Girl Kao was a native Korean living during the T'ang period. Her father surrendered to the Chinese emperor, so the Korean ruler Li Na eliminated the entire family to punish his betrayal.

34. Ibid., "Kuei-hui" [Advice and admonition], *chüan* 3, 20b. "Sang-chung chih hsing" (the [love] affair at Sang-chung) is a general expression for love affairs; see *Mao-shih* [*cheng-i*], "Yung-feng" [Odes of Yung], "Sang-chung" (*Shih-san ching chu-shu, chüan* 3, 1:314-315). "Lin-ch'iung chih pen" (Elopement from Lin-ch'iung) refers to the story of Cho Wen-chün, a young widow of the Han dynasty who eloped with the famous Han literatus Ssu-ma Hsiang-ju from her father's house in Lin-ch'iong; see Ssu-ma Ch'ien, *Shih-chi*, "Ssu-ma Hsiang-ju lieh-chuan" [Biography of Ssu-ma Hsiang-ju], *chüan* 117, 9:3000–3001.

35. Li Ch'ing, *Nü Shih-shuo*, "Ch'ung-pi" [Favor and favorite], *chüan* 4, 11a-b. Note that the image of "a hooklike crescent moon" alludes to Li Yü's lyric poem, "Tune: The Cry of Night Crow" (*Wu yeh t'i*): "Silently, I ascend the West Tower, the moon is like a hook," which is generally interpreted as "a tune of a decaying state."

36. *Chan-kuo ts'e*, "Ch'in ts'e" [Intrigues of Ch'in] III, *chüan* 5, 1:186. In this edition of the *Chan-kuo ts'e*, as well as the Chung-hua shu-chü edition of the *Shih-chi*, "Fan Chü" is printed as "Fan Sui"; for a discussion of Fan Chü's name, see Takigawa Kame-

tarō, *Shi ki kaichū kōshō* [Study of collected commentaries on the *Shih-chi*] (Taipei: Chung-cheng shu-chü ch'u-pan she, 1982), *chüan* 79, 2, the entry of "Fan Sui should be Fan Chü."

37. Hsiao T'ung, ed., *Wen-hsüan, chüan* 39, 2:545.

38. See Li Ch'ing, *Nü Shih-shuo,* "Fen-chüan" [Anger and irascibility], *chüan* 4, 31a.

39. Ibid., "Shu-te," *chüan* 1, 6a.

40. Liu Su, *Ta T'ang hsin-yü,* "Yu-t'i," *chüan* 6, 85: "Pi Kou was extremely filial. When his stepmother died, his two younger sisters, [later married to] Hsiao and Lu, were yet infants. [Pi] breast-fed them, and milk came out from his breasts. Upon his death, the two sisters cried so grievously that they fainted for a long time. They said, 'Although there is no three-year ritual for a brother, we were raised up by him, and how can we [mourn for him] just as anybody [would for a brother]]?' They therefore observed a three-year mourning period." See also Wang Tang, *T'ang yü-lin,* "Te-hsing," *chüan* 1, 9: "Yüan Lu-shan breast-fed his elder brother's son, and milk therefore came out from his breasts. Only after his nephew started eating [regular food] did his milk stop."

41. The *Women's Studies Encyclopedia* states that "gender is a cultural construct: the distinction in roles, behaviors, and mental and emotional characteristics between females and males developed by a society"; and "sex is a term that encompasses the morphological and physiological differences on the basis of which humans (and other life forms) are categorized as male and female. It should be used only in relation to characteristics and behaviors that arise directly from biological differences between men and women" (ed. Helen Tierney, [New York: Peter Bedrick Books, 1991], 153).

42. Judith Butler, "Performative Acts and Gender Constitution: An Essay in Phenomenology and Feminist Theory," in *Writing on the Body,* eds. Katie Conboy et al., 406.

43. Ibid., 403.

44. Li Ch'ing, *Nü Shih-shuo,* "Jen-hsiao," *chüan* 1, 13a-b.

45. See the *I-li* [*chu-shu*] [(Commentary on) Etiquette and ritual], "Sang-fu" [Mourning ritual], *Shih-san ching chu-shu, chüan* 29–30, 1:1100–1104. See also Wang Li, *Ku-tai han-yü* [Classical Chinese], 4 vols. (Peking: Chung-hua shu-chü, 1963), 3:932–934.

46. Li Ch'ing, *Nü Shih-shuo,* "T'ung-pien" [Erudite and eloquent], *chüan* 3, 2a.

47. For example: "King Chao of the Chou ascended the Lofty-Clouds Terrace and summoned the dancing girls Hsüan-chüan and T'i-mo. At that moment a sweet smell suddenly arose, and the two girls both had slim bodies and sweet breath" ("Jung-sheng" [Appearance and sound], *chüan* 3, 25b); "Hsi-Shih had a special fragrance all over her body" ("Jung-sheng," *chüan* 3, 25b); "In the court of Emperor Wu of the Han, the palace lady Li-chüan had soft, jadelike skin and her breath was sweeter than the orchid" ("Jung-sheng," *chüan* 3, 26a); "The Liang's daughter, Ying . . . exhaled fragrant breath and had smooth and pure skin" ("Jung-sheng," *chüan* 3, 27a); and "The imperial concubine Yang's sweat was pink, creamy, and fragrant" ("Jung-sheng," *chüan* 3, 28b).

48. Ibid., "Ju-ya," *chüan* 1, 42a.

49. Ibid., 42b.

50. Women's participation in literary or artistic creation, women's attending men's similar activities, and men's poetic communication with women are among the major themes of Li Ch'ing's *Nü Shih-shuo;* see, mainly, chapters "Ju-ya" (*chüan* 1), "Chün-ts'ai" [Outstanding talents] (*chüan* 2), "Chün-mai" [Outstanding and carefree] (*chüan* 2), "T'ung-pien" (*chüan* 3), "Ying-hui" [Prominent intelligence] (*chüan* 3), and "I-ch'iao" [Art and ingenuity] (*chüan* 3).

51. Ibid., "Ju-ya," *chüan* 1, 42b.

52. Li Ch'ing was not alone in linking female scent to women's literary creativity. It seems that a growing fashion during the Ming-Ch'ing period was for gentlemen to title their compilations of women's poetry with words such as *hsiang* and *fang,* both meaning "fragrance," or names of fragrant flowers such as orchids and plum blossoms (see Hu Wen-k'ai, *Li-tai fu-nü chu-tso k'ao* [Study of women's works from previous dynasties] [Shanghai: Shanghai ku-chi ch'u-pan she, 1985], "Index," 983–1115). For instance, famed Ming literatus T'u Lung (1542–1605) named the compilation of his daughter T'u Yao-se and daughter-in-law Shen T'ien-sun's poetry *Liu-hsiang ts'ao* [Lingering fragrance: A draft] and wrote in the preface: "They (T'u and Shen) had an agreement to print their drafts in one volume after their death. In naming the book, we followed this meaning—orchid dies, but leaves its lingering fragrance behind" (Hu, *Li-tai fu-nü chu-tso k'ao,* 173; see also Ann Waltner and Pi-ching Hsu, "Lingering Fragrance: The Poetry of Tu Yaose [T'u Yao-se] and Shen Tiansun [Shen T'ien-sun]," *Journal of Women's History* 8.4 [Winter 1997]:33–34). Also, a classified collection of Ming-Ch'ing women's lyric poems, compiled and reviewed by leading early Ch'ing scholars Hsü Shu-min, Ch'ien Yüeh, Wang Shih-chen, et al., is entitled *Chung-hsiang tz'u* [Lyric poems of collected fragrance]. The woman writer Wu Ch'i's preface (dated 1690) to this work has lines such as: "Using an oriole-shuttle to weave brocade, a scented heart often chases flower-souls; while geese fly against the cold air, the fragrant dream lingers around the cassia spirit. . . . Lines clink, piling up to form a jade mountain; words emit scent, building up a realm of collected fragrance" (Hu, *Li-tai fu-nü chu-tso k'ao,* 899).

53. See Yen Heng, *Nü Shih-shuo,* 11b, 8a, 2b, 9b, 8b.

54. For example, Chin Yüeh would "paint plum branches on a piece of paper and then stick on them the real plum blossom petals she collected from the ground" (Yen Heng, *Nü Shih-shuo,* 10a).

55. See ibid., 6a.

56. See ibid., 7b.

57. Ibid., 2b–3a.

58. See Maggie Bickford, *Ink Plum: The Making of a Chinese Scholar-Painting Genre* (Cambridge: Cambridge University Press, 1996), 28–31.

59. Ibid., 30, 16.

60. Ibid., 31.

61. See Yüan Hao-wen, "Lun shih san-shih shou" [On poetry, thirty poems], *I-shan hsien-sheng wen-chi* [Collected works of Yüan Hao-wen (I-shan)], *Ssu-pu ts'ung-k'an* ed., *chüan* 11.

62. Yüan Hao-wen, *Chung-chou chi*, quoted in Kuo Shao-yü and Wang Wensheng, *Chung-kuo li-tai wen-lun hsüan* [Selected works of Chinese literary criticism], 4 vols. (Shanghai: Shanghai ku-chi ch'u-pan she, 1979), 2:457, n. 49. In Ch'in Kuan, *Huai-hai chi*, *chüan* 10, the title of this poem is *"Ch'un-jih"* [Spring day], and *"wan-chih"* (evening branches) is *"hsiao-chih"* (morning branches); see *Chung-kuo li-tai wen-lun hsüan*, 2:457, n. 48.

63. Han Yü, *Ch'ang-li hsien-sheng wen-chi* [Collected works of Han Yü], *Ssu-pu ts'ung-k'an* ed., *chüan* 3, 1a.

64. Yen Heng, *Nü Shih-shuo*, 4a.

65. According to the stories of the twenty-four paragons of filial piety, well known during the late imperial period, Kuo Chü, a very poor man, was prepared to sacrifice his son in order to have enough food for his aging mother. Upon digging the ground, however, he found a jar of gold and the boy was thus spared. The poem by Yüan Mei's aunt reads:

> Kuo Chü the filial son is only a false name;
> He pleases his mother regardless of heavy and light.
> Killing his darling little son with no reason;
> Hurting his mother's feelings merely for food.
> Binding his son to a tree, [Teng] Po-tao broke his family line;
> Tasting the broth of his child, Yüeh Yang lost his minister position.
> Heartlessness deserves harsh punishment, past and present;
> It's unfair that Heaven would reward Kuo Chü gold!

(Quoted in Yüan Mei, *Sui-yüan shih-hua* [Poetry talks from Sui Gardens], 2 vols. [Peking: Jen-min wen-hsüeh ch'u-pan she, 1982], *chüan* 12, 1:408).

66. Yen Heng, *Nü Shih-shuo*, 3b. Lady Ch'en's given name, K'un-wei, or "female weft," was a typical female name at Yen Heng's time; see also ibid., 4a–b.

67. Judging from my reading of Ming-Ch'ing Chinese literature, a married woman had the right only to dispose of her own dowry, and it was a great virtue for a wife/mother to sell her dowry to meet the needs of household maintenance. In selling the property from her husband's side, she at least needed the husband's consent if he was alive, and, after his death, "a wife could not inherit property belonging to her deceased husband" but "only hold it in trust for his heirs" (Holmgren, *Marriage, Kinship and Power in Northern China*, 11). Since the episode does not mention Ch'en's consultation with her husband, I suspect that she is giving away her own property.

68. Li Po (701–762), "Ku-feng" [Ancient ode], No. 1, *Li T'ai-po ch'üan-chi* [Complete works of Li T'ai-po], commentary by Wang Ch'i, 3 vols. (Peking: Chung-hua shu-chü, 1977), *chüan* 2, 1:8. See also discussion of this tradition by Kuo Shao-yü and Wang Wensheng, *Chung-kuo li-tai wen-lun hsüan*, 1:87–88.

69. *Meng-tzu [chu-shu]*, I, 7, *Shih-san ching chu-shu, chüan* 1b, 2:2670.

70. Yen Heng, *Nü Shih-shuo*, 4a.

71. Ibid., 1a.

72. This wedding contest between the groom and the bride clearly alludes to two episodes in the *Shih-shuo hsin-yü* (19/9 and 27/9), both portraying a self-esteemed and out-spoken bride.

73. In his *Sui-yüan shih-hua pu-i (Supplement to Poetry Talks)*; see Mann, *Precious Records*, 112 and n. 103 for her discussion of Yüan Mei's version of the story, as well as an-other version in Wan-yen Yün Chu (1771–1833), *Kuo-ch'ao kuei-hsiu cheng-shih chi* (Correct beginnings: Women's poetry of our august dynasty).

74. See Yen Heng, *Nü Shih-shuo*, 8a.

75. Ibid.

76. See Wang Tang, *T'ang yü-lin [chiao-cheng], chüan* 3, no. 455, 1:306; see also Ou-yang and Sung, *Hsin T'ang-shu*, "Shang-kuan Chao-jung chuan" [Biography of Shang-kuan Chao-jung], *chüan* 76, 11:3488–3489.

77. See Li Ch'ing, *Nü Shih-shuo*, "Chün-ts'ai," *chüan* 2, 6b–7a.

78. The idea of a woman beautifying herself in order to please her man is expressed in pre-Ch'in classics such as in the *Shih-ching*, "Wei-feng" [Odes of Wei], "Po hsi": "Since my husband went to the east, / My head has been like the flying [pappus of the] artemisia. / It is not that I could not anoint and wash it; / But for whom should I adorn myself?" (*Mao-shih cheng-i, Shih-san ching chu-shu, chüan* 3, 1:327; trans. James Legge, *The Chinese Classics*, 4 vols., Vol. IV, *The Shih King* [Taipei: SMC Pub-lishing, 1991], 105); and in the *Chan-kuo ts'e*, "Chao ts'e" [Intrigues of Chao] I: "A gentleman dies for the one who really understands him, and a woman adorns her-self for the one who loves her" (*shih wei chih-chi che ssu, nü wei yüeh-chi che jung*) (*chüan* 18, 2:597).

79. See Yen Heng, *Nü Shih-shuo*, 2a–3b. For a detailed discussion of the Banana Gar-den Poetry Club, see Ko, *Teachers of the Inner Chambers*, 234–250.

80. See, for example, "Shih Tzu-hsien ku yu Ko-ling hsiao-ch'i Fu-ch'un shan kuan" [A brief break on the Fu-ch'un Heights while attending upon my mother-in-law Tzu-hsien for an excursion on the Ko Summit] and "Ch'u-hsia shih Chou shih ku chi ti-ssu Shih Wen-ch'ing piao-tzu yu Hsi-hu yin Hu-hsin t'ing shang" [Drinking in the Pavilion of the Lake Center while accompanying my mother-in-law Chou with my younger sister-in-law and my female cousin Shih Wen-ch'ing for an excursion on the West Lake] (1a and 2b–3a).

81. Yen Heng, *Nen-hsiang an ts'an-kao*, 2a. The last line, with the word *chih-ch'i*—miss-ing the mother—alludes to the *Shih-ching*, "Wei-feng" [Odes of Wei], "Chih-ku" [As-cending the Ku]: "Ascending the Ch'i Mountain, I am longing for my mother."

82. See *Tz'u-yüan*, s.v. *Tsan-hua ko*.

83. See *Chin-shu*, "Lieh-nü chuan," *chüan* 96, 8:2516. Hsieh Tao-yün's "gauze veil" story,

as Ann Waltner and Pi-ching Hsu point out, had long stood as an example of an accomplished wife who gave wise counsel to her family members. For instance, the
Ming poetess Shen T'ien-sun used this allusion in her poem appraising her sister-
in-law, T'u Yao-se (see Waltner and Hsu, "Lingering Fragrance," 36).

84. Ts'ai Yen was such a child prodigy of music that, at the age of six *sui*, she could tell
which string was broken on her father's zither while listening to him playing from the
next room; see, for example, Li Ch'ing, *Nü Shih-shuo*, "Ying-hui," *chüan* 3, 22a.

85. For the text of the "Hu-chia shih-pa p'ai" and a discussion of its connections with
Ts'ai Yen, see Kuo Mao-ch'ien (Sung), *Yüeh-fu shih-chi* [Anthology of music bureau
poems], "Ch'in-ch'ü ko-tz'u" [Zither lyrics] III, 4 vols. (Peking: Chung-hua shu-chü,
1979), *chüan* 59, 3:860–865.

86. *Lun-yü*, VI, 23: "The wise find joy in water; the benevolent find joy in mountains";
trans. D. C. Lau, *The Analects* (New York: Penguin, 1979), 84.

87. Ho Liang-chün, *Ho-shih yü-lin*, "Hsien-yüan," *chüan* 22, 12a.

88. Hsieh Tao-yün in particular; see, for example, *Ho-shih yü-lin*, "Yen-yü," *chüan* 4, 19a,
and "Hsien-yüan," *chüan* 22, 15b.

89. See Mann, *Precious Records*, 86–92.

90. Ibid., 93.

91. Ibid., 89, 92, 93, 83.

92. Yen Heng, *Nen-hsiang an ts'an-kao*, 3b.

93. Ibid., 1b.

94. Her attitude in this respect is quite different from that of the high-Ch'ing gentlewomen discussed in Susan Mann's *Precious Records* (see chapter 5, passim).

95. Yen Heng, *Nü Shih-shuo*, 1b. See Ellen Widmer and Kang-i Sun Chang, eds., *Writing Women in Late Imperial China* (Stanford: Stanford University Press, 1997), 5–6,
for a brief introduction to Li Yin's life and works. Hu, *Li-tai fu-nü chu-tso k'ao*, 109,
records Li Yin's *Chu-hsiao hsüan yin-ts'ao* (Draft poems from the Laughing Bamboo
Studio), with her husband, the Ming loyalist-martyr Ko Cheng-ch'i's (d. 1645) preface (1643). Ko comments that Li often "worried about the political situation with
such intense indignation that even men could not surpass it."

96. The jade tree (*yü-shu*) refers to the song "Yü-shu hou-t'ing hua" [The jade tree and
the backyard flowers] composed by Ch'en Hou-chu (r. 583–589), the last ruler of
the Ch'en dynasty (557–589); as the *Sui-shu*, "Wu-hsing chih I" [Treatise of the five
elements] records: "During the early Chen-ming reign [587–589], Hou-chu composed a new song, and it was rather sad. Its lyric reads: 'The jade tree and the backyard flowers / Flowers bloom, but cannot last.' People of the time considered the
song a bad omen, and it indeed foretold the briefness of the dynasty" (*chüan* 22,
3:637). The bronze camel [*t'ung-t'o*] is an allusion from the *Chin-shu*, "So Ching
chuan" [Biography of So Ching]: "Ching had the capability of telling the future.
Knowing that the world would be soon in a state of chaos, he pointed to the bronze

camel at the palace gate in Lo-yang, saying with a sigh: 'I'll see you in thorns!'" (*chüan* 60, 6:1648).

97. Yen Heng, *Nü Shih-shuo*, 3b. See Widmer and Chang, eds., *Writing Women in Late Imperial China*, 156, 370f., for a brief introduction to Wu Shan's life and works.

98. Yen Heng, *Nen-hsiang an ts'an-kao*, 3b.

99. Such as when mothers nurture their children with both milk and knowledge; see, for example, Li Ch'ing, *Nü Shih-shuo*, "Kuei-hui," *chüan* 3, 10b–20b.

100. Ibid., "Jen-hsiao," *chüan* 1, 9a-b.

101. Ibid., "Chün-ts'ai," *chüan* 2, 11b.

102. "Shu Ink Maiden. . . loved the ink-bamboo painting by Lady Kuan [Tao-sheng]. All her life she slept with it, and she died unmarried" (Yen Heng, *Nü Shih-shuo*, 5b).

103. Li Ch'ing, *Nü Shih-shuo*, "Ju-ya," *chüan* 1, 42b.

104. See *Shih-shuo hsin-yü*, 19/26, and Li Ch'ing, *Nü Shih-shuo*, "Yu-hui," *chüan* 4, 13a-b.

105. Li Ch'ing, *Nü Shih-shuo*, "Chün-ts'ai," *chüan* 2, 12a.

106. "Kuan-chü" [Crying ospreys], the first poem of the *Shih-ching*. "Chih chao[-fei]" [Morning (flying) pheasants], an ancient zither melody; see *Tz'u-yüan*, s.v. "Chih chao-fei." "Pai-hsüeh" [White snow], an ancient zither melody attributed to Shih K'uang, usually regarded as a representative of elite music and poetry, here probably refers to Yang Wei-chen's poetic and music works; see *Tz'u-yüan*, s.v. "Pai-hsüeh."

107. Li Ch'ing, *Nü Shih-shuo*, "Ju-ya," *chüan* 1, 44b.

108. This "glorification of romantic attachments between men and women" who were similarly cultivated and shared aesthetic tastes is obviously influenced by a late Ming intellectual ideal about gender relations. See William T. Rowe, "Women and the Family in Mid-Qing [Ch'ing] Social Thought: The Case of Chen Hongmou [Ch'en Hung-mou]," *Late Imperial China* 13.2 (December 1992):8. See also Kang-i Sun Chang, *The Late Ming Poet Chen Tzu-lung* (New Haven: Yale University Press, 1991).

109. Li Ch'ing, *Nü Shih-shuo*, "Ju-ya," *chüan* 1, 44a.

110. Yen Heng, *Nü Shih-shuo*, 1b.

111. A number of scholarly works discussed this function of the Prospect Garden in the *Hung-lou meng*. See, for example, Andrew Plaks, *Archetype and Allegory in Dream of the Red Chamber* (Princeton, NJ: Princeton University Press, 1976), 279–360; and Ying-shih Yu, "The Two Worlds of *Hung-lou meng*," *Renditions* 2 (Spring 1974).

Chapter 9: An Alien Analogue

1. On Edo imitations of the *Shih-shuo hsin-yü*, see Ōyane Bunjirō, "Edo Jidai ni okeru Sesetsu shingo ni tsuite," *Sesetsu shingo to rikuchō bungaku*, 102–105; Ma Hsing-kuo, "*Shih-shuo hsin-yü* tsai Jih-pen ti liu-ch'uan chi ying-hsiang" [Circulation and influence of the *Shih-shuo hsin-yü* in Japan], *Tung-pei Shih-ta hsüeh-pao (she-k'o pan)*

1989.3:70–74; and Wang Neng-hsien, *Shih-shuo hsin-yü yen-chiu* [Study of *A New Account of Tales of the World*] (Nanking: Kiangsu ku-chi ch'u-pan she, 1992), 253–255.

2. Later Japanese scholars acclaimed Hattori Nankaku's effort in learning the *Shih-shuo* style. For example, in his preface to Tsunota Ken, *Kinsei sōgo*, Satō Tan comments: "Hattori Nankaku compiled *Daitō seigo*, and his writing style is very much like that of the Prince Lin-ch'uan's" (2b).

3. Tei Mōichi's preface to Hattori, *Daitō seigo*, 1a–b.

4. Ibid.

5. See Sen'ichi Hisamatsu, ed., *Biographical Dictionary of Japanese Literature* (Kodansha International, in collaboration with the International Society for Educational Information, 1976), s.v. Hattori Nankaku.

6. Although Confucian values and ideals were introduced into Japan as early as the fifth century, "Confucianism did not become deeply embedded in the Japanese way of life and thought until the Tokugawa era, when the ruling family adopted Neo-Confucianism as its official philosophy and actively inculcated Confucian moral ideals into the minds of the people" (Mikiso Hane, *Premodern Japan: A Historical Survey* [Boulder: Westview Press, 1991], 27).

7. Ibid., 164. For the Tokugawa Ancient Learning School, see also John Whitney Hall et al., eds., *The Cambridge History of Japan*, 6 vols., vol. 4: *Early Modern Japan* (Cambridge: Cambridge University Press, 1988), 420–424.

8. Ogyū Sorai, *Tōmonsho*, as quoted in Tokuda Takeshi, "*Daitō seigo* ron (1)—Hattori Nankaku ni okeru *Sesetsu shingo*" [On *An Account of the Great Eastern World* [1]— *A New Account of Tales of the World* according to Hattori Nankaku], *Tōyō bungaku kenkyū* 17 (1969):96.

9. See Tokuda, "*Daitō seigo* ron (1)," 96–97; see also Hane, *Premodern Japan*, 166–167.

10. Possibly for this reason, Ogyū Sorai himself highly regarded the *Shih-shuo hsin-yü*; see Yoshikawa Kōjirō, "The *Shih-shuo hsin-yü* and Six Dynasties Prose Style," trans. Glen W. Baxter, *Harvard Journal of Asiatic Studies* 18 (1955):125, n. 2.

11. Tokuda, "*Daitō seigo* ron (1)," 98.

12. See, for example, *Shih-shuo hsin-yü*, 4/8.

13. See Mather, *Tales of the World*, xxvii–xxviii; and Ma Hsing-kuo, "*Shih-shuo hsin-yü* tsai Jih-pen," 79.

14. See Ōyane, "Edo Jidai ni okeru *Sesetsu shingo* ni tsuite," 89–91; and Ma, "*Shih-shuo hsin-yü* tsai Jih-pen," 79–83.

15. See Kawakatsu Yoshio, "Edo jidai ni okeru *Sesetsu* kenkyū no ichimen," *Tōhōgaku* 20 (1960):2–9; Ōyane, "Edo Jidai ni okeru *Sesetsu shingo* ni tsuite"; Tokuda, "*Daitō seigo* ron (1)," 84–85; and Ma, "*Shih-shuo hsin-yü* tsai Jih-pen."

16. Hattori's preface to *Daitō seigo*, 1a–b.

17. For example, Hane characterizes the major part of the Daitō period, the Heian

era, in the following terms: "Several significant developments took place during this period, among them the deterioration of the institutions and practices established by the Taika Reforms, the decline of imperial authority, the ascendancy of the Fujiwara family, the rise of the court aristocracy and its culture . . ." (*Premodern Japan,* 44).

18. See *Daitō seigo,* "Chōrei" [Favor and veneration], *chüan* 4, 17b–18a.

19. Some less influential Heian clans, including the Sugawara, the Ki, the Ōe, and two military families, the Taira (or Heike) and the Minamoto (or Genji), also appear in the *Daitō seigo,* but none of them is as extensively depicted as the Fujiwaras. The central government represented by the Fujiwaras gradually declined with the rise of military families and was replaced by the Bakufu (tent government or military government) that Minamoto no Yoritomo (1147–1199) established in Kamakura in 1185. See Hane, *Premodern Japan,* 44–85.

20. Also according to the *Daitō seigo, chüan* 3, 16a, Fujiwara no Kintō had been considered a very promising candidate for the future regent/prime minister, but he was later outdone by Fujiwara no Michinaga (966–1027), the most talented among all the Fujiwaras.

21. *Daitō seigo,* "Kenen" [Worthy beauties], *chüan* 4, 8a–b.

22. For example, when Fujiwara no Arikuni superintended the construction of the residence for Regent/Chancellor Fujiwara no Michinaga, he foresaw that Michinaga would someday wed his daughter to the emperor; therefore, he intentionally left enough space for an empress' carriage to pass through Michinaga's door. See *Daitō seigo,* "Shōgo" [Quick perception], *chüan* 3, 11a–b.

23. Hane points out that "in most instances during this period the wife and children remained with her family, while the husband visited or came to live with them; as a result the maternal grandfather and uncles exerted great influence over the children" (*Premodern Japan,* 45).

24. *Daitō seigo,* "Hinsō" [Ranking with refined words], *chüan* 3, 3b; and "Chōrei," *chüan* 4, 17b–18a.

25. See *Daitō seigo,* "Yōshi" [Appearance and manner], *chüan* 3, 19a–b.

26. Minamoto no Takakuni is considered the original author of the *Konjaku monogatari* [(Collection of) Tales of times now past]; see Hisamatsu, ed., *Biographical Dictionary of Japanese Literature,* s.v. *Konjaku monogatari.*

27. *Daitō seigo,* "Kangō" [Rudeness and arrogance], *chüan* 5, 2a–b.

28. Ibid., "Nintan" [Uninhibitedness and eccentricity], *chüan* 4, 21b.

29. See Mochizuki Shinkō, *Bukkyō dai jiten* [Grand dictionary of Buddhism], third ed., 10 vols. (Kyoto: Sekai seiten kankō kyōkai, 1954–1971), s.v. *Chū'u;* and Ting Fu-pao (1874–1952), ed., *Fo-hsüeh tai tz'u-tien* [Grand dictionary of Buddhism] (1922; reprint, Peking: Wen-wu ch'u-pan she, 1984), s.v. *Chung-yu.*

30. *Daitō seigo,* "Nintan," *chüan* 4, 24b.

31. Tadatomo's remark reminds us immediately of Kung Tzu-chen's (1792–1841) famous

essay, the "Ping-mei kuan chi" [Record of Sick Plum-Tree Hall], whose description of twisted plum branches allegorizes wretched human spirits.

32. Including *Konjaku monogatari; Gōdanshō* [Gō's remarks], attributed to Ōe no Masafusa (1041–1111); *Ōkagami* [Great mirror], a late Heian (ca. 1119) rekishi monogatari; *Jikkunshō* [Treatise of ten rules], a mid-Kamakura setsuwa collection (ca. 1252); *Tsurezuregusa* [Essays in idleness] by Yoshida Kenkō (1283–1350); etc. See Rakuhokuhōsun'an Shikka, *Daitō seigo kō* (1751 ed.); see also Tokuda Takeshi, *"Daitō seigo ron (2)," Chūgoku koten kenkyū* 16 (1969):98; Ma, *"Shih-shuo hsin-yü tsai Jih- pen,"* 72; Hisamatsu, ed., *Biographical Dictionary of Japanese Literature,* s.v. *Konjaku monogatari, Ōkagami,* and *Tsurezuregusa;* and Earl Miner, Hiroko Odagiri, and Robert Morrell, eds., *The Princeton Companion to Classical Japanese Literature* (Princeton, NJ: Princeton University Press, 1985), s.v. *Jikkunshō* and Ōe no Masafusa.

33. Hattori's preface to *Daitō seigo,* 2a.

34. Rakuhokuhōsun'an Shikka, *Daitō seigo kō,* provides a detailed comparison between the *Daitō seigo* text and the texts of its original sources; see also Ōyane, *Sesetsu shingo to rikuchō bungaku,* 103–104.

35. Yoshikawa Kōjirō, "The *Shih-shuo hsin-yü* and Six Dynasties Prose Style," 126.

36. For Hattori Nankaku's intentional imitation of the prose style of the *Shih-shuo hsin- yü* in relation to the Tokugawa Ancient Learning Scholars' study in Chinese philology, see Tokuda, *"Daitō seigo ron (1),"* 86–91.

37. Yoshikawa, "The *Shih-shuo hsin-yü* and Six Dynasties Prose Style," 128–129.

38. *Daitō seigo,* "Seiji" [Affairs of government], *chüan* 1, 18a–b.

39. Ibid., "Bungaku" [Literature and scholarship], *chüan* 2, 3a.

40. See Mather's note to this episode; see also *Shih-shuo hsin-yü,* 23/10.

41. See Rakuhokuhōsun'an, *Daitō seigo kō, chüan* 1 (not paginated).

42. See ibid.; see also Ōyane, *Sesetsu shingo to rikuchō bungaku,* 104.

43. *Lun-yü,* I, 7.

44. For a comparison between the two episodes see also Tokuda, *"Daitō seigo ron (2),"* 102–103.

45. Gail Chin, "The Gender of Buddhist Truth: The Female Corpse in a Group of Japanese Paintings," *Japanese Journal of Religious Studies* 25.3-4 (Fall 1998):282–283. Some Kamakura paintings of this motif that Chin has examined include "Kusōzu" [Pictures of the nine aspects], dated 1223, referring to nine stages of decomposition of a female corpse; and "Jindō fujō sōzu" [Picture of the unclean human path], dated from the early thirteenth century, depicting seven stages of decomposition of a female corpse.

46. *Daitō seigo,* "Gengo" [Speech and conversation], *chüan* 1, 10b.

47. See Rakuhokuhōsun'an, *Daitō seigo kō, chüan* 1.

48. The Wei-Chin frenzy about the snow is broadly reflected in the *Shih-shuo hsin-yü,*

either as the background to set forth or in a landscape description to symbolize a pure, lofty personality; see, for example, *Shih-shuo hsin-yü,* 2/71, 2/93, 4/100, 14/33, 16/6, etc; see also chapter 5.

49. *Daitō seigo,* "Shōsei" [Grieving for the departed], *chüan* 4, 4b.

50. See also Tokuda, *"Daitō seigo* ron (3)—Hattori Nankaku no ningen ninshiki to bi-ishiki" [Hattori Nankaku's understanding of human beings and his aesthetic viewpoints], *Chūgoku koten kenkyū* 17 (1970):46.

Chapter 10: New and Old

1. Hsü K'o, *Ch'ing-pai lei-ch'ao,* 13 vols. (Peking: Chung-hua shu-chü, 1984), "Fan-li" [Compilation notes], ix.

2. Chu wrote, for example: "To pursue the path of its [the Ch'ing's] evolution and the reason for its gain and loss in order to set for ourselves a mirror or a model—this we should do right away" (Ibid., Chu's "Preface," v).

3. Ibid.

4. Ibid., ix.

5. See ibid., v and vii.

6. Leo Ou-fan Lee points out that the concept of modernity was "a new mode of historical consciousness, which . . . tended to shape the cultural creativity of the May Fourth period." He observes: "In the popular May Fourth parlance, to be 'modern' means above all to be 'new' [*xin (hsin)*], to be consciously opposed to the 'old' [*jiu (chiu)*]" ("Modernity and Its Discontents: The Cultural Agenda of the May Fourth Movement," in Kenneth Lieberthal et al., eds., *Perspectives on Modern China* [An East Gate Book, 1991], 158–159).

7. Yi Tsung-k'uei, *Hsin Shih-shuo,* "Li-yen," 2a.

8. Liang was one of the most celebrated cultural heroes in the *Hsin Shih-shuo;* see "Yen-yü," *chüan* 1, 26a.

9. Liang Ch'i-ch'ao, "Hsiao-shuo yü ch'ün-chih chih kuan-hsi" [Fiction seen in relation to the guidance of society], in Kuo Shao-yü, ed., *Chung-kuo li-tai wen-lun hsüan,* 4:207. See also his "Kao hsiao-shuo chia" [Appeal to novelists], ibid., 4:217–218. For a detailed discussion of these two essays, see C. T. Hsia, "Yen Fu and Liang Ch'i-ch'ao as Advocates of New Fiction," in Adele Austin Rickett, ed., *Chinese Approaches to Literature from Confucius to Liang Ch'i-ch'ao* (Princeton, NJ: Princeton University Press, 1978), 221–257.

10. Ernest P. Young, *The Presidency of Yuan Shih-k'ai: Liberalism and Dictatorship in Early Republican China* (Ann Arbor: University of Michigan Press, 1977), 9.

11. Smith, *China's Cultural Heritage,* 289.

12. Yi, *Hsin Shih-shuo,* "Yen-yü," *chüan* 1, 25a.

13. For Hu Shih, *kuo-yü* means "a national language applicable both to speeches and writings"; see his "Wen-hsüeh kai-liang ch'u-i" [Preliminary opinions on reforming literature], *Chung-kuo li-tai wen-lun hsüan*, 4:536.

14. Yi, *Hsin Shih-shuo*, "Wen-hsüeh," *chüan* 2, 39b–40a.

15. Ibid., *chüan* 2, 40a.

16. Both were leaders of the Taiping Rebellion (1850–1864).

17. Both were leaders of the Republican Revolution (1911–1912).

18. Yi, *Hsin Shih-shuo*, "Li-yen," 1b.

19. Ibid., "Tzu-hsü" [Self-preface], 1b. *San-shih*: The *Kung-yang* Commentary divides the *Ch'un-ch'iu* records into three kinds: *so-chien shih* (what the author saw), *so-wen shih* (what the author heard of), and *so ch'uan-wen shih* (what others heard of); see *Tz'u-yüan*, s.v. *San-shih*.

20. Ts'ai Yüan-p'ei's postscript to the *Hsin Shih-shuo*.

21. Yi, *Hsin Shih-shuo*, "Tzu-hsü," 1b–2a.

22. Smith, *China's Cultural Heritage*, 39.

23. See Yi, *Hsin Shih-shuo*, "Te-hsing," *chüan* 1, 1a–2b.

24. See ibid., "Hsien-yüan," *chüan* 5, 24b.

25. See ibid., "Yen-yü," *chüan* 1, 15b, note.

26. Ibid., *chüan* 1, 15a-b.

27. See, respectively, ibid., "Wen-hsüeh," *chüan* 2, 17a-b, and "Te-hsing," *chüan* 1, 1b.

28. Ibid., "Yu-hui," *chüan* 8, 12a.

29. Ibid., *chüan* 8, 13b. This sympathy for Ch'ien seems to have been widespread. For instance, a Korean work entitled *Li-tai hui-ling* [Collected spirits from previous dynasties] also cites the "Yen Memorial," among others, as evidence for listing Ch'ien in the chapter "Chieh-i" [Integrity and righteousness] (Gest Library collection, Princeton University, *chüan* 4, 10b).

30. Yi, *Hsin Shih-shuo*, "Yu-hui," *chüan* 8, 12b–13a.

31. Ibid., "Ch'ou-hsi," *chüan* 8, 33a.

32. Ibid.

33. Ibid., "Wen-hsüeh," *chüan* 2, 34a-b.

34. Ibid., "Hao-shuang," *chüan* 4, 26a-b.

35. To be sure, Ch'ing officials such as Tseng Kuo-fan saw matters just the opposite way; see Jonathan D. Spence, *God's Chinese Son: The Taiping Heavenly Kingdom of Hong Xiuquan [Hung Hsiu-ch'üan]* (New York: W.W. Norton, 1996), 227–228.

36. *Lien* normally means "couplet," but this long *lien* contains two stanzas of three lines each, hence this English rendering.

37. Yi, *Hsin Shih-shuo*, "Shang-shih," *chüan* 5, 10a.

38. Ibid., "Li-yen," 2a. Yi also recorded Wang K'ai-yün's criticism of Tseng Kuo-fan, whose Hsiang army played the crucial role in pacifying the Taipings: "Wang K'ai-yün compiled the *Records of the Hsiang Army,* recounting its rise and anecdotes [about it]. The book reads like a compliment but means more than the words appear to express. It does not at all avoid citing the unsavory records of the [Hsiang army] generals and even launches subtle criticisms against Tseng Kuo-fan himself" ("Wen-hsüeh," *chüan* 2, 34a).

39. Ibid., "Shih-chien," *chüan* 3, 26b–27a. For the allusion of "[burning stalks are] cooking [the beans of] the same roots" (*t'ung-ken hsiang-chien*), see *Shih-shuo hsin-yü,* 4/66, about the famous "Seven-Pace Poem" (Ch'i-pu shih) attributed to Ts'ao Chih.

40. Ibid., note.

41. Ibid.

42. Ibid., "Ch'i-i," *chüan* 5, 23b–24a. *Ch'i-yün* as a technical term refers to the prosperity of the state.

43. Ibid., "Wen-hsüeh," *chüan* 2, 38b–39a.

44. Ibid., "Te-hsing," *chüan* 1, 15a, note. Yi's note to the Nan-she members refers readers to this episode for Huang's biographic information.

45. Ibid., *chüan* 1, 15a, text proper and note. Yi's note to the Nan-she members refers readers to this episode for Sung's biographic information.

46. Ibid., "Wen-hsüeh," *chüan* 2, 39a.

47. Ibid., "Hsien-yüan," *chüan* 5, 35b–36a.

48. *Li-chi* [cheng-i], "Nei-tse," *chüan* 27, *Shih-san ching chu-shu,* 2:1462.

49. Lydia H. Liu, *Translingual Practice: Literature, National Culture, and Translated Modernity—China, 1900–1937* (Stanford: Stanford University Press, 1995), 80–81.

50. Liu, *Translingual Practice,* Appendix D, "Return Graphic Loans: 'Kanji' Terms Derived from Classical Chinese," 302 and 335; see also Kao Ming-k'ai and Liu Cheng-t'an, *Hsien-tai han-yü wai-lai tz'u yen-chiu* [Studies of loanwords in modern Chinese] (Peking: Wen-tzu kai-ko ch'u-pan she, 1958).

51. *I-ching,* "Ko" [Radical change], trans. Richard John Lynn, *The Classic of Changes: A New Translation of the I Ching as Interpreted by Wang Bi* [Pi] (New York: Columbia University Press, 1994), 445.

52. See Yi, *Hsin Shih-shuo,* "Shih-chien," *chüan* 3, 27a, note to the Wang T'ao episode.

53. Yi Tsung-k'uei, *Hsin Shih-shuo,* "Yen-yü," *chüan* 1, 25b–26a.

54. See Liu, *Translingual Practice,* Appendix D, 306.

55. *Meng-tzu,* X, 1; trans. Lau, *Mencius,* 150.

56. Yi, *Hsin Shih-shuo,* "Ch'u-mien," *chüan* 7, 19a–b.

57. Ibid., "Jen-tan," *chüan* 6, 32a–b and note.

58. Ibid.

59. For Yüan Shih-k'ai's attempt to become "emperor," see Young, *Presidency of Yuan Shih-k'ai,* 210–240.

60. Lydia H. Liu categorizes *kuo-hui* (congress) and *i-yüan* (parliament) as "neologisms derived from missionary-Chinese texts" (*Translingual Practice,* Appendix A, 266 and 276) and *i-hui* (parliament) and *i-yüan* (parliamentary member) as "Sino-Japanese-European loan words in modern Chinese" (Appendix B, 293).

61. Yi, *Hsin Shih-shuo,* "Yen-yü," *chüan* 1, 24b and 26b.

62. A "Sino-Japanese-European loan word in modern Chinese" (*Translingual Practice,* Appendix B, 291).

63. Yi, *Hsin Shih-shuo,* "Yen-yü," *chüan* 1, 24b.

64. Ibid.

65. Ibid., 25b–26a.

66. Ibid., "Hao-shuang," *chüan* 4, 27a.

67. See Young, *Presidency of Yuan Shih-k'ai,* 198.

68. Yi, *Hsin Shih-shuo,* "Yen-yü," *chüan* 1, 25b.

69. Wang Shu-ch'ien, "Hsin-chiu wen-t'i" [The problem of new and old], *Hsin ch'ing-nien* 1:1 (September 1915):49–50; trans. Vera Schwarcz, *The Chinese Enlightenment: Intellectuals and the Legacy of the May Fourth Movement of 1919* (Berkeley: University of California Press, 1986), 28.

70. See Yi, *Hsin Shih-shuo,* "Tzu-hsü."

71. Yi, *Hsin Shih-shuo,* "Yen-yü," *chüan* 1, 22a.

72. About Wang Chung's scholarship, see Liang Ch'i-ch'ao, *Chung-kuo chin san-pai nien hsüeh-shu shih,* 4, 49–50, 52–53, 115.

73. Yi, *Hsin Shih-shuo,* "Wen-hsüeh," *chüan* 2, 40a-b.

74. For the rules of the "poetry bell," see *Tz'u-yü,* s.v. *Shih-chung.*

75. Ch'en Tu-hsiu, for example, declares that he would "much rather see the past culture of our nation disappear than to see our race die out now because of its unfitness for living in the modern world." See Smith, *China's Cultural Heritage,* 290.

Conclusion: The Self and the Mirror

1. The statistics on the appearance of these pronouns in the *Shih-shuo hsin-yü* are based on Chang Yung-yen, *Shih-shuo hsin-yü tz'u-tien,* s.v., respectively, *Wo, Tzu, Wu, Chi,* and *Shen.*

2. Hsü Shen, *Shuo-wen chieh-tzu* [*chu*], commentary by Tuan Yü-ts'ai, s.v., respectively, *Wo,* 632; *Tzu,* 136; *Wu,* 56–57; *Chi,* 741; and *Shen,* 388.

3. Later scholars have also noticed this Later Han/Wei-Chin consciousness of referring to one's self in a concrete differentiation from others'. Tuan Yü-ts'ai, for example, interprets Hsü Shen's definition of *wo* as "meaning to put oneself among people and then to refer to oneself" (*Shuo-wen chieh-tzu chu,* s.v. *Wo,* 632) and that of *chi* as ". . . to differentiate oneself from others. One's self is inside, and others are outside; [by using '*chi*'] we can mark and recognize this difference" (*Shuo-wen chieh-tzu chu,* s.v. *Chi,* 741).

4. See, for example, Hsü Chen-o, *Shih-shuo hsin-yü chiao-chien* [Commentary on the *Shih-shuo hsin-yü*], 2 vols. (Peking: Chung-hua shu-chü, 1984), "Preface," vi; and Chang, *Shih-shuo hsin-yü tz'u-tien,* "Preface," iii.

5. See Hsü Shen, *Shuo-wen chieh-tzu* [*chu*], s.v. *yü,* 49, and *yü,* 159.

6. See also Liu Chün's commentary.

7. See also Mather's commentary on this episode, *Tales of the World,* 71.

8. See, for example, P'ei Sung-chih's commentary on Ch'en Shou, *San-kuo chih, Shu-shu* [History of the Shu], "P'ang T'ung chuan" [Biography of P'ang T'ung], quoted from the *Hsiang-yang chi* [Record of Hsiang-yang]: "Ssu-ma Hui is a water mirror" (*chüan* 37, 4:953).

9. Quoted in P'ei Sung-chih's commentary on Ch'en Shou, *San-kuo chih, Shu-shu,* "Li Yen chuan" [Biography of Li Yen], *chüan* 40, 4:1001.

10. Such as "a spirit that is like a pond mirror" (*Ho-shih yü-lin,* "Shang-yü," *chüan* 16, 12b); "a heart that is like a clear mirror" (ibid., 21b); and "the more [a human mirror is] polished, the more starkly clear it gets" (*Chiao-shih lei-lin,* "Shang-yü," *chüan* 4, 152).

11. Wang Tang, *T'ang yü-lin* [*chiao-cheng*], "Shang-shih," *chüan* 4, no. 574, 1:391. The episode was originally quoted from Liu Su, *Sui-T'ang chia-hua* (Peking: Chung-hua shu-chü, 1979), 7; trans. Cf. Wechsler, *Mirror to the Son of Heaven,* vi.

12. Smith, *China's Cultural Heritage,* 1.

13. Frank Kermode summarizes Sainte-Beuve's notion of a classic: "It can be primarily an index of civility, or the product of individual genius, characterized by sanity, health and universality. On the basis of the first of these criteria he (Sainte-Beuve) was able to make certain discriminations, for example relegating the age of Pope to the status of secondary classic because, though it possessed civility, it lacked perpetual contemporaneity. But Virgil is a classic in both senses: a great poet and also the poet 'de la Latinité tout entière'" (*The Classic: Literary Images of Permanence and Change* [New York: Viking Press, 1975], 17–18).

14. Ch'eng Hsü, "Ch'ung-k'o *Shih-shuo hsin-yü* hsü," 1a.

15. Frank Kermode, *The Classic,* 15–16.

16. Ch'eng Hsü, "Ch'ung-k'o *Shih-shuo hsin-yü* hsü," 1a.

17. Liu Hsi-tsai, *I-kai* (Theoretical summary of art) (Shanghai: Shanghai ku-chi ch'u-pan she, 1978), *chüan* 1, 9.

18. Although T'ang *Shih-shuo* imitations, writing about T'ang, limited themselves to T'ang examples, the absence of T'ang imitations focusing on previous dynasties suggests the T'ang gentry's disappointment with the "amorality" of earlier times, the Six Dynasties in particular.

Glossary

Characters for the names of books and their authors can be found under "Selected Bibliography."

The Thirty-six Categories of the *Shih-shuo hsin-yü*

1. "Te-hsing" 德行
2. "Yen-yü" 言語
3. "Cheng-shih" 政事
4. "Wen-hsüeh" 文學
5. "Fang-cheng" 方正
6. "Ya-liang" 雅量
7. "Shih-chien" 識鑒
8. "Shang-yü" 賞譽
9. "P'in-tsao" 品藻
10. "Kuei-chen" 規箴
11. "Chieh-wu" 捷悟
12. "Su-hui" 夙惠
13. "Hao-shuang" 豪爽
14. "Jung-chih" 容止
15. "Tzu-hsin" 自新
16. "Ch'i-hsien" 企羨
17. "Shang-shih" 傷逝
18. "Ch'i-i" 棲逸
19. "Hsien-yüan" 賢媛
20. "Shu-chieh" 術解
21. "Ch'iao-i" 巧藝
22. "Ch'ung-li" 寵禮
23. "Jen-tan" 任誕
24. "Chien-ao" 簡傲
25. "P'ai-t'iao" 排調
26. "Ch'ing-ti" 輕詆
27. "Chia-chüeh" 假譎
28. "Ch'u-mien" 黜免
29. "Chien-se" 儉嗇
30. "T'ai-ch'ih" 汰侈
31. "Fen-Chüan" 忿狷
32. "Ch'an-hsien" 讒險
33. "Yu-hui" 尤悔
34. "P'i-lou" 紕漏
35. "Huo-ni" 惑溺
36. "Ch'ou-hsi" 仇隙

ai-yüan ch'i sao-jen 哀怨起騷人

Akazome 赤染

ch'a-chü 察舉

Chang Chia-chen 張嘉貞

Chang Chien 張騫

chang-hsin shih-ch'eng 仗信示誠

Chang Hsüan 張玄

Chang Hsüeh-ch'eng 章學誠

Chang-sun huang-hou 長孫皇后

Chang-sun Wu-chi 長孫無忌

Chang T'ai-yen 章太炎

Chang Wen-chu 張文柱

Chang Wen-kuan 張文瓘

Chang Wen-t'ao 張問陶

Chang Yüeh 張説

ch'ang-chi 娼妓

Chao Ch'i 趙岐

Chao Yün 趙雲

Chen-chieh 貞介

chen-shuai 真率

Ch'en Chi-ju 陳繼儒

ch'en-ching chi-mi 沉靜機密

Ch'en Fan 陳蕃

Ch'en Pao-chen 陳寶箴

Ch'en Shih-tao 陳師道

Ch'en Tu-hsiu 陳獨秀

Ch'en Yüan-lu 陳元祿（Hung-chu tz'u-jen 紅燭詞人）

cheng-chien 正諫

Cheng Cho 鄭灼

Cheng Hsüan 鄭玄

cheng-ming 正名

cheng-neng 政能

cheng-p'i 徵辟

cheng-shih 正史

Cheng Wei-chung 鄭惟忠

Ch'eng Chia-ch'eng 程家檉

ch'eng-chieh 誠節

ch'eng-chieh 懲戒

ch'eng-hsing/jōkyo 乘輿

Ch'eng Hsü 程稰

ch'eng-ming 誠明

chi 己

chi 即

chi-chien 極諫

chi-chuan t'i 紀傳體

"Chi-se lun" 即色論

ch'i-cheng 奇政

ch'i-kai 乞丐

Ch'i-lüeh 七略

"Ch'i-pu shih" 七步詩

"Ch'i-wu lun" 齊物論

ch'i-yün 氣韻

chia-yen i-hsing 嘉言懿行

ch'iang-k'ai chien ching 彊楷堅勁

chiao-yüan 教員

chieh 潔

chieh-i 節義

chieh-shuo hsiang-yü 街説巷語

chieh-t'an hsiang-yü 街談巷語

ch'ieh 且

chien-hsiung 奸雄

chien-ning 奸佞

chien-o 謇諤

chien-pen 建本

chien-ts'ai 兼材

Ch'ien Ch'ien-i 錢謙益

Ch'ien Fen 錢棻

Ch'ien-fu lun 潛夫論

Ch'ien Hsüan-t'ung 錢玄同

Ch'ien Tseng 錢曾

ch'ien-yen ching-ch'ou, wan-ho cheng-lei
　千巖競愁，萬壑爭淚

ch'ien-yen ching-hsiu, wan-ho cheng-liu
　千巖競秀，萬壑爭流

chih 智

chih-che pu yen, yen-che pu chih 知者
　不言，言者不知

chih-ch'eng 至誠

chih-ch'i 陜屺

chih-chien 指諫

chih-chien 直諫

chih-chih 質直

chih-jen 至人

chih-jen chien 知人鑒

chih-jen hsiao-shuo 志人小說

chih-jen shih 知人識

Chih Min-tu 支敏度

Chih Tun 支遁

chih-wen 至文

chih-wu 植物

chih-yen 直言

chih-yüan 志願

Ch'ih Ch'ao 郗超

ch'ih-ch'eng shih-hsin 持誠示信

ch'ih-fa 持法

Ch'ih Hsüan 郗璿

ch'ih-shen li-chia 治身理家

Ch'ih Tao-mao 郗道茂

chin-ching ch'iu-pi 金盡裘敝

Chin chu-kung tsan 晉諸公贊

Chin-hsi Tzu 金溪子

Chin Sheng-t'an 金聖嘆

Chin Ts'ai-chiang 金采江

chin tzu-shu hsiao-shuo 近子書小說

Chin Yang-ch'iu 晉陽秋

Ch'in Kuan 秦觀

ching 經

ching-liang wei-shen 精良畏慎

Ching-ling 竟陵

ching-shen 敬慎

Ching Yin 敬胤

ch'ing 卿

ch'ing 情

ch'ing-chieh lien-chieh 清介廉潔

ch'ing/cho 清/濁

ch'ing-i 清議

ch'ing-lien 清廉

ch'ing-pai 清白

ch'ing-pao 輕薄

ch'ing-t'an 清談

Ch'ing-yen 清言

Ch'ing-yen lin-yu 清言林囿

Ch'ing-yen yüan-sou 清言淵藪

chiu-p'in chung-cheng chih 九品中正制

chiu-te 酒德

chiu-yu 酒友

"Ch'iu-chih" 求志

Ch'iu Chin 秋瑾

ch'iu-ching chin-pi 裘盡金敝

Ch'iu Liang 仇亮

ch'iu wu chih miao 求物之妙

Chou I 周顗

Chou Tun-i 周惇頤

ch'ou-su 愁絲

ch'ou-su 愁思

chü 鞠

Chu Fa-t'ai 竺法汰

Chu Fa-yün 竺法蘊

Chu-hsiao hsüan yin-ts'ao 竹笑軒吟草

chü-hsien 舉賢

chü-k'ang 拘抗

Chu-ko Liang 諸葛亮

Chu-ko Tan 諸葛誕

Chu-lin ch'i-hsien 竹林七賢

Chu Shun-shui 朱舜水

Chu Tao-ch'ien 竺道潛

Chu Tao-i 竺道壹

Chu Tsung-yüan 諸宗元

chu-wei 麈尾

Chu Yüan-chang 朱元璋

ch'u/ch'u 出／處

ch'ü-hsieh kuei-cheng 去邪歸正

Ch'u-hsüeh chi 初學集

ch'ü-pieh mei-o 區別美惡

ch'u-shih heng-i 處士橫議

Ch'u Sui-liang 褚遂良

ch'u-tzu 處子

Ch'u-tz'u 楚辭

Ch'ü Yüan 屈原

chuan-chih/sensei 專制

Ch'uan-fang chi 傳芳妓

ch'uan-shen hsieh-chao 傳神寫照

Chün-chi ch'u 軍機處

chün-jen 軍人

chün-mai 俊邁

chün-ts'ai 雋才

chün-tsun ch'en-pei 君尊臣卑

chün-tzu 君子

chün-ya 雋雅

ch'un-hsin 淳信

chung-ch'i 重器

Chung-hsiang tz'u 眾香詞

Chung Hsing 鍾惺

Chung Hui 鍾會

chung-i yüan 眾議院

chung-keng 忠鯁

chung-lieh 忠烈

chung-tsu chih-chien 種族之見

Chung Yen 鍾琰

chung-yung 中庸

Chū'u 中有

ch'ung-pi 寵嬖

*d'ăk-d'ăk 濯濯

*dįwat/įwät/yüeh 悅

*d'uâi-d'âng 頹唐

*d'wâd/d'uâi/tuei 兌

*dz'uai-nguei, ts'â-ngâ / ɣap-iäp, įang-puâ / luâi-luâ, įɒng-tâ 崔巍，嵯峨/渫，揚波/
    磊砢，英多

erh-hou 而後

erh-i 而已

erh-Su lien-pi, san K'ung fen-ting 二蘇聯
    璧、三孔分鼎

Fa-chia 法家

Fan Chü 范睢

Fan Hsüan 范宣

Fan Li 范蠡

Fan Sui 范睢

fang-chin 方今

fang-cheng 方正

fei-hsing 廢興

fei-shen 非身

feng-chien 諷諫

Feng Ching 馮景

feng-yün 風雲

fu 復

Fu Ch'ang 傅暢

fu-chih 服制

fu-li 婦禮

Fu Ssu-nien 傅斯年

fu-wu 賦物

Fujiwara no Kintō 藤原公任

Fujiwara no Michinaga 藤原道長

Fujiwara no Nobunori 藤原惟規

Fujiwara no Sanetada 藤原實資

Fujiwara no Tadatomo 藤原資朝

Fujiwara no Tokihira 藤原時平

Fujiwara no Toshitsuna 藤原俊綱

Fujiwara no Yorimichi 藤原賴通

Fushimi 伏見

Genji monogatari 源氏物語

Gōdanshō 江談抄

Han Fei 韓非

Han Hsin 韓信

han-men 寒門

Han-tan Ch'un 邯鄲淳

Han-yü 韓愈

Han-yü 漢語

Hida 飛彈

Ho Ch'iao 和嶠

Ho Shao 何邵

Ho so-wen erh-lai, ho so-chien erh-ch'ü 何 所聞而來？何所見而去？

Ho Yen 何晏

Hōjō Yasutoki 北條泰時

Hou-shan shih-hua 後山詩話

Hsi K'ang 嵇康

Hsi Tsao-ch'ih 習鑿齒

Hsia Ch'ang 夏昶

Hsia Chieh 夏桀

Hsia-hou Hsüan 夏侯玄

hsia-yü 下愚

hsiang 香

Hsiang Hsiu 向秀

hsiang-yen 香艷

Hsiang Yü 項羽

hsiao-hsing 孝行

hsiao-jen 小人

hsiao-lien 孝廉

Hsiao-lin 笑林

hsiao-shuo 小説

Hsiao Ta-huan 蕭大圜

hsiao-tao 小道

Hsieh An 謝安

hsieh-ch'an 邪諂

Hsieh Chen 謝甄

Hsieh Hsüan 謝玄

Hsieh K'un 謝鯤

Hsieh Tao-yün 謝道蘊

hsien-chien 陷諫

hsien-hou 先後

hsien-hsien i-se (ken o ken toshi, iro ni kaeyo) 賢賢易色

hsien-liang 賢良

hsien-neng 賢能

hsin 信

Hsin ch'ing-nien 新青年

"Hsin-chiu wen-t'i" 新舊問題

Hsin-hsüeh 心學

Hsin-lun 新論

Hsin-wu 心無

hsing 行

hsing 形

hsing 性

hsing-chih 婞直

hsing-hua chih-chih 興化致治

hsing-ning jen 倖佞人

hsing-o 性惡

hsing-shan 性善

hsing/shen 形神

hsing shen hsiang-ch'in 形神相親

hsing-wan 興亡

hsiu-ts'ai 秀才

hsiu-tung lei-lo 休動磊落

hsiu-tz'u li-ch'eng 修辭立誠

hsiu-wen 修文

hsiung-han chieh-chien 雄悍傑健

Hsü Ching-chih 徐敬直

Hsü Chü-yüan 徐巨源

hsü-i 胥役

Hsü Hsün 許詢

Hsü Shao 許劭

Hsü Shu-hsin 徐漱馨

hsü-wang Kuai-Tan chih shuo 妄怪誕之説

Hsü Yüan-wen 徐元文

hsüan-feng 玄風

Hsüan-hsüeh 玄學

hsüan-lun 玄論

hsüan-yen 玄言

hsüan-yüan 玄遠

Hsüeh-tsan 雪贊

Hsün Hsü 荀勖

Hsün Shuang 荀爽

Hsün Ts'an 荀粲

"Hu-chia shih-pa p'ai" 胡笳十八拍

hu-wang hsing hai 忽忘形骸

Huan Ch'ung 桓沖

Huan Hsüan 桓玄

Huan-hua 幻化

Huan I 桓彝

Huan T'an 桓譚

Huan Wen 桓溫

Huang Hsien 黃憲

Huang Hsing 黃興

Huang K'an 皇侃

Huang Pai-chia 黃百家

Huang T'ing-chien 黃庭堅

Huang-fu Te-shen 皇甫德參

hui-hua 惠化

hui-tang 會黨

hui-yü 穢語

Hung Ch'eng-ch'ou 洪承疇

Hung Hsiu-ch'üan 洪秀全

Hyakusai Kawanari 百濟川成

i 義

i-ch'iao 藝巧

i-fu 亦復

I-fu 意賦

i-hsing hsieh-shen 以形寫神

i-hsiu wan-tsai 遺臭萬載

i-hsün 懿訓

i-hui 議會

i-i 亦以

i-nan ts'ao 宜男草

iro o iro toshi, ken ni kaeyo (se se i hsien)
色色易賢

i-shih hsiao-shuo 軼事小説

i-ti 夷狄

"I-wen chih" 藝文志

I-wen lei-chü 藝文類聚

i-yüan 議員

i-yüan 議院

i-yung 毅勇

jang-te 讓德

jen 仁

Jen Chan 任瞻

jen-hsiao 仁孝

jen-lun chien-shih 人倫鑒識

jen-lun chih piao 人倫之表

Jikkunshō 十訓抄

joji 助字

joji ni kenjin nashi 女事に賢人なし

jou-shun an-shu 柔順安恕

ju 乳

Ju-chia 儒家

ju-shen 辱身

ju-shih 儒士

ju-ya 儒雅

Juan Hsien 阮咸

Jung Hung 容閎

jung-sheng 容聲

Kan Pao 干寶

kang-cheng 剛正

k'ang-chih 抗直

kao-chieh 高節

kao-men 高門

Kao Ming 高明

Kao Ping 高標

Kao-shih chuan 高士傳

kao-ts'ai 高才

k'ao-cheng 考證

kashō 佳賞

katsugeki 活展

kishitsu 氣質

Ko Cheng-ch'i 葛徵奇

Kogakuha 古學派

ko-ming chu-i 革命主義

ko-ming/kakumei 革命

Konjaku monogatari 今昔物語

k'o-kuan chih tz'u 可觀之辭

"Ku-chin jen piao" 古今人表

"Ku-feng" 古風

ku hsing i i 孤行一意

Ku Shao 顧劭

Ku Yen-wu 顧炎武

k'u-jen 酷忍

k'u-miao an 哭廟案

k'u-shih 酷嗜

*kuâi-ngâ 傀俄

K'uai T'ung 蒯通

kuan-liao 官僚

Kuang-ling san 廣陵散

k'uang-chüan 狂狷

k'uang-tsan 匡贊

k'uang-wu 礦物

kuei-chien 規諫

kuei-fang chi hsiu 閨房之秀

kuei-hui 規誨

Kuei-shen lieh-chuan 鬼神列傳

kuei-te 貴德

k'uei-chien 窺諫

Kūkai 空海

kun-p'ien 棍騙

K'un-wei 坤維

kung-chih 公直

Kung Ting-tzu 龔鼎孳

Kung Tzu-chen 龔自珍

K'ung Jung 孔融

K'ung-men ssu-k'o 孔門四科

k'ung-men yu 空門友

k'ung-ming tse-shih 控名責實

K'ung Wen-chung 孔文仲

K'ung Wu-chung 孔武仲

Kuo-ch'ao kuei-hsiu cheng-shih chi 國朝閨
  秀正始集

Kuo Hsiang 郭象

kuo-hui 國會

kuo-min 國民

kuo-min hsüeh-hsiao 國民學校

Kuo T'ai 郭泰

kuo-tsu pu ju Ch'in 裹足不入秦

kuo-yü 國語

*lân-lân 爛爛

*lâng-lâng 琅琅

*lâng-lâng 朗朗

lei 類

li 禮

li 力

li-chieh 立節

li-chih kang-i 厲直剛毅

Li Ch'un-feng 李淳風

Li Chün-ch'iu 李君球

Li Ho 李賀

Li Hsiu-ch'eng 李秀成

Li-hsüeh 理學

Li Hung-chang 李鴻章

Li I-fu 李義府

Li Jun 李閏

li-ko 蘿草

li-kuo 理國

Li Ling 李陵

Li Po 李白

Li-sao 離騷

li-shen 立身

Li Ssu 李斯

Li T'ai-hsü 李太虛

Li-tai hui-ling 歷代會靈

Li T'ing-kuei 李廷珪

Li Tzu-ch'eng 李自成

Li Wei 李為

Li Yin 李因

Li Ying 李膺

Liang Ying 梁瑛（Mei-chün 梅君）

Liao-chai chih-i 聊齋志異

lien-chü 聯句

Lin-ch'iung chih pen 臨邛之奔

lin-hsia feng-ch'i 林下風氣

lin-hsün 嶙峋

Lin Ssu-huan 林嗣環

Lin Ya-ch'ing 林亞清

ling-ch'i 令器

Ling-hu Te-fen 令狐德棻

Liu Chi 劉洎

liu-fang hou-shih 流芳後世

Liu-hsiang ts'ao 留香草

Liu Hsin 劉歆

liu-hsü 柳絮

Liu I-ch'ing 劉義慶

Liu-i chü-shih 六一居士

Liu Ling 劉伶（靈）

Liu T'an 劉惔

Liu Tsun 劉遵

Liu Yü-hsi 劉禹錫

Lo Pin-wang 駱賓王

Lo-shen fu 洛神賦

Lu Chi 陸機

Lu Chien 陸堅

Lu Min-shu 陸敏樹

Lu Shih-tao 陸師道

Lu Ts'ung-p'ing 陸從平

lun-pien li-i 論辨理繹

"Lun shuo" 論說

"Lun-wen" 論文

Lun-yü chi-chieh 論語集解

lung-ching feng-ching 龍睛鳳頸

Lung-men 龍門

Mao Chi-k'o 毛際可

Mao T'i 毛媞 (An-fang 安芳)

Mei-hua shih-wu 梅花詩屋

mi-hsin 迷信

Miao-Kuan Chang 妙觀章

mieh-tsu 滅族

min-hsüan 民選

min-tsu chu-i 民族主義

Minamoto no Takakuni 源隆國

Ming-chia 名家

ming-chiao 名教

ming-ching 明鏡

ming/li 名理

ming-li nu 名利奴

ming/shih 名實

ming-shih 名士

Mo-chia 墨家

Mo Hsi 末喜

Mo-o 墨娥

mu 目

Murasaki Shikibu 紫式部

Mu-tan t'ing 牡丹亭

nai 乃

"Nei ch'u-shuo" 內儲說

Nan-she 南社

*ngam-ngam 嚴嚴

Ni Tsan 倪瓚

Nihonkoku genzai sho mokuroku 日本國現在書目錄

ning 寧

Ning T'iao-yüan 寧調元

nu-pi 奴婢

nü hsien-sheng 女先生

nü-lang shih 女郎詩

nü men-sheng 女門生

nü-tzu hsing, chang-fu hsin 女子形，丈夫心

nü wei yüeh-chi che jung 女為悦己者容

Nung-chia 農家

*ńźiät/ *lieng 熱/冷

Ōe no Masahira 大江匡衡

Ogyū Sorai 荻生徂徠

Ōkagami 大鏡

Ono no Komachi 小野小町

Ou-yang Hsiu 歐陽修

"Pa-chen t'u" 八陣圖

pa-chün 八俊

pai-hsing chih yüan 百行之源

p'ai-yu hsiao-shuo 俳優小説

P'an Yüeh 潘岳

P'ang T'ung 龐統

pao-hsi 褒錫

pao-pien 褒貶

pei 背

Pei-t'ang shu-ch'ao 北堂書鈔

P'ei Hui 裴徽

P'ei K'ai 裴楷

P'ei Wei 裴頠

pen 奔

pen/mo 本末

Pen-wu 本無

Pen-wui 本無異

P'eng Yü-lin 彭玉麟

pi 必

Pi Kou 畢構

p'i 毗

p'i-chao 辟召

P'i-pa chi 琵琶記

Pien-lin 辯林

pien-ming hsi-li 辨名析理

p'ien-neng 偏能

*pi̯ə̯u/*b'i̯u 富/腐

*pi̯ə̯u-li̯uěn / *ts'ậm-dâm / *p'i̯äu-p'iet / *yâu-ńźi̯än 不論/慘澹/飄瞥/皓然

"Pin-mei kuan chi" 病梅館記

"P'in-i" 聘義

p'in-t'i jen-lun 品題人倫

ping 並

p'ing 評

p'ing-sheng 平聲

p'ing-yün 平允

Po Chü-i 白居易

Po-jo ching 般若經

po-wu 博物

pu ch'i an-shih 不欺暗室

pu yen wai 不言外

p'u-lu ching-chin 樸露徑盡

p'u-po chou-chi 普博周給

P'u Sung-ling 蒲松齡

san-chün 三君

san-kang liu-chi 三綱六紀

san-shih 三世

san-tuo 三多

Sang-chung chih hsing 桑中之行

"Sang-fu" 喪服

Sankyō shiki 三教指歸

se/k'ung 色/空

shan-mou 善謀

"Shan-shih" 山石

shan-shui yu 山水友

shan-shuo 善說

Shan T'ao 山濤

shang-chih 上智

shang-hsin 賞心

Shang-kuan Wan-erh 上官婉兒

shang-shih 賞識

shen 身

shen 神

shen-ch'i pu pien 神氣不變

shen-ch'ing 神情

Shen Ch'üan-ch'i 沈佺期

shen-chün 神儁

shen-chün 神駿

"*shen erh-ti lun*" 神-締論

shen-feng 神鋒

shen-i 神意

shen-jen 神人

shen-ming 神明

shen-se pu pien 神色不變

shen-ssu 神似

Shen T'ien-sun 沈天孫

shen-tzu 神姿

shen-wang 神王 (旺)

shen-yü 神宇

sheng-fu 勝負

sheng-jen 聖人

sheng-ti 勝地

"Sheng wu ai-lo lun" 聲無哀樂論

Shi ki kaichū kōshō 史記會註考證

shih 士

"Shih-chih" 十志

shih-chung 詩鐘

Shih Ch'ung 石崇

shih-fei 是非

Shih-han 識含

shih-li 事理

shih-liang 識量

Shih-shuo t'i 世説體

shih ta-fu 士大夫

Shih Ta-k'ai 石達開

Shih Tao-an 釋道安

Shih-ts'ao 士操

shih-tui 實對

shih wei chih-chi che ssu 士為知己者死

shih-yu 詩友

shinsotsu 真率

Shoku yotsugi 續世繼

shu pu chin yen, yen pu chin i 書不盡言，言不盡意

shu-shih chen-liu 漱石枕流

shu-te 淑德

Shuang-ch'ing tzu 雙清子

shui-ching 水鏡

shun-chien 順諫

shuo/shui/yüeh 説

"Shuo-lin" 説林

*sįəm-sįəm 森森

*sįuk-sįuk 蕭蕭

*śįwad/śįwäi/shuei 説

*śįwat/śįwät/shuo 説

so-chien shih 所見世

so ch'uan-wen shih 所傳聞世

so-shui 所説

so-wen shih 所聞世

Sou-shen chi 搜神記

ssu-k'o p'i-shih 四科辟士

Ssu-ma Hui 司馬徽

Ssu-ma Yü 司馬昱

Ssu-ma Yüeh 司馬越

Su Che 蘇轍

Su Ch'o 蘇綽

Sugawara no Fumitoki 菅原文時

Sugawara no Michizane 菅原道真

Sui-yüan shih-hua 隨園詩話

Sun Ch'o 孫綽

Sun Ch'u 孫楚

Sun Sheng 孫盛

Sun Yat-sen 孫逸仙

Sung Chiao-jen 宋教仁

Sung Chih-wen 宋之問

ta-i 達意

Ta-jen hsien-sheng chuan 大人先生傳

Tai K'uei 戴逵

T'ai-p'ing kuang-chi 太平廣記

T'ai-p'ing t'ien-kuo 太平天國

T'ai-p'ing yü-lan 太平御覽

Takigawa Kametarō 瀧川龜太郎

tan 膽

*t'an, bįwɒng /d'am, tsˌįäng / liäm, tˌįäng 坦，平／淡，清／廉，貞

t'an-chu 談助

T'an Ssu-t'ung 譚嗣同

T'an Yüan-ch'un 譚元春

tang-jen 黨人

"Tang-ku lieh-chuan" 黨錮列傳

T'ang Hsien-tsu 湯顯祖

T'ang-Wu ko-ming 湯武革命

Tao-chia 道家

Tao-heng 道衡

Tao-hsüeh 道學

tao-tsei 盜賊

T'ao K'an 陶侃

te-i wang-hsing 得意忘形

te-i wang-yen 得意忘言

te-shih 得失

Tei Mō'ichi 鵜孟一 (Udono Shinei 鵜殿
　士寧)

t'i 題

t'i-ch'i 體氣

t'i-ming lu 題名錄

t'i/yung 體用

tien-wen 典文

t'ien-lai 天籟

T'ien-li 天理

T'ien-ming 天命

T'ien-tao 天道

"T'ien Tzu-fang" 田子方

Ting P'eng 丁澎

to-chih t'ao-ch'ing 多智韜情

Tōji 東寺

tokujin 得人

Tōmonsho 答問書

tou 都

Tsa-chia 雜家

"Tsa-chuan" 雜傳

"Tsa-shih" 雜詩

Tsa-yü 雜語

tsai 宰

ts'ai 財

ts'ai-cháng 方長

ts'ai/hsing 才/性

Ts'ai-hsing ssu-pen lun 才性四本論

Ts'ai Yen 蔡琰 (Wen-chi 文姬)

Ts'ai Yüan-p'ei 蔡元培

tsan-hua ko 簪花格

ts'an-i yüan 參議院

Ts'ao Chih 曹植

Ts'ao P'ei-ts'ui 曹佩翠

Ts'ao P'i 曹丕

Ts'ao Ts'ao 曹操

"Tse Kuo Chü shih" 責郭巨詩

tse-sheng 仄聲

Tseng Kuo-fan 曾國藩

*tś'ia/ *mieng 茶 / 茗

Tso Ssu 左思

Tso Tsung-t'ang 左宗棠

tso-wen hai-tao 作文害道

tsou-shu che 奏書者

tsu-hsiu 組修

tsun-chün pei-ch'en 尊君卑臣

tsun-hsien 尊賢

tsung-chiao 宗教

Tsung-heng chia 縱橫家

ts'ung 聰

Tsurezuregusa 徒然草

Tu Fu 杜甫

tu-hsing 獨行

tu-hua 獨化

T'u Lung 屠隆

t'u-mi 荼蘼

t'u-mu hsing-hai 土木形骸

T'u Yao-se 屠瑤瑟

Tuan Ch'eng-shih 段成式

tuan-ch'üeh 端愨

tuan-shu 短書

tui 兌

tun-hou 敦厚

tun-p'u 敦樸

tung-wu 動物

"T'ung-hsin shuo" 童心説

t'ung-ken hsiang-chien 同根相煎

t'ung-kung chien 同功繭

T'ung-meng hui 同盟會

t'ung-pao 同胞

t'ung-pien 通辯

t'ung-ts'ai 通才

tzu 子

tzu 自

Tzu-cheng yüan 資政院

Tzu-hsia 子夏

tzu hsieh-chao 自寫照

tzu-jan 自然

tzu tzu hsiang 字字香

tzu-yu 自由

tz'u 慈

tz'u-she 刺奢

tz'u-ta 辭達

Uji 宇治

wai-chiao 外交

"Wai Ch'u-shuo" 外儲説

Wan Ssu-t'ung 萬斯同

wan-wu sang-chih 玩物喪志

Wan-yen Yün Chu 完顏惲珠

Wang Chan 王澹

Wang Ch'en 王忱

Wang Ch'eng 王承

Wang Chi 王濟

Wang Chung 汪中

Wang Fu-chih 王夫之

Wang Hsi-chih 王羲之

Wang Hsien 王銑

Wang Hsien-chih 王獻之

Wang Hui-chih 王徽之

Wang Hun 王渾

Wang Jen-yü 王仁裕

Wang Jung 王戎

Wang K'ai 王愷

Wang K'ai-yün 王闓運

Wang Kuang 王廣

Wang Kung 王恭

Wang Ling 王凌

Wang Meng 王濛

Wang P'eng 王彭

Wang Shih-chen 王士禎

Wang Shu 王述

Wang Su 王肅

Wang T'an-chih 王坦之

Wang Tao 王導

Wang T'ao 王韜

Wang Tun 王敦

Wang Yang-ming 王陽明 (Shou-jen 守仁)

Wang Yen 王衍

*·wâng-ziang 汪翔

Wei-Chin feng-liu 魏晉風流

Wei-Chin feng-tu 魏晉風度

Wei-Chin shen-yün 魏晉神韻

Wei Kuan 衛瓘

Wei-lüeh 魏略

wei-shen 危身

Wei Shih 衛湜

Wei Su 危素

Wen-fu 文賦

"Wen-hsüeh kai-liang ch'u-i" 文學改良
芻議

wen-jen 文人

wen-shih 文士

wen so-wen erh-lai, chien so-chien erh-ch'ü
聞所聞而來，見所見而去

Wen T'ung 文同

wen-wang 文網

wo 我

wo-pei 我輩

wu 吾

wu 武

wu 物

wu-ch'ang chih pen 五常之本

Wu Chin 吳晉

wu-ching 物精

Wu Shan 吳山

Wu Tse-t'ien 武則天

wu-tui 晤對

wu tzu wu erh 物自物耳

Wu Wei-yeh 吳偉業

wu wu che wu wu 物物者無物

ya-su 雅俗

Yang Chi-sheng 楊繼盛

Yang Ch'iao 楊喬

Yang Chun 楊準

Yang Fu 羊孚

Yang Hsiu-ch'ing 楊秀清

Yang Mao 楊髦

Yang Mao-ch'ing 楊茂卿

Yang Pao 楊褒

"Yang-sheng chu" 養生主

"Yang-sheng lun" 養生論

Yang Shou-ch'en 楊守陳

Yeh Shih Li-wan 葉石禮紈

yen-chih 言志

"Yen chin i lun" 言盡意論

yen-chüeh 艷絕

yen/i 言／意

yen pu chin i 言不盡意

yen/shih 言／事

yen-shuo 演說

yen-ssu 閹寺

yin 印

Yin Chung-k'an 殷仲堪

Yin Chung-wen 殷仲文

Yin Hao 殷浩

Yin-yang chia 陰陽家

ying-hsung 英雄

ying-hui 穎慧

ying-wu 應物

Ying-ying 鶯鶯

Yoshida Kenkō 吉田兼好

yu-i wu-i chih-chien 有意無意之間

yu-lieh 優劣

yu-ling 優伶

Yu-ming lu 幽明錄

yu-Tao 有道

Yu T'ien-t'ai shan fu 遊天台山賦

yu/wu 有／無

Yu-yang tsa-tsu 酉陽雜俎

yü[1] 余

yü[2] 予

yü 欲

Yü Ai 庾敱

Yü Fa-k'ai 于法開

Yü Huan 魚豢

Yü Liang 庚亮

Yü-lin 語林

yü-ning 諛佞

Yü Shih-nan 虞世南

Yü Tao-sui 于道邃

yu-t'i 友悌

"Yü-tsao" 玉藻

Yüan Hao-wen 元好問

Yüan-hui 緣會

Yüan-hun chih 冤魂志

Yüan Lang 袁閬

Yüan Mei 袁枚

Yüan Shih-k'ai 袁世凱

Yüan Te-hsiu 元德秀

Yüan T'ien-kang 袁天綱

yüeh 悦

Yüeh Kuang 樂廣

Yüeh-lun 樂論

yün 孕

yung 勇

Selected Bibliography

Sections A and B incorporate part of the bibliography from Richard B. Mather, *A New Account of the World*. The texts in Sections A, B, and E are arranged in chronological order. Sections C and D are arranged alphabetically by author.

A. Texts of the *Shih-shuo hsin-yü*

T'ang hsieh-pen Shih-shuo hsin-shu ts'an-chüan 唐寫本世説新書殘卷 (Fragment of the T'ang hand copy of the *Shih-shuo hsin-shu*). Originally in 10 *chüan*. Part of an eighth-century manuscript brought to Japan perhaps as early as the ninth century and including most of *chüan* 6 (Chapters X–XIII), with the unabridged commentary by Liu Chün 劉峻. Reprinted and published by Lo Chen-yü 羅振玉, 1916.

Tōshōhon Sesetsu shinsho 唐鈔本世説新書. Reprint of the T'ang fragment, edited by Kanda Kiichirō 神田喜一郎 and Nishikawa Yasushi 西川寧. *Shoseki meihin sōkan* 書跡名品叢刊. No. 176. Tokyo, 1972.

Shih-shuo hsin-yü 世説新語. Reprint of Wang Tsao's 汪藻 edition (thirteenth century, based on Tung Fen's 董弅 edition in 1138, which is not extant). Tokyo: Sonkei Kaku 尊經閣 or Kanazawa Bunko 金澤文庫, 1929. Includes: (1) Wang Tsao, "*Shih-shuo* hsü-lu" 世説敘錄 (Preface to the *Shih-shuo*); (2) Appendix: "K'ao-i" 考異 (Alternate readings), based on an early commentary by Ching Yin 敬胤 (ca. fifth century); (3) "Jen-ming p'u" 人名譜 (Genealogical tables [of the principal families in the text]).

Shih-shuo hsin-yü. Published by Yüan Chiung 袁褧, based on Lu Yu's 陸遊 edition (1188, not extant). 3 *chüan*. Wu-chün: Chia-ch'ü t'ang 嘉趣堂, 1535.

Shih-shuo hsin-yü. Published by Ling Ying-ch'u 凌瀛初 (Ming). 8 *chüan*. Including marginalia by Liu Ch'en-weng 劉辰翁, Liu Ying-teng 劉應登, and Wang Shih-mao 王世懋, printed in three different colors.

Shih-shuo hsin-yü pu 世説新語補 (Supplement to the *Shih-shuo hsin-yü*). 20 *chüan*. Compiled by Wang Shih-chen 王世貞 in 1556. First published by Chang Wen-chu 張文柱 in 1585. An abridgment that includes 80 percent of the *Shih-shuo hsin-yü* and 30 percent of the *Ho-shih yü-lin*. Two Japanese editions, published in 1694 and 1779, incorporate the punctuation and annotations of Li Chih 李贄 and bear the title *Li Chuo-wu p'ing-tien Shih-shuo hsin-yü pu* 李卓吾評點世説新語補. These are the basis of all premodern Japanese editions.

Shih-shuo hsin-yü. Published by Chiang Huang-t'ing 蔣篁亭 sometime between 1723 and 1730, based on a collation of Lu Yu's and Yüan Chiung's texts. Not extant; the basis of the following text.

Shih-shuo hsin-yü. Published by Shen Yen 沈巖, based on Chiang's text. Shanghai: Han-fen lou 涵芬樓, 1730. Photolithographically reproduced in the *Ssu-pu ts'ung-k'an* 四部叢刊 edition, 1929, and includes Shen's collations, *Shih-shuo hsin-yü chiao-yü* 世説新語校語.

Sesetsu shōsatsu 世説鈔撮. Published by the priest Kenjō 顯常, Edo, 1763, based on Wang Shih-chen's supplemented text.

Sesetsu onshaku 世説音釋. Published by Onda Chūjin 恩田仲任, Edo, 1816, based on Wang Shih-chen's text, with glosses.

Sesetsu Sembon 世説箋本. Published by Hata Shigen 秦士鉉, Edo, 1826, based on Wang Shih-chen's text and incorporating comments by Liun Ying-teng, Li Chih, and others.

Shih-shuo hsin-yü. Published by Chou Hsin-ju 周心如, based on Yüan Chiung's edition. 6 *chüan*. P'u-chiang: Fen-hsin ko 紛欣閣, 1828. The book in Peking Library carries Li Tz'u-ming's 李慈銘 (1830–1894) original marginalia.

Shih-shuo hsin-yü. Published by Wang Hsien-ch'ien 王先謙, based on Chou Hsin-ju's edition. 3 *chüan*. Changsha: Ssu-hsien chiang-she 思賢講舍, 1891. Including: (1) Wang, "Chiao-k'an hsiao-shih" 校勘小識 (Collations) and "pu" 補 (Supplement); (2) Wang, "K'ao-cheng" 考證 (Studies on the editions); (3) Yeh Te-hui 葉德輝 (late nineteenth century), "*Shih-shuo hsin-yü* i-wen" 世説新語佚文 (Listing of "unauthorized passages"), culled from various quotations; (4) Yeh, "*Shih-shuo hsin-yü* chu yin-yung shu-mu" 世説新語註引用書目 (Bibliography of works cited in Liu Chün's commentary).

Shih-shuo hsin-yü. Reprint of Sonkei Kaku or Kanazawa Bunkō edition (Tokyo, 1929). Peking: Wen-hsüeh ku-chi k'an-hsing she, 1956. 2:1–80 including: (1) A reprint of [*T'ang hsieh-pen*] *Shih-shuo hsin-shu* [*ts'an-chüan*]; (2) Wang Li-ch'i 王利器, "*Shih-shuo hsin-yü* chiao-k'an chi" 世説新語校勘記 (Collations).

Shih-shuo hsin-yü [*chiao-chien*] 世説新語 [校箋]. Commentary by Liu P'an-sui 劉盼遂. *Kuo-hsüeh lun-ts'ung* 國學論叢 1.4 (1928):65–110.

Shih-shuo hsin-yü [*chiao-chien*] 世説新語 [校箋]. Commentary by Yang Yung 楊勇. Hong Kong: Ta-chung shu-chü, 1969.

Shih-shuo hsin-yü [*pu-cheng*] 世説新語 [補證]. Commentary by Wang Shu-min 王叔岷. Pan-ch'iao: I-wen yin-shu kuan, 1975.

Shih-shuo hsin-yü [*chien-shu*] 世説新語 [箋疏]. Commentary by Yü Chia-hsi 余嘉錫. Peking: Chung-hua shu-chü, 1983. 2nd ed., 2 vols. Shanghai: Shanghai ku-chi ch'u-pan she, 1993.

Shih-shuo hsin-yü [*chiao-chien*] 世説新語 [校箋]. Commentary by Hsü Chen-o 徐震堮. 2 vols. Peking: Chung-hua shu-chü, 1984.

B. Translations of the *Shih-shuo hsin-yü*

Sesetsu shingo 世説新語. Translated by Okada Seinoshi 岡田正之識 for the series *Kambun sōsho* 漢文叢書 (Tsukamoto Tessan 塚本哲三, general editor), Tokyo, 1925. A *kambun* translation of Wang Shih-chen's (supplemented) text, with interpretation and laconic comments based on *Sesetsu sembon*.

Sesetsu shingo. Translated by Ōmura Umeo 大村梅雄. In *Chūgoku koten bungaku zenshū* 中國古典文學全集. No. 32 in the series *Rekidai zuihitsu shū* 歴代隨筆集, Tokyo, 1959. An incomplete translation of the pre-Ming (unsupplemented) text into modern Japanese, with brief annotation.

Sesetsu shingo. Translated by Kawakatsu Yoshio 川勝義雄, Fukunaga Mitsuji 福永光司, Murakami Yoshimi 村上嘉實, and Yoshikawa Tadao 吉川忠夫. *Chūgoku koshōsetsushū* 中國古小説集 (*Sekai bungaku taikei* 世界文學大系 71, Yoshikawa Kōjirō 吉川幸次郎, general editor), Tokyo, 1964. A complete, annotated translation into modern Japanese, with appendices of biographical notes and official titles.

Sesetsu shingo. Translated by Mori Mikisaburō 森三樹三郎. In *Chūgoku koten bungaku taikei* 中國古典文學大系 9, Tokyo, 1969.

Sesetsu shingo. A selected translation with an introduction by Yagisawa Hajime 八木澤元. In *Chūgoku koten shinsho* 中國古典新書. Tokyo: Meitoku shuppansha, 1970.

Anthologie chinoise des 5ᵉ et 6ᵉ siècles: le Che-chouo-sin-yu par Lieou (Tsuen) Hiao-piao. Translated by Bruno Belpaire. Editions Universitaires, Paris, 1974. A complete translation into French with laconic annotation.

Sesetsu shingo. Translated by Mekada Makoto 目加田誠. In *Shinyaku Kambun taikei* 新譯漢文大系, 76. 3 vols. Tokyo: Meiji shoin, 1975.

Shih-shuo hsin-yü, A New Account of Tales of the World. Translated by Richard Mather. Minneapolis: University of Minnesota Press, 1976. A complete translation into English of both the text and Liu Chün's commentary, plus the translator's own annotation.

Shishuo xinyu, Kaptel 14. Translated by M. von Duhn, R. Gassmann, and R. Homann. *Asiatische Studien, Etudes Asiatiques* 30 (1976):45–78. A partial translation into German with an introduction and notes.

Sesetsu shingo. Translated by Takeda Akira 竹田晃. In *Chūgoku no koten* 中國の古典, 21. 2 vols. Tokyo: Gakushu kenkyūsha, 1983 and 1984.

Shih-shuo hsin-yü [*i-chu*] 世説新語 [譯註] ([Translation with commentary of] the *Shih-*

shuo hsin-yü). Translated from classical to modern Chinese with commentary by Hsü Shao-tsao 許紹早. Changchun: Kirin chiao-yü ch'u-pan she, 1989.

Shih-shuo hsin-yü [*hsüan-i*] 世説新語 [選譯] ([Abridged translation of] the *Shih-shuo hsin-yü*). Translated from classical to modern Chinese, with introductions to the entire book and to each of its thirty-six chapters by Liu Shih-chen 柳士鎮 and Ch'ien Nan-hsiu 錢南秀. Chengtu: Pa-shu shu-she, 1989.

Shih-shuo hsin-yü [*ch'üan-i*] 世説新語 [全譯] ([Translation of] the *Shih-shuo hsin-yü*). Translated from classical to modern Chinese, with commentary by Liu Shih-chen and Liu K'ai-hua 劉開驊. Kweiyang: Kweichow jen-min ch'u-pan she, 1996.

C. Special Studies on the *Shih-shuo hsin-yü*

Chan Hsiu-hui 詹秀惠. *Shih-shuo hsin-yü yü-fa t'an-chiu* 世説新語語法探究 (Study of the *Shih-shuo hsin-yü* grammar). Taipei: Taiwan hsüeh-sheng shu-chü, 1972.

Chang Chen-te 張振德 and Sung Tzu-jan 宋子然, eds. *Shih-shuo hsin-yü yü-yen yen-chiu* 世説新語語言研究 (Study of the *Shih-shuo hsin-yü* language). Chengtu: Pa-shu shu-she, 1994.

Chang Shu-ning 張叔寧. *Shih-shuo hsin-yü cheng-t'i yen-chiu* 世説新語整體研究 (General study of the *Shih-shuo hsin-yü*). Nanking: Nanking ch'u-pan she, 1994.

Chang Wan-ch'i 張萬起. *Shih-shuo hsin-yü tz'u-tien* 世説新語辭典 (Dictionary of the *Shih-shuo hsin-yü*). Shanghai: Shang-wu yin-shu kuan, 1993.

Chang Yung-yen 張永言. *Shih-shuo hsin-yü tz'u-tien* 世説新語辭典 (Dictionary of the *Shih-shuo hsin-yü*). Chengtu: Szechwan jen-min ch'u-pan she, 1992.

Chao Kang 趙岡. "*Shih-shuo hsin-yü* Liu chu i-li k'ao" 世説新語劉注義例考 (Study of the patterns of Liu Chün's commentary on the *Shih-shuo hsin-yü*). *Kuo-wen yüeh-k'an* 國文月刊 82 (August 1949):20–26.

Ch'en Yin-k'o 陳寅恪. "Shu *Shih-shuo hsin-yü* wen-hsüeh lei Chung Hui chuan Ssu-pen lun shih-pi t'iao hou" 書世説新語文學類鍾會撰四本論始畢條後 (Written upon reading the entry "when Chung Hui had barely finished editing his 'Treatise on four basic relations between innate ability and human nature' [*Ssu-pen lun*]" in the chapter "Literature and scholarship" in the *Shih-shuo hsin-yü*). In Ch'en Yin-k'o. *Chin-ming kuan ts'ung-kao ch'u-pien* 金明館叢稿初編. Shanghai: Shanghai ku-chi ch'u-pan she, 1980. 41–47.

Cheng Hsüeh-t'ao 鄭學弢. "Tu *Shih-shuo hsin-yü* wen-hsüeh p'ien cha-chi" 讀世説新語文學篇札記 (Notes on reading the *Shih-shuo hsin-yü*). *Hsü-chou shih-fan ta-hsüeh hsüeh-pao* 徐州師範大學學報 1982.2: 9–14.

Ch'eng Chang-ts'an 程章燦. "Ts'ung *Shih-shuo hsin-yü* k'an Chin-Sung wen-hsüeh kuan-nien yü Wei-Chin mei-hsüeh hsin-feng" 從世説新語看晉宋文學觀念與魏晉美學新風 (The Chin-Sung concept of literature and the new trends of Wei-Chin aesthetics as seen from the *Shih-shuo hsin-yü*). *Nanking ta-hsüeh hsüeh-pao* 南京大學學報 (*Jen-wen she-k'o pan*) 1989.1:51–57.

Chiang Fan 蔣凡. *Shih-shuo hsin-yü yen-chiu* 世説新語研究 (A study of the *Shih-shuo hsin-yü*). Shanghai: Hsüeh-lin ch'u-pan she, 1998.

Chou I-liang 周一良. "*Shih-shuo hsin-yü* ho tso-che Liu I-ch'ing shen-shih ti k'ao-ch'a" 世説新語和作者劉義慶身世的考察 (*Shih-shuo hsin-yü* and a study of the author Liu I-ch'ing's life). Originally published in *Chung-kuo che-hsüeh shih yen-chiu* 中國哲學史研究 1981.1. Collected in Chou I-liang, *Wei-Chin Nan-Pei ch'ao shih lun-chi hsü-pien* 魏晉南北朝史論集續編. Peking: Peking University Press, 1991. 16–22.

Chou I-liang and Wang I-t'ung 王伊同. "Ma-i *Shih-shuo hsin-yü* shang-tui" 馬譯世説新語商兌 (Discussion of Richard B. Mather's translation of the *Shih-shuo hsin-yü*). *Ch'ing-hua hsüeh-pao* 清華學報 20.2 (1990):197–256.

Chou Pen-ch'un 周本淳. "*Shih-shuo hsin-yü* yüan-ming k'ao-lüeh" 世説新語原名考略 (Brief study of the original title of the *Shih-shuo hsin-yü*). *Chung-hua wen-shih lun-ts'ung* 中華文史論叢 1980.3:43–47.

Enomoto Fukuju 榎本福壽. "Sesetsu shingo no shuho" 世説新語の手法 (Artistic technique of the *Shih-shuo hsin-yü*). *Bukkyo daigaku kenkyū kiyo* 佛教大學研究紀要 66 (1982):43–72.

Fan Tzu-yeh 范子燁. *Shih-shuo hsin-yü* 世説新語研究 (A study of the *Shih-shuo hsin-yü*). Harbin: Heilungkiang chiao-yü ch'u-pan she, 1998.

Fang I-hsin 方一新. "*Shih-shuo hsin-yü* yü-tz'u yen-chiu" 世説新語語詞研究 (A study of the *Shih-shuo hsin-yü* terminology). Ph.D. dissertation. Hangchow University, 1989.

Fu Hsi-jen 傅錫壬 "*Shih-shuo* ssu-k'o tui *Lun-yü* ssu-k'o ti yin-hsi yü shan-pien" 世説四科對論語四科的因襲與嬗變 (*Shih-shuo hsin-yü*'s continuation and variation of the four divisions in the *Analects of Confucius*). *Tan-chiang hsüeh-pao* 淡江學報 12 (March 1974):101–123.

Fukuhara Keirō 福原啓郎. "Sei Shin no kizoku shakai no fūchō ni tsuite: Sesetsu shingo no Kenshokuhen to Tashihen no kentō o toshite" 西晉の貴族社會の風潮について：世説新語の儉嗇篇と汰侈篇の檢討を通して (On the social trend of Western Chin aristocratic society: An examination of the chapters "Stinginess and meanness" and "Extravagance and ostentation" in the *Shih-shuo hsin-yü*). *Kyoto gaikokugo daigaku kenkyū ronsō* 京都外國語大學研究論叢 46 (1990):596–616.

Ho Ch'ang-ch'ün 賀昌群. "*Shih-shuo hsin-yü* cha-chi: lun *chu-wei*" 世説新語札記：論麈尾 (Jotting notes on the *Shih-shuo hsin-yü*: On the term *chu-wei*). *Kuo-li chung-yang t'u-shu kuan kuan-k'an (fu-kan)* 國立中央圖書館館刊 (復刊) 1 (1947):1–7.

Hsiao Hung 蕭虹. "*Shih-shuo hsin-yü* tso-che wen-t'i shang-ch'üeh" 世説新語作者問題商榷 (On the authorship of the *Shih-shuo hsin-yü*). *Kuo-li chung-yang t'u-shu kuan kuan-k'an* 14.1 (1981):8–24.

———. (Also under Lee, Lily Hsiao Hung). "A Study of *Shih-shuo hsin-yü*." Ph.D. dissertation. University of Sydney, 1982.

Hsü Ch'uan-wu 徐傳武. "*Shih-shuo hsin-yü* Liu-chu ch'ien-t'an" 世説新語劉注淺探 (Tentative study of Liu Chün's commentary on the *Shih-shuo hsin-yü*). *Wen-hsien* 文獻 1986.1:1–12.

Hsü Shih-ying 許世瑛. "Ts'ung *Shih-shuo hsin-yü* k'an Wei-Chin jen hsi-su ti i-pan" 從世説新語看魏晉人習俗的一斑 (An aspect of Wei-Chin customs as seen from the *Shih-shuo hsin-yü*). *Hsin she-hui yüeh-k'an* 新社會月刊 1.7 (1948):8–10.

Inami Ritsuko 井波律子. *Chūgokujin no kichi: Sesetsu shingo o chūshin toshite* 中國人の機智：世説新語を中心として (Chinese wisdom: The essence of the *Shih-shuo hsin-yü*). Tokyo: Chūōkōronsha, 1983.

Kawakatsu Yoshio 川勝義雄. "Edo jidai ni okeru *Sesetsu* kenkyū no ichimen" 江戸時代における世説研究の一面 (An aspect of the study of the *Shih-shuo hsin-yü* during the Edo period). *Tōhōgaku* 東方學 (1960):1–15.

―――. "*Sesetsu shingo* no hensan o megutte" 世説新語の編纂をめぐって (On the compilation and the editions of the *Shih-shuo hsin-yü*) *Tōhōgakuhō* 東方學報 41 (1970):217–234.

Kominami Ichirō 小南一郎. *Sesetsu shingo no bigaku: Gi Shin no sai to sei o megutte* 世説新語の美學：魏晉の才と情をめぐって (Aesthetics of the *Shih-shuo hsin-yü*: On Wei-Chin talents and emotions). In Chūgoku chūseishi kenkyūkai 中國中世史研究會, *Chūgoku chūseishi kenkyū: zokuhen* 中國中世史研究：續篇. Kyoto: Kyoto Daigaku gakujutsu shuppankai 京都大學學術出版會, 1995.

Kozen Hiroshi 興膳宏. "*Sesetsu shingo* no gunzō 世説新語の群象 (The *Shih-shuo hsin-yü* characters). *Sekai bungaku taikei* 世界文學大系 71 (1965), monthly supplement 85:2–4.

Kubo Takuya 久保卓哉. "*Sesetsu shingo* ni okeru hiyu no shosō 世説新語における比喩の諸相 (Similes and metaphors in the *Shih-shuo hsin-yü*). In *Furuta Kyōju taikan kinen Chūgoku bungaku gogaku ronshū* 古田教授退官紀念中國文學語學論集 (Collected essays on Chinese literature and linguistics in celebration of Professor Furuta's retirement). Tokyo: Tōhō shoten, 1985. 134–148.

Lin Chih-meng 林志孟. "*Shih-shuo hsin-yü* jen-wu k'ao" 世説新語人物考 (Study of the *Shih-shuo hsin-yü* characters). M.A. thesis. Chinese Cultural University, 1983.

Liu Chao-yün 劉兆雲. "*Shih-shuo* chung ti wen-hsüeh kuan-tien" 世説中的文學觀點 (Literary viewpoint in the *Shih-shuo* [*hsin-yü*]). *Sinkiang ta-hsüeh hsüeh-pao* 新疆大學學報 (*Che-hsüeh yü she-hui k'o-hsüeh pan*) 1985. 3:97–102.

―――. "*Shih-shuo* t'an-yüan" 世説探原 (Search for the origin of the *Shih-shuo hsin-yü*). Ibid. 1979.1:6–13.

Liu Yeh-ch'iu 劉葉秋 "Shih-lun *Shih-shuo hsin-yü*" 試論世説新語 (Tentative study of the *Shih-shuo hsin-yü*). In *Ku-tien hsiao-shuo pi-chi lun-ts'ung* 古典小説筆記論叢 (Collected essays on classical *hsiao-shuo* and *pi-chi*). T'ientsin: Nankai University Press, 1985. 44–59.

―――. "Yeh-hsia feng-liu tsai Chin tuo: tu *Shih-shuo hsin-yü* san-chi" 鄴下風流在晉多：讀世説新語散記 (Wei style in the Chin: Notes on reading the *Shih-shuo hsin-yü*). Ibid. 60–65.

Ma Hsing-kuo 馬興國. "*Shih-shuo hsin-yü* tsai Jih-pen ti liu-ch'uan chi ying-hsiang" 世説 新語在日本的流傳及影響 (Circulation and influence of the *Shih-shuo hsin-yü* in Japan). *Tung-pei shih-ta hsüeh-pao* 東北師大學報 (*She-k'o pan*) 1989.3:79–83.

Mei Chia-ling 梅家玲. "*Shih-shuo hsin-yü* ti yü-yen i-shu" 世説新語的語言藝術 (Lingustic art of the *Shih-shuo hsin-yü*). Ph.D. dissertation. Taiwan University, 1991.

Morino Shigeo 森野繁夫. "*Sesetsu shingo* oyobi sono chū ni mieru hyōgo—'kan' to 'sotsu'" 世説新語およびその注にみえる評語—"簡" と "率" ("Simple" and "straightforward": The two appraisal terms seen in the *Shih-shuo hsin-yü* and its commentary). *Tōhōgaku* 44 (1972):73–89.

———. "Toku *Sesetsu shingo* sakki: Bungaku hen" 讀世説新語札記：文學篇(一) (Notes on reading the *Shih-shuo hsin-yü*: "Literature and scholarship" [1]). *Chūgoku chū-sei bungaku kenkyū* 中國中世文學研究 2 (1962):38–47.

Murakami Yoshimi 村上嘉實. "*Sesetsu shingo* no kichiteki seikaku" 世説新語の機智的性格 (Witty personalities in the *Shih-shuo hsin-yü*). *Shirin* 史林 29.3 (1945):3–48.

———. "*Sesetsu shingo* ni arawaretaru kosei" 世説新語に現れたる個性 (Diverse personali-ties presented in the *Shih-shuo hsin-yü*). In *Haneda Hakushi shoju kinen tōyōshi ronsō* 羽田博士頌壽紀念東洋史論叢 (Collected essays on East Asian history in celebration of Dr. Haneda's birthday). Kyoto, 1950. 949–969.

———. "Gi Shin ni okeru toku no tayōsei ni tsuite: *Sesetsu shingo* no shisō" 魏晉における 德の多様性について：世説新語の思想 (On Wei-Chin diversity of *te*: *Shih-shuo hsin-yü*'s thought). In *Suzuki Hakushi koki kinen tōyōgaku ronsō* 鈴木博士古稀紀念 東洋學論叢 (Collected essays on East Asian studies in celebration of Dr. Suzuki's seventieth birthday). Tokyo: Meitoku shuppansha, 1972. 549–570.

Ning Chia-yü 寧稼雨. *Shih-shuo hsin-yü yü chung-ku wen-hua* 世説新語與中古文化 (*Shih-shuo hsin-yü* and medieval culture). Shih-chia chuang: Hopeh chiao-yü ch'u-pan she, 1994.

———. "*Shih-shuo hsin-yü* shih chih-jen hsiao-shuo kuan-nien ch'eng-shu ti piao-chih" 世説新語是志人小説觀念成熟的標志 (*Shih-shuo hsin-yü*: The mark of the ma-turity of the *chih-jen hsiao-shuo*). *T'ientsin shih-ta hsüeh-pao* 天津師大學報 (*She-k'o pan*) 1988.5:75–79.

———. "*Shih-shuo t'i* ch'u-t'an" 世説體初探 (Tentative study of the genre of the *Shih-shuo* [*hsin-yü*]). *Chung-kuo ku-tien wen-hsüeh lun-ts'ung* 中國古典文學論叢 6 (1987):87–105.

Ōyane Bunjirō 大矢根文次郎. *Sesetsu shingo to rikuchō bungaku* 世説新語と六朝文學 (*Shih-shuo hsin-yü* and Six Dynasties literature). Tokyo: Waseda daigaku shuppanbu, 1983.

———. "Edo Jidai ni okeru *Sesetsu shingo* ni tsuite" 江戸時代における世説新語について (*Shih-shuo hsin-yü* in the Edo period). In *Sesetsu shingo to rikuchō bungaku*. 102–105.

P'iao Ching-chi 朴敬姬. "*Shih-shuo hsin-yü* chung jen-wu p'in-chien chih yen-chiu" 世説 新語中人物品鑒之研究 (Study of character appraisal in the *Shih-shuo hsin-yü*). M.A. thesis. Taiwan Cheng-chih ta-hsüeh, 1982.

Qian, Nanxiu. "Women's Role in Wei-Chin Character Appraisal as Reflected in the *Shih-shuo hsin-yü*." In a *Festschrift* in honor of Professors Richard B. Mather and Donald Holzman, edited by David Knetchges and Paul W. Kroll. *T'ang Studies* (Fall 2000).

———. "Milk and Scent: Works about Women in the *Shishuo xinyu* [*Shih-shuo hsin-yü*] Genre," *Nan Nü: Men, Women, and Gender in Early and Imperial China* 1.2 (Fall 1999):187–236.

———. "*Daitō Seigo*: An Alien Analogue of the *Shih-shuo hsin-yü*," *Early Medieval China* 4 (1998):49–82.

———. "Being One's Self: Narrative Art and Taxonomy of Human Nature in the *Shih-shuo hsin-yü*." Ph.D. dissertation. Yale University, 1994.

——— (Also under Ch'ien Nan-hsiu) 錢南秀. "Ch'uan-shen o-tu: *Shih-shuo hsin-yü* su-tsao jen-wu hsing-hsiang ti i-shu shou-fa" 傳神阿堵：世說新語塑造人物形象的藝術手法 (Transmitting the spirit from here: Characterization of personalities in the *Shih-shuo hsin-yü*). *Wen-hsüeh p'ing-lun* 文學評論 1986.5: 104–112.

———. "Lun *Shih-shuo hsin-yü* shen-mei kuan" 論世說新語審美觀 (On the aesthetic standards of the *Shih-shuo hsin-yü*). *Chiang-hai hsüeh-k'an* 江海學刊 (*She-k'o pan*) 1982.2:122–126.

Sesetsu rinkōkai 世説輪講會. "*Sesetsu shingochū* yakkai: 'Kangōhen' 24" 世説新語注譯解：簡傲篇第二十四 (Translation and interpretation of the commentary of the *Shih-shuo hsin-yü*: Ch. 24, "Rudeness and arrogance"). *Tōyō bungaku kenkyū* 東洋文學研究 14 (1966):37–48.

———. "*Sesetsu shingochū* yakkai (2), (3), (5), (6): 'Haichōhen' 25" 排調篇第二十五 (Ch. 25, "Taunting and teasing"). *Tōyō bungaku kenkyū* 15 (1967):65–79; 16 (1968):59–66; 18 (1970):76–89; 19 (1971):64–71.

———. "*Sesetsu shingochū* yakkai (4): 'Keiteihen' 26" 輕詆篇第二十六 (Ch. 26, "Contempt and insults"). *Tōyō bungaku kenkyū* 17 (1969):100–111.

———. "*Sesetsu shingochū* yakkai (7): 'Tokugyōhen' 1" 德行篇第一 (Ch. 1, "*Te* conduct"). *Tōyō bungaku kenkyū* 20 (1972):33–58.

Tokuda Takeshi 德田武. "*Daitō seigo* ron (1): Hattori Nankaku ni okeru *Sesetsu shingo*" 大東世語論一：服部南郭における世説新語 (On *An Account of the Great Eastern World* [1]: *Shih-shuo hsin-yü* and Hattori Nankaku). *Tōyō bungaku kenkyū* 17 (1969):82–99.

———. "*Daitō seigo* ron (2): Hattori Nankaku ni okeru *Sesetsu shingo*" 大東世語論二：服部南郭における世説新語 (On *An Account of the Great Eastern World* [2]: *Shih-shuo hsin-yü* and Hattori Nankaku). *Chūgoku koten kenkyū* 中國古典研究 16 (1969):91–117.

———. "*Daitō seigo* ron (3): Hattori Nankaku no ningen ninshiki to bi-ishiki" 大東世語論三：服部南郭の人間認識と美意識 (On *An Account of the Great Eastern World* [3]: Hattori Nankaku's understanding of human beings and his aesthetic viewpoints]. *Chūgoku koten kenkyū* 17 (1970): 27–52.

Toyofuku Kenji 豊 福 健 二. *"Sesetsu* 'Kenenhen' to *Shinsho* 'Retsujoten'" 世説新語賢媛篇と晉書列女傳 (The chapter "Worthy beauties" in the *Shih-shuo hsin-yü* and the "Biographies of exemplary women" in the *History of the Chin*). In *Obi Hakushi taikyū kinen Chūgoku bungaku ronshū* 小尾博士退休紀念中國文學論集 (Collected essays on Chinese literature in celebration of Dr. Obi's retirement). Tokyo: Daiitchi gakushūsha, 1976. 263–289.

Tsung Pai-hua 宗 白 華. "Lun *Shih-shuo hsin-yü* ho Chin-jen ti mei" 論世説新語和晉人的美 (*Shih-shuo hsin-yü* and Chin aesthetics). *Hsing-ch'i p'ing-lun* 星 期 評論 10 (1941):8–11.

Utsunomiya Kiyoyoshi 宇 都 宮 清 吉. "*Sesetsu shingo* no jidai" 世説新語の時代 (The time of the *Shih-shuo hsin-yü*). *Tōhō gakuhō* 10.2 (1939). Revised for *Kandai shakai keizaishi kenkyū* 漢代社會經濟史研究 (Study of Han socioeconomic history). Tokyo, 1955. 473–521.

Wang Fang-yü 王 方 宇. Pa-ta shan-jen *Shih-shuo hsin-yü* shih" 八大山人世説新語詩 (Pa-ta shan-jen's *Shih-shuo hsin-yü* poems). *Ch'eng-ta* 成 大 22 (1975):9–20.

Wang Neng-hsien 王 能 憲. *Shih-shuo hsin-yü yen-chiu* 世説新語研究 (Study of the *Shih-shuo hsin-yü*). Nanking: Kiangsu ku-chi ch'u-pan she, 1992.

Wang Shu-min 王 叔 岷. "*Shih-shuo hsin-yü* wen-hsüeh p'ien pu-chien" 世説新語文學篇補箋 (Supplementary commentary on the chapter "Literature and scholarship" in the *Shih-shuo hsin-yü*). *Nan-yang ta-hsüeh hsüeh-pao* 南洋大學學報 8–9 (1974/1975):12–22.

Wu Chin-hua 吳 金 華. *Shih-shuo hsin-yü kao-shih* 世説新語考釋 (Interpretation of the *Shih-shuo hsin-yü* [terms]). Hofei: Anhui chiao-yü ch'u-pan she, 1994.

Yagisawa Hajime 八 木 澤 元 "*Sesetsu* kara shinsho, shingo e no hatten: *Sesetsu shingo* denpon ko" 世説から新書、新語への發展：世説新語傳本考 (From the *Shih-shuo* to the *Shih-shuo hsin-shu* and the *Shih-shuo hsin-yü*: A study of the *Shih-shuo hsin-yü* editions). *Torii Hisayasu sensei kakō kinen ronshū (Chūgoku no gengo to bungaku)* 鳥居久靖先生華甲紀念論集（中國の語言と文學）(Collected essays in celebration of Master Torii Hisayasu's sixtieth birthday) (Chinese language and literature). 1972. 99–116.

Yang I 楊 義. "Han-Wei Liu-ch'ao *Shih-shuo t'i* hsiao-shuo ti liu-pien" 漢魏六朝世説體小説的流變 (Evolution of the *Shih-shuo t'i hsiao-shuo* during the Han, Wei, and Six Dynasties). *Chung-kuo she-hui k'o-hsüeh* 中 國 社 會 科 學 1991.4:85–99.

Yang, V. T. "About *Shih-shuo hsin-yü*." *Journal of Oriental Studies* 2.2 (1955):309–315.

Yoshikawa Kōjirō 吉 川 幸 次 郎. "*Sesetsu shingo* no bunsho" 世説新語の文章 (Prose style of the *Shih-shuo hsin-yü*). *Tōhō gakuhō* 10.2 (1939):199–255. Translated into English by Glen W. Baxter, under the title "The *Shih-shuo hsin-yü* and Six Dynasties Prose Style." *Harvard Journal of Asiatic Studies* 18 (1955):124–141. Translated into Chinese (incomplete) by Chi Yung 紀 庸, under the title "*Shih-shuo hsin-yü* chih wen-chang" 世説新語之文章. *Kuo-wen yüeh-k'an* 國文月刊 64 (1948):24–27.

D. Background Works and Studies

Allport, Gordon W. "What is a Trait of Personality?" *Journal of Abnormal and Social Psychology* 25 (1931):368–372.

Allport, Gordon W., and Henry S. Odbert. "Trait-Names: A Psycho-Lexical Study." *Psychological Monograph* 47.1 (1936):i–171.

Aristotle. *Ethics (The Nicomachean Ethics)*. Trans. J. A. K. Thomson. Penguin Books, 1976.

Bickford, Maggie. *Ink Plum: The Making of a Chinese Scholar-Painting Genre*. Cambridge: Cambridge University Press, 1996.

Bol, Peter. *"This Culture of Ours": Intellectual Transitions in T'ang and Sung China*. Stanford: Stanford University Press, 1992.

Brook, Timothy. *The Confusions of Pleasure: Commerce and Culture in Ming China*. Berkeley: University of California Press, 1998.

Buber, Martin. *I and Thou*. Trans. with a prologue and notes by Walter Kaufmann. New York: Charles Scribner's Sons, 1970.

Chan, Hok-lam. *Li Chih (1527–1602) in Contemporary Chinese Historiography: New Light on His Life and Works*. Translated from *Wen-wu* and other sources with introduction, notes, and appendices. With a foreword by Frederick W. Mote. White Plains, NY: M. E. Sharpe, 1980.

Chan-kuo ts'e 戰國策 (Intrigues of the Warring States). *Ssu-pu ts'ung-k'an* ed.

Chang T'ing-yü 張廷玉 (1672–1755) et al. *Ming-shih* 明史 (History of the Ming). 28 vols. Peking: Chung-hua shu-chü, 1974.

Chang Yen-yüan 張彥遠 (fl. 847–862). *Li-tai ming-hua chi* 歷代名畫記 (Records of the masterpieces of art from previous dynasties). Peking: Jen-min mei-shu ch'u-pan she, 1963.

Chao Yi 趙翼 (1727–1814). *Nien-erh shih cha-chi* 廿二史劄記 (Jottings on reading the twenty-two histories). Peking: Chung-hua shu-chü, 1963.

Chao Yüan 趙園. *Ming-Ch'ing chih-chi shih ta-fu yen-chiu* 明清之際士大夫研究 (Study of the scholar-officials of the Ming-Ch'ing transitional period). Peking: Peking University Press, 1999.

Ch'ao Kung-wu 晁公武 (fl. mid-twelfth cent.). *Chün-chai tu-shu chih* 郡齋讀書志 (Bibliographic treatise from the Prefectural Studio). 1884. Reprint, 4 vols., Taipei: Kuang-wen shu-chü, 1967.

Chatman, Seymour. *Story and Discourse*. Ithaca: Cornell University Press, 1978.

Ch'en, Kenneth. *Buddhism in China*. Princeton, NJ: Princeton University Press, 1964.

Ch'en Shou 陳壽 (233–297). *San-kuo chih* 三國志 (Records of the Three Kingdoms). Commentary by P'ei Sung-chih 裴松之 (372–451). 5 vols. Peking: Chung-hua shu-chü, 1959.

Ch'en Yin-k'o 陳寅恪 (1890–1969). *Chin-ming kuan ts'ung-kao ch'u-pien* 金明館叢稿

初編 (Collected essays from Chin-ming studio [1]). Shanghai: Shanghai ku-chi ch'u-pan she, 1980.

———. *Chin-ming kuan ts'ung-kao erh-pien* 金明館叢稿二編 (Collected essays from Chin-ming studio [2]). Shanghai: Shanghai ku-chi ch'u-pan she, 1980.

Ch'eng Chang-ts'an. *Shih-tsu yü Liu-ch'ao wen-hsüeh* 士族與六朝文學 (The gentry and Six Dynasties literature). Harbin: Heilungkiang chiao-yü ch'u-pan she, 1998.

Ch'eng Ch'ien-fan 程千帆. *T'ang-tai chin-shih hsing-chüan yü wen-hsüeh* 唐代進士行卷與文學 (Literature and the *chin-shih* candidate literary portfolios). Shanghai: Shanghai ku-chi ch'u-pan she, 1980.

Ch'eng Ch'ien-fan and Wu Hsin-lei 吳新雷. *Liang Sung wen-hsüeh shih* 兩宋文學史 (History of Sung literature). Shanghai: Shanghai ku-chi ch'u-pan she, 1991.

Ch'eng Hao 程顥 (1032–1085) and Ch'eng I 程頤 (1033–1107). *Erh-Ch'eng i-shu* 二程遺書 (Posthumously published works of the two Ch'engs). *Ssu-k'u ch'üan-shu* ed.

Ch'eng Ming-shih 承名世. "Lun Sun Wei 'Kao-i t'u' ti ku-shih chi ch'i yü Ku K'ai-chih hua-feng ti kuan-hsi" 論孫位高逸圖的故實及其與顧愷之畫風的關係 (On the historical background of Sun Wei's *Portraits of eminent recluses* and its relationship with Ku K'ai-chih's artistic style). *Wen-wu* 文物 1965.8:15–23.

Chiang Chien-chün 江建俊. *Han-mo jen-lun chien-shih chih tsung li-tse: Liu Shao Jen-wu chih yen-chiu* 漢末人倫鑒識之總理則：劉邵人物志研究 (General principles of late Han character appraisal: A study of Liu Shao's *Jen-wu chih*). Taipei: Wen shih che ch'u-pan she, 1983.

Chiang Liang-fu 姜亮夫, ed. *Li-tai jen-wu nien-li pei-chuan tsung-piao* 歷代人物年里碑傳綜表 (Comprehensive chart of the dates and native places of [Chinese] historical figures as acquired from their epitaphs and biographies). Peking: Chung-hua shu-chü, 1959.

Chiang Tung-fu 姜東賦. "Chung-kuo hsiao-shuo kuan ti li-shih yen-chin" 中國小說觀的歷史演進 (Evolution of the Chinese perspective on *hsiao-shuo*). *T'ientsin shih-ta hsüeh-pao (She-k'o pan)* 1992.1:55–62.

Chou Hsün-ch'u 周勛初. *Wen-shih t'an-wei* 文史探微 (Inspection of subtleties of literature and history). Shanghai: Shanghai ku-chi ch'u-pan she, 1987.

———. *T'ang-jen pi-chi hsiao-shuo k'ao-so* 唐人筆記小說考索 (Study of T'ang *pi-chi hsiao-shuo*). Kiangsu: Kiangsu ku-chi ch'u-pan she, 1996.

Chou-i [cheng-i] 周易 [正義] ([Orthodox commentary on] Book of changes). *Chu* 註 commentary by Wang Pi 王弼 (226–249) and Han K'ang-po 韓康伯 (fourth century), and *shu* 疏 commentary by K'ung Ying-ta 孔穎達 (574–648). In *Shih-san ching chu-shu*. 1:5–108.

——— (Under the title *The I-ching, or Book of Changes*). Translated from Chinese into German by Richard Wilhelm. Rendered into English by Cary F. Baynes. Princeton: Princeton University Press, 1977.

Chou I-liang 周一良. *Wei-Chin Nan-Pei ch'ao shih lun-chi* 魏晉南北朝史論集 (Collected essays on the history of the Wei, Chin, Southern and Northern dynasties). Peking: Chung-hua shu-chü, 1963.

―――. "Liang-Chin Nan-ch'ao ti ch'ing-i" 兩晉南朝的清議 (Pure criticism in the Chin and Southern dynasties), *Wei-Chin Sui-T'ang shih lun-chi* 魏晉隋唐史論集2 (1983):1–9.

―――. *Wei-Chin Nan-Pei ch'ao shih cha-chi* 魏晉南北朝史札記 (Notes on reading the histories of the Wei, Chin, Southern and Northern dynasties). Peking: Chunghua shu-chü, 1985.

―――. *Wei-Chin Nan-Pei ch'ao shih lun-chi hsü-pien* 魏晉南北朝史論集續編 (Continued collection of essays on the history of the Wei, Chin, Southern and Northern dynasties). Peking: Peking University Press, 1991.

Chou-li [chu-shu] 周禮 [註疏] ([Commentary on] Book of Chou rites). *Chu* 註 commentary by Cheng Hsüan 鄭玄 (127–200), *shu* 疏 commentary by Chia Kung-yen 賈公彥 (sixth century) et al., and *shih-wen* commentary by Lu Te-ming 陸德明 (556–627). In *Shih-san ching chu-shu.* 1:31–939.

Chou Tun-i 周惇頤 (1017–1073). *Chou Yüan-kung chi* 周元公集 (Collected works of Chou Tun-i). *Ssu-k'u ch'üan-shu* ed.

Chow, Kai-wing. *The Rise of Confucian Ritualism in Late Imperial China: Ethics, Classics, and Lineage Discourse.* Stanford: Stanford University Press, 1994.

Chow, Tse-tsung. *The May Fourth Movement: Intellectual Revolution in Modern China.* Cambridge: Harvard University Press, 1960.

Chu Hsi 朱熹 (1130–1200). *Chu-tzu yü-lei* 朱子語類 (Classified quotations of Master Chu Hsi). *Ssu-k'u ch'üan-shu* ed.

Chuang-tzu [chi-shih] 莊子 [集釋] (Collected commentaries on] *Chuang-tzu*). Edited with commentary by Kuo Ch'ing-fan 郭慶藩 (1845–1891). 4 vols. Peking: Chunghua shu-chü, 1961.

――― (Under the title *The Complete Works of Chuang Tzu*). Translated by Burton Watson. New York: Columbia University Press, 1968.

Ch'un-ch'iu Kung-yang chuan [chu-shu] 春秋公羊傳 [註疏] ([Commentary on] The Kungyang commentary of the Spring and Autumn Annals). *Chieh-ku* 解詁 commentary by Ho Hsiu 何休 (129–182), and *shu* 疏 commentary by Hsü Yen 徐彥 (ninth century?). In *Shih-san ching chu-shu.* 2:2189–2355.

Ch'un-ch'iu Tso-chuan [cheng-i] 春秋左傳 [正義] ([Orthodox commentary on] The Tso commentary of the Spring and Autumn Annals). *Chu* 註 commentary by Tu Yü 杜預 (222–284), and *shu* 疏 commentary by K'ung Ying-ta 孔穎達 (574–648). In *Shih-san ching chu-shu.* 2:1697–2188.

Clunas, Craig. *Superfluous Things: Material Culture and Social Status in Early Modern China.* Cambridge: Polity Press, 1991.

Conboy, Katie, et al., eds. *Writing on the Body: Female Embodiment and Feminist Theory.* New York: Columbia University Press, 1997.

De Bary, William Theodore, et al. *Self and Society in Ming Thought*. New York: Columbia University Press, 1970.

Eagleton, Terry. *Literary Theory: An Introduction*. Minneapolis: University of Minnesota Press, 1983.

————. *Ideology: An Introduction*. London: Verso, 1991.

Egan, Ronald C. *Word, Image, and Deed in the Life of Su Shi* [*Su Shih*]. Cambridge: Council on East Asian Studies, Harvard University, 1994.

Elman, Benjamin A. "Political, Social, and Cultural Reproduction via Civil Service Examinations in Late Imperial China." *Journal of Asian Studies* 50.1 (February 1991):7–28.

————. "The Formation of 'Dao Learning' as Imperial Ideology during the Early Ming Dynasty." In *Culture and State in Chinese History: Conventions, Accommodations, and Critiques*. Eds. Theodore Huters, R. Bin. Wong, and Pauline Yu. Stanford: Stanford University Press, 1997.

Fan Ning 范寧. "Lun Wei-Chin shih-tai chih-shih fen-tzu ti ssu-hsiang fen-hua chi ch'i she-hui ken-yüan" 論魏晉時代知識分子的思想分化及其社會根源 (On Wei-Chin intellectuals' ideological division and its social origin). *Li-shih yen-chiu* 歷史研究. 1955.4:113–131.

Fan Shou-k'ang 范壽康. *Wei-Chin chih ch'ing-t'an* 魏晉之清談 (Wei-Chin pure conversation). Shanghai: Shang-wu yin-shu kuan, 1936.

Fan Yeh 范曄 (398–445). *Hou-Han shu* 後漢書 (History of the Later Han). Commentary by Li Hsien 李賢 (651–684). 12 vols. Peking: Chung-hua shu-chü, 1965.

Fang Hsüan-ling 房玄齡 (578–648) et al. *Chin-shu* 晉書 (History of the Chin). 10 vols. Peking: Chung-hua shu-chü, 1974.

Feng Yu-lan 馮友蘭. *Chung-kuo che-hsüeh shih* 中國哲學史 (History of Chinese Philosophy). 2 vols. Peking: Chung-hua shu-chü, 1961.

———— (under Fung Yu-lan). *A History of Chinese Philosophy*. Trans. Derk Bodde. 2 vols. Princeton, NJ: Princeton University Press, 1973.

Fisch, Harold. "Character as Linguistic Sign." *New Literary History* 21.3 (1990):592–606.

Foucault, Michel. *The Order of Things: An Archaeology of the Human Sciences*. New York: Vintage Books, 1973.

Fu Hsüan-ts'ung 傅璇琮. *T'ang-tai k'o-chü yü wen-hsüeh* 唐代科舉與文學 (T'ang examination system and literature). Sian: Shensi jen-min ch'u-pan she, 1986.

Gilmartin, Christina K., et al., eds. *Engendering China: Women, Culture, and the State*. Cambridge: Harvard University Press, 1994.

Goodrich, L. Carrington, and Chaoying Fang, eds. *Dictionary of Ming Biography*. New York: Columbia University Press, 1976.

Graham, A. C. *Disputers of the Tao: Philosophical Argument in Ancient China*. La Salle, IL: Open Court, 1989.

————. *Studies in Chinese Philosophy and Philosophical Literature*. Singapore: Institute of East Asian Philosophies, 1986.

Guisso, R. W. L. *Wu Tse-t'ien and the Politics of Legitimation in T'ang China*. Bellingham, WA: Program in East Asian Studies, Western Washington University, 1978.

Guisso, Richard W., and Stanley Johannesen, eds. *Women in China*. Youngstown, NY: Philo Press, 1981.

Guy, R. Kent. *The Emperor's Four Treasuries: Scholars and the State in the Late Ch'ien-lung Era*. Cambridge: Harvard University Press, 1987.

Hall, David L., and Roger T. Ames. *Thinking through Confucius*. Albany: State University of New York Press, 1987.

Hall, John Whitney, et al., eds. *The Cambridge History of Japan*. 6 vols. Vol. 4: *Early Modern Japan*. Cambridge: Cambridge University Press, 1988.

Han Fei 韓非 (d. 233 B.C.). *Han Fei Tzu [chi-chieh]* 韓非子 [集解]. Edited with commentary by Wang Hsien-shen 王先慎. *Chu-tzu chi-ch'eng* 諸子集成 ed. Peking: Chung-hua shu-chü, 1954.

Hane, Mikiso. *Premodern Japan: A Historical Survey*. Boulder: Westview Press, 1991.

Hanson, Chad. "Classical Chinese Philosophy as Linguistic Analysis." *Journal of Chinese Philosophy* 14 (1987):309–330.

————. "Qing [Ch'ing] (Emotions) 情 in Pre-Buddhist Chinese Thought." In *Emotions in Asian Thought: A Dialogue in Comparative Philosophy*, edited by Joel Markes and Roger T. Ames. Albany: State University of New York Press, 1995. 181–211.

Hegel, Robert B., and Richard C. Hessney, eds. *Expressions of Self in Chinese Literature*. New York: Columbia University Press, 1985.

Hisamatsu, Sen'ichi, ed. *Biographical Dictionary of Japanese Literature*. Kodansha International in collaboration with the International Society for Educational Information, 1976.

Ho Ch'ang-ch'ün. *Wei-Chin ch'ing-t'an ssu-hsiang ch'u-lun* 魏晉清談思想初論 (Tentative study of the thought of Wei-Chin pure conversation). Shanghai: Shanghai shang-wu yin-shu kuan, 1947.

Ho Ch'i-min 何啓民. *Chu-lin ch'i-hsien yen-chiu* 竹林七賢研究 (Study of the Seven Worthies of the Bamboo Grove). Taipei: Chung-kuo hsüeh-shu chu-tso chiang-chu wei-yüan hui, 1966.

————. *Wei-Chin ssu-hsiang yü t'an-feng* 魏晉思想與談風 (Wei-Chin thought and the trend of pure conversation). Taipei: Shang-wu yin-shukuan, 1967.

Ho Liang-chün 何良俊 (1506–1573). *Ssu-yu chai ts'ung-shuo* 四友齋叢說 (Classified accounts from the Four-Friends Studio). Peking: Chung-hua shu-chü, 1983.

Hochman, Baruch. *Character in Literature*. Ithaca: Cornell University Press, 1985.

Holcombe, Charles. "The Exemplar State: Ideology, Self-Cultivation, and Power in Fourth-Century China." *Harvard Journal of Asiatic Studies* 49.1 (June 1989):93–139.

———. *In the Shadow of the Han: Literati Thought and Society at the Beginning of the Southern Dynasties*. Honolulu: University of Hawaiʻi Press, 1994.

Holzman, Donald. "Les sept sages de la forêt des bambous et la société de leur temps." *Tʻoung pao* 44 (1956):317–346.

———. *La vie et la pensée de Hi Kʻang*. Leiden: E. J. Brill, 1957.

———. *Poetry and Politics: The Life and Works of Juan Chi (A.D. 210–263)*. Cambridge: Cambridge University Press, 1976.

Hou Wai-lu 侯外盧. *Sung-Ming li-hsüeh shih* 宋明理學史 (History of Sung-Ming Neo-Confucianism). 2 vols. Peking: Jen-min chʻu-pan she, 1984.

Hsi Kʻang 嵇康 (223–262). *Hsi Kʻang chi [chiao-chu]* 嵇康集 [校註] ([Commentary on] Collected works of Hsi Kʻang). Edited with commentary by Tai Ming-yang 戴明揚. Peking: Jen-min wen-hsüeh chʻu-pan she, 1962.

———. *Philosophy and Argumentation in Third-Century China: The Essays of Hsi Kʻang*. Translated with introduction and annotation by Robert G. Henricks. Princeton, NJ: Princeton University Press, 1983.

Hsia, C. T. "Yen Fu and Liang Chʻi-chʻao as Advocates of New Fiction." In *Chinese Approaches to Literature from Confucius to Liang Chʻi-chʻao*, edited by Adele Austin Rickett. Princeton, NJ: Princeton University Press, 1978. 221–257.

Hsiao, Kung-chuan. *A History of Chinese Political Thought*. Trans. F. W. Mote. Princeton: Princeton University Press, 1979.

Hsiao Tʻung 蕭統 (501–531), ed. *Wen-hsüan* 文選 (Selections of refined literature). Commentary by Li Shan 李善 (d. 689). 3 vols. Peking: Chung-hua shu-chü, 1977.

———. *Wen Xuan [Wen-hsüan], or Selections of Refined Literature*. Translated with annotations by David R. Knechtges. 3 vols. Princeton, NJ: Princeton University Press, 1982–1996.

Hsü Kan 徐幹 (170–217). *Chung-lun* 中論 (On the mean). *Pai-tzu chʻüan-shu* 百子全書 ed.

Hsü Shen 許慎 (30–124). *Shuo-wen chieh-tzu* 説文解字 (Interpretation of words). 1873. Reprint, Peking: Chung-hua shu-chü, 1963.

———. *Shuo-wen chieh-tzu [chu]* 説文解字 [註] ([Commentary on] Interpretation of words). Commentary by Tuan Yü-tsʻai 段玉裁 (1735–1815). 1815. Reprint, Shanghai: Shanghai ku-chi chʻu-pan she, 1981.

Hsü Sung 許嵩 (fl. 756–762). *Chien-kʻang shih-lu* 建康實錄 (Factual records of Chien-kʻang). Shanghai: Shanghai ku-chi chʻu-pan she, 1987.

Hsün Kʻuang 荀況 (313–238 B.C.). *Hsün-tzu [chi-chieh]* 荀子 [集解] ([Collected commentaries on] *Hsün-tzu*). Edited with commentary by Wang Hsien-chʻien 王先謙 (1842–1917). *Chu-tzu chi-chʻeng* ed.

———. (Under the title *Hsün-tzu: Basic Writings*). Trans. Burton Watson. New York: Columbia University Press, 1963.

Hu Shih 胡適. "Wen-hsüeh kai-liang ch'u-i" 文學改良芻議 (Preliminary opinions on re-forming literature). In *Chung-kuo li-tai wen-lun hsüan* 中國歷代文論選 (Se-lected essays of traditional Chinese literary theories), edited by Kuo Shao-yü and Wang Wen-sheng. 4 vols. Shanghai: Shanghai ku-chi ch'u-pan she, 1980. 4:528–536.

Hu Wen-k'ai 胡文楷. *Li-tai fu-nü chu-tso k'ao* 歷代婦女著作考 (Study of women's works from previous dynasties). Shanghai: Shanghai ku-chi ch'u-pan she, 1985.

Huang Tsung-hsi 黃宗羲 (1610–1695). *Huang Tsung-hsi ch'üan-chi* 黃宗羲全集 (The Complete works of Huang Tsung-hsi). 12 vols. Hangchow: Chekiang ku-chi ch'u-pan she, 1985.

———. *The Records of Ming Scholars (Ming-ju hsüeh-an* 明儒學案). A selected transla-tion edited by Julia Ching, with the collaboration of Chaoying Fang. Honolulu: University of Hawai'i Press, 1987.

Hucker, Charles O. *A Dictionary of Official Titles in Imperial China.* Taipei: Southern Materials Center, 1986.

Hui Chiao 慧皎 (Liang). *Kao-seng chuan* 高僧傳 (Biographies of eminent monks). Colla-tions and commentary by T'ang Yung-t'ung 湯用彤. Peking: Chung-hua shu-chü, 1992.

Hummel, Arthur W., ed. *Eminent Chinese of the Ch'ing Period.* 2 vols. Washington, D.C.: U.S. Government Printing Office, 1943.

Ikegami, Eiko. *The Taming of the Samurai: Honorific Individualism and the Making of Mod-ern Japan.* Cambridge: Harvard University Press, 1995.

I-li [chu-shu] 儀禮註疏 ([Commentary on] Etiquette and ritual). *Chu* 註 commentary by Cheng Hsüan 鄭玄 (127–200), *shu* 疏 commentary by Chia Kung-yen 賈公彥 (sixth century) et al. In *Shih-san ching chu-shu.* 1:941–1220.

Juan Chi 阮籍 (210–263). *Juan Chi chi* 阮籍集 (Collected works of Juan Chi). Edited by Li Chih-chün 李志鈞 et al. Shanghai: Shanghai ku-chi ch'u-pan she, 1978.

———. *Juan Pu-ping yung-huai shih [chu]* 阮步兵詠懷詩[註] ([Commentary on] Juan Chi's "Poems which sing of my innermost thoughts"). Commentary by Huang Chieh 黃節. Peking: Jen-min wen-hsüeh ch'u-pan she, 1957.

Juan Yüan 阮元 (1764–1849), ed. *Shih-san ching chu-shu* 十三經註疏 (Commentaries on the thirteen Chinese classics). 1826. Reprint, 2 vols., Peking: Chung-hua shu-chü, 1979.

Kawakatsu Yoshio 川勝義雄. *Rikuchō kizokusei shakai no kenkyū* 六朝貴族制社會の研究 (Study of the aristocratic society in the Six Dynasties). Tokyo: Iwanami shoten, 1982.

Ko, Dorothy. *Teachers of the Inner Chambers: Women and Culture in Seventeenth-Century China.* Stanford: Stanford University Press, 1994.

Ko Hsiao-yin 葛曉音. *Han-T'ang wen-hsüeh ti shan-pien* 漢唐文學的嬗變 (Evolution of literature from Han to T'ang). Peking: Peking University Press, 1990, 1995.

Ko Hung 葛洪 (284–363). *Pao-p'u tzu* 抱樸子 (The master who embraces the *p'u*). *Chu-tzu chi-ch'eng* ed.

———. *Pao-p'u tzu wai-p'ien [chiao-chien]* 抱樸子外篇 [校箋] ([Commentary on a collated edition of] *Pao-p'u tzu*, the outer chapters). Collations and commentary by Yang Ming-chao 楊明照. 2 vols. Peking: Chung-hua shu-chü, 1991.

Ku K'ai-chih 顧愷之 (341–402). "Wei Chin sheng-liu hua-tsan" 魏晉勝流畫贊 (Eulogies of the portraits of the Wei-Chin élite). In Chang Yen-yüan, *Li-tai ming-hua chi*. 117–118.

K'ung P'ing-chung 孔平仲 (*chin-shih* 1065, fl. 1065–1102) et al. *Ch'ing-chiang san K'ung chi* 清江三孔集 (Collected works of the three K'ungs from Ch'ing-chiang). *Ssu-k'u ch'üan-shu* ed.

Kuo Ch'eng-chih 郭澄之 (Chin). *Kuo-tzu* 郭子. Reconstructed by Lu Hsün in *Ku hsiao-shuo kou-ch'en*. 37–51.

Kuo Mao-ch'ien 郭茂倩 (Sung), *Yüeh-fu shih-chi* 樂府詩集 (Anthology of music bureau poems). 4 vols. Peking: Chung-hua shu-chü, 1979.

Kuo Pan 郭頒 (Chin). *Wei-Chin shih-yü* 魏晉世語. In *Wu-ch'ao hsiao-shuo ta-kuan* 五朝小說大觀. Shanghai: Sao-yeh shan-fang, 1926.

Kuo Shao-yü 郭紹虞. *Chung-kuo wen-hsüeh p'i-p'ing shih* 中國文學批評史 (History of Chinese literary criticism). Shanghai: Hsin wen-i ch'u-pan she, 1957.

Kuo Shao-yü and Wang Wen-sheng 王文生, ed. *Chung-kuo li-tai wen-lun hsüan* 中國歷代文論選 (Selected essays of traditional Chinese literary theories). 4 vols. Shanghai: Shanghai ku-chi ch'u-pan she, 1980.

Lacan, Jacques. "The Mirror Sage as Formative of the Function of the I as Revealed in Psychoanalytic Experience." In Jacques Lacan. *Ecrits: A Selection*, translated from the French by Alan Sheridan. New York: W. W. Norton, 1977. 1–7.

Lao Kan 勞榦. "Han-tai ch'a-chü chih-tu k'ao" 漢代察舉制度考 (Study of the Han selection system). In *Lao Kan hsüeh-shu lun-we chi* 勞榦學術論文集 (Collected academic essays by Lao Kan). 2 vols. Taipei: Yi-wen yin-shu kuan, 1976. 2:629–679.

Lao-tzu Tao-te ching [chu] 老子道德經 [註]. In Wang Pi 王弼. *Wang Pi chi [chiao-chu]* 王弼集 [校註], edited and collated with commentary by Lou Yü-lieh 樓宇烈. 2 vols. Peking: Chung-hua shu-chü, 1980. 1:1–193.

Lao Tzu Tao Te Ching. Translated by D. C. Lau. Penguin Books, 1963.

Lee, Leo Ou-fan. "Modernity and Its Discontents: The Cultural Agenda of the May Fourth Movement." In *Perspectives on Modern China,* edited by Kenneth Lieberthal et al. An East Gate Book, 1991. 158–177.

Legge, James, trans. *The Chinese Classics.* 5 vols. Hong Kong: Hong Kong University Press, 1960.

Li-chi [cheng-i] 禮記 [正義] ([Orthodox commentary on] Record of rites). *Chu* 註 commentary by Cheng Hsüan 鄭玄 (127–200), and *shu* 疏 commentary by K'ung Ying-ta 孔穎達 (574–648). In *Shih-san ching chu-shu*. 1:1221–2:1696.

Li chi: Book of Rites. Translated by James Legge. Edited with introduction and study guide by Ch'u Chai and Winberg Chai. 2 vols. New Hyde Park, NY: University Books, 1967.

Li Ch'ing 李清 (1602–1683). *San-yüan pi-chi* 三垣筆記 (Jottings at three ministries). Peking: Chung-hua shu-chü, 1982.

Li Yen-shou 李延壽 (fl. 627–649). *Nan-shih* 南史 (History of the Southern dynasties). 6 vols. Peking: Chung-hua shu-chü, 1975.

———. *Pei-shih* 北史 (History of the Northern dynasties). 10 vols. Peking: Chung-hua shu-chü, 1974.

Liang Ch'i-ch'ao 梁啓超 (1873–1929). *Liang Ch'i-ch'ao lun Ch'ing-hsüeh shih liang-chung* 梁啓超論清學史兩種 (Two works by Liang Ch'i-ch'ao on the history of Ch'ing learning). Collations and commentary by Chu Wei-cheng 朱維錚. Shanghai: Fu-tan ta-hsüeh ch'u-pan she, 1985. 1–90: Ch'ing-tai *hsüeh-shu kai-lun* 清代學術概論 (Survey of Ch'ing learning). 91–522: *Chung-kuo chin san-pai nien hsüeh-shu shih* 中國近三百年學術史 (History of Chinese learning of the recent three hundred years).

———. "Hsiao-shuo yü ch'ün-chih chih kuan-hsi" 論小説與群治之關係 (Fiction seen in relation to the guidance of society). In *Chung-kuo li-tai wen-lun hsüan*, edited by Kuo Shao-yü and Wang Wen-sheng. 4:207–217.

———. "Kao hsiao-shuo chia" 告小説家 (Appeal to novelists). In *Chung-kuo li-tai wen-lun hsüan*. 4:217–218.

Lieh-tzu [chi-shih] 列子[集釋] ([Collected commentaries] on *Lieh-tzu*). Edited with commentary by Yang Po-chün 楊伯峻. Peking: Chung-hua shu-chü, 1979.

Lieh-tzu [chu] 列子[註] ([Commentary] on *Lieh-tzu*). Commentary by Chang Chan 張湛 (fl. ca. 370). *Chu-tzu chi-ch'eng* ed.

——— (under the title *The Book of Lieh-tzu: A Classic of Tao*). Trans. A. C. Graham. New York: Columbia University Press, 1960, 1990.

Liu Chih-chi 劉知己 (661–721). *Shih-t'ung [t'ung-shih]* 史通通釋 ([Commentary on] Compendium of history). Commentary by P'u Ch'i-lung 浦起龍 (fl. 1730–1752). 2 vols. Shanghai: Shanghai Ku-chi ch'u-pan-she, 1978.

Liu Chün 劉峻 (462–521). *Liu Hsiao-piao chi [chiao-chu]* 劉孝標集 [校註] ([Commentary on a collated edition of] Collected works of *Liu Hsiao-piao*). Collations and commentary by Luo Kuo-wei 羅國威. Shanghai: Shanghai ku-chi ch'u-pan she, 1988.

Liu Hsi-tsai 劉熙載 (1813–1881). *I-kai* 藝概 (Theoretical summary of art). Shanghai: Shanghai ku-chi ch'u-pan she, 1978.

Liu Hsiang 劉向 (77–6 B.C.). *[Ku] Lieh-nü chuan* [古]列女傳 (Biographies of [Ancient] exemplary women). *Ts'ung-shu chi-ch'eng hsin-pien* 叢書集成新編 ed. 101:672–705.

———. *Hsin-hsü [chin-chu chin-i]* 新序 [今註今譯] ([Commentary on] New compilation of tales). Translated with commentary by Lu Yüan-chün 盧元駿. Taipei: Taiwan shang-wu yin-shu kuan, 1975.

————. *Shuo-yüan* [*shu-cheng*] 説苑 [疏證] ([Commentary on] Garden of tales). Commentary by Chao Shan-i 趙善詒. Shanghai: Huatung Normal University Press, 1985.

Liu Hsieh 劉勰 (ca. 465–522). *Wen-hsin tiao-lung* [*chu*] 文心雕龍 [註]. ([Commentary on] Literary mind and the carving of dragons). Commentary by Fan Wen-lan 范文瀾. 2 vols. Peking: Jen-min wen-hsüeh ch'u-pan she, 1978.

————. *The Literary Mind and the Carving of Dragons*. Trans. Vincent Yu-chung Shih. Hong Kong: The Chinese University Press, 1983.

Liu Hsü 劉昫 (887–946) et al. *Chiu T'ang-shu* 舊唐書 (Old history of the T'ang). 16 vols. Peking: Chung-hua shu-chü, 1975.

Liu, James J. Y. *Language—Paradox—Poetics: A Chinese Perspective*. Edited by Richard John Lynn. Princeton, NJ: Princeton University Press, 1988.

Liu Ju-lin 劉汝霖. *Han-Chin hsüeh-shu pien-nien* 漢晉學術編年 (Chronology of Han-Chin learning). 2 vols. Peking: Chung-hua shu-chü, 1987.

————. *Wei Chin Nan-Pei ch'ao hsüeh-shu pien-nien* 魏晉南北朝學術編年 (Chronology of Wei, Chin, Southern and Northern dynasties learning). Peking: Chung-hua shu-chü, 1987.

Liu, Lydia H. *Translingual Practice: Literature, National Culture, and Translated Modernity—China, 1900–1937*. Stanford: Stanford University Press, 1995.

Liu Shao 劉邵 (fl. mid-third century). *Jen-wu chih* 人物志 (Study of human abilities). Reprint of an early-sixteenth-century edition, Peking: Wen-hsüeh ku-chi k'an-hsing she, 1955.

————. *The Study of Human Abilities: The Jen wu chih of Liu Shao*. Trans. J. K. Shryock. New Haven: American Oriental Society, 1937.

Liu Shih-p'ei 劉師培 (1884–1920). *Chung-kuo chung-ku wen-hsüeh shih* 中國中古文學史 (History of medieval Chinese literature). Peking: Jen-min wen-hsüeh ch'u-pan she, 1984.

Liu Yeh-ch'iu 劉葉秋. *Wei Chin Nan-Pei ch'ao hsiao-shuo* 魏晉南北朝小説 (Wei, Chin, and Southern and Northern dynasties *hsiao-shuo*). Shanghai: Shanghai ku-chi ch'u-pan she, 1978.

Lo Tsung-ch'iang 羅宗強. *Hsüan-hsüeh yü Wei-Chin shih-jen hsin-t'ai* 玄學與魏晉士人心態 (*Hsüan-hsüeh* and the mentality of the Wei-Chin intellectual élite). Hangchou: Chekiang jen-min ch'u-pan she, 1991.

————. *Wei Chin Nan-Pei ch'ao wen-hsüeh ssu-hsiang shih* 魏晉南北朝文學思想史 (History of literary thought of Wei, Chin, Southern and Northern dynasties). Peking: Chung-hua shu-chü, 1996.

Lu Ch'in-li 逯欽立. *Hsien-Ch'in Han Wei Chin Nan-Pei ch'ao shih* 先秦漢魏晉南北朝詩 (Pre-Ch'in, Han, Wei, Chin, Southern and Northern dynasties poetry). 3 vols. Peking: Chung-hua shu-chü, 1983.

Lu Hsün 魯迅 (1881–1936). *Chung-kuo hsiao-shuo shih-lüeh* 中國小説史略 (A brief history of Chinese fiction). In *Lu Hsün ch'üan-chi* 魯迅全集 (Complete works of Lu Hsün). 10 vols. Peking: Jen-min wen-hsüeh ch'u-pan she, 1957.8:3–250.

————. *A Brief History of Chinese Fiction.* Trans. Yang Hsien-yi and Gladys Yang. Peking: Foreign Languages Press, 1976.

————, ed. *Ku hsiao-shuo kou-ch'en* 古小説鉤沉 (Collected fragments of ancient *hsiao-shuo*). Peking: Jen-min wen-hsüeh ch'u-pan she, 1951.

————. "Wei-Chin feng-tu chi wen-chang yü yao chi chiu chih kuan-hsi" 魏晉風度及文章與藥及酒之關係 (Wei-Chin style, literature, drugs, and wine). *Lu Hsün ch'üan-chi.* 3:487–503.

Lu K'an-ju 陸侃如 (d. 1978). *Chung-ku wen-hsüeh hsi-nien* 中古文學繫年 (Chronology of medieval Chinese literature). 2 vols. Peking: Jen-min wen-hsüeh ch'u-pan she, 1985.

Lü Ssu-mien 呂思勉. *Liang-Chin Nan-Pei ch'ao shih* 兩晉南北朝史 (History of two Chin, Southern and Northern dynasties). Shanghai: Shanghai ku-chi ch'u-pan she, 1983.

Lufrano, Richard John. *Honorable Merchants: Commerce and Self-Cultivation in Late Imperial China.* Honolulu: University of Hawai'i Press, 1997.

Lun-yü [cheng-i] 論語 [正義] ([Orthodox commentary on] The Analects of Confucius). Commentary by Liu Pao-nan 劉寶楠 (1791–1855). *Chu-tzu chi-ch'eng* ed.

Lun-yü [chu-shu] 論語 [註疏] ([Commentary on] The Analects of Confucius). *Chi-chieh* 集解 commentary by Ho Yen 何晏 (190–249), and *shu* 疏 commentary by Hsing Ping 邢昺 (932–1010). In *Shih-san ching chu-shu* ed. 2:2454–2536.

Lun-yü [i-chu] 論語 [譯註] ([Annotated translation of] The Analects of Confucius). Commentary and translated from classical Chinese into modern Chinese by Yang Po-chün 楊伯峻. Peking: Chung-hua shu-chü, 1980.

———— (under the title *The Analects*). Translated by D. C. Lau. Penguin Books, 1979.

Lynn, Richard John, trans. *The Classic of the Way and Virtue: A New Translation of the Tao-te ching of Laozi [Lao-tzu] as Interpreted by Wang Bi [Pi].* New York: Columbia University Press, 1999.

————. "Wang Bi and Liu Xie's *Wenxin diaolong*: Terms and Concepts" [Wang Pi and Liu Hsieh's *Wen-hsin tiao-lung*: Terms and Concepts]. Manuscript. 1997.

————, trans. *The Classic of Changes: A New Translation of the I Ching as Interpreted by Wang Bi [Pi].* New York: Columbia University Press, 1994.

Ma Chi-kao 馬積高. *Sung Ming li-hsüeh yü wen-hsüeh* 宋明理學與文學 (Sung-Ming Neo-Confucianism and literature). Changsha: Hunan Normal University Press, 1989.

Makeham, John. *Name and Actuality in Early Chinese Thought.* Albany: State University of New York Press, 1994.

Mann, Susan. *Precious Records: Women in China's Long Eighteenth Century.* Stanford: Stanford University Press, 1997.

Mao Shih cheng-i 毛詩正義 ([Commentary on] Book of songs). *Chuan* 傳 commentary by Mao Heng 毛亨 (second cent. B.C.), *chien* 箋 commentary by Cheng Hsüan 鄭玄 (127–200), and *shu* 疏 commentary by K'ung Ying-ta 孔穎達 (574–648). In *Shih-san ching chu-shu*. 1:259–629.

Mather, Richard B. "Individualist Expressions of the Outsiders during the Six Dynasties." In *Individualism and Holism: Studies in Confucian and Taoist Values*, edited by Donald J. Munro. 199–214.

———. "The Mystical Ascent of the T'ien-t'ai Mountains: Sun Ch'o's *Yu T'ien-t'ai shan fu*." *Monumenta Serica* 20 (1961):226–245.

Meng-tzu [*chu-shu*] 孟子 [註疏] ([Commentary on] *Mencius*). *Chu* 註 commentary by Chao Ch'i 趙岐 (d. 201) and *shu* 疏 commentary by Sun Shih 孫奭 (962–1033). In *Shih-san ching chu-shu*. 2:2659–2782.

Meng-tzu [*i-chu*] 孟子 [譯註] ([Annotated translation of] *Mencius*). Commentary and translated from classical Chinese into modern Chinese by Yang Po-chün 楊伯峻. 2 vols. Peking: Chung-hua shu-chü, 1960, 1981.

——— (under the title *Mencius*). Translated with an introduction by D. C. Lau. Penguin Books, 1970.

Miner, Earl, Hiroko Odagiri, and Robert Morrell, eds. *The Princeton Companion to Classical Japanese Literature*. Princeton, NJ: Princeton University Press, 1985.

Mori Mikisaburō. *Rikuchō shidaifu no seishin* 六朝士大夫の精神 (Spirit of the scholar-officials of the Six Dynasties). Kyoto: Dōbōsha, 1986.

Morohashi Tetsuji 諸橋轍次. *Dai Kan-Wa jiten* 大漢和辭典 (Comprehensive Chinese-Japanese dictionary). Tokyo: Taishūkan shoten, 1955–1960.

Mou Tsung-san 牟宗三. *Ts'ai-hsing yü ming-li* 才性與名理 ([Human] Ability and nature and names and principles). Hong Kong: 1985.

Mu K'o-hung 穆克宏. *Wei Chin Nan-Pei ch'ao wen-hsüeh shih-liao shu-lüeh* 魏晉南北朝文學史料述略 (Brief account of the historical materials of Wei, Chin, Southern and Northern dynasties literature). Peking: Chung-hua shu-chü, 1997.

Munro, Donald J. *The Concept of Man in Early China*. Stanford: Stanford University Press, 1969.

———, ed., *Individualism and Holism: Studies in Confucian and Taoist Values*. Ann Arbor: Center for Chinese Studies, University of Michigan, 1985.

Murphy, Gwendolen. *A Bibliography of English Character-Books, 1608–1700*. Oxford: Oxford University Press for the Bibliography Society, 1925.

Nanking po-wu yüan 南京博物院. "Nanking Hsi-shan ch'iao Nan-ch'ao mu chi ch'i chuan-k'o pi-hua" 南京西善橋南朝墓及其磚刻壁畫 [A Southern dynasty tomb and its brick reliefs at Hsi-shan ch'iao, Nanking], *Wen-wu* 文物 1960.8–9:37–42.

Nienhauser, William H., Jr., et al., eds. *The Indiana Companion to Traditional Chinese Literature*. Bloomington: Indiana University Press, 1986.

Ning Chia-yü. *Wei-Chin feng-tu: chung-ku wen-jen sheng-ho hsing-wei ti wen-hua i-yün* 魏

晉風度：中古文人生活行為的文化義蘊 (Wei-Chin winds and manner: The cultural connotation of the life and behavior of the medieval [Chinese] literati). Peking: Tung-fang ch'u-pan she, 1992.

Okamura Shigeru 岡村繁. "Kaku Tai Ko Shō no jimbutsu hyōron" 郭泰許劭の人物評論 (Kuo T'ai and Hsü Shao's character appraisal). *Tōhōgaku* 10 (1955):59–68.

———. "Go kan makki no hyōronteki fūki ni tsuite" 後漢末期の評論的風氣について (On the late Han trend of character appraisal). *Nagoya daigaku bungakubu kenkyū ronshū* 長崎大學文學研究論集 (1960):67–112.

Ou-yang Chien 歐陽建 (265?–300). "Yen chin i lun" 言盡意論 (On words fully expressing meanings). In *I-wen lei-chü* 藝文類聚, edited by Ou-yang Hsün 歐陽詢 (557–641). 4 vols. Shanghai: Shanghai ku-chi ch'u-pan she, 1965, 1982. *Chüan* 19, 1:348.

Owen, Stephen. *Readings in Chinese Literary Thought*. Cambridge: Harvard University Press, 1992.

Pan Ku 班固 (32–92). *Han-shu* 漢書 (History of the Han). Commentary by Yen Shih-ku 顏師古 (581–645). 12 vols. Peking: Chung-hua shu-chü, 1962.

———. *Pai-hu t'ung-i* 白虎通義 (Comprehensive interpretation of classics from White-Tiger Hall). *Ssu-pu ts'ung-k'an* ed.

P'ei-Ch'i 裴啓 (fourth century). *P'ei-tzu Yü-lin* 裴子語林 (Master P'ei's forest of tales). Reconstructed by Lu Hsün in *Ku hsiao-shuo kou-ch'en*. 5–36.

Roddy, Stephen J. *Literati Identity and Its Fictional Representations in Late Imperial China*. Stanford: Stanford University Press, 1998.

Ropp, Paul S. *Dissent in Early Modern China: Ju-lin wai-shih and Ch'ing Social Criticism*. Ann-Arbor: The University of Michigan Press, 1981.

Rowe, William T. "Women and the Family in Mid-Qing Social Thought: The Case of Chen Hongmou." *Late Imperial China* 13.2 (December 1992):1–41.

Sartre, Jean-Paul. *Being and Nothingness: An Essay on Phenomenological Ontology*. Trans. Hazel E. Barnes. New York: Philosophical Library, 1956.

Saussy, Haun. *The Problem of a Chinese Aesthetic*. Stanford: Stanford University Press, 1993.

Schwarcz, Vera. *The Chinese Enlightenment: Intellectuals and the Legacy of the May Fourth Movement of 1919*. Berkeley: University of California Press, 1986.

Seng Yu 僧祐 (fl. 515–518). *Hung-ming chi* 弘明集. 5 vols. *Ssu-pu ts'ung-k'ang* ed.

Shang-shu [cheng-i] 尚書 [正義] [(Orthodox commentary on) Book of documents]. In *Shih-san ching chu-shu*. 1:109–258.

Smeed, J. W. *The Theophrastan "Character": The History of a Literary Genre*. Oxford, NY: Clarendon Press, 1985.

Smith, Kidder, Jr., et al. *Sung Dynasty Uses of the I Ching*. Princeton, NJ: Princeton University Press, 1990.

Smith, Richard J. *China's Cultural Heritage: The Qing [Ch'ing] Dynasty, 1644–1912*. Boulder: Westview Press, 1994.

Spence, Jonathan. *God's Chinese Son: The Taiping Heavenly Kingdom of Hong Xiuquan.* New York: W. W. Norton, 1996.

———. *The Search for Modern China.* New York: W. W. Norton, 1990.

Spiro, Audrey. *Contemplating the Ancients: Aesthetic and Social Issues in Early Chinese Portraiture.* Berkeley: University of California Press, 1990.

Ssu-ma Ch'ien 司馬遷 (145–ca. 86 B.C.). *Shih-chi* 史記 (Records of the Grand Historian). *Chi-chieh* 集解 commentary by P'ei Yin 裴駰 (fifth century), *So-yin* 索隱 commentary by Ssu-ma Chen 司馬貞 (eighth century), and *Cheng-i* 正義 commentary by Chang Shou-chieh 張守節 (eighth century). 10 vols. Peking: Chunghua shu-chü, 1959.

Su Shih 蘇軾 (1036–1101). *Su Shih wen-chi* 蘇軾文集 (Complete prose of Su Shih). 6 vols. Peking: Chung-hua shu-chü, 1986.

———. *Tung-p'o I-chuan* 東坡易傳 (Tung-p'o's commentary on the *Book of Changes*). *Ssu-k'u ch'üan-shu* ed.

Sung Ch'i 宋祁 (998–1061) and Ou-yang Hsiu 歐陽修 (1007–1072). *Hsin T'ang-shu* 新唐書 (New history of the T'ang). 20 vols. (Peking: Chung-hua shu-chü, 1975).

Sung, Marina H. "The Chinese *Lieh-nü* Tradition." In *Women in China,* edited by Richard W. Guisso and Stanley Johannesen. Youngstown, NY: Philo Press, 1981. 63–74.

Takakusu Junjirō 高楠順次郎 and Watanabe Kaikyoku 渡邊海旭, eds. *Taishō shinshō daizōkyō* 大正新修大藏經 (The Taishō new compilation of the Chinese Tripitaka). 85 vols. Tokyo: Taisho issai-kyo kanko kwai, 1922–1933.

Tang, Yiming. "The Voice of Wei-Jin [Chin] Scholars: A Study of Qingtan [Ch'ing-t'an]." Ph.D. dissertation. Columbia University, 1991.

——— 唐翼明. *Wei-Chin ch'ing-t'an* 魏晉清談. Taipei: Tung-ta tu-shu yu-hsien kung-ssu, 1992.

T'ang Chang-ju 唐長儒. *Wei-Chin Nan-Pei ch'ao shih lun-ts'ung* 魏晉南北朝史論叢 (Collected essays on the history of the Wei, Chin, Southern and Northern dynasties). Peking: San-lien shu-tien, 1955.

———. *Wei-Chin Nan-Pei ch'ao shih lun-ts'ung hsü-pien* 魏晉南北朝史論叢續編(Collected essays on the history of the Wei, Chin, Southern and Northern dynasties [2]). Peking: San-lien shu-tien, 1978.

T'ang I-chieh 湯一介. *Kuo Hsiang yü Wei-Chin Hsüan-hsüeh* 郭象與魏晉玄學 (Kuo Hsiang and Wei-Chin *Hsüan-hsüeh*). Wuhan: Hupeh jen-min ch'u-pan she, 1983.

T'ang Yung-t'ung 湯用彤 (1893–1964). *Han Wei Liang-Chin Nan-Pei ch'ao fo-chiao shih* 漢魏兩晉南北朝佛教史 (History of Buddhism of the Han, Wei, Chin, and Southern and Northern dynasties). 2 vols. Peking: Chung-hua shu-chü, 1955, 1963.

———. "*Wei-Chin Hsüan-hsüeh* ho wen-hsüeh li-lun" 魏晉玄學和文學理論(Wei-Chin *Hsüan-hsüeh* and literary theories). *Chung-kuo che-hsüeh shih yen-chiu* 中國哲學史研究 1981.1:37–45.

―――. *Wei-Chin Hsüan-hsüeh lun-kao* 魏晉玄學論稿 (Preliminary studies of Wei-Chin *Hsüan-hsüeh*). Peking: Jen-min wen-hsüeh ch'u-pan she, 1957. In *T'ang Yung-t'ung hsüeh-shu lun-wen chi* 湯用彤學術論文集 (Collected academic essays of T'ang Yung-t'ung). Peking: Chung-hua shu-chü, 1983. 193–306.

―――"Wang Pi's New Interpretation of the *I ching* and *Lun-yü.*" *Harvard Journal of Asiatic Studies* 10 (1947):124–161.

T'ang Yung-t'ung and Jen Chi-yü 任繼愈. *Wei-Chin Hsüan-hsüeh chung ti she-hui cheng-chih ssu-hsiang lüeh-lun* 魏晉玄學中的社會政治思想略論 (Brief study on sociopolitical perspectives in Wei-Chin *Hsüan-hsüeh*). Shanghai: Shanghai jen-min ch'u-pan she, 1956.

Theophrastus (371–287 B.C.). *Characters*. Edited and translated by Jeffrey Rusten, I. C. Cunningham, and A. D. Knox. Cambridge: Harvard University Press, 1993.

Ting Fu-pao 丁福保 (1874–1952), ed. *Fo-hsüeh tai tz'u-tien* 佛學大辭典 (Grand dictionary of Buddhism). 1922. Reprint, Peking: Wen-wu ch'u-pan she, 1984.

T'o T'o 脫脫 (1314–1355) et al. *Sung-shih* 宋史 (History of the Sung). 9 vols. *Ying-yin jen-shou pen erh-shih liu shih* ed. Taipei: Ch'eng-wen ch'u-pan she, 1971. Vols. 35–43.

Todorov, Tzvetan. "The Origin of Genres." *New Literary History* 8 (1976):159–170.

―――. *The Poetics of Prose*. Trans. Richard Howard. Ithaca: Cornell University Press, 1977.

Ts'ao Wen-hsin 曹文心. "Chien-an hsiao-shuo k'ao pien" 建安小説考辨 (Study of Chien-an *hsiao-shuo*). *Huai-pei mei-shih yüan hsüeh-pao* 淮北煤師院學報 (*She-k'o pan*) 1988.4: 91–95.

Tsukamoto Zenryū 塚本善隆 (1898–?), ed. *Jōron kenkyū* 肇論研究 (Study of *Chao-lun*). Kyoto: Hozokan, 1955.

Tu Wei-ming. *Centrality and Commonality: An Essay on Chung-yung*. Monographs for the Society for Asian and Comparative Philosophy, No. 3. Honolulu: University of Hawai'i Press, 1976.

Tu Yu 杜佑 (735–812), *T'ung-tien* 通典 (Compendium of laws and institutions). Shanghai: Shang-wu Yin-shu kuan, 1935.

Tung Chung-shu 董仲舒 (179?–104? B.C.). *Ch'un-ch'iu fan-lu* 春秋繁露 (Luxuriant dew of the Spring and Autumn Annals). *Ssu-pu ts'ung-k'an* ed.

Tz'u-yüan 辭源 (Etymological dictionary). Revised ed. 4 vols. Peking: Shang-wu yin-shu kuan, 1979.

Vimalakirti Sutra. Trans. Burton Watson. New York: Columbia University Press, 1997.

Wan Sheng-nan 萬繩楠. *Wei-Chin Nan-Pei ch'ao wen-hua shih* 魏晉南北朝文化史 (Cultural history of the Wei, Chin, Southern and Northern dynasties). Hofei: Anhwei jen-min ch'u-pan she, 1983.

Wang Ch'i-chou 王齊洲. "Chung-kuo hsiao-shuo ch'i-yüan t'an-chi" 中國小説起源探跡 (Tracing the origin of Chinese *hsiao-shuo*). *Wen-hsüeh i-ch'an* 文學遺產 1985.1: 12–23.

Wang Ch'i-chung 王啓忠. "Shih-lun liu-ch'ao hsiao-shuo ch'uang-tso ti tzu-chüeh i-shih" 試論六朝小説創作的自覺意識 (Tentative study of the self-consciousness of Six Dynasties' *hsiao-shuo* creation). *She-hui k'o-hsüeh chi-k'an* 社會科學輯刊 1988.3: 117–120.

Wang Chung-lo 王仲犖. *Wei-Chin Nan-Pei ch'ao shih* 魏晉南北朝史 (History of the Wei, Chin, Southern and Northern dynasties). 2 vols. Shanghai: Shanghai jen-min ch'u-pan she, 1979 (Vol. I) and 1980 (Vol. II).

Wang Chung-min 王重民 (1903–1975). "Li Ch'ing Chu-shu k'ao" 李清著述考 (Study of Li Ch'ing's works). *T'u-shu kuan hsüeh chi-k'an* 圖書館學季刊 (Library science quarterly) 2.3 (1928):333–342.

———. *Chung-kuo shan-pen shu t'i-yao* 中國善本書提要 (Annotated catalog of Chinese rare books). Shanghai: Shanghai ku-chi ch'u-pan she, 1983.

Wang Ch'ung 王充 (27–91). *Lun-heng* 論衡 (Balanced discussions). *Chu-tzu chi-ch'eng* ed.

Wang Fu 王符 (ca. 85–162). *Ch'ien-fu lun* 潛夫論 (Essays by a recluse). *Chu-tzu chi-ch'eng* ed.

Wang I-t'ung 王伊同. *Wu-ch'ao men-ti* 五朝門第 (Pedigree of the Five [i.e., Six] Dynasties). 1943. Reprint, Hong Kong: Chinese University Press, 1978.

Wang Pao-hsien 王葆玹. *Cheng-shih Hsüan-hsüeh* 正始玄學. Chinan: Ch'i-lu shu-she, 1987.

Wang pi, *Wang Pi chi [chiao-shih]* 王弼集 [校釋] ([Commentary on a collated edition of] Collected works of Wang Pi). Collations and commentary by Lou Yü-lieh 樓宇烈. 2 vols. 1:1–193, *Lao-tzu Tao te ching chu* 老子道德經註 (Commentary on *Lao-tzu Tao te ching*). 1:195–210, *Lao-tzu chih-lüeh* 老子指略 (Brief interpretation of *Lao-tzu* principles). 1:211–2:590, *Chou-i chu* 周易註 (Commentary on *Chou-i*). 2:591–620, *Chou-i lüeh-li* 周易略例 (Brief examples of *Chou-i*). 2:621–637, *Lun-yü shih-i* 論語釋疑 (Interpretation of *Lun-yü*). Peking: Chung-hua shu-chü, 1980.

Wang Yao 王瑶. *Chung-ku wen-hsüeh shih lun-chi* 中古文學史論集 (Collected essays on the history of medieval Chinese literature). Shanghai: Shanghai ku-chi ch'u-pan she, 1982.

Wang Yün-hsi 王運熙 and Yang Ming 楊明. *Wei-Chin Nan-Pei ch'ao wen-hsüeh p'i-p'ing shih* 魏晉南北朝文學批評史 (History of literary criticism of Wei, Chin, Southern and Northern dynasties). Shanghai: Shanghai ku-chi ch'u-pan she, 1989.

Watson, Burton. *Chinese Rhyme-prose: Poems in the Fu Form from the Han and Six Dynasties Periods.* New York: Columbia University Press, 1971.

Wei Cheng 魏徵 (580–643) et al. *Sui-shu* 隋書 (History of the Sui). 6 vols. Peking: Chung-hua shu-chü, 1973.

Widmer, Ellen, and Kang-i Sun Chang, eds. *Writing Women in Late Imperial China.* Stanford: Stanford University Press, 1997.

Wu Hao 吳顥. *Kuo-ch'ao Hang-chün shih-chi* 國朝杭郡詩集 (Collected Hangchow poems from the reigning dynasty). 32 *chüan*. First published in 1800. Ch'ien-t'ang: Ting-shih, 1874.

Wu Hung. *The Wu Liang Shrine: The Ideology of Early Chinese Pictorial Art*. Stanford: Stanford University Press, 1989.

Wu, Laura Hua. "From *Xiaoshuo* [*Hsiao-shuo*] to Fiction: Hu Yinglin's Genre Study of *Xiaoshuo* [*Hsiao-shuo*]." *Harvard Journal of Asiatic Studies* 55.2 (December, 1995):339–371.

Yang I 楊義. *Chung-kuo ku-tien hsiao-shuo shih-lun* 中國古典小説史論 (On the history of classical Chinese *hsiao-shuo*). Peking: Chung-kuo she-hui k'o-hsüeh ch'u-pan she, 1995.

Yen Chih-t'ui 顏之推. *Yen-shih chia-hsün [chi-chieh]* 顏氏家訓 [集解] ([Collected commentaries on] Yen family instructions). Edited by Wang Li-ch'i 王利器. Shanghai: Shanghai ku-chi ch'u-pan she, 1980.

Yen Heng 嚴蘅 (1826?–1854). *Nen-hsiang an ts'an-kao* 嫩想庵殘稿 (Remnants of poems from Tender Thoughts Hermitage). 1 *chüan*. First ed. 1865. *Chüan-ching lou ts'ung-k'o pen* 娟鏡樓叢刻本 ed. Shanghai: Chü-chen fang-Sung yin-shu chü 聚珍仿宋印書局, 1920.

Yen K'o-chün 嚴可均 (1762–1843), ed. *Ch'üan shang-ku san-tai Ch'in Han San-kuo Liu-ch'ao wen* 全上古三代秦漢三國六朝文 (Complete prose from antiquity to the Six Dynasties). Reprint, 4 vols. Peking: Chung-hua shu-chü, 1958.

Yin Yün 殷芸 (473–531). *Yin Yün hsiao-shuo* 殷芸小説. *Chung-kuo ku-tien hsiao-shuo yen-chiu tzu-liao* 中國古典小説研究資料 ed. Edited with notes by Chou Leng-chia 周楞伽. Shanghai: Shanghai ku-chi ch'u-pan she, 1984.

Ying Shao 應劭 (late Han). *Feng-su t'ung-i* 風俗通義 (Comprehensive interpretation of customs). *Ssu-pu ts'ung-k'an* ed.

Yoshikawa Tadao 吉川忠夫. *Rikuchō seishin-shi Kenkyū* 六朝精神史研究 (Study of the spiritual history of the Six Dynasties). Kyoto: Dōhōsha, 1984.

———. *Gi Shin seidan shū* 魏晉清談集 (Collection of Wei-Chin *ch'ing-t'an* episodes). Tokyo: Kōdansha, 1986.

Young, Ernest P. *The Presidency of Yuan Shih-k'ai: Liberalism and Dictatorship in Early Republican China*. Ann Arbor: University of Michigan Press, 1977.

Yü Chia-hsi. *Yü Chia-hsi lun-hsüeh tsa-chu* 余嘉錫論學雜著 (Miscellaneous studies by Yü Chia-hsi). Peking: Chung-hua shu-chü, 1963.

Yü Ying-shih 余英時. *Chung-kuo chih-shih chieh-ts'eng shih-lun* 中國知識階層史論 (Historical studies of the Chinese intellectual class). Taipei: Lien-ching shih-yeh ch'u-pan kung-ssu, 1980.

———. "Individualism and the Neo-Taoist Movement." In *Individualism and Holism: Studies in Confucian and Taoist Values*, edited by Donald J. Munro. Ann Arbor: Center for Chinese Studies, University of Michigan, 1985. 121–155.

Yüan Chun 袁準 (fl. 265–274). *Ts'ai-hsing lun* 才性論 (On human ability and nature). In *I-wen lei-chü*. *Chüan* 21, 1:386.

Yüan Hsing-p'ei 袁行霈 and Hou Chung-i 侯忠義. *Chung-kuo wen-yen hsiao-shuo shu-mu*

中國文言小說書目 (Bibliography of *hsiao-shuo* in classical Chinese). Peking: Peking University Press, 1981.

Yung-jung 永瑢, Chi Yün 紀昀 et al., eds. *Ssu-k'u ch'üan-shu tsung-mu* 四庫全書總目 (also known as *Ssu-k'u ch'üan-shu tsung-mu t'i yao* 四庫全書總目提要) (Annotated catalogue of the complete collection of the Four Treasuries). 1822. Reprint, 2 vols., Peking: Chung-hua shu-chü, 1965.

Zhang Longxi. *The Tao and the Logos: Literary Hermeneutics, East and West.* Durham: Duke University Press, 1992.

Zito, Angela, and Tani E. Barlow, eds. *Body, Subject, and Power in China.* Chicago: University of Chicago Press, 1994.

Zürcher, Erik. *The Buddhist Conquest of China.* 2 vols. Leiden: E. J. Brill, 1959.

E. *Shih-shuo t'i* Works (Chronologically Arranged)

Wang Fang-ch'ing 王方慶 (d. 702). *Hsü Shih-shuo hsin-shu* 續世說新書 (Continuation of the *Shih-shuo hsin-shu*). 10 *chüan.* Recorded in *Hsin T'ang-shu,* "I-wen chih," *chüan* 59. Not extant.

Feng Yen 封演 (fl. 742–800). *Feng-shih wen-chien chi [chiao-chu]* 封氏聞見記 [校註] ([Commentary on a collated edition of] Feng's memoirs). 10 *chüan.* Compiled around 800 or later. Commentary by Chao Chen-hsin 趙貞信. Peking: Chung-hua shu-chü, 1958.

Liu Su 劉肅 (fl. 806–820). *Ta-T'ang hsin-yü* 大唐新語 (New account of the Great T'ang). 13 *chüan.* Author's preface dated 807. *T'ang-Sung shih-liao pi-chi ts'ung-k'an* 唐宋史料筆記叢刊 ed. Peking: Chung-hua shu-chü, 1984.

K'ung P'ing-chung 孔平仲 (fl. 1065–1102). *Hsü Shih-shuo* 續世說 (Continuation of the *Shih-shuo [hsin-yü]*), 12 *chüan.* Earliest extant ed. with Ch'in Kuo's 秦果 preface dated 1158. *Kuo-hsüeh chi-pen ts'ung-shu* 國學基本叢書 ed. Shang-wu yin-shu kuan.

Wang Tang 王讜 (fl. 1086–1110). *T'ang yü-lin* 唐語林 (T'ang forest of accounts). 8 *chüan.* Collated and punctuated edition. Shanghai: Shanghai ku-chi ch'u-pan she, 1978.

———. *T'ang yü-lin [chiao-cheng]* 唐語林 [校證] ([Commentary on a collated edition of] T'ang forest of accounts). Collations and commentary by Chou Hsün-ch'u 周勛初. 2 vols. Peking: Chung-hua shu-chü, 1987.

Ho Liang-chün 何良俊 (1506–1573). *Ho-shih yü-lin* 何氏語林 (Ho's Forest of Accounts). 30 *chüan.* With Wen Cheng-ming's 文徵明 preface dated 1551. *Ssu-k'u ch'üan-shu* ed.

Wang Shih-chen 王世貞 (1526–1590). *Shih-shuo hsin-yü pu* 世說新語補. (See under the same title in Section A, Texts of the *Shih-shuo hsin-yü.*) Peking Library, Library of Congress collection.

Chiao Hung 焦竑 (1541–1620) *Chiao-shih lei-lin* 焦氏類林 (Chiao's taxonomic forest). 8

chüan. Author's preface dated 1585; other prefaces, 1587. 1587 ed. Library of Congress collection.

―――. *Chiao-shih lei-lin.* 8 *chüan. Ts'ung-shu chi-ch'eng hsin-pien* 叢書集成新編 ed. 7:569–668.

―――. *Yü-t'ang ts'ung-yü* 玉堂叢語 (Collected accounts from the Jade Hall). 8 *chüan.* Author's preface dated 1618. 1618 Man-shan kuan 曼山館 ed. Library of Congress collection.

―――. *Yü-t'ang ts'ung-yü.* 8 *chüan. Yüan-Ming shih-liao pi-chi ts'ung-k'an* 元明史料筆記叢刊 ed. Peking: Chung-hua shu-chü, 1981.

Li Chih 李贄 (1527–1602). *Ch'u-t'an chi* 初潭集 (Writings on the Pond). 30 *chüan.* First ed. 1588. Ming editions collected in Peking Library, Peking Normal University Library, etc.

―――. *Ch'u-t'an chi.* 30 *chüan.* Collated and punctuated edition, 2 vols. Peking: Chung-hua shu-chü, 1974.

Hsü Shih-shuo 續世説 (Continuation of the *Shih-shuo* [*hsin-yü*]). Also titled *Nan-Pei shih hsü Shih-shuo* 南北史續世説 (Continuation of the *Shih-shuo* [*hsin-yü*] about the history of the Southern and Northern dynasties). Attributed to a T'ang writer Li Hou 李厚 (dates unknown). 10 *chüan.* With the Ming publisher Yü An-ch'i's 俞安期 preface dated 1609. *Liao-liao ko ts'ang-pen* 寥寥閣藏本 ed. Peking Library collection.

Nan-Pei shih hsü Shih-shuo. Attributed to Li Hou. Fragment of an early Ch'ing hand copy. Taiwan Central Library collection.

Li Shao-wen 李紹文 (fl. 1600–1623). *Huang-Ming Shih-shuo hsin-yü* 皇明世説新語 (Imperial Ming *Shih-shuo hsin-yü*). 8 *chüan.* First ed. with Lu Ts'ung-p'ing's 陸從平 preface dated 1610. Taiwan Central Library, Library of Congress, collections, etc. Reprint of the 1610 ed. Taipei: Hsin-hsing shu-chü, 1985.

Cheng Chung-k'ui 鄭仲夔 (fl. 1615–1634). *Ch'ing-yen* 清言 (Pure talk), or *Lan-wan chü ch'ing-yen* 蘭畹居清言 (Pure talk from the Orchid-Fields Studio), 10 *chüan,* compiled 1615. First ed. 1617. The only extant copy found in the Taiwan Central Library is included in the *Ching-shih chieh-wen* 經世捷聞 (Dispatches of the world), a 1638 collection of Cheng's four works.

Chang Yung 張墉 (fl. late Ming). *Nien-i shih shih-yü* 廿一史識餘 (Extracts from twenty-one standard histories), also named *Chu-hsiang chai lei-shu* 竹香齋類書 (Bamboo-fragrance Studio encyclopedia). 37 *chüan.* Recorded in *Ssu-k'u ch'üan-shu tsung-mu,* "Shih-pu" 史部 (History), "Shih-ch'ao lei" 史鈔類 (Historical jottings), "Ts'un-mu" 存目 (Preserved titles), *chüan* 65, 1:582. Text not seen.

Lin Mao-kuei 林茂桂 (fl. 1591–1621). *Nan-Pei ch'ao hsin-yü* 南北朝新語 (The Southern and Northern dynasties [*Shih-shuo*] *hsin-yü*). 4 *chüan.* Author's preface dated 1621. Reprint of 1621 ed. Peking: Chung-kuo shu-tien, 1990.

Yen Ts'ung-ch'iao 顏從喬 (fl. around 1639). *Seng Shih-shuo* 僧世説 (Monks *Shih-shuo* [*hsin-yü*]). 24 *chüan.* Culled from [Liang 梁] Hui Chiao 慧皎, *Kao-seng chuan* 高僧傳; [T'ang 唐] Tao Hsüan 道宣, *Hsü Kao-seng chuan* 續高僧傳, and [Sung 宋] Tsan Ning 贊寧, *Sung Kao-seng chuan* 宋高僧傳. Author's preface dated 1639; other prefaces, 1640. Wan-ch'eng 皖城 (today's Ch'ien-shan 潛山 County, Anhwei 安徽 Province): Yen-ya tzu-hang 顏衙梓行 (Yen Family Publishing House), 1640. Taiwan Palace Museum Library collection.

Liang Wei-shu 梁維樞 (1589–1662). *Yü-chien tsun-wen* 玉劍尊聞 (Distinguished accounts of the jade sword). 10 *chüan.* Author's preface dated 1654; other prefaces, 1655 or 1657. Reprint of the 1657 Tz'u-lin t'ang 賜麟堂 ed. 2 vols. Shanghai: Shang-hai ku-chi ch'u-pan she, 1986.

Li Ch'ing 李清 (1602–1683). *Nü Shih-shuo* 女世説 (Women *Shih-shuo* [*hsin-yü*]). 4 *chüan.* Compiled around early 1650s and published in early 1670s. Nanking Library collection.

———. *Nü Shih-shuo.* 5 *chüan.* With the identical print of the original 4 *chüan* plus a *chüan* of addenda (*pu-i* 補遺) and Li Ch'ing's 1676 postscript. Nanking Library collection.

Wang Wan 汪琬 (1624–1691). *Shuo-ling* 説鈴 (Bell of tales). 1 *chüan.* Ch'ing dynasty edition. Nanking University Library collection. (Also in *Chao-tai ts'ung-shu* 昭代叢書, *Hsiao-yüan ts'ung-shu* 嘯園叢書, *and Ch'ing-jen shuo-hui* 清人説薈.)

Wu Su-kung 吳肅公 (fl. 1662–1681). *Ming yü-lin* 明語林 (Ming forest of accounts). 14 *chüan. Pi lin-lang ts'ung-shu* 碧琳琅叢書 ed. With Wu's "Fan-li" 凡例 (Compilation notes) dated 1662 and his own preface dated 1681, in which he indicates that the publication was delayed for twenty years. Nanking University Library collection.

Chiang Yu-jung 江有溶 and Tsou T'ung-lu 鄒統魯 (both fl. early Ch'ing). *Ming-i pien* 明逸編 (Compilation of Ming anecdotes). 10 *chüan.* Published in early Ch'ing. Recorded in *Ssu-k'u ch'üan-shu tsung-mu,* "Tzu-pu" 子部 (Philosophers), "Hsiao-shuo chia lei" 小説家類, "Ts'un-mu" I, *chüan* 143, 2:1225. Text not seen.

Wang Cho 王日綽 (b. 1636). *Chin Shih-shuo* 今世説 (Contemporary *Shih-shuo* [*hsin-yü*]). 8 *chüan.* Author's preface dated 1683. *Chung-kuo wen-hsüeh ts'an-k'ao hsiao ts'ung-shu* 中國文學參考小叢書 ed. Shanghai: Ku-tien wen-hsüeh ch'u-pan she, 1957.

Chang Fu-kung 章撫功 (fl. early Ch'ing). *Han Shih-shuo* 漢世説. 14 *chüan.* Published in early Ch'ing. Recorded in *Ssu-k'u ch'üan-shu tsung-mu,* "Tzu-pu," "Hsiao-shuo chia lei," "Ts'un-mu" I, *chüan* 143, 2:1226. Text not seen.

Chang Chi-yung 章繼泳 (Ch'ing). *Nan-Pei ch'ao Shih-shuo* 南北朝世説 (The Southern and Northern dynasties *Shih-shuo*). 20 *chüan.* Recorded in Kuang-hsü Hang-chow Fu-chih 光緒杭州府志 (Gazetteer of the Hangchow Prefecture under the Kuang-hsü reign), "I-wen chih," "Tzu-pu," "Hsiao-shuo lei," and Yüan and Hou, ed. *Chung-kuo wen-yen hsiao-shuo shu-mu,* 366. Text not seen.

Yen Heng 嚴蘅 (1826?–1854). *Nü Shih-shuo* 女世説 (Women *Shih-shuo* [*hsin-yü*]). 1

chüan. First ed. 1865. *Chüan-ching lou ts'ung-k'e pen* 娟鏡樓叢刻本 ed. Shang-hai: Chü-chen fang-Sung yin-shu chü 聚珍仿宋印書局, 1920. Peking Library, Library of Congress collection.

Hsü K'o 徐珂 (1869–1928). *Ch'ing-pai lei-ch'ao* 清稗類鈔 (Classified records from unofficial Ch'ing historical writings). Author's preface dated 1916. 48 vols. Shang-hai: Shang-wu yin-shu kuan, 1917.

———. *Ch'ing-pai lei-ch'ao.* 13 vols. Peking: Chung-hua shu-chü, 1984.

Yi Tsung-k'uei 易宗夔 (b. 1875). *Hsin Shih-shuo* 新世説 (New *Shih-shuo* [*hsin-yü*]). First ed. 1918. Reprint of the 1922 ed. In *Ch'ing-tai chuan-chi ts'ung-k'an* 清代傳記叢刊, edited by Chou Chün-fu 周駿富. Vol. 18. Taipei: Ming-wen shu-chü, 1985.

Hattori Nankaku 服部南郭 (1683–1759). *Daitō seigo* 大東世語 (Account of the Great Eastern World). 5 *chüan*. 2 vols. Edo: Sūzanbō 嵩山房, 1750. Japan National Diet Library collection.

Rakuhokuhōsun'an Shikka 洛北方寸庵漆鍋. *Daitō seigo kō* 大東世語考 (Textual studies of *Daitō seigo*). 5 *chüan*. 1751. Waseda University Library collection.

Ōta Nanbo (Fukashi) 太田南畝 (覃) (1749–1823) and Imai Kyūsuke 今井久助 (1786–1829). *Kana Sesetsu* 假名世説 (*Tales of the World* in Kana). 2 *chüan*. Published under Shokusan sensei 蜀山先生 and Bunhōtei Sanboku 文寶亭散木. Preface dated 1824. Tōto shoshi 東都書肆, 1825. National Diet Library collection.

———. *Kana Sesetsu kōhen* 假名世説後編 (*Tales of the World* in Kana, continued edition). Recorded in Ōyane Bunjirō, "Edo Jidai ni okeru *Sesetsu shingo* ni tsuite," *Sesetsu shingo to rikuchō bungaku*, 102. Text not seen.

———. *Sesetsu shingo cha* 世説新語茶 (Tea of *Sesetsu shingo*). First ed. ca. 1770. Under the pen name Yamanote no Bakajin 山の手の馬鹿人. *Sharehon* 洒落本 ed.

Tsunota Ken 角田簡 (d. 1855). *Kinsei sōgo* 近世叢語 (Accounts of recent times). 8 *chüan*. Tsunota Ken's preface dated 1816. 4 vols. Tokyo: Shorin 書林, 1828. National Diet Library collection.

———. *Shoku Kinsei sōgo* 續近世叢語 (Continued accounts of recent times), 8 *chüan*. 4 vols. Tokyo: Shorin, 1845. National Diet Library collection.

Ōta Saijirō 太田才次郎 (fl. 1892). *Shin seigo* 新世語 (New account of the world). Preface dated 1892. Tokyo: Shorin, 1892. National Diet Library collection.

Index

389n. 42, 396nn. 54–57, 398nn. 86–88

Mann, Susan, 312, 441nn. 2–3, 448n. 73

Mao Chi-k'o, 101, 207–208, 406n. 3

Mao T'i (An-fang), 291–292, 443n. 26

Mather Richard B, 381n. 1, 382n. 3; book titles of *Shih-shuo hsin-yü*, 402n. 2; on *Chu-lin ch'i-hsien*, 395n. 45; on *chu-wei*, 392n. 12; circulation *of Shih-shuo hsin-yü* and influence in Japan, 451n. 13; editions of *Shih-shuo hsin-yü*, 382n. 4, 407n. 5; historical authenticity of *Shih-shuo hsin-yü*, 92; on *hsiao-shuo* list in *Sui Treatise*, 95–96; Liu Chün's commentary on *Shih-shuo hsin-yü*, 385n.1; men-women relationship in *Shih-shuo hsin-yü*, 141; on *ming-chiao*, 389n. 42; parodies in *Shih-shuo hsin-yü*, 136, 414n. 95; rhetoric of *Shih-shuo hsin-yü*, 163, 183–184; using *Shih-shuo* as source, 406n. 48; on *Ssu-pen lun*, 396n. 61; on Wang Tao's diplomatic talent, 390n. 58. See also *Shih-shuo hsin-yü*

Mencius, 110, 119–120, 121–122

Meng-tzu, 22. See also Mencius

metaphors: bamboo, 185; belly, 330–331; bright moon, 185; Chu-ko Liang's "Diagram of Eight Tactics," 239; clear dewdrops and new leaves, 185; cliff, 41, 181; costume, 59, 164, 343, 359; crow, 244; dragon gate (*lung-men*), 31; female body (*see* body), female cadaver, 333; flowering plum, 303–304, 443n. 20; fresh breeze, 185; glass beauty, 312; grafting plants, 327; half-cocoon, 292–293; horse, 62; ink stick, 269; inkstone, 268–269; jade mountain, 62, 181; jade-link puzzle, 295, 444n. 32; lightning, 181; locust tree, 186; mountain, 62, 179, 183; name cards, 269; orchard in spring, 82; pine tree, 40, 41,62; piping of Heaven, 73; poetry bell, 366–367; rock, 183; sambar-tail chowry (see *chu-wei*), sky, 179–180; snow, 82–83, 147, 184, 187–188, 292,

334–337; sun and moon, 181; sword, 61; water, 62, 118, 121, 122–123, 183; willow, 181,186; willow catkins, 147; wind beneath sturdy pines, 61

Minamoto no Takakuni, 326–327

Ming-chia (School of Names), 396n. 58

ming-chiao (Confucian moral teaching), 31–32; definition of, 389n. 42; versus *tzu-jan* (self-so-ness), 53–54, 64

ming/li (names and principles), 64, 66–67

ming/shih (name and actuality), 29, 63, 64, 66

Mother Chao, 144–145

Munro, Donald J., 381n. 1

Murakami Yoshimi, 412n. 76

Murasaki Shikibu, Lady, 326

Nan-k'ang, Princess, 162–163, 418n. 22

Nan-she (Southern Poetry Club), 353–354, 360

Nan-shih, 84

Neo-Confucianism: dominance of Ming-Ch'ing intellectual life, 250, 433n. 5; state orthodoxy of Tokugawa Japan, 320, 451n. 6. See also *Hsin-hsüeh; Li-hsüeh; Tao-hsüeh*

"new," republican concepts: *chuan-chih/sensei* (autocracy), 358–359; *i-hui* (national assembly), 360–363; *ko-ming/kakumei* (revolution), 358; *kuo-min* (citizens) 363–364; *p'ing-yün* (fair and proper), 363; *t'ung-pao* (compatriots), 363; *yen-shuo* (public speech), 361–363

Ni Tsan, 267–268

nine-rank system (*chiu-p'in chung-cheng chih*), 36, 390n. 56, 408n. 15

Ning Chia-yü, 18, 198n. 26, 403n. 19, 406n. 50

Ning T'iao-yüan, 354

"nominalist theory of naming," 66

nü-lang shih (girls' poetry), 304–305

Nü Shih-shuo (Li Ch'ing), 195, 248; editions and publication dates, 441n. 6. *See also* Li Ch'ing; *Shih-shuo* imitations (women)